POLITICS IN STATES AND COMMUNITIES

POLITICS
IN
STATES
AND
COMMUNITIES

Ninth Edition

THOMAS R. DYE
Florida State University

Prentice Hall, Upper Saddle River, New Jersey 07458

Library of Congress Cataloging-in-Publication Data

Dye, Thomas R.
    Politics in states and communities / Thomas R. Dye.—9th ed.
      p.   cm.
    Includes bibliographical references and index.
    ISBN 0–13–258708–4
    1. State governments—United States.   2. Local government—United
States. I. Title
JK2408.D82   1997   96–11405
320.8'0973—dc20   CIP

Editorial director: Charlyce Jones Owen
Editor-in-chief: Nancy Roberts
Acquisitions editor: Michael Bickerstaff
Editorial assistant: Anita Castro
Director of production and manufacturing: Barbara Kittle
Project manager: Joan Stone
Manufacturing manager: Nick Sklitsis
Prepress and manufacturing buyer: Bob Anderson
Creative design director: Leslie Osher
Art director: Maria Lange
Interior and cover design: Joseph Rattan Design
Photo research: Rona Tuccillo
Electronic art manager: Michele Giusti
Electronic art creation: Joseph Rattan Design
Copy editor: Rebecca J. McDearmon
Marketing manager: Chaunfayta Hightower

This book was set in 9.75/12 Sabon by NK Graphics and
was printed and bound by RR Donnelley & Sons Company.
The cover was printed by The Lehigh Press, Inc.

 © 1997, 1994, 1991, 1988, 1985, 1981, 1977, 1973, 1969 by Prentice-Hall, Inc.
Simon & Schuster/A Viacom Company
Upper Saddle River, New Jersey 07458

Printed in the United States of America

10 9 8 7 6 5 4 3 2 1

ISBN 0-13-258708-4

PRENTICE-HALL INTERNATIONAL (UK) LIMITED, *London*
PRENTICE-HALL OF AUSTRALIA PTY. LIMITED, *Sydney*
PRENTICE-HALL CANADA INC., *Toronto*
PRENTICE-HALL HISPANOAMERICANA, S.A., *Mexico*
PRENTICE-HALL OF INDIA PRIVATE LIMITED, *New Delhi*
PRENTICE-HALL OF JAPAN, INC., *Tokyo*
SIMON & SCHUSTER ASIA PTE. LTD., *Singapore*
EDITORA PRENTICE-HALL DO BRASIL, LTDA., *Rio de Janeiro*

To Joann

Contents

8 COURTS, CRIME, AND CORRECTIONAL POLICY   216

9 COMMUNITY POLITICAL SYSTEMS   260

10 STYLES OF COMMUNITY POLITICS   291

18 THE POLITICS OF BUDGETING AND TAXATION   501

PHOTO CREDITS   525

INDEX   527

PREFACE

Since its first edition, *Politics in States and Communities* has maintained certain distinguishing features:

> Its focus on *politics*
> Its *comparative* approach
> Its concern with *explanation*
> Its interest in *policy*

The ninth edition continues the development of each of these themes. The focus remains on conflicts in states and communities and the structures and processes designed to manage conflict. This "conflict management" theme emphasizes the sources and nature of conflict in society, how conflict is carried on, how key decision makers in states and communities act in conflict situations, how public policies emerge and determine "who gets what."

POLITICS

The *political conflict* theme guides the discussion of formal governmental structures: federalism, state constitutions, parties and primaries, apportionment, legislative organization, gubernatorial powers, court procedures, nonpartisanship, mayor and manager government, metropolitan government, community power, school boards and superintendents, tax systems, budget making, and so on.

This theme also guides the discussion of *timely political conflicts* in state and local politics:

> The Politics of Immigration
> Term Limit Battles
> How Congress Raised the Drinking Age
> Battles in the States over Constitutional Amendments
> "Devolution," the New New Federalism
> Coercive Federalism: Mandates and Preemptions
> Money in State Politics
> The Great Incumbency Machine
> The Lawyering of America
> Divided Government: Governors Versus Legislatures
> The War on Drugs
> Political Corruption
> "Reinventing Government"
> The Radical Style: Politics in Berkeley
> Big-City Politics

Machine and Reform Politics in Chicago
Top Bananas in the Big Apple
Busing and Racial Balancing in Schools
Affirmative Action Battles
Battles over Abortion
The Inner City: Racial Tensions and Rioting
"Reinventing" Education
Battles over School Finances
Welfare Reform in the States
Revolting Against Taxes
"No-Growth" Politics and the Nimby Syndrome

The timely case studies are designed to both improve understanding and stimulate interest in state and local politics.

COMPARISON

In each chapter, *comparative analysis* is used both to describe and to explain differences among states and communities in governmental structures, political processes, and public policy. Students observe the relative ranking of their own state on such measures as

Income
Education
Urbanization
Growth
Black and ethnic populations
Liberalism and conservatism
Reliance and federal aid
Party competition
Political participation
Interest group power
Black representation in legislatures
Professionalism in legislatures
Governors' powers
Judicial selection
Crime rates
Police protection
Prison populations
Dropout rates
SAT scores
Educational spending

Poverty and inequality

Welfare spending

Tax burdens

Abortion rates

"Rankings of the states" are presented in clear bar graphs and plots. They enable students and instructors to assess their own state's position in relation to all fifty states.

EXPLANATION

We want to know "what" is happening in American politics, but we also want to know "why." *Comparative analysis* lays the groundwork for explanation. In each chapter, recent systematic research in the social sciences is summarized for undergraduate students. Difficult theoretical questions are presented clearly and concisely for undergraduates:

Direct versus representative democracy

Politics and the popular initiative

Why federalism?

How money shifted power to Washington

Are protests effective?

The policy effects of party competition

The unpopularity of legislatures

Are legislators responsible policy makers?

Governors versus legislatures

Are school boards responsible policy makers?

Are council members responsible policy makers?

Crime and deterrence

Types of cities and forms of government

Privatization as reform

Reformism and public policy

Models of community power

Different approaches to the study of community power

Metropolitan government as marketplace

Reinventing education

Federalism and welfare policy

Controlling the use of land

Explaining state tax systems

Explaining tax revolts

What happens when a city goes bust?

The most recent systematic social science research of these topics is presented in the ninth edition.

POLICY

Public *policy* is what governments do, and state and local governments in America do many things that touch the lives of all of us. This text is divided roughly into three parts: federalism and state politics, local politics and community power, and public policy. Specific attention is devoted to policy questions in

Crime in the states

Police and law enforcement

State correctional policies

The death penalty

Abortion

The states and school desegregation

The politics of higher education

The politics of "no growth"

Housing and development policy

Poverty in America

Welfare reform in the states

Health care in the states

Types of taxes and tax politics

The politics of budgeting

Fiscal stress and cutback management

The ninth edition reflects the changing dynamics of conflict in states and communities, including:

- Immigration policy and the provision of social services to illegal immigrants
- New debates over affirmative action
- Arguments over incumbency advantages and term limits
- Partisan battles and the Republican resurgence in the states
- Controversies over the "devolution" of welfare and other functions to the states
- Arguments over federal mandates and preemptions
- Continuing disputes over the quality of education in America and educational reform
- Conflict over the "reinvention" of government and the "privatization" of governmental functions
- Arguments over "Three Strikes You're Out" and other "get-tough" anticrime measures
- The long struggles of Native Americans
- New objections to "takings" of private property through land use regulations
- Battles at the national and state levels over welfare reform and health care reform

It describes African American and Hispanic politics, the representation of these groups as well as women in city councils and mayors' offices and state legislatures and governorships, and the policy effects of the movement of minorities and women "from protest to power." It describes the growth of party competition in the states, the role of party activists in separating the parties along ideological lines, and the recent gains of the GOP in the southern states. It reviews the war on drugs and its reported effectiveness and disputes over the wisdom of legalizing drug use. It reports on political corruption in the states, and the prevalence of lawyers in legislatures, and the obstacles to judicial reform. It describes the Orange County slide into bankruptcy and warns of what happens "when a city goes bust."

Finally, the ninth edition adds "Trivia" on American states and communities—everything from state birds, songs, flowers, and nicknames, to ratings for "most livable" states and cities. Perhaps readers will find some aspects of state and community affairs entertaining as well as instructive.

If this book has a theme, it is that states and communities in America play an important role in the political life of the nation. State and local governments do more than merely provide certain services such as education, road building, or fire protection. They also perform a vital political function by helping to resolve conflicts of interests in American society.

Thomas R. Dye

POLITICS IN STATES AND COMMUNITIES

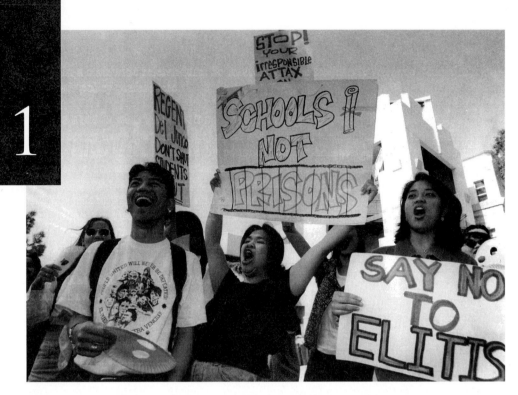

POLITICS IN STATES AND COMMUNITIES

A POLITICAL APPROACH TO STATES AND COMMUNITIES

The management of conflict is one of the basic purposes of government. Two hundred years ago, James Madison wrote that the control of "factions" was the principal function of government. He defined a faction as a number of citizens united by common interests that were opposed to the interests of other citizens "or to the permanent and aggregate interests of the community." He thought that regulating such conflict was "the principal task of modern legislation."[1] To paraphrase Madison, the management of conflict is "the principal task" of state and local government.

Politics is the management of conflict. An understanding of "politics" in American states and communities requires an understanding of the major conflicts confronting society and an understanding of political processes and governmental organizations designed to manage conflict. State and local governments do more than provide public services such as education, highways, police and fire protection, sewage disposal, and garbage collection. These are important functions of government to be sure; but it is even

---

[1]James Madison, *The Federalist*, Number 10 (New York: Modern Library, 1958).

more important that government deal with racial tensions, school disputes, growth problems, economic stagnation, minority concerns, poverty, drugs, crime, and violence. These problems are primarily *political* in nature; that is, people have different ideas about what should be done, or whether government should do anything at all.

Moreover, many of the service functions of government also engender political conflict. Even if "there is only one way to pave a street," political questions remain. Whose street will get paved? Who will get the paving contract? Who will pay for it? Why not build a school gym instead of paving the street?

So it is appropriate that a book on *politics* in states and communities deals not only with the structure and organization of state and local government, but also with many of the central policy questions confronting American society. It is true that these problems are national in scope, but they occur in our communities and our states. And much of this book is devoted to describing how these questions arise in state and local settings, and how state and local governments confront them.

A COMPARATIVE APPROACH TO STATES AND COMMUNITIES

The task of political science is not only to *describe* politics and public policy in American states and communities, but also to *explain* differences encountered from state to state and community to community through comparative analysis. We want to know *what* is happening in American politics, and we want to know *why*. In the past, the phrase "comparative government" applied to the study of foreign governments, but American states and communities provide an excellent opportunity for genuine comparative study, which is *comparing political institutions and behaviors from state to state and community to community in order to identify and explain similarities or differences*.

Comparison is a vital part of explanation. Only by comparing politics and public policy in different states and communities with different socioeconomic and political environments can we arrive at any comprehensive explanations of political life. Comparative analysis helps us answer the question *why*.

American states and communities provide excellent "laboratories" for applying comparative analysis. States and communities are not alike in social and economic conditions, in politics and government, or in their public policies. These differences are important assets in comparative study because they enable us to search for relationships between different socioeconomic conditions, political system characteristics, and policy outcomes. For example, if differences among states and communities in educational policies are closely associated with differences in economic resources or in party politics, then we may assume that economic resources or party politics help "explain" educational policies.

State politics are often affected by unique historical circumstances. (See Figure 1–1, Table 1–1.) Louisiana is distinctive because of its French–Spanish colonial background, and the continuing influence of this background on its politics today. For nine years Texas was an independent republic (1836–1845) before it was annexed as a state by Congress. Eleven southern states were involved in a bloody war against the federal government from 1861 to 1865. Hawaii has a unique history and culture, combining the influence of Polynesian, Chinese, Japanese, and haole civilizations. Alaska's rugged climate and geog-

Figure 1–1
STATE HISTORIES

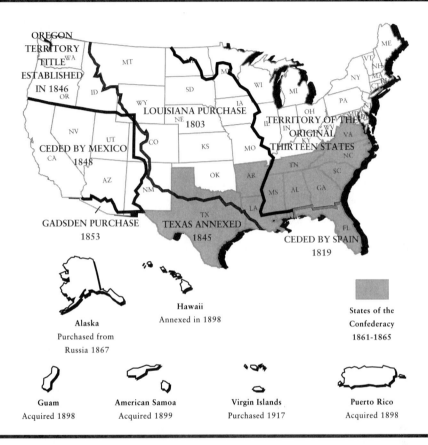

By the Treaty of Paris, 1783, England gave up claim to the thirteen original Colonies, and to all land within an area extending along the present Canadian border to the Lake of the Woods, down the Mississippi River to the 31st parallel, east to the Chattahoochie, down that river to the mouth of the Flint, east to the source of the St. Mary's, down that river to the ocean. Territory west of the Alleghenies was claimed by various states but was eventually all ceded to the nation.

In 1803 President Thomas Jefferson engineered the Louisiana Purchase from France; it was the largest acquisition of territory in U.S. history, more than doubling the size of the nation.

American invasions of Canada were failures in both the Revolutionary War and the War of 1812. In the Rush-Bagot Treaty of 1817, the border between the United States and Canada was demilitarized and fixed at the forty-ninth parallel. Later, in 1846, the British relinquished their claims to the Oregon territory south of the forty-ninth parallel.

In 1819 Spain ceded Florida to the United States in the Adams-Onis Treaty, after General Andrew Jackson and his Tennessee volunteers invaded the territory in a war with the Seminole Indians.

Following battles at the Alamo in San Antonio and at the San Jacinto River, Texas declared its independence from Mexico in 1836, but the Mexican government refused to recognize the new Republic. In 1845 Congress annexed Texas at the Republic's request, ending nine years of independence. In 1846 Congress declared war on Mexico, and following the American army's capture of Veracruz and Mexico City, forced that nation to cede the territories that became California, Nevada, Utah, Arizona, and New Mexico. Later, in 1853, the Gadsden Purchase from Mexico extended the U.S. border further south.

Beginning with South Carolina on December 20, 1860, eleven southern states seceded from the United States of America, forming their own Confederate States of America. They were readmitted to the Union following their defeat in the Civil War, after they agreed to ratify the Thirteenth Amendment, abolishing slavery (1865), and later the Fourteenth Amendment, guaranteeing equal protection of the laws (1868), and the Fifteenth Amendment, preventing denial or abridgment of the right to vote on account of "race, color, or previous condition of servitude."

Twice the size of Texas, Alaska was purchased from Russia for $7.2 million in 1867. (At the time Secretary of State William Henry Seward was criticized for his extravagance, and Alaska was dubbed "Seward's folly" and "Seward's icebox.") Hawaii was annexed to the United States by congressional resolution in 1898 without consulting its residents.

Following victories in the Spanish American War in 1898, Spain ceded Puerto Rico, and Samoa and Guam, and the Philippines, which remained as U.S. territory until granted independence in 1946. The Virgin Islands were purchased from Denmark in 1917.

Table 1–1
THE STATES OF THE UNION

State	Capital	Date Admitted to Union	Chronological Order of Admission to Union
Alabama	Montgomery	Dec. 14, 1819	22
Alaska	Juneau	Jan. 3, 1959	49
Arizona	Phoenix	Feb. 14, 1912	48
Arkansas	Little Rock	June 15, 1836	25
California	Sacramento	Sept. 9, 1850	31
Colorado	Denver	Aug. 1, 1876	38
Connecticut	Hartford	Jan. 9, 1788[a]	5
Delaware	Dover	Dec. 7, 1787[a]	1
Florida	Tallahassee	March 3, 1845	27
Georgia	Atlanta	Jan. 2, 1788[a]	4
Hawaii	Honolulu	Aug. 21, 1959	50
Idaho	Boise	July 3, 1890	43
Illinois	Springfield	Dec. 3, 1818	21
Indiana	Indianapolis	Dec. 11, 1816	19
Iowa	Des Moines	Dec. 28, 1846	29
Kansas	Topeka	Jan. 29, 1861	34
Kentucky	Frankfort	June 1, 1792	15
Louisiana	Baton Rouge	April 30, 1812	18
Maine	Augusta	March 15, 1820	23
Maryland	Annapolis	April 28, 1788[a]	7
Massachusetts	Boston	Feb. 6, 1788[a]	6
Michigan	Lansing	Jan. 26, 1837	26
Minnesota	St. Paul	May 11, 1858	32
Mississippi	Jackson	Dec. 10, 1817	20
Missouri	Jefferson City	Aug. 10, 1821	24
Montana	Helena	Nov. 8, 1889	41
Nebraska	Lincoln	March 1, 1867	37
Nevada	Carson City	Oct. 31, 1864	36
New Hampshire	Concord	June 21, 1788[a]	9
New Jersey	Trenton	Dec. 18, 1787[a]	3
New Mexico	Santa Fe	Jan. 6, 1912	47
New York	Albany	July 26, 1788[a]	11
North Carolina	Raleigh	Nov. 21, 1789[a]	12
North Dakota	Bismarck	Nov. 2, 1889	39
Ohio	Columbus	March 1, 1803	17
Oklahoma	Oklahoma City	Nov. 16, 1907	46
Oregon	Salem	Feb. 14, 1859	33
Pennsylvania	Harrisburg	Dec. 12, 1787[a]	2
Rhode Island	Providence	May 29, 1790[a]	13
South Carolina	Columbia	May 23, 1788[a]	8
South Dakota	Pierre	Nov. 2, 1889	40
Tennessee	Nashville	June 1, 1796	16
Texas	Austin	Dec. 29, 1845	28
Utah	Salt Lake City	Jan. 4, 1896	45
Vermont	Montpelier	March 4, 1791	14
Virginia	Richmond	June 25, 1788[a]	10
Washington	Olympia	Nov. 11, 1889	42
West Virginia	Charleston	June 20, 1863	35
Wisconsin	Madison	May 29, 1848	30
Wyoming	Cheyenne	July 10, 1890	44

[a] Date of ratification of U.S. Constitution.

raphy and physical isolation set it apart. Wisconsin and Minnesota reflect the Scandinavian influences of their settlers. The states of the Deep South—South Carolina, Georgia, Alabama, Mississippi, Louisiana—still reflect much of their plantation cultures. Four states—Pennsylvania, Massachusetts, Kentucky, and Virginia—call themselves "commonwealths," but this title has no legal meaning. Life in Florida is more tourist oriented than anywhere else. Michigan is the home of the automobile industry. West Virginia is noted for its mountains and its coal mines. Utah was initially settled by members of the Church of Jesus Christ of Latter-day Saints, popularly known as the Mormons, and it retains much of its distinctly Mormon culture today.

These unique historical and cultural settings help to shape state political systems and public policies. However, the mere identification of unique traits or histories does not really "explain" why politics or public policy differs from state to state. Ad hoc explanations do not help very much in developing general theories of politics. For example, only Texas has the Alamo and only New York has the Statue of Liberty, but these characteristics do not explain why New York has a state income tax and Texas does not. Students of state politics must search for social and economic conditions that appear most influential in shaping state politics over time in all the states. Despite the uniqueness of history and culture in many of our states, we must *search for generalizations* that will help to explain why state governments do what they do.

Since it is impossible to consider all the conditions that might influence state politics, we must focus our attention on a limited number of variables. We can begin with economic development—one of the most influential variables affecting state politics and public policy. Economic development is defined broadly to include three closely related components: population growth and urbanization, income, and education.

GROWTH AND URBANIZATION   The population of the United States has grown about 1 percent per year over the past few decades. But population growth is spread unevenly among the fifty states; between 1980 and 1990, Nevada, Arizona, and Florida grew by more than 30 percent, while Iowa, West Virginia, North Dakota, and Wyoming actually lost population (see Figure 1–2). Current population projections indicate that western and southern "Sunbelt" states are expected to grow 20 percent or more by the year 2000, while Massachusetts, Connecticut, and Rhode Island will actually lose population. The standard Census Bureau definition of urbanization is the percentage of population living in urban areas, that is, in incorporated cities of 2,500 or more or the urban fringe of cities of 50,000 or more. In 1790 the urban population of the United States was only 5 percent of the total population. By 1900 this figure had grown to 40 percent, and in 1990, 77.5 percent of the population lived in urban areas. Yet not all the states share this high degree of urbanization. Idaho has the smallest proportion of urban residents of any state in the nation, and New Jersey has the highest proportion.

INCOME   Rising *income* is also a component of economic development. An industrial economy means increased worker productivity and the creation of more wealth. Per capita personal income in the United States grew from $3,996 in 1970 to nearly $19,000 in 1994. This wealth was not evenly distributed throughout the states (see Figure 1–3). Per capita personal income in 1994 in Connecticut was nearly $25,000, but it was less than $15,000 in Mississippi.

Figure 1–2
POPULATION GROWTH IN THE STATES

Percent Change in State Populations 1980-1990

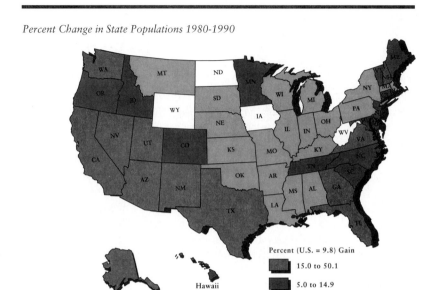

Projected Percent Change in State Populations 1990-2000

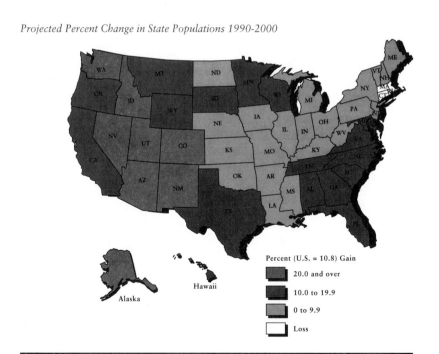

Source: Charts prepared by U.S. Bureau of the Census.

SOURCES OF DATA ON STATES AND COMMUNITIES IN THE UNITED STATES

Standard sources of data on American states and communities in tables through-out this volume include: U.S. Bureau of the Census, *Statistical Abstract of the United States,* published annually by the U.S. Government Printing Office, Wash-ington, DC; U.S. Bureau of the Census, *Census of Governments,* published after each five-year governmental census (1987, 1992, 1997, etc.) by the U.S. Govern-ment Printing Office, Washington, DC; U.S. Bureau of the Census, *Census of Population 1990,* including individual state volumes on "Numbers of Inhabi-tants," "General Population Characteristics," and "General Social and Eco-nomic Characteristics," as well as individual reports on Standard Metropolitan Statistical Areas, published by the U.S. Government Printing Office, Washington, DC; *The Book of the States,* published biennially by the Council of State Gov-ernments, Lexington, KY: *Municipal Yearbook,* published annually by the Inter-national City Managers Association, Washington, DC; U.S. Bureau of the Census, *City–County Data Book,* published every five years by the U.S. Govern-ment Printing Office, Washington, DC. Unless otherwise indicated, the social, economic, governmental, and electoral data presented in this volume are drawn from these sources.

EDUCATION   An economically developed society requires educated workers. Many economists have asserted that economic growth involves an upgrading in the work force, the development of professional managerial skills, and an increase in the volume of research. These developments obviously involve a general increase in the *educational lev-els* of the adult population. In 1970 about 11 percent of the adult population of the United States had completed four years or more of college; by 1990 that figure had risen to over 21 percent. But high levels of educational attainment do not prevail uniformly throughout the states (see Figure 1–3).

The extent to which economic development—growth and urbanization, income, and education—affects the politics of the states is an important question, which we will return to again in the chapters that follow.

STATE POLITICAL "CULTURES" AND ETHNIC INFLUENCES

Anthropologists define *culture* as customary "ways of life," including designs for living, shared values, and guides to appropriate behavior.[2] We know that states have different

---

[2]Clyde Kluckhohm, "The Concept of Culture," in *The Science of Man in the World,* Ralph Linton, ed. (New York: Columbia University Press, 1945). For an explanation of the idea of *political* culture, see Michael Thompson, Richard Ellis, and Aaron Wildavsky, *Cultural Theory* (Boulder, CO: Westview Press, 1990).

Figure 1–3
RANKINGS OF THE STATES: URBANIZATION, EDUCATION, AND INCOME

Urbanization:
Population Percentages, 1990

1.	CA
2.	NJ
3.	HI
4.	NV
5.	AZ
6.	UT
7.	RI
8.	FL
9.	IL
10.	MA
10.	NY
12.	CO
13.	MD
14.	TX
15.	CN
16.	WA
17.	OH
18.	DE
18.	NM
20.	MI
20.	OR
22.	MN
23.	VA
24.	KS
25.	PA
26.	MO
27.	LA
28.	OK
29.	AK
30.	NE
31.	WI
32.	WY
33.	IN
34.	GA
35.	TN
36.	IA
37.	AL
38.	ID
39.	SC
40.	AR
41.	ND
42.	MT
43.	KY
44.	NH
45.	NC
46.	ND
47.	MS
48.	ME
49.	WV
50.	VT

0 20 40 60 80 100

Percent Completing College, 1993

1.	CO
2.	MA
3.	CT
4.	WA
4.	NJ
6.	NH
7.	MD
8.	VA
9.	HI
10.	CA
11.	NY
12.	KS
13.	MN
14.	AK
14.	VT
16.	OR
17.	UT
18.	AZ
19.	NM
20.	TX
20.	IL
20.	DE
23.	MT
24.	GA
25.	ND
26.	OK
26.	RI
28.	ME
29.	MO
30.	WI
31.	FL
32.	OH
33.	SD
34.	MI
34.	ID
36.	PA
37.	NC
38.	WY
38.	IA
40.	NE
41.	NV
42.	MS
43.	KY
44.	SC
45.	LA
46.	AR
47.	TN
48.	AL
49.	IN
50.	WV

0 5 10 15 20 25 30 35

Personal Income per Capita, 1993

1.	CT
2.	NJ
3.	NY
4.	MA
5.	MD
6.	HI
7.	AK
8.	NV
9.	IL
10.	NH
11.	CA
12.	DE
13.	WA
14.	VA
15.	CO
16.	PA
17.	RI
18.	MN
19.	FL
20.	MI
21.	KS
22.	WI
23.	WY
24.	NE
25.	OH
26.	MO
27.	VT
28.	OR
29.	GA
30.	IN
31.	TX
32.	ME
33.	NC
34.	TN
35.	IA
36.	AZ
37.	SD
38.	ID
39.	MT
40.	AL
41.	ND
42.	OK
43.	KY
44.	SC
45.	LA
46.	NM
47.	WV
48.	UT
49.	AR
50.	MS

0 5 10 15 20 25 30
(Thousands of Dollars)

Source: Statistical Abstract of the United States, 1995.

histories, economies, climates, and rates of growth, but can the states also be distinguished by their dominant political cultures? If so, can the different political cultures of the states help explain diversity in politics and public policy? Actually, the term *culture* applies to a whole society, so we must search for important variations, or *subcultures,* that may account for political differences among the states.

One theory of American political subcultures, set forth initially by political scientist Daniel J. Elazar, attempts to identify variations in shared political values and appropriate guides to political activity.[3] These cultural differences arise among the states primarily because of different patterns of early migration and settlement and the resulting dominance of different religious and ethnic groups in a state's society. Elazar labeled these political subcultures as moralistic, individualistic, and traditionalistic (see Figure 1–4).

Figure 1–4
REGIONAL DISTRIBUTION OF POLITICAL CULTURE IN THE UNITED STATES

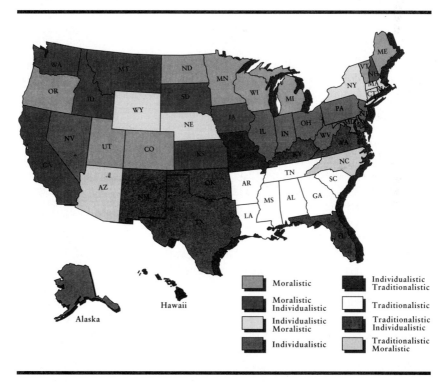

Source: Map from *American Federalism: A View from the States,* 3/e, by Daniel J. Elazar. Copyright © 1984 by Harper & Row, Publishers, Inc. Reprinted by permission of HarperCollins Publishers, Inc.

---

[3]Daniel Elazar, *American Federalism: A View from the States* (New York: Thomas Y. Crowell, 1966). For a well-developed theory of America's political subcultures, ethnic migrations, and generational changes, see Daniel Elazar, *The American Mosaic* (Boulder, CO: Westview Press, 1994).

MORALISTIC   A *moralistic* political subculture emphasizes a common public interest—honesty in government, selflessness, and a commitment to the public welfare by those who govern. Every citizen has a duty to participate in political affairs, and officeholding is looked upon as public service demanding high moral obligations. Politics should be concerned with general issues and programs, not narrow special interests or selfish office seeking. Nonpartisanship is preferred over party politics, and citizen (amateur) officeholders are preferred over professional politicians. The moralistic political subculture allows a great deal of government intervention into the social and economic life of the state or community in order to promote the "common good."

INDIVIDUALISTIC   In contrast, the *individualistic* political subculture emphasizes politics as a means of advancing the social and economic interests of groups and individuals. Political activity is undertaken for personal benefit or group advancement. Politics is based primarily on group obligations rooted in personal relationships; general political issues or public service motives are secondary. Professional politicians who look after the material interests of their own constituents are preferred to moralizing amateurs. Government intervention in private life should be minimal, although large public bureaucracies may result from efforts to give jobs (patronage) to large numbers of people.

TRADITIONALISTIC   In a *traditionalistic* political culture, a paternalistic elite plays a special and dominant role in government. The political community is ordered in a hierarchical fashion with those at the top of the social structure using government to maintain and preserve the social and economic system and their dominant role in it. Real political power is confined to a relatively small and self-perpetuating elite who generally inherit their position from family ties, social position, and wealth. *Nonelites* are not expected to be politically active; indeed, they may not even be expected to vote. Political parties have little importance; competition is usually limited to factional alignments centered on individuals or geographical areas. The primary political values are the maintenance and encouragement of traditional social and religious values. Government services are often provided on a personal, first-name basis.

CULTURE AND ETHNICITY   The location of these political subcultures throughout the American states is largely determined by the migration patterns of different ethnic and religious groups. Indeed, it appears that the *moralistic* subculture is a product of northern European, English, and German liberal Protestantism; the *individualistic* subculture is a product of southern and eastern European and Irish Catholicism; and the *traditionalist* subculture is a product of fundamentalist white Protestantism in potential conflict with large black populations.

Over time, subcultures tend to blur, owing to continued mobility of the nation's population and the impact of national cultural media—particularly television, movies, and music. There is little empirical evidence that people actually think about politics in individualistic, moralistic, or traditionalistic terms.[4]

---

[4]Peter F. Nardulli, "Political Subcultures in the American States," *American Politics Quarterly,* 18 (July 1990), 287–315.

Nonetheless, America is indeed a nation of immigrants, and patterns of immigration in the states have left their mark. A serious examination of the political effects of ethnicity might begin by observing the current distribution of people with foreign-born parentage. This distribution is shown in Table 1–2. It should come as no surprise that Canada is the leading country of origin for the states on our northern border, and Mexico is the leading country of origin for the states on our southern border. The Spanish heritage in Texas, New Mexico, Arizona, and southern California is important politically as well as culturally. Likewise the Cuban heritage in southern Florida creates the cultural background for politics in that state. Ethnicity-based political cultures throughout the nation show distinctive patterns based on the prevalence of "Anglo," "Germanic," "Nordic," "Hispanic," "Mormon," and other cultural influences.[5]

STATE POLITICAL CULTURES   Do the states exhibit separate and identifiable political cultures? That is, are there political differences among the states that cannot be accounted for by demographic characteristics, for example, race, religion, income, education? It does appear that some states have developed historical traditions of Democratic and Republican party affiliation, as well as cultural patterns of liberal and conservative politics, that are independent of any demographic features of their populations.[6] For example, Minnesota has developed a liberal and Democratic tradition, Indiana a conservative and Republican tradition, and neither can be explained by the racial, religious, or socioeconomic composition of their populations. The liberal politics of Massachusetts, Rhode Island, Vermont, and West Virginia, as well as the conservative politics of Idaho, North Dakota, and Utah, are not fully explained by characteristics of these states' populations or by specific historical events. So we attribute to "political culture" the unexplained variation in partisan affiliations and ideological predispositions that we cannot explain by social or economic factors.

LIBERALISM AND CONSERVATISM IN THE STATES

State political cultures may differ in their ideological predispositions—that is, whether they are predominantly "liberal" or "conservative." There are various ways of defining and measuring ideological predispositions. Liberal and conservative states might be identified in terms of their policy enactments. For example, "policy liberalism" might be defined as the adoption of relaxed eligibility standards for receipts of welfare and medical benefits, decriminalization of marijuana possession and an absence of the death penalty, extensive regulation of business, state ratification of the Equal Rights Amendment, and the adoption of progressive state income taxes; "policy conservatism" would be defined as the opposite of these enactments. Or liberal and conservative states might be defined in terms of their voters' self-identification in opinion surveys as "liberal," "moderate," or "conservative." A common question on opinion polls is: "How would you describe your

[5]Joel Liske, "Political Subcultures of the United States." Paper delivered at the American Political Science Association Annual Meeting, Washington, DC, 1991.

[6]Robert S. Erikson, John P. McIver, and Gerald C. Wright, "State Political Culture and Public Opinion," *American Political Science Review,* 81 (September 1987), 797–813.

Table 1–2

RACE AND ETHNICITY IN THE STATES

	Foreign-Born %	Leading Country of Origin	Black Population %	American Indian, Eskimo, Aleut	Asian, Pacific Islander	Hispanic Origin
NEW ENGLAND						
ME	19.4	Canada	0.4	0.5	0.5	0.6
NH	23.2	Canada	0.6	0.2	0.8	1.0
VT	18.2	Canada	0.3	0.3	0.6	0.7
MA	33.3	Canada	5.0	0.2	2.4	4.8
RI	32.8	Italy	3.9	0.4	1.8	4.6
CT	32.0	Italy	8.3	0.2	1.5	6.5
MIDDLE ATLANTIC						
NY	32.9	Italy	15.9	0.3	3.9	12.3
NJ	30.1	Italy	13.4	0.2	3.5	9.6
PA	18.1	Italy	9.2	0.1	1.2	2.0
DE	11.9	Italy	16.9	0.3	1.4	2.4
CENTRAL						
OH	12.3	Germany	16.9	0.3	1.4	2.4
IN	6.8	Germany	7.8	0.2	0.7	1.8
IL	19.8	Germany	14.8	0.2	2.5	7.9
MI	19.0	Canada	13.9	0.6	1.1	2.2
WI	16.9	Germany	5.0	0.8	1.1	1.9
MN	18.6	Germany	2.2	1.1	1.8	1.2
IA	10.5	Germany	1.7	0.3	0.9	1.2
MO	6.7	Germany	10.7	0.4	0.8	1.2
ND	23.6	Norway	0.6	4.1	0.5	0.7
SD	16.4	Germany	0.5	7.3	0.4	0.8
NE	13.8	Germany	3.6	0.8	0.8	2.3
KS	7.8	Germany	5.8	0.9	1.3	3.8

SOUTHEASTERN						
MD	11.6	Germany	24.9	0.3	2.9	2.6
VA	5.4	Germany	18.8	0.2	2.6	2.6
WV	4.2	Italy	3.1	0.1	0.4	0.5
NC	1.9	Germany	22.0	1.2	0.8	1.2
SC	1.9	Germany	29.8	0.2	0.6	0.9
GA	2.4	Germany	27.0	0.2	1.2	1.7
FL	18.2	Cuba	13.6	0.3	1.2	12.2
KY	2.3	Germany	7.1	0.2	0.5	0.6
TN	1.7	Germany	16.0	0.2	0.7	0.7
AL	1.9	Germany	25.3	0.4	0.5	0.6
MS	1.4	Germany	35.6	0.3	0.5	0.6
SOUTHWESTERN						
AR	1.9	Germany	15.9	0.5	0.5	0.8
LA	3.8	Italy	30.8	0.4	1.0	2.2
OK	3.6	Germany	7.4	8.0	1.1	2.7
TX	10.7	Mexico	11.9	0.4	1.9	25.5
NM	8.8	Mexico	2.0	8.9	0.9	38.2
AZ	16.8	Mexico	3.0	5.6	1.5	18.8
MOUNTAIN						
MT	17.6	Canada	0.3	6.0	0.5	1.5
ID	10.4	Canada	0.3	1.4	0.9	5.3
WY	11.4	Germany	0.8	2.1	0.6	5.7
CO	12.7	Germany	4.0	0.8	1.8	12.9
UT	12.5	United Kingdom	0.7	1.4	1.9	4.9
NV	13.9	Italy	6.6	1.6	3.2	10.4
PACIFIC						
WA	18.7	Canada	3.1	1.7	4.3	4.4
OR	14.1	Canada	1.6	1.4	2.4	4.0
CA	25.0	Mexico	7.4	0.8	9.6	25.8
AK	11.0	Canada	4.1	15.6	3.6	3.2
HI	33.4	Japan	2.5	0.5	61.8	7.3
U.S. Totals	16.5		12.1	0.8	2.9	9.0

Source: U.S. Bureau of the Census, *Census of Population 1990.*

views on most political matters? Generally do you think of yourself as liberal, moderate, or conservative?" One study collected the results of national opinion polls and then observed the responses of voters in each state.[7] Nationwide during this period 32 percent of respondents identified themselves as "conservative," 40 percent, "moderate," and 21 percent, "liberal." Figure 1–5 shows the "conservative" responses in each state: The most conservative state in terms of voter self-identification was Utah, followed by Indiana. The most liberal states were Massachusetts, New York, and New Jersey. It is interesting to note that ideological identification of the voters in the states correlates very closely with measures of policy liberalism and conservatism.

RACE AND ETHNICITY

States differ in the racial and ethnic composition of their populations. These differences account for much of the variation in the politics of states and cities throughout the nation.

Figure 1–5
LIBERALISM AND CONSERVATISM

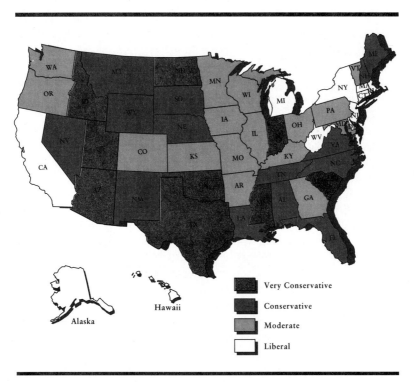

<hr />

[7]Gerald C. Wright, Robert S. Erikson, and John P. McIver, "Public Opinion and Policy Liberalism in the American States," *American Journal of Political Science,* 31 (November 1987), 980–1001.

Later we will be examining racial and ethnic cleavages in voting behavior and political participation (Chapter 4), state legislative politics (Chapter 6), community politics (Chapter 11), and civil rights policy (Chapter 14).

AFRICAN AMERICANS   In 1900, most African Americans (89.7 percent) were concentrated in the South. But World Wars I and II provided job opportunities in large cities of the Northeast and Midwest. Blacks could not cast ballots in most southern counties, but they could "vote with their feet." The migration of blacks from the rural South to the urban North was one of the largest internal migrations in our history. By 1990 only 53 percent of blacks lived in the South—still more than any other region but less of a concentration than earlier in American history. Today the nation's 33 million blacks comprise 12.5 percent of the total population of the United States. The distribution of blacks among the fifty states is shown in Table 1–2.

African American candidates have been increasingly successful in winning city and county offices and state legislative seats in the southern states and in big cities throughout the nation. (See Chapter 4 for a discussion of voting rights laws.) The largest number of black elected officials are found in the southern states. In 1989 the nation's first elected black governor, Douglas Wilder, moved into Virginia's statehouse, once the office of Jefferson Davis, president of the Confederacy. Black candidates have also been increasingly successful in winning election in large cities throughout the nation. Later in this book we will describe black representation in city councils (see Chapter 11) and in state legislatures (see Chapter 6), as well as civil rights policy (see Chapter 14).

HISPANICS   The term *Hispanic* refers to persons of Spanish-speaking ancestry and culture, regardless of race, and includes Mexican Americans, Cuban Americans, and Puerto Ricans. Today there are an estimated 27 million Hispanics or 10.1 percent of the U.S population. The largest subgroup are Mexican Americans, some of whom are descendants of citizens living in Mexican territory that was annexed to the United States in 1848 (see Figure 1–1), but most of them have come to the United States in accelerating numbers in recent years. The largest Mexican American populations are found in Texas, Arizona, New Mexico, and California (see Table 1–2). The second largest subgroup are the Puerto Ricans, many of whom retain ties to the Commonwealth and move back and forth from the island to the mainland, especially New York City. The third largest subgroup are Cubans, most of whom have fled from Castro's Cuba. They live mainly in the Miami metropolitan area. While these groups have different experiences, they share a common language and culture, and they have encountered similar difficulties in making government responsive to their needs (see Chapter 14).

NATIVE AMERICANS   It is estimated that 10 million Native Americans once inhabited the North American continent. By 1900 the Native American population had been reduced to barely a half million by wars, diseases, and forced privations inflicted upon them. Today Native Americans number about 2 million or slightly less than 1 percent of the U.S. population. Approximately half live on semiautonomous reservations in 280 federally recognized tribes, and in hundreds of native villages in Alaska. The largest concentrations of Native Americans are found in New Mexico, Oklahoma, South Dakota, Montana, and Arizona, as well as Alaska (see Chapter 14).

THE POLITICS OF IMMIGRATION

America is a nation of immigrants, from the first "boat people," the Pilgrims, to the latest Cuban *balseros* (rafters). Americans are proud of their immigrant heritage and the freedom and opportunity the nation has extended to generations of "huddled masses yearning to be free"—words emblazoned upon the Statue of Liberty in New York's harbor.

Most immigrants come to the United States for economic opportunity. Most personify the traits we typically think of as American—opportunism, ambition, perseverance, initiative, and a willingness to work hard. As immigrants have always done, they frequently take dirty, low-paying, thankless jobs that other Americans shun. When they open their own businesses, they often do so in blighted, crime-ridden neighborhoods long since abandoned by other entrepreneurs.

NATIONAL IMMIGRATION POLICY   Immigration policy is a responsibility of the national government. Today federal law recognizes several categories of legal immigrants in the United States:

- *Legal immigrants* (also "lawful permanent residents" or "permanent resident aliens"). These immigrants are admitted to the United States under a ceiling of 675,000 per year, with some admitted on the basis of job skills but most coming as family members of persons legally residing in the United States. Legal immigrants may work in the United States, and apply for citizenship after five years of continuous residence; they are eligible for all federal assistance programs.
- *Refugees and asylees.* These are persons admitted to the United States because of "a well-founded fear of persecution because of race, religion, nationality, political opinion, or membership in a social group." (Refugees are persons not yet in the United States; asylees are persons who have already arrived and apply for refugee protection.) They may work in the United States and are eligible for all federal assistance programs.
- *Parolees* (or persons enjoying "temporary protected status"). These are persons admitted to the United States for humanitarian or medical reasons or whose countries are faced with natural or man-made disasters.
- *Legalized aliens* (also called "amnesty aliens"). These formerly illegal aliens were given legal status (amnesty) under the Immigration Reform and Control Act of 1986. To qualify, they must show some evidence of having resided in the United States since 1982. They may work in the United States and are eligible for all federal assistance programs after five years.
- *Non-immigrants* (also "nonresident legal aliens"). Over 20 million people are awarded visas to enter the United States for pleasure and business. Time limits are placed on these visas usually by stamping a passport. Additionally, students, temporary workers and trainees, transient aliens, and foreign officials are eligible for temporary visas.

ILLEGAL IMMIGRATION   In theory, a sovereign nation should be able to maintain secure borders, but in practice the United States has been unwilling and unable to do so. Estimates of illegal immigration vary wildly, from the official U.S. Immigration and Naturalization Service (INS) estimate of 400,000 per year (about 45 percent of the legal immigration), to unofficial estimates ranging up to three million per year. The INS estimates that about 4 million illegal immigrants currently reside in the United States; unofficial estimates range up to ten million or more. Many illegal immigrants slip across U.S. borders or enter ports with false documentation, while many more overstay tourist or student visas (and are not counted by the INS as illegal immigrants).[8]

Border control is an expensive and difficult, but not impossible, task. Localized experiments in border enforcement have indicated that illegal immigration can be reduced by half or more with significant increases in INS personnel and technology. However, political opposition to increased border enforcement and reduced immigration comes from a variety of sources. Large numbers of Americans identify with the aspirations of people striving to come to America, whether legally or illegally. Many Americans still have relatives living abroad who may wish to immigrate. Hispanic groups have been especially concerned about immigration enforcement efforts that may lead to discrimination against all Hispanic Americans. Powerful groups that benefit from the availability of illegal immigrants, such as agriculture and the restaurant, clothing, and hospital industries, lobby in Washington to weaken enforcement efforts. Some employers prefer hiring illegal immigrants ("los indocumentados") because they are willing to work at hard jobs for low pay and few if any benefits. Foreign governments, especially Mexico, have also protested U.S. enforcement policies.

IMMIGRATION AND FEDERALISM   Although the federal government has exclusive power over immigration policy, its decisions have very significant effects on states and communities—on their governmental budgets, on the use of their public services, and even on their social character. Immigration is by no means uniform across the states. On the contrary, legal and illegal immigration are concentrated in a relatively few states. California, Hawaii, New York, Florida, and Texas have the highest proportions of legal immigrants among their populations. And these states, together with Arizona, New Mexico, Colorado, Illinois, and New Jersey, probably have the highest numbers of illegal immigrants as well. Moreover, the populations of particular cities—such as Los Angeles, Miami, El Paso, and San Antonio—may be one-third to one-half foreign born.

Federal immigration policies impose expensive unfunded mandates on the states. (For a general discussion of unfunded mandates, see Chapter 3.) Legal immigrants are fully entitled to all public assistance programs, including Aid to Families with Dependent Children, Supplemental Security Income, unemployment insurance, Medicaid, food stamps, school lunch, Head Start, job training, and housing assistance. (Although family "sponsors" may have pledged support of immigrants, and immigrants who become a "public charge" may be deported legally, these provisions of the law are almost never enforced.) Moreover, the U.S. Supreme Court has mandated that state and local governments may not exclude either legal *or illegal* immigrants from public education, and by implication from any other benefits or services available to citizens.[9] Thus, federal immigration policy heavily impacts state and local budgets, especially in California, Florida, Texas, and other states with disproportionate numbers of immigrants. Indeed, these states have tried unsuccessfully to sue the federal government to recover the costs of providing services to immigrants.

CALIFORNIA'S PROPOSITION 187   California's Proposition 187 in 1994 set off a national debate over immigration. Placed on the ballot by citizen initiative, Pro-

---

[8]American Security Council, *The Illegal Immigration Crisis* (Washington, DC: ASC, 1994).

[9]*Plyler v. Doe* 457 U.S. 202 (1982).

position 187 denies public education, nonemergency health care, and social service benefits to illegal aliens in that state. The initiative was supported by Republican Governor
Pete Wilson and opposed by his Democratic opponent, Kathleen Brown. Wilson claimed
that the state spent over $2 billion per year providing public support of over 2 million ille-
gal aliens living in California. Hispanic groups in the state feared that the passage of
Proposition 187 would lead to discrimination against legal immigrants and perhaps Hispanic American citizens generally. The denial of education and health care to children
was branded as especially mean-spirited and cruel. Following a highly spirited and well-
publicized contest over the initiative, California voters approved it by a solid 59 to 41 percent. The constitutionality of the measure is questionable—the Fourteenth Amendment
declares that no state shall "deny to any *person* within its jurisdiction the equal protection of the laws"—and its implementation has been halted by federal courts. But the vote
sent a loud message to Washington: that Californians resented the national government's
mandating state funding of benefits for illegal immigration that the national government
itself failed to control.

THE "NATIONALIZATION" OF THE STATES

We know that states differ in their histories, economies, growth rates, and ethnic and
racial compositions. Yet over time these differences are diminishing—a process that has
been labeled the "nationalization" of states.

Over time the states have become more similar in levels of economic development. Income differences among the states have diminished. As industry, people, and money
moved from the Northeast and Midwest to the South, the historic disadvantage of the
South gradually diminished.

Americans are the most mobile people in the world. Four out of every ten people move
within a five-year period! Nearly one in ten moves to a different state. As people move
about the country, distinct cultural and ethnic differences of the regions diminish. Even regional accents become less pronounced. The impact of national television, motion pictures,
and the record industry adds to the "homogenization" of state and regional cultures.

The political systems of the states are no longer as distinct as they were historically.
Years ago the Democratic party could count on "the Solid South." The more recent
political era has witnessed a stunning reversal of the South's traditional Democratic
politics, as the Republican party has grown dramatically in the region. Today the GOP
can count on winning most of the Southern states in presidential elections, and for
the first time in 1994 Republicans captured a majority of Congressional seats from the
South.

Yet the South remains "the nation's most distinctive region."[10] Eleven Southern states
fought the national government in a bloody civil war over a century ago. Slavery shaped
the early politics and economics of the South, and racial concerns have continued to influence Southern life more than in any other region. And the South remains distinctive in
many other respects, from the strength of religious fundamentalism and the popularity of
country music, to a greater sense of locality and an impressive literary tradition.

---

[10]Dewey W. Gratham, *The South in Modern America* (New York: HarperCollins, 1994), p. 6.

Although the states are gradually becoming more similar over time, in many respects there is still "enough" variation to merit comparative analysis. Interestingly, many important policy differences between the states are *not* diminishing. Throughout this book we will make comparisons among the states, and also among cities, in order to better understand politics, economics, and public policy throughout the nation.

POLICY RESPONSIBILITIES OF STATES AND COMMUNITIES

Despite the glamour of national politics, states and communities carry on the greatest volume of public business, settle the greatest number of political conflicts, make the majority of policy decisions, and direct the bulk of public programs. They have the major responsibility for maintaining domestic law and order, for educating the children, for moving Americans from place to place, and for caring for the poor and the ill. They regulate the provision of water, gas, electric, and other public utilities, share in the regulation of insurance and banking enterprise, regulate the use of land, and supervise the sale of ownership of property. Their courts settle by far the greatest number of civil and criminal cases. In short, states and communities are by no means unimportant political systems.

EDUCATION   Education is the most important responsibility of state and local governments and the most costly of all state–local functions (see Figure 1–6). States and

Figure 1–6
HOW STATE AND LOCAL GOVERNMENTS SPEND THEIR MONEY

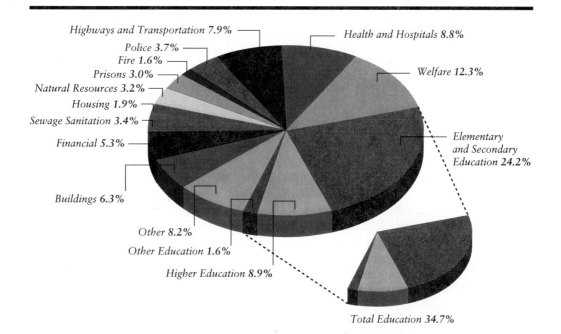

Highways and Transportation 7.9%
Police 3.7%
Fire 1.6%
Prisons 3.0%
Natural Resources 3.2%
Housing 1.9%
Sewage Sanitation 3.4%
Financial 5.3%
Buildings 6.3%
Other 8.2%
Other Education 1.6%
Higher Education 8.9%
Health and Hospitals 8.8%
Welfare 12.3%
Elementary and Secondary Education 24.2%
Total Education 34.7%

communities are responsible for decisions about what should be taught in the public schools, how much should be spent on the education of each child, how many children should be in each classroom, how much teachers should be paid, how responsibilities in education should be divided between state and local governments, what qualifications teachers must have, what types of rates and taxes shall be levied for education, and many other decisions that affect the life of every child in America. Support for higher education, including funds for state and community colleges and universities, is now a major expenditure of state governments. The federal government has never contributed more than 10 percent of the nation's total expenditures for education.

TRANSPORTATION   Transportation—more particularly, highways—is the second most costly function of state and local governments. There are over 3 million miles of surfaced roads in America, and over 180 million registered motor vehicles in the nation. States and communities must make decisions about the allocation of money for streets and highways, sources of funds for highway revenue, the extent of gasoline and motor vehicle taxation, the regulation of traffic on the highways, the location of highways, the determination of construction policies, the division of responsibility between state and local governments for highway financing administration, the division of highway funds between rural and urban areas, and other important issues in highway politics. While the federal government is deeply involved in highway construction, federal grants for highways amount to less than 30 percent of all expenditures for highways.

HEALTH AND WELFARE   States and communities continue to carry a heavy burden in the field of health and welfare—despite an extensive system of federal grants-in-aid for this purpose. States and communities must make decisions about participation in federal programs and allocate responsibilities among themselves for health and welfare programs. While the federal government itself administers Social Security and Medicare, state governments administer the largest public assistance programs—Aid to Families with Dependent Children (AFDC), Medicaid, and food stamps, as well as unemployment compensation. Within the broad outlines of federal policy, states and communities decide the amount of money appropriated for health and welfare purposes, the benefits to be paid to recipients, the rules of eligibility, and the means by which the programs will be administered. States and communities may choose to grant assistance beyond the limits supported by the national government.

CRIME   States and communities have the principal responsibility for public safety in America. State police have important highway safety responsibilities and cooperate with local authorities in the apprehension of criminals. However, community police forces continue to be the principal instrument of law enforcement and public safety. Local governments employ over a quarter of a million police in the United States today, and almost as many firefighters. Sheriffs and their deputies are still the principal enforcement and arresting officers in rural counties. States and communities also have the principal responsibility for maintaining prisons and correctional institutions. Each year over 2 million Americans are prisoners in jails, police stations, juvenile homes, or penitentiaries. More than 90 percent of these prisoners are in state and local rather than federal institutions.

CIVIL RIGHTS   The national government has defined a national system of civil rights, but these rights cannot become realities without the support of state and local authorities. States and communities must deal directly with racial problems, such as racial isolation in the public schools, job discrimination, and the existence of segregated housing patterns in the cities. They must also deal directly with the consequences of racial tension, including violence.

PHYSICAL ENVIRONMENT   Local governments have the principal responsibility for our physical environment. They must plan streets, parks, and commercial, residential, and industrial areas and provide essential public utilities for the community. The waste materials of human beings—rubbish, garbage, and sewage—exceed one ton every day per person. The task of disposal is an immense one; the problem is not only collecting it, but finding ways to dispose of it. If it is incinerated, it contributes to air pollution; and if it is carried off into streams, rivers, or lakes, it contributes to water pollution. Thus, communities are largely responsible for two of the nation's most pressing problems—air and water pollution.

TAXATION   To pay for these programs, states and communities must make important decisions about taxation: They must decide about levels of taxation and what tax burdens their citizens can carry. They must determine how much to rely upon income, sales, or property taxation. States and communities must raise over $600 billion per year and at the same time compete with one another to attract industry and commerce.

"STATES," "DISTRICTS," AND "TERRITORIES"

How did the states become states? The original thirteen states did so by ratifying the U.S. Constitution. The first new states to be admitted were Vermont in 1791 and Kentucky in 1792. States that sought admission began by petitioning Congress to allow them to elect delegates and draw up a state constitution. The Congress granted this permission in a series of enabling acts. Later, when the territorial voters approved the new constitution, the territory formally applied for admission and presented its constitution to Congress for approval. Congress accepted the application by a joint resolution of both houses, and a new star was added to the flag. The last admissions were Alaska and Hawaii in 1959.

Of course, from a political perspective, admission was not always an easy process. Long before the Civil War (or "The War Between the States" as it is still called in parts of the Old South), states were admitted roughly in pairs of free and slave states, so as not to upset the delicate balance in the U.S. Senate. Iowa and Wisconsin were admitted as free states in 1846 and 1848, while Florida and Texas were admitted in 1845 as slave states. When California was admitted as a free state in the famous Compromise of 1850, the balance was tilted toward the free states. The balance was further tipped when Minnesota was admitted in 1858 and Oregon in 1859. The Civil War followed in 1861.

Eleven states seceded from the Union that year—Alabama, Arkansas, Florida, Georgia, Louisiana, Mississippi, North Carolina, South Carolina (December 1860), Tennessee, Texas, and Virginia. Although the Supreme Court later voided the acts of secession as unconstitutional, Congress required all of these states to reapply for admission to the

Union. These states were under military occupation by United States troops. The military governments drew up new state constitutions, registered black voters, and sent black representatives to Congress. Congress required these governments to ratify the Thirteenth, Fourteenth, and Fifteenth Amendments in order to be readmitted to the Union. The "reconstructed" southern state governments did so, and all were readmitted by 1870.

When Texas was admitted in 1845, Congress granted it a special privilege: The state might, if it wished, divide itself into four states. This provision recognized that Texas was a separate nation when it chose to become a state. A conservative Congress initially rejected Arizona's constitution because it included the progressive notion of popular recall of judges; the state obligingly changed its constitution, was admitted in 1912, and then promptly amended the constitution to put recall back in. Once admitted, there was nothing the Congress could do about Arizona's recalcitrance.

THE DISTRICT OF COLUMBIA   The U.S. Constitution, Article I, Section 8, specified in 1787 that "the seat of the government of the United States" shall be in a "district not exceeding ten square miles" ceded to the federal government by the states (Maryland and Virginia). The District of Columbia was to be governed by the Congress. In defense of a separate district, Alexander Hamilton wrote:

> [Congressional control] of the seat of government . . . is an indispensable necessity. Without it not only the public authority may be insulted and its proceedings interrupted with impunity, but a dependence of the members of the general government of the state comprehending the seat of government . . . might bring the national councils an imputation of awe or influence . . . dishonorable to the government.[11]

Hamilton's language is stiff and formal, but his meaning is clear: Making Washington a state would generate undue local pressure on Congress.

Politically, Washington is heavily Democratic, liberal, and black. Its 607,000 residents are likely to support larger social welfare programs, an expanded bureaucracy, and increased federal spending. Opponents of these policies are not likely to be enthusiastic about DC representation in Congress.

The Twenty-Third Amendment, ratified in 1961, gives Washington full participation in presidential elections. Congress has also granted by law full home rule to the city so it has its own elected mayor and city council. In 1978, Congress passed another constitutional amendment that would grant the District full congressional representation and the right to vote on ratification of future constitutional amendments. However, the necessary three-quarters of the states failed to ratify this amendment. So while DC residents can vote in presidential elections, they are not represented by voting members in the U.S. Senate or House of Representatives.

Having failed to gain congressional representation by constitutional amendment, District residents and their supporters in Congress turned to a new strategy—calling on Congress to admit the District to the Union as a state. (While the Constitution specifies that Congress shall govern over "such District not exceeding ten miles square . . . as the seat of the government," presumably Congress could satisfy this constitutional mandate by reducing "the seat of the government" to a few blocks surrounding the capitol, while ad-

---

[11]Alexander Hamilton, *The Federalist*, Number 43.

mitting the bulk of the District as a state.) This strategy not only reduces the barrier in Congress from a two-thirds vote to a simple majority vote of both houses, but, more importantly, eliminates the need to secure ratification by three-quarters of the states. Nonetheless, so far Congress has refused to vote for District statehood (presumably the state would be named "Columbia").

THE COMMONWEALTH OF PUERTO RICO   Over 3 million people live on the Caribbean island of Puerto Rico. They are American citizens, and the government of Puerto Rico resembles a state government, with a constitution and an elected governor and legislature. However, Puerto Rico has no voting members of the Congress and no electoral votes in presidential elections.

The population of Puerto Rico is greater than that of twenty states; over 1 million Puerto Ricans have migrated over the years to the U.S. mainland, particularly to New York City. Median family income in Puerto Rico is the highest in the Caribbean, but it is only half that of the poorest state in the United States. The population is largely Spanish-speaking; as citizens they can move anywhere in the United States; and they have been subject to the draft in wartime. The United States seized Puerto Rico in 1898 in the Spanish-American War. In 1950, its voters chose to become a "commonwealth," and self-governing commonwealth status was officially recognized in 1952. In a 1967 plebiscite, 60 percent of Puerto Ricans voted to remain a commonwealth, 39 percent voted for statehood, and less than 1 percent voted for independence. Recent efforts to schedule another plebiscite have floundered over the specifics of each option—commonwealth, statehood, or independence.

Under "commonwealth" status Puerto Ricans pay no U.S. income tax, although local taxes are substantial. Yet, they receive all of the benefits that U.S. citizens are entitled to— Social Security, public assistance, food stamps, Medicaid, Medicare, and so forth. If Puerto Rico chose to become a state, its voters could participate in presidential and congressional elections; but its taxpayers would not enjoy the same favorable cost-benefit ratio they enjoy under commonwealth status. Some Puerto Ricans fear that statehood would dilute the island's cultural identity and force English upon them as the national language.

Statehood would grant two U.S. senators and perhaps six U.S. representatives to the island. Most of these new members would be Democrats; the island's majority party, the Popular Democratic party, is closely identified with the Democratic party. But the island's New Progressive party, identified with the Republican party, supports statehood, and many GOP leaders believe their party should appeal to Hispanic voters. If Puerto Ricans were to choose independence, a new constitution for the Republic of Puerto Rico would be drawn up by the islanders themselves.

U.S. TERRITORIES   The U.S. Virgin Islands were purchased from Denmark in 1917. Residents of the beautiful islands in the Caribbean are predominantly black, English-speaking, and poorer than most Americans on the mainland. The United States acquired Samoa and Guam from Spain in 1898; and after World War II, the United States held Wake, Midway, and the United Nations Trusteeships of the Caroline, Marianas, and Marshall Islands (the locations of some of the heaviest fighting in the Pacific). In 1903 the United States encouraged a revolution and secession of Panama from Columbia, so that the new Panamanian nation would conclude an agreement to build a canal and govern a zone five miles wide on both sides of the canal. U.S. "Canal Zone" governance was ended by a new treaty with Panama in 1978.

TRIVIA
WHAT'S IN A NAME: THE AMERICAN STATES

Alabama—Indian for tribal town, later a tribe (Alabamas or Alibamons) of the Creek confederacy.

Alaska—Russian version of Aleutian (Eskimo) word, *alakshak,* for "peninsula." "great lands," or "land that is not an island."

Arizona—Spanish version of Pimo Indian word for "little spring place," or Aztec *arizuma,* meaning "silver-bearing."

Arkansas—French variant of Kansas, a Sioux Indian name for "south wind people."

California—bestowed by the Spanish conquistadors (possibly by Cortez). It was the name of an imaginary island, and earthly paradise, in "Las Serges de Esplandian," a Spanish romance written by Montalvo in 1510. Baja California (Lower California, in Mexico) was first visited by the Spanish in 1533. The present U.S. state was called Alta (Upper) California.

Colorado—Spanish, red, first applied to Colorado River.

Connecticut—From Mohican and other Algonquin words meaning "long river place."

Delaware—Named for Lord De La Warr, early governor of Virginia; first applied to river, then to Indian tribe (Lenni-Lenape), and the state.

District of Columbia—For Columbus, 1791.

Florida—Named by Ponce de Leon on Pascua Florida, "Flowery Easter," on Easter Sunday, 1513.

Georgia—For King George II of England by James Oglethorpe, colonial administrator, 1732.

Hawaii—Possibly derived from native word for homeland, Hawaiki or Owhyhee.

Idaho—A coined name from an invented Indian meaning: "gem of the mountains," originally suggested for the Pike's Peak mining territory (Colorado), then applied to the new mining territory of the Pacific Northwest. Another theory suggests Idaho may be a Kiowa Apache term for the Comanche.

Illinois—French for Illini or land of Illini, Algonquin word meaning men or warriors.

Indiana—Means "land of the Indians."

Iowa—Indian word variously translated as "one who puts to sleep" or "beautiful land."

Kansas—Sioux word for "south wind people."

Kentucky—Indian word variously translated as "dark and bloody ground," "meadow land," and "land of tomorrow."

Louisiana—Part of territory called Louisiana by Sieur de La Salle for French King Louis XIV.

Maine—From Maine, ancient French province. Also: descriptive, referring to the mainland in distinction to the many coastal islands.

Maryland—For Queen Henrietta Maria, wife of Charles I of England.

Massachusetts—From Indian tribe named after "large hill place" identified by Capt. John Smith as near Milton, MA.

Michigan—From Chippewa words *mici gama,* meaning "great water," after the lake of the same name.

Minnesota—From Dakota Sioux word meaning "cloudy water" or "sky-tinted water" of the Minnesota River.

Mississippi—Probably Chippewa; *mici zibi,* "great river" or "gathering-in of all the waters." Also: Algonquin word, "Messipi."

Missouri—Algonquin Indian tribe named after Missouri River, meaning "muddy water."

Montana—Latin or Spanish for "mountainous."

Nebraska—from Omaha or Otos Indian word meaning "broad water" or "flat river," describing the Platte River.

Nevada—Spanish, meaning snow-clad.

New Hampshire—Named in 1629 by Capt. John Mason of Plymouth Council for his home county in England.

New Jersey—The Duke of York, 1664, gave a patent to John Berkeley and Sir George Carteret to be called Nova Caesaria, or New Jersey, after England's Isle of Jersey.

New Mexico—Spaniards in Mexico applied term to land north and west of Rio Grande in the sixteenth century.

New York—For Duke of York and Albany who received patent to New Netherland from his brother Charles II and sent an expedition to capture it, 1664.

North Carolina—In 1619 Charles I gave a large patent to Sir Robert Heath to be called Province of Carolana, from Carolus, Latin name for Charles. A new patent was granted by Charles II to Earl of Clarendon and others. Divided into North and South Carolina, 1710.

North Dakota—Dakota is Sioux for friend or ally.

Ohio—Iroquois word for "fine or good river."

Oklahoma—Choctaw coined word meaning red man, proposed by Rev. Allen Wright, Choctaw-speaking Indian.

Oregon—Origin unknown. One theory holds that the name may have been derived from that part of the Wisconsin River shown on a 1715 French map as "Ouaricon-sint."

Pennsylvania—William Penn, the Quaker, who was made full proprietor by King Charles II in 1681, suggested Sylvania, or woodland, for his tract. The king's government owed Penn's father, Admiral William Penn, £16,000, and the land being granted in part settlement, the king added the Penn to Sylvania, against the desires of the modest proprietor, in honor of the admiral.

Puerto Rico—Spanish for Rich Port.

Rhode Island—Exact origin is unknown. One theory notes that Giovanni de Verazano recorded an island about the size of Rhodes in the Mediterranean in 1524, but others believe the state was named Roode Eylandt by Adriaen Block, Dutch explorer, because of its red clay.

South Carolina—See North Carolina.

South Dakota—See North Dakota.

Tennessee—Tanasi was the name of Cherokee villages on the Little Tennessee River. From 1784 to 1788 this was the State of Franklin, or Frankland.

Texas—Variant of word used by Caddo and other Indians meaning friends or allies, and applied to them by the Spanish in eastern Texas. Also written texias, tejas, teysas.

Utah—From a Navajo word meaning upper, or higher up, as applied to a Shoshone tribe called Ute. Spanish form is Yutta, English Uta or Utah. Proposed name Deseret, "land of honeybees," from Book of Mormon, was rejected by Congress.

Vermont—From French words *vert*/green, and *mont*/mountain. The Green Mountains were said to have been named by Samuel de Champlain. The Green Mountain Boys were Gen. Stark's men in the Revolution. When the state was formed, 1777, Dr. Thomas Young suggested combining *vert* and *mont* into Vermont.

Virginia—Named by Sir Walter Raleigh, who fitted out the expedition of 1584, in honor of Queen Elizabeth, the Virgin Queen of England.

Washington—Named after George Washington. When the bill creating the Territory of Columbia was introduced in the 32d Congress, the name was changed to Washington because of the existence of the District of Columbia.

West Virginia—So named when western counties of Virginia refused to secede from the United States, 1863.

Wisconsin—An Indian name, spelled Quisconsin and Mesconsing by early chroniclers. Believed to mean "grassy place" in Chippewa. Congress made it Wisconsin.

Wyoming—The word was taken from Wyoming Valley, PA, which was the site of an Indian massacre and became widely known by Campbell's poem "Gertrude of Wyoming." In Algonquin "large prairie place."

Source: By permission of The Smithsonian Institution Press, Smithsonian Institution, Washington, DC.

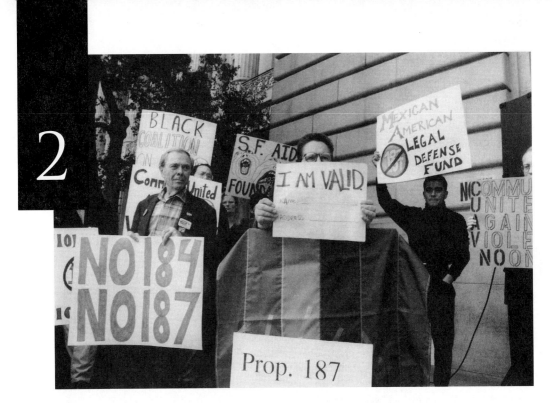

DEMOCRACY AND CONSTITUTIONALISM IN THE STATES

CONSTITUTIONAL GOVERNMENT IN THE STATES

Constitutions govern governments. They set forth the structure and organization of government; they distribute powers among branches of government; they prescribe the rules by which decisions will be made. Most important, constitutions limit the powers of government and protect the rights of citizens. All fifty states have written constitutions.

LIMITED GOVERNMENT   The true meaning of constitutionalism is limited government. Today most of the world's governments, including even the most authoritarian regimes, have written constitutions that describe the formal structure of government. But the constitutions of authoritarian regimes rarely place any restrictions on the powers of government. In the English and American political heritage, constitutionalism means that the power of government over the individual is clearly limited, that there are some aspects of life that even majorities cannot regulate, and that government itself is restrained by a higher law. Constitutional government places individual liberty beyond the reach of governments, even democratic governments. Thus if a majority of voters wanted

27

to prohibit communists, or atheists, or racists, from writing or speaking or organizing themselves, they could not do so under a constitutional government that protected free speech and press and assembly.

All fifty state constitutions limit the powers of state government and protect individual liberty. While we have come to rely principally on the U.S. Constitution for the protection of individual liberty, every state constitution also contains a bill of rights that protects individuals in each state from deprivations of personal liberty by their state government. Most of these state constitutional guarantees merely reiterate rights guaranteed to all Americans in the U.S. Constitution, but some state documents extend rights *beyond* the federal guarantees.

LEGAL STATUS   State *constitutions* are the supreme law of the state. They take precedence over any state *law* in conflict with them. Since constitutions govern the activities of governments themselves, they are considered more fundamental than the ordinary laws passed by governments.

The U.S. Constitution is the *supreme law* of the nation. State constitutions take precedence over state law, but they are subordinate to the U.S. Constitution and the laws of the United States. The U.S. Constitution mentions state constitutions only once, and it does so to assert the supremacy of the U.S. Constitution and the laws and treaties of the United States. Article VI states:

> This constitution, and the laws of the United States which shall be made in pursuance thereof; and all treaties made, or which shall be made, under the authority of the United States, shall be the supreme law of the land; and the judges in every state shall be bound thereby, anything in the constitution or laws of any state to the contrary notwithstanding.

ORIGINS OF WRITTEN CONSTITUTIONS   Probably no other people in the world are more devoted to the idea of written constitutions than are Americans. This devotion has deep roots in national traditions. In 1215 a group of English lords forced King John to sign a document, later known as the Magna Carta, that guaranteed them certain feudal rights and set a precedent for constitutional government. Although the British political tradition eventually rejected formal written constitutions, the idea of a written constitution was strongly reinforced by the experience in the American colonies. The colonies were legally established by charters given to companies establishing settlements in America. These charters became more elaborate as the colonial ventures succeeded, and depending upon a written code for the regulation of government organization and operation became strongly entrenched in the American colonies.

COLONIAL HISTORY   The charters, or "constitutions," were granted by royal action, either by recognizing proprietary rights, as in Maryland, Delaware, and Pennsylvania, or by granting royal commissions to companies to establish governments, as in Virginia, Massachusetts, New Hampshire, New York, New Jersey, Georgia, and North and South Carolina. Only in Connecticut and Rhode Island was there much popular participation in early constitution making. In these two colonies, royal charters were granted directly to the colonists themselves, who participated in drawing up the charter for submission to the Crown. The important point is that these charters, whatever their origin, were present in all the colonies, and many political traditions and expectations grew up around them.

All the colonies were subject to royal control. Yet colonists looked to their charters for protection against British interference in colonial affairs. This was particularly true in Connecticut and Rhode Island, which had elected governors and legislatures whose acts were not subjected to a royal governor's veto, nor sent to England for approval. The political importance of these early charters is illustrated by the conflict over the Fundamental Orders of Connecticut. In 1685 King James issued an order for the repeal of Connecticut's charter. In 1687 Sir Edmund Androse went to Hartford and in the name of the Crown declared the government dissolved. The charter was not surrendered, however, but hidden by Captain John Wadsworth in an oak tree, which is now displayed for sightseers. Immediately after the English revolution of 1688, the document was taken out of the "Charter Oak" and used again as the fundamental law of the colony. Succeeding British monarchs silently permitted this colonial defiance. After the Declaration of Independence, new constitutions were written in eleven states; Connecticut retained its charter as the fundamental law until 1818, and Rhode Island kept its charter until 1842. The colonial experience, together with the earlier English heritage, firmly implanted the tradition of written constitutions.

STATE CONSTITUTIONAL POLITICS   Theoretically, constitutional decision making is deciding *how to decide*. It is deciding on the rules for policy making; it is not policy making itself. Policies are to be decided later, according to the rules set forth in a constitution.

But realistically, all state constitutions not only specify organizations and processes of decision making, they also undertake to determine many substantive policy questions. Unlike the U.S. Constitution, state constitutions contain many policy mandates on topics as diverse as tax rates, utility regulation, labor–management relations, insurance regulation, debt limits, educational funding, gambling, and a host of other policy matters. In nearly every election, voters are asked to decide on proposed amendments to their state constitutions. Most of these amendments deal with policy questions about which the voters have little knowledge or information. The result, of course, is that most state constitutions have become ponderous tomes that look more like law books than constitutions. While the U.S. Constitution contains only about 8,700 words, the average state constitution contains 26,000, and some run to over 100,000 (see Table 2–1). Length itself is not the problem, but rather that these constitutions are laden with detailed policy decisions.

INTEREST GROUP INFLUENCE   Why have so many policy mandates crept into state constitutions? Inasmuch as constitutions govern the actions of governors, legislators, executive agencies, and courts, many special interest groups as well as citizen movements have sought to place their own policy preferences in constitutions. This places these preferences beyond the immediate reach of government officials, who are bound by constitutional mandates. If a policy preference is enacted into state law, it can be changed by ordinary actions of the legislature and governor. But if a policy preference is written into the state constitution, it can be changed only by extraordinary procedures—for most states a two-thirds vote in both houses of the legislature and majority approval of the

Table 2–1
GENERAL INFORMATION ON STATE CONSTITUTIONS

State or Other Jurisdiction	Number of Constitutions*	Dates of Adoption	Effective Date of Present Constitution	Estimated Length (Number of Words)	Number of Amendments	
					SUBMITTED TO VOTERS	ADOPTED
Alabama	6	1819, 1861, 1865, 1868, 1875, 1901	1901	174,000	783	556
Alaska	1	1956	1959	16,675[a]	32	23
Arizona	1	1911	1912	28,876	215	119
Arkansas	5	1836, 1861, 1864, 1868, 1874	1874	40,720	171	81[b]
California	2	1849, 1879	1879	33,350	814	485
Colorado	1	1876	1876	45,679	254	124
Connecticut	4	1818[c], 1965	1965	9,564	29	28
Delaware	4	1776, 1792, 1831, 1897	1897	19,000	(d)	123
Florida	6	1839, 1861, 1865, 1868, 1886, 1968	1969	25,100	92	65
Georgia	10	1777, 1789, 1798, 1861, 1865, 1868, 1877, 1945, 1976, 1982	1983	25,000	52[e]	39
Hawaii	1[f]	1950	1959	17,453	102	86
Idaho	1	1889	1890	21,500	189	109
Illinois	4	1818, 1848, 1870, 1970	1971	13,200	14	8
Indiana	2	1816, 1851	1851	9,377[a]	70	38
Iowa	2	1846, 1857	1857	12,500	52	49[g]
Kansas	1	1859	1861	11,865	118	90[g]
Kentucky	4	1792, 1799, 1850, 1891	1891	23,500	65	32
Louisiana	11	1812, 1845, 1852, 1861, 1864, 1868, 1879, 1898, 1913, 1921, 1974	1975	51,448	92	54

Maine	1	1819	1820	13,500	192	162[h]
Maryland	4	1776, 1851, 1864, 1867	1867	41,349	238	205[i]
Massachusetts	1	1780	1780	36,690[j]	144	117
Michigan	4	1835, 1850, 1908, 1963	1964	20,000	51	17
Minnesota	1	1857	1858	9,500	207	113
Mississippi	4	1817, 1832, 1869, 1890	1890	24,000	148	116
Missouri	4	1820, 1865, 1875, 1945	1945	42,000	132	81
Montana	2	1889, 1972	1973	11,866	32	18
Nebraska	2	1866, 1875	1875	20,048	293	197
Nevada	1	1864	1864	20,770	184	113[g]
New Hampshire	2	1776, 1784	1784	9,200	280[k]	143[k]
New Jersey	3	1776, 1844, 1947	1948	17,086	57	44
New Mexico	1	1911	1912	27,200	240	123
New York	4	1777, 1822, 1846, 1894	1895	80,000	280	213
North Carolina	3	1776, 1868, 1970	1971	11,000	35	27
North Dakota	1	1889	1889	20,564	235[l]	129[l]
Ohio	2	1802, 1851	1851	36,900	253	151
Oklahoma	1	1907	1907	68,800	293[m]	146[m]
Oregon	1	1857	1859	26,090	383[n]	(n)
Pennsylvania	5	1776, 1790, 1838, 1873, 1968(n)	1968	21,675	26	56
Rhode Island	2	1842[c]	1843	19,026[o]	102	36
South Carolina	7	1776, 1778, 1790, 1861, 1865, 1868, 1895	1896	22,500[o]	648[p]	463
South Dakota	1	1889	1889	23,300	191	99
Tennessee	3	1796, 1835, 1870	1870	15,300	55	32
Texas	5	1845, 1861, 1866, 1869, 1876	1876	76,000	518[q]	353
Utah	1	1895	1896	11,000	131	82
Vermont	3	1777, 1786, 1793	1793	6,600	208	50
Virginia	6	1776, 1830, 1851, 1869, 1902, 1970	1971	18,500	28	23
Washington	1	1889	1889	29,400	158	88
West Virginia	2	1863, 1872	1872	25,600	110	64

Table 2–1 (Continued)

State or Other Jurisdiction	Number of Constitutions*	Dates of Adoption	Effective Date of Present Constitution	Estimated Length (Number of Words)	Number of Amendments	
					Submitted to Voters	Adopted
Wisconsin	1	1848	1848	13,500	174	129g
Wyoming	1	1889	1890	31,800	102	61
American Samoa	2	1960, 1967	1967	6,000	14	7
Puerto Rico	1	1952	1952	9,281a	6	6

*The constitutions referred to in this table include those Civil War documents customarily listed by the individual states.

aActual word count.

bEight of the approved amendments have been superseded and are not printed in the current edition of the constitution. The total adopted does not include five amendments that were invalidated.

cColonial charters with some alterations served as the first constitutions in Connecticut (1638, 1662) and in Rhode Island (1663).

dProposed amendments are not submitted to the voters in Delaware.

eThe new Georgia constitution eliminates the need for local amendments, which have been a long-term problem for state constitution makers.

fAs a kingdom and a republic, Hawaii had five constitutions.

gThe figure given includes amendments approved by the voters and later nullified by the state supreme court in Iowa (three), Kansas (one), Nevada (six) and Wisconsin (two).

hThe figure does not include one amendment approved by the voters in 1967 that is inoperative until implemented by legislation.

iTwo sets of identical amendments were on the ballot and adopted in the Maryland 1992 election. The four amendments are counted as two in the table.

jThe printed constitution includes many provisions that have been annulled. The length of effective provisions is an estimated 24,122 words (12,400 annulled) in Massachusetts, and in Rhode Island before the "rewrite" of the constitution in 1986, it was 11,399 words (7,627 annulled).

kThe constitution of 1784 was extensively revised in 1792. Figures show proposals and adoptions since the constitution was adopted in 1784.

lThe figures do not include submission and approval of the constitution of 1889 itself and of Article XX; these are constitutional questions included in some counts of constitutional amendments and would add two to the figure in each column.

mThe figures include five amendments submitted to and approved by the voters which were, by decisions of the Oklahoma or U.S. Supreme Courts, rendered inoperative or ruled invalid, unconstitutional, or illegally submitted.

nCertain sections of the constitution were revised by the limited constitutional convention of 1967–68. Amendments proposed and adopted are since 1968.

oOf the estimated length, approximately two-thirds is of general statewide effect; the remainder is local amendments.

pAs of 1981, of the 626 proposed amendments submitted to the voters, 130 were of general statewide effect and 496 were local; the voters rejected 83 (12 statewide, 71 local). Of the remaining 543, the General Assembly refused to approve 100 (22 statewide, 78 local), and 443 (96 statewide, 347 local) were finally added to the constitution.

qThe number of proposed amendments to the Texas Constitution exclude three proposed by the legislature but not placed on the ballot.

Source: Book of the States, 1994–95 (Lexington, KY: Council on State Governments, 1994). Data as of January 1, 1994.

voters in a statewide referendum. So interest groups frequently strive to "constitutional-ize" their policy preferences.

CITIZENS' MOVEMENTS   Moreover, grass-roots citizen movements in the United States have frequently displayed a distrust of elected officials. Citizens have frequently sought to bind officials by constitutional mandates. Indeed, referenda on proposed state constitutional amendments confront voters in many states in almost every election. Over the years, specific constitutional amendments seeking to tell legislatures and governors what they can and cannot do have been accumulated in lengthy documents. The more detailed and specific a state's constitution, the more likely it is to require more amendments to meet changing circumstances over time, thus leading to an even longer document.

REFORMERS' INFLUENCE   Constitutional reformers and "good government" groups have sought for many years to take policy matters out of the state constitution. They argue that governors and legislators should not be bound by constitutional details, that they need flexibility in confronting new challenges, that state government should be strengthened, not weakened, in the modern era. These reform efforts have met with some success; newer state constitutions tend to be shorter than older ones.

GROWTH OF STATE CONSTITUTIONAL LAW   Along with interest groups and citizens' movements, lawyers and judges have also contributed to the growth of state constitutional law. In a significant number of cases, state court judges have interpreted their own constitutions independently of the U.S. Constitution regarding civil rights and other controversies (see "The New Judicial Federalism" in Chapter 8). An emerging body of state constitutional law is a reminder of the legal importance of state constitutions.[1]

STATE CONSTITUTIONS: AN OVERVIEW

BILL OF RIGHTS   All state constitutions have a bill of rights, which asserts the basic freedoms of speech, press, religion, and assembly. There are frequent references to basic procedural rights, such as the writ of habeas corpus, trial by jury, protection against double jeopardy and self-incrimination, prohibitions against ex post facto laws, imprisonment for debt, unreasonable searches and seizures, and excessive bail. Most of these protections merely duplicate the guarantees of the U.S. Constitution. However, frequently one finds in the state constitutions interesting "rights," which are not found in the national Constitution. For example, the Rhode Island Constitution prohibits discrimination on the grounds of gender, race, or handicap; Mississippi guarantees the right of victims of crime to speak in court and receive restitution; Indiana prohibits "unnecessary rigor" in punishment for crime. Seventeen state constitutions have "little ERAs"—equal rights amendments, guaranteeing sexual equality under law. Moreover, a *state* supreme court

---

[1]Advisory Commission on Intergovernmental Relations, *State Constitutional Law: Cases and Materials* (Washington, DC: ACIR, 1988).

may place a different interpretation on a state constitutional right than the *federal* courts place on the same guarantee in the U.S. Constitution.

SEPARATION OF POWERS   All state constitutions reflect the American political tradition of separation of powers, with separate legislative, executive, and judicial articles establishing these separate branches of government. Generally, however, state constitutions emphasize legislative power over executive power. The historical explanation for this is that governors were appointed by the king in most colonies and the early constitutions reflected the colonists' distaste for executive authority. Yet the fact that constitutions are usually written by legislatures, legislative commissions, or constitutional conventions that resemble legislatures may also explain why legislative power is emphasized. Finally, the curtailment of executive power may reflect the desires of important interest groups in the states, who would prefer to deal with independent boards and commissions in the executive branch rather than with a strong governor. (See Chapter 7 for further discussion.)

WEAK GOVERNORS   Whether the reasons are historical or political, the executive branches of most state governments are weakened and divided by state constitutions. Executive powers are divided between the governor and many separately elected executive officers—attorney general, secretary of state, treasurer, auditor, lieutenant governor, state school superintendent, and others. State constitutions also curtail executive authority by establishing a multitude of boards or commissions to head executive departments. Membership on these boards and commissions is generally for long overlapping terms, which are not coextensive with the term of the governor.

LEGISLATIVE POWERS   Only the Nebraska Constitution provides for a unicameral legislature. All other state legislatures are divided into an upper and a lower chamber—making a total of ninety-nine state legislative bodies. In many states the basis for apportioning these bodies is set forth in the state constitution. However, since the guarantee of the U.S. Constitution that no state shall deny to any person the "equal protection of the laws" takes precedence over state constitutions, federal courts require state legislative apportionment in both houses to meet the constitutional standard of one person, one vote. (See Chapter 6.)

LOCAL GOVERNMENTS   All state constitutions have provisions regarding the organization and powers of local government. Local governments are really subdivisions of state governments; they are not independent governmental bodies. State constitutions generally describe the organization of counties, cities, towns, townships, boroughs, school districts, and special districts. They may delegate responsibilities to them for public safety, police, fire, sanitation, sewage and refuse disposal, hospitals, streets, and public health. State constitutions may establish tax and debt limits for local governments, describe the kinds of taxes they may levy, and prescribe the way in which their funds may be spent. In the absence of constitutional provisions governing local governments, these subordinate units must rely upon state legislatures for their organization and powers. In recent years there has been a movement toward greater home rule for communities. More than half the states have provided for some semblance of home rule, which removes some of the internal affairs of communities from the intervention of state legislatures. Of course, when a "home rule" charter is granted to a community by an act of the legislature, it can be readily withdrawn or revised by the legislature. Constitutional home rule is a more secure grant of power to communities than legislative home rule. (See Chapter 9 for further discussion.)

INTEREST GROUP REGULATION   Since state constitutions take precedence over state laws and are more difficult to amend, interest groups prefer to see special protections written into the state's fundamental document. This prevents legislatures from meddling in important business affairs each legislative session. Even reformers sometimes support the inclusion of regulatory language in the state's constitution, out of fear that later lobbying efforts by business could easily change state laws. So most state constitutions include long sections on regulation of insurance, utilities, corporations, alcoholic beverages, railroads, mining, medicine, real estate, the state bar association, and so forth.

TAXATION AND FINANCE   All state constitutions have articles on taxation and finance. Frequently these place severe restrictions on the taxing power of state and local governments. Taxpayer groups distrust state legislatures and wherever possible seek to restrict taxing powers by constitutional mandate. Many referenda votes are designed to amend the state's constitution to limit tax burdens. (See Chapter 18.) Local governments may also be limited in state constitutions to specific tax sources and upper limits or "caps" on local taxation. Certain classes of property may be protected, such as that devoted to religious, educational, or charitable uses; government property; some agricultural or forestry land; and even "homesteads," that is, low-priced, owner-occupied homes. Some constitutions may grant tax exemptions to new industries in order to attract industrial development. Constitutions may "earmark" certain tax revenues for specific purposes; for example, gasoline taxes may be earmarked for highway use only.

DEBT LIMITATION   Most state constitutions limit debt that can be incurred by the state only or by local governments. Many states *must* have a balanced operating budget. (Although such a constitutional command does not always succeed, on the whole, state governments are less burdened by debt than is the federal government.) Local governments are frequently limited to a debt that cannot exceed a fixed percentage of the value of property in the community. Moreover, state constitutions generally require a local referendum to approve any increase in local debt. Occasionally, however, state and local governments devise ways to get around constitutional debt limits; for example, they may pledge the revenues of a new project ("revenue bonds") to pay off the debt, rather than taxes ("full faith and credit bonds"). (See Chapter 18.)

TRIVIA   According to the Vermont Constitution: "Every sect or denomination of Christians ought to observe the Sabbath or Lord's Day, and keep some sort of religious worship, which to them seem most agreeable to the revealed will of God." There are many old phrases and clauses like this in state constitutions. Commentators enjoy rummaging through state constitutions and laws to find antique provisions that have little more than symbolic meaning.

CONSTITUTIONAL CHANGE IN THE STATES

The U.S. Constitution has been amended only twenty-six times in 200 years (and the first ten amendments, the Bill of Rights, were really part of the process of ratifying the original document). But state constitutions are so detailed and restrictive that they must be amended frequently. Nearly every year state voters must consider constitutional amendments on the ballot.

Throughout the fifty states, there are now four methods of constitutional change:

1. *Legislative proposal:* Amendments are passed by the state legislature and then submitted to the voters for approval in a referendum. This method is available in all states. (However, in Delaware amendments passed by the legislature need not be submitted to the voters.)
2. *Popular initiative:* A specific number of voters petition to get a constitutional amendment on the ballot for approval by the voters in a referendum. This method is available in seventeen states.
3. *Constitutional convention:* Legislatures submit to the voters a proposal for calling a constitutional convention, and if voters approve, a convention convenes, draws up constitutional revisions, and submits them again for approval by the voters in a referendum. This method is available in at least forty-one states.
4. *Constitutional commission:* Constitutional commissions may be created by legislatures to study the constitution and recommend changes to the state legislature, or in the case of Florida (only) to submit its recommendations directly to the voters in a referendum.

LEGISLATIVE PROPOSAL   The most common method of amending state constitutions is by *legislative proposal*. Many states require that a constitutional amendment receive a two-thirds vote in both chambers of the legislature before submission to the voters; a few states require a three-fifths majority in both houses, while others require only simple legislative majorities. Some states require that a constitutional amendment be passed by two successive legislative sessions before being submitted to the voters. Every state except Delaware requires constitutional amendments proposed by the legislature to be submitted to the voters for approval in a referendum. (See Table 2–2.)

POPULAR INITIATIVE   *Popular initiative* for constitutional revision was introduced during the Progressive Era at the beginning of the twentieth century. These states usually require that an initiative petition be signed by 5, 10, or 15 percent of the number of voters in the last governor's election. (See Table 2–3.) The petition method allows citizens to get an amendment on the ballot *without the approval of the state legislature.* It is not surprising that measures designed to reduce the powers of legislators—for example, *tax limitation* measures and *term limits* for legislators—have come about as a result of citizen initiatives.

CONSTITUTIONAL CONVENTION   While there has been only one national Constitutional Convention, in 1787, there have been over 230 state constitutional conventions. State constitutional conventions are generally proposed by state legislatures, and the question of whether or not to have a convention is generally submitted to the state's voters. (Some state constitutions require periodic submission to the voters of the

Table 2–2
STATE CONSTITUTIONAL AMENDMENT BY LEGISLATURES

	Legislative Vote Required for Proposal	Consideration by Two Sessions Required	Referendum Vote Required for Ratification
Alabama	3/5	No	Majority vote on amendment
Alaska	2/3	No	Majority vote on amendment
Arizona	Majority	No	Majority vote on amendment
Arkansas	Majority	No	Majority vote on amendment
California	2/3	No	Majority vote on amendment
Colorado	2/3	No	Majority vote on amendment
Connecticut	(c)	(a)	Majority vote on amendment
Delaware	2/3	Yes	Not required
Florida	3/5	No	Majority vote on amendment
Georgia	2/3	No	Majority vote on amendment
Hawaii	(b)	(b)	Majority vote on amendment
Idaho	2/3	No	Majority vote on amendment
Illinois	3/5	No	(c)
Indiana	Majority	Yes	Majority vote on amendment
Iowa	Majority	Yes	Majority vote on amendment
Kansas	2/3	No	Majority vote on amendment
Kentucky	3/5	No	Majority vote on amendment
Louisiana	2/3	No	Majority vote on amendment
Maine	2/3	No	Majority vote on amendment
Maryland	3/5	No	Majority vote on amendment
Massachusetts	Majority	Yes	Majority vote on amendment
Michigan	2/3	No	Majority vote on amendment
Minnesota	Majority	No	Majority vote in election
Mississippi	2/3	No	Majority vote on amendment
Missouri	Majority	No	Majority vote on amendment
Montana	2/3	No	Majority vote on amendment
Nebraska	3/5	No	Majority vote on amendment
Nevada	Majority	Yes	Majority vote on amendment
New Hampshire	3/5	No	2/3 vote on amendment
New Jersey	(d)	(d)	Majority vote on amendment
New Mexico	Majority	No	Majority vote on amendment
New York	Majority	Yes	Majority vote on amendment
North Carolina	3/5	No	Majority vote on amendment
North Dakota	Majority	No	Majority vote on amendment
Ohio	3/5	No	Majority vote on amendment
Oklahoma	Majority	No	Majority vote on amendment
Oregon	Majority	No	Majority vote on amendment
Pennsylvania	Majority	Yes	Majority vote on amendment
Rhode Island	Majority	No	Majority vote on amendment
South Carolina	2/3	Yes	Majority vote on amendment
South Dakota	Majority	No	Majority vote on amendment
Tennessee	2/3	Yes	Majority vote in election

Table 2–2   (Continued)

Texas	2/3	No	Majority vote on amendment
Utah	2/3	No	Majority vote on amendment
Vermont	Majority	Yes	Majority vote on amendment
Virginia	Majority	Yes	Majority vote on amendment
Washington	2/3	No	Majority vote on amendment
West Virginia	2/3	No	Majority vote on amendment
Wisconsin	Majority	Yes	Majority vote on amendment
Wyoming	2/3	No	Majority vote in election

[a]3/4 vote at one session, or majority vote in two sessions between which an election has intervened.

[b]2/3 vote at one session or majority vote in two sessions.

[c]Majority voting in election or 3/5 voting on amendment.

[d]3/5 vote at one session or majority vote in two sessions.

Source: Book of the States, 1994–95.

question of calling a constitutional convention.) The legislature usually decides how convention delegates are to be elected and the convention organized. More important, the legislature usually decides whether the convention's work is to be *limited* to specific proposals or topics, or *unlimited* and free to write an entire new constitution.

Voters are often wary of calling a constitutional convention. Over the years voters have rejected as many constitutional convention calls as they have approved. This is true despite the fact that voters always have the option of later voting on the constitutional changes proposed by the conventions. Voters are very reluctant to approve unlimited conventions; most of these calls are rejected. Apparently they are suspicious of "reform" and fearful about "runaway" conventions changing things too much. Only one new constitution has been approved by voters in over a decade—that in Georgia in 1982.

CONSTITUTIONAL COMMISSIONS   Constitutional commissions are supposed to "study and recommend" constitutional changes. These commissions are established by the legislatures and report their recommendations back to the legislature. (Only in Florida do the recommendations of the Constitutional Revision Commission go directly to the voters for ratification and so far all of their proposals have been defeated.) Legislatures generally prefer constitutional commissions to a constitutional convention, because a commission can only study and report to the legislature. A commission can relieve the state legislature of a great deal of work. The typical commission is appointed by an act of the legislature, and its membership usually includes legislators, executive officials, and prominent citizens. Its recommendations are usually handled in the legislature like regular constitutional amendments, although they may be more sweeping than ordinary amendments.

DEMOCRACY IN THE STATES

Democracy means popular participation in government. (The Greek root of the word means "rule by the many.") But popular participation can have different meanings. To

Table 2–3

INITIATIVE, REFERENDA, AND RECALL IN THE STATES

Initiative for Constitutional Amendments (Signatures Required to Get on Ballot)[a]	Initiative for State Laws (Signatures Required to Get on Ballot)[a]	Referendum on State Laws[b]	Recall (Signatures Required to Force a Recall Election)[c]
Arizona (15%)	Alaska (10%)	Alaska	Alaska (25%)
Arkansas (10%)	Arizona (10%)	Arizona	Arizona (25%)
California (8%)	Arkansas (8%)	Arkansas	California (12%)
Colorado (5%)	California (5%)	California	Colorado (25%)
Florida (8%)	Colorado (5% secretary of state election)	Idaho	Georgia (15%)
Illinois (8%)		Kentucky	Idaho (20%)
Massachusetts (3%)		Maine	Kansas (40%)
Michigan (10%)	Idaho (10%)	Maryland	Louisiana (33%)
Mississippi (12%)	Maine (10%)	Massachusetts	Michigan (25%)
Missouri (8%)	Massachusetts (3%)	Michigan	Montana (15%)
Montana (10%)	Michigan (8%)	Missouri	Nevada (25%)
Nebraska (10%)	Missouri (5%)	Montana	North Dakota (25%)
Nevada (10%)	Montana (5% total qualified elections)	Nebraska	Oregon (15%)
North Dakota (4% of state population)	Nebraska (7%)	Nevada	Rhode Island (15%)
Ohio (10%)	Nevada (10%)	New Mexico	Washington (25%)
Oklahoma (15%)	North Dakota (2% of state population)	North Dakota	Wisconsin (25%)
Oregon (8%)	Ohio (3% electors)	Ohio	
South Dakota (10%)	Oklahoma (8%)	Oklahoma	
	Oregon (6%)	Oregon	
	South Dakota (5%)	South Dakota	
	Utah (10%)	Utah	
	Washington (8%)	Washington	
	Wyoming (15% general election)	Wyoming	

[a]Figures expressed as percentage of vote in last governor's election unless otherwise specified; some states also require distribution of votes across counties and districts.

[b]Some state legislatures are required by state constitutions to submit certain questions, such as debt authorization, to the voters. Other states allow citizens to petition for a referendum.

[c]Figures are percentages of voters in last general elections of the official sought to be recalled.

Source: Council of State Governments, The Book of the States 1994–95.

our nation's Founders, who were quite ambivalent about the wisdom of democracy, it meant that the voice of the people would be *represented* in government. "Representational democracy" means the selection of government officials by vote of the people in periodic elections open to competition in which candidates and voters can freely express themselves. (Note that "elections" in which only one party is permitted to run candidates, or where candidates are not free to express their views, do not qualify as democratic.) The

Founders believed that government rests ultimately on the consent of the governed. But their notion of "republicanism" envisioned decision making by representatives of the people, rather than direct decision making by the people themselves. The U.S. Constitution has no provision for direct voting by the people on national policy questions.

"Direct democracy" means that the people themselves can initiate and decide policy questions by popular vote. The Founders were profoundly skeptical of this form of democracy. They had read about direct democracy in the ancient Greek city-state of Athens, and they believed that "the follies" of direct democracy far outweighed any virtues it might possess. It was not until over one hundred years after the U.S. Constitution was written that widespread support developed in the American states for direct voter participation in policy making. Direct democracy developed in states and communities, and it is to be found today *only* in state and local government.

HISTORICAL DEVELOPMENT IN THE STATES   At the beginning of the twentieth century, a strong populist movement in the midwestern and western states attacked railroads, banks, corporations, and the political institutions that were said to be in their hands. The populists were later joined by progressive reformers who attacked "bosses," "machines," and parties as corrupt. The populists believed that their elected representatives were ignoring the needs of farmers, debtors, and laborers. They wished to bypass governors and legislatures and directly enact popular laws for railroad rate regulation, relief of farm debt, and monetary expansion. They believed that both the Democratic and Republican parties of their era were controlled by the trusts and monopolies. The progressives and reformers viewed politics as distasteful. They did not believe that government should be involved in resolving conflicts among competing interests or striving for compromises in public policy. Instead, government should serve "the public interest"; it should seek out the "right" answer to public questions; it should replace politicians with managers and administrators. The progressive reform movement was supported by many upper-middle-class, white, Anglo-Saxon, Protestant groups, who felt that political "machines" were catering to the votes of recent immigrants such as the Irish, Italians, eastern and southern Europeans, working-class people, Catholics, and Jews.[2] The progressive reform movement brought about many changes in the structure of municipal government. (See "Reformers and Do-Gooders" in Chapter 10.) The movement also brought about some interesting innovations in state government.

In order to reduce the influence of "politics," "parties," and "politicians," the populists and progressives advocated a wide range of devices designed to bypass political institutions and encourage direct participation by voters in public affairs. They were largely responsible for replacing party conventions with the primary elections we use today. They were also successful in bringing about the Seventeenth Amendment to the U.S. Constitution requiring that U.S. senators be directly elected by the voters, rather than chosen by state legislatures. They also supported women's suffrage, civil service, and restrictive immigration laws.

The populists and progressives were also responsible for the widespread adoption of three forms of direct democracy—the initiative, referendum, and recall. These reforms began in the farm states of the Midwest and the mining states of the West. The populists provided much of the early support for these devices, and the progressives and reformers

---

[2] See Richard Hofstadter, *The Age of Reform* (New York: Knopf, 1955).

carried them to fruition. President Woodrow Wilson endorsed the initiative, referendum, and recall, and most adoptions occurred prior to World War I.[3]

INITIATIVE   The *initiative* is a device whereby a specific number or percent of voters, through the use of a petition, may have a proposed state constitutional amendment or a state law placed on the ballot for adoption or rejection by the electorate of a state. This process bypasses the legislature and allows citizens to both propose and adopt laws and constitutional amendments. Table 2–3 lists the states that allow popular initiatives for constitutional amendments, and those that allow popular initiatives for state law. Note that Alaska, Idaho, Maine, Utah, Washington, and Wyoming permit citizen initiatives for state *laws,* but not for constitutional *amendments.*

REFERENDUM   The *referendum* is a device by which the electorate must approve decisions of the legislature before these become law or become part of the state constitution. As we noted earlier, most states require a favorable referendum vote for a state constitutional amendment (see Table 2–2). Referenda on state laws may be submitted by the legislature (when legislators want to shift decision-making responsibility to the people), or referenda may be demanded by popular petition (when the people wish to change laws passed by the legislature).

RECALL   Recall elections allow voters to remove an elected official before his or her term expires. Usually a recall election is initiated by a petition. The number of signatures required is usually expressed as a percentage of votes cast in the last election for the official being recalled (frequently 25 percent). Currently sixteen states provide for recall election for some or all of their elected officials (see Table 2–3). Although officials are often publicly threatened with recall, rarely is anyone ever removed from office through this device. A recall of a state elected official requires an expensive petition drive as well as a campaign against the incumbent. Perhaps the mere existence of recall provisions in a state constitution makes public officials more responsive to popular moods.

DIRECT VERSUS REPRESENTATIVE DEMOCRACY

The U.S. Constitution has no provision for national referenda. Americans as a nation cannot vote on federal laws or amendments to the national constitution. But voters in the *states* can express their frustrations directly in popular initiatives and referenda voting.

ARGUMENTS FOR DIRECT DEMOCRACY   Proponents of direct democracy make several strong arguments on behalf of the initiative and referendum devices:[4]

- Direct democracy enhances government responsiveness and accountability. The threat of a successful initiative and referendum drive—indeed sometimes the mere circulation of a petition—encourages officials to take the popular actions.

---

[3]See Thomas E. Cronin, *Direct Democracy: The Politics of Initiative, Referendum and Recall* (Cambridge, MA: Harvard University Press, 1989).

[4]For a balanced summary and evaluation of direct democracy in the states, see Cronin, *Direct Democracy.*

- Direct democracy allows citizen groups to bring their concerns directly to the public. Taxpayer groups, for example, who are not especially well represented in state capitols, have been able through initiative and referendum devices to place their concerns on the public agenda.
- Direct democracy stimulates debate about policy issues. In elections with important referendum issues on the ballot, campaigns tend to be more issue-oriented. Candidates, newspapers, interest groups, and television news are all forced to directly confront policy issues.
- Direct democracy stimulates voter interest and improves election-day turnout. Controversial issues on the ballot—the death penalty, abortion, gun control, taxes, gay rights, English only, and so on—bring out additional voters. There is some limited evidence that elections with initiatives on the ballot increase voter turnout by three to five percentage points over elections with no initiatives on the ballot.[5]
- Direct democracy increases trust in government and diminishes alienation. While it is difficult to substantiate such a claim, the opportunity to directly affect issues should give voters an increased sense of power.

ARGUMENTS FOR REPRESENTATIVE DEMOCRACY   Opponents of direct democracy, from our nation's Founders to the present, argue that representative democracy offers far better protection for individual liberty and the rights of minorities than direct democracy. The Founders constructed a system of checks and balances not so much to protect against the oppression of a ruler, but to protect against the tyranny of the majority. Opponents of direct democracy echo many of the Founders' arguments:

- Direct democracy encourages majorities to sacrifice the rights of individuals and minorities. This argument supposes that voters are generally less tolerant than elected officials, and there is some evidence to support this supposition. However, there is little evidence that public policy in states with the initiative and referendum is any more oppressive than public policy in states without these devices. Nonetheless, the potential of majoritarian sacrifice of the liberty of unpopular people is always a concern.
- Direct democracy facilitates the adoption of unwise and unsound policies. Although voters have rejected many bad ideas, frequently initiatives are less well drafted than legislation.
- Voters are not sufficiently informed to cast intelligent ballots on many issues. Many voters cast their vote in a referendum without ever having considered the issue before going into the polling booth.
- A referendum does not allow consideration of alternative policies or modifications or amendments to the proposition set forth on the ballot. In contrast, legislators devote a great deal of attention to writing, rewriting, and amending bills, and seeking out compromises among interests.
- Direct democracy enables special interests to mount expensive initiative and referendum campaigns. Although proponents of direct democracy argue that these devices allow citizens to bypass special-interest-group-dominated legislatures, in fact only a fairly well-financed group can mount a statewide campaign on behalf of a referendum issue. And the outcomes of the vote may be heavily influenced by paid television advertising. So money is important in both "representational" and "direct" democracy.

---

[5]Ibid., p. 227.

THE POLITICS OF STATE INITIATIVES

In theory the initiative device is ideologically neutral; both liberal and conservative groups can use this device to bypass state legislatures. During the progressive era at the beginning of the twentieth century, many liberal reforms were advanced by popular initiative. But in recent years, as the general public has moved in a conservative direction, many citizen initiative efforts have reflected conservative themes (see Table 2–4).

TAX LIMITATION INITIATIVES   The nation's "tax revolt" got its start with citizen initiatives in the states, beginning with California's Proposition 13 in 1978, and continuing in many tax limitation initiatives in other states in the years since then.

California has had a long history of citizen initiatives for constitutional change. So in 1978, in the wake of popular frustration over inflation and taxes, a Los Angeles real estate developer, Howard Jarvis, found the state's voters more than willing to support a constitutional amendment initiative to reduce property taxes. His effort was funded by real estate developers, business, and agricultural interests, but he also succeeded in organizing a statewide, grass-roots United Organization of Taxpayers to support his initiative. Opposition to Proposition 13 was led by public officials who believed the amendment would cripple public services. The political establishment was joined by the League of Women Voters, the PTA, public employee unions, teachers, and environmental groups, in making dire predictions about the impact of the amendment.

Voter turnout on election day was a record for a California June primary. Over 6.7 million California voters went to the polls to give overwhelming approval to Proposition 13 by better than a two-to-one margin. The publicity surrounding the success of Proposition 13 gave the impression that this citizen initiative was the beginning of a national tax revolt. By 1980 Democrats and Republicans across the nation were campaigning as "tax cutters." Later President Ronald Reagan would interpret it as part of a general mandate for lower taxes and less government, and as a forerunner to his own federal income tax cuts. But not all states joined in the "tax revolt."

In the years since Proposition 13, almost as many states *defeated* tax limitation referenda as passed them. (In Chapter 18 we will devote more discussion to the politics of taxation.) In the years after Proposition 13, scholars tried to distinguish between states in which the tax revolt was successful and those where it was not. It turned out that the states *with constitutional provisions for citizen initiatives* were far more likely to join the "tax revolt"—that is, to pass tax limitation constitutional amendments—than states without provisions for citizen initiatives.[6] Thus, the constitutional framework of state government has important consequences for public policy.

SOCIAL ISSUES   Crime, gambling, abortion, and civil rights are issues frequently encountered in initiative politics (see Table 2–4). In recent years the initiative process has been used to "get tough on crime," including reinstatement of the death penalty. A number of states adopted their lotteries by citizen initiative, after legislatures chose not to offend church groups opposed to gambling. However, casino gambling has been much less

---

[6]Susan B. Hansen, *The Politics of Taxation* (New York: Praeger, 1983).

Table 2–4
STATE VOTING ON SELECTED PROPOSITIONS

		For %	Against %
TAX LIMITATIONS			
Michigan (1984)	Require voter approval of new taxes	40.3	59.7
Nevada (1984)	Exempt food from sales tax	83.3	16.7
California (1986)	New local taxes require 2/3 vote	57.9	42.1
Nevada (1988)	Prohibits state income tax	81.2	17.8
Colorado (1992)	Require elections for tax increases	54.0	46.0
Nevada (1994)	Require 2/3 legislative vote and referendum for tax increase	78	22
Massachusetts (1994)	Enact graduated income tax	29	71
Montana (1994)	Require 2/3 legislative vote for tax increase	49	51
CIVIL RIGHTS			
North Dakota (1984)	Guarantee right to bear arms	80.2	19.8
New Mexico (1986)	Guarantee right to bear arms	61.7	38.3
Vermont (1986)	Equal Rights Amendment	48.4	51.6
Arizona (1988)	Make English official language	50.5	49.5
Colorado (1988)	Make English official language	61.1	38.9
Florida (1988)	Make English official language	83.9	16.1
Iowa (1992)	Equal Rights Amendment	48.0	52.0
Colorado (1992)	Deny homosexuals preferential protections against discrimination	53.0	47.0
Oregon (1992)	Require government to discourage homosexuality	43.0	57.0
Alaska (1994)	Guarantee right to bear arms	73	27
CRIME			
Oregon (1984)	Reinstate death penalty	55.6	44.4
Massachusetts (1982)	Legalize death penalty	60.1	39.9
Arizona (1982)	Prohibit bail for dangerous felons	81.0	19.0
Illinois (1982)	Prohibit bail for dangerous felons	85.3	14.7
Georgia (1988)	Compensate crime victims	52.7	47.3
Oregon (1994)	Mandatory sentences for felonies	66	34
California (1994)	Tougher sentences for repeat offenders	72	28
Colorado (1994)	No bail for violent offenders	77	23
GAMBLING			
Arkansas (1984)	Allow casino gambling	29.6	70.4
Colorado (1984)	Allow casino gambling	33.2	66.8
California (1984)	Authorize state lottery	57.9	42.1
Florida (1986)	Allow casino gambling	31.7	68.3
Florida (1986)	Authorize state lottery	63.6	36.4
South Dakota (1992)	Repeal video lottery	37.0	63.0

Table 2–4   (Continued)

Colorado (1994)	Legalize gambling at airports	7	93
Florida (1994)	Legalize casinos in limited areas	38	62
ABORTION			
Colorado (1984)	Prohibit state funds for abortion	50.4	49.6
Washington (1984)	Prohibit state funds for abortion	46.5	53.5
Rhode Island (1986)	Prohibit state funds for abortion	31.0	69.0
Arkansas (1988)	Prohibit state funds for abortion	51.9	48.1
Colorado (1988)	Prohibit state funds for abortion	39.8	61.2
Maryland (1992)	Ease restrictions on abortion	62.0	38.0
Arizona (1992)	Eliminate public funding of abortion	31.0	69.0
Wyoming (1994)	Prohibit abortion	39	61
OTHER			
New Hampshire (1982)	Change all references in state laws from "man" and "men" to "person" and "people"	16.4	83.6
California (1986)	Quarantine persons with AIDS	29.0	71.0
Oregon (1986)	Allow possession of marijuana	26.5	73.5
North Dakota (1994)	Repeal seat belt law	45	55
Oregon (1994)	Allow terminally ill to obtain lethal drugs	51	49

Note: These are selected proposition votes from recent years.

popular with the voters. The abortion issue has been raised in a number of state initiative votes over whether to allow or prohibit state funding of abortions. Colorado voted on a hotly contested initiative in 1992 that would deny homosexuals status as a protected class in civil rights laws. The initiative passed 53 to 47 percent in the statewide vote, but later was declared to be invalid by the Colorado Supreme Court.

The most publicized citizen initiative in 1994 was California's Proposition 187 prohibiting illegal aliens from receiving state-funded education, welfare, and health (except emergency) services. It also required state employees to report suspected illegal aliens to the California Department of Justice and the U.S. Immigration and Naturalization Service. Republican Governor Pete Wilson championed the proposal, while his Democratic opponent, Kathleen Brown, opposed it. California voters approved Proposition 187 by an impressive 59–41 margin, and Wilson won a solid reelection victory. A federal court later restrained implementation of the initiative; it appears to contravene the Fourteenth Amendment's command that "no person" be denied "equal protection of the law." But California voters had sent a loud message to Washington demanding responsible control of immigration.

INITIATIVE CAMPAIGNS   Over time initiative campaigns, have become more sophisticated and costly. Supporters of an initiative must first of all circulate their petitions, often using paid as well as volunteer workers to obtain the necessary signatures.[7] Television, radio, and newspaper advertising usually accompany the drive for signatures. Once on the ballot, an initiative campaign can become very expensive, with television "infomercials," celebrity endorsements, and get-out-the-vote work on election day.

Some initiative campaigns are sponsored by "special interests"—specific businesses or industries; labor unions, including government employees; religious organizations; environmental groups; and public interest groups. The gambling industry, for example, often backs "citizens' initiatives" to legalize gambling. Many of the designated sponsoring groups for petitions—for example, "Citizens for Tax Justice" (tax limits) and "Eight is Enough" (term limits)—are organized and funded by established lobbying groups that have failed to accomplish their goals through the legislative process.

Opposition campaigns to initiatives may also be well funded by organized interests. Lobbying groups that are well entrenched in state capitals—public employee unions, teachers' unions, and utility, insurance, and liquor industries (see Chapter 6)—are usually leery of citizens' initiatives. Political officeholders are also generally skeptical of citizen initiatives, even though they may occasionally endorse particularly popular ones. After all, the initiative process is designed to bypass the state capital and its power holders. A proposal in New Jersey in 1992 to adopt the initiative process was successfully defeated by a strong coalition of well-established interest groups that mounted "an unprecedented joint lobbying effort."[8] Occasionally opposition groups have resorted to the "counter initiative"—deliberately adding an initiative to the ballot that is designed to undermine support for a popular citizen initiative. There is a tendency for voters to vote against initiatives when the issues are complex and confusing. Occasionally state supreme courts have denied an initiative a place on the ballot, not only for procedural reasons, but also because in the court's opinion it violated the U.S. Constitution.

THE THREAT OF INITIATIVES   Legislatures may be goaded at times into enacting legislation by the threat of a popular initiative. Recognizing that a popular initiative may gain a position on the ballot and win voter approval, legislatures may prefer to preempt an initiative movement by writing their own version of the policy. Indeed there is some evidence that legislatures in initiative states are more sensitive to majority preferences among voters than legislatures in states without the initiative device.[9]

REFORM PROPOSALS   Reformers have argued that initiative voting is becoming too common, that multiple initiatives on the ballot overload and confuse voters, that initiatives are often poorly drafted, and that voters are often poorly informed about the real purposes and intent of an initiative. They often urge that neutral voter guides be printed by the state, summarizing arguments for and against initiative questions; that the names and affiliations of major contributors to initiative campaigns be published; and that courts scrutinize titles on initiatives to ensure that they accurately reflect their purposes and intent.

---

[7]The U.S. Supreme Court has held that a state may not prohibit financial payments for the circulation of petitions. *Meger v. Grant,* 486 U.S. 414 (1988).

[8]Council of State Governments, *Book of the States, 1994–95,* p. 286.

[9]Elizabeth A. Gerber, "Legislative Response to the Threat of Popular Initiatives," *American Journal of Political Science,* 40 (February 1996), 99–128.

TERM LIMIT BATTLES

Distrust of politicians and declining confidence in the ability of government to confront national problems fueled grass-roots movements in many states to limit the terms of public officials—both Congress members and state legislators. National opinion polls have repeatedly shown widespread popular support for term limits:

How long should members of the House and Senate serve?			
	1991	1992	1995
A maximum of 12 years	61%	67%	72%
As long as they get elected	37	31	25

But the enthusiasm of the general public for term limits was seldom matched by legislators—either in Washington or in state capitals—who are reluctant to limit their own legislative careers. Hence, citizens in states with the popular initiative and referenda turned to these instruments of direct democracy.

The U.S. Supreme Court held in 1995 that a state could not impose term limits on *members of Congress* (see below). However, states, and citizens in states with the popular initiative and referenda, can limit the terms of their own *state legislators*. Term limits, for both Congress members and state legislators, have usually won by landslide margins wherever they have appeared on referenda ballots in the states (see Table 2–5). Yet, despite their approval of state constitutional term limits, voters in these states continue to reelect incumbents.

ARGUMENTS FOR TERM LIMITS   Proponents of term limits argue that "citizen-legislators" have largely been replaced by career "professional politicians." People who have held legislative office for many years become isolated from the lives and concerns of average citizens. Career politicians respond to the media, to polls, to interest groups, but they have no direct feeling for how their constituents live. Term limits, proponents argue, would force politicians to return home and live under the laws that they make.

Proponents also argue that term limits would increase competition in the electoral system. By creating "open seat" races on a regular basis, more people would be encouraged to seek public office. Incumbents do not win so often because they are the most qualified people in their districts, but rather because of the many electoral advantages granted by incumbency itself—name recognition, campaign contributions from special interests, pork barrel and casework, office staff, and so on (see "The Great Incumbency Machine" in Chapter 6). These incumbent advantages discourage good people from challenging officeholders.

ARGUMENTS AGAINST TERM LIMITS   Opponents of term limits argue that they infringe on the voters' freedom of choice. If voters are upset with the performance

Table 2–5

VOTING ON TERM LIMITS IN THE STATES

State	Term Limit	Vote Percent	
		YES	NO
1990			
Oklahoma	Limit state legislators	67	33
Colorado	Limit Congress and state legislators	71	29
California	Limit state legislators	52	48
1991			
Washington	Limit Congress and state legislators	46	54[a]
1992			
Arizona	Limit Congress and state legislators	74	26
Arkansas	Limit Congress and state legislators	60	40
California	Limit Congress and state legislators	63	37
Florida	Limit Congress and state legislators	77	23
Michigan	Limit Congress and state legislators	59	41
Missouri	Limit Congress and state legislators	74	26
Montana	Limit Congress and state legislators	67	33
Nebraska	Limit Congress and state legislators	68	32
North Dakota	Limit Congress	55	45
Ohio	Limit Congress and state legislators	66	34
Oregon	Limit Congress and state legislators	69	31
South Dakota	Limit Congress and state legislators	63	37
Washington	Limit Congress and state legislators	52	48[a]
Wyoming	Limit Congress and state legislators	77	23
1994			
Alaska	Limit Congress (not effective unless 24 other states adopt)	63	37
Colorado	Limit Congress	52	48
Idaho	Limit Congress and state legislators	59	41
Maine	Limit Congress	63	37
Massachusetts	Limit Congress	52	48
Nebraska	Limit Congress and state legislators	68	32
Nevada	Limit Congress and state legislators (Congress limit not effective unless 24 other states adopt)	70	30
Oklahoma	Limit Congress	67	33
Utah	Limit Congress and all state and local offices	35	65[a]

[a]Only Washington and Utah voters rejected congressional term limits; Washington voters reversed their 1991 rejection in 1992.

of their state legislators, they can always "throw the rascals out." If they want to limit a legislator's term, they can do so simply by not reelecting him or her. But if voters wish to keep popular, able, experienced, and hard-working legislators in office, they should be permitted to do so. Experience is a valuable asset in state capitals; voters may legitimately desire to be represented by senior legislators with knowledge and experience in public affairs.

Opponents also argue that inexperienced legislators would be forced to rely more on the policy information supplied to them by bureaucrats, lobbyists, and staff people. Term limits, they argue, would weaken the legislature, leaving it less capable of checking the power of the special interests. But proponents counter this argument by observing that the closest relationships in state capitals develop between lobbyists and senior legislators who have interacted professionally and socially over the years, and that most powerful lobbying groups strongly oppose term limits.

SUPREME COURT REJECTION OF CONGRESSIONAL TERM LIMITS BY STATES

When the voters of Arkansas adopted a state constitutional amendment in 1992 setting term limits for their U.S. Senators and Representatives, the U.S. Supreme Court ruled in 1995 that this action violated the U.S. Constitution by setting forth qualifications for Congress members beyond those found in Article I. Only three qualifications are specified in the U.S. Constitution: age, citizenship, and residence. (The Arkansas term limit amendment actually set qualifications for eligibility for name placement on the ballot; Arkansas argued that this was a permissible exercise of power to regulate "times, places and manner of holding elections" granted to the states in Article I. But the Court dismissed this argument as an "indirect attempt to accomplish what the Constitution prohibits.") The Court held that a state cannot limit the terms of members of Congress:

> Allowing individual states to adopt their own qualifications for Congressional service would be inconsistent with the framers' vision of a uniform national legislature representing the people of the United States. If the qualifications set forth in the text of the Constitution are to be changed, that text must be amended.

Justice John Paul Stevens, writing for the majority in the controversial 5–4 decision, set forth two key arguments in opposition to state-imposed congressional term limits: first, that the power to do so is *not* among the powers reserved to the states by the Tenth Amendment, and second, that the Founders intended age, citizenship, and residency be the *only* qualifications for members of Congress.

> [Arkansas argues] that the Constitution contains no express prohibition against state-added qualifications, and that Amendment 73 is therefore an appropriate exercise of a state's reserved power to place additional restrictions on the choices that its own voters may make. We disagree for two independent reasons. First, we conclude that the power to add qualifications is not within the "original powers" of the states, and thus is not reserved to the states by the 10th Amendment. Second, even if states possessed some original power in this area, we conclude that the framers intended the Constitution to be the exclusive source of qualifications for members of Congress, and that the framers thereby "divested" states of any power to add qualifications.

But Justice Clarence Thomas, in his dissenting opinion, set forth a compelling argument on behalf of the powers reserved to the people of the states by the Tenth Amendment:

It is ironic that the Court bases today's decision on the right of the people to "choose whom they please to govern them." . . . The majority therefore defends the right of the people of Arkansas to "choose whom they please to govern them" by invalidating a provision that won nearly 60 percent of the votes cast in a direct election and that carried every Congressional district in the state.

I dissent. Nothing in the Constitution deprives the people of each state of the power to prescribe eligibility requirements for the candidates who seek to represent them in Congress. The Constitution is simply silent on this question. And whether the Constitution is silent, it raises no bar to action by the states or the people.[10]

POLITICS OF CONSTITUTIONAL REVISION

State constitutional conventions and revision commissions generally come into being in response to demands by reform-oriented "good-government" interest groups. But the activities of constitutional reformers usually spark counteractivities from interests desiring to preserve the status quo—political officeholders, party politicians, bureaucrats, and business interests, particularly those subject to state regulation.

INTEREST GROUPS   Important political interests are at stake in constitutional revision. Legislatures are understandably hesitant about calling constitutional conventions. A "runaway" convention may rearrange the balance of political power in the state. Interest groups that presently enjoy special privileges or exemptions from taxation in the state constitution have reason to fear a constitutional convention. They may stress the expense involved in such a convention or the danger that "radical reformers" may foist their dangerous ideas upon an unsuspecting public. Taxpayer groups may fear that constitutional limitations on taxing powers may be removed. Public officials may be concerned that their offices will be abolished. In other words, constitutional revision is a political thicket that discourages all but the most courageous of individuals.

REFORMERS   Reform interests—good-government groups, the League of Women Voters, and political science professors—argue that the constitution and the structure of state and local government should be simple, brief, and understandable. It should permit the legislature and the governor to make public policy. It should allocate power to the governor and the legislature commensurate with their responsibilities, and it should enable the voters to hold elected officials clearly accountable for public decisions. It should permit local governmental consolidation and community home rule. The need for frequent amendment should be eliminated.

DELEGATES   Membership in constitutional conventions as well as revision commissions is generally weighted in the direction of reform, since the calling of the convention or the establishment of a commission itself indicates the strength of reformers in the state political system. *Convention delegates* are usually elected by the voters. Nonpartisan elections (delegates run without party designation) generally maximize the number of "reformers" at the convention, while partisan elections (delegates run under party labels)

---

[10]Quotation from *U.S. Term Limits v. Thornton* (1995).

may advantage opponents of comprehensive reform.[11] *Revision commission members* are usually appointed by the governor and the legislature. A balance is frequently sought between Democrats and Republicans and between executive and legislative branch representatives; commissions also usually include representatives of business, professional, union, teacher, environmental, and civil rights groups.

The basic division within most conventions and commissions is between reformers versus preservers of the status quo. This line of division is often more pronounced than the division between Republicans versus Democrats, urban versus rural, a governor's supporters versus opponents, and so forth.[12]

CONSTITUTIONAL POLITICS IN CALIFORNIA   Reformers in California have long argued the need for a new state constitution. The current document was written in 1879 and now incorporates nearly 500 amendments. California voters are regularly asked to consider dozens of new amendments at each election. Reformers (and liberals) in the state believe that many of these citizen initiatives have overly constrained state government (for example, by limiting local government taxing powers, by requiring a two-thirds vote in the legislature to pass the state's budget, by imposing term limits on state officials, etc.).[13] A California Constitutional Revision Commission was appointed by the governor and legislature in 1994 and proceeded to give serious consideration to some very dramatic constitutional changes: the creation of a unicameral (one-house) legislature; the elimination of taxing and spending restrictions; and a requirement that citizen initiatives to change the constitution be approved in *two* consecutive elections. But the Commission eventually withdrew some of the more revolutionary changes (including a unicameral legislature), and the legislature watered down others before submitting them to the voters. California voters are likely to preserve their preference for direct democracy through the initiative and referendum.

POLITICS OF STATE CONSTITUTIONAL RATIFICATION

While new constitutions have generally moved states closer to the "reform model," the extent of change has not been very great. Since new constitutions must go to the voters for approval, reform-oriented constitution makers must be careful not to offend voters with controversial innovations. New constitutions are very vulnerable at the polls. Attempts to deal with divisive issues such as abortion, equal rights amendments, or tax limitations, often doom comprehensive revision efforts. Voters who are offended by a single provision may vote no even when all other provisions are acceptable. Different voters

---

[11]Cal Clark, Janet Clark, and Albert K. Karnig, "Voting Behavior of Chicago Democrats at the Illinois Constitutional Convention," *American Politics Quarterly,* 6 (July 1978), 325–44.

[12]Indeed, convention delegates do not usually behave in the fashion of politicians "ambitious" for higher office. See William H. Thompson, "An Analysis of the Legislative Ambitions of State Constitutional Convention Delegates," *Western Political Quarterly,* 39 (August 1976), 425–39.

[13]See Bruce E. Cain and Roger G. Noll (eds.), *Constitutional Reform in California* (Berkeley, CA: Institute of Governmental Studies, 1995).

TRIVIA
HAWKEYES, HOOSIERS, AND THE LONE STAR

One of the less important, yet sometimes very heated, issues that confront state legislatures is the selection of official nicknames for their state as well as official birds, flowers, trees, songs, and the like. If you think you know about the American states (or if you pass your driving time reading license plates), try to match the state with its official nickname without looking at the answers.

Easy Ones	*Answers*
Heart of Dixie	Alabama
Grand Canyon State	Arizona
Golden State	California
Centennial State	Colorado
Peach State, Empire State of the South	Georgia
Sunshine State	Florida
Aloha State	Hawaii
Hawkeye State	Iowa
Hoosier State	Indiana
Bluegrass State	Kentucky
Bay State, Old Colony	Massachusetts
Great Lake State, Wolverine State	Michigan
Show Me State	Missouri
Cornhusker State	Nebraska
Empire State	New York
Tar Heel State	North Carolina
Buckeye State	Ohio
Sooner State	Oklahoma
Beaver State	Oregon
Little Rhody	Rhode Island
Volunteer State	Tennessee
Lone Star State	Texas
Old Dominion	Virginia
Mountain State	West Virginia
Badger State	Wisconsin

Hard Ones	*Answers*
Land of Opportunity	Arkansas
Constitution State, Nutmeg State	Connecticut
First State, Diamond State	Delaware

Gem State	Idaho
Prairie State	Illinois
Sunflower State	Kansas
Pelican State	Louisiana
Pine Tree State	Maine
Old Line State, Free State	Maryland
North Star State, Gopher State	Minnesota
Magnolia State	Mississippi
Treasurer State	Montana
Silver State	Nevada
Granite State	New Hampshire
Garden State	New Jersey
Land of Enchantment	New Mexico
Sioux State, Flickertale State	North Dakota
Keystone State	Pennsylvania
Palmetto State	South Carolina
Coyote State	South Dakota
Beehive State	Utah
Green Mountain State	Vermont
Evergreen State	Washington
Equality State	Wyoming
None (only state with no official nickname)	Alaska

Source: Book of the States, 1988–89.

may be voting no for different reasons, but a cumulation of specific no votes on separate provisions may spell defeat for the whole document.

Generalizations about factors affecting voter support or opposition to new constitutions are difficult to derive. There is some evidence that higher socioeconomic groups give greater support to ratification than lower socioeconomic groups. But special circumstances may explain ratification outcomes more successfully than socioeconomic factors. In the successful states, partisanship was carefully avoided, the changes proposed were very modest, and state leaders of both parties publicly supported the document. Moreover, some of the more controversial items proposed were separated from the main document for separate voting.

Of course, reform interests have not yet succeeded in simplifying state constitutions or in eliminating the special privileges and exemptions contained in them. Newer constitutions, however, are somewhat shorter and more streamlined than the average state constitution. All the newer documents tend to strengthen the executive, provide for more equitable apportionment, and remove limitations on legislative power. However, there is not much hope that state constitutions will be simplified in the near future or that special exemptions and privileges will be eliminated.

Table 2–6

THE SUCCESS OF STATE CONSTITUTIONAL AMENDMENTS BY METHOD OF INITIATION

	Number of States				*Total Proposals*			
	1986–87	1988–89	1990–91	1992–93	1986–87	1988–89	1990–91	1992–93
All Methods	47	45	41	43	275	267	226	239
Legislative Proposal	46	45	41	42	243	246	197	201
Popular Initiative	9	11	10	13	18	21	29	34
Constitutional Convention	1	—	—	1	14	—	—	1
Constitutional Commission	—	—	—	1	—	—	—	3

	Percent Adopted			
	1986–87	1988–89	1990–91	1992–93
All Methods	74.3	74.0	63.3	66.1
Legislative Proposal	77.7	75.6	67.0	67.1
Popular Initiative	27.7	55.0	37.9	61.7
Constitutional Convention	57.1	—	—	0
Constitutional Commission	—	—	—	66.6

Source: Book of the States, 1994–95.

Voter approval of new state constitutions is by no means assured. Over the years, the record of voters' response to state constitutional amendment (Table 2–6) shows that voters are more accepting of individual amendments submitted to them by *state legislatures* than any other method of constitutional change. In contrast, most popular initiatives are defeated at the polls, as are most amendments proposed by constitutional conventions. These figures suggest the key role that state legislatures play in constitutional change. While it is true that many legislative proposals are merely "editorial," voters seem to prefer limited, step-by-step, constitutional change, rather than sweeping reform initiated by citizens.[14]

---

[14]For a current assessment of state constitutional revision, see Janice C. May, "State Constitutions and Constitutional Revision," in Council of State Governments, *The Book of the States, 1994–95* (Lexington, KY: Council of State Governments, 1994).

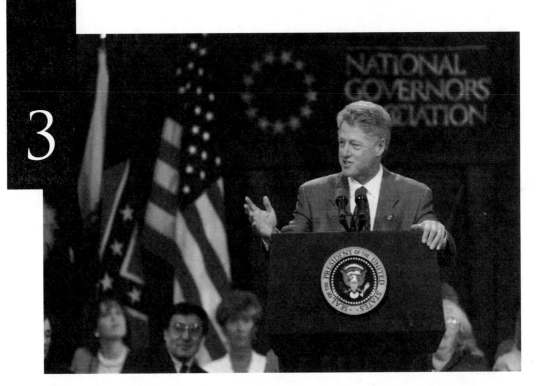

STATES, COMMUNITIES, AND AMERICAN FEDERALISM

WHAT IS FEDERALISM?

Virtually all nations of the world have some units of local government—states, republics, provinces, regions, cities, counties, or villages. Decentralization of the administrative burdens of government is required almost everywhere. But not all nations have federal systems of government.

Federalism is a system of government in which power is divided between national and subnational governments with both exercising separate and autonomous authority, both electing their own officials, and both taxing their own citizens for the provision of public services. Moreover, federalism requires that the powers of the national and subnational governments be guaranteed by a constitution that cannot be changed without the consent of both national and subnational populations.[1]

The United States, Canada, Australia, India, the Federal Republic of Germany, and Switzerland are generally regarded as federal systems. But Great Britain, France, Italy,

---

[1]Other definitions of federalism in American political science include: "Federalism refers to a political system in which there are local (territorial, regional, provincial, state, or municipal) units of government as

and Sweden are not. While these nations have local governments, they are dependent on the national government for their powers. They are considered *unitary* rather than federal systems, because their local governments can be altered or even abolished by the national governments acting alone. In contrast, a system is said to be *confederal* if the power of the national government is dependent upon local units of government. While these terms—unitary, and confederal—can be defined theoretically, in the real world of politics it is not so easy to distinguish between governments that are truly federal and those that are not. Indeed, as we shall see in this chapter, it is not clear whether the U.S. government today retains its federal character.

WHY FEDERALISM?

Why have state and local governments anyway? Why not have a centralized political system with a single government accountable to national majorities in national elections—a government capable of implementing uniform policies throughout the country?

"AUXILIARY PRECAUTIONS" AGAINST TYRANNY

The nation's Founders understood that "republican principles," while they should be nurtured and cherished, would not be sufficient in themselves to protect individual liberty. Periodic elections, party competition, voter enfranchisement, and political equality may function to make governing elites more responsive to popular concerns. But these processes do not protect minorities or individuals, "the weaker party or an obnoxious individual," from government deprivations of liberty or property. Indeed, according to the Founders, "the great object" of constitution writing was to both preserve popular government and protect individuals from "unjust and interested" *majorities.* "A dependence on the people is, no doubt, the primary control of government, but experience has taught mankind the necessity of auxiliary precautions."

Among the most important "auxiliary precautions" devised by the Founders to control government are *federalism*—dividing powers between the national and state governments—and *separation of powers*—the dispersal of power among the separate executive, legislative, and judicial branches of government.

> In the compound republic of America, the power surrendered by the people is first divided between two distinct governments, and then the portion allotted to each subdivided among distinct and separate departments. Hence a double security arises to the rights of the people. The different governments will control each other, at the same time that each will be controlled by itself.[2]

---

well as a national government, that can make final decisions with respect to at least some governmental authorities and whose existence is especially protected." James Q. Wilson, *American Government,* 4th ed. (Lexington, MA: D.C. Heath, 1989), p. 47; "Federalism is the mode of political organization that unites smaller polities within an overarching political system by distributing power among general and constituent units in a manner designed to protect the existence and authority of both national and subnational systems enabling all to share in the overall system's decision-making and executing processes." Daniel J. Elazar, *American Federalism: A View from the States* (New York: Thomas Y. Crowell, 1966), p. 2.

[2]James Madison, Alexander Hamilton, and John Jay, *The Federalist,* Number 51 (New York: Modern Library, 1958).

DISPERSING POWER   Decentralization distributes power more widely among different sets of leaders. Multiple leadership groups are generally believed to be more democratic than a single set of all-powerful leaders. Moreover, state and local governments provide a political base of offices for the opposition party when it has lost national elections. In this way state and local governments contribute to party competition in America by helping to tide over the losing party after electoral defeat so that it may remain strong enough to challenge incumbents at the next election. And finally, of course, state and local governments provide a channel of recruitment for national political leaders. National leaders can be drawn from a pool of leaders experienced in state and local politics.

INCREASING PARTICIPATION   Decentralization allows more people to participate in the political system. There are over eighty-six thousand governments in America—states, counties, townships, municipalities, towns, special districts, and school districts. Nearly a million people hold some kind of public office. The opportunity to participate doubtlessly contributes to popular support of the political system. Many people are given the opportunity to exercise political leadership; moreover, state and local governments are widely regarded as being "closer to the people." Thus, by providing more opportunities for direct citizen involvement in government, state and local governments contribute to the popular sense of political effectiveness and well-being.

IMPROVING EFFICIENCY   Decentralization makes government more manageable and efficient. Imagine the bureaucracy, red tape, and confusion if every government activity in every local community in the nation—police, schools, roads, fire fighting, garbage collection, sewage disposal, and so forth—were controlled by a centralized administration in Washington. If local governments did not exist, they would have to be invented. Government becomes arbitrary when a bureaucracy far from the scene directs a local administrator to proceed with the impossible—local conditions notwithstanding. Decentralization softens the rigidity of law.

ENSURING POLICY RESPONSIVENESS   Decentralized government encourages policy responsiveness. Multiple competing governments are more sensitive to citizen views than monopoly government. The existence of multiple governments offering different packages of benefits and costs allows a better match between citizen preferences and public policy. People and businesses can "vote with their feet" by relocating to those states and communities that most closely conform to their own policy preferences. Americans are very mobile. About four of every ten Americans moves in any five-year period: One in five moves to a different county, and one in ten to a different state. Business and industry are also increasingly mobile. Mobility not only facilitates a better match between citizen preferences and public policy, it also encourages competition between states and communities to offer improved services at lower costs.

ENCOURAGING POLICY INNOVATION   Decentralization encourages policy experimentation and innovation. Federalism may be perceived today as a "conservative" idea, but it was once viewed as the instrument of "progressivism." A strong argument can be made that the groundwork for FDR's New Deal in the 1930s was built in state policy experimentation during the Progressive Era earlier in the century. Federal programs as diverse as the income tax, unemployment compensation, countercyclical public works, Social Security, wage and hour legislation, bank deposit insurance, and food stamps all had antecedents at the state level. Indeed, the compelling phrase "laboratories of democracy" is generally attributed to the great progressive jurist, Supreme Court Justice Louis D. Brandeis, who used it in defense of state experimentation with new solutions to social and economic problems.[3] But the states cannot serve as "laboratories," and the innovative potential of federalism cannot be realized, if the states are not free to pursue a wide range of policies. Competition among governments provides additional incentives for inventiveness and innovation in public policy.[4]

MANAGING CONFLICT   Political decentralization frequently reduces the severity of conflict in a society. Decentralization is a classic method by which different peoples can be brought together in a nation without engendering irresolvable conflict. Conflicts between geographically defined groups in America are resolved by allowing each to pursue its own policies within the separate states and communities; this avoids battling over a single national policy to be applied uniformly throughout the land.

FEDERALISM'S FAULTS

Federalism is not without its faults. Federalism can obstruct action on national issues. Although decentralization may reduce conflict at the national level, it may do so at the price of "sweeping under the rug" some serious, national injustices.

PROTECTING SLAVERY AND SEGREGATION   Federalism in America remains tainted by its historical association with slavery, segregation, and discrimination. An early doctrine of "nullification" was set forth by Thomas Jefferson in the Virginia and Kentucky Resolution of 1798, asserting states' right to nullify unconstitutional laws of Congress. Although the original use of this doctrine was to counter congressional attacks on a free press in the Alien and Sedition Acts, the doctrine was later revived to defend slavery. John C. Calhoun of South Carolina argued forcefully in the years before the Civil War that slavery was an issue for states to decide and that under the Constitution of 1787, Congress had no power to interfere with slavery in the southern states or in the new western territories.

In the years immediately following the Civil War the issues of slavery, racial inequality, and black voting rights were *nationalized.* The Thirteenth, Fourteenth, and Fifteenth Amendments to the Constitution were enforced with federal troops in the southern states during Reconstruction. But following the Compromise of 1876 federal troops were withdrawn from the southern states and legal and social segregation of blacks became a "way of life" in the region. Segregation was *denationalized;* this reduced national conflict over race, but the price was paid by black Americans. Not until the 1950s and 1960s were

---

[3]David Osborne, *Laboratories of Democracy* (Cambridge, MA: Harvard Business School, 1988).

[4]The arguments for "competitive federalism" are developed at length in Thomas R. Dye, *American Federalism: Competition Among Governments* (Lexington, MA: Lexington Books, 1990). The book argues that competitive decentralized government has many advantages over centralized "monopoly" governments: greater overall responsiveness to citizen preferences; incentives for government to become efficient and provide quality services at lowest costs; restraints on the overall burdens of taxation and nonproportional taxes; encouragement of economic growth; and innovation in policies designed to improve the well-being of citizens.

questions of segregation and equality again made into national issues. The civil rights movement asserted the supremacy of national law, especially the U.S. Supreme Court's decision in *Brown* v. *Topeka*, 1954, that segregation violated the Fourteenth Amendment's guarantee of equal protection of the law, and later the national Civil Rights Act of 1964. Segregationists asserted the states' rights argument so often in defense of racial discrimination that it became a code word for racism.

Indeed, only now that *national* constitutional and legal guarantees of equal protection of the law are in place is it possible to reassess the true values of federalism. Having established that federalism will not be allowed to justify racial inequality, we are now free to explore the values of decentralized government.

OBSTRUCTING NATIONAL POLICIES   Federalism allows state and local officials to obstruct action on national problems. It allows local leaders and citizens to frustrate national policy, to sacrifice the national interest to local interests. Decentralized government provides an opportunity for local "NIMBYs" (not in my back yard) to obstruct airports, highways, waste disposal plants, public housing, and many other projects in the national interest.

ALLOWING INEQUALITIES   Finally, under federalism the benefits and costs of government are spread unevenly across the nation. For example, some states spend over twice as much on the education of each child in the public schools as other states (see Chapter 15). Welfare benefits in some states are over twice as high as in other states (see Chapter 17). Taxes in some states are over twice as high per capita as in other states (see Chapter 18). Competition among states may keep welfare benefits low in order not to encourage an in migration of poor people. Federalism allows these differences in policy to develop. Federalism is the opposite of uniformity.

THE STRUCTURE OF AMERICAN FEDERALISM

In deciding in 1869 that a state had no constitutional right to secede from the union, Chief Justice Salmon P. Chase described the legal character of American federalism:

> The preservation of the states and the maintenance of their governments, are as much within the design and care of the constitution as the preservation of the union and the maintenance of the national government. The constitution, in all of its provisions, looks to an indestructible union, composed of indestructible states.[5]

What is meant by "an indestructible union, composed of indestructible states"? American federalism is an indissoluble partnership between the states and the national government. The Constitution of the United States allocated power between two separate authorities, the nation and the states, each of which was to be independent of the other. Both the nation and the states were allowed to enforce their laws directly on individuals through their own officials and courts. The Constitution itself was the only legal source of authority for the division of powers between the states and the nation. The American

---

[5]*Texas* v. *White*, 7 Wallace 700 (1869).

federal system was designed as a strong national government, coupled with a strong state government, in which authority and power are shared, constitutionally and practically.

The framework of American federalism is determined by (1) the powers delegated by the Constitution of the national government, and the supremacy of the government; (2) the constitutional guarantees reserved for the states; (3) the powers denied by the Constitution to both the national government and the states; (4) the constitutional provisions giving the states a role in the compositions of the national government; and (5) the subsequent constitutional and historical development of federalism.

DELEGATED POWERS AND NATIONAL SUPREMACY   Article I, Section 8, of the U.S. Constitution lists eighteen grants of power to Congress. These "delegated" or "enumerated" powers include authority over matters of war and foreign affairs, the power to declare war, raise armies, equip navies, and establish rules for the military. Another series of delegated powers is related to control of the economy, including the power to coin money, to control its value, and to regulate foreign and interstate commerce. The national government has been given independent powers of taxation "to pay the debts and provide for the common defense and general welfare of the United States." It has the power to establish its own court system, to decide cases arising under the Constitution and the laws and treaties of the United States and cases involving certain kinds of parties. The national government was given the authority to grant copyright patents, establish post offices, enact bankruptcy laws, punish counterfeiting, punish crimes committed on the high seas, and govern the District of Columbia. (See Table 3–1.) Finally, after seventeen grants of express power, came the power "to make all laws which

Table 3–1
THE CONSTITUTIONAL DISTRIBUTION OF POWERS

▬▬

(ARTICLE AND SECTION NUMBERS OF THE U.S. CONSTITUTION SHOWN IN PARENTHESES)

NATIONAL POWERS
Military Affairs and Defense
Provide for the common defense (I–8)
Declare war (I–8)
Raise and support armies (I–8)
Provide and maintain a navy (I–8)
Define and punish piracies (I–8)
Define and punish offenses against the law of nations (I–8)
Make rules for the regulation of military and naval forces (I–8)
Provide for calling forth the militia to execute laws, suppress insurrections, and repel invasions (I–8)
Provide for organizing, arming, and disciplining militia (I–8)
Declare the punishment of treason (III–3)
Economic Matters
Regulate commerce with foreign nations, among the several states, and with Indian tribes (I–8)
Establish uniform laws on bankruptcy (I–8)
Coin money and regulate its value (I–8)
Regulate value of foreign coin (I–8)

Table 3–1   (Continued)

Fix standards of weights and measures (I–8)
Provide for patents and copyrights (I–8)
Establish post offices and post roads (I–8)
Taxing Powers
Levy taxes (I–8)
Contract and pay debts (I–8)
Governmental Organization
Constitute tribunals inferior to the Supreme Court (I–8, III–I)
Exercise exclusive legislative power over the seat of government and over certain military installations (I–8)
Admit new states (IV–3)
Dispose of and regulate territory or property of the United States (IV–3)
Make rules for appointments (II–2)
Implied Powers
Make necessary and proper laws for carrying expressed powers into execution (I–8)

RESERVED POWERS OF THE STATES
All powers not delegated to the national government by the Constitution, nor prohibited by the Constitution to the states, are reserved to the states "or to the people." (Amendment X)

RESTRICTIONS ON NATIONAL POWER
Economic Matters
No preference to ports of any state (I–9)
No tax or duty on articles exported from any state (I–9)
Fiscal Matters
No direct tax except by apportionment among states on population bases (I–9), now superseded as to income tax (Amendment XVI)
No money to be drawn from Treasury except by appropriation (I–9)
Social Classes
No title of nobility to be granted (I–9)
Civil and Political Rights
Congress not to establish religion or prohibit free exercise of religion (Amendment I)
Congress not to abridge freedom of speech, press, assembly, or right of petition (Amendment I)
Right to bear arms protected (Amendment II)
Restriction on quartering of soldiers in private homes (Amendment III)
No unreasonable searches or seizures (Amendment IV)
Guarantees of fair trials (Amendment V, Amendment VI, Amendment VII)
No excessive bail or cruel or unusual punishments (Amendment VIII)
No taking of life, liberty, or property without due process (Amendment V)
Voting not to be denied because of race, color, previous servitude (Amendment XV), or sex (Amendment XIX), or age if 18 or over (Amendment XXVI)
Voting not to be denied because of nonpayment of any tax (Amendment XXIV)
Suspension of habeas corpus limited (I–9)
No bills of attainder (I–9)
No ex post facto laws (I–9)

RESTRICTIONS ON THE POWERS OF THE STATES
Foreign Affairs
States not to enter into treaties, alliances, or confederation (I–10)
No compact with a foreign state, except by congressional consent (I–10)

Table 3–1   (Continued)

Military Affairs
No letters of marque and reprisal (I–10)
No standing military forces in peace without congressional consent (I–10)
No engagement in war, without congressional consent, except in imminent danger or when invaded (I–10)
Economic Matters
No legal tender other than gold or silver coin (I–10)
No separate state coinage (I–10)
No impairment of the obligation of contracts (I–10)
No emission of bills of credit (I–10)
No levying of import or export duties, except reasonable inspection fees, without consent of Congress (I–10)
Civil and Political Rights
No slavery (Amendment XIII)
No bills of attainder (I–10)
No ex post facto laws (I–10)
No denial of life, liberty, or property by state without due process of law (Amendment XIV)
No denial by state of the equal protection of the laws (Amendment XIV)
No abridgment by state of privileges and immunities of national citizenship (Amendment XIV)
No abridgment of voting rights because of race, color, or previous condition of servitude (Amendment XV)
No abridgment of voting rights because of sex (Amendment XIX)
No poll or other taxes required for voting in federal elections (Amendment XXIV)
Social Restrictions
No titles of nobility (I–10)
General Restrictions
Federal law supreme (VI)
No payment of debts for rebellion against United States or for emancipated slaves (Amendment XIV)

NATIONAL OBLIGATIONS TO THE STATES
Territorial integrity (IV–3)
Guarantee of a republican form of government (IV– 4)
Protection against foreign invasion and domestic violence (IV– 4)
Equal representation in the Senate (V)

---

shall be necessary and proper for carrying into execution the foregoing powers, and all other powers vested by this constitution in the government of the United States or in any department or officer thereof." This is generally referred to as the Necessary and Proper Clause or the Implied Powers Clause.

These delegated powers, when coupled with the National Supremacy Clause of Article VI, ensured a powerful national government. The National Supremacy Clause was quite specific regarding the relationship between the national government and the states. In questions involving conflict between the state laws and the Constitution, laws, or treaties of the United States:

> This constitution, and the laws of the United States which shall be made in pursuance thereof; and all treaties made or which shall be made under the authority of the United

States shall be the supreme law of the land; and the judges in every state shall be bound thereby, anything in the constitution or laws of any state to the contrary notwithstanding.

RESERVED POWERS   Despite these broad grants of power to the national government, the states retained a great deal of authority over the lives of their citizens. The Tenth Amendment reaffirmed the idea that the national government had only certain delegated powers and that all powers not delegated to it were retained by the states:

The powers not delegated to the United States by the constitution, nor prohibited by it to the states, are reserved to the states respectively, or to the people.

The states retained control over the ownership and use of property; the regulation of offenses against persons and property (criminal law and civil law); the regulation of marriage and divorce; the control of business, labor, farming, trades, and professions; the provision of education, welfare, health, hospitals, and other social welfare activities; and provision of highways, roads, canals, and other public works. The states retained full authority over the organization and control of local government units. Finally, the states, like the federal government, possessed the power to tax and spend for the general welfare.

POWERS DENIED TO THE NATION AND STATES   The Constitution denies some powers to both national and state governments; these denials generally safeguard individual rights. Both nation and states are forbidden to pass ex post facto laws or bills of attainder. The first eight amendments to the Constitution, "the Bill of Rights," originally applied to the federal government, but the Fourteenth Amendment, passed by Congress in 1866, provided that the states must also adhere to fundamental guarantees of individual liberty. "No state shall make or enforce any law which shall abridge the privileges or immunities of the citizens of the United States; nor shall any state deprive any person of life, liberty or property without due process of law; nor deny to any person within its jurisdiction equal protection of the laws."

Some powers were denied only to the states, generally as a safeguard to national unity, including the powers to coin money, enter into treaties with foreign powers, interfere with the obligations of contracts, levy duties on imports or exports without congressional consent, maintain military forces in peacetime, engage in war, or enter into compacts with foreign nations or other states.

THE NATIONAL GOVERNMENT'S OBLIGATIONS TO THE STATES
The Constitution imposes several obligations on the national government in its relations with the states. First of all, the states are guaranteed *territorial integrity:* No new state can be created by Congress out of the territory of an existing state without its consent. (Nonetheless, Congress admitted West Virginia to the Union in 1863 when the western counties of Virginia separated from that state during the Civil War. Later a "reconstructed" Virginia legislature gave its approval.) The national government must also guarantee to every state *"a republican form of government."* A republican government is a government by democratically elected representatives. Presumably this clause in the Constitution means that the national government will ensure that no authoritarian or dictatorial regime will be permitted to rule in any state. Apparently this clause does *not* prohibit popular initiatives, referenda, town meetings, or other forms of direct democ-

racy. The Supreme Court has never given any specific meaning to this guarantee. Each state is also guaranteed *equal representation in the U.S. Senate.* Indeed, the Constitution, Article V, prohibits any amendments that would deprive the states of equal representation in the Senate. Finally, the national government is required to *protect each state against foreign invasion and domestic violence.* The protection against foreign invasion is unequivocal, but the clause dealing with domestic violence includes the phrase "upon application of the legislature or the Executive (when the legislature cannot be convened)." Governors have called upon the national government to intervene in riots to maintain public order. But the national government has also intervened *without* "application" by state officials in cases where federal laws are being violated.

STATE ROLE IN NATIONAL GOVERNMENT   The states also play an important role in the composition of the national government. U.S. representatives must be apportioned among the states according to their population every ten years. Governors have the authority to fill vacancies in Congress, and every state must have at least one representative regardless of population. The Senate of the United States is composed of two senators from each state regardless of the state's population. The times, places, and manner of holding elections for Congress are determined by the states. The president is chosen by electors, allotted to each state on the basis of its senators and representatives. Finally, amendments to the U.S. Constitution must be ratified by three-fourths of the states.(See Figure 3–1.)

BATTLES IN THE STATES OVER CONSTITUTIONAL AMENDMENTS

The power of the states in the American federal system has been demonstrated in several battles over constitutional amendments passed by Congress. According to Article V of the U.S. Constitution, *the Constitution cannot be amended without the approval of three-fourths of the states,* either by their state legislatures or by state constitutional ratifying conventions.

THE DEFEAT OF ERA   In 1972 when Congress sent the Equal Rights Amendment (ERA) to the states for ratification, it did so with overwhelming support of both Democrats and Republicans in the House and the Senate. National opinion polls and most national leaders, including Presidents Nixon, Ford, and Carter, strongly endorsed the simple language of the proposed amendment: "Equality of rights under law shall not be denied or abridged by the United States or by any State on account of sex."

ERA won quick ratification in about half of the states. By 1978, thirty-five state legislatures had ratified ERA. (See Figure 3–2.) (However, five states voted to rescind their earlier ratification. While there is some disagreement about the validity of these "rescissions," most constitutional scholars do not believe a state can rescind its earlier ratification of a constitutional amendment; there is no language in the Constitution referring to rescissions of constitutional amendments.) Leaders of the ERA movement called upon Congress to grant an unprecedented extension of time beyond the traditional seven

Figure 3–1
THE STATES' ROLE IN CONSTITUTIONAL AMENDMENT

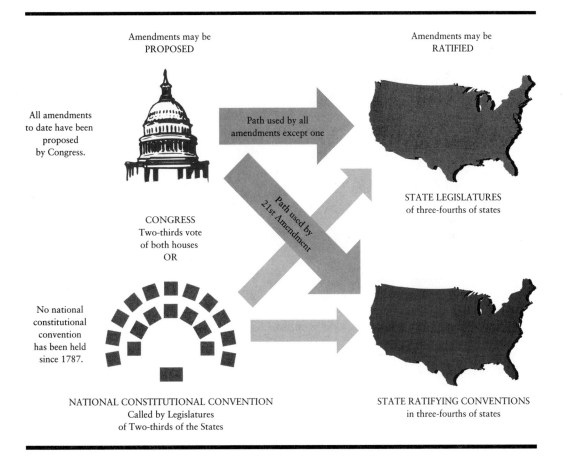

Amendments may be
PROPOSED

Amendments may be
RATIFIED

All amendments
to date have been
proposed
by Congress.

Path used by all
amendments except one

Path used by
21st Amendment

CONGRESS
Two-thirds vote
of both houses
OR

STATE LEGISLATURES
of three-fourths of states

No national
constitutional
convention
has been held
since 1787.

NATIONAL CONSTITUTIONAL CONVENTION
Called by Legislatures
of Two-thirds of the States

STATE RATIFYING CONVENTIONS
in three-fourths of states

years to continue the battle for ratification. (The Constitution, Article V, does not specify how long states can consider a constitutional amendment.) In 1978, Congress (by simple majority vote) granted ERA an unprecedented additional three years for state ratification; the new limit was 1982, a full ten years after Congress proposed the original ERA.

The "Stop ERA" movement gained strength in the states over time. Under the leadership of conservative spokeswoman Phyllis Schafly, an active group of women successfully lobbied *against* ERA in state legislatures. In spite of overwhelming support for ERA from Democratic and Republican presidents and congresses, leading celebrities from television and films, and even a majority of Americans surveyed by national polling organizations, these "ladies in pink" were influential in the defeat of ERA. (The phrase "ladies in pink" refers to a common practice of anti-ERA women lobbyists wearing pink, dressing well, baking apple pies for legislators, and otherwise adopting the traditional symbols of femininity.) Most of the lobbying against ERA in state legislatures was done by women's

Figure 3–2
ERA IN THE STATES

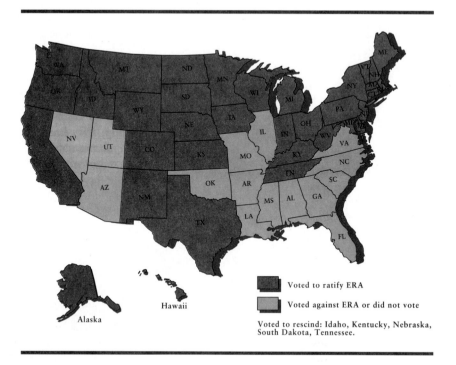

Voted to ratify ERA

Voted against ERA or did not vote

Voted to rescind: Idaho, Kentucky, Nebraska, South Dakota, Tennessee.

groups. While not as well organized as the leading feminist groups (NOW, the League of Women Voters, the Women's Political Caucus, and so on), the "ladies in pink" were very much in evidence when state legislatures considered ratification of ERA.[6]

Three-quarters of the states *must* concur in a constitutional amendment. This is a powerful tool of the states in our federal system. The wording of the Constitution cannot be altered without the approval of the states, regardless of how much support such a change in wording may have in Washington. Despite national support for ERA, the amendment fell *three states short* of ratification by the necessary thirty-eight states. Last-ditch attempts to pass ERA in states where the battle was close (Florida, Illinois, and North Carolina) failed in 1982.

THE DEFEAT OF THE DISTRICT OF COLUMBIA AMENDMENT

The Constitution grants Congress the power to govern the District of Columbia, but over time Congress has delegated considerable home rule to the District. Washington elects its own mayor and council, levies city taxes, and provides municipal services to its residents. The Twenty-third Amendment, ratified by the states in 1961, gives Washingtonians three

---

[6]See Val Burris, "Who Opposed the ERA? An Analysis of the Social Basis for Antifeminism," *Social Science Quarterly*, 64 (June 1983), 305–17.

presidential electors, but residents of the city have never had voting members of Congress. (The District's only congressional representation is its *nonvoting* delegates to the House and Senate, who may serve on committees and participate in debates on the floor.) In 1978 Congress passed and sent to the states a constitutional amendment to grant the District of Columbia two U.S. senators and as many representatives as their population would warrant if it were a state (currently one). Congress placed a seven-year time limit on ratification by the states in the amendment itself, thus preventing a time extension by simple majority vote of the House and Senate.

The DC amendment passed both houses of Congress with well over the necessary two-thirds majority and the support of both Democrats and Republicans. But opposition in the states arose quickly. Much of the opposition was political: The District was seen as predominately black, liberal, and Democratic. (Jesse Jackson would later be elected the District's nonvoting senator.) Only about 8 percent of the District's voters are registered as Republicans. The District itself has a less-than-reassuring record of self-government. (In 1995, facing municipal bankruptcy, Congress established a financial control commission with authority over the city's taxing and spending policies.) By the 1985 deadline only sixteen states, well short of the necessary thirty-eight, had ratified the amendment.

The defeat of the DC amendment led its supporters to press for a congressional vote on statehood for the District. While the Constitution clearly implies that the District "as the seat of the Government" is to be governed by Congress, they argue that Congress could reduce the size of the seat of the government to a few blocks surrounding the capitol and admit the remainder of the District as the new state of "Columbia." Statehood would accomplish the same objectives as the defeated DC amendment, giving District residents two U.S. senators and House representation. Moreover, a statehood vote only requires a simple majority of both houses, rather than the two-thirds majority required for a constitutional amendment, *and* statehood does not require ratification by three-quarters of the states. Yet, so far, the statehood strategy has failed; despite a Democratic platform pledge for DC statehood and the support of President Bill Clinton, statehood bills have failed to pass Congress.

THE SURPRISE PASSAGE OF THE TWENTY-SEVENTH AMEND-
MENT   As part of the Bill of Rights, Congress in 1789 sent to the states an amendment that would prohibit a pay raise for members of Congress until after the intervention of an election for House members. The amendment had no time limit for ratification attached to it. But only six of the original thirteen states ratified Madison's pay raise amendment, and it was largely forgotten. However, as congressional scandals mounted in the 1980s and public confidence in Congress plummeted, the old amendment was rediscovered. (By one account, a University of Texas student ran across the amendment in 1982 and realized it had no time limit. Using his own money he undertook a national campaign that resulted in twenty-six states ratifying the amendment. But he received only a "C" on his research paper.)[7] As more and more states ratified the two-hundred-year-old amendment, Congress should have realized that their behavior was under scrutiny. But Congress

---

[7]See Ruth Ann Strikland, "The Twenty-seventh Amendment and Constitutional Change by Stealth," *P.S. Political Science and Politics*, 26 (December 1993), 716–22.

proceeded in 1989 to vote itself a 50 percent pay raise, touching off a storm of protest. (Nationwide polls indicated that 82 percent of Americans opposed the pay increase.) Angry voters looked for ways to rein in an arrogant Congress. Fifteen additional states rushed to ratify Madison's amendment.

Some scholars, as well as leaders in Congress (including then House Speaker Thomas Foley), argued that ratification of the amendment after 203 years did not meet "the standard of timeliness." They argued that even though the Constitution itself placed no time limits on ratification, Article V "implied" that ratification should occur within a "reasonable" time. But when the archivist of the United States, Don Wilson, officially certified the adoption of the Twenty-seventh Amendment in 1992 as he was authorized to do by law, congressional leaders were stymied. Although they were irate over the archivist's action, they were unable to reverse it. Individual members of Congress raced to join in the popular sentiment, fearing that any effort to undo the amendment would be dealt with severely by the voters in the next election. Both houses voted nearly unanimously to endorse the amendment. The states had succeeded in administering an unexpected reprimand to Congress.

CONSTITUTIONAL AND HISTORICAL DEVELOPMENT OF FEDERALISM

The importance of formal constitutional arrangements should not be underestimated. However, the American federal system is a product of more than formal constitutional provisions. It is also shaped by court interpretations of constitutional principles and the history of disputes over state and national authority.

FEDERAL COURT AUTHORITY   The real meaning of American federalism has emerged in the heat of political conflict between states and nation. In the formative days of the new Republic, Chief Justice John Marshall, who presided over the Supreme Court from 1801 to 1835, became a major architect of American federalism. Under John Marshall, *the Supreme Court assumed the role of arbiter in disputes between state and national authority.* It was under John Marshall that the Supreme Court in *Marbury* v. *Madison* assumed the power to interpret the U.S. Constitution authoritatively.

The fact that the referee of disputes between state and national authority has been the *national* Supreme Court has had a profound influence on the development of American federalism. Since the Supreme Court is a *national* institution, one might say that in disputes between nation and states, one of the members of the two contending teams is also serving as umpire. Constitutionally speaking then, there is really *no* limitation on national as against state authority *if* all three branches of the national government—the Congress, the president, and the Court—act together to override state authority. The Constitution and the laws of the United States "made in pursuance thereof" are the supreme laws of the land, "anything in the constitution or laws of any state to the contrary notwithstanding." The Supreme Court, a national institution, through its "judicial power" interprets the Constitution and decides what laws are "made in pursuance thereof." Thus, *Marbury* v. *Madison* paved the way for the development of national power.

IMPLIED FEDERAL POWERS   Chief Justice John Marshall was also responsible for making the *Necessary and Proper Clause* the most significant grant of constitutional power to the national government. Political conflict over the scope of national power arose before the new Republic had been in operation for a year. In 1790 Alexander Hamilton, as secretary of the treasury, proposed the establishment of a national bank. Congress acted on Hamilton's suggestion in 1791, establishing a national bank to serve as a depository for national money and to facilitate federal borrowing. Thomas Jefferson considered the national bank dangerous centralization in government and objected that the power to establish a national bank was nowhere to be found in the enumerated powers of Congress. Hamilton replied that Congress could easily deduce the power to establish a bank from grants of authority in the Constitution relating to currency and other aspects of national finance, backed by the clause authorizing Congress "to make all laws which will be necessary and proper for carrying into execution the foregoing powers." Jefferson interpreted the word "necessary" to mean "indispensable," but Hamilton argued that the national government had the right to choose the manner and means of performing its delegated functions and was not restricted to employing only those means considered indispensable in the performance of its functions. The question eventually reached the Supreme Court in 1819 when Maryland levied a tax on the national bank, and the bank refused to pay it. In the case of *McCulloch* v. *Maryland,* Chief Justice John Marshall accepted the broader Hamiltonian version of the Necessary and Proper Clause:

> Let the end be legitimate, let it be within the scope of the Constitution, and all means which are appropriate, which are plainly adopted to the end, which are not prohibited but consistent with the letter and the spirit of the Constitution, are constitutional.[8]

The *McCulloch* case firmly established the principle that the Necessary and Proper Clause gives Congress the right to choose its means for carrying out the enumerated powers of the national government. Today, Congress can devise programs, create agencies, and establish national laws on the basis of long chains of reasoning from the most meager phrases of the constitutional text because of the broad interpretation of the Necessary and Proper Clause.

SECESSION AND CIVIL WAR   The Civil War was, of course, the greatest crisis of the American federal system. Did a state have the right to oppose national law to the point of secession? In the years preceding the Civil War, John C. Calhoun argued that the Constitution was a compact made by the *states* in a sovereign capacity rather than by the *people* in their national capacity. Calhoun contended that the federal government was an agent of the states, that the states retained their sovereignty in this compact, and that the federal government must not violate the compact, under the penalty of state nullification or even secession. Calhoun's doctrine was embodied in the Constitution of the Confederacy, which begins with the words "We, the people of the Confederate States, each state acting in its sovereign and independent character, in order to form a permanent federal government . . ." This wording contrasts with the preamble of the United States

---

[8]*McCulloch* v. *Maryland*, 4 Wheaton 316 (1819).

Constitution, "We, the people of the United States, in order to form a more perfect union . . ." The difference emphasizes Calhoun's thesis that the central government should be an agency of the states rather than of the people.

The issue was decided in the nation's bloodiest war. What was decided on the battlefield between 1861 and 1865 was confirmed by the Supreme Court in 1869: "Ours is an indestructible union, composed of indestructible states."[9] Yet the states' rights doctrines, and political disputes over the character of American federalism, did not disappear with Lee's surrender at Appomattox. The Thirteenth, Fourteenth, and Fifteenth Amendments, passed by the Reconstruction Congress, were clearly aimed at limiting state power in the interests of individual freedom. The Thirteenth Amendment eliminated slavery in the states; the Fifteenth Amendment prevented states from discriminating against blacks in the right to vote; and the Fourteenth Amendment declared that "No State shall make or enforce any law which shall abridge the privileges or immunities of citizens of the United States; nor shall any state deprive any person of life, liberty, or property without due process of law; nor deny to any person within its jurisdiction the equal protection of the laws." These amendments delegated to Congress the power to secure their enforcement. Yet for several generations these amendments were narrowly construed and added little, if anything, to national power.

CIVIL RIGHTS   However, after World War I, the Supreme Court began to build a national system of civil rights based upon the Fourteenth Amendment. In early cases, the Court held the Fourteenth Amendment prevented states from interfering with free speech, free press, or religious practices. Not until 1954, in the Supreme Court's desegregation decision in *Brown* v. *Board of Education* in Topeka, Kansas, did the Court begin to call for the full assertion of national authority on behalf of civil rights.[10]

The Supreme Court's use of the Fourteenth Amendment to ensure a national system of civil rights supported by the power of the federal government is an important step in the evolution of the American federal system. The controversy over federally imposed desegregation in the southern states renewed the debate over states' rights versus national authority. Despite the clear mandate of the Supreme Court in the *Brown* case, the southern states succeeded in avoiding all but token integration for more than ten years. (See Chapter 14.) Governor Faubus used the Arkansas National Guard to prevent the desegregation of Little Rock Central High School in 1957, but this opposition was ended quickly when President Eisenhower ordered the National Guard removed and sent units of the United States Army to enforce national authority. In 1962 President Kennedy took similar action when Governor Ross Barnett of Mississippi personally barred the entry of a black student to the University of Mississippi, despite a federal court order requiring his admission. Governor George Wallace of Alabama "stood in the doorway" to prevent desegregation but left his post at the doorway several hours later when federal marshals arrived. These actions reinforced the principle of national supremacy in the American federal system.

INTERSTATE COMMERCE   The growth of national power under the *Interstate Commerce Clause* is also an important development in the evolution of American feder-

---

[9]*Texas* v. *White,* 7 Wallace 700 (1869).

[10]*Brown* v. *Board of Education of Topeka, Kansas,* 347 U.S. 483 (1954).

alism. The Industrial Revolution in America created a *national* economy with a nation-wide network of transportation and communication and the potential for national economic depressions. In response to the growth of the national economy, Congress progressively widened the definition of "interstate commerce." Industrialization created interstate businesses, which could be regulated by the national government.

Yet for a time, the Supreme Court placed obstacles in the way of national authority over the economy, and by so doing created a "crisis" in American federalism. For many years, the Court narrowly construed interstate commerce to mean only the movement of goods and services across state lines, insisting that agriculture, mining, manufacturing, and labor relations were outside the reach of the delegated powers of the national government. However, when confronted with the Great Depression of the 1930s and President Franklin D. Roosevelt's threat to "pack" the Court with additional members to secure approval of his New Deal measures, the Court yielded. In *National Labor Relations Board* v. *Jones and Laughlin Steel Corporation* in 1937, the Court recognized the principle that production and distribution of goods and services for a national market could be regulated by Congress under the Interstate Commerce Clause. The effect was to give the national government effective control over the national economy, and today few economic activities are not within the reach of congressional power.

Indeed it was not until 1995 that the Supreme Court recognized any real limits to the powers granted Congress under the Interstate Commerce Clause. When Congress tried to make it a *federal* crime to carry a gun near a school in the Gun-Free School Zone Act of 1990, the Supreme Court held that it had exceeded its delegated powers. The U.S. Justice Department, which had prosecuted a Texas high school student for carrying a gun to school, argued that the act was a constitutional exercise of Congress's power over interstate commerce because "possession of a firearm in a school zone may result in violent crime and violent crime can be expected to affect the national economy." But the Court rejected this argument as "piling inference on inference . . . to convert Congressional authority under the Commerce Clause to a general police power of the sort retained by the states."[11] But it is too early to judge whether or not this decision represents a return to traditional notions of enumerated powers of Congress and retained powers of the states. The Commerce Clause remains a very broad grant of national power.

HOW MONEY SHIFTED POWER TO WASHINGTON

Over the years the national government has acquired much greater power in the federal system than the Founders originally envisioned. The "delegated" powers of the national government are now so broadly defined—particularly the power to tax and spend for the general welfare—that the government in Washington is involved in every aspect of American life. (The argument that constitutionally Congress can tax and spend only in support of its *enumerated* powers was rejected by the Supreme Court.[12]) Today there are really no segments of public activity "reserved" to the states or the people.

---

[11]*U.S.* v. *Lopez*, 63 L.W. 4343 (1995).

[12]*Massachusetts* v. *Mellon*, 262 U.S. 447 (1923).

THE EARLIEST FEDERAL AID   It is possible to argue that even in the earliest days of the Republic, the national government was involved in public activities that were not specifically delegated to it in the Constitution.[13] The first Congress of the United States in the famous Northwest Ordinance, providing for the government of the territories to the west of the Appalachian Mountains, authorized grants of federal land for the establishment of public schools, and by so doing, showed a concern for education, an area "reserved" to the states by the Constitution. Again in 1863, in the Morrill Land Grant Act, Congress provided grants of land to the states to promote higher education.

MONEY, POWER, AND THE INCOME TAX   The date 1913, when the Sixteenth Amendment gave the federal government the power to tax income directly, marked the beginning of a new era in American federalism. Congress had been given the power to tax and spend for the general welfare in Article I of the Constitution. However, the Sixteenth Amendment helped to shift the balance of financial power from the states to Washington, when it gave Congress the power to tax the incomes of corporations and individuals on a progressive basis. The income tax gave the federal government the power to raise large sums of money, which it proceeded to spend for the general welfare as well as for defense. It is no coincidence that the first major grant-in-aid programs (agricultural extension in 1914, highways in 1916, vocational education in 1917, and public health in 1918) all came shortly after the inauguration of the federal income tax.

FEDERAL GRANTS-IN-AID   The federal "grant-in-aid" has been the principal instrument in the expansion of national power. Approximately one-sixth of all state and local government revenues are currently derived from federal grants. This money is paid out through a staggering number and variety of programs. Federal grants may be obtained to assist in everything from the preservation of historic buildings, the development of minority-owned businesses, and aid for foreign refugees, to the drainage of abandoned mines, riot control, and school milk.

The largest portion of federal grant-in-aid money is devoted to health (especially Medicaid's health care for the poor) and welfare (especially Aid to Families with Dependent Children). In 1996, over 67 percent of total grant money was used for these purposes (see Table 3–2). Only 10 percent was used for highways and transit, and only about 16 percent for education, training, employment, and social services.

GRANTSMANSHIP   Federal money flows unevenly among the states. While overall about 22 percent of all state and local government revenue currently comes in the form of federal aid, the percentage is much higher in some states than others. (See Figure 3–3.)

The federal grant system is not neutral in its impact on the states, nor is it intended to be. Many grant programs are based upon formulas that incorporate various indications of need and financial ability. Federal aid is supposed to be "targeted" on national problems.[14] The effect of differential grant allocations among the states, combined with dif-

---

[13]See Daniel J. Elazar, *The American Partnership: Inter-Governmental Cooperation in Nineteenth-Century United States* (Chicago: University of Chicago Press, 1962).

[14]Robert M. Stein, "The Allocation of Federal Aid Monies: The Synthesis of Demand-Side and Supply-Side Explanations," *American Political Science Review,* 75 (June 1981), 334–43.

Table 3–2
GROWTH IN FEDERAL GRANTS-IN-AID BY FUNCTION

	Billions of Dollars				*1996*	
	1960	1970	1980	1990	B$	%
Natural resources and environment	0.1	0.4	5.4	3.7	4.0	1.6
Agriculture	0.2	0.6	0.6	1.3	0.8	0.1
Transportation	3.0	4.6	13.1	19.2	25.0	10.0
Community development	0.1	1.8	6.5	5.0	6.6	2.7
Education, employment, and social services	0.5	6.4	21.9	23.4	38.7	15.5
Health	0.2	3.8	15.8	43.9	112.6	45.2
Welfare	2.6	5.8	18.5	35.2	55.4	22.3
General government	0.2	0.5	8.6	2.3	2.2	0.1
Other	0.0	0.1	1.2	1.4	3.6	0.1
Total	7.0	24.1	91.5	135.4	248.9	100.0

Source: Budget of the United States Government 1996.

ferences among state populations in federal tax collections, is to *redistribute* federal money throughout the nation. The big winners in the federal grant game are generally rural states; the losers are the urban states.

The rush to Washington to ensure that states and cities receive their "fair share" of federal grant money, together with concerns over federal interference in the conduct of state and local government, has produced a great deal of intergovernmental lobbying at the nation's capital. The most influential organizations seeking to influence intergovernmental affairs are listed in Table 3–3. In addition to these organizations, various professional associations represent specific state and local government officials. The most notable is the International City Managers Association; others include the National Association of State Budget Officers, National Association of Attorneys General, American Association of State Highway and Transportation Officials, and American Association of School Administrators. Most individual states now maintain offices in Washington with staff committed to looking after their interests.

HOW CONGRESS RAISED THE DRINKING AGE

Nowhere among Congress's enumerated powers in the U.S. Constitution do we find the power to regulate the consumption of alcoholic beverages. Traditionally, the "reserved" powers of the states included the protection of the health, safety, and well-being of their own citizens. And every state set minimum drinking age laws of its own.

In the early 1970s most states lowered their drinking age to eighteen, influenced perhaps by the Twenty-sixth Amendment giving eighteen-year-olds the right to vote. But in

Figure 3–3
RELIANCE ON FEDERAL AID—PERCENT OF TOTAL
STATE–LOCAL REVENUE FROM FEDERAL AID

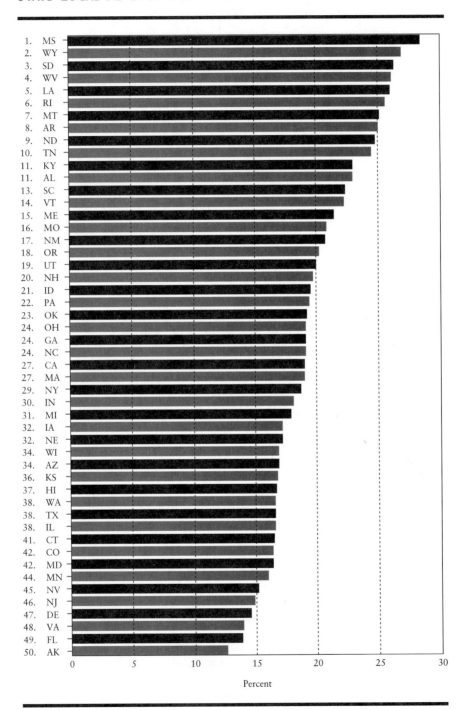

Source: Statistical Abstract of the United States, 1995.

Table 3–3

INTERGOVERNMENTAL ORGANIZATIONS

Council of State Governments
3560 Iron Works Pike
Lexington, KY 40578

U.S. Conference of Mayors
1620 Eye St. N.W.
Washington, D.C. 20006

National Governors Association
444 N. Capitol St. N.W.
Washington, D.C. 20001

National Association of Counties
440 1st St. N.W.
Washington, D.C. 20001

National Conference of State Legislatures
1560 Broadway
Denver, CO 80202

National Association of Towns and Townships
1522 K St. N.W.
Washington, D.C. 20005

National League of Cities
1301 Pennsylvania Ave. N.W.
Washington, D.C. 20004

the early 1980s, the states individually began to raise the drinking age, as part of a national movement against drunk driving. By 1984 about half of the states had changed the legal drinking age to twenty-one (such as California); other states chose nineteen (including New York, Florida, and Texas) or twenty (such as Massachusetts and Connecticut); and still other states allowed eighteen-year-olds to buy beer and wine but required a person to be twenty-one in order to buy "distilled spirits" (such as Colorado, Kansas). Only a few states (Vermont, Rhode Island, Louisiana, Hawaii) retained a general eighteen-year-old drinking age.

The minimum drinking age became a national issue largely as a result of emotional appeals by groups such as Mothers Against Drunk Driving (MADD). Politically these appeals were more effective than any scientific studies of alcohol-related deaths. Nonetheless, statistical evidence presented to Congress by the National Transportation Safety Board showed that teenagers were more likely to be involved in alcohol-related traffic deaths than nonteenagers. Indeed, drunk driving was the leading cause of death among teenagers.[15] The National Student Association, restaurant owners, and liquor industry countered that teenagers were no worse offenders than those in the twenty-one to twenty-five age group and that the selection of all teenagers for special restrictions was age discrimination. But the tragic stories told at televised committee hearings by grieving mothers of dead teenagers swept away the opposition.

Federalism arguments were also swept away. Several senators argued that a national drinking age infringed on the powers of the states in a matter traditionally under state control. However, the new law did not *directly* mandate a national drinking age. Instead, it ordered the withholding of 10 percent of all federal highway funds from any state that

---

[15]*Congressional Quarterly Weekly Report*, June 30, 1984, p. 1557.

failed to raise its minimum drinking age to twenty-one. States retained the right to ignore the national drinking age and give up a significant portion of their highway funds. This was the same approach taken by Congress in 1974 in establishing a national 55-mile-per-hour speed limit. Opponents of this device labeled it "federal blackmail" and a federal intrusion into state responsibilities. For some state officials the issue was not teen drinking but rather the preemption of state authority.

But proponents of the legislation cited the national interest in a uniform minimum drinking age. They argued that protecting the lives of young people outweighed the states' interest in preserving their authority. Moreover, teens were crossing state lines to go to states with lower drinking ages. New York, for example, with a minimum drinking age of nineteen was attracting teenagers from Pennsylvania and New Jersey, where the drinking age was twenty-one. Reports of "bloody borders" justified national action to establish a uniform drinking age. While the Reagan White House had pledged to return responsibilities to the states, it did not wish to offend the nation's mothers on such an emotional issue. Despite initial reservations, President Reagan supported the bill and signed it into law in 1984.

Constitutionally, Congress was exercising its powers to spend money for the general welfare. Congress was not *directly* legislating in an area "reserved" to the states—protection of health, safety, and well-being. Instead, Congress was threatening to withhold some *federal* highway grant monies from states that did not meet a federal requirement. Rather than infringe on states' powers, the federal law was merely "a relatively mild encouragement to the states to enact higher minimum drinking ages than they would otherwise choose." Congress had respected the powers of the states by not directly legislating a national drinking age.[16] Technically states remain free to set their own minimum drinking age. Despite heated arguments in many state legislatures, all adopted the twenty-one-year-old national drinking age by 1990. Money is power; this axiom holds true in the American federal system as in politics generally.

THE POLITICS OF GRANTS-IN-AID

From the earliest days of the Republic, American statesmen have argued over federalism. In recent years, political conflict over federalism—over the decision between national versus state and local responsibilities and finances—has tended to follow traditional "liberal" and "conservative" political cleavages. Generally, liberals seek to enhance the power of the *national* government because they believe that people's lives can be changed—and bettered—by the exercise of national governmental power. The government in Washington has more power and resources than do state and local governments, which many liberals regard as too slow, cumbersome, weak, and unresponsive. Thus liberalism and centralization are closely related in American politics.

The liberal argument for national authority can be summarized as follows:

- There is insufficient awareness of social problems by state and local governments. The federal government must take the lead in civil rights, equal employment opportunities, care for the poor and aged, the provision of adequate medical care for

---

[16]*South Dakota v. Debe*, 438 U.S. 203 (1987).

all Americans, and the elimination of urban poverty and blight. Grants-in-aid permit the government to set national goals and priorities in all levels of government without formally altering the federal structure. Thus, as problems of public assistance, urban renewal, highway construction, education, and poverty acquire national significance, they can be dealt with by the application of national resources.

- Grants-in-aid provide the necessary impetus for social change. It is difficult to achieve change when reform-minded citizens must deal with fifty state governments and over 86,000 local governments. Change is more likely to be accomplished by a strong central government.

- Finally, grants-in-aid provide an opportunity for the national government to ensure a uniform level of public service throughout the nation—for example, federal grants-in-aid help ensure a minimum level of existence for the poverty-stricken regardless of where they live. This aspect of federal policy assumes that in some parts of the nation, state and local governments are unable, or perhaps unwilling, to devote their resources to raising public service levels to minimum national standards.

Conservatives, in contrast, are skeptical about the "good" that government can do and believe that adding to the power of the national government is not an effective way of resolving society's problems. On the contrary, they argue that "government is the problem, not the solution." Excessive federal government regulation, burdensome taxation, and inflationary spending combine to restrict individual freedom, penalize work and savings, and destroy incentives for economic growth. Government should be kept small, controllable, and close to the people.

Conservative objections to federal grant-in-aid programs can be summarized as follows:

- Grass-roots government promotes a sense of self-responsibility and self-reliance. State and local government can better adapt public programs to local needs and conditions. Whenever the national government contributes financially to state or local programs, state and local officials are left with less freedom of choice than they would have had otherwise. Federal grants-in-aid are invariably accompanied by federal standards or "guidelines," which must be adhered to if states and communities are to receive their federal money. While no state is required to accept a federal grant and its restrictions, it is very difficult for states and communities to resist the pressure to accept federal money. It is sometimes said that states are "bribed" by the temptation of much-needed federal money and "blackmailed" by the thought that other states will get the money, which was raised in part by federal taxes on the state's own citizens.

- Federal grants cause state and local officials to overspend what looks to them like "free" money. Overspending on programs or services that local residents would not be willing to pay for out of their *own* tax revenues creates waste and inefficiency and contributes to the overall growth of government. Federal money is not "free": It comes from the *nation's* taxpayers. Local governments are sometimes pressured to apply for funds for projects they do not really need, simply because federal funds are available, while they may receive little or no federal assistance for more vital programs. Federal grant money is frequently provided for "new" or "innovative" or "demonstration" programs, when the real problems facing states and communities may be in traditional public services such as police, sewage, and sanitation.

- Finally, the grant-in-aid system assumes that federal officials are better judges of goals and priorities at all levels of government than are state or local officials. State and local officials do not determine what activities in their states and communities will receive federal money—federal officials determine these priorities. In many grant programs federal officials must approve each funded project—a housing project in Des Moines, a new set of welfare regulations in California, a sewage disposal system in Baton Rouge, an urban renewal project in Alabama, or a highway in North Dakota. Block grants, which allocate federal funds on a formula basis to states and communities for general purposes like "community development" or "mental health" provide more flexibility than project grants. But Congress cannot resist attaching directions for the use of these grants.

Americans are divided over the merits of these arguments. Most national opinion surveys reveal greater trust and confidence in state and local government than in the federal government, a belief that the federal government has too much power, and a greater concern about inefficiency at the federal level (see Table 3–4). But many Americans believe that the federal government can do a better job handling specific issues such as workplace safety, health care, environmental concerns, and rules for civil lawsuits. And most Americans trust the federal government more than the state government to protect civil rights. There is no way to settle these arguments about federalism; they have been heard for over 200 years in American politics.

FEDERALISM: VARIATIONS ON THE THEME

DUAL FEDERALISM (1787–1913)   For the nation's first hundred years, the pattern of federal–state relations has been described as *dual federalism*. Under this pattern, the states and the nation divided most governmental functions. The national government concentrated its attention on the "delegated" powers—national defense, foreign affairs, tariffs, commerce crossing state lines, coining money, establishing standard weights and measures, maintaining a post office and building post roads, and admitting new states. State governments decided the important domestic policy issues—slavery (until the Civil War), education, welfare, health, and criminal justice. This separation of policy responsibilities was once compared to a "layer cake,"[17] with local governments at the base, state governments in the middle, and the national government at the top.

COOPERATIVE FEDERALISM (1913–1964)   The Industrial Revolution and the development of a national economy, the income tax, which shifted financial resources to the national government, and the challenges of two world wars and the Great Depression, all combined to end the distinction between national and state concerns. The new pattern of federal–state relations was labeled *cooperative federalism*. Both the nation and the states exercised responsibilities for welfare, health, highways, education, and criminal justice. This merging of policy responsibilities was compared to a "marble cake." "As the colors are mixed in a marble cake, so functions are mixed in the American federal system."[18]

---

[17]Morton Grodzins, *The American System* (Chicago: Rand McNally, 1966), pp. 8–9.
[18]Ibid., p. 265.

Table 3–4
PUBLIC OPINION AND FEDERALISM

General[a]

TRUST AND CONFIDENCE

In which of the following people in government do you have the most trust and confidence?

Federal government	19
State government	22
Local government	37

Generally speaking, which do you trust to do a better job of running things—the federal government or your state government?

Federal government	27
State government	69

POWER

Does the federal government have too much power, do the state governments have too much power, or is the balance about right?

Federal too much	48
States too much	6
About right	38

EFFICIENCY

Which level of government do you think spends the taxpayer's dollar more wisely?

Federal government	10
State government	24
Local government	50

Specific

For each item I name, please tell me whether you trust the federal government or your state government to do a better job handling that issue:

	FEDERAL GOVERNMENT	STATE GOVERNMENT
Workplace safety	44	57
Medicare and Medicaid	46	53
Environmental rules for clean air and water	46	53
Rules for civil rights	48	53
Protect civil rights	64	37

[a]All figures in percentages of U.S. public in national opinion surveys. No Opinions and Don't Knows not shown.

Sources: See Advisory Commission on Intergovernmental Relations, *Changing Public Attitudes on Governments and Taxes* (Washington, D.C.: ACIR, annual); and Rockefeller Institute, *Bulletin 1996: The Revolution Revolution* (Albany: Rockefeller Institute, 1996), reporting surveys by ABC News/*Washington Post,* March 16–19, 1995.

The Great Depression of the 1930s forced states to ask for federal financial assistance in dealing with poverty, unemployment, and old age. Governors welcomed massive federal public works projects. In addition, the federal government intervened directly in economic affairs, labor relations, business practices, and agriculture. Through the grant-in-aid device, the national government cooperated with the states in public assistance, employment services, child welfare, public housing, urban renewal, highway building, and vocational education.

Yet even in this period of shared national-state responsibility, the national government emphasized cooperation in achieving common national and state goals. Congress generally acknowledged that it had no direct constitutional authority to regulate public health, safety, or welfare.

CENTRALIZED FEDERALISM (1964–1980)   Over the years it became increasingly difficult to maintain the fiction that the national government was merely assisting the states in performing their domestic responsibility. By the time President Lyndon B. Johnson launched the "Great Society" in 1964, the federal government clearly set forth its own "national" goals. Virtually all problems confronting American society—from solid-waste disposal and water and air pollution to consumer safety, home insulation, noise abatement, and even metric conversion—were declared to be national problems. Congress legislated directly on any matter it chose, without regard to its "enumerated powers" and without pretense to financial assistance. The Supreme Court no longer concerned itself with the "reserved" powers of the states; the Tenth Amendment lost most of its meaning. The pattern of national–state relations became centralized. As for the cake analogies, one commentator observed: "The frosting had moved up to the top, something like a pineapple upside-down cake."[19]

THE OLD "NEW FEDERALISM"

From time to time efforts have been made to reverse the flow of power to Washington and return responsibilities to state and local government. The phrase "New Federalism" originated in the administration of President Richard M. Nixon, who used it to describe General Revenue Sharing—federal sharing of tax revenues with state and local governments with few strings attached. Later, "New Federalism" was used by President Ronald Reagan to describe a series of proposals designed to reduce federal involvement in domestic programs and encourage states and cities to undertake greater policy responsibilities themselves.

GENERAL REVENUE SHARING   Although the Reagan administration ended General Revenue Sharing (GRS) in implementing *its* definition of New Federalism, the original GRS legislation in 1972 was designed as a conservative alternative to categorical grants by federal agencies for specific projects. It was argued that unrestricted federal money grants to state and local government was preferable to centralized bureaucratic decision making in Washington. GRS promised to reverse the flow of power to federal bureaucrats, end excessive red tape, and revitalize state and local governments. GRS was strongly supported by state and local government officials, who were happy to have the federal government collect tax money and then turn it over to them to spend. But revenue

---

[19]Charles Press, *State and Community Governments in the Federal System* (New York: John Wiley, 1979), p. 78.

sharing never really replaced the hundreds of categorical grant programs; it was simply an added source of state and local government revenue.[20]

The Reagan administration, confronting high federal deficits and wanting to reduce Washington's role in domestic policy, undertook a long and eventually successful effort to end General Revenue Sharing. The president argued that it was unreasonable to expect the federal government, which was running deep deficits, to turn over revenues to state and local governments, which had no deficits. (Most state and local governments are prohibited by their own constitutions and charters from having deficits in their operating budgets. Most GRS funds went for traditional services that local taxpayers should fund themselves. For several years, state and local government officials successfully lobbied Congress to restore GRS funds cut from the president's budget. But deficit pressures finally ended GRS in 1986.

BLOCK GRANTS   Another approach to cutting federal strings in grant-in-aid programs is the *block grant*. Block grants may be used by states and communities for projects decided at the local level within a broad category—"community development" or "law enforcement," for example. Federal agencies still supervise block grants, but specific projects are supposed to be decided at the local level. Obviously, block grants do not give states and communities the same freedom as revenue sharing money. But block grants provide greater flexibility than traditional project grants. State and local officials may use block-grant funds for their stated purpose without seeking the approval of federal agencies for specific projects. Congress endorsed these block grants, but the struggle between categorical grant interest (liberals and Democrats) and the consolidationists (Reagan and the Republicans) was really a draw. Many categorical grant programs were merged (notably in health services; alcohol, drug abuse, and mental health; social services; maternal and child health; community services; community development; and education), but many others remained independent.

STATE-LOCAL DEPENDENCE ON FEDERAL GRANTS   Perhaps the most important accomplishment of the Reagan administration's New Federalism was a reversal of the historical trend of the greater dependence of state and local governments on federal money. In the years prior to 1980, state and local governments had become increasingly dependent on federal grants as sources of revenue. Federal grants rose to over one-quarter of all state–local expenditures in 1980 (see Table 3–5). Total federal aid dollars continued to rise during the Reagan years, but not at the same rate as in previous years. Many state and local officials sought to blame "cutbacks in federal aid" for various troubles they encountered. It is true, of course, that federal aid declined somewhat in relative terms: as a percentage of GNP, as a percentage of total federal outlays, and most importantly as a percentage of state–local revenue. But this occurred because grants did not rise as fast as these denominators, not because of any overall "cutbacks."

However, it is not likely that presidents or Congress members or candidates for these national offices will ever be moved to restrain national power. People expect federal

---

[20]See Diel S. Wright and Alfred R. Light, "The Indeterminants of State Revenue Sharing," *Journal of Politics,* 37 (February 1977), 457–63; Richard P. Nathan et al., *Monitoring Revenue Sharing* (Washington, DC: Brookings Institution, 1975).

Table 3–5

TRENDS IN FEDERAL GRANTS-IN-AID

	Total Federal Grants	Federal Grants as a Percent of:		
	(BILLION DOLLARS)	TOTAL FEDERAL SPENDING	STATE AND LOCAL EXPENDITURES	GROSS NATIONAL PRODUCT
1950	2.3	5.3	10.4	0.8
1960	7.0	7.6	14.6	1.4
1970	24.1	12.3	19.2	2.4
1975	49.8	15.0	22.7	3.3
1980	91.5	15.5	25.8	3.4
1985	105.9	11.2	21.1	2.7
1990	136.9	11.0	18.0	3.0
1994	217.3	14.6	21.9	3.3

Source: U.S. Office of Management and Budget, *Special Analysis of the Budget 1992*, Part II–166; and Advisory Commission on Intergovernmental Relations, *Significant Features of Fiscal Federalism 1994*, vol. II, p. 30.

officials to "do something" about virtually every problem that confronts individuals, families, communities, or the nation. Politicians gain very little by telling their constituents that a particular problem is not a federal problem. Indeed, by the 1990s under Republican President George Bush as well as Democratic President Bill Clinton, the flow of federal aid dollars to the states accelerated. Reversing the trend of the 1980s, state and local government dependence on federal revenue began to rise again.

COERCIVE FEDERALISM: MANDATES AND PREEMPTIONS

Can Congress *directly* regulate the traditional functions of state and local governments? We know that Congress can influence the actions of state and local governments by offering them grants of money and then threatening to withdraw them if they do not meet federal rules, regulations, or "guidelines." But can Congress, in the exercise of its broad constitutional powers, legislate directly about traditional functions of state and local governments—schools, streets, police and fire protection, water and sewers, refuse disposal? Can the national government by law treat the states as administrative units required to carry out the mandates of Congress?

Certainly the historical answer to this question was "No." A typical nineteenth-century description of federalism by the U.S. Supreme Court asserted that the federal government could not intrude or interfere with the independent powers of state governments and vice versa:

> There are within the territorial limits of each state two governments [state and national], restricted in their spheres of action, but independent of each other, and supreme within their respective spheres. Each has its separate departments, each has its distinct laws, and each has its own tribunes for their enforcement. Neither government can intrude within the jurisdiction of the other or authorize any interference therein by its judicial officers with the action of the other.[21]

Perhaps this separation and independence never really characterized relations between the national government and the state governments. But at least state governments were viewed as independent authorities that could not be directly coerced by the national government in their traditional functions.

DIRECT CONGRESSIONAL REGULATION OF STATE AND LOCAL GOVERNMENTS   Ordinarily, Congress is careful not to give direct orders to state or local governments. Instead, Congress involves itself in state and local affairs by granting or withholding federal dollars depending on whether states and cities do what Congress wishes. In theory at least, states and cities remain independent; they *could* forgo the federal government's money and conduct their own affairs as they please. But in 1974 in amending its Fair Labor Standards Act, Congress decided to directly order state and local governments to obey minimum wage and hour legislation for all public employees. When the League of Cities, acting on behalf of all state and local governments, challenged the constitutionality of this law, the U.S. Supreme Court first ruled (five to four) that Congress could *not* order the states to do anything in matters traditionally reserved to the states.[22]

However, in its 1985 *Garcia* decision, the U.S. Supreme Court reversed itself and removed all barriers to direct congressional legislation in matters traditionally "reserved" to the states.[23] The Court dismissed the argument that the nature of American federalism and the reserved powers clause of the Tenth Amendment prevented Congress from directly legislating in state and local affairs. The Court held that it would no longer intervene to protect state powers, that judicial intervention was "unworkable," and that Congress itself should decide how far its own powers extended to state and local affairs.

CONGRESSIONAL REGULATION OF STATE TAXES   Nearly a century ago, the U.S. Supreme Court held that Congress could not levy taxes on the states or on their bonds or notes.[24] Intergovernmental tax immunity was believed to be an integral part of the Tenth Amendment's guarantee of the reserved powers of the states. The states could not tax federal bonds and the nation could not tax state bonds. But in 1987 the U.S.

---

[21]*Tarbels Case*, 13 Wall. 397 (1872). Also cited and discussed in Deil S. Wright, *Understanding Intergovernmental Relations* (Boston: Duxbury Press, 1978), p. 22.

[22]*National League of Cities v. Usery*, 426 U.S. 833 (1976).

[23]*Garcia v. San Antonio Metropolitan Transit Authority*, 105 U.S. 1005 (1985).

[24]*Pollock v. Farmers Loan and Trust Company*, 157 U.S. 429 (1895).

Supreme Court shocked state and local officials and the municipal bond market by holding that Congress could if it wished levy taxes on the interest received from state and local bonds. In a dissent, Justice Sandra Day O'Connor observed that "the Court has failed to enforce the constitutional safeguards of state autonomy and self-sufficiency that may be found in the Tenth Amendment and the Guarantee Clause, as well as in the principles of federalism implicit in the Constitution."[25]

FEDERAL PREEMPTIONS   The supremacy of federal laws over those of the states, spelled out in the Supremacy Clause of the Constitution, permits Congress to decide whether or not state laws in a particular field are preempted by federal law. *Total preemption* refers to the federal government's assumption of all regulatory powers in a particular field—for example, copyrights, bankruptcy, railroads, and airlines. No state regulations in a totally preempted field are permitted. *Partial preemption* stipulates that a state law on the same subject is valid as long as it does not conflict with the federal law in the same area. For example, the Occupational Safety and Health Act of 1970 specifically permits state regulation of any occupational safety or health issue on which the federal Occupational Safety and Health Administration (OSHA) has *not* developed a standard; but once OSHA enacts a standard, all state standards are nullified. Yet another form of the partial preemption, the *standard partial preemption,* permits states to regulate activities in a field already regulated by the federal government, as long as state regulatory standards are at least as stringent as those of the federal government. Usually states must submit their regulations to the responsible federal agency for approval; the federal agency may revoke a state's regulating power if it fails to enforce the approved standards. For example, the federal Environmental Protection Agency (EPA) permits state environmental regulations that meet or exceed EPA standards. Occasionally Congress grants preemptive relief to states in response to protests that federal regulations are incompatible with state or local conditions. For example, Congress permits states to petition the U.S. Department of Transportation to limit the size of commercial tractor-trailers on interstate highways within a state.

FEDERAL MANDATES   Federal mandates are orders to state and local governments to comply with federal laws. Federal mandates occur in a wide variety of areas—from civil rights and voter rights laws to conditions of jails and juvenile detention centers, minimum wage and worker safety regulations, air and water pollution controls, and requirements for access for disabled people. (See Table 3–6.) State and local governments frequently complain that compliance with federal "unfunded mandates" imposes costs on them that are seldom reimbursed.

REPRESENTATIONAL FEDERALISM

What is left of federalism today? If there are no real constitutional restraints on the powers of the national government, if people look primarily to the national government to

---

[25]*South Carolina v. Barker,* 485 U.S. 505 (1988).

Table 3–6
SELECTED FEDERAL MANDATES

RECENT EXAMPLES OF FEDERAL MANDATES TO STATE AND LOCAL GOVERNMENTS

- *Age Discrimination Act 1986* Outlaws mandatory retirement ages for public as well as private employees, including police, firefighters, and state college and university faculty.
- *Asbestos Hazard Emergency Act 1986* Orders school districts to inspect for asbestos hazards and remove asbestos from school buildings when necessary.
- *Safe Drinking Water Act 1986* Establishes national requirements for municipal water supplies; regulates municipal waste treatment plants.
- *Clean Air Act 1990* Bans municipal incinerators and requires auto emission inspections in certain urban areas.
- *Americans with Disabilities Act 1990* Requires all state and local government buildings to promote handicapped access.
- *National Voter Registration Act 1993* Requires states to register voters at driver's licensing, welfare, and unemployment offices.

Governors (including Bill Clinton when he was governor of Arkansas) have frequently urged Congress to halt the imposition of unfunded mandates on states and communities. In 1995 Congress agreed only to require any bill imposing unfunded costs of $50 million or more (as determined by the Congressional Budget Office) to be subject to an additional procedural vote: A majority must vote to waive a general prohibition against unfunded mandates before such a bill can come to the House or Senate floor. It is not likely that such a modest restraint will do much to alleviate the problem of unfunded mandates for states and cities.

---

solve their problems, if the national government's superior fiscal resources give it powerful leverage over states and communities, what remains of the federal division of power between states and nation? Are there any guarantees of state power remaining in our federal system?

The notion of "representational federalism" denies that there is any constitutional division of powers between states and nation and asserts that federalism is defined by the role of the states in electing members of Congress and the president. The United States is said to retain a federal system because national officials are selected from subunits of government—the president through the allocation of electoral college votes to the states, and the Congress through the allocation of two Senate seats per state and the apportionment of representatives to states based on population. Whatever protection exists for state power and independence must be found in the national political process—in the influence of state and district voters on their senators and congress members. Representational federalism does not recognize any constitutionally protected powers of the states.

FEDERALISM IN THE GARCIA DECISION   The U.S. Supreme Court appears to have adopted this notion of representational federalism, especially in its *Garcia* decision in 1985. The Court declared that there were *no* "a priori definitions of state sovereignty," *no* "discrete limitations on the objects of federal authority," and *no* protection

of state powers in the U.S. Constitution. According to the Court: "State sovereign interests . . . are more properly protected by procedural safeguards inherent in the structure of
the federal system than by judicially created limitations on federal power." The Court
rhetorically endorsed a federal system, but left it up to the national Congress, rather than
the Constitution or the courts, to decide what powers should be exercised by the states
and the national government.

In a strongly worded dissenting opinion in the *Garcia* case, Justice Lewis Powell argued
that if federalism is to be retained, the Constitution must divide powers, not the Congress.
"The states' role in our system of government is a matter of constitutional law, not legislative grace." And the Court must interpret the Constitution, protecting the powers of
the states and defining the powers of the national government. In the words of the
Supreme Court's dissenting members,

> the extent to which the states may exercise their authority . . . henceforth is to be deter-
> mined by political decision made by members of the federal government, a decision the
> Court says will not be subjected to judicial review. It does not seem to have occurred to the
> Court that *it*—an unelected majority of five justices—today rejects almost 200 years of the
> understanding of the constitutional status of federalism.[26]

FEDERALISM AND THE "CLEAR STATEMENT"   However, the Supreme
Court may be unwilling to jettison altogether the notion of federalism as the division of
power between nation and states. Justice Sandra Day O'Connor, a former Arizona legislator and appellate court judge, has been a staunch defender of federalism on the Supreme
Court. Quoting from the *Federalist* and citing the Tenth Amendment, Justice O'Connor
wrote the majority opinion in a case considering whether Congress's Age Discrimination
Employment Act invalidated a provision of the Missouri Constitution requiring judges to
retire at age 70.[27] She cited the "constitutional balance of federal and state powers" as a
reason for upholding the Missouri Constitution. Only a "clear statement" by Congress of
its intent to override a traditional state power would justify doing so. This "clear statement" rule presumably governs federal laws that may be in conflict with state laws or
constitutions. The rule does not prevent Congress from directly regulating state government activity, but it requires Congress to say unambiguously that this is its intent.

"DEVOLUTION": THE NEW NEW FEDERALISM

Controversy over federalism—over what level of government should do what—is as old
as the nation itself. Each era brings new issues and new ideas to the debate. Current debate over federalism has produced a new term, "devolution" (passing down) of responsibilities from the national government to the states. Devolution proposals generally take
one of two forms: (1) sorting out or "swapping responsibilities and revenue sources
among levels of government, and (2) consolidating various federal grant programs into
larger block grants and "devolving" greater responsibilities to the states to determine
how the monies should be spent.

---

[26]*Garcia v. San Antonio Metropolitan Transit Authority* 469 U.S. 528 (1985).
[27]*Gregory v. Ashcraft,* 11 S.Ct. 2395 (1991).

SORTING OUT RESPONSIBILITIES   Sorting out responsibilities between Washington and fifty state capitals is a recurring theme in federalism. A recent proposal, labeled the "grand swap," would shift responsibility to the states for welfare programs, including Aid to Families with Dependent Children, Supplementary Security Income, and food stamps. In return, the federal government would assume full responsibility for all health care programs, including Medicaid, which is currently the fastest-growing cost of state governments. This grand swap would probably be revenue-neutral; that is, not requiring any great shift in spending burdens. Another proposal has been to transfer the federal gasoline tax to the states along with full authority over highways and transit spending, and perhaps the elimination of the U.S. Department of Transportation. And frequently proposals are made to close down the U.S. Department of Education and rely exclusively on state and local governments for providing and funding education in America.

GREATER RELIANCE ON BLOCK GRANTS   But devolution, if it occurs at all, is more likely to take the form of more federal program consolidations into block grants, allowing greater flexibility in state expenditures of these funds. Block grants are an extension of Reagan-era "new federalism," which substituted block grants for categorical grants in a number of areas. But currently less than 10 percent of all federal aid money goes to state and local governments through block grants.

WELFARE REFORM AND DEVOLUTION   Welfare reform is not only a major domestic policy issue but also the key to the debate over devolution. As many as seventy federally funded welfare programs, including Aid to Families with Dependent Children, Medicaid, child care, and food stamps, could be consolidated into block grants, with states given broad authority to experiment with their own approaches to assisting the poor. It is doubtful that Congress would remove *all* of the strings attached to welfare money. It is likely that liberals will want to ensure that certain levels of support are guaranteed, and conservatives will want to ensure that work requirements and time limits are imposed.

But the real stumbling block to the block-grant approach to welfare is the current system of entitlements. Entitlement programs, including AFDC, Medicaid, and food stamps (which constitute well over three-quarters of all federal payments to state and local governments) give individuals the legal right to receive payments. If entitlements are continued, simply converting federal expenditures into block grants would confront the states with an open-ended, unlimited obligation to pay. The obligation would be controlled by Congress, but Congress might not provide enough money in each year's block grant to meet the obligation, presumably shifting the burden to the states.

The only way to fairly construct a welfare block grant is to eliminate the individual legal entitlement for welfare benefits. But this would be a truly revolutionary change in federal welfare policy. (The entitlement approach in AFDC dates back to 1935.) Removing entitlements would allow states themselves to determine eligibility as well as levels of support for welfare recipients. But it would also allow Congress to better control the growth of welfare costs.

POLITICAL OBSTACLES   However, it is not likely that presidents or members of Congress will ever be motivated to restrain their own power. Even if they were so inclined, popular expectation for them to "Do Something!" about virtually every problem that confronts individuals, families, or communities would pressure them into federal interventions. Politicians gain very little by telling their constituents that a particular problem is not a federal responsibility.

INTERSTATE RELATIONS—HORIZONTAL FEDERALISM

FULL FAITH AND CREDIT   The U.S. Constitution provides that "full faith and credit shall be given in each state to the public acts, records, and judicial proceedings of every other state." As more Americans move from state to state, it becomes increasingly important that the states recognize each other's legal instruments. This constitutional clause is intended to protect the rights of individuals who move from one state to another, and it is also intended to prevent individuals from evading their legal responsibilities by crossing state lines. Courts in Illinois must recognize decisions made by courts in Michigan. Contracts entered into in New York may be enforced in Florida. Corporations chartered in Delaware should be permitted to do business in North Dakota. One of the more serious problems in interstate relations today is the failure of the states to meet their obligations under the Full Faith and Credit Clause in the area of domestic relations, including divorce, alimony, child support, and custody of children. The result is now a complex and confused situation in domestic relations law.

PRIVILEGES AND IMMUNITIES   The Constitution also states: "The citizens of each state shall be entitled to all privileges and immunities of citizens in the several states." Apparently the Founding Fathers thought that no state should discriminate against citizens from another state in favor of its own citizens. To do so would seriously jeopardize national unity. This clause also implies that citizens of any state may move freely about the country and settle where they like, with the assurance that as newcomers they will not be subjected to unreasonable discrimination. The newcomer should not be subject to discriminatory taxation; nor barred from lawful occupations under the same conditions as other citizens of the state; nor prevented from acquiring and using property; nor denied equal protection of the laws; nor refused access to the courts. However, states have managed to compromise this constitutional guarantee in several important ways. States establish residence requirements for voting and holding office, which prevent newcomers from exercising the same rights as older residents. States often require periods of residence as a prerequisite for holding a state job or for admission into professional practice such as law or medicine. States discriminate against out-of-state students in the tuition charged in public schools and colleges. Finally, some states are now seeking ways to keep "outsiders" from moving in and presumably altering the "natural" environment.

EXTRADITION   The Constitution also provides that "A person in any state with treason, felony, or other crime who shall flee from justice and be found in another state, shall on the demand of the executive authority from the state from which he fled, be delivered up, to be removed to the state having jurisdiction of the crime." In other words, the Constitution requires governors to extradite fugitives from another state's justice.

TRIVIA
THE MOST LIVABLE STATES

Spirited debates are often engendered by rankings of states (or cities) by "livability." Each year the Morgan Quitno Press attracts both publicity and controversy with its livability ratings (shown below for the states). These ratings are calculated from each state's ranking on 42 separate factors ranging from crime rates, infant mortality rates, deaths by suicide, and poverty rates (negative factors) to growth in personal income, home ownership rate, job growth, percent of population graduated from college, and percent of days that are sunny.

Rank	State	Livability Rating	Rank	State	Livability Rating
1	Utah	33.26	26	Washington	25.98
2	Kansas	31.83	27	Ohio	25.69
3	Minnesota	31.76	28	Missouri	25.50
4	Iowa	31.62	29	Alaska	24.68
5	Nebraska	31.21	30	Illinois	24.57
6	Wisconsin	31.21	31	North Carolina	24.36
7	South Dakota	30.60	32	Rhode Island	24.12
8	New Hampshire	30.50	33	Michigan	24.10
9	Colorado	30.43	34	Pennsylvania	23.95
10	Virginia	30.19	35	Georgia	23.36
11	Idaho	30.14	36	Arizona	22.88
12	Connecticut	29.00	37	Texas	22.57
13	Wyoming	28.88	38	Oklahoma	22.00
14	North Dakota	28.60	39	Florida	21.86
15	Massachusetts	28.55	40	Arkansas	21.74
16	Maine	28.36	41	New Mexico	21.60
17	Vermont	27.88	42	South Carolina	21.48
18	Indiana	27.63	43	New York	21.36
19	Oregon	27.43	44	Tennessee	20.88
20	New Jersey	27.31	45	California	20.80
21	Montana	26.62	46	Kentucky	20.74
22	Delaware	26.49	47	West Virginia	20.55
23	Maryland	26.43	48	Alabama	20.02
24	Hawaii	26.38	49	Mississippi	18.83
25	Nevada	26.10	50	Louisiana	16.51

Source: State Rankings 1995 (Lawrence, KS: Morgan Quitno Press, 1995).

Governors have not always honored requests for extradition, but since no state wants to harbor criminals of another state, extradition is seldom refused. Among reasons advanced for the occasional refusals are (1) the individual has become a law-abiding citizen in his new state; (2) a northern governor did not approve of the conditions in Georgia chain gangs; (3) a black returned to a southern state would not receive a fair trial; (4) the governor did not believe that there was sufficient evidence against the fugitive to warrant his conviction in the first place.

INTERSTATE COMPACTS   The Constitution provides that "No state shall without the consent of Congress . . . enter into any agreement or compact with another state." Over one hundred interstate compacts now serve a wide variety of interests, such as interstate water resources; conservation of natural resources, including oil, wildlife, and fisheries; the control of floods; the development of interstate toll highways; the coordination of civil defense measures; the reciprocal supervision of parolees; the coordination of welfare and institutional care programs; the administration of interstate metropolitan areas; and the resolution of interstate tax conflicts. In practice, Congress has little to do with these compacts; the Supreme Court has held that congressional consent is required only if the compact encroaches upon some federal power.

CONFLICTS BETWEEN STATES   States are not supposed to make war on each other, although they did so from 1861 to 1865. They are supposed to take their conflicts to the Supreme Court. The Constitution gives the Supreme Court the power to settle all cases involving two or more states. In recent years the Supreme Court has heard disputes between states over boundaries, the diversion of water, fishing rights, and the disposal of sewage and garbage.

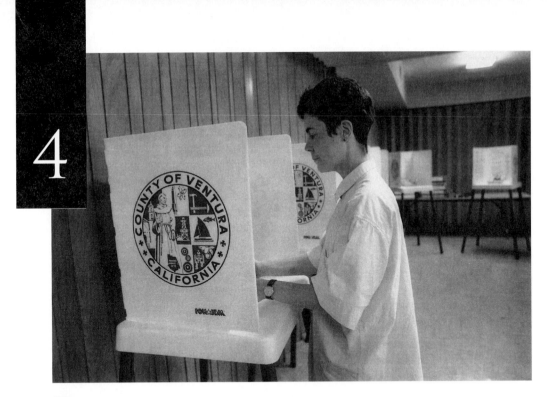

PARTICIPATION
IN STATE POLITICS

THE NATURE OF POLITICAL
PARTICIPATION

Popular participation in politics is the very definition of democracy. Individuals can participate in politics in many ways. They may run for, and win, public office; participate in marches, demonstrations, and sit-ins; make financial contributions to political candidates or causes; attend political meetings, speeches, and rallies; write letters to public officials or to newspapers; wear a political button or place a bumper sticker on a car; belong to organizations that support or oppose particular candidates or take stands on public issues; attempt to influence friends while discussing candidates or issues; vote in elections; or merely follow an issue or a campaign in the media.

This listing probably constitutes a ranking of the forms of political participation in order of frequency. (See Figure 4–1.) Only about half of the voting age population vote in presidential elections. Far fewer vote in state and local elections. Over one-third of the population is politically apathetic: They do not vote at all, and they are largely unaware of the political life of the nation.

Sustained political participation—voting consistently in election after election for state and local offices as well as Congress and the president—is very rare. One study of voter participation over ten elections (including presidential, congressional, gubernatorial, and

Figure 4–1
POLITICAL PARTICIPATION

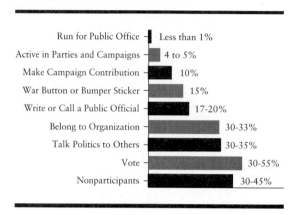

Run for Public Office	Less than 1%
Active in Parties and Campaigns	4 to 5%
Make Campaign Contribution	10%
War Button or Bumper Sticker	15%
Write or Call a Public Official	17-20%
Belong to Organization	30-33%
Talk Politics to Others	30-35%
Vote	30-55%
Nonparticipants	30-45%

state and local legislative elections) showed that only 4 percent of the voting age population voted in nine or all ten of the elections; only 26 percent voted in half of the ten elections; and 38 percent did not vote in any election.[1] Age is the best predictor of sustained political activity; older citizens are more likely than young people to be regular voters.

EXPLAINING VOTER TURNOUT

A sign of the times: A bumper sticker reads, "DON'T VOTE. IT JUST ENCOURAGES THEM." Nearly half of America's eligible voters stay away from the polls, even in a presidential election. Voter turnout is even lower in congressional elections, where turnout falls to 38 percent of the voting age population in the off years (when presidential candidates are not on the ballot). Turnouts in gubernatorial elections are roughly similar to turnouts for congressional races, rising and falling depending on whether the election is held simultaneously with a presidential election (see Figure 4–2). City and county elections, when they are held separately from national elections, usually produce turnouts of 25 to 35 percent.

IS VOTING RATIONAL?   Why is voter turnout so low? Actually, we could reverse the question and ask why people vote at all. A "rational" voter (one who seeks to maximize personal benefits and minimize costs) should vote only if the costs of voting (the time and energy spent first in registering, then in informing oneself about the candidates, and finally going to the polls on election day) are exceeded by the expected value of having the preferred candidate win (the personal benefits to be received from the winner) multiplied by the probability that one's own vote will be the deciding vote.[2] But un-

---

[1]Lee Sigelman et al., "Voting and Nonvoting: A Multi-Election Perspective," *American Journal of Political Science,* 29 (November 1985), 749–65.

[2]William H. Riker and Peter C. Ordeshook, "A Theory of the Calculus of Voting," *American Political Science Review,* 62 (March 1968), 25–42.

Figure 4–2
THE TREND IN VOTER TURNOUT

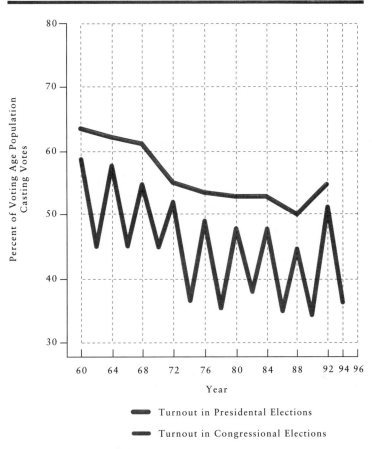

Turnout in Presidental Elections

Turnout in Congressional Elections

der this "rational" notion, not many people would vote: Few Americans receive direct personal and tangible benefits from the election of one candidate versus another. And most Americans know that the likelihood of one vote determining the outcome of the election is very remote. Yet millions of Americans vote anyway.

In order to rescue the "rational" model, political theorists have added "the intrinsic rewards of voting" to the equation.[3] These rewards include the ethic of voting, patriotism, a sense of duty, and allegiance to democracy. In other words, people get psychic rewards from voting itself rather than tangible benefits, and these psychic rewards do not depend on who wins or whether a single vote determines the outcome. So more people vote out of a sense of civic duty and commitment to democracy than on a purely rational basis.

---

[3]J. A. Ferejohn and Morris Fiorina, "The Paradox of Voting," *American Political Science Review,* 18 (March 1974), 525–36.

WHY PEOPLE STAY AT HOME   Nonetheless, millions of Americans stay at home on election day. We can apply some of the rational theorizing to understanding nonvoting in the states:

1. Registration requirements that are restrictive increase the costs of voting. By making it easier to register, states can increase voter turnout. Of the people who are registered in the nation, about three-quarters will vote in presidential elections.
2. Competition increases turnout. If a political contest appears close, more people believe that their vote might determine the outcome. Active campaigning by the candidates may not change people's minds, but it mobilizes supporters to get to the polls on election day.
3. Civic attachments and education increase voter turnout. People who believe they have a stake in the political system are more likely to vote than those who do not. Nonvoting may indicate a lack of faith in one's own power, a feeling of political impotency, or a lack of faith in the political system—a belief that it is too corrupt or too large for any single individual to make a difference.

WHO FAILS TO VOTE?   Political alienation involves a feeling that voting is useless, that nothing is really decided in an election, and that the individual cannot personally influence the outcome of political events. Political alienation explains the failure to vote by many people. Various socioeconomic factors also help to explain alienation and nonvoting (see Table 4–l). Blacks vote less frequently than whites. Hispanic Americans vote less frequently than either blacks or whites, suggesting that language differences may be a barrier to political participation. People who are working vote more frequently than the unemployed. Young people vote less often than older people. But the greatest differences in voter turnout are found among people with different educational backgrounds. Education apparently increases one's sense of civic responsibility and attachment to democratic norms.[4]

POLICY IMPLICATIONS OF NONVOTING   Do nonvoters differ significantly from voters on major policy questions? If so, then we might expect changes in government policy with a sustained increase in voter turnout. But the available evidence suggests that nonvoters generally hold policy views similar to those of voters.[5] Opinion surveys reveal that nonvoters and voters do *not* differ much on civil liberties and civil rights issues, or foreign or domestic policy issues, with the exception of a slight bias among nonvoters toward greater government spending and guaranteed jobs programs. Nonvoters are no more liberal or conservative than voters. In brief, despite a class bias in voter turnout, it is unlikely that nonvoting skews public policy in any particular direction.

OTHER FORMS OF PARTICIPATION   People who engage in other forms of participation besides voting—for example, making campaign contributions, writing or

---

[4]See John R. Bauer, "Patterns of Voter Participation in the American States," *Social Science Quarterly*, 71 (December 1990), 824–34; education is even more important in determining voter turnout in states with restrictive registration laws and lower competition levels.

[5]See Stephen Earl Bennett and David Resnick, "The Implications of Nonvoting for Democracy in the United States," *American Journal of Political Science*, 34 (August 1990), 771–802.

Table 4–1
CHARACTERISTICS OF VOTERS

Percent Reporting They Voted[a]

Total	61.3
Sex	
Male	60.2
Female	62.3
Race	
White	63.6
Black	54.0
Hispanic	28.9
Age	
18–20	38.5
21–24	45.7
25–34	53.2
35–44	63.6
45–64	70.0
65 and over	70.1
Employment	
Employed	63.8
Unemployed	46.2
Education	
8 years	35.1
High school	57.5
College	81.0

[a]Figures are for the 1992 presidential election. Some people tell pollsters that they voted when they really did not. While 61.3 percent of the voting age population reported that they voted, the actual number of votes cast was only 55.2 percent of the voting age population.

Source: Statistical Abstract of the United States, 1994, p. 257.

calling elected officials, joining and working in political organizations—are much better educated and enjoy much higher income than nonparticipants. Moreover, people who receive government middle-class benefits, such as Social Security, Medicare, and veterans' benefits, are much more active politically than those who receive poverty-tested welfare benefits such as AFDC, Medicaid, and food stamps.[6] Some political scientists contend that lower-class political "mobilization"—organizations, activity, and voter turnout—where it does occur, produces higher levels of welfare benefits.[7]

---

[6]Sidney Verba, Kay Schlozman, Henry Brady, and Norman Nie, "Citizen Activity: Who Participates? What Do They Say?" American Political Science Review, 87 (June 1993)303–18.

[7]Kim Quaile Hill, Jan E. Laghley, and Angela Hinton-Anderson, "Lower-Class Mobilization and Policy Linkage in the States," American Journal of Political Science, 39 (February 1995) 75–86.

VOTING IN THE STATES

There is a great deal of variation among the states in voter participation rates (see Figure 4–3). The turnout in presidential elections ranges from less than 45 percent of the voting population to over 70 percent. The states with the lowest turnouts are the Deep South states; the next lowest are found in the border states. Midwestern, New England, and Mountain states rank very high in voter turnout. The urban industrial states, with large metropolitan populations, tend to cluster around the middle of the rankings.

SOCIOECONOMIC EXPLANATIONS   Much of the variation among the states in voter turnout can be explained by *socioeconomic characteristics* of their population. Indeed, most of the variation in voter turnout among the states can be attributed to differences in educational level, urbanization, median family income, and percentage black.

TURNOUT POLITICS   Partisan politics has always colored the debate over registration and voting requirements. Democrats generally favor easing these requirements. They believe that doing so will bring more current nonvoters to the polls and that nonvoters are heavily drawn from groups that characteristically support the Democratic party (e.g., African American, lower income, noncollege, groups, see Table 5–3 in Chapter 5). Republican leaders are often less enthusiastic about easing voting requirements, but it is politically embarrassing to appear to oppose increased voter participation.

REGISTRATION   Voter registration is an obstacle to voting. Not only must citizens care enough to go to the polls on election day, they also must have previously registered their name and residence well before election day (usually thirty days before). Thus, registration must be accomplished at a time when interest in electoral campaigns is far from its peak. Once registered, names remain on the list unless there is a change of residence. (Prior to 1993 states periodically dropped the names of individuals who failed to vote over a prolonged period of time, a practice now banned by federal law.) Registration is designed to prevent fraud. It originated as a reform to prevent corrupt political "machines" from marching supporters from one voting booth to another on election day. Registration requires voters to identify themselves and show that they have previously registered as residents of the voting district; once they have voted, their names are checked off and they cannot vote again. Maine, Minnesota, Wisconsin, and Wyoming allow same-day registration at the polls; only North Dakota does not require registration at all.

FEDERALLY MANDATED "MOTOR VOTER" LAW   Although Congress had previously passed voting rights laws designed to protect minorities, it had never directly intervened in the general process of state election administration prior to 1993. But with strong Democratic support, Congress passed the National Voter Registration Act of 1993, popularly known as the "motor voter" act. It mandates that the states offer people the opportunity to register when they apply for a driver's license or apply for welfare services. States must also offer registration by mail, and they must accept a simplified registration form prepared by the Federal Election Commission. Finally, the act bars states from removing the names of people from registration lists for failure to vote.

Will the National Voter Registration Act have a significant effect on voter turnout in the states? States that had enacted their own motor-voter registration laws before the

Figure 4–3
Ranking of the States: Voter Participation

Presidential Election, 1992

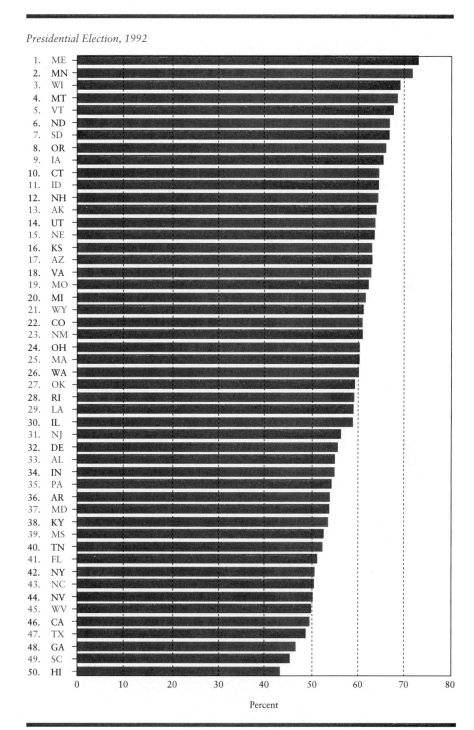

Rank	State
1.	ME
2.	MN
3.	WI
4.	MT
5.	VT
6.	ND
7.	SD
8.	OR
9.	IA
10.	CT
11.	ID
12.	NH
13.	AK
14.	UT
15.	NE
16.	KS
17.	AZ
18.	VA
19.	MO
20.	MI
21.	WY
22.	CO
23.	NM
24.	OH
25.	MA
26.	WA
27.	OK
28.	RI
29.	LA
30.	IL
31.	NJ
32.	DE
33.	AL
34.	IN
35.	PA
36.	AR
37.	MD
38.	KY
39.	MS
40.	TN
41.	FL
42.	NY
43.	NC
44.	NV
45.	WV
46.	CA
47.	TX
48.	GA
49.	SC
50.	HI

Percent

federal mandate appear to have increased their turnout rates by doing so.[8] Certainly increases in voter *registration* are predictable, but it is not clear whether the new motor-voter registrants will add significantly to *turnout* on election day. Differences among the states in turnout attributable to socioeconomic characteristics of state populations will likely continue.

REGION   Over time, differences among the states in voter turnout levels have diminished. Traditionally, turnout was low in the southern states, especially Arkansas, Florida, Georgia, Louisiana, Mississippi, South Carolina, Tennessee, Texas, and Virginia. While these states continue to rank low in turnout, they have moved closer to the other states. Federal civil rights laws, black voter mobilization, northern in-migration, and greater Republican competition may have all combined to help explain why voter participation has improved in these states.[9]

COMPETITION   Voter participation rates can also be affected by the degree of *interparty competition* in a state. The more vigorous the competition between the parties, the greater the interest of citizens in elections, and the larger the voter turnout. When parties and candidates compete vigorously, they make news and are given a large play via the mass media. Thus, a setting of competitive politics tends to have a greater amount of political stimuli available in the environment than does a setting with weak competition. People are also more likely to perceive that their votes count in a close, competitive contest, and thus they are more likely to cast them. Moreover, when parties are fighting in a close contest, their workers tend to spend more time and energy campaigning and getting out the vote.[10]

Indeed, some political scientists argue that *political mobilization* can explain most of the variation among the states in voter turnout for gubernatorial elections.[11] Political mobilization is measured by a combination of party competition, the closeness of the race, the amount of money spent campaigning, and whether or not a U.S. Senate seat was being decided in the same election.

SECURING THE RIGHT TO VOTE

The only mention of voting requirements in the Constitution of the United States as it was originally adopted is in Article I: "The electors in each state shall have the qualifications requisite for electors for the most numerous branch of the state legislature." Of course, "electors" (voters) for the most numerous branch of the state legislature are determined

---

[8]See Staci L. Rhine, "Registration Reform and Turnout Change in the American States," *American Politics Quarterly,* 23 (October 1995), 409–26; Stephen Knack, "Does Motor-Voter Work? Evidence from State Level Data," *Journal of Politics,* 57 (August 1995), 796–811.

[9]See Norman R. Lutbeg, "Differential Voting Turnout Decline in the American States," *Social Science Quarterly,* 65 (March 1984), 60–73.

[10]Studies of voter turnout *within* states (e.g., studies of voter turnout by county) confirm the importance of competition in increasing turnout. See C. Richard Hofstetter, "Inter-Party Competition and Electoral Turnout: The Case of Indiana," *American Journal of Political Science,* 17 (May 1973), 351–66.

[11]Samuel C. Patterson and Gregory A. Caldeira, "Getting Out the Vote: Participation in Gubernatorial Elections," *American Political Science Review,* 77 (September 1983), 675–89.

by *state* laws and constitutions. The effect of this constitutional provision was to leave to the states the power to determine who is eligible to vote in both state and federal elections. Over the years, however, a combination of constitutional amendments, congressional actions, and Supreme Court decisions has largely removed control over voting from the states and made it a responsibility of the national government.

ELIMINATION OF PROPERTY QUALIFICATIONS   Early in American history, voting was limited to males over twenty-one years of age, who resided in the voting district for a certain period and owned a considerable amount of land or received a large income from other investments. So great was the fear that "the common man" would use his vote to attack the rights of property that only 120,000 people out of 2 million were permitted to vote in the 1780s. Men of property felt that only other men of property had sufficient "stake in society" to exercise their vote in a "responsible" fashion. Gradually, however, Jeffersonian and Jacksonian principles of democracy, including confidence in the reason and integrity of the common man, spread rapidly in the new Republic. Most property qualifications were eliminated by the states themselves in the early nineteenth century.

FIFTEENTH AMENDMENT   The first important limitation on state powers over voting came with the ratification of the Fifteenth Amendment: "The right of the citizens of the United States to vote shall not be denied or abridged by the United States or any state on account of race, color, or previous condition of servitude." The object of this amendment, passed by the Reconstruction Congress and adopted in 1870, was to extend the vote to former black slaves and prohibit voter discrimination on the basis of race. The Fifteenth Amendment also gives Congress the power to enforce black voting rights "by appropriate legislation." Thus, the states retained their right to determine voter qualifications, *as long as they do not practice racial discrimination,* and Congress was given the power to pass legislation ensuring black voting rights.

NINETEENTH AMENDMENT   Following the Civil War many of the women who had been active abolitionists, seeking to end slavery, turned their attention to the condition of women in America. They had learned to organize, conduct petition campaigns, and parade and demonstrate, as abolitionists, and later they sought to improve the legal and political rights of women. In 1869 the Wyoming territory adopted women's suffrage; later several other western states followed suit. But it was not until the Nineteenth Amendment to the U.S. Constitution in 1920 that women's voting rights were constitutionally guaranteed.

THE "WHITE PRIMARY"   For almost 100 years after the adoption of the Fifteenth Amendment, white politicians in the southern states were able to defeat its purposes. Social and economic pressures and threats of violence were used to intimidate many thousands of would-be voters. There were also many "legal" methods of disenfranchisement.

For many years the most effective means of banning black voting was a technique known as the "white primary." So strong was the Democratic party throughout the South that the Democratic nomination for public office was tantamount to election. This meant that *primary* elections to choose the Democratic nominee were the only elections in which real choices were made. If blacks were prevented from voting in Democratic primaries, they could be effectively disenfranchised. Thus southern state legislatures resorted to the simple device of declaring the Democratic party in southern states a private club and ruling that only white people could participate in its elections, that is, in *primary* elections. Blacks would be free to vote in "official," general elections, but all whites tacitly agreed to support the Democratic, or "white man's" party, in general elections, regardless of their differences in the primary. Not until 1944, in *Smith* v. *Allright,* did the Supreme Court declare this practice unconstitutional.[12]

DISCRIMINATION   Black voting in the South increased substantially after World War II. (From an estimated 5 percent of voting age blacks registered in southern states in the 1940s, black registration rose to an estimated 20 percent in 1952, 25 percent in 1956, 28 percent in 1960, and 39 percent in 1964.) But as late as 1965 black voter turnout rate was little more than half of the white rate. In hundreds of rural counties throughout the South, no blacks were permitted to vote. Despite the Fifteenth Amendment, local registrars in the South succeeded in barring black registration by means of an endless variety of obstacles, delays, and frustrations. Application forms for registration were lengthy and complicated; even a minor error would lead to rejection, such as underlining rather than circling in the "Mr.–Mrs.–Miss" set of choices as instructed. Literacy tests were the most common form of disenfranchisement. Many a black college graduate failed to interpret "properly" the complex legal documents that were part of the test. White applicants for voter registration were seldom asked to go through these lengthy procedures.

CIVIL RIGHTS ACT OF 1964   The Civil Rights Act of 1964 made it unlawful for registrars to apply unequal standards in registration procedures or to reject applications because of immaterial errors. It required that literacy tests be in writing and made a sixth-grade education a presumption of literacy.

TWENTY-FOURTH AMENDMENT   The Twenty-fourth Amendment to the Constitution was ratified in 1964, making poll taxes unconstitutional as a requirement for voting in national elections. In 1965 the Supreme Court declared poll taxes unconstitutional in state and local elections as well.[13]

VOTING RIGHTS ACT OF 1965   In Selma, Alabama, in early 1965, civil rights organizations effectively demonstrated that local registrars were still keeping large numbers of blacks off the voting rolls. Registrars closed their offices for all but a few hours every month, placed limits on the number of applications processed, went out to lunch when black applicants appeared; delayed months before processing applications from blacks, and discovered a variety of other methods to keep blacks disenfranchised. In response to the Selma march, Congress enacted a strong Voting Rights Act in 1965. The U.S. attorney general, upon evidence of voter discrimination, was empowered to replace local registrars with federal registrars, abolish literacy tests, and register voters under simplified federal procedures.[14] However, it turned out that federal registrars were sent to

---

[12]*Smith* v. *Allright,* 321 U.S. 649 (1944).

[13]*Harper* v. *Virginia State Board of Elections,* 383 U.S. 663 (1966).

[14]*South Carolina* v. *Katzenbach,* U.S. 301 (1966).

only a small number of southern counties. Many southern counties that had previously discriminated in voter registration hurried to sign up black voters just to avoid the imposition of federal registrars. The Voting Rights Act of 1965 proved to be very effective and Congress voted to extend it indefinitely.

DILUTING MINORITY VOTES   In recent years, conflict over voting rights has centered on the effects of various institutional arrangements on minority influence in government. In 1982, Congress strengthened the Voting Rights Act by outlawing any electoral arrangements that had the *effect* of weakening minority voting power. This "effects" test replaced the earlier "intent" test which required black plaintiffs to prove that a particular arrangement was adopted with the specific intent of reducing black voting power.[15] (An "intent" test invalidates laws or practices only if they are designed to discriminate; an "effects" test invalidates laws or practices that adversely affect racial minorities regardless of the original intent.) For example, at-large elections or multimember districts for city councils, county commissions, or state legislative seats may have the effect of weakening black voting power if a white majority in such districts prevents blacks from winning office. Congress stopped short of directly outlawing such districts but established a "totality of circumstances" test to be used to determine if such districts had a discriminatory effect. The "circumstances" to be considered by the courts include whether or not there has been a history of racial polarization in voting and whether black candidates have ever won election to office in the district.[16]

AFFIRMATIVE RACIAL GERRYMANDERING   The U.S. Supreme Court requires states and cities to provide minorities with "a realistic opportunity to elect officials of their choice." In the key case of *Thornburg* v. *Gingles,*[17] the Court interpreted the Voting Rights Act Amendments of 1982 to require state legislatures to draw election district boundary lines in a way that guarantees that minorities can elect minority representatives to governing bodies. The burden of proof was shifted *from* minorities to show that district lines diluted their voting strength *to* state lawmakers to show that they have done everything possible to maximize minority representation. The effect of the Court's decision was to inspire affirmative racial gerrymandering—the creation of predominately black and minority districts wherever possible.

Racial gerrymandering dominated the redistricting process in all of the large states following the 1990 census. In many states Republican legislators allied themselves with black and Hispanic groups in efforts to create minority districts; Republicans understood that "packing" minority (usually Democratic) voters into selected districts would reduce Democratic votes in many other districts.[18] The U.S. Justice Department also pressed state legislatures to maximize the number of "majority-minority" congressional and state legislative districts. With the assistance of sophisticated computer models, state legislatures and federal courts drew many odd-shaped minority congressional and state legislative districts.

---

[15]*Mobile* v. *Bolden,* 446 U.S. 50 (1980).

[16]See Susan A. MacManus, "Racial Representation Issues," *Political Science and Politics,* 18 (Fall 1985), 759–69.

[17]*Thornburg* v. *Gingles* 478 U.S. 30 (1986).

[18]Kevin A. Hill, "Does the Creation of Majority Black Districts Aid Republicans?" *Journal of Politics,* 57 (May 1995), 384–401.

Yet the Supreme Court has expressed constitutional doubts about bizarre-shaped districts based solely on racial composition. In a controversial 5–4 decision, Justice Sandra Day O'Connor wrote: "Race gerrymandering, even for remedial purposes, may balkanize us into competing racial factions. . . . A reapportionment plan that includes in one district individuals who have little in common with one another but the color of their skin bears an uncomfortable resemblance to political apartheid."[19] (See Figure 4–4.)

INCREASED BLACK REPRESENTATION   Black representation in state and local government, as well as in the U.S. Congress, has risen dramatically in recent years. In the 104th Congress (1995–97), 37 African Americans served in the House of Representatives (35 Democrats and 2 Republicans), and one African American served in the U.S. Senate, Carol Moseley-Braun of Illinois. The numbers of blacks elected to state and local office nearly doubled between 1980 and 1995 (see Table 4–2), and new minority districts in many states boosted black representation in state legislatures. We will return to the question of minority representation in state legislatures in Chapter 6 and on city councils in Chapter 11.

Figure 4–4

AFFIRMATIVE RACIAL GERRYMANDERING

North Carolina's 12th congressional district was drawn up to be a "majority-minority" district by combining African American communities over a wide region of the state. The U.S. Supreme Court in Shaw v. Reno *(1993) ordered a court review of this district to determine whether it incorporated any common interest other than race.*

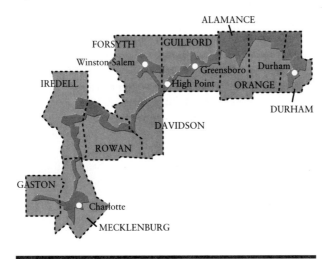

[19]*Shaw* v. *Reno* (1993).

Table 4–2
GROWTH IN NUMBERS OF BLACK ELECTED OFFICIALS

	1970	1980	1995
U.S. Congress	10	17	38[e]
State government[a]	169	309	523
City and county government[b]	719	2,871	4,819
Judicial and law enforcement[c]	213	534	922
Education[d]	368	1,232	1,682
Total	1,479	4,963	7,984

[a]Includes elected state administrators.

[b]County commissioners and council members, mayors, vice-mayors, city council members, regional officials, and other.

[c]Judges, magistrates, constables, marshals, sheriffs, justices of the peace, and other.

[d]Members of state education agencies, college boards, school boards, and other.

[e]Figure for 104th Congress, 1995–97.

Source: Joint Center for Political Studies, Washington, DC.

RACIAL POLARIZATION   Increases in the number of African American office-holders in state and local government are primarily the result of the creation of more black majority districts in cities and states. Few blacks win office in majority white city council or state legislative districts. And the federal Voting Rights Act has been responsible for the creation of more black majority districts. In legislative districts where the black population is 65 percent or more, black candidates win 98 percent of the legislative seats. Majority white districts elect black candidates to about 2 percent of their legislative seats. While a few notable black political leaders have won electoral support across racial lines, racial polarization in voting remains a fact of life.[20]

HISPANIC POWER   The progress of Hispanics in state and local politics in recent years is reflected in the election of several governors and increasing numbers of state legislators, city and county commission members, and school board members (see Table 4–3).

However, Hispanic political influence in the states is still very limited. Hispanic voter turnout is much lower than that for other ethnic groups in America. Many Hispanics are resident aliens and therefore not eligible to vote. Language barriers may also present an obstacle to full participation. Finally, Hispanic voters divide their political loyalties. Cuban Americans tend to vote Republican. They are economically very successful; they are concentrated in the Miami area, and they are now a force in city and state politics in Florida. The largest Hispanic group, Mexican Americans, tends to vote Democratic; their power is concentrated in California, Texas, Arizona, and New Mexico.

---

[20]Bernard Grofman and Lisa Handley, "The Impact of the Voting Rights Act on Black Representation in Southern State Legislatures," *Legislative Studies Quarterly,* 16 (February 1991), 111–28; Benjamin Radcliff and Martin Saiz, "Race, Turnout, and Public Policy in the States," *Political Research Quarterly* 48 (December 1995), 775–94.

Table 4–3

GROWTH IN NUMBER OF HISPANIC ELECTED OFFICIALS

	1984	1995
U.S. Congress	9	17[a]
State government	110	165
City and county government	1,276	2,023
Judicial and law enforcement	495	633
Education	1,173	2,332
Total	3,063	5,170

[a]Figure for 104th Congress (1995–97).

Source: National Association of Latino Elected and Appointed Officials. Washington, DC: *National Roster of Hispanic Elected Officials.*

VOTING AND AMERICAN YOUTH

Before 1970 only three of the fifty states permitted residents eighteen to twenty-one years of age to vote—Georgia, Kentucky, and Alaska. All other states, in the exercise of their constitutional responsibility to determine the qualifications of "electors," had set the voting age at twenty-one. The movement for eighteen-year-old voting received its original impetus in Georgia in 1944 under the leadership of Governor Ellis Arnall, who argued successfully that eighteen-year-olds were then being called upon to fight and die for their country in World War II and, therefore, deserved to have a voice in the conduct of government. However, this argument failed to convince adult voters in other states; qualifications for military service were not regarded as the same as qualifications for rational decision making in elections. In state after state, voters rejected state constitutional amendments designed to extend the vote to eighteen-year-olds.

Congress intervened on behalf of eighteen-year-old voting with the passage of the Twenty-sixth Amendment to the Constitution in 1971.[21] The states quickly ratified this amendment, during a period of national turbulence over the Vietnam War. Many supporters of the amendment believed that protests on the campuses and streets could be reduced if youthful protesters were given the vote. Moreover, Democrats believed that their party would gain from the youth vote, and liberal candidates believed that idealistic young voters would spark their campaigns.

It turns out that young people vote less often than older people. (See Table 4-1.) Moreover, young people do *not* vote as a bloc. Young voters cast their votes for most political

---

[21]Congress had earlier passed the Voting Rights Act of 1970, which (1) extended the vote to eighteen-year-olds regardless of state law; (2) abolished residency requirements in excess of thirty days; and (3) prohibited literacy tests. However, there was some constitutional debate about the power of Congress to change state laws on voting age. While Congress can end *racial* discrimination, extending the vote to eighteen-year-olds was a different matter. All previous extensions of the vote had come by constitutional amendment. Hence, Congress quickly passed the Twenty-sixth Amendment.

candidates in the same proportions as older voters. The image of the idealistic, activist student is not an accurate image of the young voter in America. Less than one-third of people aged eighteen to twenty-four are in college. More than half of this age group are working and either living with their parents or are married and living in their own households. College students may achieve greater visibility in the news media than young working people, but the bulk of young voters are not on the campus.

WOMEN IN STATE POLITICS

Traditionally women did not participate in politics as much as men. Women were less likely than men to contribute money, lobby elected officials, and run for or win public office.

Why was this so? Several explanations have been offered: (1) Women were socialized into more "passive" roles from childhood; (2) women with children and family responsibilities could not fully participate in politics; and (3) women did not have educations, occupations, and incomes equivalent to those of men. Perhaps all of these factors were at work in reducing female political participation.

WOMEN IN STATE OFFICES   Women have made impressive political gains in state politics in recent years. Today over 1,500 of the nation's 7,500 state legislators (over 20 percent) are women. Over a dozen women have served as governors of their state[22] (including Christine Todd Whitman, current Republican governor of New Jersey), and 84 of the 324 elective statewide executive offices across the country (over 25 percent) are held by women. (In the 104th Congress—1995–1997—47 women are serving in the House and 8 in the Senate.) While these figures are modest indeed, they represent significant advances over the recent past. In 1969 only 4 percent of the nation's state legislators were women. Until the election of Ella Grasso (D.–Connecticut) and Dixie Lee Ray (D.–Washington) in the late 1970s, no woman had won election to that office on her own; earlier women governors had succeeded their husbands to that office. Women are making even more rapid gains in city and county offices. The total number of women officeholders in local government has more than tripled over the last decade. This influx of women at the grass-roots level over the last decade is now contributing to the success of women in running for and winning higher state and national offices.

ELECTION CHALLENGES CONFRONTING WOMEN   Women continue to confront special challenges when running for office. In general, female candidates enjoy a slight advantage over male candidates in public perceptions of honesty, sincerity, and caring. However, women candidates are often perceived as "not tough enough" to deal with hard issues like drugs and crime. When women candidates seek to prove that they are "tough," they risk being branded with adjectives like "strident" or "abrasive."

WOMEN AND POLICY MAKING   Do greater numbers of women in state and local elected offices make any significant difference in public policy? Political scientists

---

[22]Center for the American Woman and Politics, Eagleton Institute of Politics, Rutgers University. See also "Gender" in Chapter 6, Legislators in State Politics; "Gender" in Chapter 7, Governors in State Politics; and "Women in Local Politics" in Chapter 11, Participation in Community Politics.

have attempted to learn whether or not increases in female elected officials actually bring about any significant policy changes. The evidence on this question is mixed. Male legislators support feminist positions on ERA, abortion, employment, education, and health just as often as female legislators. However, there is some evidence that women legislators give higher *priority* to these issues. Women are more likely than men to have as their "top legislative priority" bills focusing on women's and children's issues. However, state legislatures with larger percentages of women do *not* pass feminist legislation any more often than state legislatures with fewer women legislators.[23] (Women's priority issues are discussed in Chapter 14.)

There may also be gender-based attitudinal differences that affect a wide range of policy issues. For example, women state legislators may be more likely to view social problems such as crime in a larger societal context, leading them to focus on preventive and interventionist policies. Male legislators may view crime as an individual act that can be curtailed by certain swift and severe punishment. Over time as women increase their numbers in state legislatures and city councils, we might expect subtle changes in both the style and substance of policy making.[24]

INTEREST GROUPS IN STATE POLITICS

Interest groups arise when individuals with a common interest decide that by banding together and by consolidating their strength they can exercise more influence over public policy than they could as individuals acting alone. The impulse toward organization and collective action is particularly strong in a society of great size and complexity. As societies become more urban and industrial, individual action in politics gives way to collective action by giant organizations of businesspeople, farmers, professionals, and laborers, as well as racial, religious, and ideological groups.

ORGANIZED INTERESTS   Groups may be highly organized into formal organizations with offices and professional staffs within the capitals of every state: The U.S. Chamber of Commerce, the National Association of Manufacturers, the AFL-CIO, and the National Education Association are examples of highly organized interest groups that operate in every state. Other groups have little formal organization and appear at state capitals only when an issue arises of particular concern to them, for example, when motorcyclists assemble to protest mandatory helmets, or when commercial fishermen come to complain about banning of nets.

Interest groups may be organized around *occupational or economic interests* (for example, the Association of Real Estate Boards, the Association of Broadcasters, the Bankers Association, the Automobile Dealers Association, the Cattleman's Association, the Home Builders Association, the Insurance Council, the Association of Trial Lawyers), or on *racial*

---

[23]Sue Thomas, "The Impact of Women on State Legislative Policies," *Journal of Politics,* 53 (November 1991), 958–76. See also Michelle A. Saint-Germain, "Does Their Difference Make a Difference?" *Social Science Quarterly,* 70 (December 1989), 956–68.

[24]Lyn Kathlene, "Alternative Views of Crime: Legislative Policymaking in Gendered Terms," *Journal of Politics,* 57 (August 1995), 696–723.

or religious bases (for example, the National Association for the Advancement of Colored People, the Christian Coalition, the National Council of Churches, the Anti-Defamation League of B'nai B'rith), or around *shared experiences* (for example, the American Legion, the Veterans of Foreign Wars, the League of Women Voters, the Automobile Association of America), or around *ideological positions* (for example, Americans for Democratic Action, Common Cause, Americans for Constitutional Action). *Government officials* and governments themselves organize and help exert pressure on higher levels of government (for example, the National Governors' Conference, the Council of State Governments, the National League of Cities, U.S. Conference of Mayors, the National Association of Chiefs of Police, and National Association of Counties). Even the *recipients of government services* are organizing themselves (for example, the American Association of Retired Persons).

Overall, economic interests are more frequently encountered in state politics than noneconomic interests. But certainly the proliferation of active noneconomic groups in America, from the environmentalists' Sierra Club to the senior citizens' AARP and the liberal-oriented Common Cause, testifies to the importance of organization in all phases of political life. Particularly active at the state level are the businesses subject to extensive regulation by state governments. The banks, truckers, doctors and lawyers, insurance companies, the gaming industry, utilities, hospitals, and liquor interests are consistently found to be among the most highly organized groups in state capitals. Chapters of the National Education Association are also active in state capitals, presenting the demands of educational administrators and teachers. And local governments and local government officials are well organized to present their demands at state capitals.

A national survey of interest group activity in all fifty state capitals identified groups that were rated "most effective" and "effective" in the states (see Table 4–4).

PROFESSIONAL LOBBYISTS   Often groups and corporations choose to be "represented" in state capitals by professional lobbyists. Many successful professional lobbyists are former legislators, or former executive officials, or former top gubernatorial or legislative aides, who have turned their state government experience into a career. They "know their way around" the capitol. They offer their services—access to legislative and executive officials, knowledge of the lawmaking process, ability to present information and testimony to key policy makers at the right time, political skills and knowledge, personal friendships, and "connections"—to their clients at rates that usually depend upon their reputation for influence. Occasionally their compensation is tied to their success in getting a bill passed; a six-figure fee may rest on the outcome of a single vote. Some professional lobbyists are attached to law firms or public relations firms and occasionally do other work; others are full-time lobbyists with multiple clients.

Most professional lobbyists publicly attribute their success to hard work, persistence, information, and ability to get along with others: "Being prepared, personal credibility"; "Legislators know I'm going to present the facts whether they're favorable to my client or not"; "I'm a forceful advocate—determined"; "Doing my homework on the issues"; "Knowledge of the issues I'm dealing with and knowledge of the system"; "I try to understand the political pressures on elected officials." Yet in more candid moments professional lobbyists will acknowledge that their success is largely attributable to personal friendships, political experience, and financial contributions: "Close friends I made in the

Table 4–4

RANKING OF THE MOST INFLUENTIAL INTERESTS IN THE FIFTY STATES

Rank		Number of States in Which Interest Ranked:	
		MOST EFFECTIVE	MODERATELY EFFECTIVE
1	Schoolteachers' organizations (predominantly NEA)	43	5
2	General business organizations (chambers of commerce, etc.)	37	16
3	Utility companies and associations (electric, gas, water, telephones, cable TV)	23	24
4	Lawyers (predominantly trial lawyers and state bar associations)	26	14
5	Traditional labor associations (predominantly the AFL-CIO)	22	13
6	Doctors	22	12
7	Insurance: general and medical (companies and associations)	21	15
8	Manufacturers (companies and associations)	20	15
9	Health care organizations (mainly hospital associations)	15	24
10	Bankers' associations (includes savings & loan associations)	21	11
11	General local government organizations (municipal leagues, county organizations, etc.)	16	21
12	State and local government employee unions (other than teachers)	18	14
13	General farm organizations (mainly state farm bureaus)	14	20
14	Individual banks and financial institutions	14	8
15	Environmentalists	9	16
16	Universities and colleges (institutions and personnel)	7	16
17	Realtors' associations	8	12
18	Individual cities and towns	8	12
19	Gaming interests (race tracks, casinos, lotteries)	7	11
20	Contractors, builders, developers	7	10
21	Liquor, wine, and beer interests	7	10
22	Retailers (companies and trade associations)	6	11
23	Senior citizens (AARP chapters, etc.)	1	19
24	Mining companies and associations	6	7
25	Truckers and private transport interests (excluding railroads)	5	8
26	Taxpayers' interest groups	5	7
27	State agencies	5	7
28	Individual traditional labor unions (Teamsters, UAW, etc.)	6	4
29	Sportsmen/hunting and fishing (includes the NRA and anti–gun control groups)	3	10
30	Miscellaneous social issue groups (handicapped, crime victims, children and family [MADD, etc.])	2	11
31	Oil and gas (companies and associations)	3	7
32	Women and minorities (NOW, League of Women Voters, NAACP, etc.)	3	7

Table 4–4   (Continued)

33	Religious interests (churches and religious groups)	2	9
34	Miscellaneous professional occupational groups	2	9
35	Public interest/good government groups (Common Cause, PIRGs, ACLU, etc.)	4	4
36	Agricultural commodity organizations (stock growers, grain growers, etc.)	1	12
37	Railroads	2	7
38	Forest product companies	3	4

Source: From Clive S. Thomas and Ronald J. Hrebenar, in Virginia Gray and Herbert Jacob, eds., *Politics in the American States,* 6th ed. Washington, DC: CQ Press, 1996.

legislature while I served as Speaker of the House"; "I raise a lot of money for people"; "My client has the largest political action committee in the state."[25]

LOBBY REGISTRATION   It is very difficult to get a comprehensive picture of interest group activity in state capitals. Many organizations, businesses, legal firms, and individuals engage in interest group activity of one kind or another, and it is difficult to keep track of their varied activities. Most states require the registration of "lobbyists" and the submission of reports about their membership and finances. These laws do not restrain lobbying (that would probably violate the First Amendment freedom to "petition" the government for "redress of grievances"). Rather, they are meant to spotlight the activities of lobbyists. However, many hundreds of lobbyists never register under the pretext that they are not *really lobbyists,* but, instead, businesses, public relations firms, lawyers, researchers, or educational people. (There are over 3,500 registered lobbyists in Florida, for example—22 for each legislator—but an estimated 9,000 lobbyists at the state capital in Tallahassee.) Thus, only the larger, formal, organized interest groups and professional lobbyists are officially registered as lobbyists in the states.

FUNCTIONS AND TACTICS OF INTEREST GROUPS

Both interest groups and political parties organize individuals to make claims upon government, but these two forms of political organizations differ in several respects. An interest group seeks to influence specific policies of government—not to achieve control over government as a whole. A political party concentrates on winning public office in elections and is somewhat less concerned with policy questions. An interest group does not ordinarily run candidates for public office under its own banner, although it may give influential support to party candidates. Finally, the basic function of a political party in a two-party system is to organize a *majority* of persons for the purpose of governing. In contrast, an interest group gives political expression to the interests of *minority* groups.

---

[25]Quotations reported in *Tallahassee Democrat,* January 12, 1992.

Interest group techniques are as varied as the imaginations of their leaders. Groups are attempting to advance their interests when a liquor firm sends a case of bourbon to a state legislator; when the League of Women Voters distributes biographies of political candidates; when an insurance company argues before a state insurance commission that rates must be increased; when the National Education Association provides state legislators with information comparing teachers' salaries in the fifty states; when railroads ask state highway departments to place weight limitations upon trucks; or when the American Civil Liberties Union supplies lawyers for civil rights demonstrators. Let us try to classify the many techniques of interest groups under three major headings—public relations, lobbying, and campaign financing.

PUBLIC RELATIONS   Most people think of interest group tactics as direct attempts to influence decision makers, but many groups spend more of their time, energy, and resources in general public relations activities than anything else. The purpose of a continuing public relations campaign is to create an environment favorable to the interest group and its program. It is hoped that a reservoir of public goodwill can be established, which can be relied on later when a critical issue arises.

LOBBYING   *Lobbying* is defined as any communication, by someone acting on behalf of a group, directed at a government decision maker with the hope of influencing that person. Direct persuasion is usually more than just a matter of argument or emotional appeal to the lawmaker. Often it involves the communication of useful technical and political information. Many public officials are required to vote on, or decide about, hundreds of questions each year. It is impossible for them to be fully informed about the wide variety of bills and issues they face. Consequently, many decision makers depend upon skilled lobbyists to provide technical information about matters requiring action, and to inform them of the policy preferences of important segments of the population. (See "Lobbying in State Legislatures" in Chapter 6.)

The behavior of lobbyists depends on the interests they represent and the characteristics of the state political system in which they function. Some interests hire full-time lobbyists; others rely on attorneys or firms who lobby on behalf of more than one group. Still other interests rely on volunteers. Some maintain active contact with legislators or make campaign contributions. Some formulate a legislative agenda each session and trace the progress of bills in which they are interested. Indeed, one study of lobbying on behalf of the aging in four separate states revealed much variation in lobbying activity even on the same issues.[26]

Most state lobbying activity is undertaken by economic interests—finance, insurance, and real estate industries; wholesale and retail business; mining and agriculture; transportation and utilities.[27] The professions—physicians, lawyers, teachers, and others—follow next in lobbying activity. They are closely matched by governmental bodies—from cities, counties, and school districts to state bureaucracies. Public interest groups, consumer groups, and environmentalists follow, together with labor unions. Single interest and ideological groups are only intermittently active in state capitals.

---

[26]See, for example, William P. Browne, "Variations in the Behavior and Style of State Lobbyists and Interest Groups," *Journal of Politics,* 47 (May 1985), 450–68.

[27]See Kenneth G. Hunter, Laura Ann Wilson, and Gregory G. Brunk, "Societal Complexity and Interest Group Lobbying in the American States," *Journal of Politics,* 53 (May 1991), 488–503.

BRIBERY AND CORRUPTION   Lobbying in state capitals may be somewhat cruder—if not actually corrupt—than lobbying in Washington. In interviewing lobbyists and legislators in Washington, Lester Milbrath found that they considered state lobbying much more corrupt than national lobbying. "'Lobbying is very different before state legislators; it is much more individualistic. Maybe this is the reason they have more bribery in state legislatures than in Congress.' 'In the state legislatures, lobbying is definitely on a lower plane. The lobbyists are loose and hand out money and favors quite freely.' 'Lobbying at the state level is cruder, more basic, and more obvious.'"[28] Needless to say, it is difficult to document such statements. However, it seems reasonable to believe that state legislators might be more subject to the pressures and appeals of organized interest groups than members of Congress.

State legislators, unlike most members of Congress, are only part-time lawmakers. They must manage their own business, professional, and investment interests in addition to their legislative duties. They may have personal business or professional or real estate or legal ties with the same interests that are seeking to influence their legislative behavior. Such "conflicts of interests"—legislators voting in committee or on the floor on issues in which they have a personal financial interest—are not uncommon. Indeed, some interests occasionally seek to establish business or professional ties with legislators just to win their support.

Bribery is the offering of anything of value to government officials to influence them in the performance of their duties. Vote buying is illegal, but not unheard of in state capitals. Instead of bribery, organized interests may contribute to a legislator's campaign chest without mentioning any specific quid pro quo.

CAMPAIGN FINANCING   Political campaigns are very expensive, and it is always difficult for a candidate to find enough money to finance a campaign. This is true for officeholders seeking reelection as well as new contenders. It is perfectly legal for an interest group to make a contribution to a candidate's campaign fund. Ordinarily, a respectable lobbyist would not be so crude as to exact any specific pledges from a candidate in exchange for a campaign contribution. He or she simply makes a contribution and lets the candidate figure out what to do when in office to assure further contributions to the candidate's next campaign. (For further discussion, see "Money in State Politics" in Chapter 5.)

PACS IN THE STATES   Interest groups, operating through political action committees or PACs, are becoming the major source of campaign funding for state office. As campaign costs increase, reliance on PAC money increases. In large urban states such as California and New York, where campaigns for state legislature may cost $50,000 to $100,000 or more, PAC contributions are the largest source of campaign funding (see Table 4–5).

PACs are politically sophisticated contributors. They do not like to back losers. Since incumbent members of state legislatures running for reelection seldom lose (see "The Great Incumbency Machine" in Chapter 6), PAC contributions are heavily weighted in

---

[28]Quotations from legislators in Lester Milbrath, *The Washington Lobbyists* (Chicago: Rand McNally, 1963), pp. 241–43.

Table 4-5
Interest Group Campaign Contributions: Funding the Florida Senate President

As president of the Florida state senate, Democrat Pat Thomas was a favored recipient of PAC contributions in his 1992 reelection campaign. Florida law limits contributions to $500 for each election. The following is a partial list of Thomas's contributors.

Contributor	Business/Trade	Contributor	Business/Trade
Agents PAC	Insurance	Professional Fire Fighters of Fla.	Firefighters
Accredited Bond Agencies, Inc.	Bail Bonds	Funeral Directors	Funerals
American Cyanamid	Chemical	Florida Asphalt Contractors	Construction
American Family Corp.	Insurance	Florida Associated Services Inc.	Computer
American Family Life	Insurance	Florida Assn. of Surety Agents	Bail bonds
Anesthesiology PAC	Physicians	Florida Bankpac-State	Bank
Anheuser Bush Companies	Beer	Florida Beer Wholesalers	Beer
AFSCME	Public employees	Florida Business Forum Inc.	Business
American Publishers Assn.	Book publishers	Florida Chiropractic Association	Chiropractors
Associated Industries of Florida	Manufacturers	Florida CPA	CPAs
AT&T PAC-Florida	Telephone	Florida Dairy Farmers Association	Dairy farmers
Barnett People for Better Gov't	Bank	Florida Dental PAC	Dentists
Lewis Bear Co.	Wholesale	Florida Employers Insurance	Insurance
Ronnie Bergeron	Road construction	Florida Engineers	Engineers
Blue Cross/Blue Shield	Health insurance	Florida Farm Bureau	Agriculture
Calder Race Course, Inc.	Horse track	Florida Fruit and Vegetable Assn.	Agriculture
Cargill Poultry Products	Poultry	Florida Greyhound Track Owners	Dog tracks
Carson Farms	Farms	Florida Hearing Aid Society	Manufacturers
CAR PAC	Car dealers	Florida Hospital League	Hospital
Carlton, Fields PAC	Attorneys/lobbyists	Florida Medical PAC	Doctors
Centel Corp.	Telephone	Florida Osteopathic Medical Assn.	Osteopaths
Champion International Corp.	Paper	Florida Phosphate Committee	Phosphate industry
Citizens & Southern	Bank	Florida Podiatry PAC	Podiatrists
Clark, Roumelis and Associates	Engineering	Florida Premium Finance Assn.	Financial services
Coastal States Mgmt.	Energy	Florida Propane PAC	Propane gas
Coca-Cola Bottling Co.	Bottler	Florida Restaurant Assn.	Restaurants
CSX Transportation	Rail transportation	Florida RV Trade Assn.	Recreational vehicles
Eastern Airlines PAC	Airlines	Florida Shopping Center	Commercial
E. I. DuPont DeNemours & Co.	Chemical	Florida Transportation	Truckers
Everglades Agriculture PAC	Agricultural	Florida Trucking Assn.	Truckers
Exxon Corp. 500	Oil	GTE State PAC	Telephone

Source: Florida, Office of the Secretary of State

Table 4–6
PAC CONTRIBUTIONS TO STATE LEGISLATIVE RACES

	Percent of PAC Contribution Going to:			
State	INCUMBENTS	CHALLENGERS	OPEN SEAT CANDIDATES	TOTALS
California	39%	13%	23%	26%
Idaho	57%	12%	28%	31%
Minnesota	24%	8%	18%	16%
Missouri	21%	6%	9%	12%
Montana	28%	17%	9%	18%
North Carolina	49%	16%	16%	3%
New Jersey	28%	15%	15%	21%
Oregon	63%	21%	48%	43%
Pennsylvania	53%	19%	29%	35%
Washington	37%	31%	26%	33%
Wisconsin	22%	5%	14%	13%

Source: Derived from William E. Cassie, Joel A. Thompson, and Malcolm E. Jewell, "The Pattern of PAC Contributions in Legislative Elections: An Eleven-State Analysis." Paper delivered at the Annual Meeting of the American Political Science Association, Chicago, 1992. Copyright 1994–95 The Council of State Governments. Reprinted with permission from *Book of the States.*

favor of incumbents over challengers. Table 4–6 reveals the pattern of PAC contributions for state legislative races in eleven states. Note that PAC contributors in the larger states may account for as much as one-quarter to one-third of the total contributions to state legislative races.

COMPARING INTEREST GROUP POWER IN THE STATES

How do interest group systems in the states differ? Why do some states have strong, influential interest groups shaping public policy, while in other states the influence of interest groups is moderated by group competition, party rivalry, and electoral politics?

We might define overall interest group influence in a state as "the extent to which interest groups as a whole influence public policy when compared to other components of the political system, such as political parties, the legislature, the governor, etc."[29] Using this definition researchers have attempted to categorize the states as having a "dominant," "complementary," or "subordinate" interest group system, in terms of its policy impact relative to the parties and the branches of government (see Table 4–7).

---

[29]Clive S. Thomas and Robert J. Hrebenar, "Interest Groups in the States," in Virginia Gray et al., *Politics in the American States,* 5th ed. (New York: HarperCollins, 1990), p. 141.

Table 4–7

CLASSIFICATION OF THE FIFTY STATES ACCORDING TO THE OVERALL IMPACT
OF INTEREST GROUPS

	States Where the Overall Impact of Interest Groups Is:			
DOMINANT (7)	DOMINANT/ COMPLEMENTARY (21)	COMPLEMENTARY (17)	COMPLEMENTARY/ SUBORDINATE (5)	SUBORDINATE (0)
Alabama	Alaska	Colorado	Delaware	
Florida	Arizona	Connecticut	Minnesota	
Louisiana	Arkansas	Indiana	Rhode Island	
Nevada	California	Maine	South Dakota	
New Mexico	Georgia	Maryland	Vermont	
South Carolina	Hawaii	Massachusetts		
West Virginia	Idaho	Michigan		
	Illinois	Missouri		
	Iowa	New Hampshire		
	Kansas	New Jersey		
	Kentucky	New York		
	Mississippi	North Carolina		
	Montana	North Dakota		
	Nebraska	Pennsylvania		
	Ohio	Utah		
	Oklahoma	Washington		
	Oregon	Wisconsin		
	Tennessee			
	Texas			
	Virginia			
	Wyoming			

Source: Clive Thomas and Ronald J. Hrebenar, "Interest Groups in the States," in Virginia Gray and Herbert Jacob, eds. *Politics in the American States,* 6th ed. Washington, D.C.: CQ Press, 1996.

Over time interest group influence appears to be increasing in all of the states. A major factor in this strengthening of interest groups is their increasing role in campaign finance. The more money coming from interest groups to political candidates, the greater is the influence of the interest group system.

Yet interest group influence in some states is greater than in other states and our task is to search for explanations.

THE ECONOMIC DIVERSITY EXPLANATION   Wealthy urban industrial states (Connecticut, Massachusetts, Michigan, New Jersey, New York, Rhode Island) have weaker interest group systems because of the diversity and complexity of their economies. No single industry can dominate political life. Instead, multiple competing interest groups tend to balance each other, and this cancels the influence of interest groups generally. In contrast, in rural states with less economic diversity, a few dominant industries (oil and gas in Louisiana, coal in West Virginia) appear to have more influence. The reputation for influence for particular industries in these states causes them to be viewed as strong pressure group states.

THE PARTY EXPLANATION   According to political scientist Sarah McCally Morehouse, "Where parties are strong, pressure groups are weak or moderate; where parties are weak, pressure groups are strong enough to dominate the policy-making process."[30] Where competitive political parties are strong—where the parties actively recruit candidates, provide campaign support, and hold their members accountable after the election—interest groups are less powerful. Policy makers in these states look to the party for policy guidance rather than to interest groups. Interest group influence is channeled through the parties; the parties are coalitions of interest groups; no single interest group can dominate or circumvent the party. Strong party states (Connecticut, Illinois, New York, Minnesota, North Dakota, Rhode Island, Wisconsin, Massachusetts, Colorado) have weak interest group systems. Weak party states (primarily the one-party southern states) have strong interest group systems. We will discuss party competition in Chapter 5.

Strong governors and strong legislative leadership, exercising their influence as party leaders, can provide a check on the lobbying efforts of interest groups. When the special interests lose, it is usually on issues on which the governor and the party leadership have taken a clear stand.[31]

THE PROFESSIONALISM EXPLANATION   State legislatures are becoming more professional over time. In Chapter 6 we define a *professional* legislature as a well-paid, full-time, well-staffed body, as opposed to an amateur legislature, which meets only a few weeks each year, pays its members very little, and has few research or information services available to it. Professional legislatures have less turnover in members and more experience in lawmaking. Clearly, these characteristics of legislatures affect the power of interest groups. Interest groups are more influential when legislatures are *less* professional. When members are less experienced, paid less, and have little time or resources to research issues themselves, they must depend more on interest groups, and interest groups gain influence.

THE GOVERNMENTAL FRAGMENTATION EXPLANATION   It is also likely that states with weak governors, multiple independently elected state officials, and numerous independent boards and commissions have strong interest group systems. In states with fragmented executive power (Florida, South Carolina), interest groups have additional points of access and control, and executive officials do not have counterbalancing power. Strong governors (as in New York, Massachusetts, New Jersey, Connecti-

---

[30]Sarah McCally Morehouse, *State Politics, Parties and Policy* (New York: Holt, Rinehart & Winston, 1981), p. 118.

[31]See Charles W. Wiggins, Keith E. Harmun, and Charles G. Bell, "Interest-Group and Party Influence Agents in the Legislative Process: A Comparative State Analysis," *Journal of Politics* 54 (February 1992), 82–100.

cut, Delaware, and Minnesota) are better able to confront the influence of interest groups when they choose to do so. (We will discuss governors' powers in Chapter 7.)

Fortunately, we do not have to choose one explanation to the exclusion of others. Economic diversity, party strength, professionalism, and governmental fragmentation all contribute to the explanation of interest group strength in the states.

PROTEST AS POLITICAL PARTICIPATION

Organized protests—marches, demonstrations, disruptions, civil disobedience—are important forms of political activity. Protest marches and demonstrations are now nearly as frequent at state capitols and city halls as in Washington.

It is important to distinguish between *protest, civil disobedience,* and *violence,* even though all may be forms of political activity. Most *protests* do *not* involve unlawful conduct and are protected by the constitutional guarantee of the First Amendment to "peaceably assemble and petition for redress of grievances." A march on city hall or the state capitol, followed by a mass assembly of people with speakers, sign-waving, songs, and perhaps the formal presentation of grievances to whichever brave official agrees to meet with the protesters is well within the constitutional guarantees of Americans.

PROTEST   *Protest* refers to direct, collective activity by persons who wish to obtain concessions from established power holders. Often the protest is a means of acquiring bargaining power by those who would otherwise be powerless. The protest may challenge established groups by threatening their reputations (in cases in which they might be harmed by unfavorable publicity), their economic position (in cases in which noise and disruption upset their daily activity), or their sense of security (when the threat exists that the protest may turn unruly or violent). The strategy of protest may appeal especially to powerless minorities who have little else to bargain with except the promise to stop protesting.

Protests may also aim at motivating uncommitted "third parties" to enter the political arena on behalf of the protesters. The object of the protest is to call attention to the existence of some issue and urge others to apply pressure on public officials. Of course, this strategy requires the support and assistance of the news media. If protests are ignored by television and newspapers, they can hardly be expected to activate support. However, the news media seldom ignore protests with audience interest; protest leaders and journalists share an interest in dramatizing "news" for the public.

CIVIL DISOBEDIENCE   *Civil disobedience* is a form of protest that involves breaking "unjust" laws. Civil disobedience is not new: It has played an important role in American history, from the Boston Tea Party to the abolitionists who illegally hid runaway slaves, to the suffragettes who demonstrated for women's voting rights, to the labor organizers who picketed to form the nation's major industrial unions, to the civil rights workers of the early 1960s who deliberately violated segregation laws. The purpose of civil disobedience is to call attention, or to "bear witness," to the existence of injustice. In the words of Martin Luther King, Jr., civil disobedience "seeks to dramatize the issue so that it can no longer be ignored."[32] There should be no violence in true civil disobedience, and only "unjust" laws are broken. Moreover, the law is broken "openly, lovingly" with a willingness to accept the penalty. Punishment is actively sought rather than avoided, since punishment will help to emphasize the injustice of the law. The object is to stir the conscience of an apathetic majority and win support for measures that will eliminate injustices. By willingly accepting punishment for the violation of an unjust law, people who practice civil disobedience demonstrate their sincerity. They hope to shame public officials and make them ask themselves how far they are willing to go to protect the status quo.

As in all protest activity, the participation of the news media, particularly television, is essential to the success of civil disobedience. The dramatization of injustice makes news; the public's sympathy is won when injustices are spotlighted; and the willingness of demonstrators to accept punishment is visible evidence of their sincerity. Cruelty or violence directed *against* the demonstrators by police or others plays into the hands of the protesters by further emphasizing injustices.[33]

VIOLENCE   *Violence* can also be a form of political participation. To be sure, it is criminal, and it is generally irrational and self-defeating. However, political assassination, bombing and terrorism, and rioting, burning, and looting have occurred with uncomfortable frequency in American politics.

It is important to distinguish violence from protest. Peaceful protest is constitutionally guaranteed. Most protests are free of violence. Occasionally there is an implicit *threat* of violence in a protest—a threat that can be manipulated by protesters to help gain their ends. However, most protests harness frustrations and hostilities and direct them into constitutionally acceptable activities. Civil disobedience should also be distinguished from violence. The civil disobedient breaks only "unjust" laws, openly and without violence, and willingly accepts punishment without attempting escape. Rioting, burning, and looting—as well as bombing and assassination—are clearly distinguishable from peaceful protest and even civil disobedience.

NEWS MEDIA   The real key to success in protest activity is found in the support or opposition of the news media to protest group demands. Virtually all of the studies of protest activity have asserted that it is the response of "third parties," primarily the news media, and not the immediate response of public officials, that is essential to success.[34] This is a plausible finding, because, after all, if protesters could persuade public officials directly there would be no need to protest. Indeed, one might even distinguish between

---

[32]For an inspiring essay on "nonviolent direct action" and civil disobedience in a modern context, read Martin Luther King, Jr., "Letter from Birmingham City Jail," April 16, 1963.

[33]For more detailed examination of the purposes, functions, and rationale of civil disobedience, see Paul F. Power, "Civil Disobedience as Functional Opposition," *Journal of Politics,* 34 (February 1972), 37–55; and "On Civil Disobedience in Recent American Thought," *American Political Science Review,* 64 (March 1970), 35–47.

[34]Michael Lipsky, *Protest in City Politics* (Chicago: Rand, McNally, 1970); Peter K. Eisinger, "The Conditions of Protest Behavior in American Cities," *American Political Science Review,* 67 (March 1973), 11–29; Paul D. Schumaker, "Policy Responsiveness to Protest Group Demands," *Journal of Politics,* 37 (May 1975), 488–521.

"interest groups," which have a high degree of continuous interaction with public officials, and "protest groups," which do not regularly interact with public officials and must engage in protest to be heard. Furthermore, to be heard, reports of their protests must be carried in newspapers and on television.

THE EFFECTIVENESS OF PROTESTS   Several conditions must be present if protest is to be effective.[35] First of all, there must be a clear goal or objective of the protest. Protesters must aim at specific concessions or legislation they desire; generally, complex problems or complaints that cannot readily be solved by specific governmental action are not good targets for protest activity. Second, the protest must be directed at some public officials who are capable of granting the desired goal. It is difficult to secure concessions if no one is in a position to grant them. Third, the protest leaders must not only organize their masses for protest activity, but they must also simultaneously bargain with public officials for the desired concessions. This implies a division of labor between "organizers" and "negotiators."

OFFICIAL RESPONSES TO PROTESTS   Finally, we might note in this discussion the strategies available to public officials who are faced with protest activity. They may greet the protesters with smiles and reassurances that they agree with their objectives. They may dispense *symbolic* satisfaction without actually granting any tangible payoffs. Once the "crisis" is abated, the bargaining leverage of the protest leaders diminishes considerably. Public officials may dispense *token* satisfactions by responding, with much publicity, to one or more specific cases of injustice, while doing little of a broad-based nature to alleviate conditions. Or public officials may *appear to be constrained* in their ability to grant protest goals by claiming that they lack the financial resources or legal authority to do anything—the "I-would-help-you-if-I-could-but-I-can't" pose. Another tactic is to *postpone action* by calling for further study while offering assurances of sympathy and interest. Finally, public officials may try to *discredit* protesters by stating or implying that they are violence-prone or unrepresentative of the real aspirations of the people they seek to lead. This tactic is especially effective if the protest involves violence or disruption or if protest leaders have "leftist" or criminal backgrounds.

---

[35]See Michael Lipsky, "Protest as a Political Resource," *American Political Science Review,* 62 (December 1968), 1144–58.

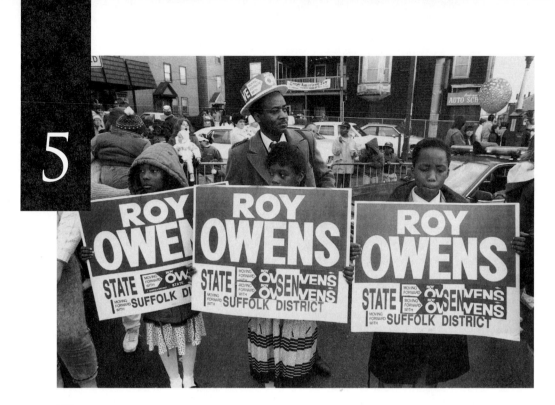

PARTIES
AND CAMPAIGNS
IN THE STATES

AMERICAN POLITICAL PARTIES
IN DISARRAY

Once upon a time, political parties were the central features on the American political landscape. Party loyalties were a way of life, passed on in families like religion. People identified themselves as Republicans or Democrats and usually voted for their party's nominees. Scholars wrote that parties were indispensable to democracy: "Political parties created modern democracy and modern democracy is unthinkable save in terms of parties."[1]

THE RESPONSIBLE PARTY MODEL   The parties were viewed as the principal instrument of majority control of public policy. "Responsible parties" were supposed to (1) develop and clarify alternative policy positions for the voters; (2) educate the people about the issues and simplify choices for them; (3) recruit candidates for public office who agreed with the parties' policy positions; (4) organize and direct their candidates'

---

[1]E. E. Schattschneider, *Party Government* (New York: Rinehart, 1942), p. 1.

campaigns to win office; (5) hold their elected officials responsible for enacting the parties' policy positions after they were elected; and (6) organize legislatures to ensure party control of policy making. In carrying out these functions, responsible parties were supposed to modify the demands of special interests, build a consensus that could win majority support, and provide simple and identifiable, yet meaningful, choices for the voters on election day. In this way, disciplined, issue-oriented, competitive parties would be the principal means by which the people would direct public policy.

PROBLEMS WITH THE MODEL   Over the years, this "responsible party" model fell into disarray, if indeed it ever accurately described American political parties. There are fundamental problems with the responsible model itself:

- *The parties do not offer the voters clear policy alternatives.* Instead, each tries to capture the broad center of most policy dimensions, where it believes most Americans can be found. There is no incentive for parties to stand on the far right or far left when most Americans are found in the center. So the parties echo each other, and critics refer to them as Tweedledee and Tweedledum.
- *Voter decisions are not motivated primarily by policy considerations.* Most voters cast their votes on the basis of candidate "image," the "goodness" or "badness" of the times, and traditional voting habits. This means there is little incentive for either parties or candidates to concentrate on issues. Party platforms are seldom read by anyone. Modern campaign techniques focus on the image of the candidate—compassion, warmth, good humor, experience, physical appearance, ease in front of a camera, and so forth—rather than positions on the issues.
- *American political parties have no way to bind their elected officials to party positions or even their campaign pledges.* Parties cannot really discipline members of Congress or state legislatures for voting against the party position. Party cohesion, where it exists, is more a product of likemindedness among Democratic or Republican legislators than it is of party control.

In addition to these underlying problems, over time parties in America weakened by various political developments:

- *The rise of primary elections.* Party organizations cannot control who the party's nominee shall be. Nominations are won in primary elections. The progressive reformers who introduced primary elections at the beginning of the twentieth century wanted to undercut the power of party machines in determining who runs for office, and the reformers succeeded in doing so. Nominees now establish personal organizations in primary elections and campaign for popular votes; they do not have to negotiate with party leaders. Of course, the party organization may endorse a candidate in a primary election, but this is no guarantee of success with the party's voters.
- *The decline of party identification.* Democratic and Republican party loyalties have been declining over the years. Most people remain registered as Democrats or Republicans in order to vote in party primary elections, but increasing numbers of people identify themselves as "independent" and cast their vote in general elections without reference to party. Split-ticket voting (where a single voter casts his or her vote for a Democrat in one race and a Republican in another) has also increased.
- *The influence of the mass media, particularly television.* Candidates can come directly into the voter's living room via television. Campaigning is now largely a me-

dia activity. Candidates no longer need party workers to carry their message from block to block.

- *The decline of patronage.* Civil service reforms, at the national, state, and even city levels, have reduced the tangible rewards of electoral victory. Party "profession-als"—who work in political campaigns to secure jobs and favors for themselves and their friends—are now being replaced by political "amateurs"—who work in political campaigns for the emotional satisfaction of supporting a "cause." Ama-teurs work intensely during campaigns, but professionals once worked year-round, off-years and election years, building party support with small personal favors for the voters. These party "regulars" are disappearing.

- *The rise of single-issue interest groups and PACs.* Parties have always coexisted with broad-based interest groups, many of whom contribute money to both Demo-cratic and Republican candidates in order to ensure access regardless of who wins. But many of the more militant single-issue groups require a "litmus test" of individ-ual candidates on single issues—abortion, gun control, and so forth. Their support and money hinge on the candidate's position on a single issue. Most PAC (political action committee) money goes directly to candidates, not to party organizations.

CONTINUING PARTY ROLE IN SELECTING CANDIDATES   De-spite these problems, the American political parties survive. They are important in the se-lection of *personnel* for public office, if not for the selection of public policy. Very few independents are ever elected to high political office. Only three governors in recent years, James Longley of Maine, Walter Hickel of Alaska, and Lowell Weicker of Connecticut, were elected as independents; there are fewer than a dozen independent state legislators in the nation; the Nebraska legislature is the nation's only nonpartisan state legislative body.

PARTY STRUCTURES   We might view political parties as three separate struc-tures. The first is the *party-in-the-electorate:* the voters who identify themselves as Demo-crats or Republicans, and who tend to vote for the candidates of their party. It is this party-in-the-electorate that appears to be in decline today. Party loyalties are weakening; more people identify themselves as "independents"; "crossover" and "ticket splitting" have increased, and more voters cast their ballots without regard to the party affiliation of the candidates. The second is the *party-in-the-government:* state and local elected offi-cials who won party nominations and appeared on the ballot as Democratic or Republi-can candidates. This party has weakened also: Party nominations are won through primary elections; party leaders have less influence over the nomination process; candi-dates communicate to the voters by television rather than through party workers; and parties have no way to bind elected officials to party positions. Nonetheless, party iden-tification and loyalty among elected officeholders (the party-in-the-government) is generally stronger than party identification and loyalty among voters (the party-in-the-electorate). (We will examine the role of parties in state legislatures in Chapter 6 and in the governorship in Chapter 7.) Finally, there is the *party organization:* party officials and workers, committee members and convention delegates, and other party activists. Years ago, many American cities were dominated by party "machines" and "bosses," but re-formers succeeded in bringing nonpartisan elections to local government in a majority of the nation's cities (see Chapter 9). Nonetheless, party organizations still flourish at the state and county level, as we will see later in this chapter.

REPUBLICAN AND DEMOCRATIC PARTY FORTUNES

Traditionally, the Democratic party held a decided edge in American state government. Figure 5–1 shows the success of Democratic gubernatorial candidates over the years. The Republican resurgence of 1994 gave the GOP a majority of governorships for the first time in thirty years. Democrats have also traditionally dominated state legislatures. Over the past half-century Democrats have controlled more state legislative bodies—both state senates and houses of representatives—than Republicans.

Figure 5–1

PARTY CONTROL OF THE GOVERNORSHIPS, 1952–1995

Democrats   Republicans

*One Independent governer in 1975 and 1995;
two Independent governors in 1989, 1991, and 1993.

PARTY IDENTIFICATION   Not only has the Democratic party traditionally been the dominant party-in-the-government in the American states, it has also enjoyed greater support in the national electorate. Over the years more Americans identified with the Democratic party than the Republican party (Table 5–1). This Democratic party preference persisted even in years when Republican presidents won landslide elections.

PARTY REGISTRATION   In states that register voters by party, the Democratic party does better in registration figures than it does in opinion polls.[2] The tendency for many independents and even some Republicans to register as Democrats is not confined to the South. (In Florida, for example, a 1994 poll showed party identifications as 33 percent Republican, 32 percent Democratic, and 34 percent independent; yet official registration figures showed 52 percent Democratic, 41 percent Republican, and 7 percent independent.) Of course, independents are spurred in many states to register with one party or another in order to participate in primary elections that are closed to all but party registrants. (See "Parties and Primaries" later in this chapter.) Voters chose to register in the dominant party for several reasons: perhaps because the dominant party's primary is more interesting insofar as the winner is more likely to go on to win office; or perhaps because people seeking political favors (like jobs, contracts, zoning decisions) wish to be identified publicly with the dominant party; or perhaps because of social pressures and a desire to be seen as a member of the dominant party. Because the Democratic party was traditionally the dominant party in most states, registration figures remain skewed toward the Democrats.

PARTY COMPETITION IN THE STATES

The ideal "responsible" party system is said to be one in which *competitive parties* present alternative programs in election campaigns, and the party winning the majority of votes captures all the power it needs to write its program into law. Moreover, in the responsible party system, the elected officials act cohesively so the voters can hold the party collectively responsible at the end of its term of office. The key to this ideal party system is the existence of competitive parties that are roughly balanced in strength.

Table 5–1

PARTY IDENTIFICATION AMONG ALL AMERICANS

	1937	1960	1972	1984	1988	1994	1996
Democrats	50	47	43	40	42	40	38
Independents	16	23	29	29	28	34	33
Republicans	34	30	28	31	30	26	29

Source: Gallup Polls. Excludes mentions of other parties and "don't knows."

[2]See Steven E. Finkel and Howard A. Scarrow, "Party Identification and Party Enrollment," *Journal of Politics*, 47 (May 1985), 620–42.

HOW MUCH PARTY COMPETITION?   In reality, however, party competition throughout the fifty states is uneven. Traditionally, dominance of the Democratic party precluded any real competition for control of upper or lower chambers of state legislatures in many states and rendered many gubernatorial races noncompetitive as well. Table 5–2 groups states according to the percentage of times between 1968 and 1994 Democrats or Republicans captured control of the governorship and upper and lower houses of the state legislature.

GROWING REPUBLICAN STRENGTH IN THE SOUTH   The recent growth of Republican party strength in the eleven southern states has shifted several of these states away from their traditional label as "one-party Democratic." For many years the southern states had been a partisan battleground in *presidential* elections, but remained solidly Democratic in *state and local* politics. Republican governors were occasionally elected, but very few Republicans served in southern state legislatures. However, Republican grass-roots strength in the South began to grow in the 1990s. By 1995 six southern states (Alabama, Mississippi, South Carolina, Tennessee, Texas, and Virginia) had Republican governors. And for the first time since Reconstruction, Republicans controlled three state legislative houses (Florida's senate, North Carolina's and South Carolina's house). Moreover, in 1995, for the first time in history, Republicans held a majority (64–61) of all U.S. House of Representatives seats from southern states. The

Table 5–2
PARTY COMPETITION IN STATE POLITICS

Traditional Democratic Advantage	Traditional Democratic but Growing Republican Strength	Competitive, Leaning Democratic	Competitive, Leaning Republican	Traditional Republican Advantage
Arkansas	Alabama	Alaska	Arizona	Indiana
Hawaii	Florida	California	Colorado	New Hampshire
Kentucky	Georgia	Connecticut	Idaho	South Dakota
Louisiana	Mississippi	Delaware	Kansas	
Maryland	North Carolina	Illinois	North Dakota	
Massachusetts	Oklahoma	Iowa	Utah	
Missouri	South Carolina	Maine	Vermont	
Nevada	Tennessee	Michigan	Wyoming	
New Mexico	Texas	Minnesota		
Rhode Island	Virginia	Montana		
West Virginia		Nebraska		
		New Jersey		
		New York		
		Ohio		
		Oregon		
		Pennsylvania		
		Washington		
		Wisconsin		

growing GOP strength in the South promises to shift more states into the "competitive" category. (These states are listed in Table 5–2 under "Traditional Democratic but Growing Republican Strength.")

DIVIDED GOVERNMENT   The frequency of divided party government in the states—where one party controls one or both houses of the legislature and the other party controls the governorship—dilutes party responsibility. In recent years, over half of the states have experienced divided party control (see "Divided Government: Governor Versus the Legislature" in Chapter 7). A unified party government—where the same party controls both houses of the legislature as well as the governorship—is presumed to be better able to enact its program into law. While many obstacles to program enactment may remain, at least party "gridlock" is avoided. More importantly, perhaps, voters are better able to attribute praise or blame for the direction of state government. Under unified party government, the dominant party cannot escape responsibility for poor performance by blaming it on the opponent party's control of one house or branch of state government.[3]

THE POLICY EFFECTS OF PARTY COMPETITION

What difference does it make in public policy whether a state has competitive or noncompetitive parties? Do states with a competitive party system differ in their approach to education, welfare, health, taxation, or highways from states with noncompetitive party systems? This is not an easy question to answer. Since historically competitive states tended to be wealthy, urban, and industrialized, and noncompetitive states poorer, rural, and agricultural, it was difficult to sort out the effects of party competition from those other socioeconomic variables. Some scholars asserted that a more competitive party system would lead to more liberal education, welfare, and taxation policies. However, available evidence indicates that education, welfare, taxation, and highway programs appear to be *more closely related* to socioeconomic factors in the states than to the degree of party competition itself.[4]

POLICY EFFECTS OF COMPETITION   The thesis that party competition produced liberal welfare programs was suggested many years ago by V. O. Key, Jr.:

> In the two-party states the anxiety over the next election pushes political leaders into serving the interests of the have-less elements of society, therefore putting the party into the countervailing power operation.

---

[3]See Kerin M. Leyden and Stephen A. Borrelli, "The Effect of State Economic Conditions on Gubernatorial Elections: Does Unified Government Make a Difference?" *Political Research Quarterly,* 48 (June 1995), 275–90.

[4]The traditional assumption that party competition had an important liberalizing effect on public policy is found in V. O. Key, Jr., *American State Politics: An Introduction* (New York: Knopf, 1956). The effect of party competition on public policy was shown in statistical analysis to be *less* influential than economic condition in Thomas R. Dye, *Politics, Economics, and the Public* (Chicago: Rand McNally, 1966). However, party competition combined with voter participation was found to have some effect on certain welfare policies in Ira Sharkansky and Richard I. Hofferbert, "Dimensions of State Politics, Economics and Public Policy," *American Political Science Review,* 63 (September 1969), 867–79.

. . . [I]n the one-party states it is easier for a few powerful interests to manage the government of the state without party interference since the parties are not representative of the
particular elements that might pose opposition to the dominant group.

. . . [O]ver the long run the have-nots lose in a disorganized politics.[5]

When these assertions were tested, however, it turned out that there were few significant *independent* relationships between party competition and levels of public taxing and
spending in the American states. Once the effects of income, urbanization, and education
are controlled, the initial relationships between competition and participation and public
policy largely disappear. Competition and participation are dependent upon levels of economic development, and so are levels of public taxing and spending; the associations between competitive politics and public policies turned out to be largely spurious. Or, as
Thomas R. Dye explains:

> Economic development shapes both political systems and policy outcomes, and most of the
> association that occurs between system characteristics and policy outcomes can be attrib-
> uted to the influence of economic development. Differences in the policy choices of states
> with different types of political systems turn out to be largely a product of differing socio-
> economic levels rather than a direct product of political variables.[6]

WHEN COMPETITION MAY NOT PRODUCE POLICY DIFFER-
ENCES   Party competition itself does not necessarily cause more liberal welfare policies.
If there is a *unimodal* distribution of voters' preferences in a state, and if the state parties
are devoid of strong organizations and ideologically motivated activists, then the party system will have little meaning for public policy. This notion can be diagrammed as follows:

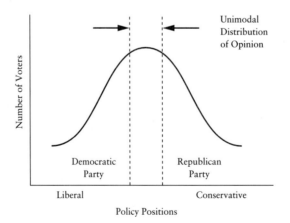

where there is unimodal distribution of opinion (most voters are found in the center) and
the parties move toward the middle position to capture the greatest number of voters.

---

[5]Key, *Southern Politics in State and Nation* (New York: Knopf, 1949), p. 307.
[6]Dye, *Politics, Economics, and the Public,* p. 293.

Table 5–3
PARTY SYSTEM CLEAVAGE STRUCTURES

Cleavage 1: Southern

BIAS:

DEMOCRAT	REPUBLICAN
Black	White
Low Income	High Income
Rural	College
	Urban

South Carolina
Mississippi
Alabama
Texas
Louisiana
Georgia
Virginia
North Carolina
Oklahoma
Florida
Tennessee

Cleavage 2: New Deal

BIAS:

DEMOCRAT	REPUBLICAN
Catholic	Protestant
Low Income	High Income
Union	College
Female	

Vermont
Maine
New Hampshire
Massachusetts
Arizona
New Mexico
Connecticut
Montana
Rhode Island
Minnesota
Colorado
Utah
Iowa
South Dakota
North Dakota
Idaho
Nebraska
Washington
Oregon

Cleavage 3: Post–New Deal

BIAS:

DEMOCRAT	REPUBLICAN
Black	White
Catholic	Protestant
Urban	High Income
Union	College
Low Income	
Female	
Jewish	

Illinois
New York
Michigan
Delaware
New Jersey
Maryland
California
Pennsylvania
Ohio
Wisconsin
Missouri
Nevada
Indiana
Kansas

Note: Arkansas, Kentucky, West Virginia, and Wyoming do not conform to these party cleavages.

Source: Robert D. Brown, Party Cleavages and Welfare Effect in the American States," *American Political Science Review*, 89 (March 1995), p. 28; reprinted with permission.

eral strength within the Democratic party increases. Blacks have assumed increasingly active and influential roles in southern Democratic party organizations, while fundamentalist white Protestants have become an increasingly active force in Republican circles.[9] The result is greater ideological cleavage between the parties.

ACTIVISTS AS POTENTIAL CANDIDATES   Party activists—people who serve on party posts as committee members or chairpersons at the city, county, or state level, or as delegates to party conventions—constitute a recruitment pool for candidates for public office. Often these people initially volunteered for party work with the expectation of eventually running for public office. Their party activity provides technical knowledge as well as personal contacts that become useful in their own future campaign. Party workers generally have voter registration lists available to them as well as information regarding ballot access, filing dates, campaign expenditure reporting, and other useful information. And, of course, party workers come into personal contact with campaign contributors. There is some evidence, however, that among party workers women are not as ambitious for public office as men, although gender differences in ambition for public office are diminishing.[10] Lawyers who volunteer as party workers are often seeking to make client contacts and enhance future opportunities to run for office.[11] .

STATE PARTY ORGANIZATIONS

State party organizations are "highly variable, elusive to find, difficult to define, and frustrating to study."[12] Indeed, both Democratic and Republican party organizations at the state and local level are ill-defined, fluid, and very often "unoccupied." As many as half of the official party positions in the nation may be vacant. Moreover, many people who hold party positions do little or nothing to help their party or its candidates.

IMPACT OF FEDERALISM   American political parties are decentralized in their organization. It is not really surprising in the American system of federalism—when only the president and vice-president have *national* constituencies, and senators, representatives, governors, state legislators, and county and city officials all have *state and local* constituencies—that the American parties are decentralized.

At the national level, the Democratic and Republican parties consist of a national committee; a House and Senate party conference; and various national clubs, such as Young Democrats and Young Republicans. There are also *fifty state parties,* which are composed of state committees and county and city organizations. This structure is tied together very

---

[9]See Harold Clarke, Frank B. Feigert, and Marianne C. Stewart, "Different Contents, Similar Packages: The Domestic Political Beliefs of Southern Local Party Activists," *Political Research Quarterly,* 48 (March 1995), 151–67.

[10]Janet Clark, Charles D. Hadley, and R. Darcy, "Political Ambition Among Men and Women State Party Leaders," *American Politics Quarterly,* 17 (April 1989), 194–207.

[11]Stephen S. Meinhold and Charles D. Hadley, "Lawyers as Political Party Activists," *Social Science Quarterly,* 76 (June 1995) 364–80.

[12]Robert J. Huckshorn, *Party Leadership in the States* (Amherst: University of Massachusetts Press, 1976), p. 1.

loosely. State parties are not very responsive to national direction, and in most states, city and county organizations operate quite independently of the state committees. State committees are generally involved in important statewide elections—governors, U.S. senators, and representatives in the smaller states. City and county committees are generally responsible for county and municipal offices, state legislative seats, and congressional seats in the larger states. The Democratic and Republican National Committees exist primarily for the purpose of holding national conventions every four years to select the party's presidential candidate. Since each level of party organization has "its own fish to fry," each operates quite independently of the other levels.

STATE LAWS GOVERN PARTIES Party affairs are governed largely by the laws of the states. Each state sets forth the conditions that an organization must meet to qualify as a political party and to get its candidates' names printed on the official election ballots. Each state sets the qualifications for membership in a party and the right to vote in the party's primary election. State laws determine the number, method of selection, and duties of various party officials, committees, and conventions. The states, rather than the parties themselves, decide how the parties shall nominate candidates for public office. Most states require that party nominations be made by direct primaries, but several states still nominate by party caucuses or conventions. Most states also attempt to regulate party finances, although with little success.

STATE COMMITTEES State party organizations officially consist of a "state committee," a "state chairman," or "chairwoman," and perhaps a small office staff working at the state capitol. Democratic and Republican state committees vary from state to state in composition, organization, and function. Membership on the state committee may range from about a dozen up to several hundred. The members may be chosen through party primaries or by state party conventions. Generally, representation on state committees is allocated to counties, but occasionally other units of government are recognized in state party organization. A state party chairman or chairwoman generally serves at the head of the state committee; these people are generally selected by the state committee, but their selection is often dictated by the party's candidate for governor.

State committees are supposed to direct the campaigns for important statewide elections—governors and U.S. senators, and congressional representatives in the smaller states. They are supposed to serve as central coordinating agencies for these election campaigns and to serve as the party's principal fund-raising organization in the state. However, the role of the state committee very often depends upon the preferences of the party's statewide candidates regarding the handling of their campaigns. Today, most candidates have their own campaign organizations to plan and execute campaign strategy. State party organizations seldom play a major role in the candidate's campaign.

State committees are not very responsive to the direction of the national committee, and in most states, city and county party organizations operate quite independently of the state committees. In other words, there is no real hierarchy of authority in state party systems.

COUNTY COMMITTEES Party organizations at the city and county level are probably the most cohesive organizations within the parties. Yet these organizations are far from disciplined groups. City or county party organizations usually include:

- An active chairperson and executive committee, plus a few associated activists, who in effect make most of the decisions in the name of the party, who raise funds, who occasionally seek out candidates (or approve the candidates who select themselves), and who speak locally for the party
- A ward and precinct organization in which only a few local committee members are active and in which there is little door-to-door canvassing or other direct voter contact
- The active participation in organizational matters of some of the party's elected public officials, who may share effective control of the organization with the official leadership of the party organization
- Financial contributors to the party and its candidates, together with leaders of local interest groups that generally ally themselves with the party.[13]

Republican and Democratic county chairpersons probably constitute the most important building blocks in party organization in America. City and county party officers and committees are chosen locally and cannot be removed by any higher party authority. In short, authority is not concentrated in any single statewide organization but is divided among many city and county party organizations.

STATE PARTY CHAIRPERSONS   Although state party organizations are weakened by decentralization, state party chairpersons are by no means political hacks. Most state chairpersons have been successful business people, lawyers, or public officials who serve in their posts without salaries to satisfy their interest in politics and public affairs. Republican chairpersons are more likely to have held important positions in business and management, while Democratic chairpersons are more likely to be lawyers who have held political office previously.

State party chairpersons can play different roles from state to state. Some see themselves as mere "political agents" of their governor; others are independently powerful. In general, chairpersons of the party out of power have more independence and power than those of the party in power. The latter are overshadowed by their governor. Party chairpersons do not hold on to their jobs very long—the average is less than three years.[14]

PARTY ORGANIZATIONS   While party attachment among voters has weakened over the years, state party organizations have strengthened.[15] Today most state party organizations maintain a permanent party headquarters in the state capital. Most have full-time staffs, including an executive director; a budget official; and public relations, fund-raising, and research people. These state party organizations help to raise campaign funds for their candidates, conduct registration drives, provide advice and services to their nominees, and even recruit candidates to run in districts and for offices where the party would otherwise have no names on the ballot. Services to candidates may include advertising and media consulting, advice on election law compliance, polling, research

---

[13]See Paul Allen Beck and Frank J. Sorauf, *Party Politics in America,* 7th ed. (New York: Harper-Collins, 1992), Chapter 2.

[14]Huckshorn, *Party Leadership,* p. 46.

[15]See James L. Gibson et al., "Assembling Party Organization Strength," *American Journal of Political Science,* 27 (May 1983), 193–222.

(including research on opponents), registration and voter identification, mailing lists, and even seminars on campaign techniques.

Yet very few local organizations have a full-time staff, or a permanent headquarters, or even a telephone listing.[16] Most rely upon volunteers—precinct and county committee members—who seldom meet in nonelection years. Few local organizations have any budget. Yet most report election year efforts at distributing campaign literature, organizing campaign events, putting up posters and lawn signs, conducting registration drives, and even some door-to-door canvassing.

Strong city and county party organizations were traditionally found in the big cities of the Northeast. (City "machines" and "bosses" are discussed at length in Chapter 10, together with the reform movements that have severely reduced their power.) While these "machines" have lost most of their "clout," local party organizations are still more visible in New York, New Jersey, and Pennsylvania than in the southern or border states.

PARTIES AND PRIMARIES

Party *primary* elections nominate most candidates for public office in America. For the nation's first century, candidates were nominated by party conventions, not primary elections, and as a result party organizations were far more influential than they are today. Primary elections were a key reform in the progressive movement of the early twentieth century. Primaries "democratized" the nomination process and reduced the power of party bosses.

FILING   Primary elections are governed by state law; anyone can *file* a petition with a minimum number of voter signatures, pay a small fee, and have his or her name placed on the primary ballot of either party for practically any public office. A candidate does *not* have to have experience in the party, or even the support of party officials, in order to file for elective office.

ENDORSEMENTS   Primaries, then, reduced the influence of party organizations in the political process. It is possible, of course, for party organizations at the city, county, or state levels to *endorse,* officially or unofficially, candidates in primary elections. The importance of endorsements varies with the strength and unity of party organizations. Where party organizations are strong at the city or county level, the word can be passed down to precinct committee members to turn out the party's faithful for the endorsed candidate. Party endorsement in a statewide race appears to have less value.

CLOSED AND OPEN PRIMARIES   Primary elections in most states are *closed*—that is, only voters who have *previously* registered as members of a party may vote in that party's primary. Only registered Democrats vote in the Democratic primary, and only registered Republicans vote in the Republican primary. Semiclosed primaries al-

---

[16]James L. Gibson et al., "Whither the Local Parties?" *American Journal of Political Science,* 29 (February 1985), 139–60.

low voters to change party registration on election day. Primaries in other states are *open*—voters can choose when they enter the polling place which party primary they wish to vote in. Alaska and Washington have *blanket* primaries in which voters can vote in *both* party primaries simultaneously. Party leaders generally prefer the closed primary because they fear *crossovers* and *raiding: Crossovers* are voters who choose to vote in the primary of the party that they usually do not support in the general election; *Raiding* is an organized attempt to cross over and try to defeat an attractive candidate running for the opposition party's nomination. However, there is no evidence that large numbers of voters connive in such a fashion. Louisiana is unique in its *nonpartisan* statewide elections: All candidates run in the same primary election. If a candidate gets over 50 percent of the vote, he or she wins the office; otherwise, the top two vote-getters run again in the general election. (See Table 5–4.)

RUNOFF PRIMARIES   In most states, the *plurality* winner of the party's primary election—the candidate receiving the most votes, whether a majority or not—becomes the party's nominee. But in ten southern states, a candidate must win a *majority* of votes in a primary election to become the party's nominee. If no candidate succeeds in winning a majority in the first primary, a *runoff primary* is held between the top two vote-getters in the first primary.

Runoff primaries are linked to the traditional one-party politics of the southern states. Runoff primaries prevent a candidate with a minority of party voters from capturing the nomination in a race with three or more contenders. Presumably the runoff primary encourages candidates to seek majority support and prevents extremist candidates from winning nominations. No one can win a nomination by relying on splits among multiple opponents.

First primary front-runners have a better-than-even chance of winning the runoff. Overall, front-runners win about two-thirds of runoff primaries for state legislative seats, although they win only slightly more than half of the runoffs for governor and U.S. senator.[17]

Run-off primaries have been attacked as racially discriminatory. In districts where there is a large but less than majority black population and a history of racial block voting, black candidates who win a plurality of votes in the first primary may be defeated in the runoff if white voters unite behind the white runner-up. (It is possible, of course, for the reverse to occur in a majority black district.) A study of local runoff primaries in Georgia suggests that black plurality winners in the first primary are somewhat less likely to win a runoff against a white runner-up (50 percent black runoff victories) than white plurality winners against a black runner-up (84 percent white runoff victories).[18] But it is not likely that the elimination of runoff primaries would significantly increase the number of black officeholders.[19]

---

[17]See Charles S. Bullock and Lock K. Johnson, "Sex and the Second Primary," *Social Science Quarterly,* 66 (December 1985), 933–42.

[18]Charles S. Bullock and A. Brock Smith, "Black Success in Local Run-off Elections," *Journal of Politics,* 52 (November 1990), 1205–20.

[19]Joseph Stewart, James F. Sheffield, and Margaret E. Ellis, "The Mechanisms of Runoff Primary Disadvantage," *Social Science Quarterly,* 76 (December 1995), 807–22.

Table 5-4

PRIMARY ELECTIONS IN THE STATES

Closed: Prior Party Registration Required	Semiclosed: Voters may register or change party on election day	Semiopen: Voters request party ballot	Open: Voter decides in which primary to vote in voting booth	Blanket	Nonpartisan	Runoff
Arizona	Colorado[a]	Alabama	Hawaii	Alaska	Louisiana	Alabama
California	Iowa[b]	Arkansas	Idaho	Washington		Arkansas
Connecticut	Kansas[a]	Georgia	Michigan			Florida
Delaware	Maine[a]	Illinois	Minnesota			Georgia
Florida	Massachusetts[c]	Indiana	Montana			Louisiana
Kentucky	New Hampshire[c]	Mississippi	North Dakota			Mississippi
Maryland	New Jersey[a]	Missouri	Utah			North Carolina
Nebraska	Ohio[b]	South Carolina	Vermont			Oklahoma
Nevada	Rhode Island[a]	Tennessee	Wisconsin			South Carolina
New Mexico	Wyoming[b]	Texas				Texas
New York		Virginia				
North Carolina						
Oklahoma						
Oregon						
Pennsylvania						
South Dakota						
West Virginia						

[a]Persons not previously voting in a party primary may register with a party on election day.

[b]Party registration may be changed on election day.

[c]Independents are permitted to change registration on election day.

Source: Book of the States 1994–95.

CONVENTIONS   State conventions continue in a handful of states. In New York and Connecticut, statewide party conventions nominate candidates; however, candidates can "challenge" the convention nominee to a primary election if the challenger receives a specified share of the convention vote (25 percent in New York, 20 percent in Connecticut).

Statewide party organizations seldom have much influence over primary outcomes. First of all, party organizations are weak or nonexistent in many counties; many ward and precinct-level positions are vacant. (Reasons for the decline of city and county party organizations are discussed in Chapter 10.) More important, traditional grass-roots efforts—telephoning, canvassing, driving voters to the polls—which were once handled by party organizations, have largely given way to mass media campaigning. Television appearances, radio commercials, and mass mailings permit candidates to take their case directly to the voters.

PROFESSIONAL MASS MEDIA CAMPAIGNS

Mass media campaigns, directed by professional public relations specialists, have replaced the party organizations' role in elections. Few candidates for governor or senator rely exclusively on the party organization to handle their campaigns. Most statewide candidates create their own campaign organizations, and increasingly these candidates are relying on professional public relations firms or consultants to manage their mass media campaigns. A whole new "image industry" has replaced the traditional role of party organizations in campaigns.

"MARKETING" CANDIDATES   If marketing, advertising, and public relations firms can sell toothpaste, why not political candidates? Indeed, today marketing and media specialists have largely taken over political campaigns for most important offices. Modern professional campaign management involves techniques that strongly resemble those employed in commercial product marketing, including the following:

1. Computerized mailing lists for fund-raising and the preparation and mailing of slick brochures to the voters.
2. Computerized voter lists that include occupation, age, race, interests, memberships, and so on, of each voter, so that special statements by the candidate can be delivered to special groups of voters.
3. Public opinion polling on a regular basis throughout the campaign, which enables candidates to identify their opponents' weaknesses as well as their own and to assess the voters' moods and opinion shifts throughout the campaign.
4. The preparation of videotapes, radio broadcasts, signs, bumper stickers, and so on, which emphasize the candidate's "theme."
5. Developing "media events" that will attract the attention of television and newspapers, for example, walking across the state, working a day in the lettuce fields, and so forth.

PUBLIC RELATIONS FIRMS   Professional public relations firms come in different sizes and shapes. Some are all-purpose organizations that plan the whole campaign; select a theme; monitor the electorate with continuous polling; produce television tapes for commercials, newspaper advertisements, and radio spots; select clothing and hairstyles for their candidates; write speeches and schedule appearances (or avoid them if the candidates cannot speak well); and even plan the victory party. Other organizations limit themselves to particular functions, such as polling or television production. Some firms specialize by party, handling only Democratic or Republican candidates; a few firms specialize by ideology, handling liberal or conservative clients. Still other firms are strictly professional, providing services to any candidate who can afford them.

POLLING   Frequently, *polling* is at the center of strategic campaign decision making. At the beginning of the campaign, polls test the "recognition factor" of the candidate and assess what political issues are uppermost in the minds of voters. Special polling techniques can determine what a "winning candidate profile" looks like in a district. The results of these polls will be used to determine a general strategy—developing a favorable "image" for the candidate and focusing on a popular campaign "theme." Early polls can also detect weaknesses in the candidate, which can then be overcome in advertising (too rich—then show him the blue jeans digging ditches; too intellectual—then show him in a hog-calling contest; and so on). Polls can tell whether the party is stronger than the candidate (then identify the candidate as loyal to the party) or whether the candidate is stronger than the party (then stress the candidate's independent thinking). During the campaign the polls can chart the progress of the candidate and even assess the effectiveness of specific themes and "media events." A "media event" is an activity generated to attract news coverage, for example, walking the entire length of the state to show "closeness to the people," or carrying around a broom to symbolize "house cleaning," or spending occasional days doing manual work on a factory or farm. Finally, polls can identify the undecided vote toward the end of the campaign and help direct the time and resources of the candidate.

NAME RECOGNITION   The first objective in a professional campaign is to increase the candidate's *name recognition* among the voters. Years ago, name recognition could only be achieved through years of service in minor public or party offices (or owning a well-known family name). Today, expert media advisors (and lots of money) can create instant celebrity. "Exposure" is the name of the game, and exposure requires attracting the attention of the news media. (As one commentator observed: "To a politician there is no such thing as indecent exposure. Obscurity is a dirty word and almost all exposure is decidedly decent.") A millionaire land developer (former Governor and now U.S. Senator Bob Graham of Florida) attracted attention by simply working a few days as ditch-digger, busboy, bulldozer operator, and so on, to identify with the "common people" and receive a great deal of news coverage.

CAMPAIGN THEMES   The emphasis of the professional public-relations campaign is on simplicity: a few themes, brief speeches, uncluttered ads, quick and catchy spot commercials. Finding the right theme or slogan is essential; this effort is not greatly different from that of launching an advertising campaign for a new detergent. A campaign theme should not be controversial. It might be as simple as "A leader you can trust"; the candidate would then be "packaged" as competent and trustworthy.

PERSONALITY, NOT POLICY   A professional media campaign generally focuses on the personal qualities of the candidate rather than his or her stand on policy issues. Professional campaigns are based on the assumption that a candidate's image is the most important factor affecting voter choice. This image is largely devoid of issues, except in very general terms, for example, "tough on crime," "stands up to the special interests," "fights for the taxpayer." Of course, there may be carefully chosen exceptions to this generalization: Republican Governor Pete Wilson of California came from behind in the polls to defeat his challenger, Democrat Kathleen Brown, by strongly endorsing a popular policy position (limiting state services to illegal immigrants). And a favorite campaign tactic is to associate one's opponent with unpopular policy positions whenever possible.

"GRASS-ROOTS" CAMPAIGNING   Door-to-door campaigning by candidates or party workers has largely disappeared from American politics. Perhaps in small towns, candidates for local office still walk through neighborhoods handing out their brochures. But grass-roots campaigning has largely been replaced with media campaigning.

MEDIA CAMPAIGNING   Media campaigning concentrates on obtaining the maximum "free" exposure on the evening news, as well as saturating television and newspapers with paid commercial advertising. To win favorable news coverage, candidates and their managers must devise attractive media events with visuals and sound bites too good for the television news to ignore. News coverage of a candidate is more credible than paid commercials. So candidates must do or say something interesting and "newsworthy" as often as possible during the campaign.

Television "spot" advertisements incur costs in both production and broadcast time. Indeed, television may consume up to three-quarters of all campaign costs; about one-third of TV costs go for production of ads and two thirds to buying time from television stations. The Federal Communications Commission requires broadcasters to make available broadcast time to political candidates at the same rates charged to product advertisers.

NEGATIVE ADS   Professional media campaigns have increasingly turned to the airing of television commercials depicting the opponent in negative terms. The original negative TV ad is generally identified as the 1964 "daisy-picking" commercial, aired by the Lyndon B. Johnson presidential campaign, which portrayed Republican opponent Barry Goldwater as a nuclear warmonger. Over time the techniques of negative ads have been refined; weaknesses in opponents are identified and dramatized in emotionally forceful thirty-second spots.

While reformers bemoan "mudslinging," negative advertising can be very effective. Such advertising seeks to "define" an opponent in negative terms. Many voters cast their ballots *against* candidates they have come to dislike. Research into the opponent's public and personal background provides the data for negative campaigning. Previous speeches or writings can be mined for embarrassing statements, and previous voting records can be scrutinized for unpopular policy positions. Personal scandals can be exposed as evidence of "character." Victims of negative ads can be expected to counterattack with charges of "mudslinging" and "dirty" politics. If candidates fear that their personal attacks on opponents might backfire, they may "leak" negative information to reporters and hope that the media will do their dirty work for them.

FREE AIR TIME   Candidates also seek free air time on public service programs and televised debates. Underfunded candidates are more dependent upon these opportunities than their more affluent opponents. Thus, well-funded and poorly funded candidates may argue over the number and times of public debates.

MONEY IN STATE POLITICS

Running for public office costs money. Running for statewide offices in large states may cost millions; but even running for city council and school board seats can cost thousands. Candidates who do not have enough personal wealth to finance their own campaigns must find contributors. Fund-raising is one of the least pleasant aspects of politics.

WHAT MONEY CAN DO   Can money buy elections? Not always, but money can make a significant difference in the outcome. Let us summarize what research has shown about the effects of campaign spending:

- Campaign spending is generally more important in contested primary elections than general elections. In primary elections there are no party labels and the electorate is more easily influenced by the kinds of campaigning that money can buy.
- "Early money"—a sizable campaign treasury available at the beginning of the campaign—is usually more valuable than money coming in later and closer to election day.
- Campaign spending in primary elections is closely related to electoral outcome where the party organizations are weak; where they are strong and they endorse a primary candidate, money is less important.[20]
- Campaign spending is more important in larger jurisdictions, where face-to-face campaigning is not possible and mass media appeals are essential.
- After a certain level of campaign spending is reached, additional expenditures do not produce the same effect. A law of diminishing returns seems to operate to reduce the impact of very heavy campaign spending.[21]
- Incumbent officeholders have a very strong advantage over challengers in soliciting and receiving campaign contributions.[22]
- However, the advantage of incumbency itself is greater than the advantage of heavy campaign spending. While it is true that incumbents have an easier time obtaining campaign contributions than challengers, only part of the advantage of being an incumbent derives from easier access to money. Most of the incumbent's advantage is in name recognition and greater news media coverage.[23]
- Candidates who outspend their opponents win in two out of three elections. Of course, the higher-spending candidates are usually incumbents, and incumbents tend to win even when they are outspent. But in elections in which there is no

---

[20]See Sarah M. Morehouse, "Money Versus Party Effect: Nominating for Governor," *American Journal of Political Science,* 34 (August 1990), 706–24.

[21]W. P. Welch, "The Effectiveness of Expenditures in State Legislative Races," *American Politics Quarterly,* 4 (July 1976), 333–56.

[22]Frank J. Sorauf, *Money in American Elections* (Boston: Scott, Foresman, 1988).

[23]Welch, "State Legislative Races."

incumbent seeking reelection, the candidate who spends the most money can be expected to win two of every three of these open-seat contests.[24]

FUND-RAISING   The need to raise millions of dollars for political campaigns, especially for costly television advertising, has stimulated the development of many new fund-raising techniques. Campaign financing has moved beyond the small, face-to-face, circle of contributing friends, supporters, and partisans. An important source of campaign money now are the political action committees, or PACs, which mobilize group financial support for candidates. PACs have been organized by corporations, unions, trade and professional associations, environmental groups, and liberal and conservative ideological groups. The wealthiest PACs are based in Washington, but PAC contributions are becoming increasingly important in state gubernatorial and legislative campaigns as well.[25] (See Table 4–5 in Chapter 4.)

Individual contributions are now sought through a variety of solicitation techniques, including direct mail to persons designated by computer programs to be likely contributors, direct telephone solicitation with recorded messages by the candidates, and live appeals by workers at telephone banks. These efforts have increased the *number* of political contributions in recent years as well as the *total amount* of political contributions.[26] About 10 percent of the population now claims to have contributed to candidates running for public office. However, contributors disproportionately represent high-income, well-educated, older, political partisans. There are, indeed, networks of contributors.[27] Some candidates have been able to tap into these networks through specialized mailing lists and telephone directories.

These specialized techniques supplement the more traditional fund-raising dinners, barbecues, fish frys, and cocktail parties. A successful fund-raising dinner usually includes an appearance by a national political figure, perhaps even the president, or an appearance by a show business celebrity. Tickets are sold in blocks to PACs and to well-heeled, individual contributors. Successful techniques may vary with the political culture of the state, for example, celebrity rock concerts in California versus barbecues in Texas.

CAMPAIGN SPENDING IN THE STATES   Campaign spending in state elections varies enormously from state to state. A gubernatorial campaign in a small state may cost only $2 to $5 million, but campaigns in California, New York, and Texas cost real money—$10 to $25 million or more.

State legislative campaigns may range in cost from $5,000 to over $500,000. Political scientist Frank Sorauf reports that California leads in campaign spending, not only because of its size, but also because of its sophisticated political culture.[28] Media consul-

---

[24]Larry Sabato, Goodbye to Good-time Charlie, 2nd ed. (Washington, DC: Congressional Quarterly Press, 1983), p. 152.

[25]Michael J. Malbin, *Money and Politics in the United States* (Washington, DC: American Enterprise Institute, 1984).

[26]Ruth S. Jones and Warren E. Miller, "Financing Campaigns," *Western Political Quarterly,* 38 (June 1985), 187–210.

[27]Ruth S. Jones and Ann H. Hopkings, "State Campaign Fund Raising," *Journal of Politics,* 47 (May 1985), 427–49.

[28]Sorauf, *Money in American Elections,* pp. 262–64.

tants, pollsters, campaign strategists, and slick television advertising have become the political norm in the Golden State.

CAMPAIGN FINANCE LAWS   Many states, as well as the federal government, have laws designed to bring greater "ethics" into political campaigning and reduce the importance of large campaign contributions. Generally these laws attempt to do one or more of the following:

- Limit the size of campaign contributions and limit the overall spending of candidates and parties
- Require financial disclosure of a candidate's personal finances as well as campaign contributions and expenditures—"Who gave it? Who got it?"
- Establish public funding of campaign expenses
- Establish regulatory agencies, or "commissions," to oversee campaign practices

The model for state laws in this area was the Federal Election Campaign Act of 1974, which placed limits on campaign contributions in presidential elections, required disclosure of campaign finances, provided for public funding of presidential elections through a tax checkoff on federal income tax returns, and established a Federal Elections Commission to supervise presidential elections and distribute public funds to candidates.

THE CONSTITUTIONAL RIGHT TO CAMPAIGN   However, reformers in the states and in Washington were surprised by the important U.S. Supreme Court decision in *Buckley v. Valeo* in 1976.[29] James L. Buckley, former U.S. Senator from New York and brother of William F. Buckley, the well-known conservative commentator, argued successfully in court that laws which limited an individual's right to participate in political campaigns, financially or otherwise, violated First Amendment freedoms. Specifically, the U.S. Supreme Court held that no government could limit an individual's right to spend money to publish or broadcast his or her own views on issues or elections. Candidates can spend as much of their own money as they wish on their own campaigns. Private individuals can spend as much as they wish to circulate their own views on elections (although their contributions to candidates and parties can still be limited). The Court, however, permitted government limitations on parties and campaign organizations and allowed the use of federal funds for financing campaigns.

Any candidate can spend unlimited personal wealth on his or her own election campaign, and individuals can spend any amount to advertise their own personal views, as long as they do not spend their money through a party or campaign organization. If anything, the personal wealth of the candidate has become an even more important qualification for successful campaigning.

WHO GAVE IT? WHO GOT IT?   All states now have some form of campaign finance reporting. Almost everyone agrees that the public should know who is contributing to a candidate's campaign and how the candidate is spending the money. The press was largely responsible for pushing these laws through the legislatures of the states, and the success of these laws largely depends on the press's publishing these campaign

---

[29]*Buckley v. Valeo*, 424 U.S. 1 (1976).

reports. Half of the states have assigned collection of reports to an existing state official, usually the secretary of state. These officials ordinarily cannot bring enforcement actions against violators themselves but must instead turn over suspected cases to state law enforcement agencies such as the attorney general. Enforcement may be weakened if the attorney general's office does not wish to embarrass fellow state officials, or if elections law enforcement is assigned a low priority relative to more serious crimes.[30] Most of the states have created independent commissions resembling the Federal Elections Commission. Appointments to these commissions are usually made by the governor, or the governor and the legislature, and membership is usually divided between the parties. Staff members perform much of the filing, auditing, and investigating for these commissions, which are empowered to investigate election law violations and turn over evidence of wrongdoing to law enforcement officials. In addition, some commissions have the power to levy civil fines on their own authority.[31]

States with campaign finance laws requiring the disclosure of the names of contributors and their occupations give us only a small peek at the real sources of funding (see Figure 5–2). The heaviest campaign contributions in state races are usually garnered from lawyers and lobbyists, political consultants, physicians, hospital and health insurance representatives, real estate developers, bankers, contractors, and unions representing

Figure 5–2

REPORTED OCCUPATIONS OF CAMPAIGN CONTRIBUTORS, FLORIDA'S GOVERNOR RACE, 1994

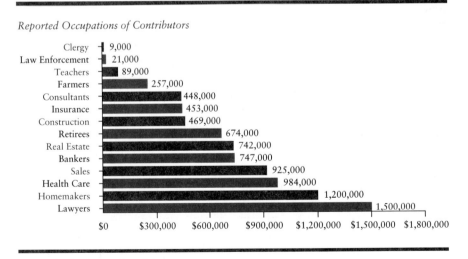

Reported Occupations of Contributors

Occupation	Amount
Clergy	9,000
Law Enforcement	21,000
Teachers	89,000
Farmers	257,000
Consultants	448,000
Insurance	453,000
Construction	469,000
Retirees	674,000
Real Estate	742,000
Bankers	747,000
Sales	925,000
Health Care	984,000
Homemakers	1,200,000
Lawyers	1,500,000

Source: Florida Elections Commission.

[30]See Robert J. Huckshorn, "Who Gave It? Who Got It?," *Journal of Politics,* 47 (August 1985), 773–89.

[31]See *Book of the States 1994–95,* pp. 236–37.

teachers and government employees. But it is not always clear from these reports who the contributing lawyers, lobbyists, and consultants represent. Moreover, big-money contributors often get around limitations on the size of individual contributions by making multiple small contributions in the names of various representatives as well as their spouses (e.g., "homemakers" in Figure 5–2) and family members.

REGULATING PACs   The Federal Election Commission prohibits PACs from contributing more than $5,000 per election to any candidate *for federal office*. Federal law preempts state laws in regulating PACs in federal elections, but states can regulate PAC contributions in state elections. Indeed, most states currently do so, with limits varying from $1,000 to $5,000 per statewide candidate per election.

PERSONAL FINANCIAL DISCLOSURE   Most states now require candidates for public office to disclose their financial assets and sources of income. Financial disclosure laws have been upheld by the courts, although opponents of these laws have argued that such laws are an "invasion of privacy." These laws vary regarding the degree of detail required and whether or not the finances of the candidate's immediate family must also be disclosed. A glance at these required financial statements will convince anyone that candidates greatly understate their assets and income.

PUBLIC CAMPAIGN FINANCING   Some states provide some public funds for candidates or parties.[32] New Jersey was the first state to undertake major financial support for candidates for governor. The arguments for such public financing are that it (1) permits less affluent candidates to run for office, (2) removes some of the advantages of wealth in office seeking, and (3) reduces the dependency of candidates on large financial contributors.[33] But there is very little evidence to support or refute these arguments.

State public campaign finance laws differ from each other and from the federal model:

- *Check-offs* versus *add-ons:* Most state campaign finance laws allow taxpayers to check off one dollar of their state income tax payments with no additional tax liability, but some states have an add-on feature that increases liability. Experience indicates that about 20 percent of state taxpayers will contribute to campaign financing if there is no additional cost to them, but only 1 to 3 percent will do so if it adds to their taxes.[34]
- Party funds or general funds: Some state campaign finance laws allow contributors to designate which party should receive their dollar, while other state laws (like federal law) provide that all contributions go to a general fund for direct distribution to candidates.[35] Allowing party preference favors the Democratic party because of its majority status.

---

[32]Including Hawaii, Idaho, Iowa, Kentucky, Michigan, Minnesota, New Jersey, North Carolina, Rhode Island, Utah, Wisconsin.

[33]See James M. Penning and Corwin Smith, "Public Funding of Gubernatorial Elections," *American Politics Quarterly,* 10 (July 1982), 315–32.

[34]Jack L. Noragon, "Political Finance and Political Reform: The Experience with State Income Tax Checkoffs," *American Political Science Review,* 75 (September 1981), 667–87.

[35]See Ruth S. Jones, "State Campaign Finance: Implications for Partisan Politics," *American Journal of Political Science,* 25 (May 1981), 342–61.

- General elections or general election plus primary elections: Most states with campaign finance laws limit funding to general elections, probably because of the added costs of funding primaries.
- Distribution of money to parties or directly to candidates: States that permit taxpayers to designate which party is to receive their contribution give these funds to party organizations. But states with general campaign funds can distribute them either to the parties or directly to the candidates.
- Gubernatorial elections only or elections for all constitutional officers and legislators: Some states subsidize only the gubernatorial election, while others subsidize all statewide elections and even state legislative campaigns.

The real stimulus to public campaign funding schemes arises from the distaste with which most politicians approach the task of soliciting contributions. Many complain that fund-raising takes more time and effort than campaigning itself. Moreover, limits on campaign spending help protect incumbents by denying their opponents the funds to overcome the advantages of incumbency.

FEDERAL TAX LAWS   Finally, the U.S. Internal Revenue Service plays an overseer role in political finance. It is a violation of federal tax laws for a candidate to use campaign contributions for personal expenses without declaring this money as personal income. Indeed, serious legal consequences for office seekers can occur when campaign funds are directed to personal use. Surplus funds may be retained in a campaign account for a future campaign, or they may be given back to contributors, or to charity, or to other candidates in the party, without incurring federal tax liability.

LEGISLATORS IN STATE POLITICS

FUNCTIONS OF STATE LEGISLATURES

If you were to ask state legislators what the job of the legislature is, they might say: "Our job is to pass laws," or "We have to represent the people," or "We have to make policy." All the answers are correct, but none by itself tells the whole story.

ENACTING LAWS   It is true that, from a *legal viewpoint*, the function of state legislatures is to "pass laws," that is, the enactment of statutory law. Legislatures may enact more than a thousand laws in a single legislative session. The average legislator introduces ten to twelve bills each year. Many are never expected to pass. They are introduced merely as a favor to a constituent or an interest group, or to get a headline in a newspaper back home.

The range of subject matter of bills considered by a legislature is enormous. A legislature may consider the authorization of $10 billion of state spending, or it may debate the expansion of the hunting season on raccoons, or it may increase teachers' salaries, or it may argue whether or not inscribing license plates with "The Poultry State" would cause the state to be called "chicken." Obviously, these considerations range from the trivial to the vital. (For more trivia, see "Trivia: Songs, Flowers, Birds, and Trees" at end of this chapter.)

CONSIDERING CONSTITUTIONAL AMENDMENTS AND GUBER-
NATORIAL APPOINTMENTS   In addition to the enactment of statutory law,
legislatures share in the process of state constitutional revision (see "Constitutional
Change in the States" in Chapter 2) and consider amendments to the U.S. Constitution.
(See "Battles in the States over Constitutional Amendments" in Chapter 3.) Many gover-
nors' appointments to high state offices require legislative approval (see "The Governor's
Managerial Powers" in Chapter 7).

APPROVING BUDGETS   Perhaps their single most important function is the
passage of the appropriation and tax measures in the state budget. No state monies may
be spent without a legislative appropriation, and it is difficult to think of any governmental action that does not involve some financial expenditure. Potentially, a legislature
can control any activity of the state government through its power over appropriations.

SERVING CONSTITUENTS   Legislators spend a great deal of time answering
requests from constituents—"servicing the district." Many letters and phone calls will
come from interest groups in their districts—business, labor, agriculture, school teachers,
municipal employees, and so on. These communications may deal with specific bills or
with items in the state budget. Other communications may come from citizens who want
specific assistance or favors—help with getting a state job, help with permits or licenses,
voicing an opinion about whom the state university should hire as a new football coach,
and so forth.[1]

OVERSEEING STATE AGENCIES   Legislative "oversight" of state agencies
and programs is another important function. Legislators frequently challenge state administrators to explain why they are doing what they do. Frequently, committee hearings
and budget hearings, in particular, provide opportunities for legislators to put administrators "through the wringer" about programs and expenditures. Often embarrassed administrators feel harassed at these meetings, but the true purpose is to remind state
administrators that elected representatives of the people are the final legal authority.

Most states now have "sunset" laws that call for their legislatures to reenact programs
every few years or else see them go out of existence (sunset). Few programs or agencies
are ever sunseted, but such laws force periodic legislative reexamination and evaluation
of the performance of state bureaucracies.

THE MAKING OF A STATE LEGISLATOR

State legislators are not "representative" of the population of their states in the sense of
being typical cross sections of them. On the contrary, the nation's 7461 state legislators
are generally selected from the better-educated, more prestiglously employed, middle-
class segments of the population.

----

[1]See Patricia K. Freeman and Lilliard E. Richardson, "Casework in State Legislatures" (Knoxville: Department of Political Science, University of Tennessee, 1993).

STATUS   Social background information on state legislators also indicates that legislators tend to come from the "upwardly mobile" sectors of the population. This places many of them among the "second-rung" elites in the status system rather than the established wealth. Although the sons and grandsons of distinguished old families of great wealth frequently enter presidential and gubernatorial politics in the states, they seldom run for the state legislature. Legislators are frequently among the middle status groups for whom politics is an avenue of upward mobility.

OCCUPATION   Legislators must come from occupational groups with flexible work responsibility. The lawyer, the farmer, or the business owner can adjust his or her work to the legislative schedule, but the office manager cannot. The overrepresented occupations are those involving extensive public contact. The lawyer, real estate agent, insurance agent, tavern owner, and merchant establish in their business the wide circle of friends necessary for political success. In short, the legislator's occupation should provide free time, public contacts, and social respectability. (See Figure 6–1.)

EDUCATION   State legislators are generally well educated. More than three-quarters of them are college educated, compared to only one-quarter of the general population.

RACE AND ETHNICITY   African Americans have made impressive gains in state legislatures in recent years. Black voter mobilization, stemming from the Voting Rights Act of 1965, and federal court enforcement of later amendments to that law, have resulted in the election of substantial numbers of black state legislators. Most African

Figure 6–1
LEGISLATORS' CAREERS

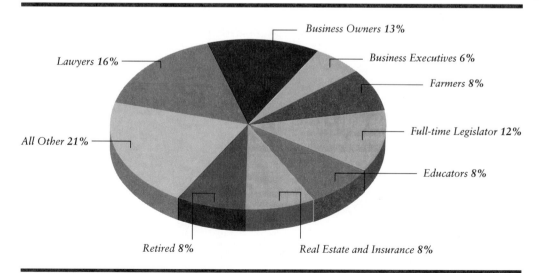

Source: National Conference of State Legislatures, 1995.

American legislators are elected from majority black districts. Southern states, with larger black populations, have the largest numbers and percentages of black state legislators (see Table 6–1).

Black legislators in the states have had a significant impact on legislative voting. Their voting on civil rights and welfare issues is clearly distinguishable in southern states.[2] White legislators, even those with substantial numbers of black constituents, are not as strong in support of these issues as black legislators.

Hispanic membership in state legislatures has also increased significantly in a number of states. The largest Hispanic delegations are found in those states with the largest Hispanic populations—New Mexico, Texas, Arizona, Colorado, and California.

GENDER   About 21 percent of the members of all state legislatures are women.[3] This is a significant increase over the scant 4 percent female legislators in 1969. (See Figure 6–2.)

Table 6–1

BLACK REPRESENTATION IN STATE LEGISLATURES

	PERCENT BLACK POPULATION	Percent Black State Legislators[a]	
		1991	1995
Nation	**12.1**	5.8	7.5
Georgia	26.9	18.2	17.8
Alabama	25.6	17.1	25.0
Maryland	26.1	16.0	19.2
Louisiana	30.6	13.2	20.8
South Carolina	30.1	12.4	18.2
Mississippi	35.6	11.5	27.1
Michigan	14.6	10.8	10.8
Illinois	16.1	10.7	12.4
North Carolina	22.1	10.6	14.1
Tennessee	16.3	9.8	12.1
Ohio	11.0	9.5	12.1
New York	16.1	9.5	12.3
Arkansas	15.9	8.9	12.6
Florida	14.2	8.8	12.5

[a]Unlisted states below 10 percent.

Source: Data supplied by National Conference on State Legislatures, Denver, CO.

[2]Mary Herring, "Legislative Responsiveness to Black Constituents in Three Southern States," *Journal of Politics,* 52 (August 1990), 740–58; for a report on the differing experiences of black legislators, see David Hedge, James Button, and Mary Spear, "Accounting for the Quality of Black Legislative Life," *American Journal of Political Science,* 40 (February 1996), 82–98.

[3]The Center for the American Woman and Politics at Rutgers University.

Figure 6–2
WOMEN IN STATE LEGISLATURES

The ten states with the highest percentages of women state legislators are:

STATE	% WOMEN	STATE	% WOMEN
Washington	39.5	Vermont	29.4
Nevada	34.9	Oregon	28.9
Colorado	31.0	Maryland	28.7
New Hampshire	30.2	Idaho	28.6
Arizona	30.0	Kansas	27.9

The ten states with the lowest percentages of women state legislators are:

STATE	% WOMEN	STATE	% WOMEN
Alabama	3.6	Mississippi	11.5
Kentucky	8.0	Pennsylvania	11.9
Louisiana	9.7	South Carolina	12.4
Oklahoma	10.7	Arkansas	12.6
Virginia	11.4	New Jersey	13.3

Source: Data supplied by Center for the American Woman in Politics, Eagleton Institute of Politics, Rutgers University.

Like their male counterparts, female legislators tend to come from politically active families, to have lived in their communities for a long time, to be representative of their district in race and ethnicity, and to enjoy somewhat higher social status than most of their constituents. Women are somewhat better represented in the New England and western states with less "professional" legislatures; the large urban industrial states with more "professional" legislatures have fewer female representatives[4] Southern states also tend to have fewer female legislators. Among the factors associated with increased representation of women are the female percentage of the labor force and the proliferation of active women's organizations in the states.[5]

Women candidates are just as successful in primary and general elections as men.[6] Voters are *not* predisposed to cast ballots either for or against female candidates.[7] Incumbency gives all officeholders an electoral advantage; since more males held office in the past, women challengers have faced the obstacle of incumbency. But women and men fare equally in races for open seats. So why are women underrepresented in state legislatures?

Fewer women than men run for state legislative seats. Scholars frequently cite women's traditional family roles of wife and mother as obstacles to a political career. Female legislative candidates with young children are very rare; newly elected women legislators are four years older on the average than newly elected male legislators—a fact generally attributed to women waiting until their children are older.[8] Many women who confront conflicts between family life and political activity choose in favor of their families. One study found that more women serve in the legislatures of states whose capitals are located close to the major population centers than in the legislatures of states whose capitals are isolated and require long commutes from home.[9]

PERSONAL WEALTH   Legislators frequently claim that public service is a financial burden. While this may be true, legislators are generally recruited from among the more affluent members of society, and they become even more affluent during their tenure. Indeed, there is evidence that (1) the average net worth of new legislators is increasing over time, and (2) the average legislator increases his or her net worth while serving in the legislature. (Net worth is the total value of all assets—houses, autos, stocks, bonds, property, etc.—after subtracting the total value of all outstanding debts—mortgages, loans, etc.) For example, in Florida the average state senator increased his or her net worth from $329,000 to $1,100,000 over a ten-year period, and the average house member increased his or her net worth from $124,000 to $433,000. In short, the average legislator more than *tripled* his or her net worth in ten years of legislative service. Asked to explain these increases in personal wealth, one legislator said, "Maybe they do well because they're achievers. That's why they win when they run for office and that's why they

---

[4]See Emmy F. Werner, "Women in State Legislatures," *Western Political Quarterly*, 21 (March 1968), 40–50; Paula J. Dubeck, "Women and Access to Political Office," *Sociological Quarterly*, 17 (March 1976), 42–52; Susan Welch, "The Recruitment of Women to Public Office," *Western Political Quarterly* (June 1978), 372–80.

[5]Wilma Rule, "Why More Women Are State Legislators," *Western Political Quarterly*, 43 (June 1990), 437–48.

[6]Susan Welch et al., "The Effect of Gender on Electoral Outcomes in State Legislative Races," *Western Political Quarterly*, 38 (September 1985), 464–75.

[7]Susan Welch and Lee Sigelman, "Changes in Public Attitudes Toward Women in Politics," *Social Science Quarterly*, 63 (June 1982), 321–22.

[8]Virginia Shapiro, "Private Costs of Public Commitments: Family Roles Versus Political Ambition," *American Journal of Political Science*, 26 (May 1982), 265–79.

[9]Carol Nechemias, "Geographic Mobility and Women's Access to State Legislatures," *Western Political Quarterly*, 38 (March 1985), 119–31.

make money."[10] But it's more likely that legislative service, and the public name recognition that comes with it, enhances one's legal practice, real estate or insurance business, as well as investment opportunities.

LAWYERS   Lawyers are overrepresented in legislative bodies at all levels of government. It is sometimes argued that the lawyer brings a special kind of skill to politics. The lawyer's occupation is the representation of clients, so he or she makes no great change in occupation when going from representing clients in private practice to representing constituents in the legislature. Lawyers are trained to deal with public policy as it is reflected in the statute books, so they may be reasonably familiar with public policy before entering the legislature. Moreover, service in the legislature can help a lawyer's private practice through free public advertising and opportunities to make contacts with potential clients.

There are also important institutional advantages for lawyers to enter state politics—specifically, the availability of a large number of highly valued "lawyers-only" posts in state government, such as judge and prosecuting attorney. Lawyers are eligible for many elective and appointive public jobs from which nonlawyers are excluded. State legislative seats are viewed by lawyers as stepping stones to these posts—appellate court judge, Supreme Court justice, attorney general, regulatory commissioner, and so on. The post-legislative careers of lawyers shows that over half go on to other public offices, compared to less than one-third of the nonlawyer legislators.[11]

Do lawyers behave any differently from nonlawyers in the legislature? Lawyers do *not* vote any differently from nonlawyers on most issues; lawyers are neutral "contractors" for parties, interest groups, constituents, and others. Generally, they do not vote together as a bloc.

However, lawyers do act together in legislatures to protect the legal profession. The opposition of trial lawyers to insurance reform, including "no-fault" insurance, and their opposition to reform of liability laws, has become a national scandal. In recent years "tort reform" (a tort is a civil wrong that results in damages) has been a major item on the agenda of state legislatures. Reform proposals include capping "pain and suffering" awards at $250,000 or $500,000; restricting the fees a trial lawyer can take from a victim's award; and ending the rule of "joint and several liability," which forces wealthy defendants to pay the total award even if they are only partially at fault. Businesses, doctors, hospitals, municipalities, and insurance companies have all lobbied heavily at state capitals for these liability law reforms. But they have generally been defeated in state legislatures. The reason: Lawyers are disproportionately represented in these bodies. And it is certainly not in the financial interest of lawyers themselves to limit jury awards or restrict their fees or prevent them from suing the deepest pockets. (See "The Lawyering of America" in Chapter 8.)

AMATEURS   Most state legislatures are still part-time bodies. There are constitutional limits to the length of legislative sessions in most states; the most common limit is

---

[10]*Tampa Tribune*, July 27, 1987.

[11]See Paul J. Hain and James E. Pierson, "Lawyers and Politics Revisited: Structural Advantages of Lawyer-Politicians," *American Journal of Political Science*, 19 (February 1975), 41–51.

sixty days per year. Most state legislatures put in fewer than 100 working days a year.[12] It is true that interim committee meetings and other legislative responsibilities may add to the duties of legislators, and over the years sessions have grown longer. But most state legislators have other occupations, and few rely on their legislative compensation alone.

In recent years, however, an increasing number of state legislators are full-time representatives. The "citizen legislator" who spends two months in the state capitol and then returns home to his or her own business or profession still predominates in the states, but the proportion of full-time legislators is now 12 percent (see Figure 6–1). Full-time legislators are even more frequent in large states with better-paid legislatures, such as California, New York, and Michigan.

PSYCHOLOGY   We know, then, that legislators differ from their constituents in certain *socioeconomic* background characteristics—social class, education, occupation. But are there *psychological* differences between legislators and their constituents that are independent of these socioeconomic differences? Years ago, political scientist John B. McConaughy succeeded in getting South Carolina state legislators to submit to extensive psychological testing.[13] The results suggested that legislators were more self-sufficient, more self-confident, more extroverted, slightly more dominant, and less neurotic than the average American. Another study of Iowa state legislators found that legislators are generally more tolerant toward others, less authoritarian, and more favorably disposed toward minority groups than a cross section of Iowa voters, even when the effects of socioeconomic backgrounds are controlled.[14] In short, there is some evidence that psychological predispositions—self-confidence, gregariousness, tolerance toward others—operate as self-selective factors in determining who will choose to make a career in political life.

GETTING TO THE STATE CAPITOL

The state legislature is a convenient starting place for a political career. About one-half of the state legislators in the nation never served in public office before their election to the legislature, and a greater percentage of new members are in the lower rather than upper chambers. The other half had only limited experience on city councils, county commissions, and school boards.

GETTING INTO POLITICS   Why does a legislator decide to run for office in the first place? It is next to impossible to determine the real motivations of political office seekers—they seldom know themselves. Legislators will usually describe their motivations in highly idealistic terms: "I felt that I could do the community a service"; "I con-

---

[12]Wayne L. Francis, "Costs and Benefits of Legislative Service in the American States," *American Journal of Political Science,* 29 (August 1985), 626–42.

[13]John B. McConaughy, "Some Personality Factors of State Legislators," in *Legislative Behavior: A Reader in Theory and Research,* eds. John C. Wahlke and Heinz Eulau (Glencoe, IL: Free Press, 1959).

[14]Ronald W. Hedlund, "Psychological Predispositions: Political Representatives and the Public," *American Journal of Political Science,* 19 (August 1973), 489–505.

sidered it a civic duty." Only seldom are reasons for candidacy expressed in personal terms: "Oh, I just think it's lots of fun." Gregariousness and the desire to socialize no doubt contribute to the reasons for some office seekers. Politics can have a special lure of its own: "It gets into your blood and you like it." Particular issues may mobilize a political career, but ideological involvement occupies a relatively unimportant place in a candidate's motives. Activity in organizations that are deeply involved in politics also leads to candidacy: "When I decided to run, I was quite active in the union." There is some evidence that political activists, including legislators, from middle- and upper-class districts are more *ideologically motivated* (running for office to correct perceived wrongs, do good, resolve issues, and so on) than political activists from working-class districts, who are more *personally motivated* (running to achieve prestige, recognition, or material rewards).[15]

POLITICAL EXPERIENCE   States with stronger parties are more likely to nominate people who have worked for the party in some previous appointed or elective office.[16] States with weaker parties are more likely to elect "amateurs" with no previous political experience. The stronger the party organization, the more likely a legislative candidate will have to serve a political apprenticeship in some local or party offices. However, as party organizations weaken, the easier it becomes for individuals with little or no prior governmental experience to win legislative seats.

RAISING CAMPAIGN MONEY   The first challenge that an aspiring legislator faces is raising money to finance the campaign. In some states with small legislative districts, nonprofessional legislatures, and largely rural constituencies, a state legislative race may cost only $10,000 to $25,000. But large urban state legislative races may cost $50,000 to $100,000 or more. On the average, senate contests cost more than house contests, and winners spend more than losers. Money allows a candidate to produce commercials, buy television and radio time, buy newspaper ads, travel around the district, and distribute bumper stickers and campaign buttons. Some state legislative candidates employ professional campaign management firms. Most state legislative campaigns are relatively amateurish, but they still cost money. When campaigns are relatively inexpensive, the candidate and his or her friends contribute most of the money. But in more expensive races, candidates may turn to PACs. Corporate, labor, environmental, and ideological PACs are becoming increasingly active in state capitals, particularly in the larger states. (See Campaign Financing in Chapter 4.) Perhaps as much as one-quarter to one-third of money for state legislative campaigns now comes from PAC contributions, most of which goes to incumbents.

FACING THE PRIMARIES   Candidates face two important obstacles when they decide to run for the state legislature: the primary and the general election. A seat in

---

[15]Quotations from state legislators interviewed by Wahlke et al., *Legislative System,* pp. 95–134. See also David J. Webber, "The Contours and Complexities of Legislator Objectives," *Western Political Quarterly,* 39 (March 1986), 93–103.

[16]Richard J. Tobin, "The Influence of Nominating Systems on the Political Experience of State Legislators," *Western Political Quarterly,* 28 (September 1975), 553–66.

the legislature depends on how much competition a candidate encounters in these elections. First, let us consider competition in the primary elections. Available evidence indicates that more than half of the nation's state legislators are *unopposed* for their party's nomination in primary elections. Many legislators who do face primary competition have only token opposition. Most primary competition occurs in a party's "sure" districts, some competition occurs in "close" districts, and there is a distinct shortage of candidates in districts where the party's chances are poor. In other words, primary competition is greater where the likelihood of victory in the general election is greater.

Some states require runoff elections when no candidate wins a majority in the first primary. Thus, some candidates face three elections on their way to the legislature—a first primary, a runoff primary, and the general election.

THE GENERAL ELECTION   The culmination of the recruitment process is in the general election, yet in many legislative constituencies one party is so entrenched that the voters have little real choice at the general election. In some districts, the minority party is so weak that it fails to run candidates for legislative seats.

"Competition" implies more than a name filed under the opposition party label. Generally a competitive election is one in which the winning candidate wins by something less than two to one. In light of this more realistic definition of competition, the absence of truly competitive politics in state legislative elections is striking. Overall, more than half of the nation's legislators are elected in *noncompetitive* general elections, where their opponents are either nonexistent or receive less than one-third of the vote. Even in competitive states, such as California, Michigan, Minnesota, New York, Pennsylvania, and Wisconsin, over half the state legislators face only token opposition in the general election.[17] Moreover, competition is *declining* over time, as more legislators are winning by lopsided margins.[18]

TURNOVER   Today about 20 to 25 percent of all state legislators are newcomers at any legislative session. (Turnover is declining over time; only a few years ago as many as one-third of state legislators were newcomers.[19]) Turnover rates vary by state, ranging from below 5 percent to above 40 percent.[20] Interestingly, it is *not* party competition that increases turnover; far more legislators voluntarily quit than are defeated for reelection. There is *less* turnover in the larger states, which have longer legislative sessions and pay their legislators more money. In other words, more "professional" legislatures have lower turnover rates than the "amateur" legislatures.

Turnover in state legislatures is diminishing as more legislators are becoming careerists. Higher pay, greater prestige, more professional staff assistance, and increased perquisites of office reduce voluntary retirements, even though sessions are longer and more work is re-

[17]David Ray and John Havick, "A Longitudinal Analysis of Party Competition in State Legislative Elections," *American Journal of Political Science,* 25 (February 1981), 119–28.

[18]Ronald Weber, Harvey Tucker, and Paul Brace, "Vanishing Marginals in State Legislative Elections," *Legislative Studies Quarterly,* 16 (February 1991), 29–47.

[19]Alan Rosenthal, "Turnover in State Legislatures," *American Journal of Political Science,* 18 (August 1974), 609–16.

[20]As reported by the National Conference of State Legislatures in *Governing* (February 1995), p. 19.

quired.[21] An increasing percentage of legislators are seeking reelection, especially in urban, industrial states, and these incumbents are remaining in office. It is still an open question, however, whether increased experience and seniority lead to more effective legislatures.

THE GREAT INCUMBENCY MACHINE

Legislators who choose to run for reelection are seldom defeated. Indeed, they are usually unopposed in the primary election, and sometimes unopposed in the general election. Potential challengers are discouraged by the record of success of incumbents.[22] *Nearly 90 percent of incumbent state legislators who seek reelection are successful.* As the *New York Times* observed, "Few things in America are as safe as a seat in the New York state legislature."[23] (The reelection rate of incumbents in New York is over 98 percent, the highest in the nation.) Aspiring newcomers in politics are advised to wait for incumbents to leave office voluntarily. Redistricting also opens up legislative seats and occasionally forces incumbents to run against each other. The likelihood of defeating an incumbent in either the primary or general election is very low.[24]

VISIBILITY   Why do incumbents win? First of all, they enjoy greater visibility and name recognition in their districts: "The reason I get 93 percent victories is what I do back home. I stay highly visible. No grass grows under my feet. I show I haven't forgot from whence I came."[25] Incumbents spend a major portion of their time throughout their term of office campaigning for reelection: "I have the feeling that the most effective campaigning is done when no election is near. During the interval between elections you have to establish every personal contact you can." Legislators regularly appear at civic clubs, social and charitable events, churches, and many other gatherings: "Personally, I will speak on any subject. I talk on everything whether it deals with politics or not." Indeed, many legislators spend more time campaigning for reelection than lawmaking. Few challengers can afford to spend two or four years campaigning.

PROFESSIONALISM   As legislatures become more professional over time—employing large professional staffs; providing offices, expense accounts, and travel budgets to legislators; and increasing their pay—incumbents acquire greater resources to assist them in servicing constituents. Constituents' services or "casework" is growing in state legislatures; legislators are increasingly involved in assisting constituents in dealing with

---

[21]David Ray, "Membership Stability in Three State Legislatures: 1893–1969," *American Political Science Review,* 68 (March 1974), 106–12; and "Voluntary Retirement and Electoral Defeat in Eight State Legislatures," *Journal of Politics,* 38 (May 1976), 426–33.

[22]Malcolm E. Jewell, "State Legislative Elections," *American Politics Quarterly,* 22 (October 1994), 483–509.

[23]Kevin Sack, "The Great Incumbency Machine," *New York Times Magazine,* September 27, 1992, p. 47.

[24]See David Breaux, "Specifying the Impact of Incumbency on State Legislative Elections," *American Politics Quarterly,* 18 (July 1990), 270–86.

[25]Quotations of legislators from William J. Keefe and Morris S. Ogul, *The American Legislative Process: Congress and the States,* 8th ed. (Englewood Cliffs, NJ: Prentice Hall, 1993).

state bureaucracies, providing information, and doing small favors at the capital. Legislators may help constituents get food stamps, sign up for unemployment compensation, obtain driver's licenses, or apply for state jobs. Over time this form of "retail" politics gradually builds a network of grateful voters.

It is no accident that the most professional state legislatures in the nation (California, Illinois, Massachusetts, Michigan, New York, Ohio, Pennsylvania, and Wisconsin) have the lowest turnover. Their legislators are given large sums to subsidize what are really campaign activities—printing and mailing of newsletters; press rooms and video studios; travel reimbursement; and aides, assistants, and secretaries who spend much of their time on constituent services.

MONEY   Finally, and perhaps most importantly, incumbents attract much more in the way of campaign contributions than challengers. Interest group contributions go overwhelmingly to incumbents. (See "Money in State Politics" in Chapter 5.) These groups are seeking access and influence with decision makers, so they direct their contributions to people in office. (For example, see the list of contributions to the reelection of the Florida senate president, Table 4–5.) Moreover, group leaders know that incumbents are rarely defeated and they do not want to antagonize incumbents by contributing to challengers. Incumbents can build a "war chest" over time; often the size of the war chest itself is enough to discourage potential challengers from entering races against them.

THE UNPOPULARITY OF LEGISLATURES

The public's disdain of politicians has fueled a movement to limit the terms of both Congress members and state legislators throughout the country. While the U.S. Supreme Court has declared state attempts to limit the terms of *Congress members* unconstitutional,[26] term limits have recently been imposed upon *state legislators* in over half of the states by amending state constitutions. Most of these term limit amendments have come about through citizens' initiatives and have won overwhelming support in referenda votes (see "Term Limit Battles" in Chapter 2). The most common limit for state senate members is eight years (two 4-year terms); state house members are often limited to six years (three 2-year terms). Most of these limits have been incorporated into state constitutions; a few have been enacted only by statute and could more easily be repealed. (See Table 6–2.)

UNPOPULAR LEGISLATURES   State legislatures, like other governmental institutions in America, have suffered a decline in popular approval in recent years. Public evaluations of legislature performance appear to be sagging everywhere. When citizens are asked in statewide polls to "rate the job [their state legislature] is doing," ratings of "fair" and "poor" regularly outnumber ratings of "excellent" and "good."

The unpopularity of state legislatures is doubtless related to the national disdain of government and politics. But economic recessions, well-publicized scandals, stalemates over policy, tax increases, an inability to deal effectively with crime or other state problems, all appear to contribute to legislative unpopularity from time to time.

Yet despite the unpopularity of state legislatures, the powers of incumbency are so

---

[26]U.S. *Term Limits v. Thornton* (1995).

Table 6–2

TERM LIMITS ON STATE LEGISLATORS

State	Constitutional (C) Statutory (S)	Limits in Years	
		SENATE	HOUSE
Arizona	C	4 2-yrs.	4 2-yrs.
Arkansas	C	2 4-yrs.	3 2-yrs.
California	C	2 4-yrs.	3 2-yrs.
Colorado	C	2 4-yrs.	4 2-yrs.
Florida	C	8-yrs.	8-yrs.
Idaho	S	8-yrs.	8-yrs.
Maine	S	4 2-yrs.	4 2-yrs.
Massachusetts	S	4 2-yrs.	4 2-yrs.
Michigan	C	2 4-yrs.	3 2-yrs.
Missouri	C	8-yrs.	8-yrs.
Montana	C	8-yrs.	6-yrs.
Nebraska	C	2 4-yrs.	
Nevada	C	3 4-yrs.	6 2-yrs.
Ohio	C	2 4-yrs.	4 2-yrs.
Oklahoma	C	12-yrs.	12-yrs.
Oregon	C	8-yrs.	6-yrs.
South Dakota	C	4 2-yrs.	4 2-yrs.
Utah	S	12-yrs.	12-yrs.
Washington	S	8-yrs.	6-yrs.
Wyoming	S	3 4-yrs	3 2-yrs.

Note: Unlisted states do not limit the terms of their state legislators.

Source: National Conference of State Legislatures.

great that individual members are regularly reelected. This apparent paradox—regular reelection of members of an unpopular legislature—helped inspire the term limit movement in the states.

FACING UP TO TERM LIMITS   Term limits will soon begin to force incumbent lawmakers to leave office. We will soon be able to assess the impact of term limits on legislature performance, that is, to evaluate some of the arguments for and against term limits. Inasmuch as some states have adopted term limits and some have not, we will soon be able to compare results from our "laboratories of democracy." For example, proponents of term limits argue that they will inspire greater competition for legislative seats and encourage more qualified people to run for office. They argue that term limits will reduce the influence of well-entrenched interest groups in state capitals and make legislatures more responsive to public opinion. Opponents of term limits believe they will weaken the power of legislatures in relation to executive branch bureaucracies. They believe that term limits will lead to less experienced legislative leadership and less professional legislatures. Within a few years, we may be able to test the validity of these arguments.

LEGISLATIVE APPORTIONMENT AND DISTRICTING

Legislative apportionment refers to the allocation of seats to specific populations. Malapportionment occurs when there are differing numbers of people in legislative districts that receive the same number of seats. Malapportionment creates inequality of representation: If one single-member district has twice the population of another, the value of a vote in the larger district is only half the value of a vote in the smaller district. Prior to 1962, malapportionment was common in American state legislatures. Small minorities of the population could elect a majority of the house or senate or both in most of the states. Generally, it was the rural voters in a state who controlled a majority of legislative seats, and it was the urban voters who were discriminated against in the value of their vote.

SUPREME COURT INTERVENTION   After years of avoiding the issue of malapportionment, the U.S. Supreme Court finally acted in 1962 in the landmark case of *Baker v. Carr*.[27] This case involved the complaint of urban residents in Tennessee where the largest district in the lower house was twenty-three times larger than the smallest district. The Supreme Court decided that such inequalities in state apportionment laws denied voters "equal protection of the laws" guaranteed by the Fourteenth Amendment and that the federal courts should grant relief from these inequalities. The Supreme Court did not decide on any firm mathematical standard of correct apportionment, holding only that "as nearly as practicable, one man's vote should be equal to another's."[28] The Supreme Court required that *both* houses of the state legislature be apportioned on the basis of population; the Court rejected the federal analogy of a senate based upon geographic units: "Legislators represent people, not trees or acres. Legislators are elected by voters, not farms or cities or economic interests."[29] State after state was forced to reapportion its legislature under the threat of judicial intervention. In addition to requiring population equality in legislative districting, the Supreme Court also required population equality in congressional districting by state legislatures. The philosophy underlying these decisions was expressed by the Court: "The conception of political equality from the Declaration of Independence to Lincoln's Gettysburg Address, to the Fourteenth, Fifteenth, Seventeenth, and Nineteenth Amendments, can mean only one thing—one person, one vote."[30]

THE IMPACT OF REAPPORTIONMENT   The reapportionment revolution of the 1960s significantly increased the representation afforded urban interests in state legislatures. Reapportionment also seemed to bring younger, better-educated, more prestigiously employed people into state legislatures. It also brought many "new" people into legislative politics—people who had little or no previous experience in public office. Some political scientists maintain that the long-term effect of reapportionment was to: (1) increase party competition in state legislatures; (2) distribute more educational and highway funds to urban areas; and (3) produce more environmental regulation.[31]

---

[27]*Baker v. Carr*, 369 U.S. 186 (1962).

[28]*Reynold v. Sims*, 84 S. Ct. 1362 (1964).

[29]*Wesberry v. Sanders*, 84 S. Ct. 526 (1964).

[30]*Gray v. Sanders*, 83 S. Ct. 801 (1963), p. 809.

[31]See Michael A. Maggiotto et al., "The Impact of Reapportionment in Public Policy," *American Politics Quarterly*, 13 (January 1985), 101–21.

STANDARDS OF EQUALITY AMONG DISTRICTS   Today there is very little inequality among legislative districts in any state, and "one person, one vote" is the prevailing form of representation. But federal courts have not always been consistent or precise in determining exactly *how equal* congressional and state legislative districts must be. In several early cases, federal courts calculated an "ideal" district by dividing the total population of the state by the number of legislative seats and then comparing all district populations to this ideal district. Variations of more than 2 percent in any district from the ideal often led to federal court invalidation of a state's redistricting plan. Later the federal courts began calculating an "overall range" by adding the deviations of the largest district and the smallest district from the ideal, disregarding the plus and minus signs. (Thus if the largest district was 2 percent larger than the ideal, and the smallest district 1 percent smaller than the ideal, the "overall range" would be 3 percent.)

With regard to *congressional* districts, the U.S. Supreme Court has required strict standards of equality. Indeed, no population inequality that "could practicably be avoided" is permitted in congressional districts; a New Jersey plan with an overall range of 0.70 percent was struck down upon presentation of evidence that the legislature could have reduced the range to 0.45.[32]

However, the U.S. Supreme Court has been somewhat more lenient in considering *state legislative* districting plans. The Court has refused to set any specific mathematical standards of equality for legislative districts. Nonetheless, districting plans with an overall range of more than 10 percent "create a prima facie case of discrimination and therefore must be justified by the state."[33] Federal courts will allow some deviations from absolute equality in order to recognize political subdivision (e.g., city, county) boundaries.

DISTRICTING   Districting refers to the drawing of boundary lines for legislative districts. While malapportionment refers to inequality in representation, *gerrymandering* refers to the drawing of district lines for political advantage. The population of districts can be equal, yet the districts drawn in such a fashion as to give advantage to one party or group over another. Consider a very simple example:

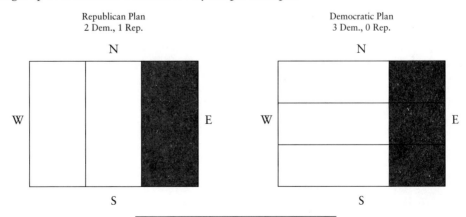

[32]*Karchev v. Daggett*, 462 U.S. 725 (1983).

[33]*Brown v. Thompson*, 462 U.S. 835 (1983).

For a city that is entitled to three representatives, the eastern third of the city is Republican while the western two-thirds is Democratic. If the Republicans draw the district lines, they will draw them along a north-south direction to allow them to win in one of the three districts; if Democrats draw the district lines, they will draw them along an east-west direction to allow them to win all three districts by diluting the Republican vote. Often, gerrymandering is not as neat as our example; district lines may twist and turn and create grotesque geographic patterns.

Gerrymandering can be accomplished by the combined methods of *splintering* and *packing.* Splintering involves dividing up and diluting a strong minority to deny it the power to elect a representative (see accompanying diagram). Packing involves the concentration of partisan voters in a single district in order to "waste" their votes in large majorities for a single representative and thereby protect modest majorities in other districts (see box, "The Original Gerrymander").

As long as districts are equal in population, partisan gerrymandering does *not* violate federal court standards for "equal protection" under the Fourteenth Amendment of the

THE ORIGINAL GERRYMANDER

The term *gerrymander* immortalizes Governor Elbridge Gerry (1744–1814) of Massachusetts, who in 1812 redistricted the state legislature to favor Democrats over Federalists. A district north of Boston was designed to concentrate and thus waste Federalist votes. The district was portrayed in a political cartoon in the *Boston Gazette* on March 26, 1812, as a "gerrymander."

U.S. Constitution. There is no constitutional obligation to allocate seats "to the contending parties in proportion to what their anticipated statewide vote will be."[34] However, the federal courts may intervene in political gerrymandering if it "consistently degrades a voter's or a group of voters' influence on the political process as a whole." This vague standard set forth by the U.S. Supreme Court opens the door to judicial intervention in particularly grievous cases of political gerrymandering.

Incumbent gerrymandering sometimes supplements traditional partisan gerrymandering. The object of incumbent gerrymandering is to protect the seats of incumbents. Often if party control of state government is divided, thus preventing the passage of a partisan gerrymander, legislators will agree to protect themselves.

THE SEATS–VOTES RELATIONSHIP   One way to determine whether partisan gerrymandering has short-changed a party is to compare the total statewide vote compiled by all of the party's candidates with the proportion of legislative seats it won.[35] For example, if a party's candidates won 55 percent of the total votes cast in all legislative elections, but won only 45 percent of the seats, we might conclude that partisan gerrymandering was to blame. This comparison is not always valid, however, especially when it is understood that a party that wins a slight majority of votes would normally be expected to win a much larger proportion of seats. For example, a party that wins 52 percent of total votes cast in all legislative elections might win 65 percent of the seats; theoretically it could win 100 percent of the seats in the unlikely event that its 52 percent of the votes was spread evenly in every legislative district. The U.S. Supreme Court has held that "a mere lack of proportionality in results in one election" cannot prove an unconstitutional gerrymander; however, the Court said that it might intervene when there is "a history of disproportionate result."[36] It is important to remember that the United States does not employ proportional representation as do many European democracies. Hence we cannot expect proportionality in the seats–votes relationship. However, extreme and persistent differences in this relationship may signal the existence of partisan gerrymandering.

AFFIRMATIVE RACIAL GERRYMANDERING   Gerrymandering designed to *dis*advantage blacks is a violation of the Equal Protection Clause of the Fourteenth Amendment of the U.S. Constitution, and it is a violation of the federal Voting Rights Act of 1965.[37] In 1982 Congress strengthened the Voting Rights Act by outlawing any electoral arrangements that had the *effect* of weakening minority voting power (see "Securing the Right to Vote" in Chapter 4). The U.S. Supreme Court obliged the states whenever possible to maximize opportunities for blacks and minority candidates to win election.[38] This apparent mandate for affirmative racial gerrymandering governed redistricting fol-

---

[34]*Davis v. Bandemer*, 106 S. Ct. 2797 (1986).

[35]See Harry Basehart, "The Seats/Vote Relationship and the Identification of Partisan Gerrymandering in State Legislature," *American Politics Quarterly,* 15 (October 1987), 484–98. See also Gerard S. Gryski, Bruce Reed, and Euel Elliot, "The Seats–Vote Relationship in State Legislative Elections," *American Politics Quarterly,* 18 (April 1990), 141–57, for an estimate of bias for each state prior to 1990 redistricting.

[36]*Davis v. Bandemer*, 106 S. Ct. 2797 (1986).

[37]*Fortson v. Dorsey,* 179 U.S. 433 (1965).

[38]*Thornbury v. Gingles,* 478 U.S. 30 (1986).

lowing the 1990 census and resulted in a significant increase in black and minority representation in many state legislatures. However, the creation of some bizarre-shaped "majority-minority" congressional districts (see Figure 4–4 in Chapter 4) led the Supreme Court to express constitutional doubts about districts that appear designed exclusively to separate the races.

MULTIMEMBER DISTRICTS   Multimember legislative districts were once very common (seventeen states had multimember districts in at least one of their legislative chambers before 1990). But court challenges and complaints by minority parties and racial minorities have restricted their use. The U.S. Supreme Court has never held multimember districts to be unconstitutional per se, as long as the population representation is equal.[39] (A two-member district, for example, should have twice the ideal district population.) However, multimember district plans that discriminate against racial minorities are unconstitutional.[40] Multimember districts provide additional opportunities for partisan gerrymandering. (In our previous example, the Democrats could simply declare the entire city a three-member district and ensure the dilution of Republican votes.) Single-member districts are strongly preferred by minorities—minority parties as well as racial minorities.

WHO DRAWS THE LINES?   Traditionally, legislatures drew up their own district lines. In most states this continues to be the case. Many legislatures employ private consultants to assist in the task, and computer mapping is now common. Legislatures generally try to protect incumbents, and the majority party frequently tries to maximize its advantages over the minority party. But in recent years, because of court challenges over apportionment (equality of population in districts) and racial gerrymandering, most legislative districting plans must be approved by courts. Reformers (Common Cause, National Municipal League, League of Women Voters) have urged state legislatures to turn over redistricting to independent nonpartisan commissions, and some states have done so. Reformers argue that partisan gerrymandering devalues voter participation, reduces competition for legislative seats, and reduces the responsiveness of legislators by creating "sure" seats. There is some evidence that independent commissions go about their task of redistricting without much regard for incumbent protection or party advantage.[41]

LEGISLATIVE ORGANIZATION AND PROCEDURE

The formal rules and procedures by which state legislatures operate are primarily designed to make the legislative process fair and orderly. Without established customs, rules, and procedures, it would be impossible for 50, 100, or 200 people to arrive at a collective decision about the thousands of items submitted to them at a legislative session. State legislatures follow a fairly standard pattern in the formal process of making laws.

---

[39]*Connor v. Johnson,* 407 U.S. 640 (1971).

[40]*White v. Regester,* 412 U.S. 755 (1973).

[41]See Harry Basehart and John Comer, "Redistricting and Incumbent Reelection in State Legislatures," *American Politics Quarterly,* 23 (April 1995), 241–53.

Figure 6–3 provides a brief description of some of the more important procedural steps in lawmaking.

PROCEDURES HAVE CONSEQUENCES   What are the political consequences of the legislative procedures described in Figure 6–3? Obviously, it is a very difficult process for a bill to become a law—legislative procedures offer many opportunities to defeat legislation. Formal rules and procedures of state legislatures lend themselves easily to those who would delay or obstruct legislation. Figure 6–3 illustrates the deliberative function of legislatures and the consequent procedural advantages given to those who would defend the status quo. Moreover, these procedures imply that the legislature is structured for deliberation and delay in decision making, rather than speed and innovation. This suggests that the legislature functions as an arbiter, rather than an initiator, of public policy, since its procedures are designed to maximize deliberation, even at the expense of granting advantage to those who oppose change.

DISORDERLINESS   As experienced legislators are fond of saying: "There are two things in the world you do not want to watch being made—sausages and laws." Lawmaking is a disorderly process, in spite of the formal procedures listed in Figure 6–3. Students often express shock and dismay when they spend some time watching or working in their legislature. After studying the formal rules, they may be unprepared for the "actual" haste, disorganization, logrolling, informality, infighting, petty jealousies, vote trading, ignorance, and ineptitude that they encounter.

WORKLOAD   Fewer than one in four bills introduced in a legislative session actually makes its way through the whole process and becomes law. In large states such as California and New York, nearly 10,000 bills may be introduced in a single legislative session, and 2,000 to 3,000 may be enacted into law. In smaller states a typical legislative session may produce 300 to 500 laws. Most bills die in committee. Many bills are introduced with no real expectation they will pass; legislators simply seek to "go on record" as working for a particular goal.

LOGJAMS   The end-of-session logjam is typically the most disorderly phase of lawmaking. In the closing days of a legislative session, hasty efforts are made to win approval for many bills and amendments that are still languishing somewhere in the legislative process. Legislative chambers sometimes become scenes of noisy confusion, with legislators voting blindly on bills described only by number. Most reformers condemn the end-of-session logjam as a source of inferior quality legislation. Other observers consider it an inevitable product of workload. For still others, the logjam is a strategy to enhance the power of legislative leaders. These leaders control the daily agenda and grant recognition to members seeking the floor; these decisions in a confused end-of-session logjam can determine whose bills get passed and whose do not. In some states in some sessions, over half of all the bills passed will be pushed through in the last few days of the session.[42]

---

[42]Harvey J. Tucker, "Legislative Logjams: A Comparative State Analysis," *Western Political Quarterly*, 38 (September 1985), 432–46.

Figure 6–3
HOW AN IDEA BECOMES LAW

A simplified chart showing the route a bill takes through the Florida Legislature. Bills may originate in either House. This bill originated in the House of Representatives.

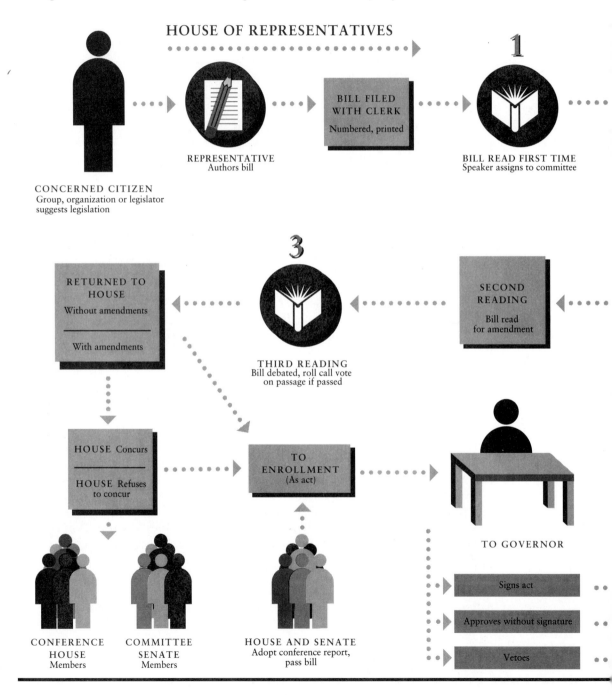

HOUSE OF REPRESENTATIVES

CONCERNED CITIZEN
Group, organization or legislator suggests legislation

REPRESENTATIVE
Authors bill

BILL FILED WITH CLERK
Numbered, printed

1

BILL READ FIRST TIME
Speaker assigns to committee

3

THIRD READING
Bill debated, roll call vote on passage if passed

RETURNED TO HOUSE
Without amendments
_____
With amendments

SECOND READING
Bill read for amendment

HOUSE Concurs
_____
HOUSE Refuses to concur

TO ENROLLMENT
(As act)

TO GOVERNOR

Signs act

Approves without signature

Vetoes

CONFERENCE HOUSE
Members

COMMITTEE SENATE
Members

HOUSE AND SENATE
Adopt conference report, pass bill

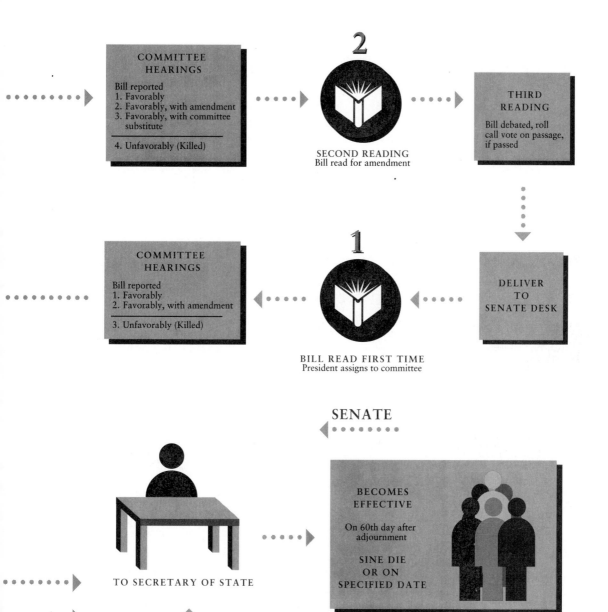

COMMITTEE HEARINGS

Bill reported
1. Favorably
2. Favorably, with amendment
3. Favorably, with committee substitute
_____
4. Unfavorably (Killed)

2

SECOND READING
Bill read for amendment

THIRD READING

Bill debated, roll call vote on passage, if passed

COMMITTEE HEARINGS

Bill reported
1. Favorably
2. Favorably, with amendment
_____
3. Unfavorably (Killed)

1

BILL READ FIRST TIME
President assigns to committee

DELIVER TO SENATE DESK

SENATE

TO SECRETARY OF STATE

BECOMES EFFECTIVE

On 60th day after adjournment

SINE DIE OR ON SPECIFIED DATE

Two-thirds vote in each house overrides veto

OFFICE OF THE CLERK
HOUSE OF REPRESENTATIVES

SESSIONS   Traditionally state constitutions limited legislative sessions to thirty or sixty days once every two years. These limits reflected the "citizen" nature of state legislatures, in contrast to the "professional" full-time congressional model of a legislature. Many observers still argue that the predominant occupation of members should *not* be "legislator," and that legislative sessions should be kept short so that citizens with other occupations can serve in the legislature. But the growing demands of legislative business have led to longer sessions.

Most states now hold annual legislative sessions; only a few are limited to biennial sessions (see Table 6–3). Twelve states place no limit on the length of sessions while thirty-two states have constitutional limits, and six states have statutory limits. The most common limit is sixty days; most legislatures convene in January and adjourn in March.

Frequently legislatures convene in "special sessions" in addition to those regularly scheduled. Special sessions may be called by the governor, or in some states by the legislative leadership, to consider special topics, for example, projected budget deficits or reapportionment. Usually these sessions are limited to the topic for which they were called.

We should remember that legislators have many duties between sessions; their work does not end when the session adjourns. Often legislative committees meet between sessions, and constituents continue to contact legislators for services.

INFORMAL RULES OF THE GAME

Partly to counteract the impact of formal rules and procedures, legislatures have developed a number of informal "rules of the game." These unwritten rules are not merely quaint and curious folkways. They support the purposes and functions of the legislature by helping to maintain the working consensus among legislators so essential to legislative output. Some rules contribute to the legislative task by promoting group cohesion and solidarity. In the words of legislators themselves: "Support another member's local bill if it doesn't affect you or your district"; "Don't steal another's bill"; "Accept the author's amendments to a bill"; "Don't make personal attacks on other members." Other informal rules promote predictability of behavior: "Keep your word"; "Don't conceal the real purpose of bills or amendments"; "Notify in advance if you cannot keep a commitment." Other rules try to put limits on interpersonal conflict: "Be willing to compromise"; "Accept half a loaf"; "Respect the seniority system"; "Respect committee jurisdiction." Finally, other rules are designed to expedite legislative business: "Don't talk too much"; "Don't fight unnecessarily"; "Don't introduce too many bills and amendments"; "Don't point out the absence of a quorum"; "Don't be too political."[43] (See also Table 6–4.)

A most important informal device is unanimous consent for the suspension of formal rules; this permits a legislature to consider bills not on the calendar, pass bills immediately without the necessary three readings, dispense with time-consuming formalities, permit nonmembers to speak, and otherwise alter procedure. Another informal rule is the

---

[43]Quotations from state legislators interviewed by John C. Wahlke et al., *The Legislative System* (New York: John Wiley, 1962), pp. 146–61.

practice in many states of passing "local bills" that would affect only one area of a state without debate or opposition when the delegation in that area unanimously supports the bill.

Most of these rules are enforced by informal sanctions. The most frequently mentioned sanction involves obstructing the bills of errant legislators by abstaining or voting against them, keeping their bills in committee, and amending their bills; more personal sanctions are using the "silent treatment," not trusting the legislator, and removing patronage and good committee assignments. Other sanctions include denial of legislative courtesies and occasionally even overt demonstrations of displeasure, such as ridicule, hissing, or laughing. The observance of rules, however, is not obtained primarily through fear of sanction so much as the positive recognition by legislators of the usefulness of rules in helping the legislature perform its chores.

LEGISLATIVE COMMITTEES

While it is most convenient to study legislative decision making by observing floor actions, particularly the division of ayes and nays, the floor is not the only locus of important legislative decisions. Committee work is essential to the legislative process. It is here that public hearings are held, lobbyists plead their case, policies are debated, legislation amended and compromised, bills rushed to the floor or pigeonholed. The function of the committee system is to reduce legislative work to manageable proportions by providing for a division of labor among legislators. However, by so doing the committees themselves often come to exercise considerable influence over the outcome of legislation. Another opportunity is provided for delay and obstruction by less than the majority of legislators, sometimes by a single committee chairperson.

FUNCTIONS   A typical legislative chamber will have between twenty and thirty standing committees that consider all bills in a particular area, such as revenue, appropriations, highways, welfare, education, labor, judiciary, or local government. Typically, a legislator will serve on three, or four, or five committees. In most state legislatures, committee assignments, including the assignment of chairpersons, are made by the speaker of the house and the president of the senate in their respective bodies. This power of appointment gives these leaders some control over the actions of committees.

Committees may decide to hold early hearings on a bill, send it to the floor with little or no revision, and recommend it favorably. Or committees may simply ignore a bill ("pigeonholing"), fail to schedule hearings on it, allow hostile witnesses to testify against it, write extensive revisions and amendments into it, and so forth. Some states reduce the power of committees by allowing bills to be considered on the floor even though they have not been reported out of committee, or by requiring that all bills be reported out either favorably or unfavorably.

PERSONNEL   Committee assignments in most legislatures are made by the leadership. Occupational background frequently determines a legislator's committee assignments. Thus, lawyers are frequently assigned to committees on the judiciary and civil and criminal law, educators to education committees, farmers to agricultural committees,

Table 6–3
THE STATE LEGISLATURES

State	Official Name	Senate		House		Salaries, 1994 (+ INDICATES ADDED PER DIEM)	Regular Sessions
		NUMBER	TERM	NUMBER	TERM		
Alabama	Legislature	35	4	105	4	Per diem	Annual
Alaska	Legislature	20	4	40	2	$24,112+	Annual
Arizona	Legislature	30	2	60	2	$15,000+	Annual
Arkansas	General Assembly	35	4	100	2	$12,500+	Biennial
California	Legislature	40	4	80	2	52,500+	Annual
Colorado	General Assembly	35	4	65	2	17,500+	Annual
Connecticut	General Assembly	36	2	151	2	16,760	Annual[a]
Delaware	General Assembly	21	4	41	2	24,900+	Annual
Florida	Legislature	40	4	120	2	22,560+	Annual
Georgia	General Assembly	56	2	180	2	10,641+	Annual
Hawaii	Legislature	25	4	51	2	32,000+	Annual
Idaho	Legislature	42	2	84	2	12,000+	Annual
Illinois	General Assembly	59	4	118	2	38,420+	Annual
Indiana	General Assembly	50	4	100	2	11,600+	Annual
Iowa	General Assembly	50	4	100	2	18,100+	Annual
Kansas	Legislature	40	4	125	2	Per diem	Annual
Kentucky	General Assembly	38	4	100	2	Per diem	Biennial
Louisiana	Legislature	39	4	105	4	16,800+	Annual[a]
Maine	Legislature	35	2	151	2	10,000+	Annual[a]
Maryland	General Assembly	47	4	141	4	28,000+	Annual
Massachusetts	General Court	40	2	160	2	30,000+	Annual
Michigan	Legislature	38	4	110	2	47,723	Annual
Minnesota	Legislature	67	4	134	2	27,979+	Biennial

State	Name						
Mississippi	Legislature	52	4	122	4	10,000+	Annual
Missouri	General Assembly	34	4	163	2	22,862+	Annual
Montana	Legislature	50	4	100	2	Per diem	Biennial
Nebraska	Legislature	49	4	Unicameral		12,000+	Annual
Nevada	Legislature	21	4	42	2	Per diem	Biennial
New Hampshire	General Court	24	2	400	2	100	Annual
New Jersey	Legislature	40	4	80	2	35,000	Annual
New Mexico	Legislature	42	4	70	2	Per diem	Annual[a]
New York	Legislature	61	2	150	2	57,500+	Annual
North Carolina	General Assembly	50	2	120	2	13,026+	Biennial
North Dakota	Legislative Assembly	53	4	106	2	Per diem	Biennial
Ohio	General Assembly	33	4	99	2	42,426	Annual
Oklahoma	Legislature	48	4	101	2	32,000+	Annual
Oregon	Legislative Assembly	30	4	60	2	13,104+	Biennial
Pennsylvania	General Assembly	50	4	203	2	47,000+	Annual
Rhode Island	General Assembly	50	2	100	2	Per diem	Annual
South Carolina	General Assembly	46	4	124	2	10,400+	Annual
South Dakota	Legislature	35	2	70	2	4,267+	Annual
Tennessee	General Assembly	33	4	99	2	16,500+	Biennial
Texas	Legislature	31	4	150	2	7,200+	Biennial
Utah	Legislature	29	4	75	2	Per diem	Annual
Vermont	General Assembly	30	2	150	2	8,160+	Biennial
Virginia	General Assembly	40	4	100	2	18,000+	Annual
Washington	Legislature	49	4	98	2	25,900+	Annual
West Virginia	Legislature	34	4	100	2	6,500+	Annual
Wisconsin	Legislature	33	4	99	2	35,070+	Annual
Wyoming	Legislature	30	4	64	2	Per diem	Annual[a]

Source: Book of the States 1994–1995, various tables.

[a]Meets annually but second session limited to specific types of legislation, usually fiscal and budgetary.

Table 6–4
Informal Legislative Norms[a]

"Highly Undesirable" Legislative Behavior
1. Concealing the real purpose(s) of a bill or purposely overlooking some portion of it in order to assure its passage.
2. Dealing in personalities in debate or in other remarks made on the floor of the chamber.
3. Being a thorn to the majority by refusing unanimous consent, etc.
4. Talking about decisions that have been reached in private to the press or anyone else.
5. Seeking as much publicity as possible from the press back home.
6. Being generally known as a spokesperson for some special-interest group.
7. Introducing as many bills and amendments as possible during any legislative session.
8. Talking on a subject coming before the legislature about which you are not completely informed.
9. Giving first priority to your reelection in all of your actions as a legislator.

---

[a]Items which at least 40 percent of Iowa House and Senate members checked as "highly undesirable." See F. Ted Hebert and Lelan E. McLemore, "Character and Structure of Legislative Norms," *American Journal of Political Science*, 17 (August 1973), 506–27.

bankers to banking committees, and so on.[44] The effect of these assignments is to further strengthen the power of special interests in the legislative process. Legislators with occupational ties to various interests dominate the committees that consider legislation dealing with those same interests.

LEGISLATIVE INSTITUTIONALIZATION

Over time political bodies develop their own rules, organizational structures, and patterns of behavior. Social scientists refer to this process as "institutionalization." In legislative bodies, institutionalization is said to occur when (1) membership stabilizes and legislators come to look upon their service as a career, (2) staffs are added, salaries increased, and internal operations expanded, and (3) rules of procedure become more complex.[45]

State legislatures have gradually become more institutionalized. We have already observed that membership turnover has diminished over time. Legislative salaries and perks are increasing over time, and incumbents enjoy a heavy advantage in seeking reelection. And we have observed that more legislators are coming to see their jobs as full-time occupations. Now we shall observe increasing institutionalization in the internal functioning of state legislatures.

---

[44]Keith E. Hamm and Ronald D. Hedlund, "Occupational Interests and State Legislative Committees." Paper delivered at the Midwest Political Science Association, Chicago, 1989.

[45]The "institutionalization" theme was first developed to understand changes in the U.S. House of Representatives by Nelson Polsby, "The Institutionalization of the U.S. House of Representatives," *American Political Science Review*, 62 (March 1968), 144–68.

PROFESSIONALISM   Some state legislatures are highly professional, while others are not. By *professional* we mean that in some legislatures the members are well paid and tend to think of their jobs as full-times ones; members and committees are well staffed and have good informational services available to them; and a variety of legislative services, such as bill drafting and statutory revision, are well supported and maintained. In other legislatures, members are poorly paid and regard their legislative work as part-time; there is little in the way of staff for legislators or committees; and little is provided in the way of legislative assistance and services. Table 6–5 groups the states by the professionalism of their legislatures.

REFORM   Reform organizations (for example, the Advisory Commission on Intergovernmental Relations, the Council on State Governments, the Eagleton Institute, and the Citizens Conference on State Legislatures) generally argue that state legislatures should be:

> *Small in size.*   This is supposed to enhance the prestige of legislative service, improve public accountability, and recruit more qualified people. The recommended size is no more than 100 members total in both upper and lower chambers. However, currently only eight state legislatures (Alabama, Arizona, Delaware, Hawaii, Nebraska, Nevada, Oregon, and Wyoming) have fewer

Table 6–5
PROFESSIONALISM IN STATE LEGISLATURES

PROFESSIONAL—Full-time, large staff, high pay, low turnover

California	Michigan	Ohio
Illinois	New York	Pennsylvania
Massachusetts	New Jersey	Wisconsin

PROFESSIONAL–CITIZEN—Moderate pay, staff, turnover, and time

Alabama	Indiana	North Carolina
Alaska	Iowa	Oklahoma
Arizona	Kansas	Oregon
Colorado	Kentucky	South Carolina
Connecticut	Maryland	Tennessee
Delaware	Minnesota	Texas
Florida	Mississippi	Virginia
Georgia	Missouri	Washington
Hawaii	Nebraska	

CITIZEN—Part-time, low pay, small staff, high turnover

Arkansas	Nevada	South Dakota
Idaho	New Hampshire	Utah
Louisiana	New Mexico	Vermont
Maine	North Dakota	West Virginia
Montana	Rhode Island	Wyoming

Source: National Conference on State Legislatures, *State Legislatures,* 20 (November 1994), 5.

than 100 total members. New Hampshire has 400 house members and 24 senators. Most states have between 150 and 200 legislators. (See Table 6–3.)

Well paid.   Annual salaries vary a great deal from state to state. The large urban industrial states generally pay their legislators more than small, rural states. (See Table 6–3.) Reformers argue that better pay would make legislators full-time professional representatives, rather than part-time amateurs who must spend time on their private business interests in order to make a living.

Well staffed.   Reformers argue that experienced, knowledgeable staffs are required to provide information, draft bills, analyze the potential impact of proposed legislation, study the governor's budget proposals, and evaluate the impact of existing programs. Less professional legislatures have only a single small "reference service" for the entire legislature; this service is mainly concerned with drafting bills with only minimal research. However, most legislatures provide professional staff for their major committees and for leadership. Some states also provide each house and senate member with year-round personal staff.

Flexible.   Reformers generally argue that legislatures should be free from constitutional restrictions, for example, restrictions on the maximum number of days they can meet annually or biennially, and restrictions on budget powers through constitutional earmarking of revenues for special purposes.

Functional.   Reformers argue that legislatures should have clear and simple procedures, well-defined committee responsibilities, published schedules for testimony, committee consideration, and floor debate, and a smooth flow of bills through the legislative process. Yet most legislatures suffer the traditional "end-of-session logjam" when many bills are passed in haste without careful consideration of their merits and other important pieces of legislation are lost in the shuffle. Most abuses of the legislative process occur in this last-minute frenzied period of lawmaking.

Well policed.   Reformers have put forward a variety of proposals to ensure the integrity of the legislative process:

1. Public financing of all state elections (only Hawaii and Minnesota provide public funds for *legislative* candidates)
2. Limitations on campaign contributions
3. Reporting of all campaign contributions
4. Registration of lobbyists and regulation of lobbying activity
5. Creation of ethics commissions
6. Sunshine laws that open all legislative activity to the media

PROFESSIONALISM AND CAREERISM   Professionalism in state legislatures encourages careerism. It encourages people who view politics as a career to seek and win a seat in the state legislature. Higher pay makes the job more attractive and allows legislators to devote all their time to politics and policy making. Year-round sessions discourage people who cannot take leave from their business or profession. Greater resources available to legislators allow them to perform more casework for constituents and to build a personal organization devoted to keeping themselves in office. Additional resources make life at the state capital more comfortable. There is less voluntary turnover in professional legislatures, and less likelihood that an incumbent will be defeated. Political scientist Alan Rosenthal writes, "One quality that distinguishes the new breed of full-time, professional politicians from the old breed of part-time, citizen legislators is ambition. The latter were content to spend a few years in legislative office and then return to private careers. The former, by contrast, would like to spend most of their careers in government and politics. They find public office appealing and the game of politics exhilarating."[46]

Careerism fosters individualism among legislators. With their own careers paramount in their calculations, professional legislators are less likely to follow the lead of the governor or party leaders. They have their own agendas to pursue. Professionalism grants some advantage to liberals and Democrats in state politics. Liberals are more likely to view government as a career, conservatives view government service as a sacrifice of business or professional time. Republicans have more difficulty finding business people willing to meet the demands of running for office and serving full time.

PROFESSIONALISM AND PUBLIC POLICY   Does it make any difference in public policy whether a legislature is "professional" or not? Reformers often *assume* that "professionalism" will result in legislatures that are "generally innovative in many different areas of public policy, generous in welfare and educational spending and services, and 'interventionist' in the sense of having powers and responsibilities of broad scope."[47] Does legislative reform, however, *really* have any policy consequences?

Unfortunately there is little systematic evidence that legislative professionalism has any direct effect on public policy. While it is true that professional legislatures spend more per person on welfare and more per pupil on education than nonprofessional legislatures, professional legislatures are found in the wealthier, urban states with well-educated populations, and these states spend more on welfare and education anyway. (See Chapter 15, "The Politics of Education," and Chapter 17, "The Politics of Poverty, Welfare, and Health.") In other words, there is little evidence that legislative professionalism *causes* increased spending for welfare and education. Instead, both legislative professionalism *and* spending for welfare and education are caused by income, urbanization, and education.

LEGISLATIVE STAFFING   Years ago, state legislatures employed only a few clerks and secretaries to handle the clerical chores and a few lawyers in a small "legislative reference service" to draft bills at the request of lawmakers. Today, the movement toward professionalism in state legislatures has created large professional staffs to serve the needs of the leadership and the standing committees. Some more "professional" legislatures have full-time professional staffs—lawyers, researchers, and speechwriters, as well as secretaries—for the house speaker, senate president, majority and minority leaders, and

---

[46]Alan Rosenthal, *Governors and Legislatures: Contending Powers* (Washington, DC: CQ Press, 1990), p. 63.

[47]Citizens Conference on State Legislatures, *The Sometimes Governments* (New York: Bantam Books, 1971), p. 77.

all standing committees; and many states now even provide full-time, year-round staff for each house and senate member. Only the less "professional" rural, small-state legislatures still depend on a small legislative reference service to serve all legislators in drafting bills and doing research.

Legislative staffs have grown rapidly over the last decade, so that today this new "legislative bureaucracy" is itself becoming an important political force. Staff members are political appointees, and they are supposed to reflect the political views of their legislator-bosses in their work. However, some "staffers" become so knowledgeable about state government, or about the state budget, or about their aspects of legislative work, that they are kept on in their jobs even when their original sponsor leaves the capital.

The staffs are expected to research issues, find out what other states are doing, assist in analyzing the budget, schedule legislative hearings, line up experts and interest groups to testify, keep abreast of the status of bills and appropriation items as they move through the legislature, maintain contact with state agencies and the governor's staff, make coffee and fetch doughnuts, write and rewrite bills, and perform other assorted chores and errands. As legislators come to rely on trusted "staffers," the "staffers" themselves become more powerful. Their advice may kill a bill or an appropriation item, or their work may amend a bill or alter an appropriation, without the legislator becoming directly involved. Often "staffers" are young, and they exercise a great deal of influence in policy making.

LEADERSHIP AND ROLE-PLAYING IN LEGISLATURES

Roles are expectations about the kind of behavior people ought to exhibit. Expectations are placed upon a legislator by fellow legislators, the legislator's party, the opposition party, the governor, constituents, interest groups, and by friends, as well as by the legislators themselves.

LEADERSHIP ROLES   Perhaps the most distinctive roles in the legislative process are those of the leadership.[48] A typical legislative chamber has a presiding officer (usually a house "speaker" and a senate "president"), a majority and a minority floor leader, a number of committee chairpersons, and a steering committee. These leaders perform functions similar to the functions of rules. First of all, leaders are expected to help make the legislative system stable and manageable. They are expected to maintain order, to know the rules and procedures, to follow the rules, and to show fairness and impartiality. Leaders are also expected to help focus the issues and resolve conflict by presenting issues clearly, narrowing the alternatives, organizing public hearings, and promoting the party or administrative point of view on bills. The majority leader is supposed to "get the administrative program through," while the minority leader develops a "constructive opposition."

Leaders are also expected to administer the legislature and expedite business. This includes "promoting teamwork," "being accessible," starting the sessions on time, keeping

---

[48]See Malcolm E. Jewell and Marcia Lynn Whicker, *Legislative Leadership in the United States* (Ann Arbor, MI: University of Michigan Press, 1994).

them on schedule, and distributing the workload. It involves communication, coordination, and liaison with the governor, the administrative departments, and the other chambers.

MEMBERS' EXPECTATIONS OF LEADERS   From the members' perspective, successful leaders are those who assist them in achieving their personal political goals. Most legislators possess a desire for reelection, as well as power and policy influence within the legislature. The relative importance of these goals will vary for each individual member. A freshman lawmaker who feels electorally insecure will have different priorities than a senior legislator from a safe district. The key to effective leadership is to understand the particular needs and goals of individual members and to respond as necessary.[49]

LEADERS' LEGISLATIVE PRIORITIES   Leaders face a difficult challenge in balancing competing priorities with limited resources. In recent years the top priorities identified by state legislative leaders across the country have been in the areas of crime and law enforcement, tax reform, education, and health care.[50] Dealing with crime has been the top priority; surveys reveal that more people name crime as the "most important problem confronting the nation" than any other concern. State legislatures have focused on keeping convicted criminals behind bars for longer periods of time, eliminating early releases due to prison overcrowding, building more prison cells, and reorganizing the juvenile justice system to handle juveniles who commit increasingly more violent crimes (see Chapter 8). Much of the recent fiscal talk in state capitols has been about tax cutting (see Chapter 18). In education, the issues include equitable distribution of school funds to achieve equality of educational opportunity across school districts (often ordered by state courts), the imposition of statewide testing of students and teachers, and experimenting with school vouchers and privately operated public schools (see Chapter 15). Health care reform is also a common topic of discussion in state legislatures. States themselves continue to worry about improving access to care while containing costs, especially the costs of Medicaid, the fastest-growing expenditure of state government (see Chapter 17). Finally, state legislative leaders across the country echo a familiar theme: They want fewer unfunded federal mandates to the states and greater control over federal programs in their state (see Chapter 3).

EXPERT ROLES   Another set of legislative roles that are commonly encountered and make important contributions to the legislative process are the "subject-matter experts." Unlike leadership roles, the roles of subject-matter experts are not embodied in formal offices. The committee system introduces specialization into the legislature, and the seniority system places at the head of the committee those persons longest exposed to the information about the committee's subject matter. Thus, subject-matter experts emerge among legislators in the fields of law, finance, education, agriculture, natural resources, local government, labor, transportation, and so on.

---

[49]Thomas H. Little, "A Systematic Analysis of Members' Environments and Their Expectations of Elected Leaders," *Political Research Quarterly*, 47 (September 1994) 733–47.

[50]National Conference of State Legislatures, *State Legislative Priorities* (Denver: NCSL, 1995).

TRUSTEES AND DELEGATES   Another way of describing roles in a legislature is to discover the legislators' orientations toward the expectations of constituents. Legislators can be classified as *trustees* (those who are guided in legislative affairs solely by their personal conscience) and *delegates* (those who are guided by instructions or wishes of their constituents). Should legislators represent their constituency or their own conscience? Actually, few legislators exhibit in their behavior a firm commitment to either one of these roles. Most legislators when facing specific issues do not see any conflict between the wishes of their constituents, their party, and their own judgment. Even when such conflict is perceived, most legislators attempt to find a compromise between conflicting demands rather than choose one role or the other exclusively. Of course, if legislators are asked how they make their decisions, they *claim* to be guided solely by their own conscience. However, this is little more than a verbalism; it reflects a heroic image of the courageous defender of the public interest, who acts out of personal virtue and conviction regardless of the consequences.

The more politically experienced legislator is more likely to assume the role of a trustee. There is some evidence that legislators who come to the office with little prior experience as public officials, and those with less service in the legislature, are more likely to respond in the manner of a "delegate," while their more experienced colleagues give "trustee" responses to interviewers.[51]

PARTY POLITICS IN STATE LEGISLATURES

While the influence of parties varies from state to state, overall, parties are perhaps the single most important influence over legislative behavior.

ONE-PARTY STATES   Traditionally the party in one-party (Democratic) states did not exercise tight party discipline over the voting of legislators. Being a Democrat in the legislature of a one-party southern Democratic state did not influence roll-call voting behavior very much. Democratic governors in these states could not depend upon party loyalty to win legislative support for their programs. However, the *minority* Republicans in these states tended to stick together.

EMERGING LEGISLATIVE PARTY CONFLICT   As Republicans won more seats in the southern and border state legislatures, party organizations and party voting within the legislatures increased. Republican legislators became more likely to organize themselves into a party caucus, to develop a party legislative program, and to vote cohesively. The emerging "threat" of a Republican opposition usually spurred the Democrats to do the same.[52]

---

[51]Charles G. Bell and Charles E. Price, "Pre-Legislative Sources of Representational Roles," *Midwest Journal of Political Science*, 13 (May 1969), 254–70. See also Corey M. Rosen, "Legislative Influence and Policy Orientation in American State Legislatures," *American Journal of Political Science*, 18 (November 1974), 681–91.

[52]See Robert Harmel and Keith E. Hamm, "Development of a Party Role in a No-Party Legislature," *Western Political Quarterly*, 39 (March 1986), 79–92. See also Cole Blease Graham and Kenny J. Whitby, "Party-Based Voting in a Southern State Legislature," *American Politics Quarterly*, 17 (April 1989) 181–93.

TWO-PARTY STATES   Within competitive states, party divisions on legislative roll-call votes are more frequent than any other divisions, including rural–urban divisions. One common measure of party influence on voting is the percentage of nonunanimous roll-call votes on which a majority of Democrats voted against the majority of Republicans. Compilations by the *Congressional Quarterly* show that the proportion of roll calls in Congress in which the two parties have been in opposition has ranged from 35 to 50 percent over the years. Party voting in competitive state legislatures such as New York, Pennsylvania, Ohio, Delaware, Rhode Island, Massachusetts, and Michigan may be even higher than it is in Congress.

LEADERSHIP VOTES   Voting along strict party lines is the norm for legislative leadership posts, notably for speaker of the house and president of the Senate. Leaders are initially selected in the majority party's caucus; all party members are then expected to support their party's choice in the official house vote that follows. Indeed, real difficulties have emerged where parties have evenly divided legislative seats in a state house. (The Indiana house once resolved the issue by agreeing to "co-speakers" who would preside on alternate days; the Florida senate once resolved the issue by agreeing to switch presidents each year of the session.) Rarely do legislators break party lines in voting on leadership posts, although considerable pressure may be placed upon some to do so where the parties are evenly or almost evenly divided. Long-term Democratic Speaker of the California House, Willie Brown, managed to swing some Republican votes his way in 1995, and to retain the speakership even though more Republicans than Democrats sat in the legislature. But this political feat is unlikely to be replicated anywhere else.

PARTY ISSUES   On what types of issues do the parties exercise their greatest influence? Parties usually display the greatest cohesion on issues involving taxation and appropriations, welfare, and regulation of business and labor—in short, the major social and economic controversies that divide the national parties. Minor bills involving the licensing of water well drillers, beauticians, or barbers do not usually become the subject matter of party votes, and only infrequently will the parties divide over such matters as the designation of an official state bird. Party influence in budgetary matters is particularly apparent, since the budget often involves issues of social welfare and class interest on which parties in many states are split. In addition, the budget is clearly identified as the product of the governor and carries the label of the party of the governor. Another type of bill that is often the subject of party voting is one involving the party as an interest group. Parties often exhibit an interest in bills proposing to transfer powers from an office controlled by one party to an office controlled by the other, or bills proposing to create or abolish non–civil service jobs. Parties display considerable interest in bills affecting the organization of local government, state administration, the civil service, registration and election laws, and legislative procedure.

SOURCES OF PARTY VOTING   What factors distinguish those states in which the party substantially influences legislative decision making from those states in which it does not?

Party cohesion is strongest in those urban industrial states in which the parties represent separate socioeconomic constituencies. Party voting occurs in those competitive states in which Democratic legislators represent central-city, low-income, ethnic, and racial constituencies, and Republican legislators represent middle-class, suburban, small-town, and rural constituencies. Party cohesion is weak in states where party alignments do not coincide with socioeconomic divisions of constituencies.

It is this division of constituencies that is the basis of party cohesion and influence in the legislature. Even within each party, members from districts typical of their party in socioeconomic attributes support the party position more often than members from districts atypical of the party. Constituency characteristics, then, help to explain not only the outcome of elections but also the behavior of the elected.

PARTY DISCIPLINE   In a few states the party leadership sets the legislative agenda, determines committee assignments, and tries to bind legislators to vote for the position taken by the party caucus. But because of the weaknesses of the parties in the electoral process (see Chapter 5), party discipline in most state legislatures is very weak. Reformers in Colorado passed a constitutional referendum specifically designed to weaken the powers of party leaders and committees in the legislative process. It requires consideration "on its merits" of every bill referred to a committee, specifies that the full house can always bring a bill out of committee, and outlaws binding party caucuses, saying that legislators cannot "commit themselves or any other member or members, through a vote in a party caucus or any similar procedure, to vote in favor of or against any bill."[53]

ARE LEGISLATORS RESPONSIBLE POLICY MAKERS?

A classic dilemma of representative government is whether the legislator should vote his or her own conscience—"the trustee"—or vote the constituency's wishes—"the delegate." Good philosophical arguments can be found to support either of these guiding principles. Nearly 200 years ago the English political philosopher Edmund Burke confronted this question directly and urged representatives to vote their own conscience about what is right for society. Burke believed that the voters should elect wise and virtuous representatives to govern *for* them—to use their own judgment in deciding issues regardless of popular demands. Even today the term *Burkean representation* refers to the willingness of a representative to ignore public opinion and decide public issues on the basis of one's own best judgment about what is right for society.

Other political philosophers stress *responsiveness* of representatives to the views of their constituents. Consider, for example, philosopher Hanna Pitkin's definition of representation: "Representation means acting in the interest of the represented, in a manner responsive to them."[54] Responsiveness connotes a deliberate effort by legislators to match their votes on public policy issues to their constituency's preferences. However, to be "responsive" to one's constituents, two conditions must be met: (1) the legislator must correctly perceive the constituents' views on the issues, and (2) the legislator must act in accord with these views. (See Figure 6–4.)

---

[53]*State Legislation*, August 1989, p. 16.

[54]Hanna Pitkin, *The Concept of Representation* (Berkeley: University of California Press, 1967), p. 154.

Figure 6–4
A MODEL OF CONSTITUENCY INFLUENCE

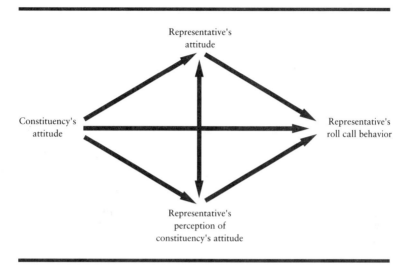

LEGISLATORS' KNOWLEDGE OF CONSTITUENTS' VIEWS   Let us consider the first condition: Do legislators know the views of their constituents on public issues? Unfortunately, the evidence is mixed. When Iowa legislators were asked to predict whether their own district would vote for or against some proposed constitutional amendments, the resulting predictions were good on some issues but poor on others.[55] Interestingly, the poorest predictions came from legislators from poor districts, suggesting that legislators have less understanding of the views of poor constituents than affluent ones. In contrast, when Florida legislators were asked to predict how both their state and district would vote on referenda on school busing and school prayer, nearly all of them made accurate predictions for both their district and the state.[56] Perhaps one explanation for these apparently conflicting findings is that legislators know their constituents' views on well-publicized, controversial, emotionally charged issues, but that legislators are poor predictors of constituent opinion on other kinds of issues.

LEGISLATORS' PERSONAL VIEWS   State legislators may indeed vote their own attitude on *most* issues coming before the legislature. A careful study of voting on welfare, tax, and consumer issues in the Texas legislature revealed that "In both houses, in every issue-area examined, the path connecting the representative's attitude with his roll-call vote is far more important than the path linking his perceptions of his constituency's attitude with his voting."[57] The explanation offered was that activities of the

[55]Ronald D. Hedlund and H. Paul Friesma, "Representatives' Perceptions of Constituency Opinion," *Journal of Politics*, 34 (August 1971), 730–52.

[56]Robert S. Erikson, Norman R. Luttbeg, and William V. Holloway, "Knowing One's District: How Legislators Predict Referendum Voting," *American Journal of Political Science*, 19 (May 1975), 231–41.

[57]Bryan D. Jones, "Competitiveness, Role Orientations, and Legislative Responsiveness," *Journal of Politics*, 35 (November 1973), 924–47.

governor and his or her staff, other legislators and legislative leaders, and outside interest groups, create "the din of the immediate legislative struggle," which "muffles" the voices from the home district. Even legislators from competitive districts were seemingly unaffected by their views of their constituents' attitudes. As expected, legislators who opted for the role of "delegate" voted what they believed to be their constituents' attitudes more than legislators who opted for the role of trustee.

In summary, the absence of direct evidence that (1) legislators know their constituents' views and (2) vote their constituents' views rather than their own views creates difficulties for the "responsiveness" theory of democracy. There is a great deal of "noise" along the lines from constituents' views to their legislator's roll-call vote.

Personal ideology rather than lobbying pressures or constituents' views is a major factor in deciding legislative votes.

> None of this denies that legislators endeavor in some decisions to please interest groups or other actors. Cowed by threats, lured by enticements, legislators often make decisions they do not believe in. In most sessions, too, they confront a few highly publicized, controversial issues; their private policy views may matter little then. Nonetheless . . . representatives have the freedom on a range of issues to weigh priorities and evaluate policy options on their merits: to decide in accord with their own private conceptions of good public policy.[58]

LOBBYING IN STATE LEGISLATURES

The influence of organized interest groups in the legislative process varies from state to state. Earlier (Chapter 4) we discussed interest groups in the fifty states and their involvement in public relations, campaign financing, and lobbying. We defined lobbying as any communication by someone acting on behalf of a group directed at a government decision maker with the hope of influencing decisions.

NARROW ISSUES   On what kinds of decisions are interest groups more likely to exercise influence? Party and constituency interests are most apparent on broad social and economic issues. On narrower issues voters are less likely to have either an interest or an opinion. The legislator is, therefore, freer to respond to the pleas of organized groups on highly specialized topics than on major issues of public interest. Economic interests seeking to use the law to improve their competitive position are a major source of group pressure on these specialized topics. Particularly active in lobbying are the businesses subject to extensive government regulation. The truckers, railroads, insurance companies, and race track and liquor interests are consistently found to be among the most highly organized and active lobbyists in state capitals. Organized pressure comes from associations of governments and associations of government employees. State chapters of the National Education Association are persistent in presenting the demands of educational administrators and occasionally the demands of the dues-paying teachers as well.

INFORMATION EXCHANGE   Legislators depend on lobbyists for much of their information on public issues. Legislators are aware of the potential bias in informa-

---

[58]Robert M. Entman, "The Impact of Ideology on Legislative Behavior," *Journal of Politics,* 45 (February 1983), 165.

tion given them by lobbyists. But the constant proximity of lobbyists to legislators facilitates information exchange.[59] Legislators *use* lobbyists, just as lobbyists use legislators:

> Typically, legislators utilize lobbyists as sources of influence in three ways: by calling upon lobbyists to influence other legislators, by calling upon lobbyists to help amass public opinion in favor of the legislator's position, and by including lobbyists in planning strategy in an effort to negotiate a bill through the legislature.[60]

THREATS   It is unwise for lobbyists to threaten legislators, for example, by vowing to defeat them in the next election. This is the tactic of an amateur lobbyist, not a professional. It usually produces a defensive response by the legislator. As one lobbyist put it: "Once you have closed the door you have no further access to the individual. Once you've threatened an individual, there is no possibility of winning in the future."[61] Even the publication of voting records of legislators by interest groups is considered an implied threat and is generally disregarded by legislators.

GETTING THE MESSAGE   Testimony at legislative committee hearings is a common form of information exchange between lobbyists and legislators. Often this testimony is the legislators' primary source of information about legislation. Direct meetings in legislators' offices are also frequent and effective. Social gatherings (where the liquor is usually furnished by the lobbyist) are more important in establishing friendships; professional lobbyists seldom bring up "business" on such occasions. Legislators are wined and dined so much during legislative sessions that attendance at social functions is sometimes viewed as a chore. The least effective method of lobbying is the submission of long letters or reports.

LOBBYING THE STAFF   One form of lobbying that is growing rapidly in importance is communication with legislative *staff* personnel. As state legislatures acquire more full-time staff for their standing committees, house and senate leaders, and majority and minority party caucuses, professional lobbyists are coming to recognize that these staff people can have as much or more to do with the specific content of bills as legislators themselves. Many of the more "modernized," "professional" state legislatures rely heavily on the advice of professional staffs. The wise lobbyist in these states cultivates friendships among staff personnel.

REGULATION OF LOBBYING   The U.S. Constitution guarantees the right "to petition the government for redress of grievances." This First Amendment right protects individuals and groups in their attempts to communicate with and influence their lawmakers. Nonetheless, lobbying is regulated in some fashion in all of the states. Most state laws require lobbyists ("anyone receiving compensation to influence legislative action") to (1) register with the clerk or secretary of the house or senate and (2) file periodic reports of direct expenditures for lobbying activity. These regulations have relatively little impact on lobbying activity; many organizations claim that they are educational or

---

[59]Christopher A. Mooney, "Peddling Information in the State Legislature: Closeness Counts," *Western Political Quarterly,* 44 (June 1991), 433–44.

[60]Harmon Zeigler and Michael A. Baer, *Lobbying: Interaction and Influence in American State Legislatures* (Belmont, CA: Wadsworth, 1969), p. 107.

[61]Ibid., p. 121.

TRIVIA
SONGS, FLOWERS, BIRDS, AND TREES

State	State Song	State Flower	State Tree	State Bird
Alabama	Alabama	Camellia	Southern Pine	Yellowhammer
Alaska	Alaska's Flag	Forget-Me-Not	Sitka Spruce	Willow Ptarmigan
Arizona	Arizona	Saguaro Cactus Blossom	Paloverde	Cactus Wren
Arkansas	Arkansas	Apple Blossom	Pine	Mockingbird
California	I Love You, California	Golden Poppy	California Redwood	California Valley Quail
Colorado	Where the Columbines Grow	Rocky Mountain Columbine	Colorado Blue Spruce	Lark Bunting
Connecticut	Yankee Doodle Dandy	Mountain Laurel	White Oak	American Robin
Delaware	Our Delaware	Peach Blossom	American Holly	Blue Hen Chicken
Florida	Swanee River	Orange Blossom	Sabal Palmetto Palm	Mockingbird
Georgia	Georgia On My Mind	Cherokee Rose	Live Oak	Brown Thrasher
Hawaii	Hawaii Ponoi	Yellow Hibiscus	Candlenut	Hawaiian Goose
Idaho	Here We Have Idaho	Syringa	White Pine	Mountain Bluebird
Illinois	Illinois	Native Violet	White Oak	Cardinal
Indiana	On the Banks of the Wabash, Far Away	Peony	Tulip Poplar	
Iowa	The Song of Iowa	Wild Rose	Oak	Eastern Goldfinch
Kansas	Home on the Range	Sunflower	Cottonwood	Western Meadowlark
Kentucky	My Old Kentucky Home	Goldenrod	Kentucky Coffee Tree	Cardinal
Louisiana	Give Me Louisiana	Magnolia	Cypress	Eastern Brown Pelican
Maine	State of Maine Song	White Pine Cone and Tassel	Eastern White Pine	Chickadee
Maryland	Maryland, My Maryland	Black-eyed Susan	White Oak	Baltimore Oriole
Massachusetts	All Hail to Massachusetts	Mayflower	American Elm	Chickadee
Michigan	Michigan, My Michigan	Apple Blossom	White Pine	Robin
Minnesota	Hail! Minnesota	Pink and White Lady's Slipper	Red Pine	Common Loon

religious in nature and not really lobbies, and they do not register. Many lobbies do not report all of their educational and public relations expenditures, but only a small portion, which they attribute directly to lobbying. Campaign contributions usually must be reported under state election laws. Of course, bribery and conspiracy may be prosecuted under criminal laws.

Mississippi	Go, Mississippi!	Magnolia	Magnolia	Mockingbird
Missouri	Missouri Waltz	Hawthorn	Dogwood	Bluebird
Montana	Montana	Bitterroot	Ponderosa Pine	Western Meadow-lark
Nebraska	Beautiful Nebraska	Goldenrod	Cottonwood	Western Meadow-lark
Nevada	Home Means Nevada	Sagebrush	Single-Leaf Pinon	Mountain Bluebird
New Hampshire	Old New Hampshire	Purple Lilac	White Birch	Purple Finch
New Jersey	Ode to New Jersey	Purple Violet	Red Oak	Eastern Goldfinch
New Mexico	O Fair New Mexico	Yucca	Pinon	Roadrunner
New York	I Love New York	Rose	Sugar Maple	Bluebird
North Carolina	The Old North State	Dogwood	Pine	Cardinal
North Dakota	North Dakota Hymn	Wild Prairie Rose	American Elm	Western Meadow-lark
Ohio	Beautiful Ohio	Scarlet Carnation	Buckeye	Cardinal
Oklahoma	Oklahoma!	Mistletoe	Redbud	Scissortailed Flycatcher
Oregon	Oregon, My Oregon	Oregon Grape	Douglas Fir	Western Meadow-lark
Pennsylvania	Hail! Pennsylvania	Mountain Laurel	Hemlock	Ruffed Grouse
Rhode Island	Rhode Island	Violet	Red Maple	Rhode Island Red
South Carolina	Carolina	Yellow Jessamine	Palmetto	Carolina Wren
South Dakota	Hail, South Dakota	Pasque Flower	Black Hills Spruce	Ringnecked Pheasant
Tennessee	The Tennessee Waltz	Iris	Tulip Poplar	Mockingbird
Texas	Texas, Our Texas	Bluebonnet	Pecan	
Utah	Utah, We Love Thee	Sego Lily	Blue Spruce	Seagull
Vermont	Hail, Vermont	Red Clover	Sugar Maple	Hermit Thrush
Virginia	Carry Me Back to Old Virginia	Dogwood	Dogwood	Cardinal
Washington	Washington, My Home	Western Rhododendron	Western Hemlock	Willow Goldfinch
West Virginia	The West Virginia Hills; This is My West Virginia; and West Virginia, My Home, Sweet Home	Big Rhododendron	Sugar Maple	Cardinal
Wisconsin	On Wisconsin!	Wood Violet	Sugar Maple	Robin
Wyoming	Wyoming	Indian Paintbrush	Cottonwood	Meadowlark

State legislatures and agencies charged with enforcement of lobbying regulations have traditionally been notorious for their neglect of their responsibilities. However, increasing professionalization of state legislatures appears to increase both their capacity and willingness to regulate lobbying.[62]

---

[62]Cynthia Opheim, "Explaining the Differences in State Lobbying Regulation," *Western Political Quarterly*, 44 (June 1991), 405–21.

LEGISLATURES IN STATE POLITICS

It seems safe to conclude that most state legislatures function as "arbiters" of public policy rather than as "initiators." Policy initiation is the function of the governor, the bureaucrat, and the interest group. It is principally these elements that develop policy proposals in the first instance; legislatures are placed in the role of responding to the stimulus provided by these groups. The structure of legislatures clearly reflects their deliberative function. Their rules and procedures and their leadership and committee systems do not lend themselves to policy initiation so much as they lend themselves to deliberation, discussion, and delay. The size and complexity of state government has reached a scale where expert knowledge rather than lay enlightenment is the crucial ingredient in policy formation. The state budget, for example, perhaps the single most important policy-making document, is drawn up by bureaucrats subordinate to the governor and modified by the governor before submission to the legislature. Legislatures make further modifications, but seldom do they undertake to rewrite an executive budget. Legislatures are still critical obstacles through which appropriation and revenue measures must pass; they are still the scenes of bloody battles over the ends for which public money is to be spent.

Yet before legislative deliberation, the agenda for decision making has already been drawn up, the framework for conflict has already been established, and the issues have already been placed in particular bills. Sophisticated lawmakers are aware of their function as arbiters rather than as initiators of public policy. As one of them put it: "We're the policy-making body of the state government, and basically we should give leadership necessary to meet the problems the state faces. But in practice it comes from the executive branch."[63]

Another general proposition about legislatures is that they function to inject into public decision making a parochial influence. Legislatures function to represent locally organized interests, interests that are manifested in local rather than statewide constituencies. Legislators have deep roots in their local constituencies. They have the religious and ethnic affiliations of their constituents, they have lived among them for most of their lives, and they meet them frequently in their businesses and clubs. The process of recruiting legislators is carried on at the local level. State legislators clearly function to represent local interests in state politics.

---

[63]Wahlke et al., *Legislative System*, p. 255.

7

GOVERNORS
IN STATE POLITICS

THE MANY ROLES OF A GOVERNOR

Governors are central figures in American state politics. People are more likely to be able to recall their governor's name than the name of any public official other than the president and vice-president of the United States. In the eyes of many citizens, governors are responsible for everything that happens in their states during their terms of office, whether or not they have the authority or the capacity to do anything about it. Governors are expected to bring industry into their states, prevent prison riots, raise teachers' salaries, keep taxes low, reduce unemployment, see that the state gets its fair share of grant money from Washington, provide disaster relief, and bring tourists into the state. Governors offer reassurance to citizens during crises and disasters—everything from floods, hurricanes, fires, and droughts, to toxic waste spills and nuclear plant accidents. These public expectations far exceed the formal powers of governors. In many ways the expectations placed upon the governor resemble those placed upon the president. Like the president, governors are expected to be their state's chief administrator, chief legislator, leader of their party, ceremonial head of their government, chief ambassador to other governments, leader of public opinion, and chief crisis manager.

CHIEF ADMINISTRATOR   As *chief administrator,* the governor must try to co-ordinate the state's bureaucracy, oversee the preparation of the state's budget, and super-vise major state programs. Governors must resolve conflicts within their administration and troubleshoot where difficulties arise. They must be concerned with scandal and endeavor to prevent it from becoming public, or act decisively to eliminate it if it does. The public will hold them responsible for any scandal in their administration, whether they were a party to it or not. The public will hold them responsible for the financial structure of the state, whether it was they or their predecessors who were responsible for the state's fiscal troubles.

Yet, as we shall see in this chapter, the formal administrative powers of a governor are severely restricted. Many of the governor's administrative agencies are headed by elected officials or independent boards or commissions, over which the governor has little or no control. Governors' powers of appointment and removal are severely restricted by state constitutions. Governors do not have control over their administration that is commen-surate with their responsibility for it.

CHIEF LEGISLATOR   As *chief legislator,* the governor is responsible for the ma-jor statewide legislative programs. There is a general public expectation that every gover-nor will put forward some sort of legislative program, even a governor committed to a "caretaker" role. The governor largely determines what public issues will be considered by the legislature. By sending bills to the legislature, governors are cast in the role of the "initiator" of public policy decisions. If they want to see their legislative proposals en-acted into law, they must also persuade legislators to support them. In other words, they must involve themselves directly in legislative decisions.

The veto power gives the governor bargaining power with the legislature. Few vetoes are overridden; in most states a two-thirds majority vote in both houses is required to override a veto. This means a governor needs only one-third plus one in either house to sustain his or her veto. So even the *threat* of a veto can force changes in a bill under con-sideration in the legislature. Moreover, in most states, the governor possesses the line-item veto, allowing the governor to veto specific items in an appropriations bill, including leg-islators' home district "pork" or "turkeys." The threat of vetoing these vote-winning pro-jects gives the governor additional bargaining power with legislators. A governor can also call special sessions of the legislature, allowing the governor to spotlight specific issues and pressure the legislature to do something.

PARTY LEADER   Traditionally governors were regarded as the head of their party in the state. But governors do not have the power to deny party nominations to recalci-trant legislators of their own party. Party nominations are won independently by legisla-tors in their own districts. Governors have no formal disciplinary powers over members of their own party. And governors may choose to emphasize their own independence from their national party to further their own electoral ambitions.

However, within the legislature, parties still count. The governor usually receives greater support for his or her program from members of his or her own party. Legislators who run for office under the same party label as the governor have a stake in his or her success. Since all who run under the party's label share its common fortunes, and since its fortunes are often governed by the strength of its gubernatorial candidate, there will al-ways be a tendency for loyal party members to support their governor. The organization of the legislature along party lines reinforces the party role of the governor. Legislative leaders of the governor's party—whether in the majority or minority—are expected to support the governor's program.

CEREMONIAL HEAD   *Ceremonial* duties occupy a great deal of a governor's time. A governor may not be able to mobilize the symbolic and ceremonial power of the office on behalf of state goals in the same way that the president can mobilize the power of that office on behalf of national goals. Nonetheless, the skillful use of symbols and ceremonies can add to a governor's prestige and popularity. These assets can in turn contribute to political power.

CHIEF NEGOTIATOR   The governor is the *chief negotiator* with other governments in the American federal system, a variation of the diplomatic role of the president. Governors must negotiate with their local governments on the division of state and local responsibilities for public programs, and with other state governments over coordinating highway development, water pollution, resource conservation, and reciprocity in state laws. Governors must undertake responsibility for negotiation with the national government as well. The governor shares responsibility with the state's United States senators in seeing to it that the state receives a "fair share" of federal contracts, highway monies, educational monies, poverty funds, and so on.

OPINION LEADER   Governors are *leaders of public opinion* in their state. They are the most visible of state officials. Their comments on public affairs make news, and they are sought after for television, radio, and public appearances. They are able to focus public opinion on issues they deem important. They may not always be able to win public opinion to their side, but at least they will be heard.

CRISIS MANAGER   Finally, governors may be called upon to *manage crises* in their states—hurricanes, floods, droughts, and other disasters. Indeed, a governor's performance in a crisis may determine his or her standing with the public.

THE MAKING OF A GOVERNOR

As the central position in American state politics, the governorship is a much sought-after office. The prestige of being called "governor" for the rest of one's life, and the opportunity to use the office as a steppingstone to the United States Senate, or even the presidency or vice-presidency of the United States, is extremely attractive to people of ambition in American politics.

VARIETIES OF BACKGROUND   Many governors have been the sons of families of great wealth, who have chosen public service as an outlet for their energies—the Roosevelts, the Harrimans, the duPonts, the Rockefellers, and the Scrantons. Others have been men who emphasized, or exaggerated, their humble beginnings—Huey Long of Louisiana, "Big Jim" Folsom of Alabama, "Pitchfork Ben" Tillman of South Carolina, "Old Gene" Talmadge of Georgia. The southern "populist" governors, however, were gradually replaced by more moderate and better educated men—Bob Graham of Florida,

Bill Clinton of Arkansas, and Jimmy Carter of Georgia. George C. Wallace of Alabama may have been the last governor in the true populist tradition.

Nelson Rockefeller was elected to four consecutive four-year terms as governor of New York, holding that post longer than anyone in history. His brother, Winthrop Rockefeller, was governor of Arkansas, and his nephew, John D. Rockefeller IV, was governor of West Virginia. Pat Brown defeated Richard Nixon in 1962 to win the governorship of California; his son, Jerry Brown, won the same office in 1974; but Kathleen Brown failed in her bid in 1994 to follow in the footsteps of her father and brother. James B. Longley of Maine was the first independent candidate to win a governorship in modern history; he was followed by independent mavericks Walter Hickel of Alaska and Lowell Weicker of Connecticut. Governors have been movie actors (Ronald Reagan of California), restaurant owners (Lester Maddox of Georgia), truck drivers (Harold Hughes of Iowa), and even country music singers (Jimmie Davis of Louisiana wrote "You Are My Sunshine"). However, the majority of governors have been *lawyers* by profession. (The predominance of lawyers in public office was explained in Chapter 6.)

AGE   Television has accented youth and good looks among state governors. It helps "image-wise" to be tall, slim, handsome, fashionable, and smiling. The median beginning age of governors has declined over the last few decades to a youngish forty-seven. Bill Clinton became the nation's youngest governor when he won that post in Arkansas in 1978.

RACE   Until Douglas Wilder's successful run for the Virginia statehouse in 1989, no state had ever elected a black governor. California came close to doing so in 1982, when Democratic Mayor Thomas Bradley of Los Angeles lost to Republican George Deukmejian by less than 1 percent of the vote. Several Hispanics have been elected governor: Jerry Abodaca of New Mexico, Raul Castro of Arizona, Toney Anaya of New Mexico, and Bob Martinez of Florida.

GENDER   As of 1996 a total of 13 women had served as governors of American states. Nellie Ross of Wyoming and Miriam "Ma" Ferguson of Texas both succeeded their husbands in office in the 1920s. Lurleen Wallace of Alabama replaced her husband, George C. Wallace, briefly in the 1960s, when he was constitutionally prohibited from another term in office. It was not until 1974 that Ella T. Grasso of Connecticut became the first woman governor whose husband had not previously held the office. Later the same year, Dixey Lee Ray of Washington accomplished the same feat. Martha Layne Collins was elected governor of Kentucky in 1983. In 1986 two women faced each other in the Nebraska governor's race, and Republican Kay Orr emerged the victor; Democrat Madeleine M. Kunin won a close race in Vermont. Lieutenant Governor Rose Mofford replaced the impeached Governor Evan Mecham of Arizona. Democrat Ann Richards's hard-fought victory in the Texas governor's race in 1990 demonstrated that women can triumph in rough, bitter personal campaigns. Richards lost to George W. Bush, the former president's son, in 1994. Two other Democratic women governors were also elected in 1990: Joan Finney in Kansas and Barbara Roberts in Oregon. Republican Christine Todd Whitman of New Jersey defeated the incumbent Democratic governor of that state in 1994. The four women who served in 1994 (Finney, Richards, Roberts, and Whitman) were the largest number of women ever to serve simultaneously as state governors.

POLITICAL EXPERIENCE   Governors usually come to their office with considerable experience in public affairs. Only about 8 percent come into the governor's chair without prior officeholding (see Table 7–1). "Promotion" from a statewide elective office—lieutenant governor and attorney general, especially—is the most well-worn path to the governorship. Many governors have experience in state legislatures: Nearly half of all governors have previously served in the legislature and about one-fifth run directly from their legislative seats. Some members of Congress and some federal cabinet officers give up their seats to run for governor—an indication of the power and prestige of the office of governor. Pete Wilson of California was the first U.S. senator in modern times to leave that body to run for governor; Lawton Chiles of Florida left the U.S. Senate and later decided to run for governor.

GUBERNATORIAL POLITICS

COMPETITION   Competition is usually strong, both in primary and general elections, for the governorship. Indeed, competition for the job has been increasing over time, especially in the southern states where Republican candidates now have an equal chance of winning governorships. Yet traditionally the Democratic party has dominated state gubernatorial politics. In 1994, for the first time in thirty years Republican governors (30) outnumbered Democratic governors (19) (see Figure 5–1).

GETTING ELECTED   What forces influence the outcome of gubernatorial elections? Are gubernatorial elections affected by national voting trends—"coattails"? Or are they more affected by conditions within the states, especially the performance of the state's economy? Or are gubernatorial elections primarily "candidate centered"—influ-

Table 7–1
POLITICAL EXPERIENCE OF GOVERNORS

Last Public Office Prior to Election as Governor	*1970–1994*
State legislature	19%
Statewide office: lieutenant governor, secretary of state, treasurer, auditor, secretary of agriculture, public service commission	27
Attorney general or law enforcement	14
Congressional	13
Administrative, federal and state	6
Local elective	5
Party office	3
Other office	4
No prior office	8

Source: From *Politics in the American States: A Comparative Analysis*, 6th ed. by Virginia Gray et al. Copyright © 1996 by Virginia Gray, Herbert Jacobs, and Robert B. Albritton. Reprinted by permission of CQ Press.

enced mostly by the personal qualities of the candidates, their handling of state issues, the strength of their own political organizations, and their success in fund-raising and campaigning?

GUBERNATORIAL VOTE CHOICE   If voters are asked "What mattered most in voting for governor?," they cite personal leadership qualities of the candidate more often than anything else (see Table 7–2). Party affiliation and agreement on issues follow in importance. Negative voting—dislike of the opponent—also plays a significant role in gubernatorial voting.

Governors are better known to the voters than any other state officials or even U.S. senators and House members. Governors receive more media attention than any other state official. This does not make governors better liked than other elected officeholders. On the contrary governors are usually rated less favorably on job performance than U.S. senators and House members.[1]

Voters do not usually hold a governor solely responsible for economic problems confronting the state. Most voters recognize that state economic conditions depend more on market factors, or on the actions of the national government, including the president, than on the governor. State (or local) officials may be held responsible for actions that make an already weak economy worse; they may expect a governor to do all that he or she can to ameliorate hard times. But few voters hold governors directly responsible for the state's economic well-being.[2]

Table 7–2

GUBERNATORIAL VOTE CHOICE

Q. "What mattered most in voting for governor?"	%	Q: "Who is to blame for the state's economic problems?"	%
Strong leadership	21.1	President	25.4
Management ability	19.7	Both president and governor	18.4
Political party	19.0	Governor	15.4
Agreement on issues	18.2	Neither	34.5
Dislike opponent	12.0		
Don't know/No answer	10.0		

Source: Gubernatorial vote choice information derived from "Economic Voting for Governor and U.S. Senator" by Robert M. Stein, in *Journal of Politics,* 52:1 (February 1990), 29–53, by permission of the author and the University of Texas Press. Based on *New York Times*/CBS News Election day surveys in 27 states in 1982, during a national economic recession.

[1]Peverill Squire and Christina Fastnow, "Comparing Gubernatorial and Senatorial Elections," *Political Research Quarterly,* 47 (September 1994), 703–20.

[2]See Robert M. Stein, "Economic Voting for Governor and U.S. Senator," *Journal of Politics,* 52 (February 1990), 29–53.

While presidential and congressional elections are influenced by national economic conditions (recessions adversely affect the vote for candidates of the party in power, while prosperity generally helps), no similar influences can be seen in state legislative or gubernatorial elections. Political scientist John E. Chubb concludes: "Voters in state elections appear to hold politicians outside of the state, specifically the president and the president's party, responsible for economic conditions, and if conditions in a state should differ from those in neighboring states, to hold the governor only minimally responsible."[3]

COATTAIL EFFECTS   There are some coattail effects in state gubernatorial and legislative elections. Gubernatorial candidates running on the same party ticket as popular presidential candidates enjoy a significant advantage. But most gubernatorial elections are held in "off years"—years in which the nation is not electing a president. Off-year elections are deliberately designed to minimize the effects of presidential voting trends on state governors' elections. Nonetheless, there is some evidence that the electoral fate of gubernatorial candidates is affected by the popularity of the president. Gubernatorial candidates of the president's party attract more votes when the president's popularity in opinion polls is high. This is true whether the candidates are incumbents or aspirants.[4] Conversely, gubernatorial candidates of the president's party suffer when the president's popularity is low. Insofar as a president's popularity is affected by national economic trends, gubernatorial candidates of the president's party can suffer from national recessions and benefit from national prosperity.

CANDIDATE EFFECTS   Despite these coattail effects, gubernatorial elections are mostly candidate centered. Governors are less closely tied to national policy issues than Congress members; governors are not called upon by the media to explain their votes in support or opposition to the president's policy positions. The outcome of gubernatorial elections depends mostly on the personal qualities of the candidates, their ability to associate themselves with popular issues, the strength of their personal political organizations, their ability to raise campaign funds, and their skills in campaigning.

REELECTION   Incumbent governors who seek reelection are usually successful. In primary elections, incumbent governors usually face *little* serious opposition.[5] In recent

---

[3]John E. Chubb, "Institutions, the Economy and the Dynamics of State Elections," *American Political Science Review,* 82 (March 1988), 151. However, for contrary evidence showing that retrospective evaluations of a state's economy affects voter choice, see Craig J. Svoboda, "Retrospective Voting in Gubernatorial Elections," *Political Research Quarterly,* 48 (March 1995), 117–34; Richard G. Nieimi, Harold W. Stanley, and Ronald J. Vogel, "State Economies and State Taxes: Do Voters Hold Governors Accountable," *American Journal of Political Science,* 39 (November 1995), 936–57.

[4]Dennis M. Simon, "Presidents, Governors and Electoral Accountability," *Journal of Politics,* 51 (May 1989), 286–304; Thomas M. Holbrook-Provow, "National Factors in Gubernatorial Elections," *American Politics Quarterly,* 15 (October 1987), 471–83.

[5]Andrew D. McNitt and Jim Seroka, "Intraparty Challenges of Incumbent Governors and Senators," *American Politics Quarterly,* 9 (July 1981), 321–40.

years the overall success rate for incumbent governors seeking reelection has averaged about 75 percent. However, governors are somewhat more vulnerable to defeat than U. S. senators (whose reelection rate is 85 percent) or House members (whose reelection rate is over 90 percent).[6] Occasionally governors are defeated, and it is interesting to try to understand these failures.

Political folklore includes the belief that any governor who raises taxes during his or her term will be defeated for reelection. But a careful study of this notion shows only a weak connection between tax increase and electoral defeat for governors.[7] Most governors who raise taxes and then seek reelection are successful! Frequently, however, those who are defeated *blame* their loss on raising taxes.

Economic conditions occasionally hurt an incumbent governor seeking reelection. Although the national economy is an important factor in presidential elections, adverse economic conditions do less harm to incumbent governors.[8] Many voters see the economy as a national issue and governors are not blamed for recessions.

CAMPAIGNING   Modern gubernatorial campaigns are quite professional: They usually involve professional public relations organizations, experienced mass media and television advertising firms, professional polling and political consultants, and sophisticated direct mail and fund-raising techniques. (See "Professional Mass Media Campaigns" in Chapter 5.) Party organizations and amateur volunteers play a very limited role in most modern campaigns in the states. The traditional barnstorming, stump-speaking, hand-shaking, and door-to-door canvassing campaigns have largely disappeared. Candidates still do these things, but the focus of the campaign is on media advertising.

Of course, campaign themes and candidate "images" must be tailored to a state's political culture and tradition. Campaign "gimmicks" are increasingly popular, particularly in state elections. Gimmicks can be as varied as the minds of advertising specialists. An example of an especially successful gimmick was the "working days" of Governor Bob Graham of Florida. Graham is a Harvard-educated, millionaire lawyer and real estate developer from Miami, whose brief career in the Florida legislature was generally perceived as unproductive. But Graham was ambitious for higher office, and he and his professional consultants realized that he must develop an image with which working people could identify. So they selected as the campaign theme for his gubernatorial race: "Bob Graham—Working for Governor," and Graham undertook during the campaign to work a full day at each of 100 different jobs. Graham's television ads showed him collecting garbage, picking oranges, herding dairy cows, and so forth, and he garnered a great deal of local television time with these colorful media events. Critics argued that Graham's

---

[6]Peverill Squire and Christina Fastnow, "Comparing Gubernatorial and Senatorial Elections," *Political Research Quarterly*, 47 (September 1994), 703–20.

[7]Susan L. Kane and Richard F. Winters, "Taxes and Voting: Electoral Retribution in the American States," *Journal of Politics*, 55 (February 1993), 22–40.

[8]Patrick J. Kenney, "The Effect of State Economic Conditions on the Vote for Governor," *Social Science Quarterly*, 64 (March 1983), 154–62.

"working days campaign" were the only days of his life that he had ever worked. But this campaign gimmick was so successful that he continued his well-publicized working days even after he won the governorship. After two terms in the state capital, Graham easily won a seat in the U.S. Senate.

MONEY   Modern mass media campaigns—with professional media advertising, opinion polls, direct mail persuasion, political consultants—are very costly. In the 1950s a typical gubernatorial campaign cost between $100,000 and $200,000; today a typical gubernatorial campaign costs $2 million to $5 million in small states and $10 million to $20 million or more in the larger states. Television advertising is the major reason for increased costs. Candidates for governor should expect to spend between $2 and $10 *per vote.*

Although money cannot buy a governorship, it is important to realize that (1) no one can mount a serious gubernatorial campaign without either personal wealth or strong financial backing by others, and (2) the heavier-spending candidate wins in two out of three elections. Most states require public reporting of campaign contributions and expenditures, and most states place limits on contributions by individuals and groups. Nonetheless, individuals can spend what they wish in order to express their personal political preferences separate from official campaigns; fund-raising political action committees (PACs) can multiply in number; and wealthy candidates can spend as much of their own money as they wish on their own campaigns. (See Chapter 5.)

POLITICAL AMBITIONS   Historically, presidents were chosen from among the ranks of America's state governors, particularly the governors of the larger states. During the cold war, the importance of international affairs in American politics detracted somewhat from the popular image of the governorship as the steppingstone to the presidency. Governors tend to be associated with domestic rather than foreign policy questions. Men such as Truman, Nixon, McGovern, Humphrey, Kennedy, Goldwater, and Johnson found the United States Senate a good place to promote their campaigns for vice-presidential and presidential nominations. For a while, scholars attributed the decline in the number of governors selected as presidential candidates to a general decline in the popularity of governors.

But in recent years, distrust of "the government in Washington" and the low esteem of Congress in the eyes of the general public have improved the presidential fortunes of governors. Georgia Governor Jimmy Carter skillfully exploited his image as an "outsider" in his successful 1976 presidential campaign. And Ronald Reagan, whose only political experience was his two terms as governor of California, reaffirmed the importance of governors in presidential politics. Massachusetts Governor Michael Dukakis lost to George Bush in 1988. (Bush had no experience in state government; he won election to Congress for two terms and then served in appointed federal posts—ambassador to China, UN ambassador, CIA director, vice-president.) But the end of the cold war brought domestic issues to the forefront of the nation's political agenda. The focus on the economy in 1992, and continuing popular distrust of Congress, paved the way for the presidential election of Arkansas Governor Bill Clinton.

PARTY TIDES   Party fortunes ebb and flow in American politics. (See "Republican and Democratic Party Fortunes" in Chapter 5.) A Republican tide swept the nation in 1994; not a single Republican incumbent governor, U.S. senator, or House member lost anywhere in the nation. For the first time in thirty years Republicans captured a majority of the nation's governorships, including eight of the nation's ten largest states.[9] Perhaps the most prominent Democratic governors ousted in 1994 were New York's Mario Cuomo and Texas' Ann Richards.

"Too Liberal, Too Long" was the campaign slogan of Republican candidate George Pataki in his successful bid to unseat three-term New York Democratic Governor Mario Cuomo. Cuomo had first been elected governor in 1982, and he had twice been considered a leading candidate for the Democratic presidential nomination. Throughout his first two terms, he had maintained public approval ratings upwards of 70 percent. He was rated highly for "leadership," "caring," and "honesty." But by 1994, more than 60 percent of New Yorkers responded in surveys that Cuomo had been governor "too long." His disapproval ratings climbed well above his approval ratings during his third term. His opposition to the death penalty upset many voters; crime was regularly named as "the number one problem facing New York state." George Pataki was a little-known state senator, who won the GOP nomination with the support of Senator Alfonse D'Amato. Much of Pataki's support came from voters who simply "disliked" Cuomo or believed it was "time for a change."

Texas has a rich Democratic history; it did not elect its first Republican governor until 1978 (although a Republican served as governor during the post–Civil War "reconstruction" era). So when the colorful Democratic governor, Ann Richards, announced the opening of her reelection campaign in 1994, in the midst of a strong economy, there were high hopes in Democratic circles that the statehouse would remain in their hands. But Republican strength had been growing over time, and the Republican nominee was George W. Bush, son of the former Texas congressman and U.S. president (who had easily won the state's presidential electors in both 1988 and 1992). Bush won by a surprising margin, 53 to 46 percent, in an election that saw a record turnout of 4.4 million voters in a gubernatorial contest. Richards won a very slight majority of women voters, and won heavy majorities of black, Hispanic, and self-identified liberal voters. But Bush won 80 percent of the votes of self-identified "conservatives," and he won 58 percent of all male voters.

EXECUTIVE POWER IN STATE GOVERNMENT

Frequently we speak of "strong" and "weak" governors. Yet it is difficult to compare the power of one governor with that of another. To do so, one must examine the constitutional position of governors, their powers of appointment and removal over state officials, their ability or inability to succeed themselves, their powers over the state budget, their legislative influence, their position in their own party and its position in state politics, and their influence over public opinion in the state.

---

[9]California (R–Wilson), Texas (R–Bush), New York (R–Pataki), Florida (D–Chiles), Pennsylvania (R–Ridge), Illinois (R–Edgar), Ohio (R–Voinovich), Michigan (R–Engler), New Jersey (R–Whitman), North Carolina (D–Hunt).

GOVERNORS, WEAK AND STRONG   In many ways the organization of American state government resembles political thinking of earlier historical eras. Jacksonian "popular democracy" brought with it the idea that the way to ensure popular control of state government was to elect separately as many state officials as possible. The Reform movement of the late nineteenth and early twentieth centuries led to merit systems and civil service boards, which further curtailed the governor's power of appointment. Many important state offices are governed by boards or commissions whose members may be appointed by the governor with the consent of the state senate but for long overlapping terms, which reduces the governor's influence over members of these boards and commissions. Not all of these trends were experienced uniformly by all fifty states, and there are considerable variations from state to state in the powers that governors have over the state executive branch. Today there are over 300 separately elected executive branch officials in the fifty states (see Table 7–3). Only Maine, New Hampshire, and New Jersey have a single statewide elected official, the governor.

EXECUTIVE REORGANIZATION   Modern public administration generally recommends a stronger governor and more centralized state executive branch. Reform and reorganization proposals usually recommend (1) four-year terms for governors with the ability to succeed themselves; (2) the elimination of many separately elected state ex-

Table 7–3
STATES WITH ELECTED EXECUTIVE OFFICIALS

Governor	50
Lieutenant Governor	42
Attorney General	43
State Treasurer	38
Secretary of State	36
State Auditor	25
Superintendent of Education	16
Agriculture Commissioner	12
Public Service Commission	9
Controller	10
Insurance Commissioner	8
Land Commissioner	5
Labor Commissioner	4
University Regents	5
Education Board	11
Railroad Commission	2
Others	
Board of Education	California
Elections Commissioner	Louisiana
Highway Commissioner	Mississippi
Tax Commissioner	North Dakota
Adjutant	South Carolina

Source: Book of the States, 1994–95.

ecutive officials and limiting the statewide ballot to governor, lieutenant governor, and attorney general; (3) elimination of boards and commissions as heads of agencies and their replacement by single, removable gubernatorial appointees; and (4) the consolidation of many state agencies into larger departments reporting directly to the governor. However, states have been slow to adopt these reforms.

POLITICAL OPPOSITION TO REORGANIZATION   Separately elected officials and independent boards and officials will be around for a long time. Political parties and public officials develop a stake in the continued existence of these elected offices. Moreover, many interest groups prefer to be governed by boards and commissions or separately elected officials. They feel they have more influence over these independent offices than those that come directly under a governor's authority. Interest groups, from educational administrators and teachers' unions, to the agriculture, insurance, real estate, and public utility industries, prefer to have direct access to executive officials. Incumbent officeholders are usually able to rally their client groups to defeat reorganization proposals that threaten their office.

TENURE POWER   Another component of a governor's influence is the ability or inability to succeed him- or herself in office. Governors with the highest "tenure power" are those who are elected for a four-year term and are permitted to succeed themselves indefinitely (see Table 7–4). Governors with the lowest "tenure power" are those who have only two-year terms. The Twenty-Second Amendment to the U.S. Constitution restricts executive tenure at the presidential level to two terms, and most states now have similar restrictions on their governors.

THE GOVERNOR'S MANAGERIAL POWERS

Governors are chief executives; they are supposed to manage state governmental bureaucracies. But aside from interviewing occasionally in response to a crisis, governors generally turn over their management chores to others. According to political scientist Alan Rosenthal, governors downplay their managerial role and avoid expending energy and power on management because "greater rewards derive from the pursuit of other functions—formulating policy, building popularity and support among the public, helping develop the state economy."[10] Managing the state bureaucracy is generally left to the governor's staff and department heads.

APPOINTMENT POWERS   Perhaps the most important managerial power is the power to appoint subordinate officials. Appointment of subordinates does not guarantee their responsibility, but there is a greater likelihood that an official appointed by a governor will be someone whose values coincide with those of the governor. Of course, gover-

---

[10]Alan Rosenthal, *Governors and Legislatures: Contending Powers* (Washington, DC: CQ Press, 1990), p. 170.

Table 7–4
TENURE PROVISIONS FOR GOVERNORS

Four-Year Term, No Restrictions on Reelection

Connecticut	Minnesota	Rhode Island
Idaho	Montana	Texas
Illinois	New York	Utah (3 terms)
Iowa	North Dakota	Wisconsin
Massachusetts		

Four-Year Term, Restricted to Two Terms

Alabama	Kentucky	North Carolina
Alaska	Louisiana	Ohio
Arizona	Maine	Oklahoma
Arkansas	Maryland	Oregon
California	Michigan	Pennsylvania
Colorado	Mississippi	South Carolina
Delaware	Missouri	South Dakota
Florida	Nebraska	Tennessee
Georgia	Nevada	Washington
Hawaii	New Jersey	West Virginia
Indiana	New Mexico	Wyoming
Kansas		

Four-Year Term, Consecutive Reelection Prohibited

Virginia

Two-Year Term, No Restrictions on Reelection

New Hampshire	Vermont

Source: Book of the States, 1994–95

nors are subject to many different pressures in exercising their appointing power; often they must pay off political debts or win the support of a political faction by their selections. Salary limitations and the shortness of tenure make it exceedingly difficult to find capable people for positions of high responsibility in state government. However, it is safe to infer that governors who can name their major department heads are stronger than governors who cannot.

COMPARING APPOINTIVE POWERS   It is possible to compare the managerial powers of governors in the fifty states by observing how many department heads the governors themselves can appoint. The *Book of the States* lists forty-six managerial functions in state government and how the heads of these functions are selected. The functions are:

Adjutant general	Employment services	Parks and recreation
Administration	Emergency management	Personnel
Agriculture	Energy	Planning
Banking	Environment	Postaudit
Budget	Finance	Preaudit
Civil rights	Fish and game	Public library
Commerce	General services	Public utility regulation
Community affairs	Health	Purchasing
Comptroller	Highways	Revenue
Computer services	Historic preservation	Social services
Consumer affairs	Insurance	Solid waste
Corrections	Labor relations	State police
Economic development	Licensing	Tourism
Education, higher	Mental health	Transportation
Education, public schools	Natural resources	Welfare
Elections administration		

Not all states have separate agencies for each of these managerial functions; on the contrary, many functions are combined in larger departments.

If the agency head is separately elected by the people (as are most attorneys general, treasurers, and secretaries of state), then the governor has little direct control over them. If the governor can appoint an agency head *without* the need for legislative approval, we can say that the governor has stronger appointive powers than if legislative confirmation of appointment is required. Indeed, agency heads themselves tend to evaluate the governor's influence largely in terms of his or her ability to appoint them to office.[11]

We have classified the states according to the number of functions over which the governors have direct control (see Table 7–5). States that have had major constitutional revisions in recent decades, such as New York and Illinois, tend to give their governor strong appointive powers. This is a reflection of the extent of management reform in these states.[12] At the other extreme, Florida's governor has weak appointive powers, not only because the secretary of state, attorney general, secretary of agriculture, superintendent of public instruction, treasurer and insurance commissioner, and controller are popularly elected, but also because major departments are headed by boards on which the governor has only one vote. Florida calls this its "cabinet system."

STATE CABINETS   State cabinets, composed of the heads of the major executive departments, advise the governors in over half of the states. Indeed, in Florida, Colorado, and New Jersey the cabinet is recognized in the state constitution and given more than just advisory powers. But most cabinets meet at the governor's discretion and function more or less in the fashion of the president's cabinet in the national government.

---

[11]F. Ted Hebert, Jeffrey L. Brudney, and Deil S. Wright, "Gubernatorial Influence and State Bureaucracy," *American Politics Quarterly,* 11 (April 1983), 243–64.

[12]See Keith J. Muller, "Explaining Variation and Change in Gubernatorial Power," *Western Political Quarterly,* 85 (September 1985), 424–31.

Table 7–5
APPOINTIVE POWERS OF GOVERNORS

Very Strong	Strong	Moderate	Weak	Very Weak
Connecticut	Arkansas	Georgia	Alaska	Florida
Delaware	California	Kansas	Arizona	Mississippi
Hawaii	Colorado	Louisiana	Alabama	South Carolina
Kentucky	Illinois	Maine	Idaho	Texas
Massachusetts	Indiana	Michigan	Missouri	
Minnesota	Iowa	Montana	Nevada	
New Jersey	Maryland	Nebraska	New Mexico	
New York	Ohio	New Hampshire	North Dakota	
North Carolina	South Dakota	Rhode Island	Oklahoma	
Pennsylvania		Utah	Oregon	
Tennessee			Washington	
Vermont			Wisconsin	
Virginia			Wyoming	
West Virginia				

Source: Calculated from information provided in *Book of States, 1994–95.*

REMOVAL POWERS   Restrictions on governors' powers of appointment are further complicated by restrictions on their powers of removal. A common statutory or constitutional provision dealing with governors' removal powers states that removal must be "for cause only"; that is, governors must provide a clear-cut statement of charges and an opportunity for an open hearing to the employee they are trying to oust. This process is often unpleasant, and governors seek to avoid it unless they have strong evidence of incompetence, fraud, or mismanagement. When a governor's removal powers are limited "for cause only," it is next to impossible to remove a subordinate for policy differences. A governor may request an officeholder to resign, even when the governor's removal power is limited, and such a request may be honored by the officeholder in preference to continued unhappy relationships with the governor's office or in fear of the governor's ability to mobilize public opinion against him or her. As a final resort, a determined governor with influence in the legislature can always oust an official by a legislative act, which abolishes the office or agency the official heads and replaces it with another; this device is sometimes called a "ripper bill."

COMPETING OFFICES   Certain elected state officials, notably the lieutenant governor and the attorney general, often use their positions to advance their own candidacy for the governorship or the U.S. Senate, thus creating further problems for a governor, particularly when their ambitions are in competition with his or her own. Lieutenant governors, of course, have few substantive duties in state government, other than the ceremonial one of presiding over the state senate. However, attorneys general have more influence—their legal opinions have great importance for a governor's program. Governors are often bound by statute to conform to the attorney general's legal opinion in interpreting state laws and constitutions.

DECLINE IN PATRONAGE   Patronage was once a major source of power for state governors. As late as the 1960s almost half of all state jobs were filled by the governor or the governor's patronage advisors from the ranks of "deserving" party workers. Party organizations were sustained with jobs in tax collection, licensing, parks, commerce, agriculture, welfare, and especially highways. The governor's office would "clear" appointments with party county chairpersons throughout the state, and patronage appointees were expected to work for the party organization at election time. Often state patronage employees held party posts themselves. Patronage was especially widespread in the older, two-party states of the East and Midwest.

However, patronage declined over the years; today more than three-quarters of all state jobs throughout the nation are covered by civil service or merit rules. In some states nearly all state workers are covered by civil service, and patronage is limited to boards, commissioners, policy-making offices, university trusteeships, and judicial posts. The patronage system was always awkward to administer; many lower-paid menial jobs were unattractive to party workers. As the influence of parties declined in electoral politics (see "American Political Parties in Disarray" in Chapter 5), governors themselves came to view patronage systems as more of a burden than a benefit to their administrations. Reform governors capitalized on the public's image of patronage as corrupt, and they gradually expanded civil service coverage. Federal law required civil service protection for state employees administering major federal grant programs in public assistance, unemployment insurance, and health care. Finally, the federal courts began to strike at patronage systems with decisions preventing governments from firing their employees for partisan political reasons.[13]

CIVIL SERVICE   Civil service systems, particularly those administered by independent civil service commissions, significantly reduce executive control over program administration. There is a persistent tendency for civil service systems to be routine, mechanical, and unimaginative. Job classification schemes, to which recruitment, qualifications, and pay scales are closely tied, become so rigid with time that executives have little flexibility in recruiting really talented people to state government. Executives whose authority to promote, hire, and fire their employees is severely curtailed can hardly be expected to obtain maximum effort and cooperation from their employees. Even the public administration experts, who originally supported the civil service movement and the removal of state jobs from the governor's authority, are beginning to recommend that the power over personnel administration be returned to the governor.

UNIONIZATION   Unions among civil service employees further complicate executive control of the bureaucracy. Today, over half of all state and local government employees are unionized. The largest public employee union in the states is the American Federation of State, County, and Municipal Employees (AFSCME). Collective bargaining agreements usually stipulate salaries and wages, pensions and benefits, grievance procedures, and seniority. These restrict executive authority over dismissals, layoffs, reorganization, elimination of positions, merit and incentive pay plans, and other actions affecting personnel.

---

[13]*Elrod v. Burns*, 96 S. Ct. 2673 (1976); *Branti v. Finkel*, 445 U.S. 507 (1980).

Unionization varies from state to state. Some state governments do not bargain collectively with their employees.[14] In these states union membership is small and state employees are not covered by labor–management contracts. Other states recognize employee unions and bargain collectively with them. In these states union membership may encompass up to 80 percent of all state employees (Hawaii, New York, and Rhode Island), and most state employees are covered by labor–management contracts.

THE GOVERNOR'S FISCAL POWERS

The state budget is the most crucial policy document in state government. Governors' control over the state budget is perhaps their most formidable power. While the legislature must enact the state budget into law, and no state monies may be spent without a legislative appropriation, in practice the greatest amount of control over state governments rests with governors and their budget staff.

BUDGET MAKING   Budget making involves bringing together the requests of all existing state agencies, calculating the costs of new state programs, estimating the probable income of the state, and evaluating these costs and income estimates in the light of program and policy objectives. The final budget document is submitted to the legislature for its adoption as an appropriations bill. No state monies can be spent without a legislative appropriation, and the legislature can make any alterations in the state budget that it sees fit. Potentially, then, a legislature can control any activity of the state government through its power over appropriations, but as a practical matter, the legislature seldom reviews every item of the governor's budget. In practice, budgets tend to reflect the views of those responsible for their preparation, namely the governor.

The most common budgetary behaviors in the states are:

Agency heads consistently request higher funds.

Governors' budget staffers consistently reduce agency requests.

The governor consistently pursues a balanced budget at higher expenditure levels than the previous year.

Legislatures approve higher appropriations but try to blame the governor if higher taxes are required.

AGENCY PRESSURE   The pressure for budget increases comes from the requests of agency officials. Most agency officials feel compelled to ask for more money each year. Requesting an increase in funds affirms the significance and protects the status of agency employees, and it assures clientele groups that new and higher standards of service are being pursued aggressively. Requested increases also give the governor's office and the legislature something to cut that will not affect existing programs. The governor's budget staff generally recognizes the built-in pressure to expand budgets. The budget staff see them-

---

[14]In 1992 the noncollective bargaining state governments were Alabama, Arizona, Colorado, Georgia, Idaho, Kentucky, Louisiana, Maryland, Mississippi, Nevada, North Carolina, North Dakota, Oklahoma, South Carolina, Tennessee, Texas, Utah, Virginia, West Virginia, Wyoming. Council of State Governments, *Book of the States 1992–93*, p. 449.

selves as "cutters." Agencies press for budgetary expansion with better programs in mind, while the governor's budget staff tries to reduce expenditures with cost cutting in mind.

RELIANCE ON STAFF   Governors must rely heavily on their budget staffs, which may be located in the governor's office or in a separate department. The budget staff may be directed by the governor's political appointee, but it should include some experienced, professional, merit employees. The budget staff must work closely with the governor in handling agency requests and developing the all-important annual budget submission to the legislature. The governor's budget makers may be the most influential group of bureaucrats in state government.

"EARMARKING"   Governors have little influence over many items of state spending. Over 50 percent of state finances come from specially earmarked funds. It is quite common to earmark in state constitutions and laws certain funds for particular purposes, such as gasoline taxes for highways. The earmarking device provides certain agencies with an independent source of income, thus reducing the governor's control over operations. What is left, "general fund expenditures," is also largely committed to existing state programs, particularly welfare and education.

"UNCONTROLLABLES"   Governors typically campaign on platforms stressing both increased service and lower taxes. Once in office, however, they typically find it impossible to accomplish both and very difficult to accomplish either one. Often new programs planned by a governor must be put aside, because of "uncontrollable" growth in existing programs. For example, additional money may be required to educate more students who are entitled to an education under existing programs; or money must be found to pay the welfare benefits of additional clients or the Medicaid costs of additional patients "entitled" to care under existing laws. These entitlement programs constitute over three-quarters of state general fund appropriations.

BALANCING THE BUDGET   Unlike the federal government, most state budgets must be balanced. This means that the governor must submit to the legislature a budget in which projected revenues are equal to recommended expenditures. And the legislature must not appropriate funds in excess of projected revenues. There are, of course, many accounting devices that allow governors and legislatures to get around the balanced budget limitation—devices known as "blue smoke and mirrors." These include "off-budget" special funds, separate state authorities, capital budgets, and so on (see Chapter 18).

Nonetheless, balanced budget requirements are a major restraint on state spending. Indeed, often revenue "shortfalls"—revenues that fall below those estimated for the year in the state budget—force the governor to order painful midyear spending cuts. Only a few states allow deficits to be carried over into the next fiscal year. And these carryover deficits force governors and legislatures to be more conservative in their spending plans for the following year.[15]

---

[15]James E. Alt and Robert C. Lowry, "Divided Government, Fiscal Institutions, and Budget Deficits," *American Political Science Review,* 88 (December 1994), 811–28.

ECONOMIC CONSTRAINTS   The most important force affecting the budget is the state's economy. When the economy is healthy, state revenues go up. Given a projected increase in revenues, governors usually recommend new programs, expanded services, more aid to local government, and so on. Occasionally governors even recommend tax reductions, although spending increases are by far the favored response to projected revenue increases. In years of prosperity, governors and legislatures expand the activities of state government, without much concern about what to do when the economy takes a downturn: "Commitments are made and clienteles are created; however, should the economy take a turn for the worse, revenues will be insufficient to keep pace with promises and expectations."[16] Indeed, when the economy falters, governors must recommend tax increases, expenditure cuts, or some combination of both. Needless to say, these are very unpleasant choices for politicians.

THE GOVERNOR'S LEGISLATIVE POWERS

The responsibility for initiating major statewide legislative programs falls upon the governor. The governor's programs are presented to the legislature in various governor's messages and in the budget. While these instruments are only recommendations, the governor can set the agenda for debate with them, and "agenda setting" is an important power. The governor takes the initiative; legislators are on the defensive; if they do not act, they must explain why. Much of the governor's power over the legislature stems from his or her power over the policy agenda.

SETTING PRIORITIES   Governors are well-advised to limit their policy agenda to a few priority issues each year, rather than sending the legislature a smorgasbord of items without any unifying goal or theme. A governor wants to develop a strong "batting average"—a reputation for getting a high percentage of his or her recommendations enacted by the legislature. Submitting multiple proposals increases the chances for defeat. Submitting only a few high-visibility proposals, and concentrating energy and power on securing their passage, usually increases the ratio of bills passed to bills submitted. But it is often difficult for governors to select their priority issues from the host of recommendations that come to them from interest groups and executive agencies. Governors can expand their policy agenda in good economic times when there are more revenues to pay for new initiatives. But in recessionary times, governors are constrained to few if any new initiatives.

PROVIDING LEADERSHIP   "What does the governor want?" is a frequent question heard in legislative debate. Leadership requires the governor to do more than simply propose legislation. The governor must also "make it happen." Governors must rally public support, packaging their proposals in a way that people will understand and support. They must make speeches and public appearances and prepare news releases highlighting their proposals. This "outside" strategy must be integrated with an "inside" strategy to persuade legislators to support the program. Governors must carefully steer

---

[16]Rosenthal, *Governors and Legislatures*, p. 133.

their proposals through the legislative process—the committee system, floor proceedings, votes on amendments, conference committees, and final passage. They must develop good working relationships with the legislative leadership and then with the rank-and-file members. They must mobilize the support of interest groups behind their proposals. Finally, governors must be willing to compromise—to take "half a loaf" and declare victory. Governors must be flexible, accepting legislative amendments when necessary to preserve the major thrust of their program.

SPECIAL SESSION   Governors can increase pressure on legislatures to act on particular recommendations by calling special sessions. The governor can specify the topics that should be considered in the special session. This device can be particularly effective if the legislature has buried one of the governor's favorite programs in the regular session. Legislators do not like to be called back from their businesses to the state capitol for a special session, so even the threat of one may force them to pass the governor's program in the regular session. Of course, legislatures can defeat a governor's program even in special session, but their actions will be spotlighted.

VETOES   The governor's veto power is a major source of power within the legislature. Only in North Carolina does the governor have no veto power at all. In some states, the veto power is restricted by giving the governor only a short time to consider a bill after it has passed the legislature, by permitting a simple majority of legislative members to override the veto, or by requiring vetoed bills to reappear at the next legislative session. In other states, governors are given longer periods of time to consider a bill, and a two-thirds vote of both houses of the legislature is required to override a veto, rather than a simple majority. (See Table 7–6.)

The veto is often the governor's principal source of bargaining power in the legislature. Veto overrides by legislatures are rare. While the possibility of override gives the legislature "the last word" in theory, in practice few governors are so weak that they cannot garner at least one-third plus one of either house to sustain a veto. Only about 5 percent of bills passed by state legislatures are vetoed by governors, and governors are overridden on less than 10 percent of their vetoes. Of course vetoes are more common when a governor faces a legislature controlled by the opposition party.[17]

The *threat* of a veto may be a more important bargaining tool than the actual exercise of the veto. A governor can threaten to veto a bill with objectionable provisions before it reaches a floor vote. Governors can negotiate from a position of strength throughout the legislative process, shaping the bill to their preferences.

Occasionally legislatures may challenge governors to veto bills. This is more likely to occur with divided party control of state government—one party controls the legislature with a governor from the opposition party. The legislature can pass a popular bill opposed by the governor and then dare the governor to veto it. Even if the governor's veto is sustained, the majority party leaders in the legislature may feel they have created an issue for the next gubernatorial election. But this strategy usually guarantees a failure to get the bill enacted into law. Legislative leaders must decide whether they want the bill passed

[17]Charles Wiggins, "Executive Vetoes and Legislative Overrides in the American States," *Journal of Politics,* 42 (November 1980), 1110–17.

Table 7–6
GOVERNORS' VETO POWERS

Votes Required to Override Veto			Line-Item Veto on Appropriations Bills	
2/3	3/5	MAJORITY	LINE-ITEM VETO	NO LINE-ITEM VETO
Alaska	Illinois	Alabama	Alaska	Alabama
Arizona	Maryland	Arkansas	Arkansas	Indiana
California	Nebraska	Indiana	Arizona	Maine
Colorado	Ohio	Kentucky	California	Maryland
Connecticut	Rhode Island	Tennessee	Colorado	Nevada
Delaware			Connecticut	New Hampshire
Florida			Delaware	North Carolina
Georgia			Florida	Rhode Island
Hawaii			Georgia	Vermont
Idaho			Hawaii	
Iowa			Idaho	
Kansas			Illinois	
Louisiana			Iowa	
Maine			Kansas	
Massachusetts			Kentucky	
Michigan			Louisiana	
Minnesota			Massachusetts	
Mississippi			Michigan	
Missouri			Minnesota	
Montana			Mississippi	
Nevada			Missouri	
New Hampshire			Montana	
New Jersey			Nebraska	
New Mexico			New Jersey	
New York			New Mexico	
North Dakota			New York	
Oklahoma			North Dakota	
Oregon			Ohio	
Pennsylvania			Oklahoma	
South Carolina			Oregon	
South Dakota			Pennsylvania	
Texas			South Carolina	
Utah			South Dakota	
Vermont			Tennessee	
Virginia			Texas	
Washington			Utah	
West Virginia			Virginia	
Wisconsin			Washington	
Wyoming			West Virginia	
			Wisconsin	
			Wyoming	

Source: Book of the States, 1994–95.

(for which they must bargain with the governor for his or her signature) or whether they want an issue for the next election.

ITEM VETO   Most governors also have the power to veto particular items in a larger appropriations bill. This allows them to pick out particular legislative spending proposals (frequently labeled "turkeys" by unsympathetic governors) and veto those proposals without jeopardizing the entire budget. In states *without* the item veto, governors may be forced to accept many legislative spending proposals in order to get a budget passed.

The line-item veto is also a powerful weapon in the governor's arsenal. The line-item veto allows the governor to take legislators' pet budget items as hostage for their support on other unrelated legislation favored by the governor. Legislators who fail to support the governor risk losing their "turkeys." Trade-offs need not be explicit. Legislators who consistently oppose the governor's programs throughout the legislative session risk losing pork for their district when the governor goes through the appropriations acts line by line.

GOVERNOR–LEGISLATURE RELATIONS   For most governors, working with the legislature is considered the most difficult and demanding part of their job.[18] "Practically all governors regard their legislature as a problem and are happy when the legislature leaves town."[19] About half of all governors have had some legislative experience before becoming governor. They may have some friends and acquaintances left over from their legislature days. And they may have greater respect for the legislative branch and greater empathy with the concerns of legislators. But many governors have little sympathy or patience with the slow and complicated legislative process.

Frequently legislators resent the exalted role of the governor. As a New York legislator remarked about Governor Cuomo: "Relating to the governor is like relating to the Pope, except that the only thing you have to kiss on the Pope is his ring."[20] Legislatures do not want to appear to be pushed around by governors. Many legislators develop a loyalty to the institution itself; they wish to preserve the independence of the legislature.

What works with the legislature? Political scientist Alan Rosenthal provides some pointers; governors should

> *Stand tall.*   This entails not only the appearance of strength and decisiveness but a willingness to punish one's enemies.
>
> *Consult members.*   Inform legislators of plans and programs and listen to their concerns.
>
> *Talk turkey.*   Communicate in legislators' language of patronage and deals, give and take, reciprocity.
>
> *Rub elbows.*   Stay in personal contact with legislators on a regular basis.
>
> *Massage egos.*   Legislators like to share center stage with the governor, to be seen at bill signings, to be invited to dinner at the governor's mansion, to have the governor praise them in public.

---

[18]Thad Beyle and Robert Dalton, *Being Governor: The View from the Office.* (Durham, NC: Duke University Press, 1983), p. 135.

[19]Rosenthal, *Governors and Legislatures,* p. 69.

[20]Ibid, pp. 47, 294, 296–98.

DIVIDED GOVERNMENT: GOVERNOR VERSUS THE LEGISLATURE

Divided government, where one party controls one or both houses of the legislature and the other party controls the governorship, is increasingly frequent in American state politics. In recent years over half of the states have experienced divided party control (see Table 7–7). The election of Republican governors in southern states with heavily Democratic legislatures helps to explain increased occurrence of divided government in the states, as well as an increased tendency of voters everywhere to split their tickets. Republican governors are more likely to face Democratic-controlled legislatures than the reverse. But divided government itself has a major impact on executive–legislature relations.

PARTISANSHIP CUTS BOTH WAYS   Party works to the advantage of governors when their party has a majority in the legislature. The governor and a legislature controlled by the same party have an incentive to produce results. This is especially true in a competitive two-party state. There is still institutional rivalry, wherein governors contend with legislatures for policy leadership. But both have an interest in compiling a record of success that the voters can attribute to everyone running under the party label in the next election.[21] But when partisan differences are added to institutional rivalry, conflict rather than cooperation is more likely to characterize relations between governor and legislature.

CONFRONTING GRIDLOCK   A governor confronting opposition party control of the legislature must spend a great deal of time bargaining and compromising with legislative leaders of the opposition party. Governors must ensure that they keep their own party's legislators behind their proposals and then either work out accommodations

Table 7–7

DIVIDED PARTY CONTROL OF STATE GOVERNMENT

	1987–1989	*1989–1991*	*1991–1993*	*1993–1995*	*1995–1997*
Unified					
Governor and majority of both houses, same party	20	19	21	22	23
Divided					
Governor and majority of one or both houses, different parties	29	30	28	27	26
Total—49 states; Nebraska nonpartisan legislature excluded					

[21]See Kevin M. Leyden and Stephen A. Borrelli, "The Effect of State Economic Conditions on Gubernatorial Elections: Does Unified Government Make a Difference?" *Political Research Quarterly*, 48 (June 1995), 275–90.

with the opposition leadership or try to chip off enough votes from less loyal opposition members to win passage of their proposals. Neither is an easy task. Party activists, including legislators, differ on ideological grounds and policy issues. Moreover, the opposing party looks forward to defeating the governor in the next election. Often one or more opposition party aspirants for the governorship are sitting in the legislature. They seek to discredit the governor, not only during the election campaign, but during his or her entire term of office. Often the opposition party in the legislature will prefer that a needed bill go down to defeat just to hurt the governor's reputation. Only a very able governor can avoid gridlock with divided party control of state government.

IMPEACHMENTS AND INVESTIGATIONS

Impeachment is a *political* process, not a legal process. While state constitutions, like the U.S. Constitution, usually define an impeachable offense as "treason, bribery, or other high crimes and misdemeanors," the political errors of impeached officials are usually more important than their legal offenses.

IMPEACHMENT, TRIAL, AND REMOVAL   All state constitutions, except Oregon's, provide for the impeachment of elected state officials by the legislature. Impeachment proceedings are initiated in the lower houses of forty-seven states, in the unicameral legislature of Nebraska, and the upper house in Alaska. Impeachment trials are held in the upper houses in forty-five states, in a special court of impeachment in Nebraska, in the lower house in Alaska, in a special commission in Missouri, and in the senate and court of appeals in New York. Most states require a two-thirds vote to convict and remove an official.

These impeachment provisions are rarely used. There appear to have been only eighteen gubernatorial impeachments since the nation's birth and eight trial convictions. When Arizona Governor Evan Mecham was impeached and convicted by the state legislature in 1988, it was the first such event in nearly sixty years. Several other governors have resigned when threatened with impeachment.[22]

EVAN MECHAM OF ARIZONA   Arizona's flamboyant Governor Evan Mecham managed to offend virtually every important political interest group in his state in his first few months in office following his election in 1986. His political troubles began with his inauguration day announcement that he was cancelling the state's Martin Luther King Jr. Day holiday. His short-lived governorship was one long publicized "gaffe" after another. He publicly blamed working women for the high divorce rate; he told a Jewish audience that the United States was a Christian nation. Less than a year after his election, a recall petition succeeded in getting the necessary 400,000 signatures, and a recall election was scheduled for 1988. In the meantime the state's attorney general

---

[22]*Book of the States*, 1988–89, p. 27. Other twentieth-century impeachments and removals include New York Governor William Sulzer in 1913; Oklahoma Governor John Walton in 1923; and Oklahoma Governor Henry S. Johnson in 1929.

indicted the governor on a series of campaign law violations. Before these charges came to trial, the state house of representatives initiated impeachment proceedings for "high crimes, misdemeanors, and maleficence in office." Mecham did not choose to go quietly, even after the house voted for impeachment. He defended himself at a bitter senate trial, during which he argued that he had committed no illegal acts and that the charges represented a vendetta against him by the press and his political enemies. Mecham was convicted by bipartisan votes in the senate and removed from office. The secretary of state, Rose Mofford, a Democrat, immediately succeeded him. The recall election was cancelled. Later in criminal court, Mecham was *acquitted* of all of the charges of campaign law violations. The jury returned the verdict in less than three hours; several jurors reportedly hugged the ex-governor.

CRIMINAL INVESTIGATIONS   Criminal investigations have led to the demise of several governors. Former Tennessee Governor Ray Blanton was convicted in 1981 for crimes committed while in office; former Maryland Governor Marvin Mandel was convicted and later pardoned for crimes committed while in office. Governor Edwin Edwards of Louisiana was acquitted in 1986 in a criminal trial; the racketeering charges temporarily undermined his support with voters and he lost a close vote in the next gubernatorial election. However, in 1991 Edwards was again elected governor in a runoff against former Ku Klux Klan member David Duke. In 1993 Republican Governor Guy Hunt of Alabama was convicted of misusing inauguration funds by the state's Democratic attorney general. The state's constitution required removal from office of anyone convicted of a felony; Hunt was replaced by Jim Folsom, Jr., the son of former Alabama Governor "Big Jim" Folsom for whom the state's prison is named.

THE GOVERNOR AS POLITICAL LEADER

The formal powers of governors—tenure, appointment and removal, budgetary, and veto powers—are not the equivalent of political influence. These formal powers can only be translated into control over public policy, legislative output, and bureaucratic performance through a governor's use of his or her own political "clout." A landslide election that carries the governor's party into control of both houses of the legislature can overcome many formal weaknesses in a governor's powers. A politically resourceful governor enjoying widespread public popularity who can skillfully employ the media to his or her advantage can overcome many constitutional weaknesses in the office.

Governors spend more time meeting the general public, attending ceremonial functions, and working with the press and television than they do managing state government and working with the legislature. They focus on these public relations tasks not only to improve their chances for reelection, but also to give themselves the political clout to achieve their goals for state government. All fifty governors have press secretaries or public information offices, some with large staffs. Press conferences, policy announcements, and other media events are carefully orchestrated for maximum coverage in the nightly news and morning papers. Increasingly, state legislatures are creating their own media offices, but media coverage of state legislatures has traditionally been very sparse.

MEDIA ACCESS   Governors are the most visible figures in state politics. An attractive governor who is skillful in public relations can command support from administrators, legislators, local officials, and party leaders through public appeals to their constituents. Politicians must respect the governor's greater access to the communications media and hence to the minds of their constituents. Effective governors not only understand the broad range of issues facing their states but also are able to speak clearly and persuasively about them.

STATE MEDIA COVERAGE   However, press and television coverage of state government suffers a great deal of neglect.[23] Governors are far more visible in the media than state legislators, but the focus of the media—even local television news broadcasts—is on national events. In many states a majority of even *daily* newspapers do not have full-time reporters assigned to the state capital.

Overall, state media, like the national media, are biased in their partisan affiliation toward the Democratic party. Democratic governors generally get more positive coverage than Republican governors. But "media savvy"—skill in working with the media—is more important than partisan affiliation in winning good media coverage. A governor who "knows what's newsworthy," puts ideas across in brief "sound bites," makes timely use of widely reported events to get into the news, "hangs around the press area in the state capitol building," and cultivates good relationships with reporters is far more likely to garner favorable media stories than a governor who is "media shy," "tongue-tied," "standoffish," self-conscious, or who "hates the press," "blames the media," and thereby encourages an adversarial relationship with them.[24]

POPULARITY   Media access and the visibility it produces provide governors with the opportunity to promote their personal popularity with the citizens of the state. The legislature is seldom as popular as the governor. Even if individual legislators are popular in their districts, the legislature as an institution is rarely very popular. (See Figure 7–1. Statewide opinion polls do not track governors' popularity as closely as national polls track the president of the United States. But opinion in most large states is regularly surveyed by private, university, and newspaper polls.) All governors have press secretaries whose responsibility it is to develop and maintain a favorable media image for the governor. Many governors devote a great deal of their personal attention to this task—massaging the capital press, organizing media events, holding town meetings, traveling about the state, and so on. There may be some tendency for legislators and interest groups to avoid direct confrontations with a popular governor. Certainly a popular governor is in a better position to advance his or her program than an *un*popular governor. But the real problem is turning personal popularity into political power.

LEADERSHIP   Governors' reputations as leaders stem not only from what they say but also from what they do. Their reputations must include a capacity to decide issues and

---

[23]William T. Gormley, "Coverage of State Government in the Mass Media," *State Government, 52* (December 1979), 46–51.

[24]Thad Beyle, G. Patrick Lynch, and Donald Ostdiek, "Perceptions of the State Media." Paper presented at the Annual Meeting of the Southern Political Science Association, Atlanta, Georgia, 1994.

Figure 7–1
GOVERNOR AND LEGISLATURES: POPULARITY RATINGS IN FLORIDA

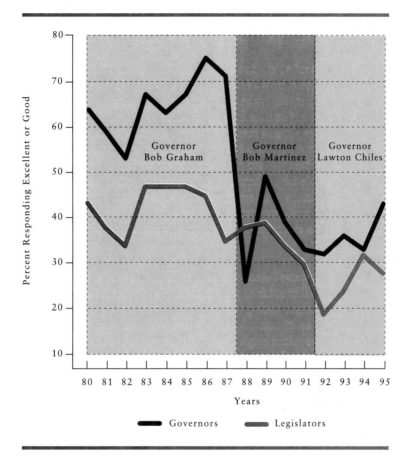

Q: "How would you rate the job [governor] [the Florida Legislature] is doing?"
Percent saying excellent or good, versus fair or poor or don't know.

to persist in the decision once it is made. A reputation for backing down, for avoiding situations that involve them in public conflict, or for wavering in the face of momentary pressures invites the governors' adversaries to ignore or oppose them. A sense of insecurity or weakness can damage a governor's power more than any constitutional limitation. Governors can also increase their influence by developing a reputation for punishing their adversaries and rewarding their supporters. Once the reputation as an effective leader is established, cooperation is often forthcoming in anticipation of the governor's reaction.

PARTY   Governors are also the recognized leaders of their state parties. In a majority of states, it is the governor who picks the state party chairperson and who is consulted on questions of party platform, campaign tactics, nominations for party office, and party finances. The amount of power that a governor derives from the position of party leader varies from state to state according to the strength, cohesion, and discipline of the state parties.

But there are limitations to the power that governors derive from their role as party leader. First of all, a governor cannot deny party renomination to disloyal members. Nominations are acquired in primary elections. Legislators must first consider constituency demands, not the voice of the governor. Second, the frequency of divided control, where governors face the legislature dominated by the opposition party, requires them to bargain with individuals and groups in the opposition party. If they have acquired a reputation for being too "partisan" in their approach to state programs, they will find it difficult to win over the necessary support of opposition party members. Finally, the use of patronage may make as many enemies as friends. There is an old political saying: "For every one patronage appointment, you make nine enemies and one ingrate."

EXPECTATIONS   It is difficult to generalize about the power of fifty state governors, especially when changes over time affect every state. Powerful governors (judged in terms of their accomplishments in office) may be followed by weak governors, even in the same state. Nevertheless, it is possible to offer a few generalizations from our studies.

First of all, governors, unlike legislators, are expected to *initiate* public policies. These policy initiatives are developed in messages, speeches, news releases, press conferences, public appearances, bills drafted by the governor's office or other executive agencies, and, most of all, in the state budget. The public *expects* governors to take the lead in solving state problems, whether they are really able to do anything about them or not.

Indeed, our second generalization is that governors do not really have sufficient powers in state government to deal effectively with the demands and expectations placed upon them. State constitutions not only divide power between the governor and legislature, but also divide the executive itself, with many separately elected officials.

OTHER EXECUTIVE OFFICES

LIEUTENANT GOVERNOR   The lieutenant governor's office in many states is looked upon as a campaign platform for the governorship. Lieutenant governors are said to have a four-year head start for the top job. The lieutenant governor's formal duties are comparable to those of the vice-president of the United States; in other words, lieutenant governors have relatively little to do. The two basic functions of the office are to serve in direct line of succession to the governor and replace him or her in the event of a vacancy in that office, and to be the presiding officer of the state senate. Since lieutenant governors generally have political ambitions of their own, they seldom make good "assistant governors" who will submerge their own interests for the success of the governor's administration. Unlike the vice-president, lieutenant governors are separately elected in most states and are sometimes members of the governor's opposition party. Some efforts have been made to reduce the boredom of the lieutenant governor's office by assigning them membership on various boards and commissions.[25]

---

[25]For a review of lieutenant governors' functions, see Daniel G. Cox, "The Subterranean Influence of Lieutenant Governors," paper presented at the Midwest Political Science Association Meeting, Chicago, 1993.

ATTORNEY GENERAL   The office of attorney general has more real powers and responsibilities than that of the lieutenant governor. Attorneys general are elected in forty-three states, and appointed in the other states, usually by the governor. Attorneys general are the chief legal counsel for their states. They represent the state in any suits to which it is a party. They act as legal counsel for the governor and for other state officials. The legal business of state agencies is subject to their supervision. The source of the attorney general's power comes from the quasi-judicial duty of rendering formal written opinions in response to requests from the governor, state agencies, or other public officials regarding the legality and constitutionality of their acts. These opinions have the power of law in state affairs unless they are successfully challenged in court. The governor and other officials are generally obliged to conform to the attorney general's legal opinion until a court specifies otherwise. Attorneys general render authoritative interpretations of state constitutions, laws, city ordinances, and administrative rulings.

The attorney general also has substantial law enforcement powers. Most states allow attorneys general to initiate criminal proceedings on their own motion, and nearly all states assign them responsibility for handling criminal cases on appeal to higher state courts or to federal courts. In some states the attorney general has supervisory powers over law enforcement throughout the state.

TREASURERS, AUDITORS, AND COMPTROLLERS   Most states have elected *treasurers,* and treasurers in other states are appointed by either the governor or the legislature. Treasurers are custodians of state funds: collecting taxes, acting as paymaster for the state, and administering the investment of state funds. The principal job of the treasurer is to make payments on departmental requisitions for payrolls and for checks to be issued to those who have furnished the state with goods and services. Generally, the department's requests for checks must be accompanied by a voucher showing the proper legislative authority for such payment. Requests for payment usually are accompanied by a statement from the auditor's or the comptroller's office that legislative appropriations are available for such payment. Thus, the treasurer's office works in close relation to another executive office of importance: that of auditor or comptroller.

The principal duty of the office of state *auditor* is that of assuring the legislature that expenditures and investment of state funds have been made in accordance with the law. This function is known as a "postaudit" and occurs after state expenditures have been made.

The primary duty of the office of the state *comptroller* is to ensure that a prospective departmental expenditure is in accordance with the law and does not exceed the appropriations made by the legislature. This "preaudit" occurs before any expenditure is made by the treasurer. Public administration experts consider the comptroller's job of preaudit to be an executive function, and they urge that the comptroller be appointed by the governor. On the other hand, the job of postaudit is essentially a legislative check on the executive, and students of public administration generally feel that the auditor should be elected or appointed by the legislature. However, there is still some confusion in state organizations about the separate functions of auditors and comptrollers—some auditors do "preauditing" and some comptrollers do "postauditing."

SECRETARY OF STATE   Another interesting state office is that of secretary of state. Thirty-six states elect secretaries of state. Like the lieutenant governor, the secretary of state has very little to do. Secretaries of state are the chief custodians of state records

TRIVIA
STATES AND THEIR CAPITALS

For each state we have listed the capital city and the largest city. You might try to identify these cities *without* first looking at their names.

State	Capital	Largest City
Alabama	Montgomery	Birmingham
Alaska	Juneau	Anchorage
Arizona	Phoenix	Phoenix
Arkansas	Little Rock	Little Rock
California	Sacramento	Los Angeles
Colorado	Denver	Denver
Connecticut	Hartford	Bridgeport
Delaware	Dover	Wilmington
Florida	Tallahassee	Jacksonville
Georgia	Atlanta	Atlanta
Hawaii	Honolulu	Honolulu
Idaho	Boise	Boise
Illinois	Springfield	Chicago
Indiana	Indianapolis	Indianapolis
Iowa	Des Moines	Des Moines
Kansas	Topeka	Wichita
Kentucky	Frankfort	Louisville
Louisiana	Baton Rouge	New Orleans
Maine	Augusta	Portland
Maryland	Annapolis	Baltimore
Massachusetts	Boston	Boston
Michigan	Lansing	Detroit

and, in the case of several states, "keepers of the great seal of the commonwealth." They keep many state documents filed in their office, including corporation papers. They also supervise the preparation of ballots and certify election results for the state. The keeping of documents and the supervision of elections does not involve much discretionary power, since these activities are closely regulated by law.

PERSONAL STAFF   All governors are permitted to maintain a small group of loyal, dedicated personal aides—the governor's staff. Many staff members previously worked in the governor's political campaign. Most work long hours in small offices for relatively low pay. Most are young. Most envision some sort of political career for them-

Minnesota	St. Paul	Minneapolis
Mississippi	Jackson	Jackson
Missouri	Jefferson City	St. Louis
Montana	Helena	Billings
Nebraska	Lincoln	Omaha
Nevada	Carson City	Las Vegas
New Hampshire	Concord	Manchester
New Jersey	Trenton	Newark
New Mexico	Santa Fe	Albuquerque
New York	Albany	New York
North Carolina	Raleigh	Charlotte
North Dakota	Bismarck	Fargo
Ohio	Columbus	Cleveland
Oklahoma	Oklahoma City	Oklahoma City
Oregon	Salem	Portland
Pennsylvania	Harrisburg	Philadelphia
Rhode Island	Providence	Providence
South Carolina	Columbia	Columbia
South Dakota	Pierre	Sioux Falls
Tennessee	Nashville	Memphis
Texas	Austin	Houston
Utah	Salt Lake City	Salt Lake City
Vermont	Montpelier	Burlington
Virginia	Richmond	Norfolk
Washington	Olympia	Seattle
West Virginia	Charleston	Charleston
Wisconsin	Madison	Milwaukee
Wyoming	Cheyenne	Casper

selves in the future; they believe the experience they are acquiring in the governor's office, and the contacts they are making, will help in their careers. The governor may have a chief of staff, an appointments secretary, a press secretary, a legal counsel, several speech-writers, one or more legislative aides, and perhaps some advisors in key policy areas—education, welfare, highways. These people are *not* civil service employees; their jobs depend directly on their value to the governor.

COURTS, CRIME, AND CORRECTIONAL POLICY

POLITICS AND THE JUDICIAL PROCESS

Courts are "political" institutions because they attempt to resolve conflicts in society. Like legislative and executive institutions, courts make public policy in the process of resolving conflict. Some of the nation's most important policy decisions have been made by courts rather than legislative or executive bodies. Federal courts have taken the lead in eliminating racial segregation, ensuring the separation of church and state, defining the rights of criminal defendants, guaranteeing individual voters an equal voice in government, and establishing the right of women to obtain abortions. These are just a few of the important policy decisions made by courts—policy decisions that are just as significant to all Americans as those made by Congress or the president. Courts, then, are deeply involved in policy making, and they are an important part of the political system in America. Sooner or later in American politics, most important policy questions reach the courts.

In resolving conflict and deciding about public policy, courts function very much like other government agencies. However, the *style* of judicial decision making differs significantly from legislative or executive decision making. Let us try to distinguish between courts as policy-making institutions and other legislative and executive agencies.

A "PASSIVE" APPEARANCE   First of all, courts rarely initiate policy decisions. Rather, they wait until a case involving a policy question they must decide is brought to them. The vast majority of cases brought before courts do not involve important policy issues. Much court activity involves the enforcement of existing public policy. Courts punish criminals, enforce contracts, and award damages to the victims of injuries. Most of these decisions are based upon established law. Only occasionally are important policy questions brought to the court. This "passive" character of the judicial process restricts the policy initiative of judges; neither legislators nor executives suffer from such restrictions.

SPECIAL RULES OF ACCESS   Courts also differ from other government agencies in that *access* to them is governed by a special set of requirements. An interested individual or group must have an attorney and sufficient money to bear the expense of the court suit. Courts must accept "jurisdiction," which means that a dispute must meet judicial criteria of a "case" or the courts cannot settle it. A case must involve two disputing parties, one of which must have incurred some real damages as a result of the action or inaction of the other. For example, individuals who object to the state welfare program cannot take their objections to a court unless they can show that the program inflicted some direct personal or property damage on them.

LEGAL PROCEDURES   The *procedures* under which judges and other participants in the judicial process operate are also quite different from procedures in legislative or executive branches of government. Facts and arguments must be presented to the courts in the specified manner. Generally these communications are quite formal, and legal skills are generally required to provide written briefs or oral arguments that meet the technical specifications of the courts. While an interest group may hire a public-relations firm to pressure a legislature, they must hire a law firm to put their arguments into a legal context. Decorum in courtrooms is rigorously enforced in order to convey a sense of dignity; seldom do legislatures or executive offices function with the same degree of decorum.

DECISIONS OF SPECIFIC CASES   Courts must limit their decisions to *specific cases*. While higher courts sometimes depart from particular cases and announce general policy positions, most courts refrain from general policy statements and limit their decisions to the particular circumstances of a case. Rarely do the courts announce a comprehensive policy in the way the legislature does when it enacts a law. Of course, the implication of a court's decision in a particular case is that future cases of the same nature will be decided the same way. This implication amounts to a policy statement; however, it is not as comprehensive as a legislative policy pronouncement, because future cases with only slightly different circumstances might be decided differently.

APPEARANCE OF OBJECTIVITY   Perhaps the most important distinction between judicial decision making and decision making in other branches of government is that judges must not appear to permit political consideration to affect their decisions. Judges must not appear to base their decisions on partisan considerations, to bargain, or to compromise in decision making. The *appearance of objectivity* in judicial decision making gives courts a measure of prestige that other governmental institutions lack. While it is true that judges have fewer direct ties with political organizations than legislators or governors, they hold political views just as everyone else, and they would be less than human if these views did not affect their decision. However, it is important that a large portion of the American public perceive judges as unaffected by personal considerations. Court decisions become more acceptable to the public if they believe that the courts have dispensed unbiased justice.

These distinctive features of the judicial process—a passive appearance, special rules of access, specialized legal procedures, decorum, focus on particular cases, and appearance of objectivity in decision making—help to "legitimize" the decisions reached by the courts; that is, they help to gain acceptance of these decisions.

FOUNDATION OF COMMON LAW   Legal traditions are influential in court decisions. English common law has affected the law of all of our states except Louisiana, which was influenced by the Napoleonic Code. English common law developed in the thirteenth century through the decisions of judges who applied their notions of justice to specific cases. This body of judge-made law grew over the centuries and is still the foundation of our legal system today. *Laws passed by legislatures take precedence over common law,* but the common law is applied by the courts when no statutory provisions are relevant. The degree to which statutory law has replaced common law varies among the states according to the comprehensiveness of state statutes and codes. Common law covers both criminal and civil law, although the common law of crimes has been replaced by comprehensive criminal codes in the states.

THE LAWYERING OF AMERICA

The United States is the most litigious society in the world. We are threatening to drown ourselves in a sea of lawsuits. Virtually every petty conflict finds its way into the courts.

The rise in the number of lawsuits in the United States corresponds to a rise in the number of lawyers. There were 285,000 practicing lawyers in the nation in 1960; by 1995 this figure had grown to over 850,000 (compared to 650,000 practicing physicians). The continuing search for legal fees by these bright professional people has brought an avalanche of civil liability suits in federal and state courts—about 15 million per year.

Lawyers are in business, and their business is conflict. Generating business means generating conflict. Just as businesses search for new products, lawyers search for new legal principles upon which to bring lawsuits. Lawyers have been successful over the years in expanding *tort* liability, that is, liability for damages incurred in a civil wrongdoing. Negligence is the most common civil wrongdoing or tort.

EXPANDED LIABILITY   Virtually any accident involving a commercial product can inspire a product liability suit. An individual who gets cut opening a can of peas can sue the canning company. Manufacturers must pay large insurance premiums to insure themselves against such suits and pass on the costs of the insurance in the price of the product. Municipal and state governments, once generally protected from lawsuits by citizens, have now lost most of their "immunity" and must purchase liability insurance for activities as diverse as recreation, street maintenance, waste collection, and police and fire protection. Real estate brokers may be sued by unhappy buyers and sellers. Homeowners and bar owners may be sued by persons injured by their guests. Hotels have paid damages to persons raped in their rooms. Coastal cities with beaches have been successfully sued by relatives of persons who drowned themselves in the ocean.

CONTINGENCY FEES   Many of these lawsuits are initiated by lawyers who charge fees on a contingency basis; the plaintiff pays nothing unless the attorney wins an award. Up to half of that award may go to the attorney in expenses and fees. Trial attorneys argue that many people could not afford to bring civil cases to court without a contingency fee contract.

THIRD-PARTY SUITS   Defendants in civil cases are not necessarily the parties directly responsible for damages to the plaintiff. Instead, wealthier third parties, who may indirectly contribute to an accident, are favorite targets of lawsuits. For example, if a drunk driver injures a pedestrian, but the driver has only limited insurance and small personal wealth, a shrewd attorney will sue the bar that sold the driver the drinks, instead of the driver. Insurance premiums have risen sharply for physicians seeking malpractice insurance, as have premiums for recreation facilities, nurseries and day care centers, motels, and restaurants.

"PAIN AND SUFFERING" AND "PUNITIVE" AWARDS   Awards in liability cases, sometimes running into tens of millions of dollars, cover much more than the doctor bills, lost wages, and cost of future care for injured parties. Most large damage awards are for *pain and suffering*. Pain and suffering awards are *added* compensation for the victim, beyond actual costs for medical care and lost wages. So also are punitive damage awards, multiples of the actual damages designed to deter and punish persons or firms found to be at fault.

"JOINT AND SEVERAL" LIABILITY   Moreover, a legal rule known as *joint and several liability* allows a plaintiff to collect the entire award from any party that contributed in any way to the accident, if other defendants cannot pay. So if a drunk driver crosses a median strip and crashes into another car leaving its driver a cripple, the victim may sue the city for not placing a guard railing in the median strip. The rule encourages trial lawyers to sue the party "with the deepest pockets," that is, the wealthiest party rather than the party most responsible for the accident. Unsophisticated juries can be emotionally manipulated into granting huge damage awards, especially against businesses, municipalities, and insurance companies.

TORT REFORM   Reforming the nation's liability laws is a major challenge confronting the nation's state governments. The most common reform proposals are capping the award for "pain and suffering" at $250,000 or $500,000; eliminating punitive damage awards; restricting the fees that lawyers can subtract from a victim's award; and ending the rule of "joint and several" liability. Perhaps the simplest reform is a "loser pays" law—a requirement that the losing party in a civil suit pay the legal fees of the winner. This would discourage frivolous suits that are often designed to force innocent parties to pay damages rather than incur even higher costs of defending themselves.

Many of these reforms are currently being considered by state legislatures across the country. The reform movement can count on support from some normally powerful groups—the insurance companies, product manufacturers, physicians and hospitals, and even municipal governments. But a major obstacle remains the trial lawyers, who are disproportionately represented in state legislatures (see Chapter 6). The American Trial Lawyers Association is bitterly opposed to reform, and they are active in every state legislature as well as Congress. The American Trial Lawyers Association was successful in defeating major liability law reform in Congress in 1995, even though the Republican "Contract with America" in the midterm Congressional election of 1994 had included a pledge to do so.

THE NEW JUDICIAL FEDERALISM

The Supremacy Clause of the U.S. Constitution (Article VI) ensures that the federal constitution supercedes state constitutions and binds the judges in every state. State constitutions cannot deny rights granted by the U.S. Constitution, and state courts may not limit federal constitutional guarantees. But state constitutions cover many topics that are not addressed in the U.S. Constitution. More importantly, state constitutions may *add* individual rights that are not found in the U.S. Constitution, and state courts may interpret state constitutional language to *expand* individual rights beyond federal constitutional guarantees. We might think of the U.S. Constitution as a floor, providing minimum protection of individual rights for all persons in the nation. But state constitutions can build upon that floor, adding individual protections for persons within their state.

"Judicial federalism" refers to state courts' exercise of their authority to interpret their own state constitutions to guarantee protections to individual rights beyond those protected by the U.S. Constitution. While this authority has always existed under the American federal system, it was seldom exercised. Historically, the remedy to civil rights violations was to be found in federal court if it was to be found at all. Civil rights attorneys almost always turned to federal courts and the U.S. Constitution to seek protection for their clients. But the new activism of state courts in interpreting their own states' constitutional guarantees has begun to change this pattern. "Forum shopping" is a common strategy of lawyers; it involves the search for a court that will be most favorably disposed to one's argument. In the past, federal courts were almost always the forum of choice for civil rights claims. But recently state courts have become the forums of choice for some claims.

Many state constitutions contain rights not explicitly found in the U.S. Constitution. For example, various state constitutions guarantee rights to privacy, rights of political participation, rights of victims of crime, rights to public information, rights to work, rights to free public education, and equal gender rights (state ERAs).

Several state supreme courts have taken the lead in extending personal liberties under their own *state constitutions*, even when the U.S. Supreme Court has declined to incorporate these same liberties within the U.S. Constitution. Some examples include:

- The Florida Supreme Court decided that the state constitutional guarantee of the right of privacy struck down laws restricting abortion, although the U.S. Supreme Court had earlier upheld similar restrictions as permissible under the U.S. Constitution (*Webster* v. *Reproduction Health Services, 1989*).
- The Texas Supreme Court (and several other states' high courts) held that the state's constitutional guarantee of equality in public education required the system of local school finance to be replaced with statewide financing that equalized educational spending throughout the state. Years earlier, the U.S. Supreme Court had decided that the U.S. Constitution did *not* include a right to equal educational funding across school districts. (*San Antonio Independent School District* v. *Rodriguez, 1973*).
- New York and Pennsylvania Supreme Courts were the first to strike down state sodomy laws (anal sexual penetration) under privacy provisions of their state constitution, although the U.S. Supreme Court had upheld a Georgia sodomy statute ruling that "there is no constitutional right to commit sodomy" (*Bowers* v. *Hardwick, 1986*).
- California's Supreme Court ruled that the state's constitution compelled the state to pay for abortions for poor women, although the U.S. Supreme Court ruled that there was no requirement in the U.S. Constitution that states fund abortions (*Harris* v. *McRae, 1980*).
- The Massachusetts Supreme Court ruled that nude go-go dancing is a protected form of free expression under the state's constitution, even though the U.S. Supreme Court had ruled that it is *not* protected by the First Amendment (*Barnes* v. *Glen Theatre Inc., 1991*).

Judicial activism by state supreme courts encourages interest groups to bring cases and amici curiae briefs (written arguments submitted by "friends of the court") to state "forums." Of course, the state strategy has significant drawbacks compared to winning at the U.S. Supreme Court level; interest groups must proceed from state to state instead of dealing with the issue once and for all in the nation's highest court. The result may be a "Balkanization" of the law from state to state. But when interest groups fail to win *expansion* of their claim to constitutional protection from the U.S. Supreme Court, we can increasingly expect to see them active at the state supreme court level.[1]

THE STRUCTURE OF COURT SYSTEMS

State courts are generally organized into a hierarchy similar to that shown in Figure 8–1. The courts of a state constitute a single, integrated judicial system; even city courts, traffic courts, and justices of the peace are part of the state judicial system.

MINOR COURTS   At the lowest level are minor courts. These may be municipal courts, magistrates courts, police courts, traffic courts, family courts, and small claims courts. They are presided over by justices of the peace, magistrates, or police judges, not all of whom are trained in the law. These courts are concerned principally with traffic

---

[1]See Donald R. Souger and Ashlyn Kuersten, "The Success of Amici in State Supreme Courts," *Political Research Quarterly*, 48 (March 1995), 31–42.

Figure 8–1

THE STRUCTURE OF STATE AND LOCAL COURTS

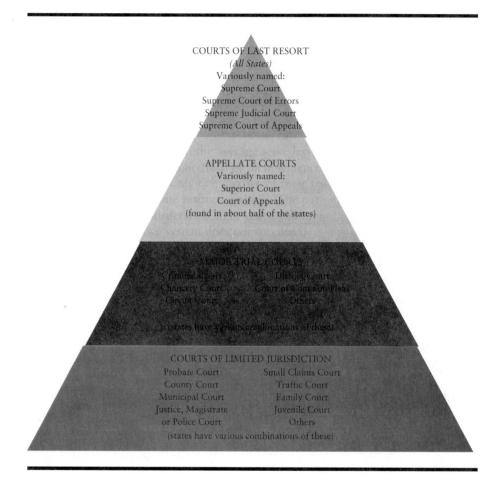

COURTS OF LAST RESORT
(All States)
Variously named:
Supreme Court
Supreme Court of Errors
Supreme Judicial Court
Supreme Court of Appeals

APPELLATE COURTS
Variously named:
Superior Court
Court of Appeals
(found in about half of the states)

MAJOR TRIAL COURTS
Criminal Court   District Court
Chancery Court   Court of Common Pleas
Circuit Court   Others

(states have various combinations of these)

COURTS OF LIMITED JURISDICTION
Probate Court   Small Claims Court
County Court   Traffic Court
Municipal Court   Family Court
Justice, Magistrate   Juvenile Court
or Police Court   Others
(states have various combinations of these)

cases, small claims, divorces and child custody, juvenile offenses, and misdemeanors, although they may hold preliminary hearings to determine whether a person accused of a felony shall be held in jail or placed under bond.

In many cities, municipal courts dispense justice in a "production line" style. Courtrooms are old, crowded, noisy, and confusing; witnesses, defendants, friends, relatives, all wait for hours for their cases to be called. Most cases are handled informally at the bench in discussions with the judge. Leniency is the rule with most judges, unless the face of the defendant is very familiar to the judge; then thirty-, sixty-, or ninety-day sentences may be imposed very quickly.

The growth of small claims courts throughout the country has helped millions of people who could not afford an attorney to bring a civil claim into the court with simplicity and low cost. Proceedings in these courts are very informal: Both sides simply "tell it to the judge." Buyers and sellers, landlords and tenants, creditors and debtors, can get a resolution to their case quickly and easily. Judge Wapner's television show, *The People's Court,* has popularized the functioning of small claims courts.

TRIAL COURTS   Major trial courts of general jurisdiction—sometimes called district courts, circuit courts, superior courts, chancery courts, county courts, criminal courts, or common pleas courts—handle major civil and criminal cases arising out of statutes, common law, and state constitutions. The geographic jurisdiction of these courts is usually the county or city; there are about 1,500 major trial courts in the United States. Juries are used in these courts, and judges are generally qualified in the law. These courts handle criminal cases involving felonies and important civil suits. Almost all cases decided by state courts originate in these major trial courts; trial courts make the initial decisions in cases carried to appellate and supreme courts and may also handle some appeals from minor courts.

SUPREME COURTS   Every state has a court of last resort, which is generally called the supreme court. These courts consist of three to nine judges, and most of their work is devoted to cases on appeal from major trial courts, although some states grant original jurisdiction to supreme courts in special types of cases. Since they consider questions of law rather than questions of fact, they sit without jury. State supreme courts are the most important and visible judicial bodies in the states. Their decisions are written, published, and distributed like the decisions of the U.S. Supreme Court. Judges can express their views in majority opinions, dissenting opinions, or concurring opinions. These courts get the most controversial cases and those with the most at stake, since these cases are most likely to be appealed all the way to the state's highest court. To relieve supreme courts of heavy case burdens, many of the more populous states maintain intermediate courts of appeal between trial courts and courts of last resort.

All state supreme courts stand atop their own state's judicial system. But some state supreme courts enjoy national reputations. Their decisions on points of law are often cited by other state supreme courts as well as by federal courts. Indeed, it is possible to identify judicial leadership among state courts by examining the number of times they are cited by other courts.[2] Supreme courts in California, New York, New Jersey, Massachusetts, and Pennsylvania enjoy superior reputations, followed by those in Illinois, Wisconsin, Washington, Michigan, Iowa, Colorado, and Minnesota.

APPEALS TO THE U.S. SUPREME COURT   Appeals from the state supreme courts may go directly to the U.S. Supreme Court on federal constitutional grounds. State supreme courts have the final word in the interpretation of *state* constitutions and laws. But many cases also raise federal constitutional questions, especially under the broad meaning of the "due process" clause and "equal protection" clause of the Fourteenth Amendment. So while most judicial appeals will end in state courts, the U.S. Supreme Court exercises general oversight through its power to accept appeals based on federal questions.

---

[2]See Gregory A. Caldereira, "On the Reputations of State Supreme Courts, *Political Behavior,* 5 (1983), 89.

THE MAKING OF A JUDGE

Political debate over methods of selecting judges in the states has been going on for many years. In writing the federal Constitution, the Founding Fathers reflected conservative views in establishing an independent federal judiciary, whose members were appointed by the president for life terms and were not subject to direct popular control. Jacksonian views of popular election were strong in the states, however, and today a majority of state judges are directly elected by the people on partisan or nonpartisan ballots.

Five different methods of selecting judges are found in the fifty states: *partisan election, nonpartisan election, appointment by the governor, legislative selection,* and the *Missouri plan* (see Table 8–1). Many states use more than one method.

Most states elect their judges, some in partisan elections and some in nonpartisan elections in which candidates for the bench do not carry party labels. In four states, judges are chosen by their legislatures, and in eight states, they are appointed by the governor. Other states have adopted the so-called Missouri plan, in which governors appoint judges on the recommendation of a select committee, and after the judge has been in office for a year or more, the voters are given the opportunity to retain or oust the appointed judge.

APPOINTMENT   The argument for selecting judges by appointment rests upon the value of judicial independence and isolation from direct political involvement. Critics of the elective method feel that it forces judges into political relationships and compromises

Table 8–1
METHODS OF JUDICIAL SELECTION IN THE STATES[a]

Partisan Election	Selection by Legislature	Nonpartisan Election	Governor Appointment	Missouri Plan
Alabama	Connecticut	Georgia	Delaware	Alaska
Arkansas	Rhode Island	Idaho	Hawaii	Arizona
Illinois	South Carolina	Kentucky	Maine	California
Mississippi	Virginia	Louisiana	Maryland	Colorado
New Mexico		Michigan	Massachusetts	Florida
New York		Minnesota	New Hampshire	Indiana
North Carolina		Montana	New Jersey	Iowa
Pennsylvania		Nevada	Vermont	Kansas
Tennessee		North Dakota		Missouri
Texas		Ohio		Nebraska
West Virginia		Oregon		Oklahoma
		Washington		South Dakota
		Wisconsin		Utah
				Wyoming

[a]States are listed by method of selection used for supreme court. In some states different methods of selection are used for different courts.

Source: Book of the States, 1994–95.

their independence on the bench. This is particularly true if judicial elections are held on a partisan rather than a nonpartisan ballot, where judges must secure nomination with the support of party leaders. Moreover, it is argued that voters are not able to evaluate "legal" qualifications—knowledge of the law, judicial temperament, skill in the courtroom, and so on. Hence, judges should be appointed, rather than elected by voters. Attorneys, bar associations, and judges themselves prefer an appointive method in which they are given the opportunity to screen candidates and evaluate legal qualifications prior to appointment.

Actually it is not possible to "take judges out of politics." Selection by appointment or by the Missouri plan removes the selection of judges from *party* politics but simply places the selection in different political hands. Instead of party leaders, the governor or the bar association become the principal actors in judicial selection. Party leaders are assumed to be familiar with the wishes of attorneys. It is not clear which system leads to "better" judges, or whether "better" judges are those more sensitive to community values or more trained in legal procedures.

INTERIM APPOINTMENT   Although most states elect their judges, in practice many judges come to the bench in elective states through the appointment procedure. The apparent paradox comes about because even in elective states, governors generally have the power to make interim judicial appointments when a judgeship is vacant because of the retirement or death of a judge between elections. Interim-appointed judges must seek election at the next regular election, but by that time they have acquired the prestige and status of a judge, and they are unlikely to be defeated by an outsider. Many members of the judiciary in elective states deliberately resign before the end of their term, if they are not seeking reelection, in order to give the governor the opportunity to fill the post by appointment. It is interesting to note that over half of the supreme court judges in states that elect their judiciary come to the bench initially by means of appointment. In practice, then, the elective system of judicial selection is greatly compromised by the appointment of judges to fill unexpired terms.

ELECTION   Few incumbent judges are ever defeated in running for reelection. The majority of judges seeking reelection are unopposed by anyone on the ballot, and very few judges seeking reelection are ever defeated. Voter interest in judicial elections is quite low.[3] Given a lack of information and interest in these election, incumbent judges have an enormous advantage. They have the prestigious title "Judge" in front of their names and some name recognition. In states with partisan elections, judges are occasionally defeated if their party loses badly.[4] But even in these partisan elections judges enjoy more stability and independence from popular control than do legislators or governors.

Very few voters know anything about judicial candidates. Indeed, one study suggests that fewer than 15 percent of voters *coming from the polls* remembered the name of one

---

[3]Philip L. Dubois, "Voter Turnout in State Judicial Elections," *Journal of Politics,* 41 (1979), 865–87.

[4]Philip L. Dubois, "The Significance of Voting Cues in State Supreme Court Elections," *Law and Society Review,* 13 (Spring 1979), 759–79.

candidate for the state supreme court, and fewer than 5 percent could remember the name of one candidate for county court.[5]

MISSOURI PLAN   The *Missouri plan* combines the elective and appointive systems of selection. The Missouri plan calls for a select committee of judges, attorneys, and laypeople to make nominations for judicial vacancies. (In various states these nominating committees are called the Judicial Nominating Commission, or the Judicial Council, or the Commission on Court Appointments, etc.) The governor appoints one of the committee's nominees to office. After the judge has served a specified time period (usually one year), the judge's name is placed on a nonpartisan ballot without any other name in opposition. "Shall judge (the name of the judge is inserted) of the (the name of the court is inserted) be retained in office? Yes ___ No ___." If voters vote yes, the judge is then entitled to a full term of office. If the voters vote no, the governor must select another name from those submitted by his nominating committee and repeat the whole process. In practice, a judge is hardly ever defeated in a retention election, in part for the same reasons that make it difficult to defeat an incumbent judge (see preceding discussion). Moreover, since "you can't beat somebody with nobody," running in a judicial retention election is the equivalent of being unopposed. Less than 1 percent of Missouri plan judges are voted out of office.[6] The effect is to place judicial selection in the hands of the judges or attorneys who compose the nominating committee and the governor, with only a semblance of voter participation. Reformers argue that the plan removes judges from politics and spares the electorate the problem of voting on judicial candidates when they know little about their professional qualifications.

WHETHER THE SELECTION METHOD MATTERS   There seems to be very little difference in the kinds of people (educational qualifications, experience, or social background) who are elevated to judgeships by different judicial selection methods (except that judges selected by state legislatures are more likely to have been state legislators).[7] However, there is some conflicting evidence on the question of whether state supreme courts selected by different methods show significant differences in judicial decision making. An early study found that courts selected by partisan or nonpartisan elections, appointed by governors or legislators, or selected under the Missouri plan, showed no clear and consistent trends in deciding for the state when it is a party to the case, or for criminal defendants, or for corporations, or for superior or inferior economic interests.[8] However, a more recent study found that in states with partisan competitive judicial elections, judges were more likely to support the death penalty.[9]

---

[5]Charles A. Johnson, Roger C. Schaefer, R. Neal McKnight, "The Salience of Judicial Candidates and Elections," *Social Science Quarterly*, 59 (September 1978), 371–78.

[6]William Jenkins, "Retention Elections: Who Wins When No One Loses," *Judicature*, 61 (August 1977), 79–86.

[7]Bradley Cannon, "The Impact of Formal Selection Processes on Characteristics of Judges—Reconsidered," *Law and Society Review*, 13 (May 1972), 570–93. An updated analysis showing that "no method of recruitment selects judges with substantially different credentials" is found in Craig F. Emmert and Henry R. Glick, "The Selection of State Supreme Court Judges," *American Politics Quarterly*, 16 (October 1988), 445–65.

[8]Burton M. Atkins and Henry R. Glick, "Formal Judicial Recruitment and State Supreme Court Decisions," *American Politics Quarterly*, 2 (October 1974), 427–49.

[9]Paul Brace and Melinda Gann Hall, "Studying Courts Comparatively," *Political Research Quarterly*, 48 (March 1995), 5–29.

RACE AND GENDER ON THE BENCH   While women comprise over half of recent law school classes, they have not yet acceded to the bench in the same proportions as men. In some states as many as one-fourth of trial judges are women, but fewer have risen to state appellate or supreme courts.[10] Even fewer blacks have won election or appointment as state court judges. While many state appellate and supreme courts have a single black member, blacks are underrepresented among judges relative to their proportions of state populations. Judicial selection method—executive appointment, partisan or nonpartisan election, merit—has *no* effect on racial or gender representation in state judiciaries.[11]

STATUS   Judges are rarely recruited from among the most prestigious high-paying law firms. Judges at the trial level may earn $80,000 to $100,000 salaries, and appellate and supreme court judges up to $125,000 or more. These incomes exceed those of the average attorney, but they are lower than salaries of senior partners at elite law firms. Moreover, judges are restricted in investments and opportunities for outside income by judicial ethics codes. While a judge enjoys status in his or her courtroom, much of the work at the trial court level is tedious and repetitious. Finally, many elite lawyers do not relish the political tasks required to secure a judgeship—garnering the support of the bar association's judicial selection panel, or attracting the nod of the governor, or worse, campaigning for the office in an election.

PARTY AFFILIATION   Traditionally Republicans fared better in capturing judgeships than in winning legislative seats or governors' chairs. Republicans did proportionately better in winning judgeships than in winning legislative seats or governorships. Most of the judges selected in nonpartisan elections refuse to identify themselves with a political party, as do nearly all the judges selected under the Missouri plan. Judges selected in partisan elections, of course, usually do not hesitate to identify themselves as Republicans or Democrats.

THE PSYCHOLOGY OF JUDGES   While most judges share a common background before coming to the bench—law school, practicing attorney, prosecutor—they are not always well prepared to assume judicial robes. The high esteem and prestige of the judiciary tend to obscure the negative aspects of the job: the requirement to remain aloof from courtroom battles, to isolate oneself, and to deal with the routines of judging. Apparently it takes several years for attorneys to adjust fully to their new roles as judges. Coping with the social and political *isolation* appears to be the most difficult problem.

> The longer you stay on the bench, the fewer close friendships you have with lawyers. . . . As you go on it becomes more and more restrictive.[12]

---

[10]See M. C. Henry, Jr., et al., *The Success of Women and Minorities in Achieving Judicial Office* (New York: Fund for Modern Courts, 1985); cited in Virginia Gray, Herbert Jacob, and Robert Albritten, eds., *Politics in the American States*, 5th ed. (Glenview, IL: Scott, Foresman, 1990), p 264.

[11]Nicholas O. Alozie, "Distribution of Women and Minority Judges," *Social Science Quarterly*, 71 (June 1990), 315–25.

[12]Quotations from Lenore Alpert, Burton M. Atkins, and Robert C. Ziller, "Becoming a Judge: The Transition from Advocate to Arbiter," *Judicature*, 62 (February 1979), 325–35.

Most judges are not paid as much as successful attorneys. After five or ten years on the bench, judges must often decide whether to step down and try to improve their personal finances or stay on with a comfortable, but not high, salary until retirement. "It's not a job for an ambitious person."

JUDICIAL DECISION MAKING: TRIAL COURTS

Social scientists know more about the behavior of federal court judges, and even state supreme court judges, than they know about the thousands of trial judges throughout the nation. This is largely because the decisions of higher courts are very visible and closely watched by lawyers and scholars. The actions of trial judges do not appear, at first glance, to have broad political impact. Nevertheless, trial court judges have enormous discretion in both civil and criminal cases. Perhaps the most dramatic and visible area of trial judge discretion is *sentencing*.

JUDICIAL DISCRETION   Trial court judges display great disparities in the sentences they give out in identical cases. As most good attorneys know, as well as many defendants with long criminal records, it matters a great deal who sits as the judge in your case. The outcome of *most* criminal cases is decided in "plea bargaining" between prosecuting attorneys and defense attorneys, where defendants agree to plead guilty to a lesser offense and the prosecution agrees not to press more serious charges or ask for stiffer penalties. However, the bargain must be approved by the judge. Wise attorneys know in advance what kinds of bargains different judges are likely to accept. It is *not* the determination of guilt or innocence that concerns judges, so much as the processing of cases, the acceptance of pleas, and sentencing. One study presented forty-eight trial judges in Wisconsin with the same hypothetical case: breaking and entering, one count, in which the defendant was a twenty-five-year-old, employed, white male without any previous record. The sentences ranged from eleven months in jail to thirty days of unsupervised probation.[13]

JUDICIAL ROLES   Different trial court judges see their roles in different ways. Four separate roles have been identified that seem to motivate county court judges.[14]

- The "game" judges: They perceive judging as difficult and challenging and get pleasure out of overcoming difficulties, meeting challenges, and presiding over a well-run courtroom. They have usually held office longer than other judges; they are more active in court proceedings; and they hand out the least severe penalties.
- The "program" judges: They enjoy delving into substantive issues and pursuing specific policy objectives. They are younger; they perceive their role as passive umpires whose main job is to keep the courtroom functioning smoothly; and their sentences are also fairly light.

---

[13]Austin Sarat, "Judging Trial Courts," *Journal of Politics,* 39 (May 1977), 368–98.
[14]Ibid.

- The "obligation" judges: They perceive their role in terms of duties, obligations, and ethical responsibilities. Obligation judges are older; they have no future political ambitions; they run a formal and businesslike courtroom; and they hand out fairly severe sentences.
- The "status" judges: They are motivated by the special prestige and status associated with the office of judge. They are young; they are ambitious for higher political or judicial office. They hand out the stiffest sentences of any judges.

The trial court judges have a difficult yet vital job to perform. They must oversee the record of a case to prevent "reversible" error—that is, to see that no legal errors have been made that would result in a conviction being reversed or appealed. At the same time they must deal with human problems at an individual level. As one judge put it: "A trial judge is a pioneer; he approaches each case without any help. He is the first to deal with problems. . . . Sometimes I don't think that appellate judges understand that."

JUDICIAL DECISION MAKING: STATE SUPREME COURTS

Conflict in state supreme courts, as measured by the number of divided opinions, is less frequent than in the U.S. Supreme Court. Dissenting votes are reported on more than half of all U.S. Supreme Court decisions, but state judges dissent in very few cases. Public disagreement is somewhat more frequent in competitive party states where judges of both parties are represented on the court.

ISSUES   Criminal appeals account for less than one-third of the workload of state supreme courts. The largest proportion of state supreme court decision making involves economic interests. A large number of cases involving economic interests result from the important role of the states in the allocation of economic resources. All states regulate public utilities, including water, electrical companies, gas companies, and public transportation companies. The insurance industry is state regulated. Labor relations and worker's compensation cases are frequently found in state courts. Litigation over natural resources, real estate, small-business regulations, gas, oil, lumber and mining, alcoholic beverage control, racing, and gambling reflects the importance of state regulation in these fields. There is a correlation between the kinds of economic litigation decided by state supreme courts and the socioeconomic environment of the state. Supreme courts in poorer, rural states spend more time on private economic litigation (wills, trusts, estates, contracts, titles, and so on), while courts in urban industrial states wrestle with corporate law and governmental regulation of large economic interests. Judges are also called upon to make decisions in political controversies—disputes over elections, appointments to government positions, and jurisdictional squabbles between governments.

PARTY   What is the impact of the party affiliation of the judges in court decision making? Party affiliation probably has little impact in decisions in lower trial courts, where much of the litigation has little to do with policy making. However, several early studies showed that party affiliation tended to correlate with state supreme court decision making.[15] Democratic judges tended to decide more frequently (1) for the administrative agency in business regulation cases; (2) for the claimant in unemployment compensation; (3) for the government in tax cases; (4) for the tenant in landlord–tenant cases; (5) for the consumer in sale-of-goods cases; and (6) for the employee in employee injury cases. And a more recent study showed that Democratic judges, especially those appointed rather than elected and those serving for long terms, were more likely to oppose the death penalty than Republican judges.[16]

ETHNICITY   What is the effect of social and ethnic group membership on judges' decisions? Judges, like other decision makers, generally belong to higher social and economic groups; white, Anglo-Saxon Protestants are disproportionately represented among state judges. One study found that judges who were members of ethnic minority groups in America were more likely to decide (1) for the defense in criminal cases, (2) for finding a constitutional violation by police or prosecutors in criminal cases, and (3) for the wife in divorce cases, than were judges with white, Anglo-Saxon backgrounds.[17]

JUDICIAL ACTIVISM VERSUS RESTRAINT   Great legal scholars have argued the merits of activism versus self-restraint in judicial decision making for more than a century.[18] The traditional restraint of state courts has been increasingly challenged in recent years by activism on the part of some state courts. As noted earlier, some state supreme courts have decided to go beyond the U.S. Supreme Court in finding new constitutional rights for citizens. And several state supreme courts have insisted on protections for criminal defendants that go beyond those provided by the U.S. Supreme Court.[19]

LIBERALS, CONSERVATIVES, AND JUDICIAL ACTIVISM   Theoretically, activist and restraintist views of the judicial role are independent of liberal or conservative ideology. That is, judicial activism could be used in support of either liberal or conservative goals; or alternatively, judicial restraint could limit the lawmaking of judges disposed to either liberal or conservative ideas. However, there appears to be a tendency for liberal judges to be more activist than conservative judges. But the major impact of ideology is *through* the role orientation of judges. Self-restraint reduces the impact of ideology on judges' decisions. Activism greatly increases the impact of judges' ideologies. Activist judges are overtly ideological in reactions to criminal appeals—activist liberal judges vote for the defendant far more frequently than activist conservative judges who tend to support the prosecution.[20]

---

[15]Stuart Nagel, "Political Party Affiliation and Judges' Decisions," *American Political Science Association,* 55 (1961), 843–51; and Sidney Ulmer, "The Political Party Variable on the Michigan Supreme Court," *Journal of Public Law,* 11 (1962), 352–62.

[16]Brace and Hall, "Studying Courts Comparatively."

[17]Stuart Nagel, "Ethnic Affiliation and Judicial Propensities," *Journal of Politics,* 24 (1962), 92–110.

[18]Jerome Frank, *Law and the Modern Mind* (New York: Coward-McCann, Inc., 1930); Benjamin N. Cardozo, *The Nature of the Judicial Process* (New Haven: Yale University Press, 1921); and Roscoe Pound, *Justice According to Law* (New Haven: Yale University Press, 1951).

[19]See John Patrick Hagan, "Patterns of Activism on State Supreme Courts," *Publius,* 18 (Winter 1988), 97–115.

[20]John M. Scheb, Terry Bowen, and Gary Anderson, "Ideology, Role Orientations and Behavior in State Courts of Last Resort," *American Politics Quarterly,* 19 (July 1991), 324–35.

SUMMARY   In summary, judicial decision making is influenced by interest group activity, political party affiliation, social and ethnic ties, religious affiliations, and the liberal and conservative views of judges. This does not mean that "judicial impartiality" is nonexistent or that judges are as free as legislators or governors to write their social and political views into the law. Judges participate in the game of politics as players as well as umpires, but they are limited by the rules of the game, the decisions of legislatures and governors, and public expectations about the way judges ought to behave.

CRIME IN THE STATES

Crime rates are the subject of a great deal of popular discussion. Crime rates are based upon the Federal Bureau of Investigation's *Uniform Crime Reports,* but the FBI reports are compiled from figures supplied by state and local police agencies. (See Table 8–2.) The FBI has established a uniform classification of the number of serious crimes per 100,000 people that are known to the police: *violent crimes* (crimes committed against persons)—murder and nonnegligent manslaughter, forcible rape, robbery, and aggravated assault; *property crimes* (crimes committed against property)—burglary, larceny, arson, and theft, including auto theft. However, one should be cautious in interpreting official crime rates. They are really a function of several factors: the tendencies of victims to report crimes to police, the adequacy of police departments in tabulating crime, and the amount of crime itself.

TRENDS IN CRIME RATES   The national crime rate has risen dramatically yet unevenly over the past few decades. From 1960 to 1975 the crime rate more than doubled, and "law and order" became an important political issue. In the early 1980s crime rates leveled off and even declined slightly from their record years. It was widely believed that the early rapid increase and later moderation was a product of age group changes in the population: The early baby boom had expanded the size of the "crime-prone" age group in the population, people fifteen to twenty-four; later, crime rates leveled off when this age group was no longer increasing as a percentage of the population. In the early

Table 8–2
CRIME RATES IN THE UNITED STATES

Offenses Reported to Police per 100,000 Population					
	1960	1970	1980	1985	1990	1995
Violent Crimes	160	360	581	557	732	689
Murder	5	8	10	8	9	8
Forcible Rape	9	18	36	37	41	37
Robbery	60	172	244	209	257	221
Assault	85	162	291	303	424	423
Property Crimes	1,716	3,599	5,319	4,651	4,903	4,611

Sources: F.B.I., *Uniform Crime Reports;* 1995 Preliminary Annual Release, May 5, 1996.

1980s many analysts were looking forward to gradual decreases in crime rates based on smaller crime-prone age groups. But by 1990 crime rates had soared upward again. The new factor in the crime rate equation appeared to be the introduction of relatively cheap "crack" cocaine. Perhaps as many as one-half of all crimes today are drug-related.

Since peaking in the early 1990s, crime rates have actually declined. Law enforcement officials attribute recent successes in crime-fighting to police "crackdowns," more aggressive "community policing," and longer prison sentences for repeat offenders, including "three strikes you're out" laws. (All are discussed later in this chapter.) In support of this claim, they observe that the greatest reductions in crime have occurred in the nation's largest cities, especially those such as New York that have adopted tougher law enforcement practices. However, while overall crime rates are down, juvenile crime is on the rise. So it is by no means certain that crime rates will not rise again in future years.

VARIATIONS AMONG THE STATES   Crime rates in some states (e.g., Florida, Arizona) are over three times greater than in other states (e.g., North Dakota, West Virginia). (See Figure 8–2.) Crime rates in the states appear related to population growth, urbanization, and economic development. Generally the urban states with more mobile populations have higher crime rates than rural states with more stable populations. Variations in crime rates among cities are even greater. Each year Miami, Atlanta, St. Louis, New Orleans, Ft. Lauderdale, New York, Detroit, Newark, Chicago, and Washington DC struggle to avoid the designation "crime capital of America." All rank high nearly every year in crime rates.

JUVENILE CRIME   While adult crime rates appear to be moderating, juvenile crime has surged upward in recent years. Indeed, murders committed by juveniles have tripled in the last decade. Yet *the juvenile system is not designed for deterrence.* Children are not held personally responsible for their actions, in the belief that they do not possess the ability to understand the nature or consequences of their behavior or its rightness or wrongness. Yet juvenile crime, most of which is committed by fifteen- to seventeen-year-olds, accounts for about 20 percent of the nation's overall crime rate. Offenders under eighteen years of age are usually processed in a separate juvenile court system, regardless of the seriousness of their crime. Only about 5 percent of all young violent offenders are tried as adults. Very few juveniles are sentenced to detention facilities for very long. Their names are withheld from publication, eliminating the social stigma associated with their crimes. Their juvenile criminal records are expunged when they become adults, so that they can begin adulthood with "clean" records.

Whatever the merits of the juvenile system in the treatment of young children, it is clear that the absence of deterrence contributes to criminal behavior among older youths—fifteen-, sixteen-, and seventeen-year-olds. Indeed these years are among the most crime-prone ages. Currently some state legislatures are considering reforms of the juvenile system, including more detention facilities, "boot camps" with intensive disciplinary training, and the transfer of older youths who commit violent crimes to the adult justice system.

VICTIMIZATION   Official crime rates understate the real amount of crime. Citizens do not report many crimes to police. "Victimization" surveys regularly ask a national sample of individuals whether they or any member of their household has been a

Figure 8–2
CRIME IN THE STATES

Offences Known to the Police per 100,000

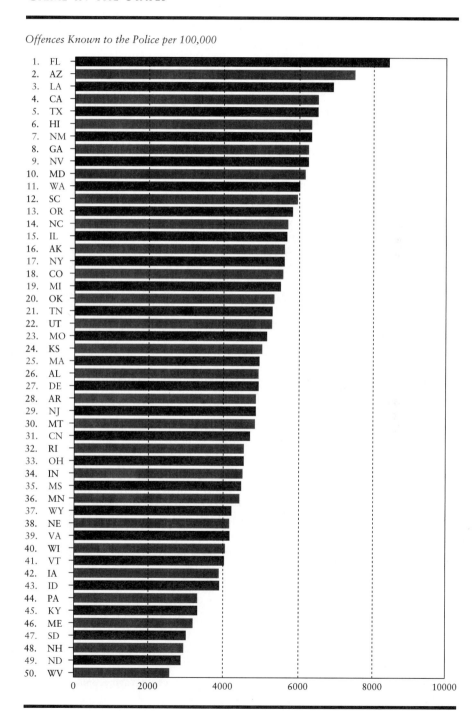

victim of crime during the past year.[21] These surveys reveal that the actual amount of crime is greater than that reported to the FBI. The number of forcible rapes is twice the number reported, burglaries and aggravated assaults and larcenies more than double, and robbery 50 percent greater than the reported rate. Only auto theft statistics are reasonably accurate, indicating that most people call the police when their cars are stolen.

Interviewees give a variety of reasons for their failure to report crime to the police. The most common reason is the feeling that police could not be effective in dealing with the crime. Other reasons include the feeling that the crime was "a private matter," that the offender was a member of the family, or that the victim did not want to harm the offender. Fear of reprisal is mentioned much less frequently, usually in cases of assaults and family crimes.

THE WAR ON DRUGS

Public policy in the United States toward drug use is inconsistent. Alcohol and cigarettes are legal products, but Congress has banned their advertising on radio and television. Marijuana has been "decriminalized" in several states, making its possession a misdemeanor comparable to a traffic offense. Yet the production and sale of marijuana remain criminal offenses in every state. The use and possession of heroin and cocaine is a criminal offense everywhere in the United States. Drug trafficking can be prosecuted in either state or federal courts. Federal drug laws are generally harsher than those of the states; the minimum federal sentence for possession of specified amounts of illegal drugs is five years.

ALCOHOL   The United States government attempted to prohibit the manufacture and sale of alcohol for only thirteen years, during "Prohibition," 1920–1933. Today, the alcoholic beverage industry is a major component of our national economy, and nearly two-thirds of the adult population drink occasionally. But according to the U.S. National Center for Health Statistics, about 5 percent of the population over eighteen averages two or more drinks each day.[22] Many of these heavy drinkers are not only dangers to themselves, but also to others, particularly on the highways. Almost half of all highway accident deaths are alcohol-related. About 1.3 million people are arrested for driving while intoxicated (DWI) each year; this is the single largest category of arrests.[23]

Alcohol is controlled in the states primarily by laws dealing with the age of the purchaser. Immediately following the passage of the Twenty-Sixth Amendment lowering the voting age to eighteen, most states dropped the legal drinking age to eighteen. But later the states reversed themselves, and today most states have returned the legal drinking age to twenty-one. In 1984 Congress required the U.S. Department of Transportation to withhold 10 percent of federal highway funds from any state that did not raise its drinking age to twenty-one (see "How Congress Raised the Drinking Age" in Chapter 3). The argument for raising the legal drinking age generally centers on the higher automobile acci-

---

[21]U.S. Bureau of Justice Statistics, *Criminal Victimization in the United States,* annual.

[22]*Statistical Abstract of the United States, 1995,* p. 145.

[23]*Statistical Abstract of the United States, 1995,* p. 206.

dent rate for young people and the dangers of "drinking and driving." The states have also tried to deal directly with the drunk driving by all age groups by setting specific blood alcohol concentration (BAC) standards for intoxication, usually 0.10; increasing the penalties for driving while intoxicated (DWI); and even holding bars legally accountable if their patrons are found DWI.

MARIJUANA   The medical evidence on the health effects of marijuana is mixed; conflicting reports have been issued about whether or not it is more dangerous than alcohol.[24] Estimates of the number of "regular" marijuana users are roughly comparable to estimates of the number of heavy drinkers—about 5 percent of the adult population. Marijuana users are younger than the general population. Decriminalizing marijuana use does not make its production or sale legal, but makes its possession (generally an ounce or less) a civil offense, much like a traffic offense.

COCAINE   The burgeoning market for cocaine currently challenges law enforcement efforts. Cocaine is not regarded as physically addictive, although the psychological urge to continue use of the drug is strong. It is made from coca leaves and imported into the United States. At one time, its high cost and use by celebrities made it the drug of choice in middle- and upper-class circles. In the 1980s a cheap yet potent version, "crack," spread rapidly in the nation's cities. The health problems associated with cocaine are fairly serious, as reported by the National Institute on Drug Abuse.[25] Death, although rare, can occur from a single ingestion.

TRAFFICKING   Crime associated with drug trafficking is a serious national problem, whatever the health effects of various drugs. The world of drug trafficking is fraught with violence. Sellers rob and murder buyers and vice versa; neither can seek the protection of police or courts in their dealing with the other.

It is very difficult to estimate the total size of the drug market, but $20 to $25 billion per year is a common figure.[26] This would suggest that the drug business is comparable in size to one of the ten largest U.S. industrial corporations. More important, perhaps, drugs produce huge profit margins: A kilo of cocaine purchased in Colombia may cost only $3,600; when sold in the United States, that kilo may retail for $80,000 to $120,000.[27] The price of smuggling a single, easily concealable kilo may run to $15,000. These huge profits allow drug traffickers to corrupt police and government officials as well as private citizens in the United States and other nations.

DRUG POLICY   Antidrug efforts can be divided into three categories: interdiction, enforcement, and education.

Interdiction: Efforts to seal U.S. borders against the importation of drugs have been frustrated by the sheer volume of smuggling. Each year increasingly large drug shipments

---

[24]For a summary of this evidence and references to the relevant health literature, see Richard C. Schroeder, *Politics of Drugs* (Washington, D.C.: CQ Press, 1980).

[25]Ibid., p. 148.

[26]*Congressional Quarterly Weekly Report,* June 25, 1988.

[27]Ethan A. Nadelmann, "U.S. Drug Policy," *Foreign Policy* (Spring 1988), 83–108.

are intercepted by the U.S. Drug Enforcement Administration, the U.S. Customs Service, the Coast Guard, and state and local agencies. Yet each year the volume of drugs entering the country seems to increase. Drug "busts" are considered just another cost of business to the traffickers. It is not likely that the use of U.S. military forces to augment other federal agencies can succeed in sealing our borders. American pressure against Latin American governments to destroy coca crops and assist in interdiction has already resulted in strained relationships. Our neighboring countries wonder why the U.S. government directs its efforts at the suppliers, when the demand for drugs arises within the United States itself.

Enforcement: The FBI and state and local law enforcement agencies already devote great effort to combating drugs; an estimated 40 percent of all arrests in the United States are drug-related. Federal and state prisons now hold a larger percentage of the nation's population than ever before. Sentences have lengthened for drug trafficking, and prisons are overcrowded as a direct result of drug-related convictions. Drug testing in government and private employment is increasing, but unless it is random it is not very useful, and some courts have prevented random testing of individuals without their consent.

Education: Efforts at educating the public about the dangers of drugs have inspired many public and private campaigns, from former First Lady Nancy Reagan's "Just say no" to Jesse Jackson's "Up with hope, down with dope" to D.A.R.E. (drug abuse resistance education) programs in local communities. But it is difficult to evaluate the effects of these efforts. The number of people arrested for drug offenses in the United States remains at over one million per year.[28] Reported drug use is down, yet there appears to be no significant reduction in the availability of drugs on the street.

FEDERAL POLICY   Congress created a cabinet-level "drug czar," a National Drug Control Policy Director, in 1988 to develop and coordinate antidrug policy in the United States. The national "war on drugs" has included funds for federal prison construction and more courts and prosecutors; grants for state and local drug law enforcement; increased money for border control for the Coast Guard, Customs Service, Immigration and Naturalization Service; authorization for use of U.S. military in drug enforcement; and additional funds for the Drug Enforcement Administration. Congress added funds for treatment programs in states and cities.

DRUGS AND CRIME   Police officials are convinced that drugs cause crime—not just violation of drug laws, but robbery, burglary, assault, and murder. Indeed, drug use among persons arrested for nondrug crimes is very high; reports from various cities indicate that half to two-thirds of all persons arrested for nondrug crimes test positive for drug use.[29] But this does not necessarily mean that drugs cause crime. A majority of criminals may use drugs, but the vast majority of drug users do not commit other crimes.

WHO'S WINNING THE WAR ON DRUGS?   The U.S. government's National Institute on Drug Abuse regularly surveys Americans to ask whether they have ever

---

[28]Office of National Drug Control Policy, *National Drug Control Strategy* (Washington, D.C.: Government Printing Office, 1994), p. 104.

[29]*Statistical Abstract of the United States, 1995,* p. 207.

used particular drugs and whether they have used them in the past year or month. These surveys suggest that about 5 percent of the U.S. population have used an illicit drug in the previous thirty days (see Figure 8–3). Marijuana is the most commonly used illicit drug, followed by cocaine.

According to the survey evidence, the numbers of people using illicit drugs has declined in recent years. However, the U.S. Drug Enforcement Administration (DEA) reports increased numbers of drug seizures each year. There appear to be no significant reductions in the volume of drugs entering the country or reaching the streets.

Educational campaigns against drugs may actually reduce the number of casual users, or these campaigns may signal that drug use is socially unacceptable and inhibit respondents from admitting use even in anonymous interviews. Perhaps the reported reduction in drug use over the years reflects both effects.

The most common interpretation of the poll results showing reduced drug use, and the law enforcement data showing continued volume of drug availability, is that *casual* use is down but daily use by *hard-core* addicted persons remains high.

LEGALIZATION?   The failure of antidrug policies to produce any significant reductions in drug supply or demand, coupled with the high costs of enforcement and the

Figure 8–3
REPORTED DRUG USE IN THE PAST MONTH

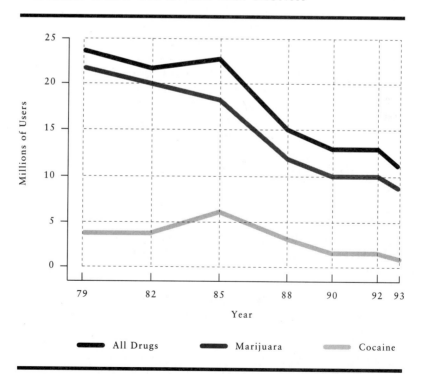

Source: Office of the National Drug Control Policy, *National Drug Control Strategy* (Washington, DC: Government Printing Office, 1994).

loss of civil liberties, has caused some observers to propose the legalization of drugs and government control of their production and sales. "Prohibition" failed earlier in the century to end alcohol consumption, and the crime, official corruption, and enormous cost of futile efforts to stop drinking eventually forced the nation to end Prohibition. Similarly it is argued that the legalization of drugs would end organized crime's profit monopoly over the drug trade, raise billions of dollars by legally taxing drugs, end the strain on relations with Latin American nations caused by efforts to eradicate drugs, and save additional billions in enforcement costs, which could be used for education and treatment.[30] If drugs were legally obtainable under government supervision, it is argued that many of society's current problems would be alleviated: the crime and violence associated with the drug trade, the corruption of public officials, the spread of diseases associated with drug use, and the many infringements of personal liberty associated with anti-drug wars.

But even the suggestion of drug legalization offends Americans who believe that legalization would greatly expand drug use in the country. Cheap, available drugs would greatly increase the numbers of addicted persons, creating a "society of zombies" that would destroy the social fabric of the nation. Cocaine and heroin are far more habit-forming than alcohol, and legalization would encourage the development of newer and even more potent and addictive synthetic drugs. Whatever the health costs of drug abuse today, it is argued that legalization would produce public health problems of enormous magnitude.[31] Cocaine is very cheap to produce; the current $5 to $10 cost of a "hit" is mostly drug dealer profit; legalization even with taxation might produce a 50¢ "hit." Whatever the damages to society from drug-related crime and efforts to prohibit drugs, the damages to society from cheap, available drug usage would be far greater.

FEDERALISM AND LAW ENFORCEMENT

The public demand to DO SOMETHING! about crime inspires political officeholders in Washington as well as those in state capitols and city halls. Neither Democrats nor Republicans in Washington are willing to risk their political futures by restricting the federal government's role and telling their constituents that crime control is principally a state and local responsibility.

TRADITIONAL DIVISION OF POWERS   Traditionally the federal government's responsibilities were limited to the enforcement of a relatively narrow range of federal criminal laws, including laws dealing with counterfeiting and currency violations; tax evasion, including alcohol, tobacco, and firearm taxes; fraud and embezzlement; robbery or theft of federally insured funds, including banks; interstate criminal activity; murder or assault of a federal official; and federal drug laws. While some federal criminal laws overlapped state laws, most criminal activity—murder, rape, robbery, assault, burglary, theft, auto theft, gambling, sex offenses, and so on—fell under state jurisdiction.

---

[30]Ethan A. Nadelmann, "The Case for Legalization," *The Public Interest* (Summer 1988), 3–31.

[31]John Kaplan, "Taking Drugs Seriously," *The Public Interest* (Summer 1988), 32–50.

FEDERALIZING CRIME FIGHTING   Pressure has mounted in recent years for greater federal involvement in crime fighting. President Clinton and many Democrats and Republicans in Congress pushed for a major federal crime-fighting package with a broad range of new provisions:

- Federal grants to cities to place an additional 100,000 police officers on the beat, with an emphasis on community crime prevention. Liberals succeeded in earmarking some grant money for community drug treatment, midnight sports programs, and alternatives to incarceration.
- Federal grants to states for expansion of prison facilities.
- New federal crimes subject to the death penalty, including kidnapping, hostage taking, drive-by shootings, and carjackings. (However, the Supreme Court is unlikely to allow the death penalty to be imposed for any crime other than first-degree murder.)
- Limit death row inmate appeals to one federal habeas corpus petition to be submitted within one year of the final state appeal.

Over time, Congress has made more and more offenses *federal* crimes. Today federal offenses range from drive-by shootings to obstructing sidewalks in front of abortion clinics. (In 1995 the U.S. Supreme Court struck down a *federal* law prohibiting the carrying of a gun near a school, declaring the law to be beyond the powers delegated to Congress in Article I of the Constitution.[32]) The greatest impact of federal legislation is found in drug-related crime. Federal as well as state laws prohibit drug trafficking; offenders may be tried in either federal or state courts.

The U.S. Department of Justice, headed by the Attorney General, handles all criminal prosecutions for violation of federal laws. The federal government's principle investigative agencies are the Federal Bureau of Investigation (FBI) and the Drug Enforcement Administration (DEA), both units of the Department of Justice, and the Bureau of Alcohol, Tobacco and Firearms (ATF) in the Treasury Department. Efforts to combine these federal law enforcement agencies have consistently floundered in bureaucratic turf battles.

CONTINUED DOMINANCE OF STATES IN LAW ENFORCEMENT
Yet despite growing federal activity in law enforcement, state and local governments continue to bear the major burden of fighting crime in America. (See Table 8–3.) About 10 million people are arrested and charged with a crime in the United States each year. But only about 50,000 people are prosecuted for crimes by federal authorities in federal courts.

POLICE PROTECTION IN THE STATES

State, county, and municipal governments are all directly involved in law enforcement. Every state has a central law enforcement agency, sometimes called the state police, state troopers, state highway patrol, or even Texas Rangers. At one time, state governors had only the National Guard at their disposal to back up local law enforcement efforts, but

---

[32]*U.S. v. Lopez* (1995).

Table 8–3

CRIMINAL JUSTICE ACTIVITY BY LEVEL OF GOVERNMENT

	Federal	*State and Local*
FULL-TIME PERSONNEL (1,000)		
Law Enforcement	65	735
Judicial	22	203
Corrections	22	534
PRISONERS		
Number (1,000) present in institutions at end of year (excludes local jails and juvenile detention centers)	56.7	732.6
EXPENDITURES		
Total (1990) B$	10.1	64.9

Source: Statistical Abstract of the United States, 1995, p. 210.

the coming of the automobile and intercity highway traffic led to the establishment in every state of a centralized police system. In addition to patrolling the state's highways, these centralized agencies now provide expert aid and service for local police officers and strengthen law enforcement in sparsely populated regions. Most of the states have given their central police agencies full law enforcement authority in addition to highway duties: They may cooperate with local authorities in the apprehension of criminals, or even intervene when local authorities are unable or unwilling to enforce the law. The size and influence of these agencies vary from state to state. On the whole, however, state police forces constitute a very small proportion of the total law enforcement effort in America. About 15 percent of all law enforcement officers are state police, 5 percent are federal officers, and the remaining 80 percent are city and county officers. Law enforcement in the nation is principally a *local* responsibility.

THE COUNTY SHERIFF   Historically, the county sheriff has been the keystone of law enforcement in the United States. Sheriffs and their deputies are still the principal enforcement and arresting officers in the rural counties and in the unincorporated fringe areas of many urban counties. In addition, the sheriff serves as an executive agent for county and state courts in both civil and criminal matters, and maintains the county jail for the retention of persons whose trials or sentences are pending or who are serving short sentences. The sheriff's office is a political one; in every state except Rhode Island the sheriff is an elected official. Reliance upon the sheriff's office for law enforcement is a characteristic of rural states. Since city police forces usually assume the sheriff's law enforcement duties within the boundaries of cities, the sheriff's office has seriously atrophied in most urban states; often the sheriff is reduced to a process server for the courts.

CITY POLICE   Urban police departments are the most important instruments of law enforcement and public safety in the nation today. City police officers vastly outnumber all other state and county law enforcement officers combined. The urban police department does more than merely enforce the law; it engages in a wide range of activities for social control.

POLICE AND CRIME   The total number of police officers nationwide has grown to about 1.3 million—about 25 full-time police officers per 10,000 population. This figure includes all city, county, state, federal, and specialized law enforcement agencies. But police protection varies considerably among the fifty states, with some states providing over 30 police officers per 10,000 population, and other states providing fewer than 20 (see Figure 8–4). But the number of officers has *not* kept abreast of crime. On the contrary, the number of police officers relative to the number of reported crimes has declined steadily. This decline is unique to police personnel, as growth in the number of other state and local employees has generally exceeded the growth of their workload.

POLICE AND LAW ENFORCEMENT

Police perform at least three important functions in urban society—law enforcement, keeping the peace, and furnishing services. Actually, law enforcement may take up only a small portion of a police officer's daily activity, perhaps only 10 percent. The service function is far more common—attending accidents, directing traffic, escorting crowds, assisting stranded motorists, and so on. The function of peace keeping is also very common—breaking up fights, quieting noisy parties, handling domestic or neighborhood quarrels, and the like. It is in this function that police exercise the greatest discretion in the application of the law. In most of these incidents blame is difficult to determine, participants are reluctant to file charges, and police must use personal discretion in handling each case.

Police are on the front line of society's efforts to resolve conflict. Indeed, instead of a legal or law enforcement role, the police are more likely to adopt a peace-keeping role. Police are usually lenient in their arrest practices; that is, they use their arrest power less often than the law allows. Rather than arresting people, the police prefer first to reestablish order. Of course, the decision to be more or less lenient in enforcing the law gives the police a great deal of discretion.

POLICE "CULTURE"   What factors influence police decision making? Probably the first factor to influence police behavior is the attitude of the other people involved in police encounters. If people adopt a cooperative attitude, display deference and respect for the officers, and conform to police expectations, they are much less likely to be arrested than those who show disrespect or use abusive language toward police.[33] Formal police training emphasizes self-control and caution in dealing with the public, but on-the-job experiences probably reinforce predispositions toward distrust of others. The element of danger in police work makes police officers naturally suspicious of others. They see many of the "worst kind" of people, and they see even the "best kind" at their worst.

---

[33]Stuart A. Scheingold, "Cultural Cleavage and Criminal Justice," *Journal of Politics*, 40, 865–97.

Figure 8–4
POLICE PROTECTION IN THE STATES

Police Officers per 10,000 Population

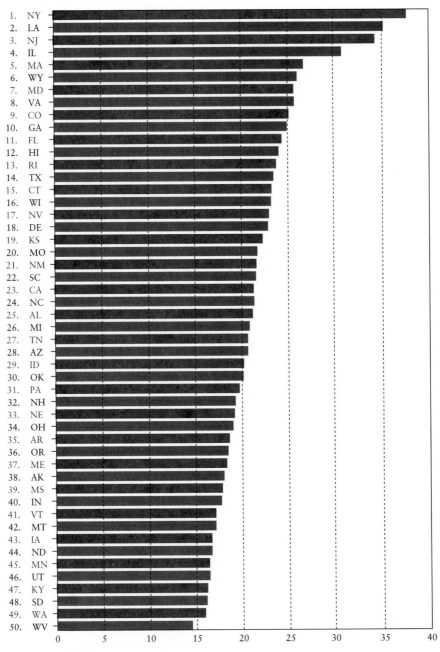

POLICE AND CRIME REDUCTION   Does increased police protection significantly reduce crime? The common assumption is that increased numbers of police officers and increased police expenditures can significantly reduce crime in cities. However, unfortunately, it is very difficult to produce firm evidence to support this assumption. So many other factors may affect crime rates in cities—size, density, youth, unemployment, race, poverty, and so on—that police activity appears insignificant.

COMMUNITY POLICING   Most police activity is "reactive": typically two officers in a patrol car responding to a radio dispatcher who is forwarding reports of incidents. Police agencies frequently evaluate themselves in terms of the number and frequency of patrols, the number of calls responded to, and the elapsed time between the call and the arrival of officers on the scene. But there is little evidence that any of these measures affect crime rates or even citizens' fear of crime or satisfaction with the police.

An alternative strategy is for police to become more "proactive": typically by becoming more visible in the community by walking or bicycling the sidewalks of high crime areas; learning to recognize individuals on the streets and winning their confidence and respect; deterring or scaring away drug dealers, prostitutes, and their customers by a police presence. But this "community policing" is often expensive and potentially more dangerous for police officers.

POLICE CRACKDOWNS   Police crackdowns—beefed up police actions against juvenile gangs, prostitutes, and drug traffickers; the frisking of likely suspects on the street for guns and drugs; and arrests for (often ignored) public drinking, graffiti, and vandalism—can reduce crime only if supported by the community as well as prosecutors and judges. Crime rates, even murder rates, have been significantly reduced during periods of police crackdowns in major cities.[34] But these efforts are often sporadic; enthusiasm ebbs as jails fill up and the workload of prosecutors and courts multiplies.

CITIZEN ACTION   Anticrime efforts by private citizens have risen dramatically over the last decade. Today there are over one million private security guards, overseeing businesses, banks, airports, stores, hotels, and residential communities. (In effect, this force doubles the size of the nation's police force.) Improved security devices are now found in virtually all commercial establishments—from gas stations and neighborhood convenience stores to banks and schools. Millions of Americans live in communities with security gates and guards and millions more have installed security systems in their houses. Citizen patrol groups and "town watch" associations have multiplied.

POLICE EFFICIENCY   Most crimes are never solved. This is particularly true of property crimes like burglary; these crimes seldom produce eyewitnesses or other useful information. On average across the nation police claim to solve about 14 percent of burglaries; this is their official "clearance rate." Police "clear" only about 50 percent of all violent crimes, and 70 percent of murders. (See Table 8–4.) Most clearances occur in cases in which the victim and perpetrators know each other.

---

[34]For a summary, see John J. DiIulio, Jr., "Arresting Ideas: Tougher Law Enforcement Is Driving Down Crime," *Policy Review* (Fall 1995), 12–16.

Table 8–4
CRIME AND ARREST

	Percent of Crimes Cleared by Arrest
Murder	70.0
Rape	52.1
Robbery	25.6
Aggravated Assault	56.8
Burglary	13.5
Larceny/Theft	19.7

Source: National Center for Policy Analysis, "Crime Pays, But So Does Imprisonment," Dallas: National Center for Policy Analysis, 1992. Calculated from Federal Bureau of Investigation, *Crime in the United States, Uniform Crime Reports,* annual issues (Washington, DC: Government Printing Office).

About 12 million people are arrested each year, and many more millions of traffic citations are issued. But even this huge number is less than the 14 million crimes reported to police and the 20 to 30 million crimes estimated from victimization surveys.

THE POLITICS OF PROSECUTION

Prosecution is also part of the political process. Legislatures and governors enact policy, but its enforcement depends upon the decisions of prosecutors as well as judges. Political pressures are most obvious in the enforcement of controversial policies—gambling laws, Sunday closing laws, liquor rules, laws against prostitution, and other laws that are contrary to the interests of significant segments of the population. Prosecution also involves decision making about the allocation of law enforcement resources to different types of offenses—traffic violations, juvenile delinquency, auto theft, assault, burglary, larceny, and robbery. Decisions must be made about what sections of the city should be most vigorously protected and what segments of the population will be most closely watched. The public prosecutor, sometimes called the district attorney (D.A.) or state's attorney, is at the center of diverse pressures concerning law enforcement.

The political nature of the prosecutor's job is suggested by the frequency with which this job leads to higher political office. Prosecuting attorney is often a steppingstone to state and federal judgeships, congressional seats, and even the governorship. Ambitious D.A.s, concerned with their political future, may seek to build a reputation as a crusader against crime and vice, while at the same time maintaining the support and friendship of important interests in the community.

The political power of prosecutors stems from their discretion in deciding (1) whether or not to prosecute in criminal cases, and (2) whether prosecution will be on more serious or less serious charges. Prosecutors may decide simply to drop charges ("nol-pros") when they feel adequate proof is lacking, or when they feel that police have committed a procedural error that infringed on the defendant's rights, or when they feel that the resources of their office would be better allocated by pursuing other cases. About half of all felony arrests result in dismissal of charges against the defendant. Prosecutors may also engage in "plea bargaining"—reducing the charges from more serious to less serious crimes in exchange for defendants' promises to plead guilty. Or prosecutors may reduce charges because they believe it will be easier in court to obtain a guilty verdict on the lesser charge.

Are there any checks on the power of prosecutors? In principle, the *grand jury* is supposed to determine whether evidence presented to it by the prosecutor is sufficient to warrant the placing of a person on trial in a felony case. Ideally, the grand jury serves as a check against the overzealous district attorney, and as a protection for the citizen against unwarranted harassment. However, in practice, grand juries spend very little time deliberating on the vast majority of the cases.[35] A typical grand jury spends only five to ten minutes per case, primarily listening to the prosecutor's recommendation as to how the case should be decided. Over 80 percent of the cases may be decided on an immediate vote, without discussion among jurors, and almost always with unanimous votes. Finally, and most importantly, grand juries follow the recommendations of prosecutors in over 98 percent of the cases presented to them. The prosecutor controls the information submitted to grand juries, instructs them in their duties, and is usually perceived by jurors as an expert and relied on for guidance. In short, there is no evidence that grand juries provide much of a check on the power of prosecutors.

CRIME AND THE COURTS

Society needs the protection of the police, but it is equally important to protect society *from* the police. Arbitrary searches, seizures, and arrests; imprisonment without hearing or trial; forced confessions; beatings and torture; tainted witnesses; excessive punishments; and other human rights violations are all too common throughout the world. The courts function to protect citizens accused of crime as well as to mete out punishment for criminal behavior.

UNREASONABLE SEARCHES AND SEIZURES   Individuals are protected by the Fourth Amendment from "unreasonable searches and seizures" of their private "persons, houses, papers, and effects." The amendment lays out specific rules for searches and seizures of evidence: "No warrants shall issue but upon probable cause, supported by Oath or affirmation, and particularly describing the place to be searched, and the persons or things to be seized." Judges cannot issue a warrant just to let the police see if an individual has committed a crime; there must be "probable cause" for such issuance. The indiscriminate searching of whole neighborhoods or groups of people is unconstitutional and is prevented by the Fourth Amendment's requirement that the place to be searched must be specifically described in the warrant. This requirement is meant to prevent "fishing expeditions" into an individual's home and personal effects on the possibility that some evidence of unknown illegal activity might crop up.

However, the courts permit the police to undertake many other "reasonable" searches

---

[35]The following discussion relies on evidence presented by Robert A. Carp, "The Behavior of Grand Juries: Acquiescence or Justice," *Social Science Quarterly,* 55 (March 1975), 853–70.

without a warrant: searches in connection with a valid arrest, searches to protect the safety of police officers, searches to obtain evidence in the immediate vicinity and in the suspect's control, searches to preserve evidence in danger of being immediately destroyed, and searches with the consent of a suspect. Indeed, most police searches today take place without a warrant under one or another of these conditions. The Supreme Court has also allowed automobile searches and searches of open fields without warrants in many cases. The requirement of "probable cause" has been very loosely defined; even a "partially corroborated anonymous informer's tip" qualifies as probable cause to make a search, seizure, or arrest.

SELF-INCRIMINATION AND RIGHTS TO COUNSEL   Freedom from self-incrimination originated in English common law; it was originally designed to prevent persons from being tortured into confessions of guilt. It is also a logical extension of the notion that individuals should not be forced to contribute to their own prosecution, that the burden of proof rests upon the state. The Fifth Amendment protects people from both physical and psychological coercion.

The Supreme Court under Justice Earl Warren greatly strengthened the Fifth Amendment protection against self-incrimination and the right to counsel in a series of rulings in the 1960s:

> *Gideon* v. *Wainwright* (1963)—Equal protection under the Fourteenth Amendment requires that free legal counsel be appointed for all individual defendants in all criminal cases.
>
> *Escobedo* v. *Illinois* (1964)—Suspects are entitled to confer with counsel as soon as a police investigation focuses on them or once "the process shifts from investigatory to accusatory."
>
> *Miranda* v. *Arizona* (1966)—Before questioning suspects, a police officer must inform them of all their constitutional rights, including the right to counsel (appointed at no cost to the suspect, if necessary) and the right to remain silent. Although suspects may knowingly waive these rights, the police cannot question anyone who at any point asks for a lawyer or declines "in any manner" to be questioned.

THE EXCLUSIONARY RULE   Illegally obtained evidence and confessions may not be used in criminal trials. If police find evidence of a crime in an illegal search, of if they elicit statements from suspects without informing them of their rights to remain silent or to have counsel, the evidence or statements produced are not admissible in a trial. This exclusionary rule is one of the more controversial procedural rights that the Supreme Court has extended to criminal defendants. The rule is also unique to the United States; in Great Britain evidence obtained illegally may be used against the accused, although the accused may bring charges against the police for damages.

The rule provides enforcement for the Fourth Amendment guarantee against unreasonable searches and seizures, as well as the Fifth Amendment guarantee against compulsory self-incrimination and the guarantee of counsel. The exclusionary rule initially applied only in federal cases, but in *Mapp* v. *Ohio* (1961) the Supreme Court extended it to *all* criminal cases in the United States. A "good faith exception" is made "when law enforcement officers have acted in objective good faith or their transgressions have been minor."

PLEA BARGAINING   Most convictions are obtained by guilty pleas. Indeed, about 90 percent of the criminal cases brought to trial are disposed of by guilty pleas before a judge, not trial by jury. The Constitution guarantees defendants a trial by jury (Sixth Amendment), but guilty pleas outnumber jury trials by ten to one.

Plea bargaining, in which the prosecution either reduces the seriousness of the charges, drops some but not all charges, or agrees to recommend lighter penalties in exchange for a guilty plea by the defendant, is very common. Some critics of plea bargaining view it as another form of leniency in the criminal justice system that reduces its deterrent effects. Other critics view plea bargaining as a violation of the Constitution's protection against self-incrimination and guarantee of a fair jury trial. Prosecutors, they say, threaten defendants with serious charges and stiff penalties to force a guilty plea. Still other critics see plea bargaining as an under-the-table process that undermines respect for the criminal justice system.

It is very fortunate for the nation's court system that most defendants plead guilty. The court system would quickly break down from overload if any substantial proportion of defendants insisted on jury trials.

CRIME AND DETERRENCE

Can punishment deter crime? This is a difficult question to answer. First of all, we must distinguish between *deterrence* and *incapacity*. *Incapacity* can be imposed by long terms of imprisonment, particularly for habitual offenders; the policy of "keeping criminals off the streets" does indeed protect the public for a period of time, although it is done at a considerable cost. The object of *deterrence* is to make the certainty and severity of punishment so great as to inhibit potential criminals from committing crimes.

DETERRENCE THEORY   In theory, deterrence is enhanced by:

1. The *certainty* that a crime will be followed by costly punishment. Justice must be sure.
2. The *swiftness* of the punishment following the crime. Long delays between crime and punishment break the link in the mind of the criminal between the criminal act and its consequences. And a potential wrong-doer must believe that the costs of a crime will occur within a meaningful time frame, not in a distant, unknowable future. Justice must be swift.
3. The *severity* of the punishment. Punishment that is perceived as no more costly than the ordinary hazards of life on the streets which the potential criminal faces anyhow will not deter. Punishment must clearly outweigh whatever benefits might be derived from a life of crime in the mind of potential criminals. Punishment must be severe.

These criteria for an effective deterrent policy are ranked in the order of their probable importance. That is, it is most important that punishment for crime be certain. The severity of punishment is probably less important than its swiftness or certainty.

AN ECONOMIC VIEW OF CRIME   Economists view crime as a product of rational calculations by people of the expected benefits and expected costs of their criminal acts. The reason we have so much crime is that crime pays—its benefits outweigh its costs. Economists believe that if you increase the cost of something (crime), less of it will be consumed (there will be fewer crimes). Their own studies confirm the deterrent effect of both the certainty and severity of punishment.[36]

CURRENT POLICIES DO NOT DETER   However, virtually all social scientists agree that the current system of criminal justice in America is *not* a serious deterrent to crime. Punishment for crime is neither certain, swift, nor severe. Indeed, the criminal justice system itself, by failing to deter crime, is principally responsible for the fact that *crime in the United States is more common than in any other advanced industrial nation of the world.*

The best available estimates of the *certainty* of punishment for serious crime suggest that very few crimes actually result in jail sentences for the perpetrators. About 14 million serious crimes were reported to police in 1992, but only 2.4 million persons were arrested for these crimes (see Figure 8–5). Some of those arrested were charged with committing more than one crime, but it is estimated that police clear less than 20 percent of reported crimes by arresting the offender. Prosecutors do not charge about half of the persons ar-

Figure 8–5
CRIME AND PUNISHMENT

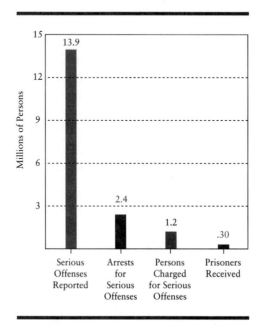

Source: Statistical Abstract of the United States, 1994.

[36]See Gordon Tullock, "Does Punishment Deter Crime?" *The Public Interest* (Summer 1974), 11.

rested for serious offenses. Some offenders are handled as juveniles; some are permitted to plead guilty to minor offenses; others are released because witnesses fail to appear or evidence is weak or inadmissible in court. Of the persons charged with serious offenses by prosecutors, only about 25 percent receive jail sentences for their crimes. Convicted felons are three times more likely to receive probation instead of a prison sentence. Thus, even if punishment could deter crime, our current criminal justice system does *not* ensure punishment for crime.

SOCIAL HETEROGENEITY THEORY   Of course, there are many other conflicting theories of crime in America. For example, it is sometimes argued that this nation's high crime rate is a product of its social heterogeneity—the multiethnic, multiracial character of the American population. Low levels of crime in European countries, Japan, and China are often attributed to their homogeneous populations and shared cultures. Blacks in the United States are both victims and perpetrators of crime far more frequently than whites. While blacks constitute only about 12 percent of the population, they account for over 30 percent of all persons arrested for serious crimes (see Table 8–5). A larger segment of the black population is in the young crime-prone age (fifteen to twenty-four years), and these youths are more likely to live outside husband–wife families. It is argued that "the streets" of the nation's black inner cities produce a subculture that encourages crime.

"CRIME OF PASSION" THEORY   It is also argued that crime is irrational, that is, the criminal does not weigh benefits against potential costs before committing the act. Many acts of violence are committed by persons acting in blind rage—murders and aggravated assaults among family members, for example. Many rapes are acts of violence, inspired by hatred of women, rather than efforts to obtain sexual pleasure. More murders occur in the heat of arguments than in the commission of other felonies. These are crimes of passion rather than calculated acts. Thus, it is argued, no rational policies can be devised to deter these irrational acts.

Table 8–5
ARRESTS BY AGE, SEX, AND RACE

	Percent of Total Arrests
Male	80.5
Female	19.5
White	66.9
Black	31.1
Native American, Asian, other	2.0
Under 18	23.1
18–24	27.5
25–44	47.6
45–54	5.4
55 and over	2.4

Source: Statistical Abstract of the United States, 1995, pp. 206–7.

PROTECTING INDIVIDUAL LIBERTY   Finally, we must recognize that the reduction of crime is not the overriding value of American society. Americans cherish individual liberty. Freedom from repression—from unlawful arrests, forced confession, restrictions on movement, curfews, arbitrary police actions, unlimited searching of homes or seizures of property, punishment without trial, trials without juries, unfair procedures, brutal punishments—is more important to Americans than freedom from crime. Many authoritarian governments boast of low crime rates and criminal justice systems that ensure certain, swift, and severe punishment, but these governments fail to protect the personal liberties of their citizens.

STATE PRISONS AND CORRECTIONAL POLICIES

The United States has experienced an explosive growth in its prison population in recent years. Millions of Americans each year are brought to a jail, police station, or juvenile home or prison. The vast majority are released within hours or days. There are, however, over one million inmates in state and federal prisons in the United States. These prisoners are serving time for serious offenses. Ninety percent had a record of crime before they committed the act that led to their current imprisonment. An additional 450,000 persons are temporarily residing in city or county jails at any one time across the country. The rate of incarceration (prisoners per 100,000 population) in the United States is one of the highest in the world. (See Figure 8–6.)

Why are so many people behind bars? Because they have committed so many crimes. The crime rate in the United States is also one of the highest in the world. Indeed, the number of prisoners in the United States *relative to the numbers of crimes* is no higher than in other industrialized nations.

PRISONERS IN THE STATES   States differ a great deal in the number of prisoners and the proportion of their populations behind bars. (See Figure 8–7.) As might be expected, prisoner populations generally reflect the crime rate in the states; higher crime rate states have larger proportions of their population in prison.

Another cause of increased prison populations in the states is an increase in the length of criminal sentences. In recent years many states have attempted to "get tough on crime" by legislating longer sentences for particular crimes, specifying mandatory minimum sentences for crimes, eliminating judicial variation in sentences, adding years to the sentences given repeat or "habitual" criminals, and abolishing parole.

THE FAILURE OF REHABILITATION   For many years the prevailing philosophy in corrections was that of rehabilitation. In deciding sentences judges were free to consider not only the crime, but personal characteristics of the defendant. State criminal codes stated broad ranges of sentences for various crimes, for example, two to ten years. Moreover, judges in many states had the option of imposing "indeterminant" sentences (e.g., not less than one nor more than five years) and leaving the decision concerning how long a prisoner would serve to parole boards. While in prison, individuals were expected to "rehabilitate" themselves through education, job training, counseling, and

Figure 8–6
GROWTH IN PRISON POPULATION

Total Number of Prisoners in Federal and State Correctional Institutions

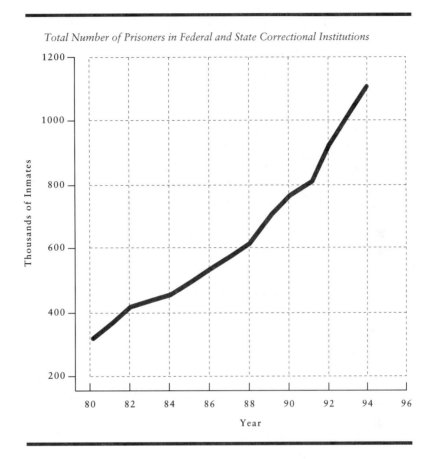

other programs. Prisons were called "correctional institutions" to reflect their therapeutic value.

Over time it became increasingly difficult to maintain the fiction that prisons were designed to rehabilitate people. Over 80 percent of all felonies are committed by repeaters—individuals who have had prior contact with the criminal justice system and were not corrected by it. Over two-thirds of all prison admissions are "recidivists"—people returned to prison for new crimes. Almost half have had three or more prior prison sentences.[37] Reformers generally recommend more education and job training, more and better facilities, smaller prisons, halfway houses where offenders can adjust to civilian life before parole, more parole officers, and greater contact between prisoners and their families and friends. But there has never been any convincing evidence that these investments

[37]Bureau of Justice Statistics, *Survey of State Prison Inmates* (1994).

Figure 8–7
Prisoners in the States

State and Federal Prisoners Sentenced to More Than One Year per 100,000 Population

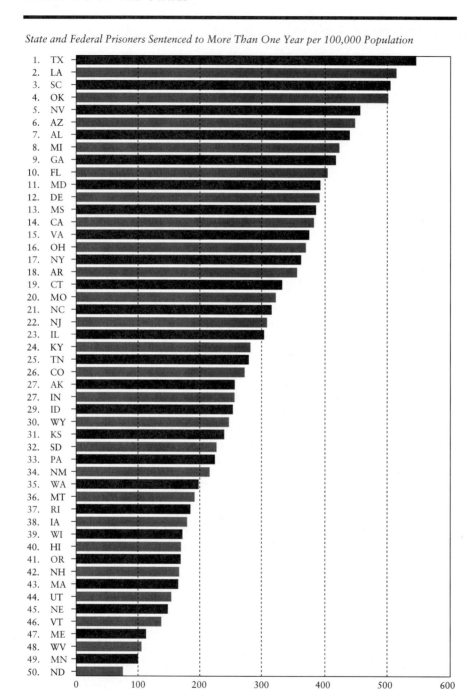

1. TX
2. LA
3. SC
4. OK
5. NV
6. AZ
7. AL
8. MI
9. GA
10. FL
11. MD
12. DE
13. MS
14. CA
15. VA
16. OH
17. NY
18. AR
19. CT
20. MO
21. NC
22. NJ
23. IL
24. KY
25. TN
26. CO
27. AK
27. IN
29. ID
30. WY
31. KS
32. SD
33. PA
34. NM
35. WA
36. MT
37. RI
38. IA
39. WI
40. HI
41. OR
42. NH
43. MA
44. UT
45. NE
46. VT
47. ME
48. WV
49. MN
50. ND

Source: U.S. Bureau of Justice Statistics.

reduce what criminologists call "recidivism," the offenders' return to crime. There is no evidence that people *can* be "rehabilitated," no matter what is done. Even the maintenance of order *within* prisons and the protection of the lives of guards and inmates have become serious national problems.

Prison life does little to encourage good behavior. For the most part, inmates spend their days in idleness—watching television, weight lifting, walking and talking in the yard. "Meaningful educational, vocational, and counseling programs are rare. Strong inmates are permitted to pressure weaker prisoners for sex, drugs, and money. Gangs organized along racial and ethnic lines are often the real 'sovereign of the cellblocks.'"[38] About 55 percent of the nation's overall prison population is black; about 94 percent are male. Most of the nation's 1,300 state prisons and 70 federal prisons have more inmates than their rated capacity. Most state prison systems, like the Federal Bureau of Prisons, operate maximum security institutions for high-risk inmates who have proven too violent to mix with the general prison population.

DETERRENCE AND INCAPACITATION   At least two other theories of punishment have competed with rehabilitation in guiding the criminal justice system. We have already described the theory of deterrence—punishment should be certain, swift, and severe, and it should be known and predictable. Clearly indeterminant sentencing and discretion given parole boards does *not* serve the goal of deterrence. Rather deterrence is served by making prison sentences predictable (certain) and long (severe). Potential lawbreakers are supposed to say to themselves, "If you can't serve the time, don't do the crime." Throughout the 1980s states enacted amendments to their criminal codes specifying *determinant sentences* for various crimes. The discretion of judges was restricted. Variation in sentencing was reduced (although not eliminated); judges were obliged by law to mete out sentences based on the crime and the number of previous convictions amassed by the defendant. Greater uniformity of sentencing also served the goal of reducing arbitrary, unfair, and discriminatory sentencing. For many crimes, deterrence was also strengthened by long *mandatory minimum* sentences. For example, many states enacted mandatory one-, two-, or three-year prison terms for the use of a gun in the commission of a felony.

But many mandatory minimum sentence laws focused on drug offenses. And the "war on drugs" in the state and federal law enforcement agencies directed resources away from investigation and prosecution of property crimes, and even violent crimes, toward drug offenses.[39] The result was that prisons soon filled with drug offenders; today over half of the nation's prisoners are incarcerated for drug offenses.

PRISON OVERCROWDING   The effect of longer sentences, combined with higher crime rates and more prisoners, has been to create mammoth prison overcrowding. Overcrowding contributes directly to unsanitary and dangerous prison living conditions; overcrowding is associated with assaults, rapes, homicides, suicides, and riots. Prison staff are also placed at risk by overcrowding and the violence it produces.

---

[38]John J. DiIulio, Jr., "Punishing Smarter," *Brookings Review* (Summer 1989), 8.

[39]See David W. Rasmussen and Bruce L. Benson, *The Economic Anatomy of the Drug War* (Latham, MD: Rowan and Littlefield, 1994).

Federal courts have determined that prison overcrowding is a violation of the U.S. Constitution's Eighth Amendment prohibition against "cruel and unusual punishments." (Simple crowding per se is not unconstitutional; federal courts must also find evidence of adverse effects of overcrowding.) Virtually all of the states confront federal court orders to reduce prison overcrowding at one or more of their prisons or their entire prison system. Most state prison systems are near, at, or over their capacity to house prisoners.

EARLY RELEASES   As a result of overcrowding, most states have had to resort to *early release* programs. Sentences of prisoners are automatically reduced and those near the end of their terms are let go first. Some states deny early release to certain violent offenders. Nonetheless, violent criminals on the average serve less than half of their sentences, and nonviolent offenders less than one-third of their sentences. In some states, due to prison overcrowding, inmates serve only one-quarter of their sentences.[40] In many states, early release programs have become institutionalized. The national average prison time actually served by convicted murderers is eight years, eight months (see Figure 8–8).

Thus, the criminal justice system does not succeed in incapacitating criminals for very long. Indeed, it is estimated that about 20 percent of all violent crimes and 30 percent of property crimes are committed by *persons who would still have been in prison on an earlier conviction if they had served their full sentence.*[41] These "avertable" crimes are

Figure 8–8
VIOLENT CRIME SENTENCES VERSUS TIME SERVED

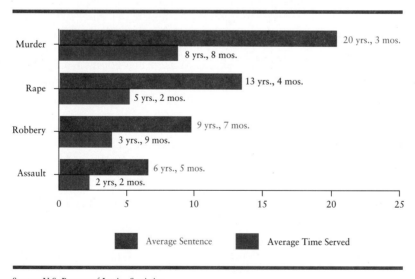

Source: U.S. Bureau of Justice Statistics.

---

[40]Richard B. Abell, "Beyond Willie Horton: The Battle of the Prison Bulge," *Policy Review,* 47 (Winter 1989), 32–35.

[41]DiIulio, "Punishing Smarter," pp. 3–12.

increasing over time as early release is used more and more to relieve prison over-crowding.

BUILDING MORE PRISONS   States have been compelled to build more pris-ons in recent years. But taxpayers are understandably upset with the prospects of spend-ing $50,000 to $75,000 for each new prison bed, and $10,000 to $20,000 per year to keep a prisoner behind bars. But if the costs of incarceration are weighed against its ben-efits, taxpayers may feel better about prison construction and maintenance. A prisoner's "rap sheet" may list only three or four convictions and a dozen arrests. But interviews with offenders suggest the typical convict has committed hundreds of crimes. Various studies have attempted to estimate the dollars lost to society in the crimes committed by the typical convict in a year.[42] Estimates run from $200,000 to $400,000. This means that a year of crime may be ten to twenty times more costly to society than a year of incar-ceration.

"THREE STRIKES YOU'RE OUT"   The "revolving door" syndrome, with its heavy toll in crimes committed by persons previously convicted of crimes, has led to a nationwide movement to impose minimum 25-years-to-life sentences on crim-inals convicted of a third felony or third violent felony crime. A California citizens' initiative in 1994, Three Strikes You're Out, illustrates the popularity of this crack-down with voters; it passed 72 to 28 percent. The initiative was begun by a father whose eighteen-year-old daughter had been murdered by a parolee. Some of these initiatives are broadly written to include all felony convictions and therefore often encompass drug offenders, bad-check writers, and other nonviolent criminals. Other initiatives specify three *violent* felony convictions and thus target a smaller population of repeat crimi-nals. In 1995, Congress mandated life sentences for federal defendants convicted of their third violent felony. But longer prison sentences exacerbate the problem of prison over-crowding.

Efforts are now under way in many states to lower the cost of prison facilities. Not all prisoners need to be housed in maximum security institutions; nonviolent criminals can be safely housed in less costly minimum security facilities. "Privatization" can also dra-matically lower the costs of maintaining prisoners. States and counties can contract with private companies to both build and maintain prisons at much lower costs than govern-ment itself requires to perform these functions.

THE FAILURE OF PROBATION AND PAROLE   In addition to the nearly 1 million people behind bars, an additional 2.8 million are currently on probation and 600,000 on parole for serious crimes. But parole and probation have been just as ineffec-tive as prison in reducing crime. Even though persons placed on probation are considered less dangerous to society than persons imprisoned, studies indicate that nearly two-thirds of probationers will be arrested and over one-half will be convicted for a serious crime committed *while on probation.*

---

[42]See Abell, "Beyond Willie Horton," pp. 32–35.

The function of parole and postrelease supervision is (1) to procure information on the parolee's postprison conduct and (2) to facilitate and graduate the transition between the prison and complete freedom. These functions are presumably oriented toward protecting the public and rehabilitating the offender. However, studies of recidivism indicate that up to three-quarters of persons paroled from prison will be rearrested for serious crimes. There is no difference in this high rate of recidivism between persons released under supervised parole and those released unconditionally. Thus, it does not appear that parole succeeds in its objectives.

THE DEATH PENALTY

Perhaps the most heated debate in criminal justice today concerns capital punishment. Opponents of the death penalty argue that it is "cruel and unusual punishment" in violation of the Eighth Amendment of the U.S. Constitution. They also argue that the death penalty is applied unequally. A large proportion of those executed have been poor, uneducated, and nonwhite.

In contrast, there is a strong sense of justice among many Americans that demands retribution for heinous crimes—a life for a life. The death penalty dramatically signifies that society does not excuse or condone the taking of innocent lives. It symbolizes the value that society places on innocent lives. A mere jail sentence for murder devalues the life of the innocent victim. In most cases, a life sentence means less than ten years in prison under the current parole and probation policies of most states. Convicted murderers have been set free, and some have killed again. Moreover, prison guards and other inmates are exposed to convicted murderers who have "a license to kill," because they are already serving life sentences and have nothing to lose by killing again.

FURMAN V. GEORGIA AND UNFAIR APPLICATION   Prior to 1972, the death penalty was officially sanctioned by about one half of the states. Federal law also retained the death penalty. However, no one had actually suffered the death penalty since 1967, because of numerous legal tangles and direct challenges to the constitutionality of capital punishment. In 1972, the Supreme Court ruled that capital punishment *as it was then imposed* violated the Eighth and Fourteenth Amendment prohibitions against cruel and unusual punishment and due process of law. The decision was made by a narrow 5–4 vote of the justices, and the reasoning in the case is very complex. Only two justices—Brennan and Marshall—declared that capital punishment itself is cruel and unusual. The other three justices in the majority—Douglas, White, and Stewart—felt that death sentences had been applied unfairly: A few individuals were receiving the death penalty for crimes for which many others were receiving much lighter sentences. These justices left open the possibility that capital punishment would be constitutional if it was specific for certain kinds of crime and applied uniformly.

THE DEATH PENALTY REINSTATED   After *Furman* v. *Georgia,* most states rewrote their death-penalty laws to try to ensure fairness and uniformity of application.[43] Generally, these laws mandate the death penalty for murders committed during rape or robbery, hijacking or kidnapping; murders of prison guards; murder with torture; multiple murders; and so on. Two trials would be held: one to determine guilt or innocence and another to determine the penalty. At the second trial, evidence of "aggravating" and "mitigating" factors would be presented; if there were aggravating factors but no mitigating factors, the death penalty would be mandatory. In 1976, in *Gregs v. Georgia, Profit v. Florida,* and *Jurek v. Texas,* the Supreme Court upheld state laws that were carefully written to ensure fairness and due process in the application of the death penalty. The Court declared that capital punishment itself was not "cruel or unusual" within the meaning of the Eighth Amendment; that the authors of the Constitution did not consider it cruel or unusual; and that the reenactment of the death penalty by so many state legislators was evidence that the death penalty was not considered cruel or unusual by contemporary state lawmakers.

FEW EXECUTIONS   Despite these new laws, very few executions have been carried out. Over 2,700 prisoners are awaiting execution on "death row," but fewer than 225 persons were executed in eighteen states from 1976 through 1993. Texas, Florida, Louisiana, and Georgia led the states in the number of executions. California has had the highest number of prisoners on death row (nearly 400), but it carried out only two executions prior to 1994.

With less than 1 percent of death sentences actually carried out over the past decade, the death penalty cannot possibly be a deterrent to murder. Respect for the court system is eroded when the decisions of juries and judges are frustrated by convicted murderers. As trial judges and juries continue to impose the death penalty, and appellate courts continue to grant stays of execution, the number of prisoners on death row grows. The few who have been executed have averaged ten years' delay between trial and execution.

RACIAL BIAS?   The U.S. Supreme Court is especially sensitive to arguments based on racial discrimination. Defense lawyers have challenged the death penalty in several states by attempting to prove that racial bias infects the application of capital punishment. While white murderers are just as likely to receive the death penalty as black murderers, there are statistical disparities in sentencing between killers of whites and killers of blacks. If the *victim* is white, there is a greater chance that the killer will be sentenced to death than if the victim is black. But in 1987 the U.S. Supreme Court ruled (in a 5–4 decision) that statistical disparities in the race of the victim do not by themselves bar the

---

[43]States *with* death penalty: Alabama, Arizona, Arkansas, California, Colorado, Connecticut, Delaware, Florida, Georgia, Idaho, Illinois, Indiana, Kentucky, Louisiana, Maryland, Mississippi, Missouri, Montana, Nebraska, Nevada, New Hampshire, New Jersey, New Mexico, North Carolina, Ohio, Oregon, Oklahoma, Pennsylvania, South Carolina, South Dakota, Tennessee, Texas, Utah, Vermont, Virginia, Washington, and Wyoming. States with *no* death penalty: Alaska, Hawaii, Iowa, Kansas, Maine, Massachusetts, Michigan, Minnesota, New York, North Dakota, Rhode Island, West Virginia, Wisconsin, and the District of Columbia. As of 1994.

TRIVIA
PACKING A GUN IN THE STATES

The federal "Brady Law" requires a seven-day waiting period for the purchase of a handgun. This law is named for James S. Brady, former press secretary to President Ronald Reagan, who was severely wounded in the 1981 attempted assassination of the president. Brady and his wife, Sarah, championed the bill for many years before its adoption in 1993. Under the law's provisions, handgun dealers must send police agencies a form completed by the buyer (which is already required in most states); police agencies have seven days to make certain the purchaser is not a convicted felon, fugitive, drug addict, or mentally ill person, before the handgun can be transferred to the buyer.

Even if the Second Amendment's guarantee of "the right to bear arms" protects a citizen's right to own a gun (and many constitutional scholars argue that it only protects the rights of states to form militias), it does not protect the right to carry a hidden gun—a "concealed weapon." Indeed, nine states and the District of Columbia prohibit citizens from doing so. An additional sixteen states require citizens to go before a judge or a police official and prove that they have a specific need to carry a handgun before a concealed-weapon license can be issued. However, in recent years a number of states have relaxed their laws to allow any law-abiding citizen to obtain a concealed-weapon license. Previously convicted felons and mental incompetents are denied licenses everywhere, and some states require proof of training with a firearm. It is estimated that about 4 percent of the U.S. population is licensed to carry a concealed weapon. Polls suggest that about half of all U.S. households own a gun.

death penalty; there must be evidence of racial bias against a particular defendant in order for the Court to reverse a death sentence.[44]

DOES THE DEATH PENALTY DETER?   The death penalty as it is employed today—inflicted on so few and so many years after the crime—has little deterrent effect. However, it gives prosecutors some leverage in plea bargaining with murder defendants. They may choose to plead guilty in exchange for a life sentence, when confronted with the possibility that the prosecutor may win a conviction and the death penalty in a jury trial.

PUBLIC OPINION AND CAPITAL PUNISHMENT   Much of the debate in the states over the death penalty, however, has *not* centered on the question of deterrence. Opponents of the death penalty call it "murder" and contend that it is morally in-

---

[44]*McCluskey v. Kemp*, 481 U.S. 279 (1987).

STATE CONCEALED-WEAPON LAWS

CITIZENS PROHIBITED FROM CARRYING HANDGUNS

District of Columbia	Missouri	Ohio
Illinois	Nebraska	Wisconsin
Kansas	New Mexico	
Kentucky	North Carolina	

HANDGUNS PERMITTED UPON SHOWING SPECIFIC NEED

Alabama	Iowa	Nevada
California	Louisiana	New Jersey
Colorado	Maryland	New York
Delaware	Massachusetts	Rhode Island
Hawaii	Michigan	South Carolina
Indiana	Minnesota	

HANDGUNS PERMITTED WITH CITIZEN LICENSE

Alaska	Mississippi	Tennessee
Arizona	Montana	Texas
Arkansas	New Hampshire	Utah
Connecticut	North Dakota	Virginia
Florida	Oklahoma	Washington
Georgia	Oregon	West Virginia
Idaho	Pennsylvania	Wyoming
Maine	South Dakota	

NO RESTRICTIONS
Vermont

defensible for the state to take away life. Proponents of the death penalty say that the unwillingness of the state to impose capital punishment implies that little value is placed upon the lives of innocent victims. Public opinion now favors the death penalty by over 3 to 1. Only for a few years during the mid-1960s did public opinion oppose the death penalty, and then only by a small margin. With increases in the crime rate in the 1970s, heavy majorities swung back in favor of capital punishment. Public support for capital punishment remains high today.

9

COMMUNITY POLITICAL SYSTEMS

COMMUNITIES AS SETTINGS FOR POLITICS

American communities come in different shapes and sizes, and community politics come in a variety of styles. Generalizing about community politics is perhaps even more difficult than generalizing about American state politics. There are more than 86,000 local governments in the United States. These include cities, municipalities, townships, counties, and a host of other school districts and special districts. (See Table 9–1.) Two-thirds of the American people live in urban units of local government known as "municipalities," including "cities," "boroughs," "villages," or "towns." Other Americans are served by county or township governments. Moreover, there are over 250 metropolitan areas in the United States; these are clusterings of people and governments around a core city of 50,000 or more residents. These metropolitan areas range in size up to the New York area, which has 600 local governments and 18 million people. In short, one may conceive of community political systems as rural counties, towns, and villages, cities of all sizes, or even sprawling metropolitan areas.

MANAGING CONFLICT   Community political systems serve two principal functions. One is that of supplying goods and services—for example, police protection or sewage disposal—that are not supplied by private enterprise. This is the "service" func-

Table 9–1

LOCAL GOVERNMENTS IN THE UNITED STATES

	1952	1962	1972	1982	1987	1992
Counties	3,502	3,043	3,044	3,041	3,042	3,043
Municipalities	16,807	17,997	18,517	19,076	19,200	19,296
Townships	17,202	17,144	16,991	16,734	16,691	16,666
School Districts	67,355	34,678	15,781	14,851	14,721	14,586
Special Districts	12,340	18,323	23,885	28,588	29,532	33,131
Total (including States and National Government)	116,756	91,185	78,269	82,341	83,186	86,743

Source: U.S. Bureau of the Census, *Census of Governments, 1992*

tion. The other function is the "political" one, that of *managing conflict* over public policy. Of course, the "political" and the "service" functions of local governments are often indistinguishable in practice. A mayor who intervenes in a dispute about the location of a park is managing a local government service, namely recreation, at the same time that he or she is managing political conflict about whose neighborhood should get the most benefit from the new park. In the day-to-day administration of the service functions of local government, officials must decide a variety of political questions. Where are the facilities to be located? (Often the question is where *not* to locate facilities, since many neighborhoods avoid having public facilities for fear that they will displace families, attract "undesirables," or depress local property values.) How are public services to be paid for? Which agency or official will be in charge of a particular service? What policies or practices will govern the provision of this service? What level of service will be provided?

Occasionally, students are led to believe that local governments should be less "political" than state or national governments. Many people feel that it would be best to eliminate "politics" from local government. However, politicians who respond to political considerations, in contrast to service considerations, are not necessarily sacrificing the welfare of the community. It is not always true that the community is best served by treating the service function of government as if it were more important or more worthy of government attention than the political one. A politician who undertakes to arrange political compromises and balance competing interests in a community is performing a very important function. Helping people with different incomes, occupations, skin colors, religious beliefs, and styles of living to live together in a reasonably peaceful fashion is a vital task.

SOURCES OF COMMUNITY CONFLICT   What are the sources of community conflicts? Human diversity is the source of all political conflict—differences among people in wealth, occupation, education, ethnicity, race, religion, and style of living. In the United States, there are many rural communities, small towns and cities, and compact suburbs with relatively homogeneous populations. In these communities, there are few differences among citizens that create permanent lines of cleavage or that run very deep. Some conflicts occur in these communities, of course, but groupings of forces are usually temporary. In contrast, in most large cities and metropolitan areas there are many different kinds of people living closely together, and there are more lasting cleavages, or "fault lines," which tend to open when controversial issues arise. These cleavages are readily recognized in disputes among upper-, middle-, and lower-income groups; ethnic groups; labor and management interests; property owners and nonproperty owners; families with children and those without; suburbanites and city dwellers; and traditional political party divisions.[1] Increasingly in America's large cities, *race* is becoming the major source of conflict.

COPING WITH DISSATISFACTION   How do individuals cope with community problems? If you are dissatisfied with the way things are going in your community, you have three choices: (1) resign yourself to the situation, do nothing, and just tolerate it; (2) move away and find a community that provides more satisfactions; (3) stay and make an attempt to change things. Political scientists tend to focus their attention on the people who try to change things, implying that this is the only way to respond rationally to community problems. However, economists have developed theories of residential mobility that focus on the individual's choice of community based on a rational calculation of personal costs and benefits.[2] (The theory is most applicable to metropolitan areas where many different kinds of communities are available.) There are recognized negative "push" factors—crime, congestion, noise, overcrowding, racial conflict—and positive "pull" factors—more space, larger houses, better shcools, "nice" playmates for the children—both of which affect decisions to move. One might move to the suburbs "for the kids," or move to the city to be close to good restaurants, fine entertainment, cultural events, and specialty shops, or to reduce the trip to work. One can choose among suburbs by balancing residential amenities and services against land costs and taxes. In short, economists emphasize rational calculations and freedom of choice, which they assume most citizens possess.

How do people actually respond to community dissatisfactions? There is some evidence to suggest that, in the face of community problems:[3]

- Higher-status whites tend either to become politically active or to move out, with political activity somewhat more common.
- Lower-status whites tend to move out rather than become politically active.

---

[1] For some empirical support for these speculations, see Gordon S. Black, "Conflict in the Community: A Theory of the Effect of Community Size," *American Political Science Review,* 68 (September 1974), 1245–61; see also Timothy A. Almy, "Residential Locations and Electoral Cohesion," *American Political Science Review,* 67 (September 1973), 914–23, who argues that conflict is greater in communities where different social groups are residentially segregated.

[2] The widely cited classic essay is Charles M. Tiebout, "The Pure Theory of Local Expenditure," *Journal of Political Economy,* 64 (October 1956), 416–24.

[3] John M. Orbell and Toru Uno, "A Theory of Neighborhood Problem Solving: Political Action versus Residential Mobility," *American Political Science Review,* 66 (June 1972), 471–89; William E. Lyons and David Lowery, "Citizen Response to Dissatisfaction in Urban Communities," *Journal of Politics,* 51 (November 1989), 841–68.

- Blacks are more likely to become politically active than to move out, probably because of the increased difficulties most blacks face in residential relocation.
- City residents are more likely to move out, whereas suburbanites are more likely to become politically active.
- People who have been generally satisfied with the past performance of their local government, as well as people who have invested in home ownership or local businesses, are more likely to become politically active to solve a current problem, rather than to move out or do nothing.
- Dissatisfied affluent residents may chose to "privatize" the community services that distress them. The most common example is the choice of private schools over the public school system, but occasionally residents and businesses also turn to private police protection, security services, garbage collection, and so on.

Overall, the tendency to "move away" from urban problems has greatly accentuated the difficulties of the nation's largest central cities. Many of these cities are actually declining in population—losing middle-class residents to their surrounding suburbs. We will return to this problem in Chapter 12, but it is important to know how individual citizens as well as governments cope with community problems.

EIGHTY-SIX THOUSAND GOVERNMENTS: WHAT THEY ALL DO

Local government is not mentioned in the U.S. Constitution. Although we regard the American federal system as a mixture of federal, state, and *local* governments, from a constitutional point of view, local governments are really parts of state governments. Communities have no right to self-government in the U.S. Constitution. All of their governmental powers legally flow from state laws and constitutions. Local governments—cities, townships, counties, special districts, and school districts—are creatures of the state, subject to the obligations, privileges, powers, and restrictions that state governments impose upon them. The state may create or destroy any or all units of local government. To the extent that local governments can collect taxes, regulate their citizens, and provide services, they are actually exercising *state* powers delegated to them by the state in either its constitution or its laws.

Different units of government are assigned different responsibilities by each of the states, so it is difficult to generalize about what each of these types of local governments is supposed to do. Indeed, even in the same state, there may be overlapping functions and responsibilities assigned to cities, counties, school districts, and special districts. Nevertheless, let us try to make some generalizations about what each of these types of government does, realizing of course that in any specific location the pattern of governmental activity may be slightly different:

Counties

—Rural: keep records of deeds, mortgages, births, marriages; assess and levy property taxes; maintain local roads; administer elections and certify election results to state; provide law enforcement through sheriff; maintain criminal court; maintain a local jail; administer state welfare programs.

—Urban: most of same functions as rural counties (except police and court systems, which often become city functions), together with planning and control of new subdivisions; mental health; public health maintenance and public hospitals; care of the aged; recreation, including parks, stadiums, and convention centers; and perhaps some city functions.

Cities

—provide the "common functions" of police, fire, streets, sewage, sanitation, and parks; over half of the nation's large cities also provide welfare services and public education. (In other cities welfare is handled by county governments or directly by state agencies, and education is handled by separate school districts.)

School districts

—organized specifically to provide public elementary and secondary education; community colleges may be operated by county governments or by special districts with or without state support.

Townships

—generally subdivisions of counties with the same responsibilities as their county.

Special districts

—may be as large as the Port Authority of New York and New Jersey with billions in diversified assets. However, special districts are usually established for mass transit, soil conservation, libraries, water and irrigation, mosquito control, sewage disposal, airports, and so on.

The fifty states vary a great deal in the numbers of local governments they authorize. (See Figure 9–1.) Hawaii is the nation's most centralized state: There are only eighteen local governments in the Aloha State; fourteen of these are special districts without taxing power; three are counties; and one is the city of Honolulu. In contrast, there are 6,627 local governments in Illinois, including 1,279 cities, 102 counties, 1,434 townships, 1,029 school districts, and 2,783 special districts.

COUNTY GOVERNMENTS: RURAL AND URBAN

All states, with the exception of Connecticut and Rhode Island, have organized *county* governments. In Louisiana, counties are called "parishes," and in Alaska they are called "boroughs." It is difficult to generalize about the powers of the nation's 3,402 counties. The legal powers, organization, and officers of counties vary a great deal. Perhaps it would be best to begin a description of county government by distinguishing between *rural* and *urban* counties. Obviously there is a great deal of difference between Los Angeles County with 8.5 million people; Cook County, Chicago, with 5.2 million; and Harris County, Houston, with 2.8 million; and the 725 rural counties in the nation with populations of 10,000 or less.

Figure 9–1
LOCAL GOVERNMENTS IN THE STATES

All Local Governmental Units

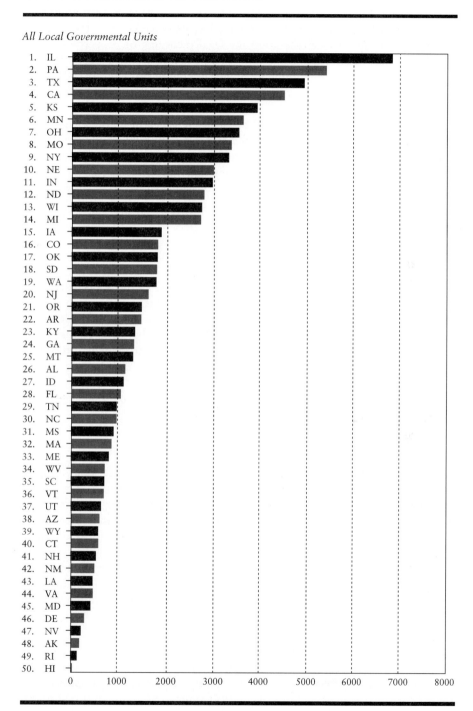

Source: *Statistical Abstract of the United States, 1994*, p. 295.

RURAL COUNTIES   Traditionally, the rural county was the most important unit of local government: It handled such essential matters as law enforcement, courts, schools, roads, elections, poor relief, and the legal recording of property deeds, mortgages, wills, and marriages. Rural communities competed with each other for the location of the county seat, because the community named as county seat won social and political prestige, county jobs, a county fair, and preferential treatment in county roads and public buildings. Moreover, many rural dwellers identify themselves as "coming from" a particular county. The county seat attracted retail business: Farm markets were generally located in county seats, where a farmer could transact both public and private business. Rural county government provided an arena for a folksy, provincial, individualistic, "friends and neighbors" type of politics. Rural county government was the province of amateurs rather than experts or professionals. Decision making was personalized and informal. Often rural counties resemble urban counties about as much as the old-fashioned country store resembles a modern supermarket.

URBAN COUNTIES   County government in urban areas is acquiring many of the responsibilities of city governments. Urban counties may provide traditional "city services" to the unincorporated areas of the county, that is, to the areas not within the boundaries of cities, and occasionally to cities as well. This is particularly true of the county governments located in large metropolitan areas (see Table 9–2). Urban county governments generally provide all of the services of traditional rural counties together with a host of additional contemporary government services, from mass transit facilities and airports to sports stadiums and convention centers (see Table 9–3).

THE STRUCTURE OF COUNTY GOVERNMENT

Although county governments may differ markedly in their organization, they generally have (1) a governing body variously called the "county commissioners," "county board," "board of supervisors," or even "judges," which is composed of anywhere from three to fifty elected members; (2) a number of separately elected officials with countrywide jurisdictions, such as sheriff, county attorney, auditor, recorder, coroner, assessor, judge, treasurer, and so on; (3) a large number of special boards or commissions which have authority over various functions, whose members may be elected or appointed by the county commissioners or may even include the county commissioners in an ex officio capacity; and (4) an appointed county bureaucracy in planning, transportation, health, welfare, libraries, parks, and so on.

TRADITIONAL COUNTY COMMISSION STRUCTURE   Traditionally county governments have been organized around the commission structure (see top of Figure 9–2). Over half of the nation's counties still operate under this structure. Typically there are three or five county commissioners, elected for overlapping four-year terms, and a large number of separately elected county officials. There is no single person responsi-

Table 9–2

URBAN COUNTIES OF ONE MILLION OR MORE PERSONS

County	Population (millions)
Arizona	
Maricopa (Phoenix)	2.0
California	
Alameda (Oakland and Berkeley)	1.2
Los Angeles	8.6
Orange (South of Los Angeles)	2.3
San Diego	2.4
Santa Clara (San Jose)	1.4
Florida	
Broward (Ft. Lauderdale)	1.2
Dade (Miami)	1.8
Illinois	
Cook (Chicago)	5.3
Michigan	
Oakland (North of Detroit)	1.1
Wayne (Detroit)	2.1
Minnesota	
Hennepin (Minneapolis)	1.0
Missouri	
St. Louis	1.0
New York	
Bronx (part of New York City)	1.2
Kings (part of New York City)	2.3
Nassau (part of New York City)	1.3
New York (part of New York City)	1.5
Queens (part of New York City)	1.9
Suffolk (part of New York City)	1.3
Ohio	
Cuyahoga (Cleveland)	1.4
Pennsylvania	
Alleghenny (Pittsburgh)	1.4
Philadelphia	1.6
Texas	
Bexar (San Antonio)	1.2
Dallas	1.9
Harris (Houston)	2.8
Tarrant (Fort Worth)	1.1
Washington	
King (Seattle)	1.4

Source: U.S. Bureau of the Census.

Table 9–3
COUNTY FUNCTIONS

Traditional, Rural	Contemporary, Urban
Property tax assessment and collection	Mass transit
Election administration	Airports
Judicial administration, including civil	Libraries
and criminal courts, probate, etc.	Water supply and sewage disposal
Recording of deeds, mortgages, and other	Water and air pollution control
legal instruments	Building and housing code enforcement
Recording of vital statistics, including	Natural resource preservation
births, deaths, and marriages	Planning and land use control
Local roads and bridges, construction and	Community development and housing
maintenance	Parks and recreation
Law enforcement (sheriff and coroner)	Stadiums, convention and cultural centers
County jail maintenance	Public health, including clinics
Administer state welfare and social	Public hospitals
service programs	Disaster preparedness together with
Other: county fairs, agricultural extension	traditional functions
service	

ble for administration of county functions. The commissioners may supervise some functions themselves and share supervision of other functions with other elected officials. Thus, for example, both the elected sheriff and the county commissioners share responsibility for the county jail, with the sheriff supervising day-to-day operations, but the commissioners deciding on its construction, repair, and financing. The commissioners usually decide on the property tax *rate* (or "millage," with one mill equal to one-tenth of a percent) to be imposed on property owners (subject to maximums usually set by the state legislature). But the tax *assessor* determines the value of each parcel of property in the county against which the rate is to be applied. And in some counties a separate tax *collector* actually sends out the tax bills and undertakes to collect the revenue. A separate *treasurer* may maintain the county's financial accounts and write the checks. Thus, responsibility for county government is fragmented and dispersed.

Reformers view this traditional structure of county government as lacking in efficiency and accountability. Governmental functions are usually in the hands of untrained nonprofessional county officeholders. County jobs are awarded to "friends and neighbors and relatives." Few voters, even in small rural counties, know enough about what goes on in various offices in the "county courthouse" to hold individual officers responsible for their administration. Typically, independently elected county officials are returned to office term after term with little or no opposition. Only the sheriff's race in rural counties stirs up much interest.

COUNTY ADMINISTRATOR STRUCTURE   Urbanization and the proliferation of county functions usually result in demands for more professional administration of county government. When county commissioners find that they cannot cope with the

Figure 9–2
STRUCTURES OF COUNTY GOVERNMENT

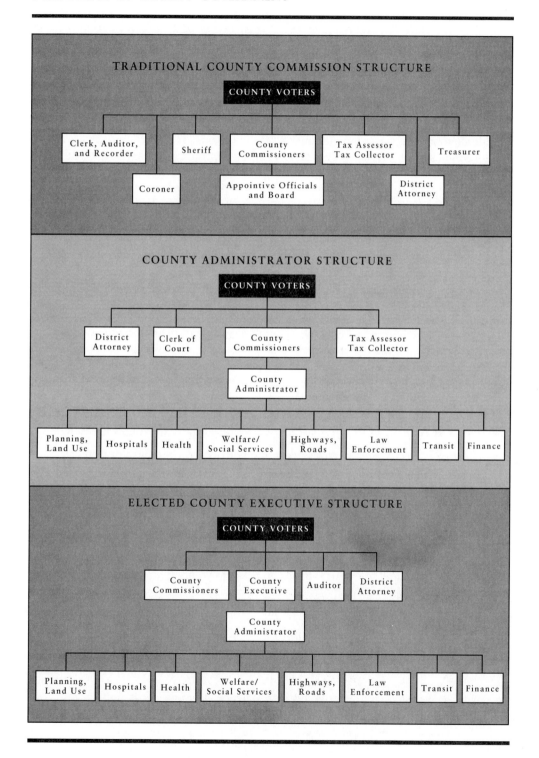

volume and complexity of county business, they often seek professional assistance. The *county administrator* or county-manager structure of government offers a solution. It is based on the council-manager form of city government (see "Forms of City Government" later in this chapter). An appointed county administrator, responsible to the commission, is placed in charge of the various county departments and agencies. The commission makes policy and appoints the administrator to *implement* policy. The administrator prepares the budget for the commission's approval and then implements it; the administrator hires and fires department heads and reports back regularly to the commission on county business. It seldom works out as neatly as it appears on the organization chart, but the use of the county administrator plan has grown rapidly throughout the United States in recent years.

Voters lose some direct control over county functions with the adoption of the county administrator structure. And county commissioners themselves are usually obliged to go through the county administrator to influence activities in a county department. But the advantage is the professional leadership, administrative efficiency, and functional account-ability that the structure brings to county government. The role of the administrator is similar to that of a city manager (see "City Managers in Municipal Politics" in Chapter 11).

ELECTED COUNTY EXECUTIVE STRUCTURE   A few counties in the United States have adopted a governmental structure that features an *elected* "county executive." Voters elect *both* a county commission and a separate county executive officer, who exercises formal responsibility over county departments. The elected county executive usually appoints the county administrator subject to approval of the commission. This structure envisions the separation of legislative and executive powers, much like American state and national governments. The elected county executive, like the county administrator, has won approval in many urban counties over recent years.

COUNTY OFFICIALS   Typically, county officials have the following duties:

Commissioners: elected governing body with general responsibility for all county functions; most commissions have three to seven members with election by the county's voters at large.

Sheriff: maintains jail; furnishes law enforcement and unincorporated areas; carries out orders of the county court.

Auditor: maintains financial records; authorizes payment of county obligations.

County or district attorney: serves as chief prosecuting attorney; conducts criminal investigations and prosecutes law violators.

Coroner: conducts medical investigations to determine cause of death; maintains county morgue.

Tax collector: collects taxes.

Treasurer: maintains and disperses county funds; makes county fiscal reports.

Clerk: registers and records legal documents including deeds, mortgages, subdivision plats, marriages, divorces, births; certifies election returns.

Tax assessor: determines value of all taxable property in the county.

The many separately elected county officials are generally considered an obstacle to the emergence of strong executive leadership at the county level. The ability of county governments to assume more important functions and responsibilities, particularly in urban areas, probably hinges upon a reorganization of county government to provide for stronger executive leadership.

TOWNSHIPS   Another interesting unit of local government is the "township," which is found in about half of the states—the northern states from New England to the Midwest. Southern and western states have made little use of this unit of government. Townships are subdivisions of counties and perform many of the functions of county governments at a grass-roots level—elections, road repair, tax administration, fire protection, and even law enforcement through local justices of the peace. Townships are unincorporated, which means they do not have charters from state governments guaranteeing their political independence or authorizing them to provide many municipal services. The jurisdiction of townships may extend over many square miles of sparsely populated rural territory. About 40 million people, or one-fifth of the U.S. population, live under township governments today.

Township governments vary considerably in their powers and organization. Perhaps it would be best to classify them as "rural townships," and "urban townships." Rural townships outside of New England have lost much of their vitality in recent years. The school district consolidation movement (see Chapter 15) has centralized the control of public schools at the county level or in school districts that span villages and townships.

Some urban townships appear to have a brighter future as units of government than do rural townships. This is particularly true in certain suburban areas of larger cities where metropolitan growth has enveloped township governments. Some states, Pennsylvania for example, have authorized urban townships to exercise many of the powers and provide many of the services previously reserved to city governments.

THE NEW ENGLAND TOWN   In the New England states, the "town" is a significant unit of local government, with long traditions and deep roots in the political philosophy of the people of the region. In fact, the New England "town meeting" is often cited by political philosophers as the ideal form of *direct* democracy as distinguished from *representative* democracy. For the town meeting was, and to some extent still is, the central institution of "town" government. The New England town included a village and all of its surrounding farms. The town meeting was open to all eligible voters; it was generally an important social as well as political event. The town meeting would levy taxes, make appropriations, determine policy, and elect officers for the year. Between town meetings, a board of selected officials would supervise the activities of the town—schools, health, roads, care of the poor, and so on. Other officers include town clerk, tax assessors and collectors, justices of the peace, constables, road commissioners, and school board members. Although the ideal of direct democracy is still alive in many smaller New England towns, in the large towns, the pure democracy of the town meeting has given way to a representative system (representative town meeting government), in which town meeting members are elected prior to the town meeting. Moreover, much of the determination of the towns' financial affairs, previously decided at town meetings, has now been given over to elected officials, and many towns have appointed town managers to supervise the day-to-day administration of town services.

CITIES AS "MUNICIPAL CORPORATIONS"

Legally speaking, cities are "municipal corporations" that have received charters from state governments setting forth their boundaries, governmental powers and functions, structure and organization, methods of finance, and powers to elect and appoint officers and employees. The municipal *charter* is intended to grant the powers of local self-government to a community. Of course, the powers of self-government granted by a municipal charter are not unlimited. A state can change its charter or take it away altogether, as it sees fit. Cities, like other local governments, have only the powers that state laws and constitutions grant them. They are still subdivisions of the state. And, of course, state laws operate within the boundaries of cities. In fact, municipal corporations are generally responsible for the enforcement of state law within their boundaries. However, they also have the additional power to make local laws, "ordinances," which operate only within their boundaries.

DILLON'S RULE   Perhaps the most serious limitation on the powers of cities is the fact that American courts have insisted upon interpreting the powers granted in charters very narrowly. The classic statement of this principle of restrictive interpretation of municipal powers was made by John F. Dillon many years ago and is now well known as "Dillon's rule":

> It is a general and undisputed proposition of law that a municipal corporation possesses and can exercise the following powers, and no others: first, those granted in express words; second, those necessarily or fairly implied in or incident to the powers expressly granted; third, those essential to the accomplishment of the declared objects and purposes of the corporation—not simply convenient, but indispensable. Any fair, reasonable, substantial doubt concerning the existence of power is resolved by the courts against a corporation, and the power is denied.[4]

STATE LEGISLATORS RETAIN LOCAL POWERS   The restrictive interpretation of the powers of cities leads to rather lengthy city charters, since nearly everything a city does must have specific legal authorization in the charter. The city charter of New York, for example, is several hundred pages long. City charters must cover in detail such matters as boundaries, structure of government, ordinance-making powers, finances, contracts, purchasing, bonds, courts, municipal elections, property assessments, zoning laws and building codes, licenses, franchises, law enforcement, education, health, streets, parks, public utilities, and on and on. Since any proposed change in the powers, organization, or responsibilities of cities requires an act of a state legislature amending the city's charter, state legislatures are intimately involved in local legislation. This practice of narrowly interpreting city charters may appear awkward, but its effect is to increase the power of state legislators in city affairs. State legislators from cities acquire power because legislatures usually grant a local legislator the courtesy of accepting his or her views on local legislation that affects only that legislator's constituency.

---

[4]John F. Dillon, *Commentaries on the Laws of Municipal Corporations*, 5th ed. (Boston: Little, Brown, 1911), p. 448.

SPECIAL ACT CHARTERS   State legislative control over cities is most firmly entrenched in *special act* charters. These charters are specially drawn for the cities named in them. Cities under special act charters remain directly under legislative control, and specific legislative approval for that city and that city alone must be obtained for any change in its government or service activities. Such charters give rise to local acts dealing with small details of city government in a specially named city, for example, "that West Fall River be authorized to appropriate money for the purchase of uniforms for the park policy." Under special act charters, laws that apply to one city do not necessarily apply to others.

GENERAL ACT CHARTERS   In contrast, *general act* charters usually classify cities according to their size and then apply municipal laws to all cities in each size classification. Thus, a state's municipal law may apply to all cities of less than 10,000 people, another law to all cities with populations of 10,000–25,000, another to cities with 25,000–50,000 people, and so on. These general act charters make it difficult to interfere in the activities of a particular city without affecting the activities of all cities of a similar size category. Yet in practice there are often exceptions and modifications to general act legislation. For example, since legislators know the populations of their cities, they can select size categories for municipal law that apply to only one city.

OPTIONAL CHARTERS   *Optional charter* laws provide cities with some choice in the structure and organization of their governments. Such laws generally offer a choice of governmental forms: strong mayor and weak council, weak mayor and strong council, commission, city manager, or some modification of these.

HOME RULE   *Home rule* charters are designed to give cities the power to adopt governmental forms and provide municipal services, as they see fit, without state legislative interference. Home rule charters may be given to cities by state constitutions or by legislative enactments; legislative home rule is considered less secure, since a legislature could retract the grant if it wished to do so. Beginning with Missouri in 1875, more than half the states have included in their constitutions provisions for the issuance of home rule charters. About two-thirds of the nation's cities with populations over 200,000 have some form of home rule.

The intended effect of home rule is to reverse "Dillion's rule" and enable cities to "exercise all legislative powers not prohibited by law or by charter." In other words, instead of preventing a city from doing anything not specifically authorized, home rule permits the city to do anything not specifically prohibited. The theory of home rule grants sweeping powers to cities; however, in practice, home rule has not brought self-government to cities.

Home rule provisions in state constitutions range from those that grant considerable power and discretion over local affairs, to provisions that are so useless that no city has ever made use of them. First of all, these constitutional provisions may be too cumbersome or vague for effective implementation. In some states, cities feel that it is easier to use the general law charters, particularly if they provide for optional forms of government, than to use the cumbersome procedures for obtaining home rule.

Another important limitation on home rule is the distinction between "self-enforcing" and "non–self-enforcing," or "permissive," home rule provisions in state constitutions. Non–self-enforcing home rule provisions merely permit the state legislature to grant home rule to its cities; cities cannot acquire home rule without legislative action. Only about a dozen states have "self-enforcing" home rule provisions, which enable cities to bypass the state legislature and adopt home rule for themselves.

Finally, home rule may be limited by court interpretations of the language of the constitutional provisions granting power to home rule in cities. Constitutional provisions may grant to home rule cities the power to make "all laws and ordinances relating to municipal concerns," or the "powers of local self-government," or all powers "in respect to municipal affairs." Of course, ordinances passed under home rule authority cannot be in conflict with state law. Courts must distinguish between municipal and statewide concerns. In cases where doubt exists, legal traditions of municipal law require that courts resolve the doubt in favor of the state and against local powers of home rule. State legislatures can intervene in local affairs in home rule cities by simply deciding that a particular matter is of statewide concern.

POLITICS OF HOME RULE   The politics of home rule often pits reform groups, city mayors, and administrators against state legislators and large municipal taxpayers. State legislators are generally wary of giving up their authority over cities. Rural legislators have little reason to support city home rule, and even city legislators seldom welcome proposals to give up their authority over local bills. Sometimes city employees with good access to the legislature will oppose giving a mayor or a city manager too much control over their employment. Taxpayer groups may fear that home rule will give the city the ability to increase taxes. Local bills may be pictured as a distraction to legislators by reformers, but many legislators enjoy the power that it brings them in local affairs and welcome the opportunity to perform legislative services for their constituents. And so, even with reapportionment adding to the number of urban legislators, the League of Women Voters, good-government groups, and mayors may still be frustrated in their attempts to achieve genuine home rule for American cities.

COURTS RETAIN LOCAL POWERS   Courts figure prominently in municipal politics. This is because of the subordinate position of the municipal corporation in the hierarchy of governments, and legal traditions, such as Dillon's rule, which narrowly interpret the power of local governments. The power of courts over municipal affairs grants leverage to defenders of the *status quo* in any political battle at the local level. Proponents of a new municipal law or municipal service not only must win the battle over whether a city *ought* to pass the new law or provide the new service but also must win the legal battle over whether the city *can* pass the law or provide the service. Limitations and uncertainties abound about the validity of local enactments. Legal challenges to the authority of the city to pass new regulations or provide new services are frequent. The city attorney becomes a key official because he or she must advise the city about what it can or cannot do. Not only must the city obey the federal constitution, but it is also subject to the restraints of the state constitution, state laws, its municipal charter, and of course, Dillon's rule. The result is to greatly strengthen courts, attorneys, and defenders of the status quo.

FORMS OF CITY GOVERNMENT

American city government comes in various structural packages (see Figure 9–3). There are some adaptations and variations from city to city, but generally one can classify the form of city government as mayor-council, commission, council-manager, town meeting, or representative town meeting. Over half of American cities operate under mayor-council governments; most other cities have adopted council-manager government (see Table 9–4).

MAYOR-COUNCIL   The nation's largest cities tend to function under the *mayor-council* plan. This is the oldest form of American city government and is designed in the American tradition of separation of powers between legislature and execuve. One may also establish subcategories of "strong" or "weak" mayor forms of mayor-council government. A strong mayor is one who is the undisputed master of the executive agencies of city government and who has substantial legislative powers in the form of budget making, vetoes, and opportunity to propose legislation. Only a few cities make the mayor the sole elected official among city executive officers; it is common for the mayor to share powers with other elected officials—city attorney, treasurer, tax assessor, auditor, clerk, and so on. Yet many mayors, by virtue of their prestige, persuasive abilities, or role as party leader, have been able to overcome most of the weaknesses of their formal office.

In recent years, large cities have been adding to the formal powers of their chief executives. Cities have augmented the mayors' role by providing them with direction over budgeting, purchasing, and personnel controls; and independent boards and commissions and individual councilmen have relinquished administrative control over city departments in many cities. Moreover, many cities have strengthened their mayors' position by providing them with a chief administrative officer, "CAO," to handle important staff and administrative duties of supervising city departments and providing central management services.

COMMISSION   The *commission* form of city government gives both legislative and executive powers to a small body, usually consisting of five members. The commission form originated at the beginning of the century as a reform movement designed to end a system of divided responsibility between mayor and council. One of the commission members is nominally the mayor, but he or she has no more formal powers than the other commissioners. The board of commissioners is directly responsible for the operation of city departments and agencies. In practice, one commission member will become responsible for the management of a specific department, such as finance, public works, or public safety. As long as the council members are in agreement over policy, there are few problems; but when commissioners differ among themselves and develop separate spheres of influence in city government, city government becomes a multiheaded monster, totally lacking in coordination. The results of a commission form of government were generally so disastrous that the reform movement abandoned its early support of this form of government in favor of the council-manager plan.

COUNCIL-MANAGER   The *council-manager* form of government revived the distinction between legislative "policy making" and executive "administration" in city

Figure 9–3
FORMS OF CITY GOVERNMENT

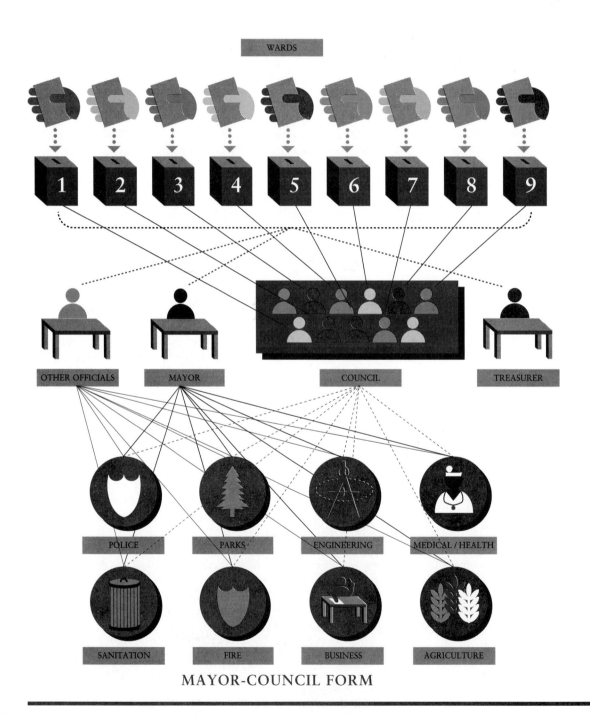

WARDS

1 2 3 4 5 6 7 8 9

OTHER OFFICIALS   MAYOR   COUNCIL   TREASURER

POLICE   PARKS   ENGINEERING   MEDICAL / HEALTH

SANITATION   FIRE   BUSINESS   AGRICULTURE

MAYOR-COUNCIL FORM

COUNCIL-MANAGER FORM

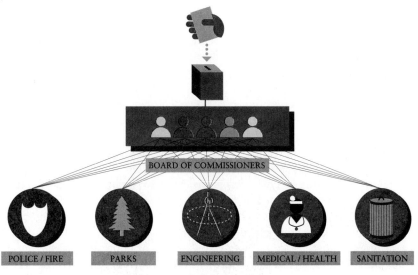

COMMISSION FORM

Table 9–4

AMERICAN CITIES: FORMS OF GOVERNMENT

	Number	*Percent*
Mayor-council	3,800	53
Council-manager	2,683	38
Commission	172	2
Town meeting	411	6
Representative town meeting	79	1

Source: International City Managers' Association, *Municipal Yearbook 1992,* Washington: ICMA, 1992. Table 1–1.

government. Policy-making responsibility is vested in an elected council, and administration is assigned to an appointed professional administrator known as a manager. The council chooses the manager who is responsible to it. All departments of the city government operate under the direction of the manager, who has the power to hire and fire personnel within the limits set by the merit system. The council's role in administration is limited to selecting and dismissing the city manager. The plan is based on the idea that policy making and administration are separate functions, and that the principal task of city government is to provide the highest level of services at the lowest possible costs—utilities, streets, fire and police protection, health, welfare, recreation, and so on. Hence, a professionally trained, career-oriented administrator is given direct control over city departments.

TOWN MEETING AND REPRESENTATIVE TOWN MEETING

Town-meeting and representative town-meeting governments are currently found in Connecticut, Maine, Massachusetts, New Hampshire, and Vermont. Most town meetings are held in response to the issuance of a warrant (agenda) by an elected town clerk and/or by the elected town council. The town meeting is open to all residents and it possesses full legislative authority. A town meeting may be called once or twice a year. In most town meetings, the passage of the annual budget is the most important item of business.

Town meetings usually choose a board to oversee business between meetings. Voters separately elect a town clerk, treasurer, assessor, constable, school board, and other officers. The town meeting may also elect a finance committee to prepare the budget.

While the town meeting has been celebrated by many political philosophers as "pure democracy," the reality is much less than full participatory democracy. Attendance at town meetings is usually less than 10 percent of the town's voters. In larger towns, the participation rate may be only 1 or 2 percent of the voters. The idealized town meeting democracy is really governance by a very small group of political activists. Special interest groups can easily pack a town meeting. Senior citizens attend these meetings in disproportionate numbers. And employees, members of the volunteer fire company, school teachers, and business and civic association members are also overrepresented. Of course, attendance increases when controversial items are on the agenda. And in many town-meeting governments, a decision can be overturned by citizen initiative and referendum.[5]

Representative town-meeting government (RTM) is a hybrid political institution that seeks to combine features of the open town meeting with representative government. In RTM the voters elect a relatively large number of persons to vote at meetings, yet voters retain the right to attend and speak at town meetings themselves. However, in practice the number of candidates for town-meeting members is frequently equal to or even smaller than the number of town-meeting members to be elected. Town clerks often must recruit people to become town-meeting members. In theory representative town-meeting members should be more attentive than townspeople because they accepted the responsibility of public office. But attendance is also a problem in RTM government.

TYPES OF CITIES AND FORMS OF GOVERNMENT

Let us examine the social, economic, and political forces shaping the struture of city government—that is, the conditions associated with the selection of one of the principal forms of government.

SIZE OF CITY   First of all, council-manager government is closely associated with the *size* of cities. Large cities show a distinct preference for the more "political" form of mayor-council government in contrast to the more "efficient" form of council-manager government. (See Table 9–5.) All cities over 1 million population have the mayor-council form of government. Only a few large cities have council-manager government. The council-manager form of government is most popular in the middle-sized cities—those with populations of 25,000 to 250,000 people. Probably, cities with fewer than 10,000 residents do not have sufficient resources to justify hiring a trained professional city manager nor, in all probability, do they have the administrative problems requiring the expertise of such an individual. Thus, small cities, like large cities, tend to rely upon mayor-council government, although probably for different reasons.

POLITICAL CONFLICT   What explains the absence of council-manager government in large cities? A common explanation is that the political environment of large cities is so complex, with many competing interests, that these cities require strong *political* leardership that can arbitrate struggles for power, arrange compromises, and be directly responsible to the people for policy decisions. A large city requires a political form of government that can resolve the conflicting claims of diverse interests. This implies that in smaller cities there are fewer competing interests. A professional city manager would have less difficulty in accepting cues about correct behavior in a small city than in a large city with its complex political structure. There is a greater degree of consensus on policy direction in a smaller city; therefore, such a city requires a professional administrator rather than a political negotiator. The question is whether or not political skill or admin-

---

[5]See Joseph F. Zimmerman, "The New England Town Meeting: Pure Democracy in Action?" *Municipal Yearbook 1984* (Washington, DC: International City Mangers' Association, 1984), pp. 102–6.

Table 9–5
FORMS OF GOVERNMENT IN AMERICAN CITIES

Population Size	Number of Cities Reporting	Council-Manager		Mayor-Council		Commission		Town Meeting	
		NUMBER	PERCENT	NUMBER	PERCENT	NUMBER	PERCENT	NUMBER	PERCENT
Over 1 million	6	0	0	6	100.0	0	0	0	0
500,000 to 1 million	17	5	29.4	12	70.6	0	0	0	0
250,000 to 500,000	34	15	44.1	17	50.0	2	5.9	0	0
100,000 to 250,000	113	67	59.3	41	36.3	5	4.4	0	0
50,000 to 100,000	280	162	57.9	104	37.1	9	3.2	5	1.8
25,000 to 50,000	616	340	55.2	226	36.7	30	4.9	20	3.2
10,000 to 25,000	1545	666	43.1	705	45.6	54	4.0	120	7.8
Under 10,000	4432	1295	29.2	2705	61.0	77	1.7	355	8.0

Source: International City Managers' Association, *Municipal Yearbook 1986.*

istrative expertise is more important in a city, and there is reason to believe that larger cities require political skills more than professional administration.

GROWTH RATE   Growing cities face more administrative and technical problems than cities whose population is stable. There is a strong relationship between population *growth* and council-manager government. A rapidly growing city faces many administrative problems in providing streets, sewers, and the many other services required by an expanding population. This creates a demand for a professional administrator.

In contrast, the mayor-council form of government is associated with cities having relatively stable populations, in which administrative and technical problems are not quite so pressing, and political conflict is more likely to be well-defined and persistent. Council-manager government is more popular in the rapidly growing cities of the West and the South; mayor-council government is preferred in cities in the East and Midwest.

SOCIAL CLASS   Council-manager cities tend to be *middle-class* cities. Cities with large proportions of working-class residents, low-income families, and ethnic minorities prefer mayor-council government.[6]

Why is it that middle-class communities prefer the manager form of government while working-class communities prefer a mayor-council government? Middle-class citizens, those in white-collar jobs with good educations and reasonably high incomes, are more likely to want government conducted in a businesslike fashion, with a council serving as a board of directors and a city manager as the president of a "municipal corporation." These goals are not necessarily shared by labor, low-income, ethnic, and minority groups, which may prefer a government that grants small favors, dispenses patronage jobs, awards representation and "recognition" to minority groups, and can be held directly responsible by the voters at election time. In a campaign for city-manager government, one usually finds business leaders, newspapers, and civic associations supporting the plan, and labor unions and minority group organizations far less enthusiastic. Party organizations and professional politicians often oppose this plan. Its support generally comes from white-collar, high-income, well-educated, white neighborhoods, and its opposition from low-income, blue-collar, black, and ethnic neighborhoods.

PARTY COMPETITION   Communities with well-organized *competitive party systems* are less likely to have manager government than one-party communities or communities in which the formal party organization is weak. It is sometimes argued that the introduction of the manager plan decreases party activity in communities, but it is also true that the presence of strong party organizations may be a significant factor in the defeat of manager plans. Thus, manager government may depress party activity, or strong parties may kill off manager government, or both; but whatever the case, manager government appears incompatible with strong partisan politics in a community.

---

[6]Thomas R. Dye and Susan MacManus, "Predicting City Government Structure," *American Journal of Political Science,* 20 (May 1976), 257–72.

REGION   Cities in the Northeast and Upper Midwest are more likely to have the mayor-council form of government as well as partisan elections. Cities in the South and West are more likely to have council-manager governments and nonpartisan elections. This regional pattern emerges as the strongest single correlate of local government structure.[7] This strong correlation between *region* and governmental structure is explained in part by the fact that southern and western cities are younger, growing cities without any history of strong party organizations; whereas northeastern and upper midwestern cities are older, stable cities with histories of strong party "machines." However, geographic region itself, apart from these other social and political factors, may also explain governmental form. In other words there may be some "imitation" effect within regions that is separate from the effects of other causal factors.

NONPARTISAN ELECTIONS

Most of America's cities use the nonpartisan ballot to elect local officials. Reformers believed that nonpartisanship would take the "politics" out of local government and raise the caliber of candidates for elected offices (see Chapter 10). They believed that nonpartisanship would restrict local campaigning to local issues and thereby rule out extraneous state or national issues from local elections. They also believed that by eliminating party labels, local campaigns would emphasize the qualifications of the individual candidates rather than their party affiliations.

Nonpartisanship is found in both large and small cities. Nonpartisanship is even more widespread than council-manager government. However, there is a tendency for these two forms to be related: 83 percent of all council-manager cities have nonpartisan ballots, while only 65 percent of all mayor-council cities are nonpartisan (see Table 9–6). Party politics is still the prevailing style of local elections in eastern cities, except for New England. Elsewhere in the nation nonpartisanship prevails. The nonpartisan ballot is more likely to be adopted in homogeneous middle-class cities, where there is less social cleavage and smaller proportions of working-class and ethnic group members.

Do nonpartisan elections remove politics? To what extent has nonpartisanship succeeded in removing "politics" from local government? Of course, if "politics" is defined as conflict over public policy, then "politics" has certainly not disappeared with the elimination of party labels. There is no evidence that eliminating party ballots can reduce the level of community conflict. If we define "politics" to mean "partisanship," that is, *party* politics, then nonpartisanship can remove party influences from local government.

Apparently several types of political systems can be found in nonpartisan cities. First of all, in some nonpartisan cities, parties continue to operate effectively behind the scenes in local affairs. *Disguised party politics* is most likely to be found in big cities of the Northeast and Midwest, in states where political parties are strong and competitive. In these cities persons who are known Democratic and Republican candidates run in officially "nonpartisan" elections.

---

[7]See Paul G. Farnhorn and Stephen N. Bryant, "Form of Local Government," *Social Science Quarterly,* 66 (June 1985), 386–400.

Table 9–6
AMERICAN CITIES: TYPE OF ELECTIONS

	Percent	
	PARTISAN	NONPARTISAN
ALL CITIES	25.5	74.5
POPULATION GROUP		
Over 1,000,000	0.0	100.0
500,000–1,000,000	25.0	75.0
250,000–499,999	18.8	81.3
100,000–249,999	17.3	82.7
50,000–99,999	18.5	81.5
25,000–49,999	25.7	74.3
10,000–24,999	30.1	69.9
5,000–9,999	27.3	72.7
2,500–4,999	24.1	75.9
Under 2,500	18.0	82.0
GEOGRAPHIC DIVISION		
New England	27.7	72.3
East Atlantic	88.1	11.9
East North Central	29.1	70.9
West North Central	3.8	96.2
South Atlantic	9.5	90.5
East South Central	17.6	82.4
West South Central	12.8	87.2
Mountain	5.7	94.3
Pacific Coast	2.3	97.7
METROPOLITAN STATUS		
Central city	24.9	75.1
Suburb	30.9	69.1
Independent city	18.1	81.9
FORMS OF GOVERNMENT		
Mayor-council	35.2	64.8
Council-manager	16.7	83.3
Commission	27.2	72.8
Town meeting	23.5	76.5
Rep. town meeting	34.1	65.9

Source: International City Managers' Association, *Baseline Data Report: Profile of the City Council* (Washngton, DC: ICMA, 1992).

Another type of nonpartisan political system is one in which the major parties are inactive, but clear *coalitions* of socioeconomic groups emerge that resemble the national Democratic and Republican parties. These opposing coalitions may involve liberal, labor, Catholic, and black groups on one side; and conservative, business, Protestant, middle-class groups on the other.

Nonpartisan systems may feature the activities of independent community *groups* and organizations. Frequently, these groups are civic associations led by newspapers, chambers of commerce, or neighborhood associations. These organizations may "slate" candidates, manage their campaigns, and even exercise some influence over them while they are in office. These organizations are not usually as permanent as parties, but they may operate as clearly identifiable political entities over the years.

In still another type of nonpartisan political system, neither parties, nor coalitions, nor groups play any significant role, and there are no local slate-making associations. Individual candidates select themselves, collect their own money, and create their own temporary campaign organizations. Voting does not correlate with issues, or party identification, or socioeconomic groups, but instead tends to follow a *friends and neighbors* pattern. Indeed, voting in local nonpartisan elections often depends on factors such as incumbency, name recognition, position on the ballot (the first name on the list gets more votes), and very brief personal contacts (a handshake at the office or factory, or a door-to-door canvass, or even a telephone call).

POSSIBLE REPUBLICAN ADVANTAGE   Does nonpartisanship increase Republican influence in city government? It is sometimes arued that the removal of party designations from local elections hurts Democrats by disengaging their traditional support from urban voters—the low-income, labor, ethnic, and black groups that traditionally vote the Democratic ticket. Moreover, the well-educated, high-income groups and interests that are normally Republican have a natural edge in organization, communication, and prestige in the absence of parties. Republicans also have better turnout records in nonpartisan elections. Surveys of local officials elected under partisan and nonpartisan systems tend to confirm that nonpartisanship results in the election of more Republicans. However this Republican advantage in nonpartisan elections is very modest; it appears to be limited to smaller cities and cities that are dominated by Democrats.[8]

NONPARTISAN CANDIDATES   Does nonpartisanship result in "better-qualified" candidates winning public office? Of course, the answer to this question depends upon one's definition of better qualified. Nonpartisanship does result in more high-income, "respectable," older, white Anglo-Saxon Protestants with prestige jobs running for public office.[9] Working-class candidates are disadvantaged by nonpartisanship for several reasons. First, nonpartisanship reduces the turnout of labor, low-income, eth-

---

[8]Susan Welch and Timothy Bledsoe, "The Partisan Consequences of Nonpartisan Elections," *American Journal of Political Science*, 30 (February 1986), 128–39.

[9]Carol A. Cassel, "Social Background Characteristics of Nonpartisan City Council Members," *Western Political Quarterly*, 38 (September 1985), 495–501.

nic, Democratic voters and, consequently, increases the influence of well-educated, high-income, white, Anglo-Saxon, Protestant Republican voters who continue to come to the polls in nonpartisan elections. In addition, nonpartisanship means that recruitment of candidates will be left to civic associations, or ad hoc groups of one kind or another, rather than to Democratic or Republican party organizations. This difference in recruitment and endorsement practices tends to give an advantage to middle-class candidates. Working-class candidates seldom have the organizational ties or memberships that would bring them to the attention of civic associations that recruit in nonpartisan elections. In contrast, in partisan big-city politics, being a member of a working-class, ethnic, or minority group may be a positive advantage. Parties traditionally try to "balance the ticket" with candidates who represent various groups in rough proportion to their voting strength. This practice of having a balanced party ticket with Irish, Italian, Polish, Jewish, and black names on the ballot is thought to add strength to the entire party ticket, since voters will be asked to vote for the party rather than for the individual candidates.

INCUMBENT ADVANTAGE   Nonpartisanship appears to contribute to the reelection of incumbent council members, particularly when nonpartisanship is combined with at-large elections. Incumbent council members are reelected on the average about 80 percent of the time. When incumbents *are* defeated, they tend to suffer defeat in a group as a result of intensive community conflict.[10] Incumbents are more likely to have a name that is known to the voters. Incumbent council members in partisan cities are not reelected as often as incumbents in nonpartisan cities. This suggests that it is difficult to hold public officials accountable in nonpartisan elections. The voter does not have the opportunity to hear organized criticisms of incumbent officeholders from an opposition party. When the only challenge to an incumbent officeholder is an unknown name on the ballot, he or she is more likely to be reelected than if he or she is challenged by a candidate backed by an opposition party. The higher rates of reelection in nonpartisan systems suggest that accountability is harder to achieve where party labels are absent.

AT-LARGE AND DISTRICT ELECTIONS

At-large elections are designed to promote a citywide approach to municipal problems among council members. Roughly 60 percent of American cities elect their council members at-large, about 10 percent by districts, and 30 percent by a combination of at-large and district constituencies. (There is always some confusion in counting cities as having at-large or ward elections, not only because some cities have "combination" elections with some council members elected by district and others at-large, but also because some cities *elect* council members at-large yet require that they *reside* in the districts they are supposed to represent.)

---

[10]John J. Kirlen, "Electoral Conflict and Democracy in Cities," *Journal of Politics,* 37 (February 1975), 262–69.

THE CASE FOR AT-LARGE ELECTIONS   Traditionally reformers believed that district constituencies encourage parochial views, neighborhood interests, "log-rolling," and other characteristics of "ward politics." These "undesirable" characteristics occur because council members are responsible to local majorities in the particular sections or wards from which they are elected. In contrast, council members elected at-large are responsible to citywide majorities; this should encourage impartial, communitywide attitudes. Moreover, in council-manager cities, it is argued that the manager can be more effective in serving the "general good" of the whole community if the manager is responsible to council members elected at-large rather than by districts. (Of manager cities, 70 percent elect council members at-large, compared to only 50 percent of mayor-council cities.)

MINORITY OPPOSITION   Minorities, who might be able to capture some council seats if these seats are elected by district, may oppose at-large elections if they feel unable to influence council members elected by communitywide majorities. Blacks especially have raised objections to at-large elections in predominantly white cities and counties. Council members and commissioners elected at-large by white majorities are perceived by many black voters as unresponsive to minority concerns.

CIVIL RIGHTS TESTS   The use of at-large elections to discriminate against racial minorities in their ability to participate in the political process and elect candidates of their own choice clearly violates the Equal Protection Clause of the Fourteenth Amendment and the federal Voting Rights Act. The U.S. Supreme Court in *Mobile* v. *Bolden* (1980) held that at-large elections are *not* unconstitutional in the absence of any evidence of discriminatory intent.[11] However, Congress amended the Voting Rights Act in 1982 to substitute a *results test* for the more difficult to prove *intent test* in assessing discrimination. But Congress stopped short of declaring all at-large elections discriminatory and illegal. Instead Congress established a "totality of circumstances" test to be used in deciding whether the at-large elections resulted in racial discrimination. The elements to be considered by the federal courts are:[12]

- A history of official discrimination. (This test applies primarily to southern states.)
- A record of racial polarization in voting.
- Unusually large election districts.
- The existence of candidate slating by parties or groups, and whether minority members have been slated.
- The extent to which minorities have been adversely affected by local government decisions.
- Whether political campaigns have been characterized by racial appeals.
- The extent to which minority group members have been elected to office.

The federal courts are prepared to evaluate the use of at-large elections in each community by these tests.[13]

---

[11]*Mobile v. Bolden*, 446 U.S. 55 (1980).

[12]For a discussion of federal court applications of these tests, see Susan A. MacManus and Charles S. Bullock, "Racial Representation Issues," *PS*, 18 (Fall 1985), 759–69.

[13]*Thornburgh v. Gingles*, 106 S. Ct. 2752 (1986).

FEDERAL COURT INTERVENTION   Federal court cases in recent years involving at-large elections suggest that it is becoming increasingly difficult for cities, counties, and even school districts to defend exclusive reliance on at-large elections. Civil rights groups have effectively utilized the "totality of circumstances" test to invalidate at-large elections across the country and especially in southern states. In some cases federal courts have ordered district elections for all officials, and in other cases federal courts have accepted combination plans—some council members elected by district and some at-large. The U.S. Supreme Court does *not* require proportional representation for minorities, that is, a council that is 20 percent black if the city's population is 20 percent black. However, lower federal courts have tended to compare the black proportion of the council with the black proportion of residents in determining whether the "totality of circumstances" suggests discrimination.

TREND TOWARD MIXED DISTRICTS   These constitutional challenges have led to a shift away from exclusively at-large electoral districts and toward greater reliance on a combination of at-large and district representation on city councils. Combination plans—for example, three council members elected at-large and four by districts on a seven-member council—have been favorably received by federal courts. The percentage of all U.S. cities using combination electoral plans is rising rapidly; at-large plans, although still in use in a majority of cities, are being abandoned.[14]

MINORITY REPRESENTATION   Until recently, blacks were significantly *underrepresented* on city councils that elected their members at-large. In the 1970s several studies reported that blacks won fewer than 50 percent of the seats they deserved (based on their percentage of a city's population) in *at-large* cities, compared to 85 to 100 percent of the seats they deserved in cities that elected council members *by districts*.[15] However, by the late 1980s, black representation on city councils throughout the nation had increased dramatically, and it no longer made much difference in black representation whether councils were elected at-large or by district.[16] For cities with more than 10 percent and less than 50 percent black population, black representation on city councils is only slightly below black population percentages, and the difference between at-large and district elections is minuscule. For cities with black populations over 50 percent, "then it is whites who need district representation to obtain their proportion share of council seats."[17]

---

[14]International City Managers Association, *Baseline Data Report,* 19 (6) Nov./Dec. 1987).

[15]Albert K. Karnig, "Black Representation on City Councils," *Urban Affairs Quarterly,* 12 (December 1976), 223–43; Thomas R. Dye and Theodore P. Robinson, "Reformism and Black Representation on City Councils," *Social Science Quarterly,* 59 (June 1978).

[16]Susan Welch, "The Impact of At-Large Districts on the Representation of Blacks and Hispanics," *Journal of Politics,* 52 (November 1990), 1050–76. See also Charles S. Bullock and Susan M. MacManus, "Municipal Electoral Structure and the Election of Councilwomen." *Journal of Politics,* 53 (February 1991), 75–89.

[17]Ibid, p. 1072.

TRIVIA
THE 100 LARGEST GOVERNMENTS IN THE UNITED STATES

GOVERNMENTS RANKED BY TOTAL REVENUES

(States in capital letters; city and county governments in lowercase. Eighteen local governments are larger than the smallest state government, #68 South Dakota.)

Rank	Jurisdiction	Revenue ($ billions)	Population
1	CALIFORNIA	$100	30,380,000
2	NEW YORK	$75	18,058,000
3	New York City, NY	$45	7,322,564
4	TEXAS	$37	17,349,000
5	PENNSYLVANIA	$36	11,961,000
6	OHIO	$35	10,939,000
7	NEW JERSEY	$29	7,760,000
8	FLORIDA	$28	13,277,000
9	ILLINOIS	$28	11,543,000
10	MICHIGAN	$26	9,368,000
11	MASSACHUSETTS	$20	5,996,000
12	NORTH CAROLINA	$18	6,737,000
13	WISCONSIN	$18	4,955,000
14	WASHINGTON	$17	5,018,000
15	VIRGINIA	$15	6,286,000
16	MINNESOTA	$15	4,432,000
17	GEORGIA	$15	6,623,000
18	INDIANA	$14	5,610,000
19	MARYLAND	$14	4,860,000
20	Los Angeles County, CA	$13	8,863,164
21	LOUISIANA	$12	4,252,000
22	CONNECTICUT	$12	3,291,000
23	MISSOURI	$12	5,158,000
24	TENNESSEE	$11	4,953,000
25	KENTUCKY	$11	3,713,000
26	ALABAMA	$11	4,089,000
27	OREGON	$10	2,922,000
28	SOUTH CAROLINA	$10	3,560,000
29	ARIZONA	$10	3,750,000
30	COLORADO	$9	3,377,000
31	OKLAHOMA	$8	3,175,000
32	IOWA	$8	2,795,000
33	Los Angeles, CA	$7	3,485,398
34	ALASKA	$6	570,000
35	MISSISSIPPI	$6	2,592,000

36	ARKANSAS	$6	2,372,000
37	KANSAS	$6	2,495,000
38	NEW MEXICO	$6	1,548,000
39	WEST VIRGINIA	$5	1,801,000
40	HAWAII	$5	1,135,000
41	UTAH	$5	1,770,000
42	Washington, DC	$5	606,900
43	Chicago, IL	$5	2,783,726
44	NEVADA	$4	1,284,000
45	MAINE	$4	1,235,000
46	NEBRASKA	$4	1,593,000
47	RHODE ISLAND	$4	1,004,000
48	Philadelphia, PA	$3	1,585,577
49	San Francisco City/ County, CA	$3	723,959
50	Metropolitan Dade County, FL	$3	1,937,094
51	IDAHO	$3	1,039,000
52	NEW HAMPSHIRE	$3	1,105,000
53	DELAWARE	$3	680,000
54	MONTANA	$3	808,000
55	Fairfax County, VA	$2	818,584
56	Orange County, CA	$2	2,410,556
57	San Diego County, CA	$2	2,498,016
58	Detroit, MI	$2	1,027,974
59	NORTH DAKOTA	$2	635,000
60	WYOMING	$2	460,000
61	Baltimore, MD	$2	736,014
62	VERMONT	$2	567,000
63	Memphis, TN	$2	610,337
64	Nassau County, NY	$2	1,287,348
65	Boston, MA	$2	574,283
66	Houston, TX	$2	1,630,553
67	Montgomery County, MD	$2	757,027
68	SOUTH DAKOTA	$2	703,000
69	San Bernardino County, CA	$2	1,418,380
70	Santa Clara County, CA	$2	1,497,577
71	Metro Nashville/ Davidson, TN	$2	488,374
72	Cook County, IL	$2	5,105,067
73	Jacksonville, FL	$2	635,230
74	Sacramento County, CA	$1	1,041,219
75	Alameda County, CA	$1	1,279,182
76	San Diego, CA	$1	1,110,549
77	San Antonio, TX	$1	935,933
78	Suffolk County, NY	$1	1,321,864

79	Dallas, TX	$1	1,006,877
80	Prince George's County, MD	$1	729,268
81	Westchester County, NY	$1	874,866
82	Harris County, TX	$1	2,818,199
83	Baltimore County, MD	$1	692,134
84	Riverside County, CA	$1	1,170,413
85	Denver City/County, CO	$1	467,610
86	Phoenix, AZ	$1	983,403
87	Erie County, NY	$1	968,532
88	Austin, TX	$1	465,622
89	Clark County, NV	$1	741,459
90	Seattle, WA	$1	516,259
91	Maricopa County, AZ	$1	2,122,101
92	Cuyahoga County, OH	$1	1,412,140
93	Hillsborough County, FL	$1	834,054
94	Wayne County, MI	$1	2,111,687
95	Hennepin County, MN	$1	1,032,431
96	Indianapolis, IN	$1	731,327
97	Milwaukee County, WI	$1	959,275
98	Honolulu City/County, HI	$1	836,231
99	Contra Costa County, CA	$1	803,732
100	Monroe County, NY	$1	713,968

10

STYLES
OF COMMUNITY
POLITICS

MACHINES AND BOSSES

Machine politics has gone out of style. Machines—tightly disciplined party organizations, held together and motivated by a desire for tangible benefits rather than by principle or ideology and run by professional politicians—emerged in the nation's large cities early in the nineteenth century. This style of city politics has historical importance. Between the Civil War and the New Deal, every big city had a machine at one time or another, and it is sometimes easier to understand the character of city politics today by knowing what went on in years past. A more important reason for examining the machine style of politics is to understand the style of political organization that employs personal and material rewards to achieve power. These kinds of rewards will always be important in politics, and the big-city machine serves as a prototype of a style of politics in which ideologies and issues are secondary and personal friendships, favors, and jobs are primary.

The political machine was essentially a large brokerage organization. Its business was to get votes and control elections by trading off social services, patronage, and petty favors to the urban masses, particularly the poor and the recent immigrants. To get the money to pay for these social services and favors, it traded off city contracts, protection, and privileges to business interests, which paid off in cash. Like other brokerage organizations, a great many middlemen came between the cash paid for a franchise for a trolly line or a construction contract and a Christmas turkey sent by the ward chairman to the Widow O'Leary. However, the machine worked. It performed many important social functions for the city.

PERSONAL ATTENTION   First of all, it personalized government. With keen social intuition, the machine recognized the voter as a person, generally living in a neighborhood, who had specific problems and wants. The machine provided individual attention and recognition. As Tammany Hall boss George Washington Plunkitt, the philosopher king of old-style machine politics, explained:

> I know every man, woman, and child in the 15th district, except them that's been born this summer—and I know some of them, too. I know what they like and what they don't like, what they are strong at and what they are weak in, and I reach them by approachin' at the right side. . . . I don't trouble them with political arguments. I just study human nature and act accordin'.[1]

WELFARE   The machine also performed functions of a welfare agency.

> What tells in holdin' your grip on your district is to go right down among the poor families and help them in the different ways they need help. I've got a regular system for this. If there's a fire in Ninth, Tenth, or Eleventh Avenue, for example, any hour of the day or night, I'm usually there with some of my election district captains as soon as the fire engines. If a family is burned out I don't ask whether they are Republicans or Democrats, and I don't refer them to the Charity Organization Society, which would investigate their case in a month or two and decide they were worthy of help about the time they are dead from starvation. I just get quarters for them, buy clothes for them if their clothes were burned up, and fix them up till they get things runnin' again. It's philanthropy, but it's politics, too— mighty good politics. Who can tell how many votes one of these fires bring me? The poor are the most grateful people in the world, and let me tell you, they have more friends in their neighborhoods than the rich have in theirs.[2]

EMPLOYMENT   The machine also functioned as an employment agency. In the absence of government unemployment insurance or a federal employment service, patronage was an effective political tool, particularly in hard times. Not only were city jobs at the disposal of the machine, but the machine also had its business contacts:

> Another thing, I can always get a job for a deservin' man. I make it a point to keep on the track of jobs, and it seldom happens that I don't have a few up my sleeve ready for use. I know every big employer in the district and in the whole city, for that matter, and they ain't in the habit of sayin' no to me when I ask them for a job.[3]

FRIENDSHIP   It was not so much the petty favors and patronage that won votes among urban dwellers, as it was the sense of friendship and humanity that characterized

---

[1] William L. Riordan, *Plunkitt of Tammany Hall* (New York: McClure, Phillips & Co., 1905), p. 46.
[2] Ibid., p. 52.
[3] Ibid., p. 53.

the "machine" and its "boss."[4] The free turkeys, and bushels of coal were really only tokens of this friendship. As Jane Addams, the famous settlement house worker, explained:

> On the whole, the gifts and favors were taken quite simply as evidence of genuine loving kindness. The alderman is really elected because he is a good friend and neighbor. He is corrupt, of course, but he is not elected because he is corrupt, but rather in spite of it. His standard suits his constituents. He exemplifies and exaggerates the popular type of a good man. He has attained what his constituents secretly long for.[5]

ASSIMILATION   The machine also played an important role in educating recent immigrants and assimilating them into American life.[6] Machine politics provided a means of upward social mobility for ethnic group members, which was not open to them in businesses or professions. City machines sometimes met immigrants at dockside and led them in groups through naturalization and voter registration procedures. Machines did not keep out people with "funny" sounding names but instead went out of the way to put these names on ballots. Politics became a way "up" for the bright sons of Irish and Italian immigrants.

"GETTING THINGS DONE"   Finally, for businesses, and particularly for public utilities and construction companies with government contracts, the machine provided the necessary franchises, rights of way, contracts, and privileges. As Lincoln Steffens wrote: "You cannot build or operate a railroad, or a street railway, gas, water, or power company, develop and operate a mine, or cut forests or timber on a large scale, or run any privileged business, without corrupting or joining in the corruption of government."[7] The machine also provided the essential protection from police interference, which is required by illicit businesses, particularly gambling. In short, the machine helped to centralize power in large cities. It could "get things done at city hall."

THE DECLINE OF MACHINES   The era of the political machine has passed. Big-city political organizations have radically altered their style of operation. Federal and state welfare agencies now provide the basic welfare services that the bosses used to provide. Patronage jobs do not look as attractive in an affluent economy, and today civil service examinations cover most governmental jobs anyhow. The middle class was excluded from machine politics, and much of the opposition to the machine came from the middle class. As the middle class grew in American society (today white-collar workers outnumber blue-collar workers), opposition to the machine grew in every city. Middle-class voters supported reform movements and good-government crusades. They often succeeded in replacing the machine with professional city managers, civil service, and reorganized

---

[4]Edward C. Banfield and James Q. Wilson, *City Politics* (Cambridge, MA: Harvard-M.I.T. Press, 1963), chap. 9.

[5]Jane Addams, *Democracy and Social Ethics* (New York: 1902), p. 254; also cited by Banfield and Wilson, *City Politics*, p. 118.

[6]See Elmer E. Cornwell, Jr., "Bosses, Machines, and Ethnic Groups," *Annals of the American Academy of Political and Social Science* (May 1964), 27–39.

[7]Lincoln Steffens, *Autobiography* (New York: Harcourt, Brace & World, 1931), p. 168.

city government. They supported city administrations pledged to eliminate corruption and exercise economy and efficiency in government.

Political machines were never very efficient, even by their own standards. Machines frequently made poor use of their patronage and perquisites. Jobs were frequently handed out to personal friends and family members without regard to whether they worked hard in elections to produce additional votes for the machine.[8] Even the Daley organization in Chicago failed to allocate its "perks" according to strict vote-getting requirements.[9] In short, political machines were not always very good at machine politics—trading patronage and perks for votes and power.

MACHINE AND REFORM POLITICS IN CHICAGO

DALEY: LAST OF THE BOSSES   For over two decades Mayor Richard J. Daley governed Chicago in the style of traditional politics. (When Mayor Daley himself was asked about his "machine," he replied, "Organization, not machine. Get that. Organization, not machine.") In Chicago, few others understood so well the labyrinths of formal and informal power. Daley won election to six four-year terms as mayor of Chicago, beginning in 1955. He remained the captain of his old Eleventh Ward Democratic committee, and he was chairman of the Cook County Democratic committee. He picked candidates' slates,

The late Richard J. Daley, generally regarded as the last of the big-city bosses, won six four-year terms as Mayor of Chicago. When he died in office in 1976, the Chicago "machine" began to lose its clout.

---

[8]Michael Johnson, "Patrons and Clients, Jobs and Machines: A Case Study of the Uses of Patronage," *American Political Science Review,* 73 (June 1979), 385–98.

[9]Kenneth R. Mladenka, "The Urban Bureaucracy and the Chicago Political Machine," *American Political Science Review,* 74 (December 1980), 991–98.

ran the patronage machinery, and worked his will on nearly all of Chicago's city council. Illinois Democratic governors were usually responsive to his wishes, and Chicago's nine-member delegation to the U.S. House of Representatives also acted promptly on Daley's recommendations. The Cook County Democratic delegation to the Illinois legislature was firmly in his hands. No presidential candidate could ignore Daley's political "clout," either in the Democratic National Convention or in the general election. Daley may have been the most successful mayor in America, not only for his political acumen, but also for his ability to manage a great metropolis.[10]

CONFLICT MANAGEMENT   As a political broker, Daley was seldom the initiator of public policy. His approach to policy questions was more like that of an arbitrator between competing interests. When political controversies developed, Daley waited on the sidelines without committing himself, in the hope that public opinion would soon "crystallize" behind a particular course of action. Once the community was behind a project—and this determination Daley made himself after lengthy consultations with his political advisors—he then awarded his stamp of approval. This suggests that in policy matters many political "bosses" were not so much bosses as referees among interested individuals and groups. The boss was really *a*political when it came to policy matters. He was really more concerned with resolving conflict and maintaining his position and organization than he was with the outcome of public policy decisions. Boss Daley's politics: "Don't make no waves; don't back no losers."

THE MACHINE LOSES CLOUT   When Mayor Daley died in office in 1976, a lackluster machine replacement, Michael Bilandic, tried unsuccessfully to fill the shoes of the nation's most successful "boss." However, the once powerful Cook County Democratic committee gradually lost its direction, leadership, and "clout." Mayor Bilandic failed to hold together the coalition of white ethnic groups, blacks, Catholics, labor unions, and city employees, which were the backbone of the machine. In 1978 Bilandic fired a Daley appointee, Jane Byrne, from her post as the city's commissioner on consumer affairs. Byrne accused Bilandic of collusion in allowing taxi fare increases in the city, and she announced her intention to oppose Bilandic in the 1979 mayor's race. Initially, observers gave her little chance of defeating the official machine candidate in the Democratic primary. However, a huge snowfall paralyzed the city for weeks, and Bilandic's administration was not very competent in handling the emergency. Perhaps more importantly, the machine itself seemed to fall apart without the leadership of Daley. On election day, Jane Byrne captured most of the city's predominantly black wards—traditionally machine strongholds. Byrne sounded like a reformer in public, but she privately reminded many old Daley supporters that she was an old and trusted friend of "hizzoner." Byrne emerged from the close contest as Chicago's first female mayor. Party regulars pledged to support her, and she promised to work with the Cook County Democratic committee. Nevertheless, it was clear to all that Chicago's once powerful machine was in disarray.

---

[10]For an excellent description of the functions of Mayor Daley's political organization in Chicago, see Edward C. Banfield, *Political Influence* (Glencoe, IL: The Free Press, 1961). For a hostile account of Mayor Daley, see Mike Royko, *Boss: Richard J. Daley of Chicago* (New York: E. P. Dutton, 1971).

BLACKS SPLIT FROM THE MACHINE   As the machine stumbled, the city's black voters became increasingly restless. Mayor Byrne's administration was attacked as unresponsive to black demands. Finally, in the 1983 Democratic mayoral primary the black community, under the leadership of Congressman Harold Washington, split from the Democratic machine. The machine went into the 1983 election hopelessly fractured. Mayor Byrne sought reelection and claimed control over city job holders; state attorney Richard M. Daley, son of the late mayor, challenged Byrne's control of the machine and called upon old loyalties to the family name; and Harold Washington worked hard to register and mobilize the city's black residents, 40 percent of Chicago's total population. The resulting split in the Democratic primary was: Washington, 37 percent; Byrne, 33 percent; Daley, 30 percent.

The general election campaign was a bitter one. The Republican candidate, businessman Bernard Epton, sensed an opportunity to become the city's first Republican mayor. He struck hard at Washington's weaknesses. Washington had once been convicted for failing to file federal income tax returns, and his license to practice law had once been suspended for accepting payments for services not performed. Several prominent white Democratic machine politicians deserted the Democratic candidate. Race dominated the campaign. Voter turnout in Chicago's 1983 mayoral election was a record 82 percent of registration. Washington won with 51.4 percent. He had the near-unanimous support of black voters combined with just enough "Lakefront liberal" white voters to provide a thin margin of victory. But most white voters, including the white ethnic voters who provided the machine with its traditional base of support, case their ballots against the black Democratic nominee.[11]

HAROLD WASHINGTON   Harold Washington was raised in Chicago machine politics. His father was a Democratic precinct captain, lawyer, and minister on Chicago's South Side. Harold inherited his father's law practice and his position in the Democratic party machine. Washington served in the Illinois state legislature for sixteen years prior to his election to Congress in 1980. Despite his background in machine politics, Washington battled endlessly with the white ethnic remnants of the machine. He pledged to end machine politics in Chicago and to "heal the divisions that have plagued us. . . . Chicago is one city."[12]

RACIAL POLITICS   The demise of the old Daley political machine allowed racial divisions to surface as the major force in the city's political life. Harold Washington faced formidable opposition among many white city workers, police officers and firefighters, and a majority of white council members elected from wards. The leader of white ethnic forces was Alderman Edward Vrdolyak, chairman of the Cook County Democratic committee, Mayor Daley's old post. Council meetings became scenes of bitter confrontations between Mayor Washington and Alderman Vrdolyak and his forces. Indeed, the struggle for power resulted in near paralysis of city business, as personnel appointments, election

---

[11]Michael B. Preston, "The Election of Harold Washington," *P.S. Political Science* (Summer 1983), 486.

[12]*Time*, April 25, 1983, p. 24.

administration, and financial decisions were drowned in political controversy. As council meetings deteriorated from parliamentary pandemonium to near fistfights, the courts were called upon to resolve many city issues.

Mayor Washington's campaign theme, "It's our turn," was widely interpreted among white municipal job holders as a threat to replace them with blacks. But the dreams of blue-collar, white ethnics in Chicago to revive the old machine were dashed in 1987 when Mayor Washington defeated Edward Vrdolyak in the Democratic primary for mayor. Washington won with the support of almost all of the city's black voters combined with 15 percent of the white voters. Vrdolyak's blue-collar supporters also lost control of the city council.

Harold Washington's personal popularity among blacks and Hispanics and a significant portion of affluent, liberal whites was a major factor in his success as mayor. The city itself was almost evenly divided between white and black residents, with Hispanics comprising a smaller but important constituency. Washington's popularity, together with the gradual decline of the white percentage of the city's population, led many observers to believe that Chicago had seen its last white mayor. But Washington's untimely death in 1988 brought a new administration to the city.

OLD NAME, NEW STYLE   Richard M. Daley is the eldest son of the former mayor and long-time boss of Chicago's politics, Richard. J. Daley. His father found him a job in the city attorney's office and later persuaded an incumbent state senator to give up his seat so that young "Richie" could start a political career. At the state capital, young Daley was unswervingly loyal to his father's machine. But after the mayor's death, and the personal tragedy of the death of a severely handicapped child, Richard M. Daley began to emerge as his own man.

Following Washington's death, Eugene Sawyer, another black former machine politi-

Richard M. Daley, son of the late "Boss" Daley, won election to the Chicago Mayor's office once occupied by his father, but he did so by projecting the image of a "reform" rather than a "machine" candidate.

cian, became acting mayor. But black Alderman Timothy Evans won the support of most of the city's black political organizations. Sawyer came under intense pressure to drop out of the mayor's race in 1989 in order to avoid splitting the black vote. But Sawyer saw himself as the legitimate heir to Harold Washington's political coalition. Sawyer remained in the Democratic primary fight, while Evans announced that he would run as an independent in the general election and face the Democratic nominee. Everyone assumed that racial voting would predominate in both the primary and general elections, and Sawyer and Evans accused each other of destroying black unity.

Daley won the Democratic primary against Sawyer with 56 percent of the vote. He held on to white ethnic voters who had so long supported his father, won the Hispanic vote, and won back many white liberals who were convinced the younger Daley stood for reform.

Race also divided the voters in the general election. Daley won with 55 percent of the vote compared to 41 percent for Evans and 4 percent for Vrdolyak. But polls suggested that Daley won 91 percent of the white vote and Evans 95 percent of the black vote.[13] Very few voters crossed racial lines. Hispanics (16 percent of the population and about 7 percent of the electorate) supported Daley.

DALEY, THE REFORMER   As mayor, Daley presented himself not as a "politician" but rather as a "manager" trying to reform a costly, unresponsive city bureaucracy. While critics claim that Daley's image as a reformer is only a cover for his political ambition, Daley's growing popularity in the job indicates that governmental reform is good politics. Chicago's voters seem to agree. Daley won the Democratic primary in 1991 with 63 percent of the vote (surpassing the best primary showing ever posted by his father), and then won an overwhelming 71 percent of the vote in the general election.

Daley's efforts to reform the city bureaucracy present an ironic twist to the long history of machine and reform politics in Chicago. Daley's father had overstaffed city hall with patronage appointees who worked his precincts at election time. But over time, the courts had given most city workers civil service protection as a "reform" of patronage practices. The result was a bloated bureaucracy unresponsive to either the mayor or the council. "You get elected mayor to make decisions, and then you find out the bureaucracy is against you," complained Daley. "Their attitude is 'we're going to be here when you leave!'"[14] Daley has pushed to contract out to private firms—to "privatize"—many city functions, from janitorial services and parking fine collections to towing of abandoned cars. And he has imposed modern data management and accounting practices on city agencies.

Privatization efforts are bitterly opposed by Chicago's public employee unions, especially the American Federation of State, County and Municipal Employees (AFSCME). By pursuing privatization, Daley has cut the political ties between the city's employee unions and the mayor's office, a strategy his father would never have considered. But the "Son of Boss" has put together a new political coalition, consisting of the city's white ethnic groups and its rapidly growing Hispanic population. Black leaders charge that Daley's

---

[13]New York Times, April 5, 1989.

[14]Quoted in U.S. News and World Report, March 23, 1992, p. 41.

privatization schemes have disproportionately impacted black employees, who were concentrated in service and maintenance jobs, those easiest to privatize. But the black community has been divided since the death of Harold Washington. And Daley's style is to appeal to *taxpayers:* "Minorities are taxpayers. You go out to a homeowner—who is black, Hispanic, female, or Asian—and they pay taxes!"[15]

REFORMERS AND DO-GOODERS

A reform style of politics appeared in the United States shortly after the Civil War to battle the "bosses." Beginning in 1869, scathing editorials in the *New York Times* and cartoons by Thomas Nast in *Harper's Weekly* attacked the "Tammany Society" in New York City, a political organization that controlled the local Democratic party. William M. Tweed was president of the board of supervisors of New York County and undisputed boss of "Tammany Hall," as the New York County Democratic committee was called, after its old meeting place on Fourteenth Street. This early reform movement achieved temporary success under the brilliant leadership of Samuel J. Tilden, who succeeded in driving the "Tweed Ring" out of office and went on in 1876 to be the only presidential candidate ever to win a majority of popular votes and then be denied the presidency through the operation of electoral college. George William Curtis, editor of *Harper's Weekly;* E. L. Godkin, editor of the *Nation;* and Senator Carl Schurz of Missouri laid the foundations for a style of reform politics that continues to have great influence in American cities.[16]

Early municipal reform is closely linked to the Progressive movement in American politics. Leaders such as Robert M. La Follette of Wisconsin, Hiram Johnson of California, Gifford Pinchot of Pennsylvania, and Charles Evans Hughes of New York backed municipal reform at the local level as well as the direct primary and direct election of senators and women's suffrage at the national level. In 1912 social worker Jane Addams, who labored in slums and settlement houses, sang "Onward Christian Soldiers" at the Progressive party convention that nominated Teddy Roosevelt for president. Lincoln Steffens wrote in *The Shame of the Cities* ". . . St. Louis exemplified boodle; Minneapolis, police graft; Pittsburgh, a political industrial machine; and Philadelphia (the worst city in the country), general civic corruption."[17]

SOCIAL BASES OF REFORM   From its beginning, reform politics was strongly supported by the upper-class, Anglo-Saxon, Protestant, longtime residents of cities whose political ethos was very different from that which the new immigrants brought with them. The immigrant, the machine that relied upon his vote, and the businessman who relied upon the machine for street railway and other utility franchises, had formed an alliance in the nineteenth century that had displaced the native, old

---

[15]Quoted in Charles Mahtesian, "Taking Chicago Private," *Governing* (April 1994), 26–31.

[16]See Richard J. Hofstadter, *The Age of Reform* (New York: Knopf, 1955); and Lorin Peterson, *The Day of the Mugwump* (New York: Random House, 1961).

[17]Lincoln Steffens, *The Shame of the Cities* (New York: Sagamore Press, 1957), p. 10.

family, Yankee elite that had traditionally dominated northern cities. This upper-class elite fought to recapture control of local government through the municipal reform movement.

Machine politicians catered to ethnic groups, organized labor, blue-collar workers, and other white working-class elements of the city. The reform politician appealed to the upper- and middle-class affluent Americans who were well educated and public-service minded. Reform was popular among liberals, newspaper reporters, college professors, and others who considered themselves "intellectuals."

REFORM GOALS   Reform politics included a belief that there was a "public interest" that should prevail over competing, partial interests in a city. The idea of balancing competing interests or compromising public policy was not part of the reformers' view of political life. Rather, the reform ethos included a belief that "politics" was distasteful. Enlightened people should agree on the public interest; municipal government is a technical and administrative problem rather than a political one. City government should be placed in the hands of those who are best qualified, by training, ability, and devotion to public service, to manage public business. These best-qualified people can decide on policy and then leave administration to professional experts. Any interference by special interests in the politicies or administration of the best-qualified people should be viewed as corruption.

The objectives of early reform movements were:

- *Eliminate corruption.* The elimination of corruption in public office, and the recruitment of "good people" (educated, upper-income individuals who were successful in private business or professions) to replace "politicians" (who were no more successful than their constituents in private life and who were dependent upon public office for their principal source of income).
- *Nonpartisanship.* The elimination of parties from local politics by nonpartisan elections.
- *Manager government.* The establishment of the council-manager form of government, and the separation of "politics" from the "business" of municipal government.
- *At-large districts.* The establishment of at-large citywide constituencies in municipal elections in lieu of "district" constituencies in order to ensure that an elected official would consider the welfare of the entire city in public decision making and not merely his or her own neighborhood or "ward."
- *Short ballot.* The reorganization of local government to eliminate many separately elected offices (the "short-ballot" movement) in order to simplify the voters' task and focus responsibility for the conduct of public affairs on a small number of top elected officials.
- *Strong executive.* The strengthening of executive leadership in city government— longer terms for mayors, subordination of departments and commissions to a chief executive, and an executive budget combined with modern financial practices.
- *Merit system.* The replacement of patronage appointments with the merit system of civil service.
- *Home rule.* The separation of local politics from state and national politics by home-rule charters and the holding of local elections at times when there were no state and national elections.

All these objectives were interrelated. Ideally, a "reformed city" would be one with the manager form of government, nonpartisan election for mayor and council, a home-rule charter, a short ballot, at-large constituencies, a strong executive, a merit service personnel system, and honest people at the helm. Later, the reform movement added comprehensive city planning to its list of objectives—official planning agencies with professional planners authorized to prepare a master plan of future development for the city. The National Municipal League incorporated its program of reform into a *Model City Charter*, which continues today to be the standard manual of municipal reform.[18] There is reason to believe that the early reformers also opposed immigration (which was very logical, of course, since the immigrant was the backbone of machine politics). Many persons active in municipal reform at the time supported the passage of the Immigration Act of 1921, reducing immigration to a trickle and establishing quotas heavily weighted in favor of Anglo-Saxon Protestant immigrants and against southern and eastern European Catholic immigrants.[19]

REFORM POLITICS TODAY   Political divisions in American cities do not always take the form of upper classes versus lower classes. On the contrary, in urban politics, one often finds upper-class liberal reformers allied with minorities, notably blacks, in opposition to the white working-class and ethnic voters. Democratic reformers in municipal politics are generally liberal Democrats in national politics, while Republican reformers are frequently supporters of the progressive wing of that party.

Reformers are generally amateurs in politics, in contrast to the professional politicians who constitute the regular party organizations. The "amateur" is more motivated by the ideological and psychological rewards of mixing in government and public affairs; in contrast, the "professional" is interested in tangible rewards—jobs, contracts, public offices. Reformers do not deal with the personal problems confronting individuals but rather with the broad social problems confronting groups or classes. Reformers view government as an instrument for achieving broad social reforms and not merely as a source of jobs, buildings and civic improvements, or upward social mobility for gifted individuals from the lower classes. The politics of reform is frequently more ideological than pragmatic. Appeals are made to lofty principles, rather than material welfare. All of this, of course, is in direct contrast to the machine style of politics.

---

[18]National Municipal League, *Model City Charter* (Chicago: National Municipal League, 1961).

[19]Andrew D. White, first president of Cornell University, summarized early reform thinking when he wrote in 1890: "What is this evil theory? It is simply that the city is a political body; that its interior affairs have to do with national political parties and issues. My fundamental contention is that a city is a corporation; that as a city it has nothing whatever to do with general political interests; that party political names and duties are utterly out of place there. The questions in a city are not political questions. They have reference to the laying out of streets; to the erection of buildings; to sanitary arrangements, sewerage, water supply, gas supply, electrical supply; to the control of franchises and the like; and to provisions for the public health and comfort in parks, boulevards, libraries and museums. The work of a city being the creation and control of the city property, it should logically be managed as a piece of property by those who have created it, or a real substantial part in it, and who can therefore feel strongly their duty to it. Under our theory that a city is a political body, a crowd of illiterate peasants, freshly raked in from Irish bogs, or Bohemian mines, or Italian robber nests, may exercise virtual control." Andrew D. White, "The Government of American Cities," in *Forum* (1890); reprinted in Edward C. Banfield, *Urban Government: A Reader in Administration and Politics* (Glencoe, IL: The Free Press, 1961).

THE TRIUMPH OF REFORM?

The machine style of politics has largely disappeared from the urban scene.

REASONS FOR THE MACHINE'S DECLINE   Parties in general are losing their appeal to many Americans. Increasing proportions of voters are identifying themselves as "independents," rather than as Democrats or Republicans. (See Chapter 5.) Party offices (precinct committee, ward chairperson, county committee, and so on) are vacant in many cities and counties. The general decline in parties has contributed to the decline of machine politics. Several additional factors might be cited as contributing to the decline of machine politics:

- *The decline in European immigration* and the gradual assimilation of white ethnic groups—Irish, Italians, Germans, Poles, Slavs.
- *Federal social welfare programs,* which undercut the machine's role in welfare work—unemployment insurance, workers' compensation, social security, and public assistance.
- *Rising levels of prosperity* and higher educational levels, which make the traditional rewards of the machine less attractive.
- *The spread of middle-class values* about honesty, efficiency, and good government, which inhibit party organizations in purchases, contracts, and vote buying, and other cruder forms of municipal corruption.
- *New avenues of upward social mobility* that have opened up the sons and daughters of working-class families, and higher education, which has allowed many to join the ranks of professionals, corporate executives, educators, and so on so that the party machine is no longer the only way "up" for persons at the bottom of the social ladder.
- *Structural reforms* such as nonpartisanship, better voting procedures, city-manager government, and—most important of all—civil service, which have weakened the party's role in municipal elections and administration.

THE OLD PATRONAGE   Patronage was once very useful in maintaining a party organization, attracting voters, financing the party, ensuring favorable government actions for party requests, and maintaining discipline within the party's ranks. But patronage jobs have been restricted over the years by the merit system in every state government and most large city governments as well. Many lower-level municipal jobs are not as valuable as they once were, as federal welfare programs and expanded opportunities for urban minorities provide alternatives to poor-paying patronage jobs.

THE NEW PATRONAGE   However, if we define *patronage* to include a wide range of tangible benefits—construction contracts, insurance policies, printing and office supplies, architectural services, and other government contracts for goods or services—then patronage may still be important in many communities. Competitive bidding by potential government contractors is required in most states and cities, but it is not difficult to "rig" the process. The fact that the firms that do much of their business with government are also the largest contributors to political campaigns cannot be coincidence. Another source of patronage is the power of courts to appoint referees, appraisers, receivers in bankruptcies, and trustees and executors of estates; these plums require little work and produce high fees for attorneys who are "well connected." Few cities have ever been able to remove zoning from politics: Rezoning property from lower-value classifications (single-family residential) to higher-value classifications (apartments, commercial, industrial) is one of the most important "goodies" available to municipal governments. In addition, municipal construction permits, inspection, and licensing can be slow and cumbersome, or fast and painless, depending on the political resources of the builder-developer.[20]

PERSISTENCE OF MATERIAL REWARDS IN POLITICS   Something resembling "machine" politics—political organizations held together and motivated by a desire for tangible benefits rather than principle or ideology—continues to thrive in many cities and rural counties. Most machines may not be as centralized, disciplined, or powerful as in a previous era, but as long as the need to personalize government exists—as long as individuals value small favors, appreciate personal intervention on their behalf with government agencies, need assistance in finding their way around city halls and county courthouses, and require help in filing for benefits, obtaining bonds, registering complaints, dealing with the bureaucratic demands of government—political organizations will still have a role to play.

THE PERSONALIZED MACHINES   Some big-city mayors have been successful in building personal political organizations centered on the mayor's office. They have expanded their supply of patronage jobs by enlarging the mayoral office staff and creating public authorities and agencies that are directly responsible to the mayor's office. Appointees to these fairly high-paying staff and administrative positions form the nucleus of the mayor's personal campaign organization. A resourceful mayor can augment his or her immediate staff people ("the palace guard") with appointments to city economic development authorities, community rehabilitation agencies, housing authorities, and other quasi-governmental bureaucracies. Many of these bureaucracies are federally funded and their top posts can be filled by an astute mayor using "creative" personnel practices.[21]

THE NEIGHBORHOOD POLITICIAN   In many large cities, elements of the old ward politics survive in particular neighborhoods. The neighborhood politician, perhaps a state senator or city council member, still strolls the sidewalks, glad-handling constituents, and promising to find a job for someone, fix a street light, and see about uncollected trash. Indeed, the modern neighborhood politician may enter each constituent's name in the office computer system and keep track of individual requests and favors rendered.[22] It still matters to many voters that their representative grew up in the neighborhood, still lives there, can be contacted day or night, knows their names, and gives personal attention to their problems.

---

[20]See also Raymond E. Wolfinger, "Why Political Machines Have Not Withered Away and Other Revisionist Thoughts," *Journal of Politics*, 34 (May 1972), 365–98.

[21]See Alan D. Gaetano, "The Rise of the New Urban Political Machine," Paper presented at the Midwest Political Science Association Meeting, 1986.

[22]John F. Persimos, "Ward Politics 21st-Century Style," *Governing* (October 1989), 46–50.

Reformism and Public Policy

What are the policy consequences of reform government? Traditionally, political scientists assumed that the reform of city government would bring about changes in public policy. Reform was expected to result in better public services, lower tax rates, and more professional administration. However, *assumptions* regarding the impact of structural changes on public policy are not a substitute for *systematic investigation* of the actual linkages between political structures and public policies.

Sorting Out the Effect of Reform　　It is not easy to distinguish *independent* effects of reform on public policy from the effects of other urban characteristics associated with reform—smaller size, southern and western regions, less ethnicity, more middle-class residents. Urban conditions such as population density, income, poverty, mobility, home ownership, and property value are *more* influential than the structure of government in determining levels of taxing and spending. However, despite the overriding importance of social and economic conditions in shaping municipal policy, the structure of government—reformed versus unreformed—does have *some* interesting effects on public policy.

Reform, Taxing, and Spending　　The first important systematic study of the policy consequences of reformism found that reformed cities tended to tax and spend *less* than unreformed cities. Cities with manager governments were *less* willing to spend money for public purposes than cities with mayor-council governments.[23] But socioeconomic conditions had an even more important impact than reform on tax and spending policies. For example,

- The more middle class the city, measured by income, education, and occupation, the lower the general tax and spending levels.
- The greater the home ownership in a city, the lower the tax and spending levels.
- The larger the percentage of racial and ethnic minorities in the population, the higher the city's taxes and expenditures.

Reform and Responsiveness　　What turned out to be an even more important finding was the difference in *responsiveness* of the two kinds of city governments—reformed and unreformed—to the socioeconomic composition of their populations. *Reformed* cities (cities with manager governments, at-large constituencies, and nonpartisan elections) appeared to be *un*responsive in their tax and spending policies to differences in income and educational, occupational, religious, and ethnic characteristics of their populations. In contrast, unreformed cities (cities with mayor-council governments, ward constituencies, and partisan elections) reflected class, racial, and religious composition in their taxing and spending decisions.

---

[23]Robert L. Lineberry and Edmund P. Fowler, "Reformism and Public Policy in American Cities," *American Political Science Review*, 61 (September 1967), 701–16. See also David R. Morgan and John P. Pelissero, "Urban Policy: Does Political Structure Matter?" *American Political Science Review*, 74 (December 1980), 999–1005.

Reformism tends to reduce the importance of race, class, home ownership, ethnicity, and religion in city politics. It tends to minimize the role that social conflicts play in public decision making. In contrast, mayor-council governments, ward constituencies, and partisan elections permit social cleavages to be reflected in city politics and public policy to be responsive to socioeconomic factors. These findings suggest that reformed cities have gone a long way toward accomplishing the reformist goal—that is, "to immunize city governments from 'artificial' social cleavages—race, religion, ethnicity, and so on." Thus, political institutions seem to play an important role in policy formation:

> ... a role substantially independent of a city's demography. . . . Nonpartisan elections, at-large constituencies, and manager governments are associated with a lessened responsiveness of cities to the enduring conflicts of political life.[24]

In short, reformism makes city governments less responsive to citizens' needs.[25]

REFORM AS AN OBSTACLE TO CIVIL RIGHTS GROUPS   The assertion that reformism lessens the responsiveness of city governments is reinforced by observing the responses of cities to civil-rights-group activity. Political scientist Albert K. Karnig measured the strength of civil rights groups—the National Association for the Advancement of Colored People (NAACP), the National Urban League, the Congress of Racial Equality (CORE), and the Southern Christian Leadership Conference (SCLC)—in 417 cities.[26] He correlated the strength of these organizations with policies generally associated with the needs of poor and black people—low-rent housing, community-action programs, and neighborhood youth-corps programs. In general, he found the presence of civil rights organizations was related to increased community efforts in these areas. More importantly, however, he found that *reformed governments were less responsive* to civil rights groups in these policy areas than unreformed governments. The associations between civil-rights-group activity and policies favoring the poor and the black were *lower* in cities with nonpartisan elections, manager governments, and at-large elections. This evidence suggests that blacks and other urban minorities have little to gain through reformism.

AFRICAN AMERICANS AND REFORM   Indeed, to many African American leaders it seems that the triumph of reform politics came just when blacks were finally beginning to gain control of municipal government in many big cities. Civil service is perceived as an obstacle to blacks finally receiving their "fair share" of municipal patronage. Relatively few city managers are African Americans (see "City Managers in Municipal Politics" in Chapter 11). These structural reforms, together with the reform emphasis on economy and efficiency in government and its deemphasis on "politics," all combine to frustrate black communities in many cities.

---

[24]Lineberry and Fowler, "Reformism and Public Policy," p. 715. See also William Lyons, "Reform and Response in American Cities," *Social Science Quarterly,* 59 (June 1978), 118–32.

[25]See also Susan Blackall Hansen, "Participation, Political Structure and Concurrence," *American Political Science Review,* 69 (December 1975), 1181–99.

[26]Albert K. Karnig, "Private Regarding Policy, Civil Rights Groups, and the Mediating Impact of Municipal Returns," *American Journal of Political Science,* 19 (February 1975), 91–106.

PRIVATIZATION AS REFORM

Conservatives have mounted their own reform movement in state and local government, centering on the notion of the "privatization" of public services. Traditionally conservatives have sought to restrain the growth of government:

> The bigger the government the greater the force for even bigger government. Budgets will expand, resulting in the appointment of more officials and the hiring of more workers. These will go to work at once to enlarge their budgets, do less work, hire still more workers, obtain better-than-average raises, and vote for more spending programs, while encouraging their constituents and beneficiaries to do the same. The forecast seems ominous: Sooner or later everyone will be working for government.[27]

Occasionally citizens revolt against the trend toward ever larger governments by voting for tax limitation proposals or threatening to move to lower tax jurisdictions. But according to the proponents of privatization, "a more educated, critical, and sophisticated" approach to controlling the growth of government is needed, namely the privatization of government services wherever and whenever possible.

PRIVATIZATION   In the broadest sense privatization includes the shifting of many responsibilities *from* government *to* the private marketplace. "Load shedding" implies that government should sell off many of its enterprises—for example, housing projects, airports, stadiums—to private individuals or firms who would operate them more efficiently and effectively. But privatization has also generally come to mean greater reliance on private providers of governmental services functioning in a competitive marketplace and giving individuals greater choice in services.

Privatization recognizes a distinction between government *provision* of a service and government *production* of a service. Governments may decide to *provide* citizens with certain goods and services—for example, schools, police and fire protection, garbage collection, bus transportation, street maintenance, and so on—but not necessarily *produce* these services directly through government bureaucracies—public schools, municipal police and fire departments, municipal garbage collection, city-owned buses, city street maintenance departments, and so on. Rather, a variety of other methods of "service delivery" are available that rely more on private, competitive producers and individual choice.

HOW TO PRIVATIZE   The following are among the more common methods of privatizing the provision of government services:

- *Contracting:* Governments contract with private organizations to provide a publicly funded service. Private firms compete to win and keep the contracts by providing quality services at low costs.
- *Franchising:* Governments grant exclusive contracts for a certain period of time to a private firm to provide a monopoly service—for example, cable television or garbage collection. The private firm collects fees directly from citizens under contractual terms agreed to by the government. The franchise firm may pay a fee to

---

[27]E. S. Savas, *Privatizing the Public Sector* (New York: Chatham House, 1982), p. 25.

the government for the privilege. Government may terminate the franchise for poor performance or excessive fees charged to citizens.

* *Grants:* Governments provide direct grants of money to private firms or nonprofit organizations conditioned on their providing low-cost services to citizens. Grants are typically made to hospitals and health facilities, libraries and cultural centers, and low-cost housing projects, among others.

* *Vouchers:* Vouchers are given directly to citizens who qualify for them, allowing these citizens to exercise free choice in selecting the producers of the service. Unlike grants, in which the government chooses the producers of the service, vouchers give citizens the power to choose the producer. Producers compete to attract citizens who have vouchers; the vouchers are later turned in to the government by producers for cash. For example, rent vouchers to the poor or homeless allow them to select housing of their choice; grants to public housing organizations oblige the poor and homeless to seek shelter in specific projects. Education vouchers (see Chapter 15) would allow parents to choose any school, public or private, for their children. Schools would compete to attract pupils, cashing in their accumulated vouchers.

* *Interjurisdictional agreements:* Governments may contract with other governments to provide certain services more efficiently and on a larger scale than they could provide themselves. Strictly speaking, this is not privatization, but the idea of seeking the most efficient producers is offered as a reform.

Privatization proponents also recommend greater reliance on private market provision of services that government may require citizens to obtain (such as auto insurance), greater reliance on voluntary service and charitable organizations functioning with the cooperation of government; and finally the encouragement of indivudal self-help that might reduce the need for governmental services.

Surveys of the extent of privatization in city government services suggest that many cities have succeeded in contracting out services for

Vehicle towing and storage
Commercial solid waste disposal
Residential solid waste disposal
Day care facilities
Street light operation
Traffic signal installation/maintenance
Street repairs
Bus system operation
Ambulance service
Airport operation
Hospitals operations/management

roughly in that order of frequency.[28] A few cities and counties have even experimented with privatization of jail operations, building and grounds maintenance, data processing, tax billing, deliquency tax collection, and other functions traditionally performed by government employees.

---

[28]*Municipal Yearbook 1987* (Washington DC: ICMA, 1988), pp. 43–53.

THE POLITICS OF PRIVATIZATION   Privatization is usually defended as a cost-saving measure—a way of reducing the waste, inefficiency, and unresponsiveness of "bloated municipal bureaucracies." It is argued that private contractors, operating in a competitive marketplace, can provide the same services at much lower costs than government bureaucracies. At the same time, privatization strengthens private enterprise.

Of course, privatization is usually opposed by powerful political groups—especially municipal employees and their unions and teachers' unions and public school administrators. They argue that the cost savings of privatization are often exaggerated and that the savings come at the price of reduced quality and/or a failure to serve all of the people. There is also concern about the loss of public control of services through privatization and a belief that government contractors and franchises can become at least as arrogant and unresponsive as government bureaucracies.

Some reformers acknowledge that privatization is not a cure-all. David Osborne writes that "privatization is one answer, but not *the* answer."

> The most important issue is not "public" vs. "private." It is monopoly vs. competition. Sometimes, when governments contract with private companies to pick up the garbage or run a prison, they wind up with monopolies, and their costs skyrocket. Private monopolies are just as inefficient as public monopolies. Defense contractors are an example. So are private utilities, which are in fact more expensive than publicly owned utilities.[29]

Government's job, according to Osborne, is to determine whether a particular function can best be produced by government employees; private contractors; or nonprofit, voluntary organizations. Governments cannot hand over the responsibility of *governance* to others; governments still make the policy decisions and provide the financing.

NEW REFORMS: "REINVENTING GOVERNMENT"

The current thrust of reform in government is focused on overcoming "the bankruptcy of bureaucracy"—the waste, inefficiency, impersonality, and unresponsiveness of large government organizations.[30] Today's reform efforts are largely devoted to overcoming the unanticipated results of the early Progressive reform movement that created the civil service and professionalized city and state and school administrations.

ENTREPRENEURIAL GOVERNMENT   People are angry at government at all levels. People believe governments are spending more but delivering less; they are frustrated with bureaucracies over which they have little control and tired of politicians who raise taxes and cut services. According to the new reformers: "Our fundamental problem today is not too much government or too little government . . . [but] the wrong kind of

---

[29]David Osborne, "Privatization: One Answer, Not *The* Answer," *Governing* (April 1992), 83.

[30]David Osborne and Ted Gaebler, *Reinventing Government: How the Entrepreneurial Spirit Is Transforming the Public Sector* (New York: Addison-Wesley, 1992), p. 12.

government. We do not need more government or less government, we need better government."[31]

The problem is perceived as one of overcoming "the routine tendency to protect turf, to resist change, to build empires, to enlarge one's sphere of control, to protect projects and programs regardless of whether or not they are any longer needed." The solution is the "entrepreneurial" government that "searches for efficient and effective ways of managing."

REINVENTING GOVERNMENT   How is the "entrepreneurial spirit" to be encouraged in government? In their widely read and cited book, *Reinventing Government*, the reformist authors set out ten principles of government entrepreneurialship:

- *Steer rather than row.* Separte policy decisions (steering) from service delivery (rowing). Government should focus on steering while relying more on private firms to deliver services. Government should be a catalyst.
- *Empower people rather than simply deliver services.* Governments should encourage communities and neighborhoods to undertake ownership and control of public services. Government should be community-owned.
- *Inject competition into service delivery.* Competition between public and private agencies, among private contractors, or between different governments encourages efficiency, innovation, and responsiveness. Government should be competitive.
- *Make government organizations mission-driven rather than rule-driven.* Do not prescribe how government organizations should go about doing things by prescribing rules, procedures, and regulations; but rather set goals and encourage government organizations to find the best ways to achieve them. Government should be mission-driven.
- *Encourage governments to be results oriented.* Government bureaucracies should be measured in terms of their results, not their size, numbers, or services. Government should fund outcomes, not inputs.
- *Focus on the needs of customers, not the bureaucracy.* Governments should treat citizens as if they were customers, responding to their needs, "putting them in the driver's seat." Government should be customer-driven.
- *Encourage governments to earn money through user charges.* Charging the users of government services, whenever possible, is fair; it raises revenues and balances demands for services. Governments should be enterprising.
- *Practice prevention rather than cure.* Problems from fires to ill-health are cheaper to address through prevention than services. Government should be anticipatory.
- *Decentralize government organizations.* Decentralization increases flexibility, effectiveness, innovation, morale, and commitment. Government should be decentralized.
- *Use market incentives to bring about change rather than command and control.* Market mechanisms are preferred over regulations. Government should be market oriented.

Note that these are guiding principles, rather than recommendations for changes in the structure of state or local government. Unlike earlier reformers who focused on structural

---

[31]Ibid., pp. 23–24.

changes, today's reformers are more concerned about *how* governments go about their tasks.

POLITICS OF REINVENTION   The principles of "reinvention" are identified with the "neoliberal" ("new" liberals) and Democrats who acquired influence in state and local politics in the 1980s. A recognized leader of the movement was Arkansas Governor Bill Clinton who was widely praised for his innovative efforts in education and economic development in that state.[32] Clinton served for serveral years as chair of the Democratic Leadership Confernce (DLC), designed to move the national Democratic party toward a more moderate, centrist position that could win back the support of white middle-class voters in presidential elections. Upon entering the Oval Office, Clinton commissioned Vice President Al Gore to head a National Performance Review specifically committed to "reinventing" the federal government.[33]

But political opposition to the new reform arises from many of the core constituency groups of the Democratic party—government employees, teachers' unions, environmental groups, and black leaders and organizations. Jesse Jackson once described the DLC derisively as "Democrats for the Leisure Class." Government employees and their unions are concerned about the antibureaucratic thrust of many of the new reforms; they fear a loss of the government sector jobs to private contractors. Likewise teachers' unions have been concerned with the reformers' focus on government performance, fearing that it means competence testing of students and teachers (see Chapter 15). Blacks and other minority groups fear that the focus on efficiency and productivity will overshadow concerns about equity. User fees and charges often place heavy burdens on the poor.

Support for "reinvention" is strong in the business community. Business interests have long bemoaned bloated government bureaucracies and senseless rules and regulations. High-tech companies have an added interest in selling governments computer hardware and software designed to make governmental operations more efficient. Major management consulting firms, like Peat Marvick and Price Waterhouse, are anxious to win contracts from state and local governments to proceed with reinvention. And many elected state and local officials understand the political appeal to taxpayers of efforts to reinvent government. Various "cookbooks" are now available to assist them in these efforts.[34]

POLITICAL CORRUPTION

Corruption is an ever-present theme in American political life. We all know that "politics is corrupt," but with the exception of some well-publicized cases we really do not know *how* much corruption takes place. Corruption *may* be more widespread in state and local politics than in national politics, because state and local officials avoid the spotlight of the national news media.

---

[32]See Thomas Osborne, *Laboratories of Democracy* (Boston: Harvard Business School, 1988), chap. 3, "Arkansas: The Education Model."

[33]See National Performance Review, *Creating a Government That Works Better and Costs Less* (Washington DC: Government Printing Office, 1994).

[34]In addition to Osborne and Gaeber, *Reinventing Government*, see National Commission on State and Local Government Public Service, *Hard Truths/Tough Choices: An Agenda for State and Local Government Reform* (Washington DC: Government Printing Office, 1993).

DEFINING CORRUPTION   One major problem in studying corruption is defining the term. What is "corrupt" to one observer may be "just politics" to another or merely "an embarrassment" to someone else.

One attempt to sort out some of the ambiguities of "corruption" focused on four components.[35]

- *The use of official position.* If officials use their public post in the illegal activity, it is considered *more* corrupt than if officials commit an illegal act outside of their official duties.
- *The donor's relation to the official.* If the donor is a constituent, the favor performed is *less* likely to be perceived as corrupt than if the favor was performed for a non-constituent. Using one's office to directly steal from the public treasury for one's own personal enrichment is "corrupt"; but using one's influence to obtain costly favors from other government agencies for one's hometown constituents is not.
- *The favor rendered by the official.* If the favor rendered by the official is very special, it is more likely to be considered corrupt than if it is a routine type of constituent service. (Routine calls by legislators to executive agencies to check on the status of contracts for firms located in the legislator's district are not usually considered corrupt, even when the firms are large campaign contributors.)
- *The size and nature of the payoff.* If the payoff is very large and occurs near the date of the favor, it is considered more corrupt than if the payoff is modest and is separated in time from the favor. Finally, money given for personal use is considered more corrupt than money given for campaign expenses.

For example, here is a list of hypothetical acts that state senators in twenty-four states were asked to rate as more or less corrupt, together with the percentage of senators who viewed each act as corrupt.[36]

- The driveway of the mayor's home being paved by the city crew—95.9 percent.
- A public official using public funds for personal travel—95.2 percent.
- A state assembly member, while chairman of the public roads committee, authorizing the purchase of land he or she had recently acquired—95.1 percent.
- A legislator accepting a large campaign contribution in return for voting "the right way" on a legislative bill—91.9 percent.
- A judge with $50,000 worth of stock in a corporation hearing a case concerning that firm—78.8 percent.
- A presidential candidate promising an ambassadorship in exchange for campaign contributions—71.1 percent.
- A secretary of defense owning $50,000 in stock in a company with which the Defense Department has a million-dollar contract—58.3 percent.
- A member of Congress who holds a large amount of stock (about $50,000 worth) in Exxon working to maintain the oil depletion allowance—54.9 percent.
- A member of Congress using seniority to obtain a weapons contract for a firm in his or her district—31.6 percent.
- A public official using influence to get a friend or relative admitted to law school—23.7 percent.

---

[35]John G. Peters and Susan Welch, "Political Corruption in America: A Search for Definitions and a Theory," *American Political Science Review,* 72 (September 1978), 974–84.

[36]Ibid., p. 978.

The line between unethical behavior and criminal activity is a fuzzy one. Unethical behavior includes lying and misrepresentation; favoritism toward relatives, friends, and
constituents; conflicts of interest, in which public officials decide issues in which they have
a personal financial interest. Not all unethicial behavior is criminal conduct. But bribery
is a criminal offense—soliciting or receiving anything of value in exchange for the performance of a governmental duty.

HOW MUCH CORRUPTION?   It is difficult to estimate the extent of corruption in American politics, in part because public officials do not usually volunteer information on their own corrupt behavior! The U.S. Justice Department reports on *federal*
prosecutions of public officials for violations of criminal statutes (see Figure 10–1). These
figures do not include state prosecutions, so they do not cover all of the criminal indictments brought against public officials each year. (And, of course, they do not tell us how

Figure 10–1
FEDERAL PROSECUTIONS OF PUBLIC
CORRUPTION

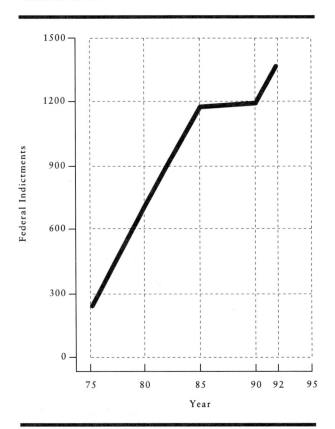

Source: Statistical Abstract of the United States, 1995, p. 214.

much corruption went undetected.) Nonetheless, these figures indicate that now over one thousand public officials are indicted and convicted of criminal activity each year.

EXPLAINING CORRUPTION   Why do some government officials engage in corruption? We can think of at least three reasons: (1) for personal gain, that is, simply to enrich themselves; (2) to benefit friends, constituents, or ethnic groups with contracts, jobs, and aid; and (3) to bring coordination to fragmented government by exchanging favors simply "to get things done." Often we think of activities under these last two categories as less corrupt than efforts to achieve personal gain. Corruption for personal gain is less acceptable. Yet such corruption is almost an American tradition. Politicians over the years could echo Tammany Hall's George Washington Plunkitt, "I seen my opportunities and I took 'em."[37]

Political corruption is more common in some cities and states than in others. Generally corruption is measured by federal prosecutions because it is more common in large cities and larger states. Competitive parties tend to dampen corruption somewhat, suggesting that strong opposition parties perform a watchdog function. Gambling is closely associated with official corruption. But the size of government bureaucracies appears to be the strongest determinant of corruption: As government grows, so do the opportunities for corruption.[38]

PROSECUTING CORRUPTION   Investigating and prosecuting state and local government officials for corrupt activity was once the exclusive responsibility of the state attorney general's office using state laws. But today U.S. attorneys have largely taken over this responsibility. Acting under broad federal statutes—federal laws dealing with mail fraud, tax fraud, and the RICO Act (Racketeer Influenced and Corrupt Organizations)—federal prosecutors have largely displaced state prosecutors in dealing with official corruption.[39] Federal prosecutors have the vast resources of the FBI, the Internal Revenue Service, the Postal Inspection Service, and a myriad of other federal agencies to assist them in investigations. Moreover, U.S. attorneys have great discretion in their investigatory and prosecutory decisions. U.S. attorneys, unlike regional directors of other federal departments, are nominated by the president and confirmed by the U.S. Senate. They are not only free from state or local influence, they are also free from interference from federal elected officials. They can initiate lengthy and complex investigations, convene federal grand juries, obtain indictments, arrange plea bargains with defendants, and build "pyramid" cases against prominent officials. ("Pyramid building" consists of dropping or reducing charges against lower-level figures in exchange for their testimony implicating higher officials.) Federal prosecutors generally pride themselves on their ability to prosecute prominent state and local officials. And well-publicized successful prosecutions often provide a springboard for their own political ambitions.

The great discretion given U.S. attorneys, combined with partisan politics and their own personal ambitions, can lead to selective use of federal laws against prominent officials. Indeed, the possibility of "targeting" by a federal prosecutor should inspire caution in even the most honest state and local officials. Cleaning up political corruption in state

---

[37]Riordan, *Plunkitt of Tammany Hall*, p. 3

[38]These findings are set forth in Kenneth J. Meier and Thomas M. Holbrook, "I Seen My Opportunities and I Took 'Em: Political Corruption in the American States," *Journal of Politics*, 54 (February 1992), 135–55.

[39]See Arthur Maass, "Public Policy by Prosecution," *The Public Interest* (Fall 1987), 107–27.

and local government is *not* an enumerated or implied power of the federal government. This is one more activity that has shifted from the state to the national level and undermined earlier ideas of the American federalism (see Chapter 3). The states have a special interest in policing their own political processes. The principal responsibility for attacking corruption should rest with the states themselves and the people who elect state and local officials.

VOTER REACTION   Do voters punish officials for corrupt activities? Not always. Voters sometimes reelect officials who have been convicted of criminal offenses. There are various reasons for the continued voter support of corrupt politicians. First of all, *charges* of corruption are so frequent in election campaigns that voters disregard information about improprieties in office. Or voters may perceive both candidates as more or less corrupt and simply make their voting choices on other factors. Second, if voters believe that officials' corrupt acts were designed to benefit their district or their race or their ethnic group, they may support them despite (or even because of) their corrupt acts. Third, corrupt politicians may be popular with their constituents, whether personally or because of their stand on issues; constituents may knowingly ignore corruption because they value the representation more. There are many other issues besides "honesty in government."[40]

THE "REDEMPTION SCAM"   A strategy of some disgraced officeholders today is to publicly acknowledge one's past errors, claim personal redemption, go on television talk shows, and ask voters to accept a restored and chastised candidate. Mayor Marion Barry of Washington, DC, was tried and convicted on cocaine charges arising out of a sting operation that videotaped him at a D.C. hotel in 1991. His initial response: "Who are you going to believe—me or the videotape?" But after serving a jail term and enduring nationwide ridicule, he made a strong political comeback and recaptured the mayor's chair in 1994. He campaigned on his own redemption: "God has made it possible for me to overcome many obstacles. I stand here with you stronger and wiser and better than ever before."[41]

THE RADICAL STYLE: POLITICS IN BERKELEY

Imagine a city council meeting held in a theater, with hundreds of enraged participants shouting political obscenities at each other, in a fierce debate over a resolution dealing with Israel's policy toward the Palestinians. Welcome to Berkeley, California, where a radical political style has displaced both traditional machine and liberal reform politics. If you believe that land reform in Nicaragua, or U.S. nuclear weapons policy, or hunger in Somalia might be beyond the scope of municipal government, you would be adjudged guilty of "sandbox politics" (thinking locally instead of globally) in Berkeley. Moreover,

---

[40]For some tests about voter reaction to corruption, see Barry S. Rundquist, Gerald S. Strom, and John G. Peters, "Corrupt Politicians and Their Electoral Support," *American Political Science Review,* 71 (September 1977), 954–63.

[41]Quoted in *Governing* (February 1995), p. 7.

in dealing with garbage collection or traffic control, it is more important that you devise "envrionmentally correct, politically progressive solutions." For Berkeley thinks of itself as a beacon of "progressive" (radical) politics, an inspiring example for Madison, Wisconsin, and Burlington, Vermont, and eventually every other city in the world.[42]

Early in this century, Berkeley was a leader in reform politics, having adopted council-manager government in 1923. Home of the University of California, for many years Berkeley reflected the liberal reform politics so popular among academics. It developed fair housing laws, a school integration plan, public housing and citywide planning, all well in advance of other cities in the nation. But in the 1960s the Vietnam War "radicalized" politics in Berkeley. Anti-American and revolutionary romanticism replaced liberal politics; "revolutionary violence" was promoted as the path to "soulful socialism in Berkeley." Tom Hayden, now California state representative, organized the Berkeley Liberation Front, and in 1969 the first radical was elected to the Berkeley city council, Ronald Dellums, now a U.S. Congressman. By 1975 radicals had become the dominant force in Berkeley politics. They created a strongly disciplined organization, Berkeley Citizens' Action, renamed themselves "progressives," and set about the task of bringing socialism to Berkeley and the world.

One of their earliest programs centered on establishing "community control" over the police. A series of police department resignations and shake-ups followed. Crime rates rose dramatically, as did drug sales and use. By the late 1980s Berkeley was challenging much larger American cities for the dubious honor of having the highest crime rate in the nation.

The radical agenda for Berkeley included a vigorous rent control program and stringent building regulation that virtually shut down private construction and real estate investment in the city. Wealth was to be "expropriated" in favor of "the people." The result was a disastrous decline in available housing and a rapid increase in homelessness. The radical response to these developments was to call for more public housing and to blame Washington when not enough funds were forthcoming for this purpose.

Berkeley's school system had once been regarded as one of California's finest. Berkeley had adopted a voluntary school desegregation plan in the early 1960s. But when radicals won control of the school board, they undertook to replace racial integration with "cultural nationalism"—the development of separate schools where black students would study black culture and Hispanic students would study Hispanic culture. These schools were eventually closed by the federal courts, but the resulting turmoil led one-quarter of Berkeley parents—black, white, and Hispanic—to send their children to private schools.

Distinguishing features of the radical political style include:

- Diverting the community's attention from local to national and international political issues.
- Abusing democratic processes by disruptive and violent behavior at public meetings under the guise of participating democracy.
- Tolerating violent behavior by leftist and minority groups and rationalizing such behavior.

---

[42]See Joseph P. Lyford, "The Lessons of Berkeley," *The Center Magazine* (March 1980), 54–63; Peter Collier and David Horowitz, "Slouching Towards Berkeley: Socialism in One City," *The Public Interest* (Winter 1989), 47–68; Gail L. Zellman and Steven L. Schlossman, "The Berkeley Youth Wars," *The Public Interest* (Summer 1986), 29–41.

- Stressing conflict rather than seeking consensus on the radical assumption that revolutions require continuing class struggle.

Elements of radical or "progressive" politics are identifiable in many cities.

It is no coincidence that the cities that have flirted with radical politics are university locations. Neither the faculty nor the students have a strong identification with real city
problems—crime, garbage, streets, sewers, and so on. University life fosters abstract thinking about politics, and the temporary residential status of students and many faculty
undermines responsibility for the long-term future of the community. Universities are independently funded; administrators, faculty, and students do not have to worry about the
economic foundation of the community. And, of course, liberal to radical politics are popular among faculty, students, and the nonstudents who settle on the fringes of universities.

TRIVIA
THE MOST LIVABLE CITIES

Each year *Money* magazine ranks the three hundred largest U.S. metropolitan areas according to "The Best Places to Live Today." The rankings are based on scores attributed
to each city based on forty-one factors, from low crime rate, clean air and water, plenti-
ful health care, and quality schools, to low taxes, inexpensive housing, low unemployment, arts and recreation, and good weather.

AND THE WINNERS ARE . . .

Top Ten Overall

Gainesville, FL	Ft. Lauderdale, FL
Rochester, MN	Salem, NH/Havenhill, MA
Jacksonville, FL	Raleigh/Durham, Chapel Hill, NC
Seattle, WA	Las Vegas, NV
Ocala, FL	Naples, FL

Five Best Places in

MIDWEST	WEST	NORTHEAST	SOUTH
Rochester, MN	Seattle, WA	Salem, NH	Gainesville, FL
Madison, WI	Las Vegas, NV	Manchester, NH	Jacksonville, FL
Sioux Falls, SD	Pueblo, CO	Nashua, NH	Ocala, FL
Lafayette, IN	San Francisco, CA	Fitchburg, MA	Ft. Lauderdale, FL
Grand Forks, ND	Greeley, CO	Middlesex County, MA	Raleigh/Durham, Chapel Hill, NC

Source: Based on rankings by *Money*, September 1995.

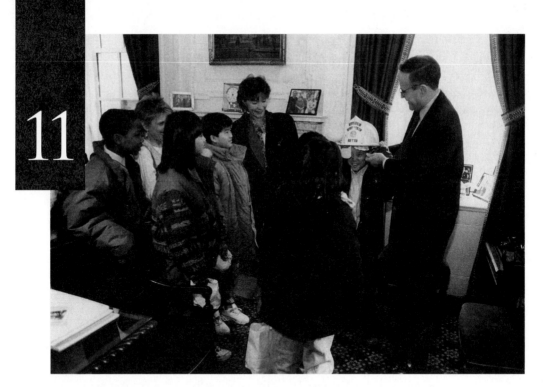

PARTICIPATION IN COMMUNITY POLITICS

CITIZEN PARTICIPATION

Ideally, democracy inspires widespread citizen participation in government—as voters, community activists, neighborhood association and interest group members, party workers, and candidates for public office. But in fact, rarely do many citizens participate actively in community politics.

A "communitarian" view praises the many values of direct citizen participation in community affairs, not just by voting, but perhaps more importantly, by participating in groups and forums, working with neighbors to solve the problems of the community. This view asserts that where neighbors talk about community affairs in face-to-face meetings, they learn from one another, become more tolerant of different people with different views, create bonds of friendship, and look to common solutions to their problems. Communitarians of the left in American politics call for "participatory democracy" as a means of finding meaning in life; communitarians of the right echo Tocqueville's praise of town meetings and call for increased community "volunteerism."

But in reality relatively few people are interested in community affairs. They are busy at their jobs and professions, concerned with raising their children, and more interested in watching sports on television than broadcasts of city council meetings. And it may be naive to believe that community political activism always engenders tolerance, respect, and common efforts to resolve problems. Often, increased participation inspires rancorous conflict, intolerant popular policy initiatives, and even violence. Indeed, a surge of participation, with resulting conflicting claims upon a government that cannot satisfy everyone, may simply engender cynicism and disrespect toward government. Citizen activists are not always well-informed even on the issue on which they are most vociferous. Activism—particularly neighborhood NIMBY activity ("not in my backyard" opposition to community projects)—may paralyze local government, preventing it from effectively addressing communitywide problems.[1]

DIRECT CITIZEN INVOLVEMENT   Can participation in community government be increased, and if so, what might be the effect of doing so? An elaborate, long-term study of neighborhood-based citizen participation programs of five cities (Birmingham, Dayton, Portland, St. Paul, and San Antonio), with ten matching cities serving as a comparison group, concluded that "a rebirth of urban democracy" is both desirable and possible.[2]

Among the study's conclusions:

- Citizens who participate in community politics are more likely to feel that local government is responsive to their needs.
- Higher levels of community participation generate higher levels of tolerance.
- Organized citizen groups force elected officials to be more responsive to neighborhood concerns. While relatively weak in affecting citywide issues, neighborhood groups are very effective in neighborhood issues.
- The development of neighborhood groups tends to dilute the influence of business organizations on community affairs, forcing them to negotiate with neighborhoods.
- However, the development of citizen groups in a city does not necessarily increase overall participation rates. Nor does it necessarily increase the influence of African Americans or Hispanics or low-income residents.
- People can be uninterested in community politics, not because they are alienated or apathetic, but because they have other more compelling interests in life.

VOTERS IN LOCAL ELECTIONS   Voter turnout in local elections is substantially lower than in state or national elections. While 55 percent of the nation's eligible voters may cast ballots in a presidential election, voter turnouts of 25 to 35 percent are typical in local elections.

Nonpartisanship in local elections depresses voter turnout substantially. Voter turnout for municipal elections in nonpartisan cities averages closer to 25 percent, compared to

---

[1]Arguments over value of direct citizen participation are as old as democracy itself. See "Direct Versus Representative Democracy" in Chapter 2. And see Samuel P. Huntington, *American Politics: The Promise of Disharmony* (Cambridge: Harvard University Press, 1981); and Thomas R. Dye and Harmon Zeigler, *The Irony of Democracy,* 10th ed. (Belmont, CA: Wadsworth, 1996).

[2]Jeffrey M. Berry, Kent E. Portney, and Ken Thompson, *The Rebirth of Urban Democracy* (Washington DC: Brookings Institution, 1993).

over 35 percent for partisan cities. Partisan campaigns heighten voter turnout, in part because of the greater interest they generate and in part because of the role of party workers in getting out to vote.

Voter participation in local government can be further reduced by holding municipal elections at odd times of the year when no other state or national elections are being held. Approximately 60 percent of the nation's cities hold municipal elections that are completely independent of state or national elections. A common rationale for holding municipal elections at times other than state or national elections is to separate local issues from state or national questions, but the real effect of scheduling local elections independently is to reduce voter turnout and to increase the influence of groups who vote more regularly.

Voter turnout in cities with a mayor-council form of government is higher than in cities with a council-manager plan. In summary, nonpartisanship, council-manager government, and separate municipal elections—all part of the municipal "reform" movement— operate to reduce voter turnout and probably strengthen the influence of middle-class voters at the polls.

Voter turnout in municipal elections is also affected by the social character of cities. Social cleavages, especially race, increase voter turnout. Mayoral elections in which the racial or ethnic backgrounds of the candidates are well publicized inspire heavy voter turnout. Social homogeneity, on the other hand, is associated with lower voter interest.

CORRELATES OF VOTER TURNOUT   In summary, voter turnout in municipal elections can be described as follows:

Lower voter turnout is expected with	*Higher voter turnout is expected with*
• Nonpartisan electoral systems	• Partisan elections with competitive parties
• Council-manager form of government	• Strong mayor form of government
• City elections held separately from state or national elections	• City elections held concurrently with state and national elections
• Small or middle-sized cities	• Large cities
• Middle-class, homogeneous cities	• Ethnic, heterogeneous cities

LOCAL REFERENDA VOTING   *Referenda voting* is an important aspect of local politics—an aspect not found at the national level. City charters frequently require that referenda be held on all proposals to increase indebtedness or to increase property taxation. Over three-quarters of American cities have referenda provisions in their charters. (See Table 11–1.) Recall elections are permitted in over half of all American cities. (See Chapter 2 for definitions of initiative, referenda, and recall elections.)

HOMEOWNERS VERSUS RENTERS   Referenda votes provide us with an excellent opportunity to examine the factors influencing voter attitudes toward local government and to test some theories about voting behavior on local issues. Many voters in local referenda will try to maximize family income by weighing the benefits that will come to them from a bond issue against the amount of the tax that will fall on them as a result of the expenditure. Non–property owners, having nothing to lose by the expenditure and

Table 11-1
CITIES WITH INITIATIVE, REFERENDUM, AND RECALL

Form of Government	Initiative	Referendum	Recall
Mayor-council	36.8%	71.4%	52.9%
Council-manager	58.8	82.9	70.4
Commission	36.5	76.1	59.4

Source: International City Managers' Association, *Municipal Yearbook 1994*, p. 12.

something to gain, however small, can be expected to favor the passage of bond and expenditure referenda. (Renters seldom realize that landlords will pass the tax increase on to them in higher rent.) Homeowners are more likely to oppose public expenditures that are financed from property taxes than nonhomeowners.

"PUBLIC-REGARDINGNESS"   Among homeowners, support for local public expenditures often *increases* with education, wealth, and income. This tendency of upper-class, liberal voters to support recreational, cultural, environmental projects (e.g., parks, museums, stadiums, libraries, art centers) was once labeled "public-regardingness."[3] But it is not clear whether upper-class voters are more civic minded, or whether the costs to them of these projects are a relatively small percentage of their income and they have the leisure time to make use of these civic facilities.

BIG-CITY POLITICS

Traditionally Democrats have dominated politics in the nation's large central cities, even while their surrounding suburbs have usually been governed by Republicans. Social groups that normally vote Democratic—white ethnic groups, Catholics and Jews, African Americans, union members, low-income families—tend to be concentrated in big cities (see "Identifying Party Cleavages in the States" in Chapter 5). Since the formation of the modern "New Deal" Democratic party coalition under President Franklin D. Roosevelt in the 1930s, most big cities in the United States have been governed by Democrats. This has been true whether the city's electoral system has officially been partisan (e.g., New York, Chicago, Philadelphia, Boston) or nonpartisan (e.g., Los Angeles, Detroit, Miami).

---

[3]Early arguments over public-regardingness are found in James Q. Wilson and Edward C. Banfield, "Public Regardingness as a Value Premise in Voting Behavior," *American Political Science Review*, 58 (December 1964), 876–87; and Roger Durand, "Ethnicity, Public-Regardingness and Referenda Voting," *Midwest Journal of Political Science*, 16 (May 1972), 259–68. More recent evidence that wealth and income lead citizens to be more supportive of public services is found in Evel Elliot, James Regens, and Barry Sheldon, "Exploring Variation in Public Support for Environmental Protection," *Social Science Quarterly*, 76 (March 1995), 41–52.

SPLITS AMONG URBAN DEMOCRATS   Political cleavages *within* the Democratic party have been a driving force in big-city politics over the years. Political conflict in many of America's largest cities has centered on differences between working-class, Catholic, white ethnic (especially Irish, Italian, Polish) Democrats *versus* upper-class, white, liberal Protestants and Jews, allied with black Democratic voters. These factions within the Democratic party have frequently battled over such issues as affirmative action hiring in city government, busing in schools to achieve racial balance, and the behavior of police and prosecutors in crime control. And they have often differed over the burdens of public spending for welfare, health, and public housing—with working-class white ethnics, who are often homeowners and property tax payers, opposed to higher taxes and spending for these services; and upper-class liberals and blacks, many of whom are renters whose property taxes are hidden in rent payments, supporting these expenditures (see "Minorities in Local Politics" later in this chapter).

Occasionally Democratic party organizations have been strong enough to hold these diverse Democratic groups together. Traditional party "machines" would slate candidates for city office with an eye to racial and ethnic group balance. But as these party machines lost influence over time (see "Machines and Bosses" in Chapter 10), intraparty factional conflict—especially between working-class white ethnics and blacks—intensified in many cities.

The growing Hispanic vote in many of America's largest cities adds another potentially unstable element to the Democratic party coalition. Both African Americans and Hispanics have suffered discrimination in a predominantly white, "Anglo" society, and both have higher-than-average rates of poverty and unemployment and lower median family incomes. But a number of studies have shown this coalition to be unstable, occasionally engaging in competition over city jobs, language issues, and representation (e.g., as in Chicago, Denver, Miami).[4] In triethnic cities, whites are more likely to ally themselves with Hispanics than with blacks. Nonetheless some big-city mayors (e.g., Dinkins in New York, Bradley in Los Angeles, Cisneros in San Antonio, and Pena in Denver)[5] were able to build successful black–Hispanic coalitions during their tenure in office.

REPUBLICAN BIG-CITY RESURGENCE?   Splits among urban Democrats, combined with continuing big-city ills—huge deficits, violent crime, racial conflict—have opened up new opportunities for Republican candidates. Despite overwhelming Democratic registration, big-city voters have recently elected a number of Republican mayors to cope with urban problems. Republican prosecuting attorney Rudolph Giuliani, was elected mayor of New York in 1994, the first Republican to govern that city in over twenty years (see "Top Bananas in the Big Apple" later in this chapter). Richard Riordan, a multimillionaire lawyer-businessman, was elected mayor of Los Angeles in 1994, the first Republican to hold that office in twenty years. Other Republicans and some conservative

---

[4]See Raphael Sonenshein, "Bi-Racial Coalition Politics in Los Angeles," *P.S*, 19 (September 1986), 582–90; "The Dynamics of Bi-Racial Coalitions, *Western Political Quarterly*, 42 (June 1989), 333–53; and Rufus Browning, Dale Rogers Marshall, and David Tabb, *Protest Is Not Enough* (Berkeley: University of California Press, 1984).

[5]See also Kent L. Tedin and Richard W. Murray, "Support for Biracial Political Coalitions Among Blacks and Hispanics," *Social Science Quarterly*, 75 (December 1994), 772–89.

Democrats (e.g., Edward Rendell in Philadelphia) have won unexpected victories in heavily Democratic cities in recent elections. Certain common themes have driven their campaigns: a crackdown on crime, cutting the size of the city bureaucracy, reducing city deficits, easing tax burdens, and stimulating the city's economy. But it is not clear yet whether these Republican inroads in big-city politics are temporary responses to voter frustration or a more permanent resurgence of Republican strength.

GETTING INTO COMMUNITY POLITICS

Political ambition is the most distinguishing characteristic of elected officeholders at all levels of government. The people who run for and win public office are not necessarily the most intelligent, best-informed, wealthiest, or most successful business or professional people. At all levels of the political system, from presidential candidates, members of Congress, governors, and state legislators, to city council and school board members, it is the most politically ambitious people who are willing to sacrifice time, family and private life, and energy and effort for the power and celebrity that comes with public office.

Most politicians publicly deny that personal ambition is their real motivation for seeking public office. Rather they describe their motives in highly idealistic terms— "civic duty," "service to community," "reform the government," "protect the environment." These responses reflect the norms of our political culture: People are not supposed to enter politics to satisfy *personal* ambitions, but rather to achieve *public* purposes. Many politicians do not really recognize their own drive for power—the drive to shape their community according to their own beliefs and values. But if there were no personal rewards in politics, no one would run for office.

POLITICAL ENTREPRENEURSHIP   The talent required is that of *political entrepreneurship*—the ability to sell oneself to others as a candidate, to raise money from contributors, to organize people to work on one's behalf, to communicate and publicize oneself through the media. Political parties no longer recruit candidates; candidates recruit themselves. Interest groups do not recruit candidates; candidates seek out interest groups to win their support.

PROFESSIONALIZATION   Politics is becoming increasingly professionalized. "Citizen-politicians"—people with business or professional careers who get into politics part time or for short periods of time—are being driven out of political life by career politicians—people who enter politics early in life as a full-time occupation and expect to make it their career.[6] Politics is increasingly demanding of time and energy. At all levels of governments, from city council to state legislatures to the U.S. Congress, political work is becoming full time and year-round. It is not only more demanding to *hold* office than it was a generation ago, but also far more demanding to *run* for office. Campaigning has become more time-consuming, more technically sophisticated, and much more costly over time.

---

[6]Alan Ehrenhalt, *The United States of Ambition: Politicians, Power and the Pursuit of Office* (New York: Random House, 1991), p. 22.

OCCUPATIONS   Traditionally, city council members and county commissioners were local business people who were respected in the community and active in civic organizations. They were likely to own small businesses and to have many contacts among constituents—retail merchants, real estate brokers, insurance agents, and so on. (Seldom do executives of large corporations concern themselves with local affairs, although they may encourage lower-management personnel to do so.) The part-time nature of traditional community governance, combined with only nominal pay and few perks of office, made local office holding a "community service." It attracted people whose business brought them into close contact with the life of the community and allowed them spare time to attend to community affairs.

These civic-minded small business people are still politically dominant in many small towns and rural counties throughout the nation. But they are gradually being replaced by lawyers, government employees, teachers, and professional officeholders in medium to large cities. In these cities, council pay is higher, the work more time-consuming, greater celebrity attaches to council membership (television interviews, newspaper stories, deference, and respect), and greater opportunities exist for political advancement.

> Full-timers drive part-timers out of circulation. The city councilman who spends his days building political coalitions, meeting with constituents, and cultivating financial support sets a standard of political sophistication that colleagues pretty much have to meet if they are going to stay effective or even stay in office. Once a city council attracts its full-time members, it is on the way to becoming a de facto full-time institution, even if it does not think of itself as one.[7]

POLITICAL BIAS IN RECRUITMENT   As a result of the increasing professionalization of local politics, liberals and Democrats are more likely to win office. Increasing demands of time and energy attract people for whom politics is more important and more rewarding than business or professional success. Older business and professional leaders, who once managed city affairs on a part-time basis while still tending to their businesses and professions, tended to be conservative and Republicans. But these part-time, civic-minded business leaders are gradually being replaced by younger people for whom politics is a career.

> Serving in city government in Concord used to be easy work. Businessmen did it in their spare time. As the city grew, governing it became a demanding, time-consuming job. The Republican merchants and insurance brokers who used to do it no longer wanted to take the time. In their place came political professionals, and all the professionals, over an entire decade, were Democrats.[8]

CITY COUNCILS: TERMS AND ELECTIONS   In most American cities, especially those with nonpartisan at-large elections, getting elected to city council is a do-it-yourself project. Most party organizations and civic associations are unreliable as sources of money and workers. Candidates must mobilize their own resources and created their own organizations. It is generally unwise to challenge an incumbent; over 80

[7]Ibid., p. 14.
[8]Ibid., p. 7.

percent of all incumbent council members seeking reelection are returned to office. When vacancies occur, there are likely to be many candidates in the race. Since local races lack the visibility of national or statewide races, most focus on the personality, style, or image of the candidate. Even when local issues divide the candidates, most voters in local elections will be unaware of the candidates' stands on these issues.

WINNING ELECTIONS   In this fluid setting, electoral success depends on (1) the social acceptability of candidates relative to the community (especially their race and ethnic background); (2) their personal recognition in the community (name recognition, contacts from business, church, civic activity, etc.); and (3) their political resources (endorsements by newspapers and civic associations, access to political contributors, people willing to serve as volunteer workers, etc.). These factors are especially important for first-time candidates.[9] In subsequent campaigns, candidates develop more stable political followings.

NONPARTISANSHIP   Most American cities elect their council members in nonpartisan elections (see Table 9–5). This reflects the success of the reform movement (described in Chapter 10) and the widespread acceptance of the idea of nonpartisanship in municipal government.

COUNCIL SIZE   Most city councils have five or seven members, but large city councils with up to twenty-two members are found in the larger, older cities of the Northeast and Midwest (see Table 11–2).

COUNCIL TERMS   Four-year terms for council members are most frequent, but some council members are elected for two- or three-year terms. In most cities, council member terms overlap, so that some council seats are filled at every municipal election. Presumably overlapping terms ensure continuity in the deliberations of the council.

AT-LARGE VERSUS DISTRICT ELECTIONS   About 60 percent of American cities currently elect their council members at large and an additional 30 percent elect council members from a combination of at-large and district constituencies. At-large elections, where council candidates face the entire city electorate, are part of the package of "reform" government, together with nonpartisanship and manager government. However, at-large elections are increasingly coming under court scrutiny. Depending on the "totality of circumstances" in the community, at-large elections may adversely affect the voting rights of minorities. (See Chapter 9).

RUNOFF ELECTIONS   Do majority runoff requirements in nonpartisan municipal elections pose a disadvantage for minority and women candidates? It is sometimes claimed that minority candidates who win a plurality of votes in the first-round election are later defeated in the runoff by a coalition of antiminority voters. But systematic stud-

---

[9]See Joel Lieske, "The Political Dynamics of Urban Voting Behavior," *American Journal of Political Science,* 33 (February 1989), 150–74.

Table 11-2
CITY COUNCILS

	Average Size of Council	Council Terms (%)		
		TWO YEARS	THREE YEARS	FOUR YEARS
Total	6.5	29.5	9.5	60.0
SIZE OF CITY				
Over 1 million	12	50.0	0	50.0
500,000 to 1 million	13	40.0	0	60.0
250,000 to 500,000	9	33.3	0	66.7
100,000 to 150,000	8	19.5	2.6	77.9
50,000 to 100,000	8	28.1	2.6	68.4
25,000 to 50,000	7	25.8	6.2	65.6
10,000 to 25,000	6	28.0	12.5	57.5
5,000 to 10,000	6	29.1	11.8	57.6
Under 5,000	5	32.1	8.2	59.0

Source: International City Managers' Association, *Baseline Data Report: Profile of the City Council,* 1992.

ies of this issue fail to produce any evidence to support this minority disadvantage claim regarding runoff elections. Indeed, on the average, first-round front-runners win runoffs twice as often as they lose (However, *incumbents* who are forced into runoffs lose more often than their challengers.) Blacks and women who win first-round elections are just as likely to win runoffs as white males.[10]

FRIENDS AT CITY HALL   A surprising number of council members are initially *appointed* to their office to fill the unexpired terms of resigning members. Those appointees are likely to be personal friends of council members or to have held some other city job. Finally, 80 percent of incumbents running for reelection are successful. Voluntary retirement is the most common exit from community politics. Political scientist Kenneth Prewitt observes that

> The election system provides advantages to those citizens who already have social and political resources; to those favorably located in the network of friendships which play such an important part in city politics; to those whose apprentice roles identify them as likely candidates for political office; to those who have natural organizational ties and support; and, finally, to those already in office if they choose to stand for reelection.[11]

[10]See Charles S. Bullock and Loch K. Johnson, "Runoff Elections in Georgia," *Journal of Politics,* 47 (August 1985) 937–46; Arnold Fleischmann and Lana Stein, "Minority and Female Success in Municipal Runoff Elections," *Social Science Quarterly,* 68 (June 1987), 378–85.

[11]Kenneth Prewitt, *The Recruitment of Political Leaders: A Study of Citizen-Politicians* (Indianapolis: Bobbs-Merrill, 1970), p. 148.

WOMEN IN LOCAL POLITICS

Women's participation in local politics has risen dramatically in recent years. Today, of the approximately 19,000 municipal council members serving in cities with populations over 10,000, over 3,700 or almost 20 percent are women.[12] As late as 1975 this figure was estimated to be only about 4 percent. Women occupy about 15 percent of mayors' offices across the country. Women have served as mayors of Chicago (Jane Byrne), San Francisco (Diane Feinstein), Dallas (Annette Strauss), Houston (Kathy Whitmire), Ft. Worth (Kay Granger), Cincinnati (Bobbie Stern), Pittsburgh (Sophie Masloff), San Diego (Maureen O'Conner), Washington, DC (Sharon Pratt Kelly), and many other major cities.

WHY LOCAL POLITICS?   Why have women taken a more active role in community politics? The increase in women's political participation has taken place at all levels of government, with more women serving in Congress[13] and in state legislatures (see Chapter 6). The movement of women into politics generally is attributed to the movement of women into the work force and the changing cultural values redefining women's role in American society. At the local level, women may find fewer obstacles to political officeholding than at the state or national level. Local offices do not require women to move away from their home communities to the state capital or to Washington. Women candidates, unlike men, are seldom relieved of all of their home responsibilities when running for or occupying political office.[14] Moreover, campaigns for local office do not require as much money as state or congressional campaigns. Fund-raising has been a traditional obstacle to women candidates, although that barrier is diminishing relative to men over time. There is also a long tradition of women in volunteer community organizations, from hospitals and welfare agencies to cultural centers and neighborhood associations. Upon reexamining their traditional community roles, many women decided to use the knowledge and experience gained in volunteer work to move into elective politics:

> After devoting considerable time and energy to organizational life and civic activities, voluntary community service, or political party work, [a] woman sees it as only reasonable that she should be moving into elective or appointive positions of public responsibility.[15]

POLICY CONSEQUENCES   What are the policy consequences of increased women's representation on city councils? The best available evidence suggests that there are no significant policy differences between men and women council members, even on feminist issues.[16] For example, political scientist Susan Gluck Mezey found that both men and women on Connecticut councils supported abortions, day-care centers, and rape cri-

---

[12]Center for the American Woman in Politics, Eagleton Institute of Politics, Rutgers University, 1995.

[13]See Thomas R. Dye, *Politics in America*, 2nd ed. (Englewood Cliffs, NJ: Prentice Hall, 1997), Chap. 10.

[14]Ruth B. Mandel, *In the Running: The New Woman Candidate* (New Haven, CT: Ticknor and Fields, 1981), pp. 63–97.

[15]Ibid., p. 13.

[16]Susan Gluck Mezey, "Support for Women's Rights Policy," *American Politics Quarterly*, 6 (October 1978), 485–96. See also Albert K. Karnig and B. Oliver Walter, "Election of Women to City Councils," *Social Science Quarterly*, 56 (March 1976), 605–13.

sis centers. Typical liberal and conservative identifications were better predictors of how council members stood on issues than gender itself. Thus, increasing female representation in local government may not result in major policy changes.[17]

MINORITIES IN LOCAL POLITICS

Local politics is the entry level in the American political system for minorities as well as women. Currently about half of the one-hundred largest cities in the United States have minority or women mayors. All but a few of these cities have had minority or women mayors in the recent past.

MINORITY MAYORS   Black mayors have served in many cities with majority white populations, including New York, Chicago, Los Angeles, and Philadelphia, as well as cities with majority black populations, including Detroit, Washington, DC and New Orleans.

The success of blacks and Hispanics in city politics, especially in majority white and Anglo cities, suggests that race is becoming less important as a criterion in voter choice for municipal leadership. However, voting patterns in city elections in which black and white candidates face each other indicate a continuing residue of racial politics. Black voters continue to cast their votes solidly for black candidates in these elections; white voters continue to give majority support to white candidates. The swing vote in these black–white election confrontations usually rests with 30 to 40 percent of white voters who are prepared to support qualified black candidates.

Successful black candidates in majority white cities have generally emphasized racial harmony and conciliation. They have stressed broad themes of concern to all voters—regardless of race. They have built coalitions that cut across racial, ethnic, and economics lines; many have worked their way up the ranks of local organizations. They have avoided identification as "protest" candidates.

MINORITIES ON COUNCILS   Until recently blacks were generally underrepresented on city councils across the country. That is to say, blacks held a smaller proportion of seats on city councils than the black percentages of city populations. But the steady rise in the number of black city council members and county commissioners over the last twenty years (see Figure 11–1) has brought black representation to rough proportionality in most American cities. In cities in which blacks constitute 10 to 50 percent of the population, black representation on city councils generally reflects the black population percentage (see Figure 11–2). In cities in which the black population constitutes a majority (over 50 percent), black representation on city councils usually exceeds the black population percentage.[18]

---

[17]However, assertions of "gender cleavage" in municipal politics, based on observations of a single city where men supported economic development projects and women opposed them, can be found in Paul Schumaker and Nancy Elizabeth Burns, "Gender Cleavages and the Resolution of Local Policy Issues," *American Journal of Political Science,* 32 (November 1988), 1070–95.

[18]Susan Welch, "The Impact of At-Large Elections on the Representation of Blacks and Hispanics," *Journal of Politics*, 52 (November 1990), 1050–76.

Figure 11–1
BLACK ELECTED OFFICIALS

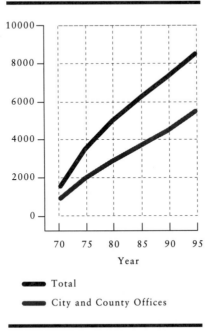

Source: Data from *Statistical Abstract of the United States, 1995*, p. 282.

In contrast, Hispanic representation on city councils is significantly below the Hispanic population percentages. Earlier we observed that Hispanic voter turnout was significantly lower than that for other social groups (see Chapter 4). Lower voter turnout among Hispanics is frequently attributed to cultural and language barriers and the resident alien status of many Hispanics. These factors together with some structural features of reform government, including at-large elections, continue to create barriers to political mobilization of Hispanics.[19]

POLICY CONSEQUENCES: EMPLOYMENT   What are the policy consequences of increasing black representation on city councils? Perhaps the most obvious consequence is increased black *employment* in city jobs. Black employment at all levels of city administration—professional and managerial, police and fire, office and clerical, service and maintenance—tends to increase with increases in the black population of the

[19]See Rufus P. Browning, Dale Rodgers Marshall, and David H. Tabb, *Protest Is Not Enough* (Berkeley: University of California Press, 1984); Rodney E. Hero, "Hispanics in Urban Government," *Western Political Quarterly*, 43 (June 1990), 403–14; Jerry L. Polinard, Robert D. Wrinkle, and Thomas Longovia, "The Impact of District Elections on the Mexican American Community," *Social Science Quarterly*, 72 (September 1991), 609–14.

Figure 11-2
MINORITY POPULATION AND REPRESENTATION ON CITY COUNCILS

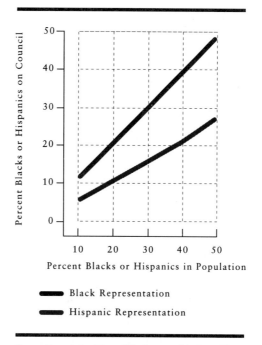

Black Representation

Hispanic Representation

Source: Data derived from "The Impact of At-Large Elections on the Representation of Blacks and Hispanics" by Susan Welch in *Journal of Politics* volume 52:4, pp. 1063, 1070; by permission of the author and the University of Texas Press.

city, as we might expect.[20] But the single most important determinant of black employment in administrative and professional positions is the proportion of blacks elected to city councils.[21] The employment of blacks in service and maintenance jobs does not require political representation. However, to get important city jobs, blacks must first win political power.[22]

---

[20]Peter K. Eisinger, "Black Employment in Municipal Jobs," *American Political Science Review,* 76 (June 1982), 380–92.

[21]Thomas R. Dye and James Renick, "Political Power and City Jobs," *Social Science Quarterly,* 62 (September 1981), 475–86. See also Matthews Hutchins and Lee Sigelman, "Black Employment in State and Local Government," *Social Science Quarterly,* 62 (March 1981), 79–87.

[22]For an argument that black and Hispanic *mayors* do *not* increase minority city employment, but that black and Hispanic *council* members do so, see Brinck Kerr and Kenneth Mladenka, "Does Politics Matter?" *American Journal of Political Science,* 38 (November 1994), 918–43.

POLICE POLICIES   Urban police departments have long been a focus of concern for minorities. Police policies have come under scrutiny for contributing to racial tensions, triggering riots, blocking minority aspirations, and shaping minority perceptions of justice. Many black mayors have campaigned on explicit pledges to reform police departments and adopt policies designed to make police responsive and sensitive to the concerns of minorities. The adoption of minority-oriented police policies, including increases in the number of minority police officers, has occurred with increases in black population percentages in cities, regardless of whether cities elect black mayors and council members. However, there is some evidence that the election of black mayors results in (1) accelerated recruitment of black police officers and (2) the adoption of citizen review boards to oversee police actions.[23]

TAXING AND SPENDING   To date there is *no* evidence that cities with greater black representation on city councils, or even cities with black mayors, pursue significantly different taxing, spending, or service policies than do cities with little or not black representation. This is really not surprising; black city leaders face the same problems as white city leaders in raising revenue, fighting crime, improving housing, reducing congestion, removing garbage, and so on. It is possible, of course, that black residents *feel* better about a city government that includes some black faces, and it is even possible that black neighborhoods might receive better *delivery* of urban services under black leadership. However, the overall problems of cities may remain unaffected by substituting black leadership for white leadership.

ATTITUDES AT CITY HALL   The presence of blacks on city councils is important for city politics even if there is little impact on taxing and spending policies. Blacks in city government improve the image of that government among black residents; it helps to link minorities to city hall, to provide role models, and to sensitize white officials to minority concerns. "When minorities talk to the city council now, council members nod their head rather than yawn."[24]

COUNCIL MEMBERS: RESPONSIBLE POLICY MAKERS?

The policy-making role of council members varies a great deal from city to city. Council members have more formal power in commission or weak-mayor forms of government, where the council itself sometimes appoints officials, prepares the budget, supervises departments, and performs other administrative tasks. However, in other cities—particularly strong mayor or manager cities—the council merely oversees city affairs. In these cities, the function of the council may be principally the representation of the interests of

---

[23]Grace Hall Saltzstein, "Black Mayors and Police Policies," *Journal of Politics*, 51 (August 1989), 525–44.

[24]Browning, Marshall, and Tabb, *Protest Is Not Enough*. p. 41.

local constituents—forwarding complaints, making inquiries, pushing for new sidewalks or streetlights, and so forth.

Council members do *not* usually serve as either general policy innovators or general policy leaders. The role of the council is largely passive, granting or withholding approval in the name of the community when presented with proposals from a leadership outside of itself. The outside leadership is usually the manager, city departments, planning commission, citizen groups, or private enterprise.[25]

In confronting community problems, councils frequently appoint special study commissions, or contract with private consulting firms, in order to obtain their reports and recommendations. In many cases, the council knows what should be done about the problem even before the commission or the consultants render a report. But the council wants the support of independent and prestigious groups before initiating community projects.

Some council members have little interest in a political career and serve out of a sense of public service (frequently at considerable personal expense in time and energy). "Volunteerism" is probably most prevalent in suburban, small, and middle-class communities. Volunteers see their service as a sacrifice, and they are relatively immune from direct constituency pressure. Threats to oust them as to the next election have little meaning. "I don't really give a damn whether I am reelected for not" is a common response. Moreover, the attitude of "volunteerism" results in councils that are "(a) more likely to vote against what they see as majority opinion; (b) less likely to feel under pressure from the public; (c) less likely to consider the upcoming election when choosing among policy alternatives; (d) less likely to facilitate group access to the council, and (e) less likely to perform services to constituents."[26]

The problem of political accountability in local politics is further aggravated by several factors:

1. *The frequency of appointment to elected office.* It is probable that as many as one-quarter of the nation's council members initially come into office by appointment rather than election. They are appointed, usually by the mayor, to fill unexpired terms.
2. *The effective constituency is very small.* Given the low turnout in municipal elections, and the small constituencies served by a council member, only a very few votes may elect a person to office. A council member's personal friends, immediate neighbors, business associates, fellow church members, and acquaintances at the Rotary Club may be enough for election.
3. *Limited contact with citizens.* Few citizens know how to contact city officials, and even fewer citizens actually do so.[27] Moreover, citizen-initiated contacts are closely related to socioeconomic status, with higher-status individuals far more likely to contact city officials about a problem than middle- or lower-status persons.

---

[25]Of course, council members themselves are not likely to agree that their role is a passive one. They like to think of themselves as policy innovators—people of vision and leadership—who follow their own convictions in public affairs regardless of what other want them to do.

[26]See Kenneth Prewitt, "Political Ambitions, Volunteerism, and Electoral Accountability," *American Political Science Review,* 64 (March 1970), 5–17.

[27]Elaine B. Sharp, "Citizen-Initiated Contacting of Government Officials and Socio-Economic Status," *American Political Science Review,* 76 (March 1982), 109–15.

4. *The infrequency of electoral defeat.* Incumbents running for reelection are hardly ever defeated. It is estimated that 80 percent of incumbent council members running for reelection are returned to office.[28] When they are defeated, it is frequently in groups, when several incumbents are turned out of office at once owing to a specific community controversy.

5. *The frequency of voluntary retirement from elected office.* The vast majority of council members voluntarily retire from office, over half of them after two terms. Officeholders simply conclude that the obligations of office exceed the rewards.

All these factors, together with the attitude of volunteerism, tend to distance municipal government from direct citizen control.

CITY COUNCILS AND PUBLIC POLICY

Despite this evidence of a lack of electoral accountability in local politics, some factors may compel council members to reflect the will of their constituents in policy making. First of all, volunteerism is becoming less prevalent over time, especially in large cities with competitive, partisan elections. We know that big-city council members are more likely to be attorneys and professional politicians, to aspire to higher office, and to spend more time on city affairs; we might infer from this that they would be more directly concerned with their constituents' views.

SHARED BELIEFS   Moreover, council members tend to reflect, in their own socioeconomic background, the characteristics of their constituents. This does not *ensure* that council members share the same attitudes as their constituents on all matters; indeed, the experience of being a public official itself can help to shape a council member's views and give a different perspective on public affairs than the constituents'. However, if council members have deep roots in their communities (many social contacts and group memberships; shared socioeconomic, ethnic, racial, and religious characteristics with their constituents), they may reflect these in their policy making, whether they are consciously aware of these "constituency influences" or not. The effects of shared community life may be very influential in shaping decision making in small, homogeneous communities where uniformity of outlook may amount to compulsion. In short, although "electoral accountability" may have little direct influence over council members, "belief sharing" may still assure some congruence between the views of community residents and the views of their representatives.[29]

COMMON COMMUNITY ENVIRONMENT   There are strong relationships between a community's socioeconomic environment, the perceptions and attitudes of its council members, and the public policies that are adopted. The "policy maps" of city council members (their perceptions of community conditions and goals for the future) are

---

[28]John J. Kirlin, "Electoral Conflict and Democracy in American Cities," *Journal of Politics,* 37 (February 1975), 262–69.

[29]See David R. Morgan, "Political Linkage and Public Policy: Attitudinal Congruence Between Citizens and Officials," *Western Political Quarterly* (June 1973), 209–23.

usually in accord with public-spending decisions.[30] In short, council members' attitudes seldom stray far from the constraints placed upon them by their communities' populations, needs, and resources.

CITY MANAGERS IN MUNICIPAL POLITICS

When council-manager government was first introduced as part of the municipal reform movement, managers were expressly admonished not to participate in community "politics." Early supporters of manager government believed in the separation of "politics" from "administration."[31] Politics, not only *party* politics but *policy* making as well, should be the exclusive domain of the elected city council. The manager was hired by the council to carry out its policy directives, and the manager could be removed by the council by majority vote at any time. This belief in the separation of policy making from administration was intended to produce "nonpolitical," efficient, and economical government, which middle-class supporters of the reform movement valued so highly. Popular control of government was to be guaranteed by making the manager's tenure completely dependent upon the will of the elected council.

However, after a few years of experience with manager government in America, it became increasingly apparent to the managers themselves that they could not escape responsibility for policy recommendations. It turned out to be very difficult in practice to separate policy making from administration. The first code of ethics of the International City Managers' Association (ICMA) stated flatly that "no manager should take an active part in politics." Managers agreed that they should stay out of partisan politics and election campaigns, but there was a great deal of debate about the role of managers in community policy making. In 1938, the ICMA revised its code of ethics to recognize the positive role of managers in policy leadership.[32]

MANAGERS AS POLICY LEADERS   Today, we are likely to find varying role orientations among city managers. Some see themselves as "policy managers," providing community leadership through their recommendations to their councils on a wide variety of matters. They believe they should innovate and lead on policy matters. Others see themselves as "administrative managers," restricting themselves to the supervision of the municipal bureaucracy and avoiding innovative policy recommendations, particularly in controversial areas. Ambivalent about innovation and leadership on policy matters, these managers avoid involvement in community issues.

Probably a majority of professionally trained city managers see themselves as "policy managers." Better-educated managers who have had experience in different cities and

---

[30]Heinz Eulau and Kenneth Prewitt, *The Labyrinths of Democracy* (Indianapolis: Bobbs-Merrill, 1973); Heinz Eulau and Robert Eyestone, "Policy Maps of City Councils and Policy Outcomes," *American Political Science Review,* 62 (March 1968), 143. See also Judith V. May, "Urban Legislators and Public Policy," a review essay in *Urban Affairs Quarterly,* 10 (June 1975), 487–96.

[31]Leonard D. White, *The City Manager* (Chicago: University of Chicago Press, 1927).

[32]See Harold A. Stone, Don K. Price, and Kathryn H. Stone, *City Manager Government in the United States* (Chicago: Public Administration Service, 1940).

who aspire to move to larger cities and assume greater responsibilities are unlikely to settle for a restricted, administrative role. However, managers without professional training in city administration or those with engineering degrees, who have lived most of their lives in their own communities and who expect to remain there, may be more likely to accept a fairly narrow administrative role.[33]

MANAGERS AS ADMINISTRATORS

While most managers see themselves as policy leaders, most council members see managers in their traditional role of administrators. This means that prudent managers will not wish to *appear* to be policy makers even when they are. They seek to have others present their policy proposals to the community and avoid the brasher methods of policy promotion. Like any successful politician, city managers try to avoid taking public stands on the more, controversial issues facing the community. Their dependence upon the council for their jobs prevents them from being too extreme in policy promotion. Managers can push their councils, but they can seldom fight them with any success. Open disputes between the manager and the council are usually resolved by the dismissal of the manager. Managers who assume strong policy-leadership roles have shorter tenures than those who do not.

Nevertheless, the manager is the most important policy initiator in most council-manager cities. Most managers determine the agenda for city council meetings. This permits them to determine the kinds of issues to be raised and the policy options to be considered. The council may not accept everything recommended by the manager, but the manager's recommendations will be given serious consideration. The city manager is the major source of information for most council members. The manager prepares the city budget; writes formal reports on city problems, defining the problems and proposing solutions; and advises and educates the council privately as well as publicly.

MANAGERS IN A DUAL ROLE

Thus, managers really have two important roles in community politics: administration and policy making. The administrative role involves the supervision of the municipal bureaucracy; this role requires administrative skills and technical expertise. Managers direct their personal staff, develop and control the city budget, and appoint and remove department heads. In most council-manager cities, managers try to guard these powers from direct council interference; these powers are the managers' most important formal resources.

HOW COUNCIL MEMBERS VIEW MANAGERS

What kind of managers do mayors and council members want? Doubtlessly, some mayors and council members want to retain a larger policy role for themselves and resent a manager who wants to run the show. These elected officials might try to recruit "administrative managers" by avoiding applicants with forceful personalities, high professional qualifications, and experience in other cities. However, we have already suggested that many council members are "volunteers" who prefer a passive role in policy making—approving or disapproving propos-

---

[33]See Timothy A. Almy, "Local-Cosmopolitanism and U.S. City Managers," *Urban Affairs Quarterly,* 10 (March 1975), 243–77.

als brought before them by the manager and others. A weak manager can lengthen council meetings and significantly increase the council's workload. So we should not be surprised to find many council members welcoming policy leadership from the manager (as long as the manager avoids the appearance of dominating the council). Indeed, one study indicates that a majority of council members "expect the manager to take the lead" in budget decisions, hiring and firing personnel, reorganization of city departments, wage and salary negotiations, community improvements, and cooperative proposals with other communities.[34] Only in planning and zoning do council members say they want to retain leadership. Presumably these council members would try to recruit well-educated, professionally trained, experienced, and mobile managers to their community. However, past manager-council relations in a community may affect recruitment. Some communities may undergo cycles in council-manager relations: A council resentful of a strong manager replaces him or her with a weak one, only to find that their workload increases, decisions are postponed, complaints of inaction accumulate; and the council decides to find a new, stronger manager.

PROFESSIONALISM   Today, most city managers are professionals who have been trained in university graduate programs in public administration. They are familiar with budgeting and fiscal administration, public personnel management, municipal law, and planning. They tend to move from city to city as they advance in their professional careers. They may begin their careers as a staff assistant to a city official and then move to assistant city manager, then manager of a small town, and later perhaps of a larger city. About three-quarters of all city manager appointments are made from outside the city, and only about one-quarter are local residents, which indicates the professionalism of city management. The average tenure of managers who resigned or were removed from office has been about five years. One in ten managers reports having been fired at least once. Most of these found another job within six months but reported using up their savings or severance pay to survive between jobs. The three principal reasons given for having been fired were "poor working relationship with council," "politics," and "change in the council." All of these reasons might be termed *political*.

MAYORS IN CITY POLITICS

Today, more than ever before, the nation's cities need forceful, imaginative political leadership. The nation's major domestic problems—race relations, poverty, violence, congestion, poor schools, fiscal crisis—are concentrated in cities. Mayors are in the "hot seat" of American politics; they must deal directly with these pressing issues. No other elected official in the American federal system must deal face-to-face, eyeball-to-eyeball with these problems.

LIMITED POWERS   The challenges facing big-city mayors are enormous; however, their powers to deal with these challenges are restricted on every side. Executive power in major cities is often fragmented among a variety of elected officials—city treasurer,

---

[34]Alan L. Saltzstein, "City Managers and City Councils: Perceptions of the Division of Authority," *Western Political Quarterly*, 27 (June 1974), 275–87.

city clerk, city comptroller, district attorney, and so on. The mayor may also be required to share power over municipal affairs with county officials. Many city agencies and functions are outside the mayor's formal authority: Independent boards and commissions often govern important city departments—for example, the board of education, board of health, zoning appeals board, planning commission, civil service board, library board, park commission, sewage and water board, and so on. Even if the mayor is permitted to appoint the members of the boards and commissions, they are often appointed for a fixed term, and the mayor cannot remove them. The mayor's power over the affairs of the city may also be affected by the many special district governments and public authorities operating within the city, including public housing, urban renewal, sewage and water, mass transit, and port authority. Traditionally, school districts have been outside the authority of the mayor or city government. Mayors' powers over city finances may even be restricted—they may share budget-making powers with a board of estimate, and powers over expenditures with an elected comptroller or treasurer. Civil service regulations and independent civil service boards can greatly hamper mayors' control over their own bureaucrats. The activities of federal and state agencies in a city are largely beyond the mayor's control.

SELECTING MAYORS   The method of selecting mayors also influences their powers over city affairs. Some mayors are not directly elected by the people of their cities. (See Table 11–3.) These mayors are selected by their city councils or commissions and generally have little more power than other council members or commissioners. Their job is generally ceremonial: They crown beauty queens, dedicate parks, lay cornerstones, and lead parades. Larger cities and mayor-council cities generally elect their mayors. Mayors may be elected for anything from one to five years, but two-year and four-year terms are most common in American cities.

Table 11-3

THE MAYORS: METHOD OF SELECTION AND TERM OF OFFICE

	Method of Selection[a]		Term[b]		
	DIRECTLY ELECTED	SELECTED BY COUNCIL	ONE YEAR	TWO YEAR	FOUR YEAR
Total	77.7	20.9	11.1	41.4	44.7
BY FORM OF GOVERNMENT					
Mayor-Council	98.0	1.9	2.1	33.9	62.5
Council-Manager	61.8	35.5	21.7	51.3	23.2
Commission	69.2	29.1	9.6	20.2	60.5

[a]Percentages do not equal 100 because 1.4% of cities reported selected their mayor by some other method, including rotation of council members and council members receiving most votes in election.

[b]Percentages do not equal 100 because 2.6% of mayors elected for three years and 0.2% for five or more years.

Source: International City Managers' Association, Municipal Yearbook 1988.

LEGISLATIVE POWERS   Mayors' legislative powers also vary widely. Of course, in all cities they have the right to submit messages to the council and to recommend policy. These recommendations will carry whatever prestige the mayor possesses in the community. Moreover, in council-manager and commission cities, mayors usually are themselves members of the council. In these cities where mayors are chosen by the council, they generally have voting power equal to that of other council members. In about one-third of mayor-council cities, the mayor also serves on the council; in about half of the mayor-council cities the mayor presides over meetings of the council and can cast a tie-breaking vote. In most cities where the mayor is *not* a member of the council, the mayor enjoys veto power over council-passed ordinances. The veto power distinguishes between "strong-mayor" and "weak-mayor" cities.

ADMINISTRATIVE POWERS   Another distinction between "strong" and "weak" mayors is made on the basis of their powers of administration. Weak mayors have very limited appointing powers and even more limited removal powers. They have little control over separately elected boards and commissions or separately elected offices, such as clerk, treasurer, tax assessor, comptroller, and attorney. The council, rather than the mayor, often appoints the key administrative officers. No single individual has the complete responsibility for law enforcement or coordinating city administration.

POLITICAL POWERS   In summary, a mayor's ability to provide strong leadership in his or her city is limited by fragmented authority, multiple elected officials, limited jurisdiction over important urban services, civil service, state or federal interference, and constraints placed upon that power by "reform" and "good-government" arrangements. Nevertheless, even though it is recognized that mayors have few formal powers to deal with the enormous tasks facing them, it is frequently argued that mayors can and should exercise strong leadership as "political brokers"—mediating disputes, serving as a channel of communications, bringing conflicting groups together for reasonable discussions of their differences, and suggesting solutions that diverse groups can accept in coping with the city's problems. In other words, the "ideal" mayor overcomes limited formal powers by skill in persuasion, negotiation, and public relations. Each "success" in resolving a particular problem "pyramids" the mayor's prestige and influence, and he or she eventually accumulates considerable informal power. The mayor can then direct energy and power toward accomplishing one or more of the numerous goals set for mayors: reducing racial tensions, providing effective law enforcement, speeding redevelopment and renewal of downtown areas and the relocation of persons living there, improving public schools, constructing low-cost housing, cleaning up the urban environment, finding ways to move people and things about the city speedily and efficiently, and, most of all, finding ways to finance these goals.

But this "ideal" city leadership requires that the mayor possess certain minimum resources.[35]

---

[35]Jeffrey L. Pressman, "Preconditions of Mayoral Leadership," *American Political Science Review,* 66 (June 1972), 511–24.

- Sufficient financial and staff resources in the mayor's office and in city government generally
- City jurisdiction over social-program areas—education, housing, urban renewal, etc.
- Mayor's jurisdiction within city government over these areas
- A salary that enables the mayor to spend full time on the job
- Friendly newspapers or television stations supportive of the mayor and his or her goals
- Political groups, including a political party, that the mayor can mobilize to attend meetings, parades, distribute literature, etc., on his or her behalf

Most mayors do not have the formal authority sufficient to deal with the many challenges facing city government. Successful mayors must rely chiefly upon their own personal qualities of leadership: their powers to persuade, to sell, to compromise, to bargain, and to "get things done." Mayors are not usually expected to initiate proposals for new programs or to create public issues. Nor is their primary concern the administration of existing programs, although they must always seek to avoid scandal and gross mismanagement, which would give their administrations a bad public "image." They must rely upon other public agencies, planners, citizens' groups, and private enterprise to propose new programs, and they can usually rely upon their department heads and other key subordinates to supervise the day-to-day administration of city government. Mayors are primarily promoters of public policy: Their role is to promote, publicize, organize, and finance the projects that others suggest.

TOP BANANAS IN THE BIG APPLE

New York City, "The Big Apple," is the largest municipal government in the nation. Its annual expenditures exceed those of forty-eight of the states (only the states of New York and California have larger budgets) as well as every other city in the nation. The mayoralty of New York may be the toughest executive job in the nation after the presidency itself.

WORMS IN THE BIG APPLE   From the early days of the Tammany Hall machine, through the flamboyant mayoralties of Jimmy Walker and Fiorello LaGuardia, to the liberal visions of Mayors Robert Wagner and John Lindsay, the city's political organizations catered to the needs (and won the votes) of the city's large needy population. No other city provided such a range of free services and recreation: libraries, parks, and playgrounds; scores of city hospitals; museums and zoos; antipoverty programs and day-care centers; drug-treatment programs; and a costly but tuition-free City University of New York, open to any high school graduate. No other city was as generous in salary and retirement benefits to such a large number of city employees. As a result of these many expensive services and benefits, the per capita cost of running New York City was, and still is, higher than any other city in the nation, except Washington, DC.

For years, under Mayors Robert Wagner and John Lindsay, the city's comptroller, Abraham Beame, managed to postpone fiscal disaster by budgeting gimmickry. Like many cities, New York is required by the state constitution to maintain a balanced budget—obviously an unenforceable requirement. Comptroller Beame simply shifted current expenses, salaries, and supplies to the capital construction budget, which covers long-term building projects for which the city can borrow money. Other strategies included deliberately overestimating revenues, establishing semi-independent city "authorities" that could borrow money, asking the state and federal governments for "advances" on grants-in-aid, and draining various trust funds. In 1973, Abraham Beame was elected mayor.

NEAR BANKRUPTCY   The real financial crunch came in the fall of 1975. New York City banks insisted that the city balance its budget and undertake a long-range program to reduce its debts. The banks would no longer lend the city money unless the city displayed greater fiscal responsibility. The city was unable to borrow money; outstanding debts were falling due, and there was not enough cash to pay city employees, welfare recipients, or bondholders. For several hours New York City teetered on the verge of default and bankruptcy until the city's teachers union agreed to lend the city enough money from its pension fund to struggle through for a few more weeks. New York Governor Hugh Carey succeeded in getting the New York State legislature to create a Municipal Assistance Corporation ("Big Mac") to convert short-term city debt into long-term debt and to sell to the public bonds that could be backed by specific city revenues. Initially, New York's request for federal aid was met with strong presidential opposition. Republican President Gerald Ford quickly perceived a campaign issue for 1976—liberal Democratic fiscal irresponsibility leads to bankruptcy. The New York *Daily News* headlined the president's stand: "FORD TO CITY: DROP DEAD."

Eventually, all of the participants in New York's fiscal crisis were forced to come to an agreement. The federal government agreed to provide the city with over $2 billion in annual revolving credit; sales taxes in the city were increased to 8 percent (the highest in the nation); the banks, which were holding city bonds, were forced to accept delays in principal and interest payments; the city was obliged to make additional budget cuts, eliminating city jobs, holding down wages, and imposing tuition at the City University; the unions were obliged to accept additional work force cuts and to invest some of their pension funds in New York City bonds. But few observers really believed that New York could manage its problems.

ENTER ED KOCH   Then in 1977 New York voters chose Ed Koch as mayor over the incumbent Abraham Beame. Ed Koch had worked his way through the City College of New York selling shoes. He fought in Germany in World War II and returned to New York University law school. He lived in the Greenwich Village section of the city and became active in liberal, reform Democratic politics. Koch served five terms in Congress before entering the mayor's race.

Ed Koch's approach to city government was simple enough: "Don't spend what you don't have." Despite his record as a big-spending, liberal congressman, Koch cut city spending growth. To critics who charged that his spending cuts hurt the poor, he replied: "If you have a healthy city financially, who benefits? The *poor*. Because if you have an unhealthy city, who leaves? The middle-class. The poor *can't* leave."[36]

The mayor was concerned about crime in the city. He added to the police force and created new trial courts to reduce delays in judicial proceedings. He tried unsuccessfully to

---

[36]*Time,* June 15, 1981, p. 26.

get pretrial jailing without bail of the most dangerous criminals. He tells the story of the judge who got mugged but announced that this would not affect his courtroom decisions. According to Koch, an old lady shouted, "Then mug him *again.*"

THE GOOD YEARS

Before Ed Koch moved into Gracie Mansion, New York City had been described by scholars and journalists as "ungovernable." But whatever else his critics said about him, few would claim that Ed Koch did not govern New York City during his twelve years in office. He presented the city's first balanced budget in many years. The Municipal Assistance Corporation gradually improved its standing in the financial community; later the city itself was able to sell its bonds again on the open market. The city became less dependent on federal aid throughout the 1980s.

"How'm I doin?" was Mayor Koch's trademark question. He used it on call-in talk shows, a public appearances, and in direct confrontation on the streets of New York with his constituents. Usually the reply was "Great!" and Koch's reelection votes confirmed that he was one of the nation's most popular mayors. In 1985 Koch was reelected by an unprecedented 78 percent of the vote.

Like many of America's big cities, racial tension pervades virtually every urban problem in New York. Ed Koch boasted of a long record on behalf of civil rights and social justice. Yet blacks and Jewish leaders in New York, including Ed Koch, had frequently battled over affirmative action quota systems and racial set-asides. Koch did not hesitate to publicly attack blacks with whom he disagreed. He pleaded for calm and understanding during racially threatening periods, notably the highly publicized shooting of four black youths on a subway by Bernard Goetz, and the highway death of a black man trying to run from attacking white teenagers in the Howard Beach section of Queens. Yet his opposition to the presidential candidacy of Jesse Jackson in 1988 marked his final break with the city's black voters.

DAVID DINKINS: A CALMING VOICE?

Perhaps after twelve years of aggressive, combative leadership, it was understandable that New York voters should seek a calm, reassuring, conciliatory voice. David Dinkins offered a marked contrast to the contentious Ed Koch.

Dinkins's father was a barber and later a realtor in Trenton, New Jersey, where young David went to public schools. Following a brief stint in the Marine Corps, he enrolled in Howard University in Washington, DC, and graduated cum laude in 1950 in mathematics. He returned to New York to attend Brooklyn Law School and quickly became involved in Harlem politics under the tutelage of his father-in-law, a New York state assemblyman, J. Raymond Jones, known as the "Harlem Fox." Dinkins practiced law and slowly worked his way up the patronage ladder. He replaced his father-in-law as Harlem party leader in 1967, a position he held for the next twenty years. He suffered a minor setback when an investigation revealed he had paid no city income taxes for four years. In a courageous talk in 1985 Dinkins challenged Louis Farrakhan, the controversial leader of the Nation of Islam, for his attacks on Jews. After Farrakhan described Dinkins as a "traitor" to his race, Dinkins was assigned police protection.

Dinkins's calm demeanor appealed to New Yorkers after twelve years of boisterous irreverence from Ed Koch. More importantly, Dinkins avoided the confrontational racial style of Jesse Jackson. Dinkins reassured whites and Hispanics that he would represent *all* of the city, not just its black residents.

Dinkins's reassuring style fit well with New York City's demographics— roughly 25 percent black, 10 percent Hispanic, and 55 percent white. In the hard-fought 1989 Democratic primary, Dinkins won virtually all of the black vote, a majority of the Hispanic vote, and one-third of the white vote in defeating Ed Koch's unprecedented bid for a fourth term as mayor. Koch took his loss in good grace, immediately endorsing Dinkins in the general election.

In the general election Dinkins confronted the first formidable candidate put forward by the Republican party in New York City in several decades—Rudolph W. Giuliani. Giuliani, a former federal prosecutor, had won fame by winning cases against drug lords and Wall Street financiers. During the campaign Giuliani launched hard-hitting personal attacks on Dinkins, especially citing his failure to pay city income taxes. While neither candidate raised racial issues, voters tended to divide along racial lines—with Dinkins winning virtually all of the black vote, most of the Hispanic vote, and enough white liberal votes to win comfortably.

While Dinkins demonstrated his ability to bring together a broad coalition of blacks, Hispanics, white liberals, and union supporters to win office, actually governing the nation's largest city proved more difficult. Faced with looming budget deficits, Dinkins raised city taxes and cut services. Yet, at the same time, he acquiesced to the teachers' union's demands for large salary increases. He was equally ambivalent in handling the city's racial tensions, sometimes taking the lead in denouncing racism, while at other times seeming to ignore racial and ethnic conflicts. Dinkins mishandled serious racial conflict in the mostly Jewish section of Crown Heights in Brooklyn, losing the confidence and support of many Jewish voters citywide.

RUDOLPH GIULIANI: GETTING TOUGH   In 1993, Rudolph Giuliani successfully exploited Dinkins's perceived weakness on crime control, to defeat the incumbent mayor and become New York's first Republican mayor in a generation. Giuliani had been educated in Catholic schools in New York and had graduated from New York University Law School in 1968. He had built a career as a hardnosed federal prosecuting attorney. He successfully prosecuted top mafia crime family heads, exposed massive fraud and bribery in New York's parking-violations bureau, and won indictments against prominent Wall Street investors for insider trading. Although frequently accused of grandstanding, his tough-guy approach won him widespread support in a city obsessed with crime.

In both mayor's races against David Dinkins, 1989 and 1993, Giuliani campaigned largely on his anticrime reputation. But in a city racked by racial conflict, crime is often a code word for race. As racial tensions mounted during Dinkins's term, especially following violence in the largely Jewish Crown Heights section of Brooklyn, many white liberal voters decided to desert the Democratic party and support Giuliani. As in 1989, the vote in 1993 divided largely along racial lines, but this time Giuliani won an estimated 75 percent of the white vote, enough to overcome Dinkins's near-unanimous support by black voters.

Although Giuliani finally made it to Gracie Mansion, he must still work with a Democratic-controlled city council, as well as large black and Hispanic minority populations deeply suspicious of him. The city's huge deficits and bloated bureaucracy remain a challenge to Gouliani's efforts to "reinvent" government. (New York has over 200,000 full-time city employees, the largest municipal workforce in this nation; its eleven city-owned hospitals have three times the number of workers per patient as private hospitals; over one million of the city's seven million inhabitants are on welfare rolls.) But the mayor's initial success in crime fighting—New York has led all other big cities in crime rate reductions in recent years—has won him some much-needed political support in dealing with the city's financial and bureaucratic problems. Yet the city remains "a heartbeat away" from the bankruptcy crisis it faced twenty years earlier.

INTEREST GROUPS IN CITY POLITICS

Interest group activity may be more influential in community politics than in state or national political affairs. Since the arena of local politics is smaller, the activities of organized interest groups may be more obvious at the local level.

THE CIVIC ASSOCIATIONS   At the local level, interest groups frequently assume the form of *civic associations*. Few communities are too small to have at least one or two associations devoted to civic well-being, and larger cities may have hundreds of these organizations. Council members usually name civic associations (service clubs, citizens' commissions, improvement associations) as the most influential groups or organizations that are active and appear before the council.[37] This does not necessarily mean that economic interests or taxpayer associations are less active than civic associations, but probably that civic associations are the predominant style of organized interest group activity at the local level. Business people, reform groups, taxpayer associations, merchants, service clubs, developers, and so on organize themselves into civic associations for action at the local level. Civic associations generally make their appeals in terms of "the welfare of the community," "the public interest," "civic responsibility," "making Janesville a better place to live." In other words, civic associations claim to be community-serving rather than self-serving. Members belong to these groups as a hobby, because of the sense of prestige and civic participation they derive from membership. Occasionally, of course, participation in civic associations can be a steppingstone to local office.

TAXPAYER GROUPS   Organized *taxpayer groups* generally stand for lower taxes and fewer governmental activities and services. Their most enthusiastic support comes from the community's larger taxpayers, generally business people with large investments in commercial or industrial property in the community.

ENVIRONMENTAL AND "GROWTH-MANAGEMENT" GROUPS
Environmental groups and opponents of residential and commercial development have become major forces in community politics throughout the nation. These groups are gen-

---

[37]Betty Zisk, Heinz Eulau, and Kenneth Prewitt, "City Councilmen and the Group Struggle," *Journal of Politics,* 27 (August 1965), 632. See also Betty Zisk, *Local Interest Politics: A One-Way Street* (Indianapolis: Bobbs-Merrill, 1973).

erally opposed to community growth, although they employ the term "growth management" to imply that they do not necessarily oppose all growth. But they are generally opposed to highway construction, street widening, tree cutting, increased traffic, noise and pollution, commercial or industrial development, or anything else that offends their aesthetic preferences. These groups generally reflect liberal reformist view of upper-middle-class residents who are secure in their own jobs and own their own homes. Indeed, restrictions on new housing construction directly benefit them by increasing the value of existing property. Municipal government offers many tools to restrict growth—planning regulations, zoning laws, building permits, environmental regulations, developmental charges and restrictions, street and utility access, and so on. (For further discussion, see Chapter 16.) Often environmental, "growth-management" groups combine with neighborhood associations to oppose specific developmental projects.

NEIGHBORHOOD GROUPS   *Neighborhood associations* frequently spring up when residents perceive a threat to their property values. They may be formed to oppose a rezoning that would allow new business and unwanted traffic in their neighborhood, or to oppose a new mobile home park, or to petition for stoplights or sidewalks or pothole repairs. Sometimes neighborhood associations will fight to keep out "undesirables," whose presence they feel will reduce property values. Neighborhood groups may protest the location of low-income housing, halfway houses for parolees, or mental health facilities. Neighborhood associations may also lead the fight *against* development, where residents will be displaced or their lifestyle threatened. They may oppose road building, urban renewal, or industrial and commercial development in or near their neighborhood. The NIMBY (not in my backyard) forces may be closely identified with "growth-management" efforts to slow or halt development. This posture places them in opposition to the local growth-oriented "power structure." (See Chapter 13.)

BUSINESS GROUPS   Traditionally *business interests* were the most influential of all groups in community politics. Many business people or "economic notables" occupied an important role in the structure of community decision making or "the power structure." (See Chapter 13.) Business interests are also represented in local politics by organized groups: The chamber of commerce and the junior chamber of commerce, or "Jaycees," are found in nearly every community, representing the general views of business. The program of the chamber of commerce is likely to be more general than the interests of particular sectors of the business community—banks, utilities, contractors, real estate developers, downtown merchants, or bar and club owners. The chamber or the Jaycees can be expected to support lower taxes and more economy and efficiency in government operations. They are also active "promoters" of community growth and business activity. They can be expected to back civic improvements so long as it does not raise the tax rate too much. "Service to the community" creates a "favorable image," which the chamber and business people are anxious to cultivate.

Generally, the active members of the chamber of commerce or the Jaycees are younger business owners in the community who are still on their way "up" in business. Owners of larger businesses, banks, utilities—the "big powers" in the community—are more likely to function informally in the community's power structure than to take an overt role in organized interest group activity.

The so-called service clubs—the Lions, Kiwanis, Rotarians, and others—are basically for business people. Their interests are likely to be more social than political, but their service projects often involve them in political activity and their meetings provide an excellent opportunity for speechmaking by political candidates.

The businesses most active in community affairs are those most directly affected by policies of local government, such as department stores, banks, utilities, contractors, real estate developers, bar and club owners, and television and newspaper interests.

BANKS   Banks often own, or hold the mortgages on, downtown business property. They have an interest in maintaining business, commercial, and industrial property values. Banks are also interested in the growth and prosperity of the city as a whole, particularly large business enterprises who are their primary customers. Banks are influential because they decide who is able to borrow money in a community and under what conditions. Banks are directly involved in local governments in financing municipal bond issues for public works, school buildings, and so on, and in pledging financial backing for urban renewal projects. Banks are also influential in land development, for they must provide the financial backing for real estate developers, contractors, businesses, and home buyers; hence they are interested in business regulation, taxation, zoning, and housing.

CONTRACTORS   Contractors are vitally interested in city government because the city has the power of inspection over all kinds of construction. Local governments enforce building, plumbing, electric, and other codes, which are of great interest to contractors. Some contractors, particularly road-grading and surfacing companies, depend on public contracts, and they are concerned with both city policy and the personnel who administer this policy. While municipal contracts are generally required by law to be given to the "low bidder" among "responsible" contractors, definitions about what is or is not a "low bid," and who is or who is not a "responsible" contractor, make it important for contractors to maintain close and friendly relationships with municipal officials. It is no accident that builders, contractors, and developers are a major source of campaign contributions for local office seekers.

REAL ESTATE DEVELOPERS   Real Estate developers are particularly interested in planning, zoning, and subdivision control regulations and urban renewal programs. (These are discussed at length in Chapter 16.) Developers of residential, commercial, and industrial property must work closely with city government officials to coordinate the provision of public services—especially streets, sewage, water, and electricity. They must also satisfy city officials regarding planning and zoning regulations, building codes, fire and safety laws, and environmental regulations. Today, real estate developers must be highly skilled in governmental relations.

NEWSPAPERS   Newspapers are an important force in community politics. The influence of the press would be relatively minor if its opinions were limited to its editorial pages. The influence of the press arises from its power to decide what is "news," thereby focusing public attention on the events and issues that are of interest to the press. Newspaper writers must first decide what proportion of space in the paper will be devoted to local news in contrast to state, national, and international news. A big-city paper may give local news about the same amount of space that it gives to national or foreign news. Suburban or small-town papers, which operate within the circulation area of a large metropolitan daily, may give a greater proportion of the news space to local events than to national and international affairs. Crime and corruption in government are favorite targets for the press. Editors believe that civic crusades and the exposure of crime and corruption help sell newspapers. Moreover, many editors and writers believe they have a civic responsibility to use the power of the press to protect the public. In the absence of crime or corruption, newspapers may turn to crusades on behalf of civic improvements—like a city auditorium or cultural center.

The politics of newspapers can be understood in part by some insight into the economics of the newspaper business. Newspapers get two-thirds of their revenue from advertising. Over the years the newspapers' percentage of all advertising dollars has declined in the face of stiff competition from television. Many big-city newspapers have either merged or gone out of business because of a lack of sufficient advertising revenue to offset increasing costs; it was not a lack of readers that brought about their collapse. Moreover, it is important to know that downtown department stores provide the largest source of advertising revenue. Big-city newspapers have been hurt by the flight of the middle class to the suburbs and the declining role of downtown department stores in retail sales in the metropolitan area. In metropolitan affairs, one can expect big-city newspapers to support the position of downtown interests. This means support for urban renewal, mass transit, downtown parking, and other pro–central-city policies in metropolitan affairs. On the other hand, suburban daily and weekly newspapers are supported by the advertising from suburban shopping centers, and they can be expected to take a pro-suburban position on metropolitan issues.

Newspapers are more influential in the absence of strong party organizations, which would compete with newspapers as channels of communication to the voters. Nonpartisanship, lengthy ballots, and numerous referenda all contribute to the influence of newspapers. Any situation that tends to obscure candidates or issues to the voter contributes to the power of newspapers, since the voter is obliged to rely upon them for information. Newspapers doubtlessly have more influence in local than in state or national politics because of (1) the relative importance in local politics of middle-class groups who read newspapers, (2) the relative obscurity of local politics to voters in their reliance upon newspapers for information about local affairs, and (3) the relative weakening of party affiliations in local politics.

CHURCHES   Any listing of influential interest groups in local politics should include the community's churches and church-related organizations. Ministers, priests, rabbis, and leaders of religious lay groups are frequently participants in community decision making. The Catholic Church and its many lay organizations are vitally concerned with the operation of parochial schools. Protestant ministerial associations in large cities may be concerned with public health, welfare, housing, and other social problems. Ministers and church congregations in small towns may be concerned with the enforcement of blue laws, limitations on liquor sales, prohibitions on gambling, and other public policies relative to "vice" and public morality.

THE POWER OF MUNICIPAL UNIONS

No one has a greater personal stake in municipal government than municipal employees—police, firefighters, street crews, transit employees, welfare workers, sanitation workers, clerks, secretaries. There are over 15 million state and local government employees in the nation (4.5 million state employees, and 10.7 million employees of cities, counties, school districts, and special districts). Their rate of voter turnout in municipal elections is very high, and they are politically influential in small towns and suburbs whether they are organized into unions or not.

MUNICIPAL EMPLOYEE UNIONS   Over one-third of the nation's state and local government employees are unionized. Municipal employee unions are more influential in large cities, where fragmentation of authority and public acceptance of union activity encourage unions to assert their employees' interests. In New York City, for example, associations of teachers, police, firefighters, transit workers, social workers, sanitation workers, and so on, have a great deal of political clout. Employee work stoppages and other forms of protest occur frequently, even though state law prohibits strikes of municipal employees. The American Federation of State, County, and Municipal Employees, the International Association of Fire Fighters, and the American Federation of Teachers, all AFL-CIO unions, are directly concerned with organization and collective bargaining in public employment. In addition, certain other unions, such as the Transport Workers Union, are organized to bargain on behalf of both public and private employees. In the absence of union representation, public employees may form "professional associations," such as the Fraternal order of Police and, of course, the National Education Association.

LABOR RELATIONS   Most state laws today recognize the right of municipal employees to organize unions and bargain collectively with municipal officials over wages, hours, and conditions of work. However, in contrast to *private* employees, *public* employees are generally prohibited by law from striking. Instead, most state laws stipulate that public employee labor disputes are to go to arbitration—that is, be submitted to neutral third parties for decision. Decisions of arbitrators (or arbitration boards consisting of equal representation from employees and employers, together and with neutral members) may or may not be binding on both the city and union, depending on specific provisions of each state's laws. However, many public employee unions throughout the country have rendered "no-strike" laws practically useless in a heated labor dispute. Police, firefighters, teachers, sanitation workers, and others have struck in many large cities and there have been statewide strikes as well. Unions can nullify no-strike laws by simply adding another demand—no legal prosecution of strikers or union leaders—as a condition of going back to work.

STRIKES   Strikers that threaten the health and safety of a community are qualitatively different from strikes that shut down private business enterprise and threaten only economic dislocation. Strikes of police, firefighters, hospital workers, or sanitation workers, for example, must be ended quickly for the safety of the community; this brings great pressure to bear on public officials to satisfy the demands of strikers, even at the risk of creating serious financial problems for the city.

WAGES AND BENEFITS   State and local employees, who for generations were paid wages below those for comparable jobs in private enterprise, now at least match private employees in salaries, benefits, pensions, and so on. Theoretically, public employee unions should be very effective in raising wages. It might be reasoned that: (1) Elected government officials are less constrained than private employers by profit and loss considerations, and more likely to grant union demands; and (2) unlike employees in the private sector, public employees participate in electing their own bosses, placing additional pressure on them to succumb to union demands. Empirical research does suggest that unionized municipal workers earn more than nonunionized municipal workers.[38] But unions may have even greater impact on raising fringe benefits (retirement, health benefits, vacations, etc.) and ensuring job security of government employees.

POLITICAL CLOUT   Unions in the *private* sector of the American economy have been in steep decline in recent decades; today less than 13 percent of the private work force is unionized. But unions in the *public* sector have grown dramatically; in 1990, 37 percent of all employees in federal, state, and local governments were union members. The American Federation of State, County and Municipal Employees (AFSCME) is the nation's second largest union, after the Teamsters, and it adds members each year. Most of its membership is concentrated in ten states—New York, Ohio, Pennsylvania, Michigan, Illinois, Wisconsin, Massachusetts, Minnesota, Connecticut, and Hawaii.

Government employee unions can usually be counted on to lend strong support for tax increases at all levels of government: "The AFSCME protects the personnel levels, the bureaucrats and the budgets of government agencies. The union makes a good ally when you're lobbying for a tax increase or to retain public services."[39]

Government employee unions are vigorous opponents of privatization (see Chapter 10). The AFSCME objects strongly to the idea that private contractors can provide services more efficiently than municipal bureaucracies. Moreover, the union claims that privatization "diminishes government accountability to citizens."

---

[38]For a summary of research on this topic, see Gregory B. Lewis and Lana Stein, "Unions and Municipal Decline," *American Politics Quarterly,* 17 (April 1989), 208–22.

[39]Quoted in John F. Persimos, "Can AFSCME Parley Its Savvy into Another Decade of Growth?" *Governing* (July 1989), 48.

METROPOLITICS: CONFLICT IN THE METROPOLIS

THE METROPOLIS: SETTING FOR CONFLICT

Three out of every four Americans live in population clusters called *metropolitan areas*. What is a metropolitan area? The U.S. Census Bureau calls a metropolitan area a "Metropolitan Statistical Area" (MSA) and defines it as a city of 50,000 or more people together with adjacent counties that have predominantly urban populations with close ties to the central city. (See Figure 12–1.)

Some metropolitan areas adjoin each other, creating a continuous urban environment over an extended area. One such "megalopolis" is the New York–Northern New Jersey–Long Island area, encompassing parts of three states, nine MSAs, and nearly 20 million people. The U.S. Census Bureau calls such an area a "Consolidated Metropolitan Statistical Area" (CMSA) and defines it as two or more adjoining MSAs with at least 1 million people in which a large number of workers commute between the MSAs. Nearly half of the nation's population lives in the thirty-seven metropolitan areas with 1 million or more people. (See Table 12–1.)

The states have become "metropolitanized." Today thirty-five states have more than half of their populations concentrated in metropolitan areas. (See Figure 12–2.)

Table 12–1

METRO-AMERICA: METROPOLITAN AREAS WITH ONE MILLION OR MORE
RESIDENTS

New York	19.6	St. Louis	2.5	Indianapolis	1.4
Los Angeles	14.5	Minneapolis	2.5	New Orleans	1.3
Chicago	8.2	San Diego	2.5	San Antonio	1.3
Washington/Baltimore	6.7	Pittsburgh	2.4	Orlando	1.2
San Francisco	6.3	Phoenix	2.3	Buffalo (NY)	1.2
Philadelphia	5.9	Tampa	2.1	Providence (RI)	1.2
Boston	5.5	Denver	2.0	Charlotte (NC)	1.2
Detroit	5.2	Cincinnati	1.8	Hartford (CT)	1.2
Dallas/Ft. Worth	4.0	Milwaukee	1.8	Salt Lake City	1.1
Houston	3.7	Portland (OR)	1.8	Rochester	1.1
Miami/Ft. Lauderdale	3.2	Kansas City	1.6	Greensboro	1.0
Seattle/Tacoma	2.9	Sacramento	1.5	Nashville	1.0
Atlanta	2.9	Norfolk (VA)	1.4		
Cleveland	2.8	Columbus (OH)	1.4		

Source: U.S. Bureau of the Census, 1995.

The very definition of metropolitan life involves *large numbers* of *different* types of people living *close together* who are socially and economically *dependent* upon one another.[1] *Numbers, density, heterogeneity,* and *interdependence* are said to be distinguishing characteristics of metropolitan life. It is not difficult to envision a metropolitan area as a large number of people living together; we can see these characteristics in metropolitan life from a map or an airplane window. However, it is more difficult to understand the heterogeneity and interdependence of people living in metropolitan areas.

HETEROGENEITY   The modern economic system of the metropolis is based upon a highly specialized and complex division of labor. Highly specialized jobs account for much of the heterogeneity in urban populations. Different jobs produce different levels of income, dress, and styles of living. People's jobs shape the way they look at the world and their evaluations of social and political events. In acquiring their jobs, people attain a certain level and type of education that also distinguish them from those in other jobs with different educational requirements. Differences in educational level in turn produce a wide variety of differences and opinions, attitudes, and styles of living. Metropolitan living concentrates people with all these different economic and occupational characteristics in a very few square miles.

ETHNIC AND RACIAL DIVERSITY   Ethnic and racial diversity are also present. In the nineteenth and early twentieth centuries opportunities for human betterment in the cities attracted immigrants from Ireland, Germany, Italy, Poland, and Russia.

---

[1]See John Bollens and Henry Schmandt, *The Metropolis* (New York: Harper & Row, 1985).

Figure 12–1
STANDARD METROPOLITAN STATISTICAL AREAS

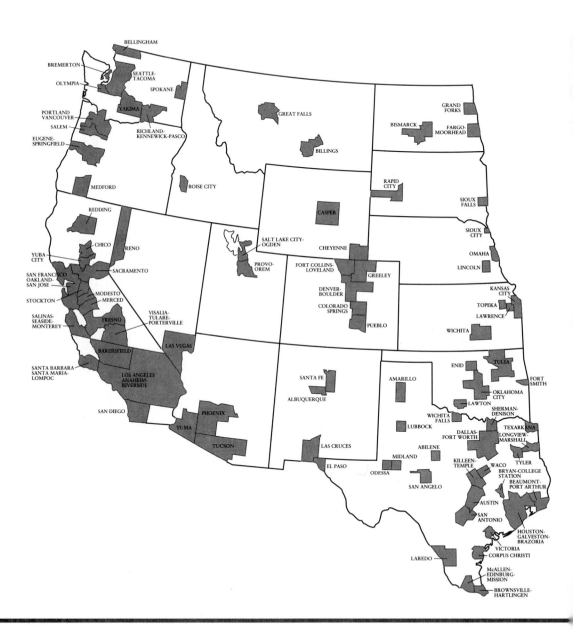

Source: U.S. Bureau of the Census.

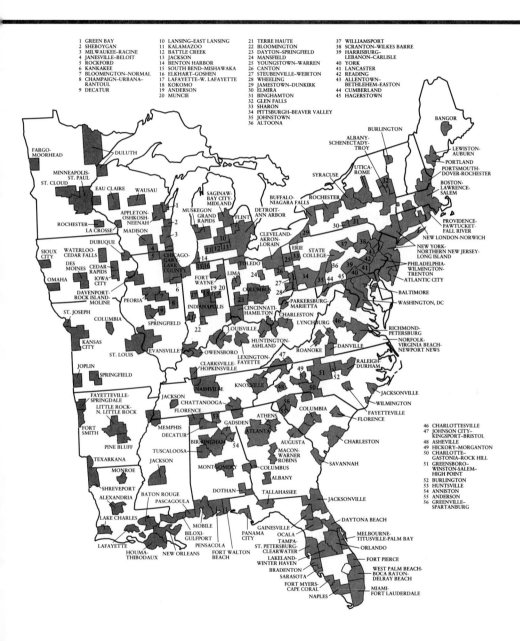

African Americans in search of opportunities migrated to cities from the rural South. Today America's cities attract waves of immigrants from Mexico and other Latin American countries, Asia and the Philippines, and Haiti and other less developed nations of the world. Newcomers to the metropolis bring with them different needs, attitudes, and ways of life. The "melting pot" tends to reduce some of this diversity over time, but the pot does not "melt" people immediately, and there always seem to be new arrivals.

INTERDEPENDENCE   Yet despite social and economic differences, urban dwellers are highly dependent upon one another in their daily activities. Suburbanites, for example, rely upon the central city for food, clothing, newspapers, entertainment, hospitalization, and a host of other modern needs. More importantly, they rely upon the central city for employment opportunities. Conversely, the central city relies upon the suburbs to supply its labor and management forces. Downtown merchants look to the entire metropolitan area for consumers. This interdependence involves an intricate web of economic and social relationships, a high degree of communication, and a great deal of daily physical interchange among residents, groups, and firms in a metropolitan area. Just as specialization produces diversity among people, it also produces interdependence and the need for coordinated human activity.

FRAGMENTED GOVERNMENT   Another characteristic of metropolitan areas is "fragmented" government. Suburban development, spreading out from central cities, generally ignored governmental boundaries and engulfed counties, townships, towns, and smaller cities. Some metropolitan areas even spread across state lines, and four metropolitan areas of the United States—Detroit, San Diego, El Paso, and Laredo—adjoin urban territory in Canada and Mexico. This suburbanization has meant that hundreds of governments may be operating in a single metropolitan area. Thus, while metropolitan areas are characterized by social and economic interdependence, and consequently require coordinating mechanisms, metropolitan government is generally "fragmented" into many smaller jurisdictions, none of which is capable of governing the entire metropolitan area in a unified fashion.

POTENTIAL FOR CONFLICT   The metropolis presents a serious problem in *conflict* management. Because a metropolitan area consists of a large number of different kinds of people living closely together, the problem of regulating conflict and maintaining order assumes tremendous proportions. Persons with different occupations, incomes, and educational levels are known to have different views on public issues. People well equipped to compete for jobs and income in a free market view government housing and welfare programs differently than others not so well equipped. People at the bottom of the social ladder look at police—indeed, governmental authority in general—differently from the way those on higher rungs do. Homeowners and renters usually look at property taxation in a different light. Families with children and those without children have different ideas about school systems. And so it goes. Differences in the way people make their living, in their income and educational levels, in the color of their skin, in the way they worship, in their style of living—all are at the roots of political life in the metropolis.

Figure 12–2

Metropolitanization in the States

Metropolitan Population Percentage

Source: U.S. Bureau of the Census.

Cities Versus Suburbs

Suburbs account for most of the growth of America's metropolitan areas. Very few large *central cities* are growing in size; on the contrary, many are losing population (see Table 12–2). Metropolitan areas are growing because their *suburbs* are growing.

Suburbanization   America's suburbanization was a product of technological advances in transportation—the automobile and the expressway. In the nineteenth century an industrial worker had to live within walking distance of his or her place of employment. This meant that the nineteenth-century American city crowded large masses of people into relatively small central areas, often in tenement houses and other high-density neighborhoods. However, modern modes of transportation—first the streetcar, then the private automobile, and then the expressway—eliminated the necessity of workers living close to their jobs. The same technology that led to the suburbanization of residences also influenced commercial and industrial location. Originally industry was tied to waterways or railroads for access to suppliers and markets. This dependence was reduced by the development of motor truck transportation, the highway system, and the greater mobility of the labor force. Many industries located in the suburbs, particularly light industries, which did not require extremely heavy bulk shipments that could only be handled by rail

Table 12–2

Cities with Largest Percentage Loss in Population, 1980–1995

City	1995 (000)	1980 (000)	Change (%)
1. Gary, IN	117	152	−23
2. Newark	268	329	−18
3. Detroit	1,012	1,203	−16
4. St. Louis	384	453	−15
5. Pittsburgh	367	424	−13
6. Flint, MI	139	160	−13
7. Cleveland	503	574	−12
8. New Orleans	490	558	−12
9. Warren, MI	142	161	−12
10. Buffalo	323	358	−10
11. Chicago	2,768	3,005	−8
12. Kansas City, KS	147	161	−8
13. Baltimore	726	787	−8
14. Philadelphia	1,553	1,688	−8
15. Washington, DC	585	638	−8

Source: Bureau of the Census, U.S. Dept. of Commerce.

or water. When industry and people moved to the suburbs, commerce followed. Giant suburban shopping centers sprang up to compete with downtown stores. Thus, metropolitan areas become decentralized over time as people, business, and industry spread themselves over the suburban landscape.[2]

CITY–SUBURBAN DIFFERENCES   Social, economic, and racial conflict can be observed at all levels of government, but at the metropolitan level, it is most obvious in the conflict that occurs between central cities and their suburbs. At the heart of city–suburban conflict are the differences in the kinds of people who live in cities and suburbs. City–suburban conflict is at the heart of "the metropolitan problem"; that is, the failure to achieve metropolitanwide consensus on public policy questions affecting the entire metropolitan area and the failure to develop metropolitan government institutions. Social, economic, and racial differences between cities and suburbs are major obstacles to the development of metropolitanwide policies and government institutions.[3]

Of course, generalizing about cities and suburbs is a dangerous thing. Although we will talk about some common characteristics of cities and suburbs, students are cautioned that individual suburbs may be quite different from one another (just as there are wide differences between social and economic groups living in central cities). There are, for example, industrial suburbs, residential suburbs, black suburbs, wealthy suburbs, working-class suburbs, and so forth.[4] Nevertheless, a clear perception of the social distance between cities and suburbs is important in understanding metropolitan politics.

SOCIAL CLASS   Cities and suburbs can be differentiated, first of all, on the basis of *social class*—the occupation, income, and educational levels of their population. The cultured class of an earlier era established "country" living as a symbol of affluence; widespread prosperity has made possible mass imitation of the aristocracy by an upwardly mobile middle-class population. The suburbs house greater proportions of white-collar employees, college graduates, and affluent families than any other sector in American life.

Status differentials in favor of suburbs are more pronounced in larger metropolitan areas; status differentials in smaller metropolitan areas are not as great as in larger areas, and sometimes even favor the city rather than the suburbs. However, on the whole, suburban living reflects middle-class values.

FAMILISM   Cities and suburbs can also be differentiated on the basis of "*familism,*" or lifestyle. Perhaps the most frequently mentioned reason for a move to the suburbs is "the kids." Family after family list consideration of their young as the primary cause for their move to suburbia. A familistic, or child-centered, lifestyle can be identified in certain social statistics. A larger percentage of suburban families have children under eighteen than city families. In addition, the single-family, free-standing home has become symbolic of familistic living in an affluent society. The nonfamilistic lifestyle is characteristic

[2]Lewis Mumford, *The City in History* (New York: Harcourt, Brace, & World, 1961), p. 34.

[3]Richard Child Hill, "Separate and Unequal: Government Inequality in the Metropolis," *American Political Science Review,* 68 (December 1974), 1557–68.

[4]Kenneth Jackson, *Crabgrass Frontier: The Suburbanization of the United States* (New York: Oxford University Press, 1985).

of the central city where there are proportionately fewer children and more apartment living.

RACE   Perhaps the most important difference between cities and suburbs is their contrasting *racial composition*. The nonwhite percentage of all U.S. suburbs is about 6 percent, in contrast to a nonwhite percentage for all central cities of 22 percent. (See Table 12–3.)

POVERTY   Low-income, low-education, unskilled populations are concentrated in the central cities. Social problems are also concentrated in central cities—racial imbalance, crime, violence, inadequate education, poverty, slum housing, and so on. By moving to the suburbs, white middle-class families not only separate themselves from blacks and poor people but also place physical distance between themselves and the major social problems that confront metropolitan areas. This permits them, for the time being, to avoid the problems associated with poverty.

PARTIES   In general, large cities are much more Democratic than their suburban rings, which generally produce more Republican votes. While temporary shifts may occur from one election to another, this general pattern of Democratic cities and Republican suburbs is likely to prevail for the near future. As long as the national Democratic party represents central-city, low-income, ethnic, labor, and racial constituencies, and the Republican party represents middle-class, educated, managerial, white, Anglo-Saxon Protestant constituencies, the political coloration of cities and suburbs is likely to be different.

Table 12–3
CITIES AND SUBURBS OF METROPOLITAN AREAS IN THE UNITED STATES

	Metropolitan Areas			Outside Metropolitan Areas
	TOTAL	CITIES	SUBURBS	
Total population (000)	192,726	77,844	114,882	55,984
Percent of U.S. total	76.2	31.5	44.7	23.8
Growth: percent population increase 1980–1990	11.6	7.5	15.7	2.2
Age: percent under 18	25.3	24.7	25.7	26.6
Race: percent black	13.0	22.1	6.9	8.7
Home ownership: percent owning home	58.4	49.1	68.1	80.6
Percent families with children	33.2	30.0	35.6	34.8
Median home value	$89,100	$71,600	$99,000	$50,100

Source: U.S. Bureau of the Census, Census of Population 1990.

SCHOOLS   City and suburban social differences are also reflected in the divergent public policies of city and suburban governments. First of all, there is some evidence that the child-centered character of suburban living produces higher educational expenditures in suburbs than in cities. Suburban parents with high hopes and plans for their children's occupational success tend to focus more concern upon the school system and spend more money on it per pupil than city residents. (Of course, in smaller metropolitan areas, where social and lifestyle differences between city and suburb are minimal, differences between city and suburb in educational expenditures are very slight and occasionally run opposite from the expected direction.)

COSTS OF GOVERNMENT   Large central cities show substantially higher operating expenditures per capita than their suburbs. The maintenance of a large physical plant for the entire metropolitan area requires city residents to make higher per capita operating expenditures than those required for suburbanites. In addition, many living costs in suburban communities are shifted from public to private spending (private septic tanks instead of public sewers, private instead of public recreation, and so on). Differences in the public services provided by city and suburban governments are greatest in the area of police protection, recreation, and health. This reflects a concentration in the city of people who are likely to require these public services, in contrast to the suburbs.

TAXES   The tax bill in suburbs is only slightly lower than in central cities. Taxes had much to do with the migration of the "pioneer" suburbanites, those who moved to the suburbs in the 1930s and 1940s. At that time, suburban living offered a significant savings in property taxation over what were thought to be heavy city taxes. However, the tax advantage of the suburbs turned out partly to be a "self-denying prophecy": The more people who fled to the suburbs to avoid heavy taxes, the greater the demand for public services in these new suburban communities, and the higher suburban taxes became to meet these new demands. Yet, the tax bill in most suburbs remains lower than in central cities. The difference in tax burden between city and suburb would be even greater if suburbanites did not choose to spend more per pupil in education than city residents, which produces higher school taxes in the suburbs. The suburbs also manage to limit their indebtedness more than cities, and most of the indebtedness incurred by the suburbs is for school rather than municipal purposes.

EXCEPTIONS   Finally, it should be noted that differences between city and suburb in smaller metropolitan areas do not appear to be as great as differences between cities and suburbs in larger metropolitan areas. In fact, all these generalizations about cities and suburbs are, indeed, generalizations. Individual cities and suburbs can be found that do not conform to these national patterns.

THE CASE FOR METROPOLITAN CONSOLIDATION

"The metropolitan problem" is often defined as a problem of "fragmented" government—that is, the proliferation of governments in metropolitan areas and the lack of coordination of public programs. The objective of the metropolitan reform movement of the last thirty years has been to reorganize, consolidate, and enlarge government jurisdictions. The goal is to rid metropolitan areas of "ineffective multiple local jurisdictions" and "governments that do not coincide with the boundaries of the metropolis."[5]

PUBLIC SERVICE   Many advantages are claimed for metropolitan governmental reorganization. First of all, the reorganization and consolidation of metropolitan governments is expected to bring about *improved public services* as a result of centralization. Consolidation of governments is expected to achieve many economies of large-scale operations and enable government to provide specialized public services, which "fragmented" units of government cannot provide. For example, larger water treatment plant facilities can deliver water at lower per gallon costs, and larger sewage disposal plants can handle sewage at a lower per gallon cost of disposal.

The problem with this argument is that most studies show that larger municipal governments are *un*economic and fail to produce improved services. Only in very small cities (with populations under 25,000) can economies of scale be achieved by enlarging the scope of government. In cities of over 250,000, further increases in size appear to produce *dis*economies of scale and lower levels of public service per person.

COORDINATION   Second, it is argued that metropolitan consolidation will provide the necessary *coordination of public services* for the metropolis. Study after study reported that crime, fire, traffic congestion, air pollution, water pollution, and so on do not respect municipal boundary lines. The transportation problem is the most common example of a coordination problem. Traffic experts have pleaded for the development of a balanced transportation system in which mass transit carries many of the passengers currently traveling in private automobiles. Yet mass transit requires decisive public action by the entire metropolitan area. Certainly, the city government is in a poor position to provide mass transit by itself without the support of the suburbanites who will be riding on it.

EQUALITY   The third major argument for metropolitan consolidation stresses the need to eliminate *inequalities in financial burdens* throughout the metropolitan area. Suburbanites who escaped many city taxes continue to add to the cities' traffic and parking problems, use city streets and parks, find employment in the cities, use city hospitals and cultural facilities, and so on. By concentrating the poor, uneducated, unskilled minorities in central cities, we also saddle central cities with costly problems of public health and welfare, crime control, fire protection, slum clearance, and the like—all the social problems that are associated with poverty and discrimination. We concentrate these costly problems in cities at the same time that middle-class tax-paying individuals, tax-paying commercial enterprises, and tax-paying industries are moving into the suburbs. Thus, metropolitan-government fragmentation often succeeds in segregating financial needs from resources. The result is serious financial difficulty for many central cities.

---

[5]John Harrigan, *Political Change in the Metropolis* (Boston: Little, Brown, 1985).

RESPONSIBILITY   It is also argued that metropolitan government will *clearly establish responsibility for metropolitanwide policy.* One of the consequences of "fragmented" government is the scattering of public authority and the decentralization of policy making in the metropolis. This proliferation in the number of autonomous governmental units reduces the probability of developing a consensus on metropolitan policy. Each autonomous unit exercises a veto power over metropolitan policy within its jurisdiction; it is often impossible to secure the unanimity required to achieve metropolitan consensus on any metropolitanwide problem. An opponent of any particular solution need only find, among the countless independent governmental bodies whose consent is required, one that can be induced to withhold its consent in order to obstruct action. The dispersion of power among a large number of governmental units makes it possible for each of them to reach decisions without concern for the possible spillover effects, which may be harmful to other governments or residents of the metropolis.

THE CASE FOR "FRAGMENTED" GOVERNMENT

Suburb "bashing" is a common theme among central-city politicians, city newspaper columnists, and many reform-minded scholars who would prefer centralized metropolitan government.[6] But the suburbs house nearly half of the nation's population and it is important to try to understand why so many suburbanites prefer "fragmented" government. Many citizens do not look upon "the optimum development of the metropolitan region" as a particularly compelling goal. Rather, there are a variety of social, political, and psychological values at stake in maintaining the existing "fragmented" system of local government.

IDENTITY   First of all, the existence of separate and independent local governments for suburbs plays a vital role in developing and maintaining a sense of community *identity.* Suburbanites identify their residential community by reference to the local political unit. They do not think of themselves as residents of the "New York metropolitan region," but rather as residents of Scarsdale or Mineola. Even the existence of community problems, the existence of a governmental forum for their resolution, and the necessity to elect local officials heighten community involvement and identity. The suburban community, with a government small in scale and close to home, represents a partial escape from the anonymity of mass urban culture. The institutional apparatus of government helps the suburban community to differentiate itself from "the urban mass" by legislating differences in the size and design of buildings, neighborhood and subdivision plans, school policies, types and quality of public services, and tax expenditure levels.

---

[6]For an excellent analysis of the political values of scholars who study urban problems, see Brett W. Hawkins and Stephen L. Percy, "On Anti-Suburban Orthodoxy," *Social Science Quarterly,* 72 (September 1991), 478–90.

ACCESS   The political advantages of a fragmented suburbia cannot easily be dismissed. The existence of many local governments provides *additional forums* for the airing of public grievances. People feel better when they can publicly voice their complaints against governments, regardless of the eventual outcome of their grievance. The additional points of access, pressure, and control provided by a decentralized system of local government give added assurance that political demands will be heard and perhaps even acted upon. Opportunities for individual participation in the making of public policy are expanded in a decentralized governmental system.

EFFECTIVENESS   Maintaining the suburb as an independent political community provides the individual with a sense of *personal effectiveness* in public affairs. The individual can feel a greater sense of manageability over the affairs of a small community. A smaller community helps relieve feelings of frustration and apathy which people often feel in their relations with larger bureaucracies. Suburbanites feel that their votes, their opinions, and their political activities count for more in a small community. They cling to the idea of grass-roots democracy in an organizational society.

INFLUENCE   Fragmented government clearly offers a larger number of groups the opportunity to *exercise influence* over government policy. Groups that would be minorities in the metropolitan area as a whole can avail themselves of government position and enact diverse public policies. This applies to blacks in the central city as well as to whites in the suburbs. Fragmented government creates within the metropolitan area a wide range of government policies. Communities that prefer, for example, higher standards in their school system at higher costs have the opportunity to implement this preference. Communities that prefer higher levels of public service or one set of services over another or stricter enforcement of particular standards can achieve their goals under a decentralized governmental system. Communities that wish to get along with reduced public services in order to maximize funds available for private spending may do so.

SCHOOLS   Racial imbalance and the plight of central-city schools are important forces in maintaining the political autonomy of suburban school systems in the nation's large metropolitan areas. Many suburbanites left the central city to find "a better place to raise the kids," and this means, among other things, better schools. As we have already observed, suburbs generally spend more on the education of each child than central cities. Moreover, the increasing concentration of blacks in central cities has resulted in racial imbalance in center-city schools. Efforts to end de facto segregation within the cities frequently involve busing school children into and out of ghetto schools in order to achieve racial balance. In Chapter 14 we will discuss de facto segregation in greater detail. However, it is important to note here that independent suburban school districts are viewed by many suburbanites as protection against the possibility that their children might be bused to inner-city schools. Autonomous suburban school districts lie outside the jurisdiction of city officials. While it is possible that federal courts may some day order suburban school districts to cooperate with cities in achieving racial balance in schools, the political independence of suburban schools helps to assure that their children will not be used to achieve racial balance in city schools.

METROPOLITAN GOVERNMENT AS MARKETPLACE

Fragmented metropolitan government means many different mixes of municipal services, public schools, and tax levels in the same metropolitan area. So why can't people "shop around" among local communities and move into the community where the mix of services, schools, and taxes best suits their individual preferences?

THE TIEBOUT MODEL   Economist Charles Tiebout argues that the existence of many local governments in the same area, all offering "public goods" (public schools, police and fire protection, water and sewer, refuse collection, streets and sidewalks) and various "prices" (taxes), provides a competitive and efficient government marketplace.[7] Families can choose for themselves what public goods they want at what price by simply moving to the community that best approximates their own preferences. Both families and businesses can "vote with their feet" for their preferred "bundle" of municipal services and taxes. Local governments must compete for residents and businesses by offering high-quality public services at the lowest possible tax rates. This encourages efficiency in local government.

MOBILITY?   The Tiebout model of efficient local government assumes that metropolitan residents have a high degree of *mobility,* that is, they can move anywhere in the metropolitan area anytime they wish. The major criticism of this model is that many metropolitan residents do not enjoy unlimited mobility. The poor are limited by meager financial resources from "shopping" for the best governmental services. And minorities often confront barriers to residential mobility regardless of their economic resources.

EQUITY?   Moreover, the Tiebout model in its original formulation ignores the interdependence of the metropolis. Many public services are metropolitanwide in scope—urban expressway, mass transit, clean air and water, public health and hospitals, for example. These services cannot be provided by small local governments. Suburbanites use public facilities and services of cities when they work in the city or go to the city for entertainment. If they do not share in the costs of these services and facilities, they become "free riders," unfairly benefiting from services paid for by others. The major social problems of the city—poverty, racial tension, poor housing, crime and delinquency—are really problems of the entire metropolis.[8]

SATISFACTION?   Yet the Tiebout model is correct in asserting that there is a great variety of lifestyles, housing types, governmental services and costs *within* large metropolitan areas, and that most families take this into account when choosing a place of residence. And judging by the subjective evaluations of residents, many different types of

---

[7]Charles Tiebout, "A Pure Theory of Local Expenditures," *Journal of Political Economy,* 64 (October 1956), 416–24.

[8]Bollens and Schmandt, *The Metropolis.*

neighborhoods are judged satisfactory by the people living in them. Quality-of-life studies usually ask respondents how "satisfied" they are with their neighborhoods. These studies reveal that people living in *all* types of neighborhoods express satisfaction with them. Indeed, even lower-income people living in substandard housing or areas considered slums by outsiders report being satisfied. (However, attachment to friends and relatives is a major source of their satisfaction, rather than governmental services.)[9] The fact that residents of many different kinds of communities express satisfaction with them lends implicit support to the Tiebout model. There is also evidence that business locational decisions within the metropolis are influenced by the "bundle" of governmental services and taxes offered by local governments.[10]

"SOLUTIONS" TO THE METROPOLITAN PROBLEM

Let us examine various strategies for metropolitan governmental consolidation in connection with the values of suburban independence and the need for coordinating governmental activity in metropolitan areas.

ANNEXATION   The most obvious method of achieving governmental consolidation in the metropolitan area would be for the central city to annex suburban areas. *Annexation* continues to be the most popular integrating device in the nation's metropolitan areas. Not all cities, however, have been equally successful in annexation efforts. Opposition to central-city annexation is generally more intense in the larger metropolitan areas. The bigger the metropolis, the more one can expect that suburbanites will defend themselves against being "swallowed up" or "submerged" by the central city. Central cities in smaller urbanized areas experience more success in annexing people than cities in large urbanized areas. Yet size does not appear to be the most influential factor affecting annexation success. Actually, the "age" of a city seems more influential than its size in determining the success of annexation efforts. Over three-fourths of the area and population annexed to central cities in the nation in the last two decades have been in newer cities of the West and South. City boundary lines in "older" metropolitan areas are relatively more fixed than in "newer" areas. Perhaps the immobility of boundaries is a product of sheer age. Over time, persons and organizations adjust themselves to circumstances as they find them. The longer these adjustments have been in existence, the greater the discomfort, expense, and fear of unanticipated consequences associated with change.[11]

---

[9]See Barrett A. Lee, "The Urban Unease Revisited: Perceptions of Local Satisfaction Among Metropolitan Residents," *Social Science Quarterly,* 62 (December 1987), 611–29; Craig St. John and Frieda Clark, "Race and Social Class Differences in the Characteristics Desired in Residential Neighborhoods," *Social Science Quarterly,* 65 (September 1984), 803–13.

[10]See Mark Schneider, "Suburban Fiscal Disparities and the Location Decisions of Firms," *American Journal of Political Science.* 29 (August 1985), 587–605.

[11]See Arnold Fleischmann, "The Politics of Annexation," *Social Science Quarterly,* 67 (March 1986), 128–41; Gary J. Miller, *Cities by Contract: The Politics of Municipal Incorporation* (Cambridge, MA: MIT Press, 1981).

CITY-COUNTY CONSOLIDATION   Three-quarters of the nation's metropolitan areas lie within single counties. From the standpoint of administration, there is much to be said for *city–county consolidation*. It would make sense administratively to endow county governments with the powers of cities and to organize them to exercise these powers effectively. Yet, important political problems—problems in the allocation of influence over public decision making—remain formidable barriers to strong county government. Suburbanites are likely to fear that consolidation will give city residents a dominant voice in county affairs. Suburbanites may also fear that city–county consolidation may force them to pay higher taxes to help support the higher municipal costs of running the city. (Actually, county governments usually do provide more benefits to city than suburban residents, while receiving more tax revenues from suburbanites than city residents.[12]) Suburbanites may not welcome uniform, countywide policies in taxation or zoning or any number of other policy areas. Suburbanites who had paid for their own wells and septic tanks will hardly welcome the opportunity to help pay for city water or sewer services. Suburbanites with well-established, high-quality public school systems may be unenthusiastic about integrating their schools with city schools in a countywide system, and so on. A variety of policy differences may exist between city and suburb, which will reflect themselves in any attempt to achieve city–county consolidation.

SPECIAL DISTRICTS   One of the more popular approaches to metropolitan integration is the creation of *special districts or authorities* charged with administering a particular function or service on a metropolitanwide or at least an intermunicipal level, such as a park, sewage, water, parking, airport, planning, other district, or authority. (See Figure 12–3.)

Figure 12–3
SPECIAL DISTRICT GOVERNMENTS BY FUNCTION

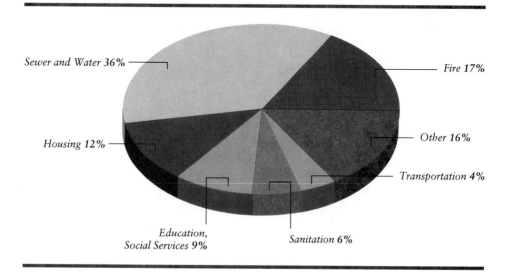

Sewer and Water 36%

Fire 17%

Other 16%

Housing 12%

Transportation 4%

Education, Social Services 9%

Sanitation 6%

[12]See Brett W. Hawkins and Rebecca M. Hendrick, "Do County Governments Reinforce City–Suburban Inequalities," *Social Science Quarterly*, 25 (December 1994), 755–71.

Because the special district or authority leaves the social and governmental *status quo* relatively undisturbed, important integrative demands are met with a minimum of resistance with this device. The autonomy of suburban communities is not really threatened, loyalties are not disturbed, political jobs are not lost, and the existing tax structure is left relatively intact. Special districts or authorities may be preferred by suburban political leaders when they believe it will lessen the pressure for annexation by the central city. Special districts or authorities may also be able to incur additional debt after existing units of government have already reached their tax and debt limits. Thus, special districts or authorities may be able to operate in an area wider than that of existing units of governments and at the same time enable governments to evade tax or debt limits in financing a desired public service. The nation's largest special districts—New York's Metropolitan Transportation Authority, Boston's Massachusetts Bay Transportation Authority, Washington's Metro Area Transit Authority, Los Angeles County Transportation Commission, Port Authority of New York and New Jersey—collect and spend billions of dollars each year.

Yet, experience in the cities that have relied heavily upon special districts or authorities has suggested that these devices may create as many problems as they solve. Many special districts and authorities are governed by a quasi-independent board or commission, which, once established, becomes largely immune from popular pressures for change. These agencies may be quite independent of other governmental jurisdictions in the metropolis; their concerns might be water, air or water pollution control, city planning, and so on. Remoteness from popular control or close political responsibility often results in the professional administrators of these authorities exercising great power over their particular function. While authorities and special districts are supposed to be nonprofit governmental agencies, they often act very much like private enterprises, concentrating their resources on those activities that produce revenue and ignoring equally important non-revenue-producing responsibilities. Independent authorities often borrow money, collect tolls and services charges, and otherwise control their own finances in a manner very much like a private business. The structure of these districts and authorities usually confuses the voters and makes it difficult for the average citizen to hold officials of these agencies responsible for their decisions. Moreover, since these special districts and authorities are usually created for a single purpose, they often come to define the public interest in terms of the promotion of their own particular function—recreation, mass transit, water, parks, and so on—without regard for other metropolitan concerns. This "single-mindedness" can lead to competition and conflict between authorities and other governmental agencies in the region. Sooner or later, the problem of coordinating the activities of these independent authorities of special districts arises. Thus, even from the point of view of administrative efficiency, it is not clear whether the special district or authority, with its maze of divided responsibility, reduces or compounds the problem of governmental coordination in the metropolis in the long run.

INTERJURISDICTIONAL AGREEMENTS   Another approach to metropolitan integration is the *interjurisdictional agreement*. Voluntary cooperative agreements between governments in a metropolitan area are common. Agreements may take the form of *informal*, verbal understandings that might involve, for example, the exchange between welfare departments of information on cases, or cooperation among police departments in the apprehension of a lawbreaker, or agreements among local fire departments to come to the assistance of each other in the event of a major fire. Agreements may also be *formal* interjurisdictional agreements among governments, perhaps to build and operate a major facility such as a garbage incinerator or a sewage treatment plant. Interjurisdictional agreements may provide for (1) one government performing a service or providing a facility for one or more other governments on a contractual basis, (2) two or more governments performing a function jointly or operating a facility on a joint basis, or (3) two or more local governments agreeing to assist and supply mutual aid to each other in emergency situations.

One of the attractions of interjurisdictional agreements is that they provide a means for dealing with metropolitan problems on a voluntary basis while retaining local determination and control. Interjurisdictional agreements do not threaten the existence of communities or governments. They do not threaten the jobs of incumbent public officials. Yet at the same time they enable governments to achieve the economies and provide the specialized services that only a larger jurisdiction can make possible.

COUNCILS OF GOVERNMENT   Metropolitan councils of governments (COGs) are another form of integration in metropolitan areas. Metropolitan councils are associations of governments or government officials that provide an opportunity for study, discussion, and recommendations regarding common metropolitan problems. Not governments themselves, these COGs have no power to implement decisions but must rely instead upon compliance by member governments. Metropolitan councils provide an arena where officials of metropolitan governments can come together regularly, discuss problems, make recommendations, and, hopefully, coordinate their activities.[13]

Although COGs started slowly, the federal government provided the major stimulus to their acceptance by making federal planning funds available for metropolitanwide planning agencies. Today, most metropolitan areas have *some* organization functioning as a metropolitan council of government.

Generally, COG's strive for unity in their decisions because their recommendations must be acted upon by member governments who are unlikely to implement proposals they oppose. The result, for the most part, is that studies and recommendations of COGs are likely to be rather bland. It is very difficult for these councils to deal with the really divisive issues in the metropolis. Since councils have no authority to act upon metropolitan problems, they may be, in the words of Bollens and Schmandt, a "toothless tiger or—even worse—a protector of the inadequate status quo."[14]

---

[13]The best-known councils of government include the Metropolitan Regional Council (New York), Southern California Association of Governments (Los Angeles), Northeast Illinois Planning Commission (Chicago), Southeast Michigan Council of Governments (Detroit), Associated Bay Area Governments (San Francisco), Metropolitan Washington Council of Governments (Washington), East-West Gateway Council (St. Louis), Northeast Ohio Areawide Coordinating Agency (Cleveland).

[14]See Bollens and Schmandt, *The Metropolis,* pp. 379–80.

THE POLITICS OF METROPOLITAN CONSOLIDATION

City officials—mayors, managers, and council members–usually provide the public stimulus for annexation. Their immediate goal is to expand the tax base of the city; over the long run they seek growth and revenues. They do not want to see the city cut off from new residential, industrial, and commercial development on the rim of the metropolis. Their primary strategy is to cultivate political support for various annexation efforts by offering city services—especially water and sewer, fire and police protection, street lighting and sidewalks—at reasonable prices to residents of areas targeted for annexation. Sometimes builders and developers can be enticed to offer land for annexation in exchange for city water, sewer, or streets. Cities with active managers and planners are more likely to have continuous annexation programs.

City business interests, with capital already invested in downtown land, buildings, and enterprises, are usually strong supporters of annexation. These city power structures are growth oriented (see Chapter 13). If the city government is cut off from new sources of revenue, the costs of city government will increasingly fall on the shoulders of downtown business. The downtown Chambers of Commerce, the city newspaper, and the downtown civic (reform) organizations can all be expected to support the expansion of the city.

POLITICAL OPPOSITION   Political opposition to annexation and city expansion is usually centered among suburban municipal officials and residents. They see continued value in "fragmentation"—a sense of community identity, access to government, personal influence in a smaller governmental setting, insulation from city dwellers whose lifestyles they do not share, and perhaps a desire to maintain racial isolation. They also fear higher tax rates in the city, and they may not feel that the additional services offered by city government are worth the added cost. County or township officials may take the lead in urging residents not to sign annexation petitions and to vote "no" if an election is held; they may also challenge annexation petitions and votes in the courts.

Political realities have frequently overwhelmed the "logic" of metropolitan consolidation. These political realities are deeply rooted in the social, economic, lifestyle, and racial differences between cities and suburbs described earlier. The record of consolidation referenda shows more defeats than victories.[15] Yet reformers have not been inhibited by the dismal record thus far, and consolidation proposals of various kinds are under discussion in a great many urban areas.

Consolidation involves considerable disruption for public officials—redesigning governmental structure, reordering the authority of various offices, combining offices and agencies, and enlarging the magnitude of government operations. Unless a *large* majority of community influentials are *very* dissatisfied with the current state of affairs and are mo-

---

[15]Vincent L. Marando and Carl Whitley, "City-County Consolidation: An Overview of Voter Response," *Urban Affairs Quarterly,* 8 (December 1972), 181–203.

tivated to actively support consolidation, there is little chance that consolidation efforts will be successful.[16]

CONSOLIDATION COMMISSIONS   Consolidation efforts usually begin with the formation of a charter commission to determine the form of the new consolidated government and write a charter for it. Usually the commission includes representatives of both the city and county governments to be consolidated, together with some "citizen" representatives. Sometimes the establishment of the commission itself is the subject of a referendum; interestingly, referenda to establish a commission tend to pass more often than not, even though the final vote on consolidation is likely to be negative. Establishing a charter commission is more easily obtainable than consolidation itself.

CONSOLIDATION REFERENDA   The critical point of the consolidation battle is the referenda vote on the acceptance of the new consolidated-government charter. The form of the vote depends on state law: A "double majority" vote requirement means that a majority "yes" vote must be obtained within the city *and* within the area outside of the city; a "double-count majority" vote requirement means that the vote of city residents is counted twice—once for the city and again for the county because they are also county residents. It is much easier for consolidation to win under the "double-count" requirement. Consolidation campaigns are usually managed by reform groups especially selected for the purpose. They are typically mass-media-oriented campaigns rather than the grassroots organizational, ward- and precinct-level campaigns of party organizations. Voter turnout is only slightly heavier than that of ordinary municipal elections—ranging from 30 percent to 60 percent. Contrary to the public pronouncements of reformers, a high turnout does *not* help passage; indeed, there is a slightly better chance of success if turnout is low.

Most consolidation proposals are defeated by *county* residents, that is, suburbanites. The average voter turnout level of suburbanites is much higher than city dwellers, and the percentage of "no" votes is much greater in the suburbs than in the city. Thus, overall voter response to consolidation proposals tends to support the notion that suburbanites prefer to maintain their identity and autonomy, their own governmental institutions, and their insulation from city people and problems. They do *not* want the improved public services, coordinated policies, or shared financial burdens that reformers urge upon them. While fear of higher taxes plays a role in suburban opposition, there appear to be many other social and psychological factors at work in helping to preserve suburban autonomy.

The fear of being "submerged" into a large, impersonal, unresponsive government is evidenced by the interesting fact that proposed consolidation charters that stipulate many elected representatives and separately elected administrators (sheriff, tax assessor, and so on) do better at the polls than the "streamline," governmental charters preferred by re-

---

[16]For an interesting comparison of elite roles in successful (Jacksonville) and unsuccessful (Tampa) consolidation campaigns, see Thomas A. Henderson and Walter A. Rosenbaum, "Prospects for Consolidating Local Government: The Role of Elites in Electoral Outcomes," *American Journal of Political Science,* 17 (November 1973), 695–720.

formers. In other words, a "Jacksonian" consolidation charter has a better chance of passage than one with a small legislative body and single strong executive.

RACE   Race is an increasingly important issue in consolidation campaigns. Most successful consolidation efforts have occurred in the South. A common appeal to suburbanites in the South is to vote to join the city in order to "save" it from black majority rule by "diluting" the black vote. However, the issue is complex and cuts both ways. Suburbanites may simply decide to stay out of a consolidated government precisely because it would include many central-city blacks. Blacks were traditionally expected to vote "yes" for economic reasons—to bring valuable suburban property into the tax base of the city. However, black support for consolidation will certainly turn to opposition if it appears that blacks will lose power in the outcome.[17]

REFORM   Political support for consolidation is usually greatest among civic and business organizations and newspapers. Their arguments for consolidation are familiar— improved services, better coordination, more equal financial burdens, and clearer lines of responsibility. Moreover, consolidation offers an opportunity to reorganize local government: The new government may offer a manager form of government, a reduction in the number of elected officials, and a more orderly structure for the delivery of municipal services.

THE TAX ISSUE   Does city–county consolidation save the taxpayers' money? Reformers have been *unable* to produce any convincing evidence that consolidation either improves governmental services or reduces governmental costs. Indeed, in careful study of this important question, employing a before-and-after research design in similar "experimental" and "control" cities, researchers found "no measurable impact" from consolidation on governmental costs of services.[18] This study focused on Florida's Jacksonville/Duval County, which consolidated their governments, and Tampa/Hillsbourgh County, which did not. Both metropolitan areas are similar in socioeconomic composition, both operate under the same state laws, and both have the same mayor-council form of government. Yet an examination of property taxes, total expenditures, and policy protection in both cities from 1955 through 1981 (Jacksonville/Duval County consolidated in 1969) showed *no* significant short-term or long-term differences between these two areas.

A RECORD OF FAILURE   Most consolidation efforts fail. Only about one-quarter of the consolidation proposals that come to a vote are approved. These have all been single counties. Most have been in medium-size or smaller metropolitan areas. There have been no adoptions in the Northeast or Midwest; all consolidations have taken place in the South or West. Successful consolidations have always involved some unique politi-

---

[17]See Richard L. Engstrom and W. E. Lyons, "Black Control or Consolidation: The Fringe Response," *Social Science Quarterly,* 53 (June 1972), 161–68.

[18]J. Edwin Benten, "City County Consolidation and Economics of Scale," *Social Science Quarterly,* 65 (March 1985), 190–98.

cal factors. Often it is necessary to allow some offices to remain separate in order to secure political support for consolidation, for example, retaining a separate sheriff's office and city police force, or retaining separate school districts.[19]

"METRO" GOVERNMENT   The American experience with federalism at the national level has prompted consideration of federated governmental structures for metropolitan areas. A "metro" government with authority to make metropolitanwide policy in selected fields might be combined with local control over functions that are "local" in character. Metropolitan federation, in one form or another and at one time or another, has been proposed for many major metropolitan regions in the nation. Yet, with the exception of Toronto, Miami, and Nashville,[20] proposals for metropolitan federation have been consistently rejected by both voters and political leaders. While metropolitan federation promises many of the advantages of governmental consolidation listed earlier—administrative efficiency, economy of large-scale operation, elimination of financial inequalities, and public accountability for metropolitanwide policy—it seriously threatens many of the social, political, and psychological values in the existing "fragmented" system of local government in the metropolis. Metropolitan federation also poses a problem discussed earlier, that of deciding what is a "metropolitan" problem. In order to allocate functions to a "metro" government in a federation arrangement, one must first determine what is a metropolitan problem in which all the citizens of the area have a responsibility.

THE CONCENTRATION OF SOCIAL PROBLEMS IN THE INNER CITY

The nation's largest cities have become the principal location of virtually all of the social problems confronting our society—poverty, homelessness, racial tension, family instability, drug abuse, delinquency, and crime. (Some of these problems are discussed in other chapters—crime in Chapter 8, racial issues in Chapter 14, education in Chapter 15, and poverty and homelessness in Chapter 17.) But it is important to note here that these problems are all made worse by their concentration in the inner city. This concentration is a relatively recent occurrence; as late as 1970 there were higher rates of poverty in rural America than in the cities.

JOBLESSNESS   Why has the "inner city" become the locus of social problems? It has been argued that changes in the labor market from industrial goods-producing jobs to professional, financial, technical, and service jobs is increasingly polarizing the labor

---

[19]See Vincent L. Marando, "City County Consolidation: Reform Regionalism Referenda and Requiem," *Western Political Quarterly,* 32 (December 1979), 409–21.

[20]See Edward Sofen, *The Miami Metropolitan Experiment* (Bloomington: University of Indiana Press, 1963); Edward Sofen, "The Politics of Metropolitan Leadership: The Miami Experience," *Midwest Journal of Political Science,* 5 (February 1961), 18–38; Brett W. Hawkins, *Nashville Metro* (Nashville, TN.: University of Vanderbilt Press, 1966); Brett W. Hawkins, "Public Opinion and Metropolitan Reorganization in Nashville," *Journal of Politics,* 28 (May 1966), 408–18.

market into low-wage and high-wage sectors.[21] The decline in manufacturing jobs, together with a shift in remaining manufacturing jobs and commercial (sales) jobs to the suburbs, has left inner-city residents with fewer job opportunities. The rise in joblessness in the inner cities has in turn increased the concentration of poor people, added to the number of poor single-parent families, and increased welfare dependency.

MIDDLE-CLASS FLIGHT   At the same time, inner-city neighborhoods have experienced an out-migration of working-class and middle-class families. The number of inner-city neighborhoods in which the poverty rate exceeds 40 percent has risen sharply.[22] The loss of working- and middle-class families creates further social instability. In earlier decades most inner-city adults were employed, and they invested their income and time in their neighborhoods, patronizing churches, stores, schools, and community organizations. Their presence in the community provided "role models" for youth. But their out-migration has decreased contact between the classes, leaving the poorest members of the community isolated and "truly disadvantaged." Inner-city residents now lack not only nearby jobs, but also access to job information, social learning through working role models, and suitable (for example, employed) marriage partners.

THE TRULY DISADVANTAGED   It is argued that joblessness and poverty are much more demoralizing when concentrated in the inner city. Neighborhoods that have few legitimate employment opportunities, inadequate job information networks, and poor schools not only weaken the work ethic, but also give rise to illegal income-producing activities in the streets—drugs, crime, and prostitution. A jobless family living in a neighborhood where these ills are concentrated is influenced by the behaviors, beliefs, and perceptions of the people around them. These "concentration effects" make things worse. Moreover, the deterioration of inner-city neighborhoods saps the vitality of local businesses and public services, leading to fewer and shabbier movie theaters, restaurants, markets, parks, and playgrounds. Inner-city schools are particularly disadvantaged: As educational requirements for good jobs are rising, the quality of education available in the inner city is eroded by the concentration of children from poverty-impacted and disintegrating families. The fiscal burden on city governments increases: The cost of services to the inner city rises at the same time that the tax base is eroded by out-migrating businesses and working residents.

THE INNER CITY: RACIAL TENSIONS AND RIOTING

The concentration of social problems in the inner city not only adds to their severity, but also removes them from direct observation by most Americans. Only when the inner city erupts in rioting and violence do many Americans turn their attention to the racial ten-

---

[21]See William Julius Wilson, *The Truly Disadvantaged* (Chicago: University of Chicago Press, 1987).

[22]See Christopher Jencks and Paul E. Peterson, eds., *The Urban Underclass* (Washington, DC: Brookings Institution, 1991).

sions, family breakdowns, joblessness, welfare dependency, crime and drugs, poor schools, and hopelessness that permeate so many core areas of our nation's large cities. And often the attention of policy makers, the media, and the general public is fleeting—it is "politics as usual" after the rioting has been quelled, with inner-city dwellers left to pick up the charred pieces.

THE URBAN RIOTS OF THE SIXTIES

Domestic violence is not new to American cities. Three early riots—Watts in Los Angeles in 1965, and Newark and Detroit in 1967—were major civil disorders. Detroit was the worst of these outbreaks: A week of rioting left forty-three dead and more than 1000 injured. Whole sections of the city were reduced to charred ruins and smoke. Over 1300 buildings were totally demolished and 2700 businesses sacked. Detroit's upheaval began when police raided an after-hours club and arrested the bartender and several customers for selling and consuming alcoholic beverages after authorized closing hours. A force of 15,000 city and state police, National Guardsmen, and finally federal troops fought to quell the violence. Most of the looted retail businesses were liquor stores, grocery stores, and furniture stores. Many black merchants scrawled "Soul Brother" on their windows in an attempt to escape the wrath of the mobs. Eventually, homes and shops covering a total area of fourteen square miles were gutted by fire. Firefighters were stoned and occasionally shot by ghetto residents. Of the forty-three persons who were killed during the riot, thirty-three were black and ten were white. Police officers killed 20 persons, and National Guard and Army troops an additional 10; one Guardsman, one firefighter, and one private security guard were among the dead.[23]

President Lyndon Johnson appointed a National Commission on Civil Disorder to study the nature and causes of urban rioting. Among the commission's conclusions were the following:

> Typically, rioting was a result of a complex relationship between underlying grievances and one or more "triggering" incidents. For example, grievances about allegedly abusive police practices . . . were often aggravated in the minds of many blacks by incidents involving the police, or the inaction of municipal authorities on complaints about police action.
>
> Many grievances in the black community resulted from discrimination, prejudice, and powerlessness which blacks often experience. . . .
>
> Characteristically, the typical rioter was not a hoodlum, habitual criminal, or riffraff. . . . Instead, he was a teenager or young adult, a life-long resident of the city in which he rioted, a high school drop-out and almost invariably underemployed or employed in a menial job. He was proud of his race, extremely hostile to both whites and middle-class blacks, and highly distrustful of the political system and of political leaders.
>
> . . . Some rioters shared neither the conditions nor the grievance of their neighbors; some coolly and deliberately exploited the chaos created by others; some may have been drawn into the melee merely because they identified with, or wished to emulate, others.[24]

---

[23]National Advisory Commission on Civil Disorders, *Report* (Washington, DC: Government Printing Office, 1968), p. 107.

[24]Ibid., p. 4.

NATIONAL RESPONSE   Many new "Great Society" social welfare programs were already under way at the time of these early riots. The War on Poverty produced a myriad of new federal programs in education, welfare, health care, and housing. While some of these programs were later abandoned, notably the federal Office of Economic Opportunity and its local antipoverty "community action" agencies, nonetheless many important policy innovations grew to become major programs today. Later, we will describe Head Start and other federal educational programs (Chapter 15); federal transportation and housing programs (Chapter 16); and Medicare, Medicaid, and welfare programs (Chapter 17).

But responsibility for the nation's "urban policy" remains divided between federal departments (for example, the Department of Health and Human Services, the Department of Education, the Department of Housing and Urban Development, the Department of Labor, the Department of Transportation, etc.) and between federal and state governments. Indeed, there is no clear agreement on what "urban policy" encompasses, inasmuch as the problems of cities include virtually every problem confronting the nation.

Despite the dramatic growth of federal social welfare programs and expenditures over the past three decades, there was little noticeable improvement in conditions in the inner city. The Detroit experience was particularly disillusioning: Its inner city is a more depressed and dangerous place today than when the riots erupted in 1967. Its population plummeted from 1.6 million to 1 million as middle-class blacks and whites fled. Its crime rate soared 60 percent between 1976 and 1991, and it lost over one-third of its jobs. Efforts to stem the flight of the middle class and stabilize neighborhoods were largely ineffective. Thousands of abandoned apartments, stores, and business locations litter the inner city. If anything, the rioting accelerated the worsening of conditions.

THE LOS ANGELES RIOTS—1992   The Los Angeles riots in 1992 were a bloody reminder that racial conflict and social misery in the nation's inner cities have not disappeared. The city's "Rodney King" riot was the nation's worst urban rioting of the twentieth century. It left over fifty people dead and many square miles of charred desolation in south-central Los Angeles. The triggering event was the not-guilty verdict rendered by a predominately white jury in suburban Simi Valley in the case of four white Los Angeles police officers accused of beating a black motorist, Rodney King. The case had attracted national attention owing to the fact that the beating had been videotaped and shown many times on national television. The verdict was regarded by both blacks and whites nationwide as a serious miscarriage of justice. Many blacks in the inner city regarded it as white support for continued police brutality and a signal to express their outrage. Within hours of the verdict black youth in south-central Los Angeles

> began throwing stones and bottles at passing cars. The mob swelled. They hauled two white motorists from their cars and stomped them. Then Reginald Oliver Denny, 36, a gravel-truck driver with long blond hair, drove into the melee. Five men grabbed him, kicked him, smashed him on the head with a fire extinguisher and stole his wallet. For nearly an hour panicked drivers drove around him. A news chopper filmed the assault, possibly even encouraged it. T. J. Murphy, 30, an aerospace engineer, saw the beating on TV and drove to the scene. He found Denny, eyes swollen shut, in the cab of his truck. With the help of three other African-Americans, Murphy shielded the critically injured trucker and got him to a hospital.

. . . the violence rippled outward. Drivers jumped from cars and fled. Shouting kids smashed windows, tromped on hoods and roofs, torched the abandoned vehicles. They turned to a liquor store, small shops, a gas station. Before long, flames and black smoke engulfed the neighborhood. And the LAPD was nowhere in sight. . . .

Looters of all races owned the streets, storefronts and malls. Throughout the city black merchants spray-painted their doors and awnings or put signs in their windows to distinguish them from white and Asian shops. Sometimes it worked: mostly it didn't. . . .[25]

IN THE ASHES   Despite a great deal of political rhetoric following urban rioting, neither Congress nor the president has responded with any clear solutions to the problems of the inner city. And it may be that these problems are largely beyond the reach of government policy: The breakdown of families, the drug culture, the loss of inner-city jobs, and racial and ethnic tensions have all proven to be highly resistant to anything government does. In later chapters we will examine government efforts in welfare, health, homelessness, housing, and education.

Rioting intensifies racial distrust and conflict. Black psychologist Halford Fairchild believes that "violence has laid bare the city's inter-ethnic competition and hostility. The potential exists for urban warfare where the battle lines are drawn according to skin color, language, and ethnicity."[26]

Governments may be more effective in controlling riots than in ameliorating their underlying conditions. Police reforms may have a more direct effect on the outbreak of rioting than anything else cities can do. Police departments that maintain close relationships with minority communities, train officers in benign conflict-resolution tactics, vigorously investigate and publish charges of police brutality, and endeavor to anticipate and respond quickly to events that might trigger riots may minimize unrest in their cities.

---

[25]*Newsweek,* May 11, 1992, pp. 30–38.

[26]*New York Times,* November 11, 1992, p. 19.

TRIVIA
URBAN STRESS: RATING METROPOLITAN AREAS

Psychologists argue that favorable living conditions do not always produce feelings of personal well-being. While there are no direct measures of psychological well-being for metropolitan areas, there are reliable data for important indicators of psychological and social stress: alcoholism, suicide, divorce, and crime. Combining metropolitan rankings on these four measures produces the results presented below. It turns out that western and southern metropolitan areas, known for their mild climates and easy living, ranked high on these measures of stress. Many of the lowest-stress cities were in the Northeast and Midwest.

Lowest Stress Metro Areas

1. State College, PA
2. Grand Falls, ND
3. St. Cloud, MN
4. Rochester, MN
5. McAllen/Pharr/ Edinburg, TX
6. Altoona, PA
7. Bloomington, IN
8. Provo/Oren, UT
9. Utica, NY
10. Akron, OH
11. Sheboygen, WI
12. Lancaster, PA
13. Paterson/Clifton/ Passaic, NJ
14. Bismarck/ND
15. Allentown/Bethlehem/ Easton, PA
16. Lafayette/West Lafayette, IN
17. Nassau/Suffolk, NY
18. Poughkeepsie,NY
19. Albany/Schenectady/ Troy, NY
20. Lawrence, KS
21. New Bedford/Fall River, MA
22. Bloomington/Normal, IL
23. Wheeling, WV
24. Cumberland, MD
25. Wausau, WI

Highest Stress Metro Areas

1. Tucson, AZ
2. Tacoma, WA
3. Stockton, CA
4. Riverside/San Bernardino, CA
5. Houston, TX
6. New York, NY
7. Tampa/St. Petersburg/ Clearwater, FL
8. Bakersfield, CA
9. Ocala, FL
10. Sacramento, CA
11. Orlando, FL
12. Oklahoma City, OK
13. Phoenix, AZ
14. Fort Lauderdale/ Hollywood, FL
15. West Palm Beach/Boca Raton, FL
16. Los Angeles/Long Beach, CA
17. San Francisco/ Oakland, CA
18. Jacksonville, FL
19. Odessa, TX
20. Panama City, FL
21. North Little Rock/ Little Rock, AR
22. Lakeland/Winter Haven, FL
23. Miami, FL
24. Las Vegas, NV
25. Reno, NV

Source: As reported by Robert Levine, "City Stress Index," *Psychology Today* (November 1988), 53–58.

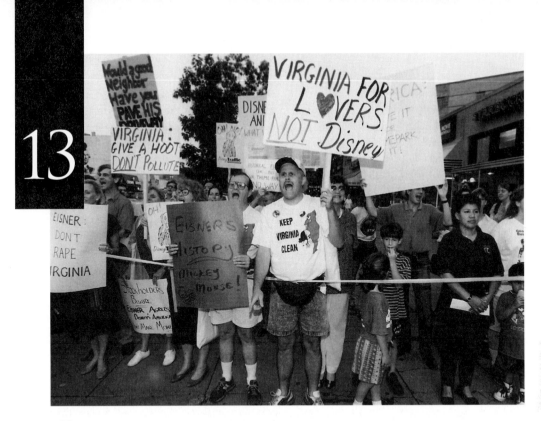

13

COMMUNITY
POWER STRUCTURES

MODELS OF COMMUNITY POWER

Who runs this town? Do the elected public officials actually make the important decisions? Or is there a "power structure" in this community that really runs things? If so, who is in the power structure? Are public officials "gofers" who carry out the orders of powerful individuals who operate "behind the scenes"? Or are community affairs decided by democratically elected officials acting openly in response to the wishes of many different individuals and groups? Is city government of the people, by the people, and for the people? Or is it a government run by a small "elite," with the "masses" of people largely apathetic and uninfluential in public affairs?

Social scientists have differed over the answers to these questions. Some social scientists, whom we shall refer to as "elitists," believed that power in American communities is concentrated in the hands of relatively few people, usually top business and financial leaders. They believe that this "elite" is subject to relatively little influence from the "masses" of people. Other social scientists, whom we shall refer to as "pluralists," believe that power is widely shared in American communities among many leadership groups who represent segments of the community and who are held responsible by the people through elections and group participation. Interestingly, both elitists and pluralists seem to agree that decisions are made by small minorities in the community. Direct, widespread, individual citizen participation in community decision making is more of an ideal than a reality. *Elitists describe a monolithic structure of power,* with a single leadership group making decisions on a variety of issues. *Pluralists describe a polycentric structure of power,* with different leaders active in different issues and a great deal of competition, bargaining, and sharing of power among them.

Most "real" communities will probably fall somewhere in between—that is, along a continuum from the monolithic elite model of power to a diffused and polycentric pluralist model. Many social scientists are neither confirmed "elitists" nor "pluralists," but they are aware that different structures and power may exist in different communities. Yet these ideal models of community power may be helpful in understanding the different ways in which community power can be structured.

THE ELITE MODEL OF COMMUNITY POWER

European social theory has long been at odds with democratic political writers about the existence and necessity of elites. The Italian political theorist, Gaetano Mosca, in his book *The Ruling Class,* wrote, "In all societies . . . two classes of people appear—a class that rules and a class that is ruled."[1] For Mosca, elitism is explained by the nature of social organization. Organization inevitably results in the concentration of political power in the hands of a few. Organized power cannot be resisted by an unorganized majority in which each individual ". . . stands alone before the totality of the organized minority. A hundred men acting uniformly in concert, with a common understanding, will triumph over a thousand men who are not in accord and can therefore be dealt with one by one."[2] Since organized power will prevail over individual effort in politics, sooner or later, organizations will come to be the more important actors in political life. And organizations cannot function without leaders. In the words of European sociologist Robert Michels, "He who says organization, says oligarchy."[3] The masses are permanently incapable of running or controlling political organizations. They must give that power to active, expert, and interested leadership groups. The idea that economic elites will tend to dominate in politics is also found in a great deal of social theory. Mosca wrote that the ruling class will possess ". . . some attribute real or apparent which is highly esteemed or very influential in the society in which they live." Needless to say, in a capitalist society, control over business and financial resources generally makes one "highly esteemed and very influential."

POWER IN "MIDDLETOWN"   One of the earliest studies of American communities, the classic study of Middletown, conducted by sociologists Robert and Helen

---

[1]Gaetano Mosca, *The Ruling Class* (New York: McGraw-Hill, 1939), p. 50.
[2]Ibid., p. 51.
[3]Robert Michels, *Political Parties* (Glencoe, IL: The Free Press, 1949).

Lynd in the mid-1920s and again in the mid-1930s, confirmed a great deal of elitist thinking about community power.[4] The Lynds found in Muncie, Indiana, a monolithic power structure dominated by the owners of the town's largest industry. Community power was firmly entrenched in the hands of the business class, centering on, but not limited to, the "X family."[5] The power of this group was based upon its control over the economic life in the city, particularly its ability to control the extension of credit. The city was run by a "small top group" of "wealthy local manufacturers, bankers, the local head managers of . . . national corporations with units in Middletown, and . . . one or two outstanding lawyers." Democratic procedures and governmental institutions were so much window dressing for business control. The Lynds described the typical city official as a "man of meager calibre" and as "a man whom the inner business control group ignores economically and socially and uses politically." Perhaps the most famous quotation from the Lynds' study was a comment by a Middletown man made in 1935:

> If I'm out of work, I go to the X plant; if I need money I go to the X bank, and if they don't like me I don't get it; my children go to the X college; when I get sick I go to the X hospital; I buy a building lot or house in the X subdivision; my wife goes downtown to buy X milk; I drink X beer, vote for X political parties, and get help from X charities; my boy goes to the X YMCA and my girl to their YWCA; I listen to the word of God in X subsidized churches; if I'm a Mason, I go to the X Masonic temple; I read the news from the X morning paper; and, if I'm rich enough, I travel via the X airport.[6]

POWER IN "REGIONAL CITY"   One of the most influential studies of community politics was sociologist Floyd Hunter's *Community Power Structure,* a study of Atlanta, Georgia.[7] According to Hunter, no one person or family or business dominated "Regional City" (a synonym for Atlanta), as might be true in a smaller town. Instead, Hunter described several tiers of influentials, with the most important community decisions reserved for a top layer of the business community. Admission to the innermost circle was based primarily on one's position in the business world. These top decision makers were not formally organized but conferred informally and passed down decisions to government leaders, professional personnel, civic organizations, and other "figure heads." Hunter explained that the top power structure only concerned itself with major policy decisions; there were other substructures—economic, governmental, religious, ed-

---

[4]Robert S. Lynd and Helen M. Lynd, *Middletown* (New York: Harcourt Brace & World, 1929); and *Middletown in Transition* (New York: Harcourt Brace & World, 1937). Other classic community studies include W. Lloyd Warner et al., *Democracy in Jonesville* (New York: Harper & Row, 1949); and August B. Hollingshead, *Elmtown's Youth* (New York: John Wiley, 1949).

[5]The "X family," never identified in the Lynds' books, was actually the Ball family, glass manufacturers. As late as 1975 the Ball family exercised a controlling influence over the Ball Corporation, Ball Brothers Foundation, Ball Memorial Hospital, Muncie Aviation Corp., and Muncie Airport, Inc.; and E. F. Ball served as a director of American National Bank and Trust of Muncie, Borg-Warner Corp., Indiana Bell Telephone Co., Merchants National Bank of Muncie, and Wabash College. Ball State University in Muncie is named for the family.

[6]Lynd and Lynd, *Middletown in Transition*, p. 74.

[7]Floyd Hunter, *Community Power Structure* (Chapel Hill: University of North Carolina Press, 1953).

Figure 13-1
POWER IN "REGIONAL CITY"

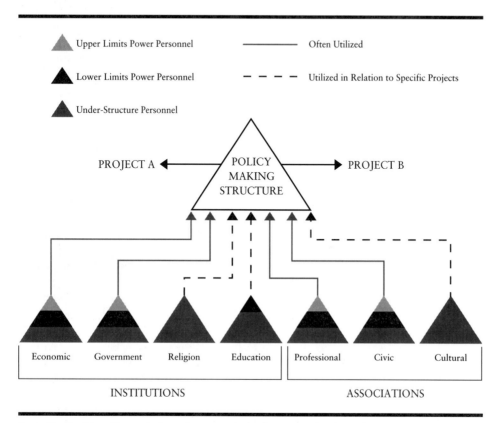

Source: Reprinted from *Community Power Structure: A Study of Decision Makers,* by Floyd Hunter. Copyright © 1953 by the University of North Carolina Press. Used by permission of the publisher.

ucational, professional, civic, and cultural—that communicated and implemented the politics. (See Figure 13-1.) These substructures

> . . . are subordinate, however, to the interests of the policy makers who operate in the economic sphere of community life in Regional City. The institutions of the family, church, state, education, and the like draw sustenance from economic institutional sources and are thereby subordinate to this particular institution more than any other. . . . Within the policy forming groups the economic interests are dominant.[8]

Top power holders seldom operated openly. "Most of the top personnel in the power group are rarely seen in the meetings attended by the associational understructure personnel in Regional City."[9]

---

[8]Ibid., p. 94.
[9]Ibid., p. 90.

In Hunter's description of community decision making, decisions tended to flow *down* from top policy makers, composed primarily of business and financial leaders, to civic, professional, and cultural association leaders, religious and education leaders, and government officials, who implemented the program; and the masses of people had little direct or indirect participation in the whole process. Policy did not go *up* from associational groupings or from the people themselves. According to Hunter, elected public officials are clearly part of the lower-level institutional substructure, which "executed" policy rather than formulated it. Finally, Hunter found that this whole structure was held together by "common interests, mutual obligations, money, habit, delegated responsibilities, and in some cases, by coercion and force."

THE PLURALIST MODEL OF COMMUNITY POWER

Political science had largely ignored the study of community power prior to the publication of Floyd Hunter's *Community Power Structure*. While sociologists had been developing an important body of literature on community power even before the Lynds' safari to darkest Indiana in the 1920s, community politics remained a "lost world" for political scientists.[10] Political science had been preoccupied with the municipal reform movement, the structure of local government, and the administrative problems of economy and efficiency; they had largely ignored informal structures of power and decision making. Hunter's findings were very discomforting. They suggested that in reality American communities were not governed very democratically. Hunter's research challenged the notion of popular participation in "grass-roots" democracy and raised doubts as to whether or not the cherished values of Jeffersonian democracy were being realized in community life. While admitting that "none of us [political scientists] has moved in with such a study in dynamics of power in a metropolitan community," leading political scientists were willing to assert on the basis of their own "administrative experience" that Hunter's study was "at best . . . incomplete at worst . . . invalid."[11] Political scientists believed that much more competition, access, equality, and popular participation occurred in community politics than the work of the Lynds, Hunter, and others implied.

MULTIPLE, COMPETITIVE, INTEREST GROUPS   Modern pluralism does not mean a commitment to "pure democracy," where all citizens participate directly in decision making. The underlying value of individual dignity continues to motivate contemporary pluralist thought, but it is generally recognized that the town-meeting type of pure democracy is not really possible in an urban industrial society. To modern pluralists, individual participation has come to mean membership in *organized groups*. Interest groups become the means by which individuals gain access to the political system. Government is held responsible, not directly by individuals, but by organized interest groups and political parties. Pluralists believe that competition between parties and organized

---

[10]See Lawrence J. R. Herson, "The Lost World of Municipal Government," *American Political Science Review*, 51 (June 1957), 330–45.

[11]Herbert Kaufman and Victor Jones, "The Mystery of Power," *Public Administration Review*, 14 (Summer 1954), 205–12.

groups, representing the interests of their citizen members, can protect the dignity of the individual and offer a viable alternative to individual participation in decision making.

The pluralist model of community power stresses the fragmentation of authority, the influence of elected public officials, the importance of organized group activity, and the role of public opinion and elections in determining public policy. Who rules in the pluralist community? "Different small groups of interested and active citizens in different issue areas with some overlap, if any, by public officials, and occasional intervention by a large number of people at the polls."[12]

POWER IN NEW HAVEN   Perhaps the most influential of the pluralist community studies was Robert A. Dahl's *Who Governs?*, a detailed analysis of decision making in New Haven, Connecticut. Dahl chose to examine sixteen major decisions on redevelopment and public education in New Haven and on nominations for mayor in both political parties for seven elections. Dahl found a polycentric and dispersed system of community power in New Haven, in contrast to Hunter's highly monolithic and centralized power structure. Influence was exercised from time to time by many individuals, each exercising power over some issue but not over others. When the issue was one of urban renewal, one set of individuals was influential; in public education, a different group of leaders was involved. Business elites, who were said by Hunter to control Atlanta, were only one of many different influential groups in New Haven. According to Dahl,

> The economic notables, far from being a ruling group, are simply one of many groups out of which individuals sporadically emerge to influence the politics and acts of city officials. Almost anything one might say about the influence of the economic notables could be said with equal justice about a half dozen other groups in the New Haven community.[13]

The mayor of New Haven was the only decision maker who was influential in most of the issue areas studied, and his degree of influence varied from issue to issue:

> The mayor was not at the peak of a pyramid but at the center of intersecting circles. He rarely commanded. He negotiated, cajoled, exhorted, beguiled, charmed, pressed, appealed, reasoned, promised, insisted, demanded, even threatened; but he most needed support and acquiescence from other leaders who simply could not be commanded. Because he could not command them, he had to bargain.[14]

DIFFERENT APPROACHES TO THE STUDY OF COMMUNITY POWER

Social scientists have used different methods to study community power. To some extent these different methods explain the different *findings* of elitists and pluralists. Sociologists, including the elitists, study the entire social structure of the community, and they view power as a by-product of social and economic position. Persons in a position to con-

---

[12]Aaron Wildavsky, *Leadership in a Small Town* (Totowa, NJ: Bedminster Press, 1964), p. 8.

[13]Robert Dahl, *Who Governs?* (New Haven: Yale University Press, 1961), p. 72.

[14]Ibid., p 204.

trol the social and economic life of the community are said to have political power whether they exercise it or not. In contrast, pluralists define power as participation in decision making. Persons are said to have power only when they participate directly in a particular community decision.

PLURALIST OBJECTIONS TO ELITIST METHODS   Pluralists object to the presupposition that people who control economic resources are necessarily in positions of power:

> . . . nothing categorical can be assumed about power in any community. . . . If anything, there seems to be an unspoken notion among pluralist researchers that at bottom nobody dominates in a town, so that their first question is not likely to be, "Who runs this community?," but rather, "Does anyone at all run this community?" The first query is somewhat like, "Have you stopped beating your wife?," in that virtually any response short of total unwillingness to answer will supply the researchers with a "power elite" along the lines presupposed by the stratification theory.[15]

REPUTATION VERSUS REALITY   The pluralists also attack the use of certain sociological methods in community research. According to the pluralists, the interview technique inquires about the *reputation* of power rather than about the *reality* of power. By asking people what they think about power distributions in the community, elitist researchers are at best only conducting a public-opinion poll about power. They are asking about beliefs and reputations, rather than observing actual behavior.

GENERALIZED VERSUS SPECIFIC POWER   Moreover, elitist researchers' concern for social structure, the persistence through time of power relations, lead them to phrase their questions about influence and leadership in general terms rather than to tie them to specific issues or decisions. For example, Hunter asked the following question:

> Suppose a major project were before the community, one that required decision by a group of leaders whom nearly everyone would accept. Which persons would you choose to make up this group—regardless of whether or not you know them personally?

However, pluralists argue that general power rankings can be misleading:

> Most of the reputational researchers, by their failure to specify scopes in soliciting reputations for influence, assume that the power of their leader-nominees is equal for all issues. . . . This is an exceedingly dubious assumption. It is improbable, for instance, that the same people who decide which houses of prostitution are to be protected . . . also plan the public school curriculum.[16]

---

[15]Nelson Polsby, "How to Study Community Power: The Pluralist Alternative," *Journal of Politics*, 21 (1960), 476.

[16]Raymond E. Wolfinger, "Reputation and Reality in the Study of Community Power," *American Sociological Review*, 25 (1960), 636–44.

POTENTIAL FOR POWER VERSUS EXERCISE OF POWER   Pluralists argue that the "reputational technique" results in confusing *status* with *power*. Respondents may offer names of persons who have high status and are well known in the community even though such persons may not actually wield power. A related problem confuses *potential for power* with the *exercise of power*. Respondents may nominate persons who occupy high formal positions in industry or government and could conceivably exercise a great deal of power but who, as a matter of practice, do not. Pluralists believe that the potential for power is not power itself, unless it is actually exercised over specific community decisions.

UNITY VERSUS COMPETITION   Finally, the pluralists argue that elitist researchers usually do not inquire about the existence of unity among the "elite." It is unreasonable to expect that members of the elite *always* agree on everything and that they *always* impose their ideas on unwilling masses. On the other hand, a "ruling elite" should have some common attitudes and interests that are distinguishable from the attitudes and interests of nonelites.[17] The question remains, however, *how much* unity among leaders is required in order to verify the existence of an elite? The fault in elitist methodology is that they seldom attempt to test for any commonality of attitudes or interests among elite members. Instead, they infer unity of interest from similarity in the class or status background of elite members. Yet ample evidence is available that business and financial leaders disagree on many things.

ELITIST OBJECTIONS TO PLURALIST METHODS   Pluralist methods of research, however, are not above criticism either. To the pluralist, power means participation in decision making; it means the activities of individuals in relation to other individuals. In Dahl's words: "*A* has power over *B* to the extent that he can get *B* to do something that *B* would not otherwise do."[18] Dahl conceives of power primarily in terms of the behavior of individuals at a specific point in time. His unit of analysis is the individual actor and not the social system. This is a very critical difference in conceptual starting places, and this difference leads directly to contrasting methodologies.

Because the pluralist defines power as a decision-making activity, it follows that pluralist research into power involves the "decisional technique," that is, a careful examination of a series of concrete public decisions. To study community power, pluralists first select a number of "key public decisions" that have received widespread publicity in the community. Then they identify the people who took an active part in making these decisions and obtain a full account of their actual behavior while these decisions were being made. The methodology involves reportorial techniques that have characterized case studies in political science for many years.

NONCOMPARABLE CASE STUDY METHOD   But, like that of the elitists, the pluralists' definition of power and their methods of study help to determine their find-

---

[17]Robert Dahl, "Critique of the Ruling Elite Model," *American Political Science Review,* 52 (December 1958), 463–69.

[18]Robert Dahl, "The Concept of Power," *Behavioral Science,* 2 (July 1957), 202.

ings and conclusions.[19] First, the case study approach, to which the pluralists are committed, predisposes the researcher to regard each decision as unique. By examining power in relation to a particular decision, one's findings about power are likely to be tied to particular decisional situations. It is not surprising that the pluralist researchers, after compiling a series of separate case studies, conclude that the exercise of power is situational, that different people exercise power over different decisions, and that generalizations about the exercise of power in different issue areas are unwarranted. The case study method predisposes the researcher to see power in situational terms.

NON-DECISION MAKING   The pluralist approach also implies that political power is completely reflected in open public decisions. No doubt power is exercised in resolving the well-publicized public issues, but is this the whole story of community power? Power is also exercised when social or political values or institutions limit public consideration to only those issues that are relatively unthreatening to the power holders.[20] A is exercising power over B when A succeeds in suppressing issues that might in their resolution be seriously detrimental to A's preferences. In other words, elites exercise power when they prevent issues from becoming public controversies. This exercise of power is known as "*non*–decision making."[21] The pluralist researcher who concentrates his or her attention on open "concrete decisions" may overlook the possibility that public decision making has been deliberately limited to relatively noncontroversial matters, notwithstanding the fact that there are serious latent conflicts in a community.

PUBLIC VERSUS PRIVATE DECISIONS   Pluralist methodology not only overlooks nondecisions, but also overlooks private decisions. Pluralist methodology assumes that the significant community decisions are made publicly; yet there is ample evidence that many of the most important decisions in a community are private decisions. Land use and development decisions, industrial-location and employment decisions, housing decisions, and many other important economic decisions that profoundly affect every aspect of community life are largely private decisions made with little public visibility. How can pluralists legitimately exclude these kinds of decisions from their analyses? They cannot claim that such decisions are not made. Their only recourse is to distinguish between *public* and *private* decisions and to claim that their interest is in *public* decisions. In other words, their only recourse is to narrow the scope of political science

[19]Thomas J. Anton, "Power, Pluralism, and Local Politics," *Administrative Science Quarterly,* 7 (March 1963), 425–57; Peter Bachrach and Morton S. Baratz, "Two Faces of Power," *American Political Science Review,* 56 (December 1962), 947–53.

[20]Bachrach and Baratz, "Two Faces of Power," pp. 947–53; Peter Bachrach and Morton S. Baratz, "Decisions and Nondecisions," *American Political Science Review,* 57 (September 1963),632–42.

[21]For an interesting debate over the concept of non–decision making, see Geoffrey Debnam, "Nondecisions and Power: The Two Faces of Bachrach and Baratz," and Peter Bachrach and Morton S. Baratz, "Power and Its Two Faces Revisited," *American Political Science Review,* 69 (September 1975), 889–904; see also Richard M. Merelman, "On the Neo-Elitist Critique of Community Power," *American Political Science Review,* 62 (June 1968), 451–60; Raymond Wolfinger, "Nondecisions and the Study of Local Politics," *American Political Science Review,* 65 (December 1971), 1063–80.

to public decision making. By arbitrarily limiting their subject matter, they can escape the responsibility for dealing with private decisions.

CONTRASTING INTERPRETATION OF FINDINGS   Even pluralist researchers report that very few people exercise influence in community affairs. Dahl and others acknowledge that the total number of people involved in concrete public decisions is a very small minority of the community. All pluralist researchers recognize that persons exercising leadership in each issue area are of higher social status than the rest of the community. These middle- and upper-class people possess more of the skills and qualities required of leaders in a democratic system.

In short, neither the elitist nor the pluralist model of community power is the equivalent of the American ideal of grass-roots democracy—a government of, by, and for the people, in which individuals decide their own future and all have an equal voice in the affairs of their communities.

SYSTEMIC POWER AND STRATEGIC ADVANTAGE

All known societies have some system of ranking their members. Sociologists use the term *stratification* to refer to the classification of individuals and their ranking along a superiority–inferiority scale. The United States Constitution guarantees legal and political equality of individuals, especially in its Equal Protection Clause; but in most other dimensions of society—income and wealth, occupation and institutional position, social status and lifestyle—we recognize differences among individuals and rank these differences according to their desirability.

The American system of stratification tends to be diamond shaped: a small upper class, a large middle class, and a somewhat smaller lower class. The advantage of numbers—an important source of power in the electoral system—accrues to the middle class, not the lower class. All other sources of power are distributed unequally from top to bottom:

- *Economic power.* The top stratum enjoys great wealth and income and control of corporations, banks, and other economic enterprises. The middle stratum has job skills, occupational positions, and moderate amounts of personal wealth and income. The lower stratum is largely economically dependent. Individuals in this stratum receive more governmental revenues than they produce.
- *Institutional position.* The top stratum occupies positions of authority in institutions that organize society's resources—corporations, banks, utilities, television networks and stations, newspapers, foundations, universities, law firms, civic and cultural organizations. The middle stratum occupies middle- and lower-level positions in these same organizations and may also occupy key positions in government, unions, recreational associations, and churches. The bottom stratum is seldom organized at all. Indeed, most organizations claiming to represent the poor are run by middle- and upper-class people.
- *Social status and lifestyle.* The top stratum enjoys education, travel, leisure, clubs, and a social and cultural life that is widely envied. The middle classes try to emulate the upper-class lifestyles and succeed to a limited degree. But lower-class lifestyle is restricted; goals are immediate and limited, and activities are protective or escapist.

DECISION MAKING AND STRATIFICATION   Community decision making takes place within a stratified social system. It defies common sense to argue, as pluralists do,[22] that community decisions are *unaffected* by the stratification of economic power, institutional position, and lifestyle. Public officials—mayors, council members, commissioners, school board members, authority directors, and board members—as well as managers, administrators, and public employees, civic association officers, and interest group officers, all function within the larger stratified society. They must maintain and enhance their own income, position, and lifestyle; and their behavior will be patterned by the system of stratification.

Power is exercised in open public decisions *and* in the distribution of advantages and disadvantages among individuals and groups within society. *Systemic power* refers to outcomes that are attributed to the stratification system's distribution of advantages and disadvantages. *Strategic advantage* refers to the power that the top stratum enjoys because of its income and wealth, positional authority, and status and lifestyle.[23]

ANTICIPATED REACTIONS   Systemic power may take many forms. Power is being exercised when public officials or administrators base their own behavior on the anticipated reactions of powerful people within the community. *A* has power over *B* if *B* modifies his or her conduct because of fear of *A*'s reaction or a need to stay in *A*'s good graces to obtain some future benefit. Note that *A* and *B* do not have to communicate directly. *A* may not even know what *B* is doing (or not doing) to win favor; there is no open public decision. The strength of this power relationship is determined by the distribution of wealth and income, position, and lifestyle in the larger society, and the desire of public officials and administrators to maintain and enhance their share of these benefits now or in the future.

AGENDA SETTING   In agenda setting, power is being exercised in the selection of topics or problems to be addressed by government. Power is being exercised when someone suppresses an issue that might adversely affect their interests if it came up for a public vote on the council. This is a direct yet covert exercise of power. But power is also being exercised by groups who regularly succeed in getting their issues placed on a crowded agenda when there is competition for the space. Power is also being exercised when other groups are unable to attract public attention to their problems or articulate their problems and present their case for public action.

OPPORTUNITY COSTS   With opportunity costs, power is being exercised when the costs of political success are higher for some groups than others. Persons in the top social stratum must expend a smaller proportion of their total resources than persons in the bottom social stratum to achieve a political goal. "The weak must struggle while the

---

[22]See Nelson W. Polsby, *Community Power and Political Theory,* 2nd ed. (New Haven: Yale University Press, 1980).

[23]See Clarence N. Stone, "Systemic Power in Community Decision-Making: A Restatement of Stratification Theory," *American Political Science Review,* 74 (December 1980), 978–90.

strong have only to ask."[24] Public officials and administrators frequently ask business and community leaders "what things need doing?" The poor, by contrast, frequently need protests, marches, or direct action to call attention to their concerns. "The truly powerful are often able to achieve their aims with little effort, whereas those who are less powerful must make a much greater effort to achieve the same results."[25]

The disadvantaged in society often appear passive and quiescent. The pluralist researcher is obliged to conclude that they confront no serious problems or concerns. But quiescence may only signify that the poor are not well positioned to act on their grievances. With few resources, they cannot undertake costly battles that they are likely to lose. Indeed, when the poor *do* act politically, it is usually on behalf of some immediate and tangible benefit, rather than long-range or fundamental change. It is logical for the poor to spend their limited political resources for short-term goals with some likelihood of success.

MOBILIZATION OF BIAS   In a case of mobilization of bias, power is exercised in the way the political system is organized. Some forms of organization make it difficult for some issues to be raised and difficult for government to address some problems. For example, it is difficult for local governments to adopt policies that redistribute income from rich to poor; any community that taxed the rich heavily in order to generously support the poor would drive out its wealthy residents and attract large numbers of poor. Competition between communities and the ability of both rich and poor to move freely among communities prevent local governments from adapting highly redistributive policies.

It is true that the governmental system is based upon the principle of equality—equal protection of the laws, one-person–one-vote, and majority rule. This means that if an issue becomes a highly publicized, open public decision made by the elected governmental body, it is likely that public officials will be influenced by majority opinion. But the upper stratum enjoys an advantage when decisions have low public visibility, when public officials are least accountable to the general public, and when these officials are free to pursue their own private interests.

ECONOMIC POWER IN COMMUNITIES

Great power derives from control of economic resources. Most of the nation's economic resources are controlled by national institutions—industrial corporations, banks, utilities, insurance companies, investment firms, and the national government. Most of the forces shaping life in American communities arise outside of these communities; community leaders cannot make war or peace, or cause inflation or recession, or determine interest rates or the money supply.

CONTROL OF LAND USE   But there is one economic resource—land—which *is* controlled by communities. Land is a valuable resource: Capital investment, labor and management, and production must be placed somewhere. Traditionally, community

---

[24]Ibid., p. 981.
[25]Ibid.

power structures were composed primarily of economic elites whose goals were to maximize land values, real estate commissions, builders' profits, rent payments, and mortgage interest, as well as to increase revenues to commercial enterprises serving the community. Communities were traditionally dominated by mortgage-lending banks, real estate developers, builders, and landowners. They were joined by owners or managers of local utilities, department stores, attorneys and title companies, and others whose wealth was affected by land use. Local bankers who financed the real estate developers and builders were often at the center of the elite structure in communities. Unquestionably these community elites competed among themselves for wealth, profit, power, and preeminence. But they shared a consensus about intensifying the use of land. Corporate plants and offices, federal and state office buildings, and universities and colleges all contributed to the increased land values, not only on the parcels used by these facilities but also on neighboring parcels.

GROWTH AS SHARED ELITE VALUE   Growth was the shared elite value. The community elite was indeed a "growth machine."[26] Economic growth expands the work force and disposable income within the community. It stimulates housing development, retail stores, and other commercial activity. The economic elite understands that they all benefit, albeit to varying degrees, when economic growth occurs within the community. Not only must a community compete for new investments, but it must also endeavor to prevent relocation of investments it already has.

ELITE STRIVING FOR CONSENSUS   Community economic elites strive for consensus. They believe that community economic growth—increased capital investment, more jobs, and improved business conditions—benefit the entire community. According to Paul E. Peterson, community residents share a common interest in the economic well-being of the city:

> Policies and programs can be said to be in the interest of cities whenever the policies maintain or enhance the economic position, social prestige, or political power of the city as a whole.[27]

Community economic elites themselves would doubtlessly agree with Peterson. He adds that the interests of the city as a whole are closely bound to its export industries. These industries add net wealth to the community at large, while support and service industries merely transfer wealth within the community.

> Whatever helps them prosper redounds to the benefit of the community as a whole—perhaps four or five times over. It is just such an economic analysis (of the multiplier effect of export industries) that has influenced many local government policies. Especially the smaller

---

[26]See Harvey Molotch, "The City as Growth Machine," *American Journal of Sociology,* 82 (September 1976), 309–30; and "Capital and Neighborhood in the United States," *Urban Affairs Quarterly,* 14 (March 1979) 289–312.

[27]Paul E. Peterson, *City Limits* (Chicago: University of Chicago Press, 1981), p. 20.

towns and cities may provide free land, tax concessions, and favorable utility rates to in-coming industries.[28]

The less economically developed a community, the more persuasive the argument on be-half of export industries.

GROWTH AS GOOD POLITICS   Economic elites expect local government officials to share in the growth consensus. Economic prosperity is necessary for protect-ing the fiscal base of local government. Growth in local budgets and public employment, as well as governmental services, depends upon growth in the local economy. Govern-mental growth expands the power, prestige, and status of government officials. Moreover, economic growth is usually good politics. Growth-oriented candidates for public office usually have larger campaign treasuries than antigrowth candidates. Growth-oriented candidates can solicit contributions from the community power structure. Finally, ac-cording to Peterson, most local politicians have "a sense of community responsibility." They know that if the economy of the community declines, "local business will suffer, workers will lose employment opportunities, cultural life will decline, and city land values will fall."[29]

POLITICAL POWER IN COMMUNITIES

But consensus on behalf of economic growth is sometimes challenged by other commu-nity interests. However much the economic elite may strive for consensus, some people do not like growth, and they are willing to use political power to stop it.

OPPOSITION TO GROWTH   Indeed, it has become fashionable in upper-middle-class circles today to complain loudly about the problems created by growth—congestion, pollution, noise, unsightly development, or the replacement of green spaces with concrete slabs. People who already own their houses and do not intend to sell them, people whose jobs are secure in government bureaucracies or tenured professorships, people who may be displaced from their homes and neighborhoods by new facilities, peo-ple who see no direct benefit to themselves from growth, and businesses or industries who fear the new competition that growth may bring to the community, all combine to form a potentially powerful *counter-elite*.[30]

Not all of the opposition to growth is upper-middle-class in character. Students of com-munity power have described the struggle of blacks and low-income neighborhood groups in opposing urban renewal and downtown city development. However, this liter-ature suggests that traditional community elites are likely to be successful against this kind of opposition. We might speculate that the "growth machine" elites are more concerned about opposition from educated, affluent, upper-middle-class, "growth-management"

---

[28]Ibid., p. 23.

[29]Ibid., p. 29.

[30]For a parallel argument, see Heywood T. Sanders and Clarence N. Stone, "Developmental Politics Reconsidered," *Urban Affairs Quarterly,* 22 (June 1987), 521–39; and Mark Schneider, "Undermining the Growth Machine," *Journal of Politics,* 54 (February 1992), 214–30.

homeowners than they are about opposition from minority, low-income neighborhood groups.

NO-GROWTH MOVEMENTS

No-growth movements (or, to use the current euphemism, "growth-management" movements) are *not* mass movements. They do *not* express the aspirations of workers for jobs or renters for their own homes. Instead, they reflect upper-middle-class lifestyle preferences of educated, affluent, articulate homeowners. Growth brings ugly factories, cheap commercial outlets, hamburger stands, fried chicken franchises, and "undesirable" residents. Even if new business or industry would help hold down local taxes, these affluent citizens would still oppose it. They would rather pay the higher taxes associated with no growth than change the appearance or lifestyle of their community. They have secure jobs themselves and own their homes; they are relatively unconcerned about creating jobs or building homes for less affluent citizens.

No-growth movements challenge traditional economic elites in many large and growing cities in the West and South. The no-growth leaders may themselves have been beneficiaries of community growth only five or ten years ago, but they quickly perceive their own interest in slowing or halting additional growth. Now that they have climbed the ladder to their own success, they are prepared to knock the ladder down to preserve their own style of living.

TOOLS TO RESTRICT GROWTH

Municipal government offers the tools to challenge the growth elite. (See Chapter 16.) Communities may restrict growth through zoning laws, subdivision control restrictions, utility regulations, building permits, and environmental regulations. Opposition to street widening, road building, or tree cutting can slow or halt development. Public utilities needed for development—water lines, sewage disposal facilities, fire houses, and so on—can be postponed indefinitely. High development fees, "impact fees," utility hookup charges, or building permit fees can all be used to discourage growth. Environmental laws, or even "historic preservation" laws, can be employed aggressively to halt development.

PLURALISM AND ELITISM RECONCILED?

Elitist and pluralist models of community power have inspired great debate in the social sciences over the years. But can these models be reconciled? Perhaps our best understanding of community power comes about through diversity in theories and methods of study. Students of community power are better advised to ask "What can each model tell us about community power?" rather than "What are the shortcomings of each model?" Elitist and pluralist models might be reconciled in several ways.

ELITISM IN DEVELOPMENTAL POLICIES

First of all, elitist and pluralist models of community decision making may each be more accurate in separate policy areas. The influence of traditional community economic elites—mortgage bankers, real estate developers, builders and land owners—is more likely to be felt in *developmental policies*. These include efforts to attract industry, build streets and highways, improve airports, renew depressed areas, construct convention centers, and so on. The earliest studies of the activities of community power structures appear to describe developmental policy making. The elitist model of community power accurately describes the private and public influence of the community's economic leadership over developmental policies.

Reputations for power in the community are often made in developmental politics. This should not really surprise us. Job, home, and business are viewed by most people as the most important aspects of their lives. Those people in the community who are in a position to influence job opportunities, home building, and industrial and commercial developments are viewed by most residents as "powerful." So when residents are asked to make general judgments about power in their community, they name bankers, developers, builders, and business people. They do not usually name school board members, civic association officers, neighborhood activists, police or fire chiefs, minority group leaders, or even city council members. These persons may be active in other areas of policy making, but most citizens understand that the really important developmental policies—policies that directly affect jobs, houses, and business—will be largely determined by the community's economic elite.

ELITISM IN REDISTRIBUTIONAL POLICIES   *Redistributional policies* are not designed to add to the net economic well-being of the whole community, but to benefit low-income residents by redirecting the economic resources of the community. Most redistributional policies in the United States—social security, welfare, medical care, unemployment compensation—are undertaken by state and national governments. Local governments are only occasionally called upon to decide redistributional questions. Many cities provide low-income housing, indigent hospital care, shelters for the homeless, and other services that are only partially covered by state or federal funds.

Redistribution policies seldom involve community economic elites directly. They have an interest in keeping redistributional questions *out* of local politics, since their resolution may jeopardize members' wealth and income. Elites may manipulate the local policy agenda to exclude redistributional issues and ensure the "unpolitics" of local poverty, through the now familiar tactic of non–decision making. In addition, Peterson argues that the absence of redistributive issues in local politics "is seldom due to the suppressive activities of an organized economic elite," but rather a product of American federalism and the assignment of responsibility for health and income maintenance programs to state and national levels of governments.[31]

Redistributive demands are occasionally raised in community politics, despite the structure of American federalism and the preferences of community economic elites.[32] Riots, protests, rent strikes, demonstrations, and other public manifestations of discontent are threatening to elites. If nothing else, unrest adversely affects the reputation of the community in its efforts to attract new industry. Economic elites cannot altogether ignore redistributive demands.

PLURALISM IN ALLOCATIONAL POLICIES   *Allocation policies* describe the broad range of traditional public services provided by local government—schools,

---

[31]Peterson, *City Limits*, p. 38.

[32]Paul K. Eisenger, "The Conditions of Protest Behavior in American Cities," *American Political Science Review,* 67 (March 1973), 11–29; Michael Lipsky, *Protest in City Politics* (Chicago: Rand McNally, 1970); Clarence Stone, *Economic Growth and Neighborhood Discontent* (Chapel Hill: University of North Carolina Press, 1976).

streets, sewer, water and utilities, garbage collection, and parks and recreation, and so on. There are, of course, frequent distributional arguments over the provisions of these services. Occasionally the quality of these services becomes a developmental issue when potential investors express a concern about them. But, overall, these allocational policies are developmentally and distributionally neutral.

Economic elites are seldom directly interested or active in allocation policy. The allocational policy arena is pluralist in character. Decisions about police and fire protection, street maintenance, garbage collection, sewage disposal, school attendance boundaries, recreation, libraries, public buildings, and the like are usually made by elected public officials or professional managers employed by them. Council members, managers, school board members, and superintendents are responsive to the expressed demands of many varied and often competing groups within the community. Participation in decision making is open to anyone who attends public meetings, gathers petitions, or writes letters to the editor. Interest and activity rather than economic resources are the key to leadership in allocational policy. Access is based upon information about the issues, knowledge of the political process, and organizational and public relations skills. Community organizations are instruments by which individuals magnify their voices in public affairs. No single group of people dominates decision making in *all* of their service functions of a community's city, county, and school district governments. Elected officials are very sensitive to the opinions of their constituents on service questions. Allocational policies are material and divisible, so allocative policies can easily reflect compromises among competing groups. These are the familiar characteristics of pluralist politics.

Much of what takes place in local government—at commission meetings, public hearings, school board meetings, and in the offices of city managers and school superintendents—involves allocational policies. It is easy for pluralist scholars studying local government to mistake allocational politics for the whole of community politics. This error is facilitated by a narrow and traditional definition of political science as the study of *government* and the consequent exclusion of community social structure from the purview of pluralist studies. Allocational policies are the "key public decisions" studied by pluralist researchers, and governmental bodies are the locus of their studies.

PLURALISM AND ORGANIZATIONAL POLICIES   *Organizational policies* encompass decisions about the structure of decision making in the community. These polices include the composition, terms, and legal activity of school boards, city and county commissions, city managers, school superintendents, independent authorities and boards, and other elected officials. Typical issues may include whether or not to have a city manager, a mayor-council, or a commission form of government, at-large or district elections, partisan or nonpartisan elections, an elected or appointed school superintendent, and so forth. Personnel and employment policies may also be considered organizational—that is, who gets elected to community office and who gets hired by the city. Sometimes these questions become redistributional when issues of minority or low-income representation are raised. Sometimes these questions are intertwined with allocational issues, as when incumbents are charged with poor performance on the job.

Economic elites are usually only interested bystanders in organizational politics. While it is true that their "class interests" would appear to place them on the side of the upper-class reformers, we know that bankers, developers, and builders had little difficulty in dealing with big-city machines. Indeed, machines were often better in "getting things done at City Hall"—that is, moving growth projects to completion—than reformed administrations (see Chapter 10). There is no question that economic elites thrived under urban political machines.

Likewise, current disputes over organizational policies—the representation of blacks and other minorities in elected offices and municipal jobs—do not threaten economic interests. While the rhetoric of urban black politics frequently calls for massive income redistribution, the reality of black city administrations is quite different. Whatever fears white propertied elites may have had years ago about black power in the nation's cities should now be put to rest. There is no evidence that the nation's black mayors are hostile to economic growth and development.

DIFFERENT MODELS FOR PUBLIC AND PRIVATE DECISIONS
Another way to reconcile elitist and pluralist models of community power is to recognize that some community decisions are public, that is, made by governmental bodies, while others are private, made by real estate developers, banks and mortgage companies, builders and land owners, investors and business people. Private decisions may have as much or even more impact on life in a community than decisions made by government. The pluralist model may be best suited for understanding public decision making, while the elite model may better describe private decision making. Indeed, many pluralists now acknowledge that economic elites have a "privileged position" regarding decisions that are vital to society.[33] If we are to understand the full range of decisions that shape the community—public and private—we will have to consider both public and private power. This requires an integration of studies of governmental decision making with studies of systemic forces—economic power, institutional position, social status, and lifestyle.

DIFFERENT MODELS PORTRAY DIFFERENT COMMUNITIES Finally, power structures may vary across communities. Some communities may have more concentrated, pyramidal structures of power dominated by economic elites, while other communities may have diffused and multicentered power structures with competing citizens' groups, neighborhood associations, developers, environmentalists, and so forth. For example, large communities with a great deal of social and economic diversity, a competitive party system, and a variety of well-organized competing interest groups may tend to have *pluralist* decision-making systems. On the other hand, small communities with homogeneous populations, a single dominant industry, nonpartisan elections, and few competing organizations may have power structures resembling the *elite* model.

---

[33]Charles E. Lindbloom, Politics and Markets (New York: Basic Books, 1977), chap. 13.

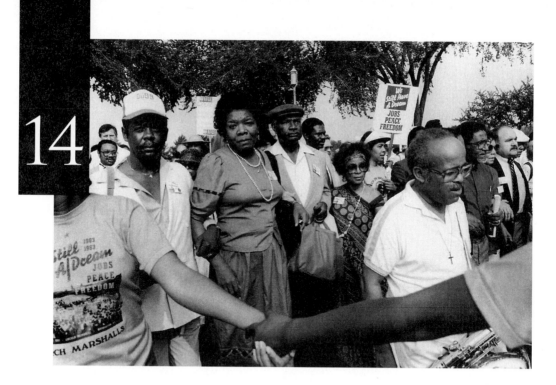

POLITICS AND CIVIL RIGHTS

FROM PROTEST TO POWER

African Americans and Hispanics have made significant progress in urban politics in recent years. The progress of these minorities in city government has important implications for the future of the American political system, because these are the two largest minority groups in the country. Minorities were almost totally excluded from significant influence in city politics prior to the 1960s. We have already discussed increases in black representation in city councils (Chapter 11) and state legislatures (Chapter 6), and black political power in the nation's largest cities is a recognized fact of American politics. As former Atlanta Mayor Andrew Young said, "It's like the old preacher says: we ain't what we oughta be; we ain't what we gonna be; but thank God we ain't what we was."[1]

VARIATION IN RESPONSIVENESS TO URBAN MINORITIES One important test of a democratic system is its responsiveness to the demands of newly mo-

---

[1]Quotation in Rufus P. Browning, Dale Rogers Marshall, and David H. Tabb, *Protest Is Not Enough: The Struggle of Blacks and Hispanics for Equality in Urban Politics* (Berkeley: University of California Press, 1984), p. 17.

bilized groups. Comparative studies of city governments suggest that there are significant variations in their responsiveness to the demands of newly mobilized minority groups. In an important study of ten California cities over a twenty-year period, appropriately titled *Protest Is Not Enough*, the authors observed that:

> In some cities, quite remarkable levels of responsiveness to minority interests were achieved, and minority representatives came to occupy positions of authority and respect.
>
> In other cities, relationships between white and minority leaders were more manipulative and co-operative, though significant concessions to minority interests were made.
>
> And in still other cities, established interests successfully resisted minority demands and efficiently excluded minority representation from influence.[2]

CONDITIONS FOR SUCCESS   What determines the success or failure of minorities to gain influence in urban politics? The conditions associated with minority success were:

The absolute size of minority groups in the city.

The size of supportive groups, especially white liberals.

A strategy of combining protests with a willingness to form electoral coalitions.

Protests by themselves produced only limited results. Extreme protests delayed progress.

Protest alone is insufficient to bring about lasting political change. Protest must be accompanied by political mobilization, the formation of electoral coalitions, and winning public office.

> We know that protest is not enough. . . . Protest must be translated into electoral organizing, the traditional political activity of recruiting candidates, controlling the number who run, and developing support and coalitions.[3]

POLICY CONSEQUENCES   Do city government policies change as a result of minority incorporation into the political system? Black elected officials in cities perceive poverty and unemployment as more severe problems than do white officials in the same cities; and black officeholders are more likely to add race relations and racial balance in the distribution of city jobs and services to the policy agenda.[4] Another consequence of the election of blacks to public office, especially the mayor's office, is an increase in political participation among black citizens.[5]

But many city government policies, especially taxing and spending policies, are severely constrained by economic conditions and by limits and mandates set by the state and fed-

---

[2]Ibid., p. 8.

[3]Ibid., p. 213.

[4]Carmine Scavo, "Racial Integration of Local Government Leadership in Small Southern Cities," *Social Science Quarterly*, 71 (June 1990), 362–72.

[5]Lawrence Bobo and Franklin D. Gilliam, Jr., "Race, Sociopolitical Participation, and Black Empowerment," *American Political Science Review*, 84 (June 1990), 377–86.

eral governments.[6] So it is unrealistic to expect major shifts in these policies to accompany the election of blacks or Hispanics to city office. The policies that respond to minority representation in city government are those that deal directly with minority presence in government. Broad taxing and spending policies are largely *unaffected* by minority influence in government. Examples of the kind of policy changes directly attributable to minority representation in government include the creation of police review boards, the appointment of more minorities to city boards and commissions, increasing use of minority contractors, and a general increase in the number of programs oriented toward minorities. Perhaps the most significant policy impact of minority representation on city councils is an increase in the number of minorities in city employment and their employment in higher-grade positions.[7]

THE STRUGGLE AGAINST SEGREGATION

The Fourteenth Amendment of the U.S. Constitution declares:

> All persons born or naturalized in the United States, and subject to the jurisdiction thereof, are citizens of the United States and of the State wherein they reside. No State shall make or enforce any law which shall abridge the privileges or immunities of citizens of the United States; nor shall any State deprive any person of life, liberty, or property, without due process of law; nor deny to any person within its jurisdiction the equal protection of the laws.

The language of the Fourteenth Amendment and its post–Civil War historical context leave little doubt that its original purpose was to achieve the full measure of citizenship and equality for American blacks. Some "radical" Republicans were prepared in 1867 to carry out the revolution in southern society that this amendment implied. Under military occupation, southern states adopted new constitutions that awarded the vote and full civil liberties to blacks, and southern states were compelled to ratify the Thirteenth, Fourteenth, and Fifteenth Amendments to the U.S. Constitution. Blacks were elected to southern state legislatures and to the Congress; the first black to serve in Congress, Hiram R. Revels, took over the U.S. Senate seat from Mississippi previously held by Confederate President Jefferson Davis.

However, by 1877 Reconstruction was abandoned. The national government was not willing to carry out the long and difficult task of really reconstructing society in the eleven states of the former Confederacy.[8] In what has been described as the "Compromise of 1877," the national government agreed to end military occupation of the South, give up its efforts to rearrange southern society, and lend tacit approval to white supremacy in

---

[6]See Paul Peterson, *City Limits* (Chicago: University of Chicago Press, 1981).

[7]See Kenneth R. Mladenka, "Blacks and Hispanics in Urban Politics," *American Political Science Review*, 83 (March 1989), 165–91; Thomas R. Dye and James Renick, "Political Power and City Jobs: Determinants of Minority Employment," *Social Science Quarterly*, 62 (September 1981), 475–86.

[8]C. Vann Woodward, *Reunion and Reaction: The End of Reconstruction* (Boston: Little, Brown, 1951).

that region. In return, the southern states pledged their support of the Union, accepted national supremacy, and agreed to permit the Republican candidate, Rutherford B. Hayes, to assume the presidency after the disputed election of 1876.

"SEPARATE BUT EQUAL"   The Supreme Court adhered to the terms of the compromise. The result was an inversion of the meaning of the Fourteenth Amendment so that by 1896 it had become a bulwark of segregation. State laws segregating the races were upheld so long as persons in each of the separated races were treated equally. The constitutional argument on behalf of segregation under the Fourteenth Amendment was that the phrase "equal protection of the laws" did not prevent state-enforced *separation* of the races. Schools and other public facilities that were "separate but equal" won constitutional approval.[9] This separate but equal doctrine remained the Supreme Court's interpretation of the Equal Protection Clause of the Fourteenth Amendment until 1954.

As a matter of fact, of course, segregated facilities, including public schools, were seldom if ever equal, even with respect to physical conditions. In practice, the doctrine of segregation was "separate and *un*equal." The Supreme Court began to take notice of this after World War II. While it declined to overrule the segregationist interpretation of the Fourteenth Amendment, it began to order the admission of individual blacks to white public universities, where evidence indicated that separate black institutions were inferior or nonexistent.[10]

NAACP   Leaders of the newly emerging civil rights movement in the 1940s and 1950s were not satisfied with court decisions that examined the circumstances in each case to determine if separate school facilities were really equal. The National Association for the Advancement of Colored People (NAACP), led by Roy Wilkins, its executive director, and Thurgood Marshall, its chief counsel, pressed for a court decision that segregation itself meant inequality within the meaning of the Fourteenth Amendment, whether or not facilities were equal in all tangible respects. In short, they wanted a complete reversal of the "separate but equal" interpretation of the Fourteenth Amendment, and a holding that laws *separating* the races were unconstitutional.

The civil rights groups chose to bring suit for desegregation in Topeka, Kansas, where segregated black and white schools were equal with respect to buildings, curricula, qualifications and salaries of teachers, and other tangible factors. The legal strategy was to prevent the Court from ordering the admission of a black because *tangible* facilities were not equal and to force the Court to review the doctrine of segregation itself.

BROWN V. TOPEKA   On May 17, 1954, the Court rendered its decision in *Brown* v. *Board of Education of Topeka, Kansas:*

> Segregation of white and colored children in public schools has a detrimental effect upon the colored children. The impact is greater when it has the sanction of law, for the policy of separating the races is usually interpreted as denoting the inferiority of the Negro group. A sense of inferiority affects the motivation of a child to learn. Segregation with the sanction

---

[9]*Plessy v. Ferguson*, 163 U.S. 537 (1896).

[10]*Sweatt v. Painter*, 339 U.S. 629 (1950); *McLaurin v. Oklahoma State Regents*, 339 U.S. 637 (1950).

of law, therefore, has a tendency to retard the educational and mental development of Negro children and to deprive them of some of the benefits they would receive in a racially integrated school system.[11]

The symbolic importance of the original *Brown* v. *Topeka* decision cannot be overestimated. While it would be many years before any significant number of black children would attend formerly segregated white schools, the decision by the nation's highest court undoubtedly stimulated black hopes and expectations. Black sociologist Kenneth Clark writes:

> This [civil rights] movement would probably not have existed at all were it not for the 1954 Supreme Court school desegregation decision which provided a tremendous boost to the morale of Negroes by its *clear* affirmation that color is irrelevant to the rights of American citizens. Until this time the Southern Negro generally had accommodated to the separatism of the black from the white society.[12]

STATE RESISTANCE

The Supreme Court had spoken forcefully in the *Brown* case in 1954 in declaring segregation unconstitutional. From a constitutional viewpoint, any state-supported segregation of the races after 1954 was prohibited. Article VI of the Constitution declares that the words of that document are "the supreme law of the land . . . anything in the constitution or laws of any state to the contrary notwithstanding." From a political viewpoint, however, the battle over segregation was just beginning.

SEGREGATION IN THE STATES   In 1954 the practice of segregation was widespread and deeply ingrained in American life. Seventeen states required the segregation of the races in public schools. These seventeen were:

Alabama	North Carolina	Delaware
Arkansas	South Carolina	Kentucky
Florida	Tennessee	Maryland
Georgia	Texas	Missouri
Louisiana	Virginia	Oklahoma
Mississippi		West Virginia

The Congress of the United States required the segregation of the races in the public schools of the District of Columbia.[13] Four additional states—Arizona, Kansas, New Mexico, and Wyoming—authorized segregation upon the option of local school boards. (See Figure 14–1.)

---

[11]*Brown v. Board of Education of Topeka, Kansas,* 347 U.S. 483 (1954).

[12]Kenneth B. Clark, *Dark Ghetto* (New York: Harper & Row, 1965), pp 77–78.

[13]The Supreme Court also ruled that Congress was bound to respect the equal protection doctrine imposed upon the states by the Fourteenth Amendment as part of the due process clause of the Fifth Amendment. *Bolling v. Sharpe,* 347 U.S. 497 (1954).

Figure 14–1
SEGREGATION LAWS IN THE UNITED STATES IN 1954

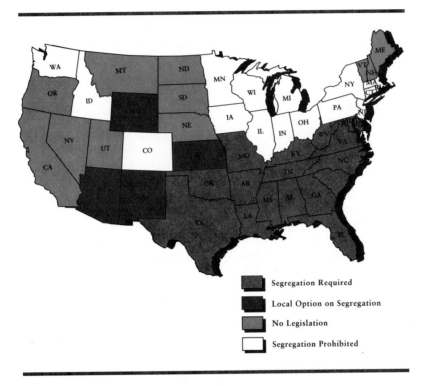

- ■ Segregation Required
- ■ Local Option on Segregation
- ▨ No Legislation
- □ Segregation Prohibited

Thus, in deciding *Brown* v. *Topeka*, the Supreme Court struck down the laws of twenty-one states and the District of Columbia in a single opinion. Such a far-reaching decision was bound to meet with difficulties in implementation. The Supreme Court did not order immediate nationwide desegregation, but instead it turned over the responsibility for desegregation to state and local authorities under the supervision of federal district courts.

The six border states with segregated school systems—Delaware, Kentucky, Maryland, Missouri, Oklahoma, and West Virginia—together with the school districts in Kansas, Arizona, and New Mexico that had operated segregated schools, chose not to resist desegregation. The District of Columbia also desegregated its public schools the year following the Supreme Court's decision.

RESISTANCE   Resistance to school integration was the policy of the eleven states of the Old Confederacy. Refusal of a school district to desegregate until it was faced with a federal court injunction was the most common form of delay. Other schemes included state payment of private school tuition in lieu of providing public schools, amending compulsory attendance laws to provide that no child shall be required to attend an integrated school, requiring schools faced with desegregation orders to cease operation, and the use of pupil-placement laws to avoid or minimize the extent of integration.[14] State officials also attempted to delay desegregation on the grounds that it would endanger public safety.[15] On the whole, those states that chose to resist desegregation were quite successful in doing so during the ten-year period from 1954 to 1964. Ten years after *Brown* v. *Topeka,* only about 2 percent of the black schoolchildren in the eleven southern states were attending integrated schools.

FEDERAL FUNDS   In the Civil Rights Act of 1964, Congress finally entered the civil rights field in support of court efforts to achieve desegregation. Among other things, the Civil Rights Act of 1964 provided that every federal department and agency must take action to end segregation in all programs and activities receiving federal financial assistance. It was specified that this action was to include termination of financial assistance if states and communities receiving federal funds refused to comply with federal desegregation orders. Acting under the authority of Title VI, the U.S. Office of Education (now the Department of Education) required all school districts in the seventeen formerly segregated states to submit desegregation plans as a condition of federal assistance. Progress toward desegregation was speeded up.

UNITARY SCHOOLS   The last vestige of legal justification for delay in implementing school desegregation collapsed in 1969 when the Supreme Court rejected a request by Mississippi school officials for a delay in implementing school desegregation plans in that state. The Supreme Court declared that every school district was obligated to end dual school systems "at once" and "now and hereafter" to operate only unitary schools.[16] The effect of the decision—fifteen years after the original *Brown* case—was to eliminate any further legal justification for the continuation of segregation in public schools.

BUSING AND RACIAL BALANCING IN SCHOOLS

In *Brown* v. *Board of Education of Topeka, Kansas,* the Supreme Court found that segregation had "a tendency to retard the educational and mental development of Negro children and to deprive them of some of the benefits they would receive in a racially integrated school system." The U.S. Civil Rights Commission reported that even when segregation was "de facto," that is, a product of segregated housing patterns and neighborhood schools rather than direct discrimination, the adverse effects on black students were still significant.[17] In northern urban school districts, the commission reported, pre-

---

[14]State laws that were obviously designed to evade constitutional responsibilities to end segregation were struck down in federal courts; but court litigation and delays slowed progress toward integration.

[15]The Supreme Court declared that the threat of violence was not sufficient reason to deny constitutional rights to black children and again dismissed the ancient interposition arguments. *Cooper* v. *Aaron,* 358 U.S. 1 (1958).

[16]*Alexander* v. *Holmes County Board of Education,* 396 U.S. 19 (1969).

[17]United States Commission on Civil Rights, *Racial Isolation in the Public Schools,* 2 vols. (Washington, DC: Government Printing Office, 1967). See also James S. Coleman, *Equality of Educational Opportunity* (Washington, DC: Government Printing Office, 1966).

dominantly black schools were less likely to have good libraries or advanced courses in sciences and languages than predominantly white schools and more likely to have over-crowded classrooms, poorly trained teachers, and teachers who were dissatisfied with their school assignments.

RACIAL BALANCE   Ending racial isolation in the public schools frequently in-volves busing schoolchildren into and out of segregated neighborhoods. The objective is to achieve a racial "balance" in public schools, so that each has roughly the same per-centages of blacks and whites as are found in the total population of the entire school dis-trict. Indeed, in some large cities where blacks comprise the overwhelming majority of public school students, desegregation may require city students to be bused to the suburbs and suburban students to be bused to the core city.

FEDERAL COURT SUPERVISION   Federal district judges enjoy wide free-dom in fashioning remedies for past or present discriminatory practices by governments. If a federal district court anywhere in the United States finds that any actions by govern-ments or school officials have contributed to racial imbalances (e.g., in drawing school district attendance lines), the judge may order the adoption of a desegregation plan to overcome racial imbalances produced by official action. A large number of cities have come under federal district court orders to improve racial balances in their schools through busing.

In the important case of *Swan* v. *Charlotte-Mecklenburg Board of Education,* the Su-preme Court upheld (1) the use of racial balance requirements in schools and the assign-ment of pupils to schools based on race, (2) "close scrutiny" by judges of schools that are predominantly of one race, (3) gerrymandering of school attendance zones as well as "clustering" or "grouping" of schools to achieve equal balance; and (4) court-ordered busing of pupils to achieve racial balance.

> Absent a constitutional violation there would be no basis for judicially ordering assignment of students on a racial basis. All things being equal, with no history of discrimination, it might well be desirable to assign pupils to schools nearest their homes. But all things are not equal in a system that has been deliberately constructed and maintained to enforce racial segregation. The remedy for such segregation may be administratively awkward, in-convenient, and even bizarre in some situations and may impose burdens on some; but all awkwardness and inconvenience cannot be avoided when remedial adjustments are being made to eliminate the dual school system.[18]

The Court was careful to note, however, that racial imbalance in schools is not itself grounds for ordering these remedies, unless it is also shown that some present or past gov-ernmental action contributed to the imbalance.

CROSS-DISTRICT BUSING   In the absence of any governmental actions contributing to racial imbalance, states and school districts are *not* required by the Four-teenth Amendment to integrate their schools. Thus, for example, where central-city

---

[18]*Swan* v. *Charlotte-Mecklenburg County Board of Education,* 402 U.S. 1 (1971).

schools are predominantly black, and suburban schools are predominantly white, owing to residential patterns, cross-district busing is not constitutionally required, unless it is shown that some official action brought about these racial imbalances. The Supreme Court threw out a lower federal court order for massive busing of students between Detroit and fifty-two suburban school districts. Although Detroit city schools are 70 percent black, none of the Detroit-area school districts segregated students within their own boundaries. Chief Justice Burger, writing for the majority, said:

> The constitutional right for the Negro respondents residing in Detroit is to attend a unitary school system in that district. Unless petitioners drew the district lines in a discriminatory fashion, or arranged for the white student residing in the Detroit district to attend schools in Oakland or Macomb counties, they were under no constitutional duty to make provision for Negro students to do so.[19]

In a strong dissent, Justice Thurgood Marshall wrote:

> In the short run it may seem to be the easiest course to allow our great metropolitan areas to be divided up each into cities—one white, the other black—but it is a course, I predict, our people will ultimately regret.

This important decision means the largely black central cities, surrounded by largely while suburbs, will remain de facto segregated because there are not enough white students living within the city to achieve integration.

WHEN IS DESEGREGATION COMPLETE?   Many school districts in the South and elsewhere have operated under federal court supervision for many years. How long should court supervision continue, and what standards are to be used in determining when desegregation has been achieved once and for all? In recent years the Supreme Court under Chief Justice Rehnquist has undertaken to free some school districts from direct federal court supervision. Where the last vestiges of state-sanctioned discrimination have been removed "as far as practicable," the Supreme Court has allowed lower federal courts to dissolve racial balancing plans even though imbalances due to residential patterns continue to exist.[20]

CONTINUING RACIAL SEPARATION AND "WHITE FLIGHT"
Minority students now comprise the overwhelming majority of public school pupils in many large cities (including Detroit, Philadelphia, Boston, Atlanta, Chicago, Baltimore, Cleveland, Memphis, New Orleans, Newark, Richmond, St. Louis, and Washington, DC). In some cities, where extensive busing has been employed, "white flight" from the public schools is so widespread that the schools have ended up more segregated than before busing was imposed.[21] Currently *over two-thirds of all black public school pupils in*

---

[19]*Milliken* v. *Bradley,* 418 U.S. 717 (1974).

[20]*Oklahoma City Board of Education* v. *Dowell,* 498 U.S. 237 (1991).

[21]Michael W. Giles et. al., "The Impact of Busing on White Flight," *Social Science Quarterly,* 55 (September 1974), 493–501. See also George M. Metcalf, *From Little Rock to Boston: The History of School Desegregation* (Westport, CT: Greenwood Press, 1985).

the United States attend schools that are predominately black.[22] The most racially segregated schools are found in Illinois, Michigan, New York, New Jersey, and Pennsylvania (in that order) with over half of their black pupils attending schools that are 90 to 100 percent black.

QUALITY EDUCATION   The continuation of racial isolation in public schools has caused many educators to focus on the quality of education in predominately minority schools. According to the NAACP: "At the present time, we are more concerned with the quality of education. This has to take precedence over whether the schools are integrated. Having said that, we still support desegregation efforts and busing as a means to that end."[23]

MARTIN LUTHER KING, JR., AND THE CIVIL RIGHTS MOVEMENT

The initial objective of the civil rights movement in America was to prevent discrimination and segregation as practiced by or supported by *governments,* particularly states, municipalities, and school districts. However, even while important victories for the civil rights movement were being recorded in the prevention of discrimination by governments, particularly in the *Brown* case, the movement began to broaden its objectives to include the elimination of discrimination in all segments of American life, private as well as public.

The Constitution does not govern the activities of private individuals. It is the laws of Congress and the states that govern the conduct of private individuals. When the civil rights movement turned to combating private discrimination, it had to carry its fight into the legislative branch of government. The federal courts could help restrict discrimination by state and local governments and school authorities, but only Congress, state legislatures, and city councils could restrict discrimination practiced by private owners of restaurants, hotels and motels, private employers, and other individuals who were not government officials.

MARTIN LUTHER KING, JR.   The leadership in the struggle to eliminate discrimination and segregation from private life was provided by a young black minister, Martin Luther King, Jr. King's father was the pastor of one of the South's largest and most influential congregations, the Ebenezer Baptist Church in Atlanta, Georgia. Martin Luther King, Jr., received his doctorate from Boston University and began his ministry in Montgomery, Alabama. In 1955 the black community of Montgomery began a year-long boycott with frequent demonstrations against the Montgomery city buses over segregated seating practices. The dramatic appeal and the eventual success of the boycott in Mont-

---

[22]Howard University School of Education, as reported in *New York Times,* December 14, 1993, p. A11.

[23]Statement by National Association for the Advancement of Colored People, reported in *New York Times,* December 14, 1993, p. A11.

gomery brought nationwide attention to its leader and led to the creation in 1957 of the Southern Christian Leadership Conference.

NONVIOLENT DIRECT ACTION   Under King's leadership the civil rights movement developed and refined political techniques for minorities in American politics, including *nonviolent direct action.* Nonviolent direct action is a form of protest that involves breaking "unjust" laws in an open, "loving," nonviolent fashion. The general notion of civil disobedience is not new; it played an important role in American history from the Boston Tea Party to the abolitionists who illegally hid runaway slaves, to the suffragettes who demonstrated for women's voting rights, to the labor organizers who formed the nation's major industrial unions, to the civil rights workers of the early 1960s who deliberately violated segregation laws. The purpose of nonviolent direct action is to call attention, or to "bear witness," to the existence of injustice. In the words of Martin Luther King, Jr., civil disobedience "seeks to dramatize the issue so that it can no longer be ignored."

There should be no violence in true civil disobedience, and only "unjust" laws are broken. Moreover, the law is broken "openly, lovingly," with a willingness to accept the penalty. Punishment is actively sought rather than avoided, since punishment will help to emphasize the injustice of the law. The object is to stir the conscience of an elite and win support for measures that will eliminate the injustices. By willingly accepting punishment for the violation of an unjust law, one demonstrates the strength of one's convictions. The dramatization of injustice makes news; the public's sympathy is won when injustices are spotlighted; and the willingness of demonstrators to accept punishment is visible evidence of their sincerity. Cruelty or violence directed against the demonstrators by police or others plays into the hands of the protestors by further emphasizing the injustices they are experiencing.

Martin Luther King, Jr., in his famous "Letter from Birmingham City Jail," explained:

> In no sense do I advocate evading or defying the law as the rabid segregationist would do. This would lead to anarchy. One who breaks an unjust law must do it *openly, lovingly* (not hatefully as the white mothers did in New Orleans when they were seen on television screaming, "nigger, nigger, nigger") and with a willingness to accept the penalty. I submit that an individual who breaks a law that conscience tells him is unjust, and willingly accepts the penalty by staying in jail to arouse the conscience of the community over its injustice, is in reality expressing the very highest respect for law.[24]

MARCHES IN BIRMINGHAM AND WASHINGTON   Perhaps the most dramatic confrontation between the civil rights movement and the southern segregationists occurred in Birmingham, Alabama, in the spring of 1963. In support of a request for desegregation of downtown eating places and the formation of a biracial committee to work out the integration of public schools, Martin Luther King, Jr., led several thousand Birmingham blacks in a series of orderly street marches. The demonstrators were met with strong police action, including fire hoses, police dogs, and electric cattle prods.

---

[24]Martin Luther King, Jr., "Letter from Birmingham City Jail," April 16, 1963.

Newspaper pictures of blacks being attacked by police and bitten by dogs were flashed all over the world. More than 25,000 demonstrators, including Dr. King, were jailed.

The Birmingham protest set off demonstrations in many parts of the country; the theme remained one of nonviolence, and it was usually whites rather than blacks who resorted to violence in these demonstrations. The culmination of the nonviolent philosophy was a giant, yet orderly, march on Washington, held on August 28, 1963. More than 200,000 blacks and whites participated in the march, which was endorsed by various labor leaders, religious groups, and political figures. The march ended at the Lincoln Memorial where Martin Luther King, Jr., delivered his most eloquent appeal, "I Have a Dream":

> I have a dream. It is a dream deeply rooted in the American dream. I have a dream that one day this nation will rise up and live up and live out the true meaning of its creed: "We hold these truths to be self-evident; that all men are created equal."
>
> I have a dream that one day on the red hills of Georgia the sons of former slaves and the sons of former slaveowners will be able to sit down together at the table of brotherhood.
>
> I have a dream that one day even the state of Mississippi, a desert state sweltering with the heat of injustice and oppression, will be transformed into an oasis of freedom and justice.
>
> I have a dream that my four little children will one day live in a nation where they will not be judged by the color of their skin but by the content of their character. . . .[25]

It was in response to this march that President John F. Kennedy sent a strong civil rights bill to Congress, which was passed after his death—the landmark Civil Rights Act of 1964.

THE CIVIL RIGHTS ACT OF 1964

The Civil Rights Act of 1964 passed both houses of Congress by better than a two-thirds favorable vote; it won the overwhelming support of both Republican and Democratic members of Congress. It was signed into law on July 4, 1964. It ranks with the Emancipation Proclamation, the Fourteenth Amendment, and *Brown* v. *Topeka* as one of the most important steps toward full equality for blacks in America. Among other things, the Civil Rights Act of 1964 provides:

- That it is unlawful to discriminate or segregate persons on the grounds of race, color, religion, or national origin in any place of public accommodation, including hotels, motels, restaurants, movies, theatres, sports areas, entertainment houses, and other places which offer to serve the public. This prohibition extends to all establishments whose operations affect interstate commerce or whose discriminatory practices are supported by state action. (Title II)
- That each federal department and agency shall take action to end discrimination in all programs or activities receiving federal financial assistance in any form. This action shall include termination of financial assistance. (Title VI)
- That it shall be unlawful for any employer or labor union with twenty-five or more persons after 1965 to discriminate against any individual in any fashion in em-

---

[25]Martin Luther King, Jr., August 28, 1963, at the Lincoln Memorial, Washington DC.

ployment, because of his race, color, religion, sex, or national origin, and that an Equal Employment Opportunity Commission shall be established to enforce this provision by investigation, conference, conciliation, persuasion, and, if need be, civil action in federal court. (Title VII)[26]

FAIR HOUSING   For many years "fair housing" had been considered the most sensitive area of civil rights legislation. Discrimination in the sale and rental of housing was the last major civil rights problem on which Congress took action. Discrimination in housing had not been mentioned in any previous legislation; even the comprehensive Civil Rights Act of 1964 made no reference to housing. Prohibiting discrimination in the sale or rental of housing affected the constituencies of northern members of Congress more than any of the earlier, southern-oriented legislation. The prospects for a fair housing law were not very good at the beginning of 1968. When Martin Luther King, Jr., was assassinated on April 4, however, the mood of the nation and of Congress changed dramatically, and many felt that Congress should pass a fair housing law as a tribute to the slain civil rights leader. The Civil Rights Act of 1968 prohibited the following forms of discrimination:

- Refusal to sell or rent a dwelling to any person because of race, color, religion, or national origin.
- Discrimination against a person in the terms, conditions or privileges of the sale or rental of a dwelling, or advertising the sale or rental of a dwelling indicating a preference or discrimination based on race, color, religion or national origin.

The act applied to all apartments and houses, rented or sold by either real estate developers or by private individuals who used the services of real estate agents. It exempted private individuals who sold their own home without the services of a real estate agent, provided they did not indicate any preference or discrimination in advertising in the sale or rental of a house.

---

[26]Opponents of the Civil Rights Act of 1964 argued that Congress unconstitutionally exceeded its delegated powers when it prohibited discrimination and segregation practiced by *privately owned* public accommodations and *private* employers. Nowhere among the delegated powers of Congress in Article I of the Constitution, or even in the Fourteenth or Fifteenth Amendments, is Congress specifically given the power to prohibit discrimination practiced by *private* individuals. In reply, supporters of the act argued that Congress has the power to regulate interstate commerce. Instead of relying upon the Fourteenth Amendment, which prohibits only *state-supported* discrimination, Congress was relying on its powers over interstate commerce. In unanimous opinions in *Heart of Atlanta Motel* v. *United States* and *Katzenbach* v. *McClung* in December 1964, the Supreme Court upheld the constitutionality of the Civil Rights Act. The Court held that Congress could, by virtue of its power over interstate commerce, prohibit discrimination in any establishment that serves or offers to serve interstate travelers or that sells food or goods previously moved in interstate commerce. This power over commerce included not only major establishments, like the Heart of Atlanta Motel, but also the family-owned Ollie's Barbecue serving a local clientele. *Heart of Atlanta Motel* v. *United States*, 379 U.S. 241 (1964); *Katzenbach* v. *McClung*, 379 U.S. 294 (1964).

AFFIRMATIVE ACTION BATTLES

Although the gains of the civil rights movement were immensely important, they were primarily gains in *opportunity*, rather than in *results*. The civil rights movement of the 1960s did not bring about major changes in the conditions under which most blacks lived in America. Racial politics today center on the actual inequalities between blacks and whites in incomes, jobs, housing, health, education, and other conditions of life.

CONTINUING INEQUALITIES   The issue of inequality is often posed today as differences in the "life chances" of blacks and whites. Figures can reveal only the bare outline of the life chances in American society (see Table 14–1). The average income of a

Table 14-1
MINORITY LIFE CHANCES

	Median Income of Families			
	1975	1980	1985	1993
White	14,268	21,904	29,152	39,300
Black	8,779	12,674	16,786	21,542
Hispanic	9,551	14,716	19,027	23,654
	Percentage of Persons Below Poverty Level			
White	9.7	10.2	11.4	12.2
Black	31.3	32.5	31.3	33.1
Hispanic	26.9	25.7	29.0	30.6

	Percentage of Persons Over 25 Completing	
	HIGH SCHOOL	COLLEGE
White	79	22
Black	65	11
Hispanic	51	9

	Unemployment Rate		
	1980	1985	1994
White	6.3	6.2	5.2
Black	14.3	15.1	10.6
Hispanic	10.1	10.5	9.7

Source: Statistical Abstract of the United States, 1995.

black family is less than 60 percent of the average white family's income. Nearly 32 percent of all black families are below the recognized poverty line, while less than 11 percent of white families live in poverty. The unemployment rate for blacks is over twice as high as that for whites. Blacks are less likely to hold prestigious white-collar jobs in professional, managerial, clerical, or sales work. They do not hold many skilled craft jobs in industry but are concentrated in operative, service, and laboring positions. The civil rights movement opened up new opportunities for black Americans. But equality of *opportunity* is not the same as *absolute* equality.

POLICY CHOICES   What public policies should be pursued to achieve equality in America? Is it sufficient that government eliminate discrimination, guarantee "equality of opportunity," and apply "color-blind" standards to both blacks and whites? Or should government take "affirmative action" to overcome the results of past unequal treatment of minorities—that is, preferential or compensatory treatment to assist minority applicants for university admissions and scholarships, job hiring and promotion, and other opportunities for advancement in life?

The early emphasis of government policy, of course, was nondiscrimination. This approach began with President Harry Truman's decision to desegregate the armed forces in 1948 and was carried through to Title VI and Title VII of the Civil Rights Act of 1964 to eliminate discrimination in federally aided projects and private employment. Gradually, however, policy shifted from the traditional aim of *equality of opportunity* through nondiscrimination alone to affirmative action to establish "goals and timetables" to achieve greater *equality of results* between blacks and whites. While avoiding the term *quota,* the notion of affirmative action tests the success of equal opportunity by observing whether minorities achieve admissions, jobs, and promotions in proportion to their numbers in the population.

CONSTITUTIONAL ISSUES—THE BAKKE CASE   The constitutional question posed by "affirmative action" programs is whether or not they discriminate against whites in violation of the Equal Protection Clause of the Fourteenth Amendment. The U.S. Supreme Court first dealt directly with this question in *Regents of the University of California* v. *Bakke* (1978). The Court struck down a special admissions program for minorities at a state medical school on the grounds that it excluded a white applicant because of his race and violated his rights under the Equal Protection Clause.[27] Allan Bakke applied to the University of California Davis Medical School two consecutive years and was rejected; in both years black applicants with significantly lower grade point averages and medical aptitude test scores accepted through a special admissions program that reserved sixteen minority places in a class of one hundred.[28] The University of California did not deny that its admission decisions were based on race. Instead, it argued that its

---

[27]*Regents of the University of California* v. *Bakke,* 438 U.S. 265 (1978).

[28]Bakke's overall grade point average was 3.46, while the average for special admission students was 2.62. Bakke's MCAT scores were verbal–96, quantitative–94, science–97, general information–72; while the average MCAT scores for special admissions students were verbal–34, quantitative–30, science–37, general information–18.

racial classification was "benign," that is, designed to assist minorities, not to hinder them. The Supreme Court held that race and ethnic origin *may* be considered in reviewing applications to a state school without violating the Equal Protection Clause. However, the Court held that a *separate* admissions program for minorities with a specific quota of openings that were unavailable to white applicants violated the Equal Protection Clause. The Court ordered Bakke admitted to medical school and the elimination of the special admissions program. It recommended that California consider an admissions program developed at Harvard that considered disadvantaged racial or ethnic background as a "plus" in an overall evaluation of an application but did not set numerical quotas or exclude any persons from competing for all positions.[29]

AFFIRMATIVE ACTION AS A REMEDY FOR PAST DISCRIMINATION   The Supreme Court has generally approved of affirmative action programs when there was evidence of past discriminatory practices. In *United Steelworkers of America* v. *Weber* (1979), the Supreme Court approved a plan developed by a private employer and a union to reserve 50 percent of higher paying, skilled jobs for minorities.[30] In *United States* v. *Paradise* (1987), the Court upheld a rigid 50 percent black quota system for promotions in the Alabama Department of Safety, which had excluded blacks from the ranks of state troopers prior to 1972 and had not promoted any blacks higher than corporal prior to 1984. In a 5–4 decision, the majority stressed the long history of discrimination in the agency as a reason for upholding the quota system. Whatever burdens were imposed on innocent parties were outweighed by the need to correct the effects of past discrimination.[31]

CASES QUESTIONING AFFIRMATIVE ACTION   Yet the Supreme Court has continued to express concern about whites who are directly and adversely affected by government action solely because of their race. In *Firefighters Local Union* v. *Stotts* (1984), the Court ruled that a city could not lay off white firefighters in favor of black firefighters with less seniority.[32] In *Richmond* v. *Crosen* (1989), the Supreme Court held that a minority set-aside program in Richmond, Virginia, which mandated that 30 percent of all city construction contracts must go to "blacks, Spanish-speaking, Orientals, Indians, Eskimos, or Aleuts" violated the Equal Protection Clause of the Fourteenth Amendment.[33]

AFFIRMATIVE ACTION AND "STRICT SCRUTINY"   It is important to note that the Supreme Court has never adopted the color-blind doctrine first espoused by Justice John Harlan in his *dissent* from *Plessy* v. *Ferguson*—that "our constitution is

---

[29]The Bakke case did *not* affect overall minority enrollments in law schools and medical schools. Black and Hispanic enrollments continued to rise until the 1980s, when economic conditions appeared to have an adverse effect on minority enrollments. See John Gruhl and Susan Welch, "The Impact of the Bakke Decision on Black and Hispanic Enrollments in Medical and Law Schools," *Social Science Quarterly*, 71 (September 1990), 458–73.

[30]*United Steelworkers* v. *Weber*, 443 U.S. 193 (1979).

[31]*United States* v. *Paradise*, 480 U.S. 149 (1987).

[32]*Firefighters Local Union* v. *Stotts*, 465 U.S. 561 (1981).

[33]*Richmond* v. *Crosen*, 109 S. Ct. 706 (1989).

color-blind and neither knows nor tolerates classes among cities." If the Equal Protection Clause requires that the laws of the United States and the states be truly color-blind, then *no* racial preferences, goals, or quotas would be tolerated. This view has occasionally been expressed in recent minority dissents, and concurring opinions.[34]

However, the Court has held that racial classifications in law must be subject to "strict scrutiny." This means that race-based actions by government—any disparate treatment of the races by federal, state, or local public agencies—must be found necessary to remedy past proven discrimination, or to further clearly identified, compelling, and legitimate government objectives. Moreover, it must be "narrowly tailored" so as not to adversely affect the rights of individuals. In striking down a federal construction contract "set-aside" program for small businesses owned by racial minorities, the Court expressed skepticism about governmental racial classifications: "There is simply no way of determining what classifications are 'benign' and 'remedial' and what classifications are in fact motivated by illegitimate notions of racial inferiority or simple racial politics."[35]

Yet the membership of the Supreme Court appears to be closely split over the meaning and use of "strict scrutiny" in affirmative action cases.[36] And the Court's cumulative decisions about affirmative action have not provided the nation with a clear or coherent interpretation of the Constitution. Generally, affirmative action programs are *more likely to be found constitutional* when (a) they are adopted as a remedy to past proven discrimination, (b) they serve a clearly identified, compelling, and legitimate government objective, (c) they are "narrowly tailored" to achieve this objective; and (d) they do not absolutely bar majority members from participation.

PUBLIC OPINION TOWARD AFFIRMATIVE ACTION   Most Americans, black and white, support "affirmative action" when it is defined as encouragement, training, and education for qualified minorities and women (see Table 14–2). However, black and white opinion differs sharply over preferences and "quotas" in hiring, promotions, and admissions. Whites oppose such measures by more than two to one, while blacks support them by comparable margins. But both blacks and whites oppose preferences for "less qualified" minorities over "more qualified" whites.

Aware of the popular opposition to "preferences" and "quotas," affirmative action programs are usually couched in more favorable terms—"goals," "ethnic representation," and "diversity." Yet, over time, increasing resentment among whites toward preferential treatment of minorities has weakened political support for affirmative action programs across the country.

---

[34]See Justice Antonin Scalia's dissent in *Johnson* v. *Transportation Agency of Santa Clara County,* 480 U.S. 616 (1987).

[35]*Aderand Construction* v. *Pena* (1995).

[36]Several major cases have split the Court 5 to 4, including *Aderand Construction* v. *Pena* (1995). At least two justices (Scalia and Thomas) believe that the Constitution requires a color-blind standard: "Under our Constitution, the Government may not make distinctions based on race." Three justices (O'Connor, Rehnquist, and Kennedy) apparently require "strict scrutiny" of racial distinctions by governments. And four justices (Stevens, Ginsburg, Souter, and Breger) appear willing to accept racial distinctions that are "benign" toward minorities even if these distinctions place an "incidental burden on some members of the majority."

Table 14-2

PUBLIC OPINION ON AFFIRMATIVE ACTION: A CLOSER LOOK

Do you favor or oppose the following?

	ALL	BLACKS	WHITES
Companies making special efforts to find qualified minorities and women and then encouraging them to apply for jobs.			
Favor	73	87	71
Oppose	24	12	12
Providing job training programs for minorities and women to make them better qualified for jobs?			
Favor	82	94	80
Oppose	17	6	18
Providing special education classes for minorities and women to make them better qualified for college?			
Favor	25	90	73
Oppose	22	9	24
Establishing quotas that require businesses to hire a certain number of minorities and women?			
Favor	35	66	30
Oppose	63	31	68
Establishing quotas that require schools to admit a certain number of minorities and women as students?			
Favor	39	20	35
Oppose	52	27	61
Favoring a well-qualified minority applicant over an equally qualified white applicant when filling a job in a business that has few minority workers?			
Favor	48	51	47
Oppose	44	42	45
Favoring a minority who is less qualified than a white applicant when filling a job in a business that has few minority workers?			
Favor	13	22	11
Oppose	84	68	86

Source: As reported in *USA Today*, March 24, 1995.

OPPOSITION TO PREFERENCES   Opponents of affirmative action argue that government racial classifications violate the fundamental principle of equality under the law. "To pursue the concept of racial entitlement even for the most admirable and benign of purposes is to reinforce and preserve for future mischief the way of thinking that produces race slavery, race privilege, and race hatred. In the eyes of the government, we are just one race here. It is American."[37] It is argued that America cannot "make up" for past discrimination, by "discrimination in the opposite direction." It is "unfair" to discriminate against the current generation of white workers and students to compensate for a history of discrimination in which they did not participate. Some early supporters of affirmative action have come to believe that race-conscious programs are no longer necessary, that disadvantages in society today are more class-based than race-based, and that if preferences are to be granted at all they should be based on economic disadvantage, not race. Moreover, misgivings have been expressed by some African Americans about unfair stigmatizing of the supposed beneficiaries of affirmative action—a resulting negative stereotyping that "stamps minorities with a badge of inferiority and may cause them to develop dependencies or to adopt an attitude that they are 'entitled' to preferences."[38] White resentment against the perceived unfairness of affirmative action aggravates racial conflict, creating an "angry white male" backlash that erodes support for civil rights generally.

ARGUMENTS FOR CONTINUING AFFIRMATIVE ACTION   Yet most Americans agree that discrimination still exists in American society, even if they do not agree on what should be done about it. Many supporters of affirmative action would ideally prefer a society in which "our children will one day live in a nation where they will not be judged by the color of their skin but by the content of their character." Martin Luther King, Jr.'s dream remains the ultimate goal for the nation. But they see race-conscious policies as a continuing necessity to remedy current discrimination and the effects of past discrimination. America is not now nor has it ever been a "color-blind" society. "If we abandon affirmative action we return to the old white boy network."[39] They perceive affirmative action as a necessary tool in achieving equality of opportunity.

THE CALIFORNIA CIVIL RIGHTS INITIATIVE   The rethinking of affirmative action was inspired by a citizen's initiative placed on the ballot in California by popular petition. The California Civil Rights Initiative would add the following key phrase to that state's constitution.

> Neither the state of California nor any of its political subdivisions or agents shall use race, sex, color, ethnicity or national origin as a criterion for either discriminating against, or granting preferential treatment to, any individual or group in the operation of the State's system of public employment, public education or public contracting.

Supporters argue that this initiative leaves all existing federal and state civil rights protections intact. It simply extends the rights of specially protected groups to all of the state's citizens. The only preferences that are prohibited are those based on race, sex, color, ethnicity, and national origin. It does *not* restrict the state from granting preferential treatment to individuals based upon socioeconomic disadvantage or physical disability or veterans' status or other legitimate criteria.

---

[37]Concurring opinion of Justice Antonin Scalia, *Aderand Construction* v. *Pena* (1995).

[38]Concurring opinion of Justice Clarence Thomas, *Aderand Construction* v. *Pena* (1995).

[39]Quote from Connie Rice of the NAACP, reported in *U.S. News and World Report*, February 13, 1995, p. 35.

HISPANIC POWER

The term *Hispanic* refers to persons of Spanish-speaking ancestry and culture, including Mexican Americans, as well as Puerto Ricans and Cubans. In 1995 there were over 27 million Hispanics in the United States, comprising 10 percent of the U.S. population. (There were 33 million blacks, making up 12.6 percent of the population.) The largest subgroup of Hispanics are Mexican Americans, some of whom are descendants of citizens living in the Mexican territory that was annexed to the United States in 1848. Most however, have come to the United States in accelerating numbers in recent years. The largest Mexican American populations are found in Texas, Arizona, New Mexico, and California. (See Figure 14–2.) The second largest subgroup are Puerto Ricans, many of whom retain ties to the commonwealth and move back and forth from the island to the mainland, especially New York City. The third largest subgroup are Cubans, most of whom have fled from Castro's Cuba. They live mainly in the Miami metropolitan area. While these groups have different experiences, they share a common language and culture, and they have encountered similar difficulties in making government responsive to their needs.

In recent years Hispanics have served as governors in Florida, Arizona, and New Mexico, and as mayors in Miami, Denver, San Antonio, and several other large cities. However, overall Hispanic political influence in state and local politics does not match Hispanic population percentages.[40] Hispanic voter turnout is lower than for other ethnic groups in America. Many Hispanics are still resident aliens and therefore not eligible to vote. Language barriers may also present an obstacle to full participation. Finally, Hispanic voters divide their political loyalties. The largest Hispanic groups, Mexican Americans, tend to vote Democratic; their power is concentrated in California, Texas, Arizona, and New Mexico. Cuban Americans and other political refugees from Marxist guerrilla wars in Central and South America tend to vote Republican. These groups are economically very successful; they are concentrated in the Miami area, and they are now a major force in city and state politics in Florida. In Miami, Los Angeles, and other cities with large Hispanic populations *and* large black populations, competition and conflict, rather than minority coalition building, have often characterized relations between these groups.[41]

NATIVE AMERICANS AND TRIBAL GOVERNMENT

Christopher Columbus erred in his estimate of the circumference of the globe. He believed he had arrived in the Indian Ocean when he first came to the Caribbean. He mis-

---

[40]See F. Chris Garcia, ed., *Latinos in the Political System* (Notre Dame, IN: Notre Dame University Press, 1988); Rudolpho O. dela Garza et al., *Latino Voices: Mexican, Puerto Rican, and Cuban Perspectives in American Politics* (Boulder: Westview Press, 1992).

[41]See Paula D. McClain and Albert K. Karnig, "Black and Hispanic Political Competition," *American Political Science Review*, 84 (June 1990), 535–45.

Figure 14–2

HISPANIC AMERICANS: SOCIAL AND ECONOMIC CHARACTERISTICS

Origins

Puerto Rico 10.6%

Mexico 63.6%

Other 21.1%

Cuba 4.7%

STATES WITH HISPANIC POPULATION OVER 10 PERCENT

New Mexico	38.2%	Colorado	12.9%
California	25.8	New York	12.3
Texas	25.5	Florida	12.2
Arizona	18.8	Nevada	10.4

CITIES WITH MAJORITY HISPANIC POPULATIONS

East Los Angeles CA	94.7%	Miami FL	62.5%
Laredo TX	93.9	San Antonio TX	55.6
Hialeah FL	87.6	Oxnard CA	54.4
El Monte CA	72.5	Pomona CA	51.3
El Paso TX	69.0	Corpus Christi TX	50.4
Santa Ana CA	65.2	Salinas CA	50.6

MEDIAN FAMILY INCOME 1991, U.S. AVERAGE $35,353

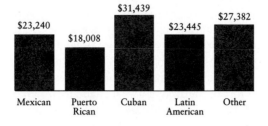

$23,240 $18,008 $31,439 $23,445 $27,382

Mexican   Puerto Rican   Cuban   Latin American   Other

PERSONS BELOW POVERTY LEVEL 1991, U.S. AVERAGE 12.1 %

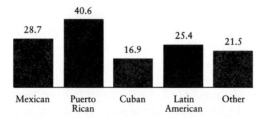

28.7   40.6   16.9   25.4   21.5

Mexican   Puerto Rican   Cuban   Latin American   Other

Source: Statistical Abstract of the United States, 1994.

took the Arawaks for people of the East Indies, calling them "Indios," and this Spanish word passed into English as Indians—a word that came to refer to all Native American peoples. But at the time of the first European contacts, these peoples had no common identity; there were hundreds of separate cultures and languages thriving in the Americas. Although estimates vary, most historians believe that 7 to 12 million people lived in the land that is now the United States and Canada; 25 million more lived in Mexico; and 60 to 70 million lived in the Western Hemisphere, a number comparable to Europe's population at the time.

In the centuries that followed, the native population of the Americas was devastated by warfare, famine, and, most of all, by epidemic diseases brought from Europe. Overall, the native population fell by 90 percent, the greatest human disaster in world history. Smallpox was the most devastating disease, followed by measles, bubonic plague, influenza, typhus, diphtheria, and scarlet fever. The superior military technology of Europeans, together with skill in exploiting hostilities between tribes, gradually overcame native resistance. By 1910, there were only 210,000 Native Americans in the United States. Their population has slowly recovered to the current 1.8 million.

THE TRAIL OF BROKEN TREATIES   In the Northwest Ordinance of 1787, Congress, in organizing the western territories of the new nation, declared that:

> The utmost good faith shall always be observed toward the Indians. Their lands and property shall never be taken from them without their consent.

And later, in the Intercourse Act of 1790, Congress declared that public treaties between the United States government and the independent Indian "nations" would be the only legal means of obtaining Indian land. As president, George Washington forged a treaty with the Creeks: In exchange for land concessions, the United States pledged to protect the boundaries of the "Creek Nation" and allow the Creeks themselves to punish all violators of their laws within these boundaries. This semblance of legality was reflected in hundreds of treaties to follow. (And indeed, in recent years some Indian tribes have successfully sued in federal court for reparations and return of lands obtained in violation of the Intercourse Act of 1790 and subsequent treaties.) Yet, Indian lands were constantly invaded by whites. The resulting Indian resistance would typically lead to wars that would ultimately result in great loss of life among warriors and their families and the further loss of tribal land. The cycle of invasion, resistance, military defeat, and further land concessions, continued for a hundred years.

INDIAN WARS   The "Indian wars" were fought between the Plains Indian tribes and the U.S. Army between 1864 and 1890. Following the Civil War, the federal government began to assign boundaries to each tribe and created a Bureau of Indian Affairs (BIA) to "assist and protect" Indian peoples on their "reservations." But the reservations were repeatedly reduced in size until subsistence by hunting became impossible. Malnutrition and demoralization of the native peoples were aided by the mass slaughter of the buffalo; vast herds, numbering perhaps as many as seventy million, were exterminated over the years. The most storied engagement of the long war occurred at the Little Big Horn River in South Dakota on June 25, 1876, where Civil War hero General George

Armstrong Custer led elements of the U.S. Seventh Calvary to destruction at the hands of Sioux and Cheyenne warriors led by Chief Crazy Horse, Sitting Bull, and Gall. But Custer's Last Stand inspired renewed army campaigns against the Plains tribes; the following year Crazy Horse was forced to surrender. In 1881 destitute Sioux under Chief Sitting Bull returned from exile in Canada to surrender themselves to reservation life. Among the last tribes to hold out were the Apaches, whose famous warrior, Geronimo, finally surrendered in 1886. Sporadic fighting continued until 1890, when a small, malnourished band of Lakota Sioux were wiped out at Wounded Knee Creek.

FEDERAL POLICIES TOWARD TRIBAL AFFAIRS   The Dawes Act of 1887 governed federal Indian policy for decades. The thrust of the policy was to break up tribal lands, allotting acreage for individual homesteads in order to assimilate Indians into the white agricultural society. Farming was to replace hunting, and tribal life and traditional customs were to be shed for English language and schooling. But this effort to destroy Indian culture never really succeeded. While Indian peoples lost over half of their 1877 reservation land, few lost their communal ties or accumulated much private property. The Dawes Act remained federal policy until 1934, when Congress finally reversed itself in the Indian Reorganization Act of 1934 and reaffirmed tribal ownership of land. Life on the reservations was often disparate. Indians suffered the worst poverty of any group in the nation, with high rates of infant mortality, alcoholism, and other diseases. The BIA, notoriously corrupt and mismanaged, encouraged dependency, and regularly interfered with Indian religious affairs and tribal customs.

THE AMERICAN INDIAN MOVEMENT   The civil rights movement of the 1960s inspired a new activism among Native American groups. The American Indian Movement (AIM) was founded in 1968 and attracted national headlines by occupying Alcatraz Island in San Francisco Bay. Violence flared in 1972 when AIM activists took over the site of the Wounded Knee battle and fought with FBI agents. Several tribes succeeded in federal courts and Congress to win back lands and/or compensation for lands taken from them in treaty violations. Indian culture was revitalized, and Vine Deloria's *Custer Died for Your Sins* and Dee Brown's *Bury My Heart at Wounded Knee* became national bestsellers.

NATIVE AMERICANS TODAY   Today about 2 million people—less than 1 percent of the nation's population, identify themselves as American Indians. About 800,000 of these people live on tribal reservations and trust land, the largest of which is the Navaho and Hopi enclave in southwestern United States (see Figure 14–3). Yet these peoples remain the poorest and least healthy in America, with high incidences of infant mortality, suicide, and alcoholism. Approximately half of all Indians live below the poverty line.

TRIBAL GOVERNMENT   The U.S. Constitution (Article I, Section 8) grants Congress the full power "to regulate Commerce . . . with the Indian Tribes." States are prevented from regulating or taxing Indian tribes or extending their courts' jurisdiction over them, unless authorized by Congress. The Supreme Court recognizes Native Americans "as members of quasi-sovereign tribal entities"[42] with powers to regulate their own

---

[42] *Morton v. Mancari*, 417 U.S. 535 (1974).

Figure 14–3
NATIVE AMERICAN RESERVATIONS AND TRUST LAND

Source: U.S. Bureau of the Census, 1990 *Census of Population: American Indian and Alaska Native Areas; Indian Land Areas,* U.S. Dept. of the Interior, Bureau of Indian Affairs, 1993.

internal affairs, establish their own courts, and enforce their own laws, all subject to congressional supervision. Thus, for example, many Indian tribes chose to legalize gambling, including casino gambling, on reservations in states that otherwise prohibited the activity. As American citizens, Indians have the right to vote in state as well as national elections. Indians living off of reservations have the same rights and responsibilities as anyone else. Indians enrolled as members of tribes and living on reservations are entitled to certain benefits established by law and treaty. The Bureau of Indians Affairs (BIA) in the Department of Commerce continues to supervise reservation life.

AMERICANS WITH DISABILITIES

Throughout most of our nation's history, little thought was given to making public or private buildings or facilities accessible to blind, deaf, or mobility-impaired people.[43] But in 1990 Congress passed the sweeping Americans with Disabilities Act (ADA), which prohibits discrimination against the disabled in private employment, government programs, public accommodations, and telecommunications. The act is vaguely worded in many of its provisions, requiring "reasonable accommodations" for the disabled that do not involve "undue hardship." But the ADA mandates that:

1. The disabled cannot be denied employment or promotion if, with "reasonable accommodation," they can perform the duties of the job.
2. The disabled cannot be denied access to government programs or benefits. New buses, taxis, and trains must be accessible to disabled persons, including those in wheelchairs.
3. The disabled must enjoy "full and equal" access to hotels, restaurants, stores, schools, parks, museums, auditoriums, and the like. To achieve equal access, owners of existing facilities must alter them "to the maximum extent feasible"; builders of new facilities must ensure that they are readily accessible to disabled persons unless doing so is structurally impossible.

These federal mandates for accommodations of the disabled were not accompanied by any federal funds to employers or state and local governments to implement them (see "Coercive Federalism: Mandates and Preemptions" in Chapter 3).

GENDER EQUALITY

Until recently, gender issues had been determined largely by *state* laws, particularly laws governing marriage, divorce, employment, and abortion. State laws frequently differentiated between the rights and responsibilities of men and women. Women had many special protections in state laws, but often these protections limited opportunities for advancement and encouraged dependence upon men.

---

[43]See Joseph P. Shapiro, *No Pity: People with Disabilities Forging a New Civil Rights Movement* (New York: Times Books/Random House, 1993).

EMPLOYMENT   Traditionally, state laws governing employment considered women as frail creatures in need of special protections against long hours, heavy work, night work, and so on. Moreover, states did not guarantee equal pay and promotion opportunities for women or bar sexual discrimination in employment. However, Title VII of the federal Civil Rights Act of 1964 prevents sexual (as well as racial) discrimination in hiring, pay, and promotions. The Equal Employment Opportunity Commission, which is the federal agency charged with eliminating discrimination in employment, has established guidelines barring stereotyped classifications of "men's jobs" and "women's jobs." State laws and employer practices that differentiate between men and women in hours, pay, retirement age, and so on have been struck down.

GENDER CLASSIFICATIONS   Over the years the Supreme Court ruled that states could no longer set different ages for men and women to become legal adults[44] or purchase alcoholic beverages;[45] women could not be barred from police or firefighting jobs by arbitrary height and weight requirements;[46] insurance and retirement plans for women must pay the same monthly benefits even though women on the average live longer;[47] and schools must pay coaches in girls' sports the same as coaches in boys' sports.[48] However, all-male and all-female schools are still permitted;[49] and Congress may draft men for military service without drafting women.[50] Gender protection under the Equal Protection Clause was also extended to men: The Supreme Court struck down a state law that allowed wives to obtain alimony from husbands but did not permit husbands to obtain alimony from wives.[51]

EDUCATION   Title IX of the Federal Education Act Amendment of 1972 dealt with sex discrimination in education. This federal law barred discrimination in admissions, housing, rules, financial aid, faculty and staff recruitment, pay, and—most troublesome of all—athletics. The latter problem has proven very difficult because men's football and basketball programs have traditionally brought in the money to finance all other sports and have received the largest share of school athletic budgets.

THE EARNINGS GAP   Yet women's earnings on average remain substantially below men's earnings. In 1994 for example, women earned only about 72 percent of what men earned. Despite federal laws barring direct gender discrimination in employment, the existence of a "dual" labor market, with male-dominated "blue-collar" jobs distinguishable from female-dominated "pink-collar" jobs, continues to be a major obstacle to economic equality between men and women. These occupational differences can be attributed to cultural stereotyping, social conditioning, and training and education that

---

[44]*Stanton v. Stanton*, 421 U.S. 7 (1975).

[45]*Craig v. Boren*, 429 U.S. 191 (1976).

[46]*Dothland v. Raulinson*, 433 U.S. 321 (1977).

[47]*Arizona v. Norvis*, 103 S. Ct. 3492 (1983).

[48]*E.E.O.C. v. Madison Community School District*, 55 U.S.L.W. 2644 (1987).

[49]*Vorcheheimer v. Philadelphia School District*, 430 U.S. 703 (1977).

[50]*Rostker v. Goldberg*, 453 U.S. 57 (1981).

[51]*Orr v. Orr*, 440 U.S. 268 (1979).

narrow the choices available to women. While significant progress has been made in recent years in reducing occupational sex segregation, nonetheless, many observers doubt that sexually differentiated occupations will be eliminated soon.

COMPARABLE WORTH   As a result of a growing recognition that the wage gap is more a result of occupational differentiation than direct discrimination, some feminist organizations have turned to another approach—the demand that pay levels in various occupations be determined by "comparable worth" rather than by the labor market. *Comparable worth* means *more* than paying men and women equally for the same work; it means paying the same wages for jobs of comparable value to the employer. It means that traditionally male and female jobs would be evaluated by governmental agencies or courts to determine their "worth" to the employer, perhaps by considering responsibilities, effort, knowledge, and skill requirements. Jobs adjudged to be comparable would have equal wages. Government agencies or the courts would replace the labor market in the determination of wage rates.

To date the U.S. Equal Employment Opportunity Commission has rejected the notion of comparable worth and declined to recommend wages for traditionally male and female jobs. And so far the federal courts have refused to declare that different wages in traditionally male and female occupations are evidence of sexual discrimination in violation of federal law. However, some state governments and private employers have undertaken to review their own pay scales to determine if traditionally female occupations are underpaid.

BATTLES OVER ABORTION

Arguments over abortion touch on fundamental moral and religious principles. Proponents of legalized abortion, who often refer to themselves as "pro-choice," argue that a woman should be permitted to control her own body and should not be forced by law to have unwanted children. They cite the heavy toll in lives lost in criminal abortions and the psychological and emotional pain of an unwanted pregnancy. Opponents of abortion, who often refer to themselves as "pro-life," generally base their belief on the sanctity of life, including the life of the unborn child, which they believe deserves the protection of law—"the right to life." Many believe that the killing of an unborn child for any reason other than the preservation of the life of the mother is murder.

EARLY STATE LAWS   Historically, abortions for any purpose other than saving the life of the mother were criminal offenses under state law. About a dozen states acted in the late 1960s to permit abortions in cases of rape or incest, or to protect the physical health of the mother, and in some cases her mental health as well. Relatively few legal abortions were performed under these laws, however, because of the red tape involved—review of each case by several concurring physicians, approval of a hospital board, and so forth. Then, in 1970, New York, Alaska, Hawaii, and Washington enacted laws that in effect permitted abortion at the request of the woman involved with the concurrence of her physician.[52]

---

[52]See Christopher Z. Mooney and Mei-Hsien Lee, "Legislating Morality in the American States: Pre-*Roe* Abortion Reform," *American Journal of Political Science*, 39 (August 1995), 599–627.

ROE V. WADE   The U.S. Supreme Court's decision in *Roe* v. *Wade* was one of the most important and far-reaching in the Court's history.[53] The Supreme Court ruled that the constitutional guarantee of "liberty" in the Fifth and Fourteenth Amendments included a woman's decision to bear or not to bear a child. The Supreme Court ruled that the word *person* in the Constitution did not include the unborn child. Therefore, the Fifth and Fourteenth Amendments to the Constitution, guaranteeing "life, liberty and property," did not protect the "life" of the fetus. The Court also ruled that a state's power to protect the health and safety of the mother could not justify *any* restriction of abortion in the first three months of pregnancy. Between the third and sixth months of pregnancy, a state could set standards for abortion procedures in order to protect the health of women, but a state could not prohibit abortions. Only in the final three months could a state prohibit or regulate abortion to protect the unborn.

REACTIONS IN THE STATES   The Supreme Court's decision did not end the controversy over abortion. Congress declined to pass a constitutional amendment restricting abortion or declaring that the guarantee of life begins at conception. However, Congress banned the use of federal funds under Medicaid (medical care for the poor) for abortions (except to protect the life of a woman, and later, in cases of rape and incest). The Supreme Court upheld the constitutionality of federal and state laws *denying tax funds for abortions.*[54] While women retained the right to an abortion, the Court held that there was no constitutional obligation for governments to pay for abortions; the decision about whether to pay for abortions from tax revenues was left to Congress and the states.[55] However, efforts by the states to directly restrict abortion ran into Supreme Court opposition.[56]

ABORTIONS IN THE STATES   About 1.6 million abortions are performed each year in the United States. This is about 44 percent of the number of live births. About 85 percent of all abortions are performed at abortion clinics; others are performed in physicians' offices or in hospitals, where the cost is significantly higher. Most of these abortions are performed in the first three months; about 10 percent are performed after the third month. Abortion is more frequent in some states (New York, Nevada, New Jersey, California) than in other states (Utah, Idaho, West Virginia, Wyoming, South Dakota). (See Figure 14–4.)

Why are abortions more frequent in some states than in others? A careful study of this question by political scientist Susan B. Hansen revealed that abortion rates were *not* related to unwanted pregnancies, that is, the "demand" for abortions.[57] Rather, abortion

---

[53]*Roe* v. *Wade*, 410 U.S. 113 (1973).

[54]*Harris* v. *McRae*, 448 U.S. 297 (1980).

[55]For a review of state funding of abortions, see Kenneth J. Meier and Deborah R. McFarlane, "The Politics of Funding Abortion," *American Politics Quarterly*, 21 (January 1993), 81–101.

[56]*Planned Parenthood of Missouri* v. *Danforth*, 428 U.S. 52 (1976); *Bellotti* v. *Baird*, 443 U.S. 622 (1979); *Akron* v. *Akron Center for Reproductive Health*, 103 S. Ct. 2481 (1983).

[57]Susan B. Hansen, "State Implementation of Supreme Court Decisions: Abortion Rates Since *Roe* v. *Wade*," *Journal of Politics*, 42 (1980), 372–95.

Figure 14–4
ABORTION RATES IN THE STATES

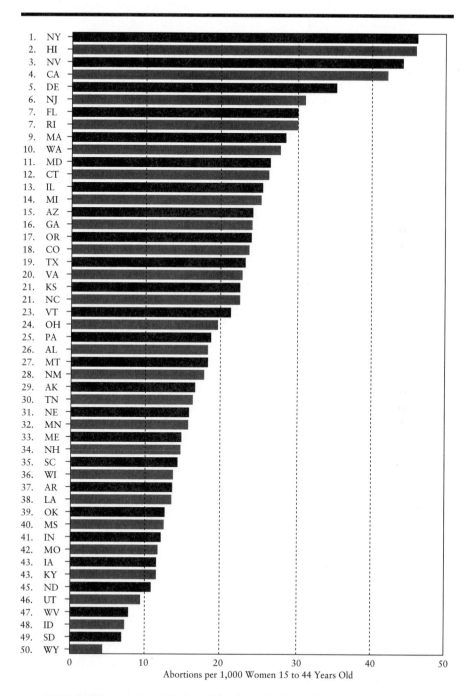

Abortions per 1,000 Women 15 to 44 Years Old

Source: Statistical Abstract of the United States, 1995, p. 85.

rates were related to state policies affecting the availability of abortion services, that is, to government policies affecting the "supply" of abortions. Among the reported findings were that abortion rates are higher in states that permitted abortion before *Roe v. Wade;* some states with low abortion rates (Utah and Idaho) have large Mormon populations; and greater state legislative support for abortion facilities and health services leads to higher abortion rates.

STATE RESTRICTIONS   Opponents of abortion won a victory in the *Webster* case in 1989 when the Supreme Court upheld a Missouri law sharply restricting abortions.[58] The right to abortion under *Roe v. Wade* was not overturned, but narrowed in application. The effect of the decision was to return the question of abortion restrictions to the states for decision.

The Court held that Missouri could deny public funds for abortions that were not necessary for the life of the woman and could deny the use of public facilities or public employees in performing or assisting in abortions. More important, the Court upheld the requirement for a test of "viability" after twenty weeks and a prohibition of an abortion of a viable fetus except to save a woman's life. The Court recognized the state's "interest in the protection of human life when viability is possible."

ABORTION BATTLES IN THE STATES   Contentious debates over abortion continue in virtually all state capitals. Various legal restrictions on abortions have been passed in the states, including (1) *denial of public financing:* prohibitions on public financing of abortions; (2) *viability tests:* requirements for a test of viability and prohibitions on the abortion of a viable fetus; (3) *conscience laws:* laws granting permission to doctors and hospitals to refuse to perform abortions; (4) *fetal disposal:* laws requiring humane and sanitary disposal of fetal remains; (5) *informed consent:* laws requiring physicians to inform patients about the development of the fetus and the availability of assistance in pregnancy; (6) *parental notification:* laws requiring that parents of minors seeking abortion be informed; (7) *spousal verification:* laws requiring spouses to be informed; (8) *hospitalization requirement:* laws requiring that late abortions be performed in hospitals; (9) *clinic licensing:* laws setting standards of cleanliness and care in abortion clinics; (10) *gender selection:* laws prohibiting abortion based on the gender of the fetus.

REAFFIRMING ROE V. WADE   Abortion has become such a polarizing issue that pro-choice and pro-life groups are generally unwilling to search out a middle ground. Yet the current Supreme Court appears to have chosen a policy of affirming a woman's right to abortion while upholding modest restrictions.

Pennsylvania is a state where pro-life forces won the support of the governor and legislature for a series of restrictions on abortion—physicians must inform women of risks and alternatives; a twenty-four-hour waiting period is required; minors must have consent of parents or a judge; spouses must be notified. These restrictions reached the Supreme Court in the case of *Planned Parenthood of Pennsylvania v. Casey* in 1992.[59]

---

[58] *Webster v. Reproductive Health Services,* 492 U.S. 490 (1989).
[59] *Planned Parenthood v. Casey,* 112 S. Ct. 2791 (1992).

Justice Sandra Day O'Connor took the lead in forming a moderate, swing bloc on the Court; her majority opinion strongly reaffirmed the fundamental right of abortion:

> Our law affords constitutional protection to personal decisions relating to marriage, procreation, contraception, family relationships, child rearing, and education . . . These matters, involving the most intimate and personal choices a person may make in a lifetime, choices central to personal dignity and autonomy, are central to the liberty protected by the Fourteenth Amendment. . . . A woman's liberty is not so unlimited, however, that from the outset the State cannot show its concern for the life of the unborn, and at a later point in fetal development the State's interest in life has sufficient force so that the right of the woman to terminate the pregnancy can be restricted. We conclude the line should be drawn at viability, so that before that time the woman has a right to choose to terminate her pregnancy. . . .

Justice O'Connor went on to establish a new standard for constitutionally evaluating state restrictions: They must not impose an "undue burden" on women seeking abortion or place "substantial obstacles" in her path. All of Pennsylvania's restrictions were upheld except spousal notification.

The likelihood of states adopting restriction on abortion appears to be related to the size of their Catholic populations. It is in the states with large Catholic populations that pro-choice and pro-life forces are well organized and active in lobbying legislatures.[60]

---

[60]See Robert E. O'Conner and Michael B. Berkman, "Religious Determinants of State Abortion Policy," *Social Science Quarterly,* 76 (June 1995), 447–59.

15

THE POLITICS
OF EDUCATION

GOALS IN EDUCATIONAL POLICY

The primary responsibility for American public education rests with the fifty state governments and their local school districts. It is the largest and most costly of state functions.

In 1647 the Massachusetts colonial legislature first required towns to provide for the education of children out of public funds. The rugged individualists of earlier eras thought it outrageous that one person should be taxed to pay for the education of another person's child. They were joined in their opposition to public education by those aristocrats who were opposed to arming the common people with the power that knowledge gives. However, the logic of democracy led inevitably to public education. The earliest democrats believed that the safest repository of the ultimate powers of society was the people themselves. If the people make mistakes, the remedy was not to remove power from their hands, but to help them in forming their judgment through education. Congress passed the Northwest Ordinance in 1787 offering land grants for public schools in the new territories and giving succeeding generations words to be forever etched on grammar school cornerstones: "Religion, morality, and knowledge being necessary to good government and the happiness of mankind, schools and the means for education shall ever be encouraged." When American democracy adopted universal suffrage, it affected every aspect of American life, and particularly education. If the people were to be granted the right of suffrage, they must be educated to the task. This meant that public education had to be universal, free, and compulsory.

If there ever was a time when schools were only expected to combat ignorance and illiteracy, that time is far behind us. Today, schools are expected to do many things: resolve racial conflict and build an integrated society; improve the self-image of minority children; inspire patriotism and good citizenship; offer various forms of recreation and mass entertainment (football games, bands, choruses, cheerleaders, and the like); teach children to get along well with others and appreciate multiple cultures; reduce the highway accident toll by teaching students to be good drivers; eliminate unemployment and poverty by teaching job skills; end malnutrition and hunger through school lunch and milk programs; produce scientists and other technicians to continue America's progress in science and technology; fight drug abuse and educate children about sex and sexually transmitted diseases; and act as custodians for teenagers who have no interest in education but are not permitted to work or roam the streets unsupervised. In other words, nearly all the nation's problems are reflected in demands placed on schools. And, of course, these demands are frequently conflicting.

EDUCATIONAL PERFORMANCE MEASUREMENT

Too often educational reports focus on "inputs"—measures of resources expended on education—rather than "outputs"—measures of an educational system's performance. Professional educators frequently resist performance measurement, especially comparisons between states or school districts. (The National Education Association's popular "Rankings of the States" focuses exclusively on enrollment, staff, and expenditure measures.) It is true that many performance measures, especially test scores, are controversial; many commentators argue that they do not measure the qualitative goals of education or that they are biased in one fashion or another. Certainly all interested citizens will welcome future refinements in educational performance measurement. But we cannot ignore performance simply because our measures are unrefined. We need to make reasoned use of the best available comparative measures of educational performance.

THE DROPOUT RATE   Certainly one measure of an educational system's performance is its ability to retain and graduate its students. National studies have consistently shown that high school dropouts tend to experience more unemployment and earn less over a lifetime than high school graduates. Yet often schools fail to convince young people that staying in school is a worthwhile endeavor.

The conflict over dropouts begins with arguments over how to measure the dropout rate. The U.S. Department of Education currently counts high school dropouts in two ways:

1.   Persons who are recorded by the schools as having stopped attending during the tenth, eleventh, and twelfth grades in a single year, as a percentage of total attendance.

This measure produced an annual figure of about 4 percent in 1994 down from 6 percent in 1980. This measure is preferred by professional educators because it is low and because educators themselves collect the data.

2.   Persons age sixteen to nineteen years old who are not attending school and have not graduated from high school, as a percentage of all sixteen- to nineteen-year-olds.

This measure produced an annual figure of 13 percent in 1994, down from 16 percent in 1980. This measure is often overlooked by school administrators because it is so high. Another figure that is seldom mentioned by school administrators is the 26 percent of nineteen-year-olds who have not graduated from high school.

The good news is that high school dropout rates are declining over time, however they are measured. Even so, dropout rates differ by race and ethnicity; the percentage of white sixteen- to nineteen-year-olds not attending or not graduated from school is about 12 percent; for blacks it is about 16 percent, and for Hispanics about 33 percent.[1] Dropout rates are higher than the national average in southern states and states with large Hispanic populations.

CONTROVERSIES OVER TESTING   Performance testing of students is another controversial issue in educational circles. Professional educators argue that the acquisition of verbal and quantitative skills is not the only, or even perhaps the most important, product of public education. Educators often criticize the tests as culturally biased, unfair to minorities, or otherwise flawed. Nonetheless, public sentiment is strongly in favor of testing students' basic skills. Governors and state legislators have pressured educational administrators to engage in more testing. Cross-national studies have attempted to evaluate the performance of American students over time, and to compare their performance with that of students of other nations (Table 15–1). The results of these tests, showing U.S. students ranking well below students of other advanced nations, has added urgency to calls on the national and state levels for added emphasis on basic skills.

SAT SCORES   For many years critics of modern public education cited declining scores on standardized tests, particularly the Scholastic Aptitude Test (SAT) required by many colleges and universities, as evidence of the failure of the schools to teach basic reading and mathematics skills. SAT scores declined dramatically during the 1960s and

---

[1]*Statistical Abstract of the United States, 1995*, p. 173.

Table 15–1

INTERNATIONAL PROFICIENCY SCORES IN SCIENCE AND MATHEMATICS

	Science			*Mathematics*	
RANK	NATION	PERCENT CORRECT	RANK	NATION	PERCENT CORRECT
1	South Korea	78	1	South Korea	73
2	Taiwan	76	2	Taiwan	73
3	Switzerland	74	3	Switzerland	71
4	Hungary	73	4	Russia	70
5	Russia	71	5	Hungary	68
6	Slovenia	70	6	France	64
7	Italy	70	7	Italy	64
8	Israel	70	8	Israel	63
9	Canada	69	9	Canada	62
10	France	69	10	Scotland	61
11	Scotland	68	11	Ireland	61
12	Spain	68	12	Slovenia	57
13	**United States**	67	13	Spain	55
14	Ireland	63	14	**United States**	55
15	Jordan	57	15	Jordan	40

Note: Scores for thirteen-year-old students on International Assessment of Educational Progress test in 1992 made as comparable as possible. Notable nonparticipating nations, Germany and Japan, are likely to have ranked high.

Source: U.S. Department of Education, *Learning Mathematics and Learning Science, 1992.*

1970s, ironically during a period in which per pupil educational spending was rising and the federal government initiated federal aid to education. (See Figure 15–1.) When the decline ended in 1982, it was attributed to increasing emphasis on basic skills and standardized testing. But changes in these test scores are also a function of how many students take the test. During the declining years, increasing numbers of students were taking the test—students who never aspired to college in the past and whose test scores did not match those of the earlier, smaller group of college-bound test takers. In recent years SAT scores have remained fairly stable, but no significant improvements have been recorded.

Professional educators and school administrators generally oppose efforts to evaluate state educational performance by comparing average SAT scores. In addition to the objections to testing previously mentioned, educators argue that only college-bound students usually take the test, rather than all of the students in a school system. In some states over 75 percent of graduating students take the test, while in twenty-two states fewer than 20 percent do so. Average scores are higher when only a small select group takes the test. Table 15–2 ranks those states in which more than 40 percent and less than

Figure 15–1
SAT SCORE TRENDS

Source: *Statistical Abstract of the United States, 1995*, p. 175, updated by the author.

40 percent of graduating students took the SAT, by average combined verbal and quantitative scores. (The percentages of students taking the test are shown in parentheses.) Oregon and New Hampshire are ranked highest among states with 50 percent or more
students taking the test.

EDUCATIONAL REFORM

How can the quality of education be improved? Systematic research over the last two
decades has made it clear that money alone does not guarantee good educational performance. The early landmark work of sociologist James Coleman, *Equality of Educational
Opportunity* (popularly known as the Coleman report), demonstrated that pupil expenditures, teacher salaries, classroom size, facilities, and materials were *un*related to student
achievement.[2] Student success is more closely related to characteristics of the home envi-

---

[2]James S. Coleman et al., *Equality of Educational Opportunity* (Washington, DC: Government Printing Office, 1966).

Table 15–2

EDUCATIONAL PERFORMANCE BY STATE

	Dropout Rate[a]			Average SAT Scores[b]	
RANK	STATE	RATE	RANK	STATE	SCORE (PERCENT TAKING)
1	Nevada	14.9	1	Oregon	947 (51)
2	Arizona	14.3	2	Washington	937 (48)
3	California	14.3	3	New Hampshire	935 (70)
4	Florida	14.2	4	Alaska	934 (47)
5	Georgia	14.1	5	Maryland	909 (64)
6	Tennessee	13.6	6	Connecticut	908 (81)
7	North Carolina	13.2	7	Massachusetts	907 (80)
8	Kentucky	13.0	8	California	902 (45)
9	Rhode Island	12.9	9	Vermont	901 (68)
10	Alabama	12.6	10	New Jersey	898 (70)
11	Texas	12.5	11	Delaware	897 (68)
12	Missouri	12.2	12	Maine	896 (68)
13	Louisiana	11.9	13	Virginia	896 (65)
14	South Carolina	11.9	14	Texas	893 (47)
15	Mississippi	11.7	15	New York	892 (74)
16	Indiana	11.4	16	Hawaii	889 (57)
17	Delaware	11.2	17	Florida	889 (48)
18	Maryland	11.0	18	Rhode Island	888 (70)
19	Oregon	11.0	19	Indiana	882 (58)
20	Arkansas	10.9	20	Pennsylvania	880 (70)
21	New Mexico	10.8	21	North Carolina	865 (60)
22	West Virginia	10.6	22	Georgia	854 (65)
23	Illinois	10.4	23	South Carolina	844 (58)
24	Virginia	10.4			
25	Washington	10.2			
26	New York	10.1			

States with Less Than 40 Percent Taking SAT

STATE	SCORE (PERCENT TAKING)
North Dakota	1107 (5)
Iowa	1099 (5)
Minnesota	1085 (9)
Utah	1076 (4)
Wisconsin	1073 (9)
South Dakota	1068 (5)
Kansas	1060 (9)
Nebraska	1050 (9)
Illinois	1048 (13)
Missouri	1045 (9)
Tennessee	1040 (12)
Mississippi	1038 (4)

Continuation of Dropout Rate column:

RANK	STATE	RATE
27	Michigan	9.9
28	New Hampshire	9.9
29	Oklahoma	9.9
30	Alaska	9.6
31	Colorado	9.6
32	Idaho	9.6
33	Massachusetts	9.5
34	Pennsylvania	9.4
35	New Jersey	9.3
36	Connecticut	9.2
37	Ohio	8.8
38	Vermont	8.7
39	Kansas	8.4
40	Maine	8.4
41	Utah	7.9

Table 15–2 (Continued)

42	Montana	7.1	Michigan	1033 (11)
43	South Dakota	7.1	Alabama	1029 (8)
44	Hawaii	7.0	Oklahoma	1027 (9)
45	Wisconsin	6.9	Louisiana	1021 (9)
46	Nebraska	6.6	New Mexico	1015 (11)
47	Iowa	6.5	Montana	1009 (21)
48	Wyoming	6.3	Arkansas	1005 (6)
49	Minnesota	6.1	Wyoming	1001 (10)
50	North Dakota	4.3	Kentucky	999 (11)
			Colorado	980 (29)
			Idaho	979 (15)
			Ohio	975 (23)
			Arizona	944 (27)
			West Virginia	932 (17)
			Nevada	917 (30)

ᵃPercentage of sixteen- to nineteen-year-olds not attending and not graduated from high school 1992.

Source: U.S. Department of Education.

ᵇCombined verbal and quantitative scores.

Source: College Boards, 1995.

ronment than to those of the schools. However, Coleman later demonstrated that student achievement levels are higher in schools in which there is a high expectation for achievement, an orderly and disciplined learning environment, an emphasis on basic skills, frequent monitoring of student progress, and teacher–parent interaction and agreement on values and norms.[3] These factors help explain why students from the same family backgrounds perform better in private and Catholic schools than in public schools.[4]

A Nation At Risk   Educational reform was given impetus by an influential 1983 report by the National Commission on Excellence in Education entitled "A Nation At Risk."[5]

> Our nation is at risk. Our once unchallenged prominence in commerce, industry, science, and technological innovation is being overtaken by competitors throughout the world. . . .
>
> If an unfriendly foreign power had attempted to impose on America the mediocre educational performance that exists today, we might well have viewed it as an act of war.

The commission's recommendations set the agenda for educational policy debate in the states. Among the many recommendations were these:

---

[3]James S. Coleman et al., *High School Achievement* (New York: Basic Books, 1982).

[4]James S. Coleman and Thomas Hoffer, *Public and Private High Schools* (New York: Basic Books, 1987).

[5]National Commission on Excellence in Education, *A Nation At Risk* (Washington, DC: Government Printing Office, 1983).

- A minimum high school curriculum of four years of English, three years of mathematics, three years of social science, and one-half year of computer science.
- Four to six years of foreign language study beginning in the elementary grades.
- Standardized tests for achievement for all of these subjects.
- More homework, a seven-hour school day, and a 200- to 220-day school year.
- Reliable grades and standardized tests for promotion and graduation.
- "Performance-based" salaries for teachers and rewards for "superior" teaching.

PERFORMANCE TESTING   Many state legislatures responded to the commission's report and the demand for greater achievement in basic skills by requiring minimum competence testing (MCT) in the schools. MCTs may be used as diagnostic tools to determine the need for remedial education, or minimum scores may be required for promotion or graduation. Currently, about half of the states require students to pass a minimum competence test to receive a high school diploma. These tests usually require performance at an eighth- or ninth-grade level.

Minimum competence tests force schools and teachers to place greater emphasis on the "basics." Professional educators have been less enthusiastic about testing than citizen groups and state legislators. Educators contend that testing leads to narrow "test-taking" education rather than broad preparation for life. Testing requires teachers to devote more time to coaching students on how to pass an exam rather than preparing them for productive lives after graduation.

But the most serious opposition to testing has come from minority group leaders who charge that the tests are racially biased. Average black student scores are frequently lower than average white student scores, and a larger percentage of black students than white students are held back from promotion and graduation by testing. Some black leaders charge that racial bias in the examination itself, as well as racial isolation in the school, contributes to black–white differences in exam scores. Denying a disproportionate number of black students a diploma because of the schools' failure to teach basics may be viewed as a form of discrimination. However, to date, federal courts have declined to rule that testing itself is discriminatory, as long as sufficient time and opportunity have been provided to all students to prepare for the examination.

TESTING TEACHER COMPETENCY   Professional education groups have opposed teacher competency tests on the grounds that standardized tests cannot really measure competency in the classroom. The National Education Association has opposed all testing of teachers; the American Federation of Teachers is willing to accept competency testing only for new teachers. The Educational Testing Service (which prepares the GRE, LSAT, and other standardized national examinations) offers a National Teacher Examination (NTE), which measures general knowledge, basic comprehension, and mathematical skills. Today, only a few states have adopted teacher competency tests, but the results have been disquieting. Large numbers of experienced teachers have failed the tests.

PAY AND RECRUITMENT   Another concern of the National Commission on Excellence in Education was the inability of the teaching profession to attract quality students. The average SAT scores of education majors are lower than the average scores of other students. It should not be surprising that education fails to attract many top students when average starting salaries for teachers nationwide are less than 75 percent of the average starting salaries for other graduates. Years ago, when women were excluded from many other professions, teaching attracted women of high ability even though salaries were low. But today, with expanded opportunities for women, the teaching profession cannot expect to attract quality graduates without offering competitive salaries.

MERIT PAY   Few state legislators are willing or able to raise all teachers' salaries to the level of other professionals. The adoption of "merit pay" provides a less costly option, yet one that promises to reward good teaching. Ideally, merit pay would help retain exceptional teachers and encourage quality teaching, without rewarding mediocrity through general (across-the-board) salary increases to all teachers. But the professional education groups fear that merit pay will become a substitute for adequate teachers' salaries. They also argue that there are no objective criteria for measuring "merit" in classroom teaching. Using student test scores would unfairly penalize teachers who taught disadvantaged students. And teacher scores on "pencil-and-paper" tests do not really measure classroom performance. And of course, the subjective allocation of merit pay by principals and superintendents is potentially arbitrary. In short, merit pay plans often founder on an age-old question: What is good teaching?

EDUCATIONAL GOALS   The president and the nation's governors have generally agreed on the *goals* for American education. In 1991 President George Bush and the nation's governors, including Arkansas Governor Bill Clinton, agreed in *America 2000* to strive toward the following goals by the year 2000.[6]

- All children in America will start school ready to learn.
- The high school graduation rate is to increase to at least 90 percent.
- American students will leave grades four, eight, and twelve having demonstrated competency in challenging subject matter, including English, mathematics, science, history, and geography. (This recommendation endorses the National Assessment of Educational Progress, emphasizing standardized testing of basic skills.)
- U.S. students will be first in the world in science and mathematics achievement. (See Table 15–1.)
- Every adult American will become literate.
- Every school in America will be free of drugs and violence and will offer a disciplined environment conducive to learning.

"REINVENTING" EDUCATION

It is unlikely that the United States will reach its educational goals without a comprehensive restructuring of education. Simply spending more money on the current system of public education in the nation does not promise much in terms of improved performance. Nor do the imposition of tougher standards, more required courses, more hours in

---

[6]U.S. Department of Education, *America 2000* (Washington, DC: Government Printing Office, 1991).

schools, and other top-down mandates from states to the schools.[7] Rather, good perfor-mance is associated with the sharing of high expectations among parents, teachers, and pupils; a mutual determination of goals, methods, and disciplinary standards among teachers, administrators, and parents; close monitoring of student progress by teachers and parents; and frequent interaction between parents and principals and teachers.[8] But the problem is how to bring about these conditions.

PARENTAL CHOICE   "Choice" is a key word in the movement to restructure public education. Parental choice among schools is designed to do more than benefit only those parents who take the time and effort to choose the best schools for their children. It is also designed to foster competition for pupils among schools and thereby improve ed-ucation for everyone. It sends a message to educators to structure their schools to give parents what they want for their children or risk losing enrollment and funding.

SCHOOL-BASED MANAGEMENT   The current fad in public education is "school-based management"—decentralized decision making in individual schools by principals, teachers, parents, and community members, rather than central offices of school districts. It is designed to give flexibility to people closest to the students and to foster within the community a sense of ownership and responsibility for the quality of ed-ucation. Presumably principals, teachers, and parents at each school would decide about goals, curriculum, discipline, and perhaps even personnel. But it seldom works out that way. School-based councils often end up in conflict with central school district adminis-trators, elected school boards, state and federal regulations, budgetary restrictions, and so on. Principals and teachers often feel that it takes time away from teaching, or requires additional efforts to reach community consensus.

MAGNET SCHOOLS   Another common reform proposal is the "magnet school." High schools might choose to specialize, some emphasizing math and science, others the fine arts, others business, and still others vocational training. Some schools might be "adopted" by business, professional organizations, or universities. Magnet schools, with reputations for quality, specialized instruction, are frequently recommended for inner-city areas in order to attract white pupils and reduce racial isolation.

CHARTER SCHOOLS   Yet another reform that has been advanced in a limited number of states is the "charter" school. Community educational groups, including pub-lic school teachers and parents, sign a "charter" with their school district or state educa-tion department to establish their own school. They receive waivers from most state and school district regulations to enable them to be more innovative; in exchange for this flex-ibility they promise to show specific student achievement. Minnesota was the first state,

---

[7]See John E. Chubb and Terry M. Moe, "Politics, Markets, and the Organization of Schools," *American Political Science Review,* 82 (December 1988), 1065–87; and their *Politics, Markets, and America's Schools* (Washington, DC: Brookings Institution, 1990).

[8]James S. Coleman and Thomas Hoffer, *Public and Private High Schools* (New York: Basic Books, 1987).

in 1991, to permit charter schools and about a dozen states have followed suit; but relatively few charter schools have been established anywhere.

PRIVATIZED PUBLIC SCHOOLS   A more radical version of the charter school is the privately contracted public school, where a private profit-making corporation contracts with the school district to provide schooling for its pupils, thus replacing the public schools. Private firms usually promise to provide pupil education at a lower cost to school districts than the districts regularly incur in providing schools themselves. The private firms make their profits from cost savings in instructional delivery and program management. And they usually promise to produce better results—higher test scores, fewer dropouts, more employable graduates. So far only limited experiments have taken place throughout the country.

But privatization is bitterly opposed by public school administrators, public school teachers, and especially teachers' unions. They argue that profit-making entrepreneurs do not have the community's best interest at heart, that private firms teach only test-taking skills at the expense of broader educational goals, and that there is no hard evidence so far that private firms can produce better educational results.

EDUCATIONAL VOUCHERS   An even more controversial version of parental choice involves educational vouchers that would be given to parents to spend at any school they choose, public or private. State governments would redeem the vouchers submitted by schools by paying specified amounts—perhaps the equivalent of the state's per pupil educational spending (the U.S. average was over $5,500 in 1994). All public and private schools would compete equally for students, and state education funds would flow to those schools that enrolled more students. Competition would encourage all schools to satisfy parental demands for excellence. Racial or religious or ethnic discrimination would be strictly prohibited in any private or public school receiving vouchers. Providing vouchers for private school education would be most effective for children from poor or disadvantaged homes. These children currently do not have the same option as children from more affluent homes of fleeing the public schools and enrolling in private academies.

OPPOSITION TO VOUCHERS   Yet there is strong opposition to the voucher idea. The most vocal opposition comes from professional school administrators and state educational agencies. They argue that giving parents the right to move their children from school to school disrupts educational planning and threatens the viability of schools that are perceived as inferior. It may lead to a stratification of schools into popular, magnet schools that would attract the best students, and less popular schools that would be left with the task of educating students whose parents were unaware or uninterested in their children's education. Other opponents of choice plans fear that public education might be undermined if the choice available to parents includes the option of sending their children to private, church-related schools. Public education groups are fearful that vouchers will divert public money from public to private schools. As governor of Arkansas, Bill Clinton endorsed the notion of choice, but only *within* the public school system.[9]

---

[9]Bill Clinton and Al Gore, *Putting People First* (New York: Times Books, 1992), p. 86.

CALIFORNIA VOTES TO REJECT VOUCHERS   The educational choice movement was dealt a major setback in 1993 when California voters soundly defeated a citizens' initiative known as Proposition 174, Parental Choice in Education. Professional educators, teachers' unions, and liberal groups joined together to mount an expensive, highly publicized campaign to defeat the measure. Proposition 174 promised to "empower parents" by granting each schoolchild a "scholarship" (voucher) equal to about one-half of the average amount of state and local government aid per pupil in California (about $2,600). The money was to be paid directly to the schools in which parents chose to enroll their children. Either public or private schools could qualify as "scholarship-redeeming schools"; schools that discriminated on the basis of race, ethnicity, color, or national origin would not be eligible.

Opposition groups, including the powerful California Teachers Association, argued that the proposal would create "a two-tier system of schools, one for the haves, one for the have-nots." They portrayed vouchers as "an entitlement program offering wealthy families a private-school subsidy for their children, paid for by the taxpayers," noting that there was no means test for the vouchers. About 10 percent of California's schoolchildren were in private schools already; their parents would enjoy an immediate windfall benefit from the program. Opponents warned that public education would suffer grievously if both money and gifted students were removed from public schools. Although only half of the costs of educating a public school student would go into a voucher, it was argued that public schools would face financial difficulties from the implementation of the program. The initial costs of vouchers for pupils already attending private schools posed a major financial problem. No one could accurately estimate how many pupils would eventually transfer from public to private schools. Finally, opponents made inroads in the electorate by warning that taxpayers' money would go to religious schools and noting that the content of instruction and credentials of teachers were unregulated in the proposal.

THE LIMITED FEDERAL ROLE IN EDUCATION

Traditionally, education in America was a community responsibility. But today state governments have taken major responsibility for public education. The federal government remains largely an interested spectator in the area of educational policy. While it has taken the lead in guaranteeing racial equality in education, and separating religion from public schools, it has never assumed any significant share of the costs of education. The federal state of educational spending has never exceeded 10 percent. (See Table 15–3.)

EARLY FEDERAL AID   The federal government's role in education, however, is a longstanding one. In the famous Northwest Ordinance of 1787, Congress offered land grants for public schools in the new territories. Then in 1862 the Morrill Land Grant Act provided grants of federal land to each state for the establishment of colleges specializing in agricultural and mechanical arts. These became known as "land-grant colleges." In 1867 Congress established a U.S. Office of Education, which became the Department of Education in 1979. The Smith-Hughes Act of 1917 set up the first program of federal

Table 15–3

SOURCES OF FUNDS FOR EDUCATION IN THE UNITED STATES

	Percentage of Educational Expenditures by Source			
	1965	1975	1985	1992
Federal	9.4	10.0	8.6	6.9
State	29.5	33.8	38.8	42.0
Local	35.1	30.8	25.6	29.1
Private	26.0	25.3	27.0	22.0

Source: Statistical Abstract of the United States, 1994, p. 154.

grants-in-aid to promote vocational education and enabled schools to provide training in agriculture, home economics, trades, and industries. In the National School Lunch and Milk programs, begun in 1946, federal grants and commodity donations are made for nonprofit lunches and milk served in public and private schools. In the Federal Impacted Areas Aid Program, begun in 1950, federal aid is authorized in "federally impacted" areas of the nation. These are areas where federal activities create a substantial increase in school enrollments or a reduction in taxable resources because of federally owned property. In response to the Soviet Union's success in launching "Sputnik," the first satellite into space in 1957, Congress became concerned that the American educational system might not be keeping abreast of advances made in other nations, particularly in science and technology. In the National Defense Education Act (NDEA) of 1958, Congress provided financial aid to states and public school districts to improve instruction in science, mathematics, and foreign languages.

ELEMENTARY AND SECONDARY EDUCATION (TITLE I)   The Elementary and Secondary Education Act of 1965 marked the first large breakthrough in federal aid to education. Yet even ESEA was not a *general* aid-to-education program—one that would assist all public and private schools in school construction and teachers' salaries. The main thrust of ESEA is in "poverty-impacted" schools, instructional materials, and educational research and training. The Education Consolidation and Improvement Act of 1981 consolidated ESEA and related education programs into a single "Title I" block grant allowing the states greater discretion in how federal funds can be spent for compensatory education. This remains the largest federal aid-to-education program, accounting for over 60 percent of federal elementary and secondary education spending.

However, it is difficult to demonstrate that federal aid programs improve the quality of education in America.[10] Indeed, during the years in which federal aid was increasing, student achievement scores were *declining* (see Figure 15–1). Raising the educational achievement levels of America's youth depends less on the amount spent than on how it is spent.

---

[10]See Brian Jendryka, "Failing Grade for Federal Aid," *Policy Review* (Fall 1993), 77–81.

Presidents and Congress are often tempted to direct state educational policies from Washington. To date, however, the goals set forth at national conferences have not been enacted into law, although Congress has considered proposals to make instruction in basic subjects and national testing a prerequisite to federal educational aid to the states.

ORGANIZING PUBLIC EDUCATION IN THE STATES

The fifty state governments, by means of enabling legislation, establish local school districts and endow them with the authority to operate public schools. There are about 15,000 local school boards, and 85,000 board members, who are chosen usually, but not always, by popular election. State laws authorize these boards to levy and collect taxes, borrow money, engage in school construction, hire instructional personnel, and make certain determinations about local school policy.

STATE SUPERVISION   Yet, in every state, the authority of local school districts is severely limited by state legislation. State law determines the types and rates of taxes to be levied, the maximum debt that can be incurred, the number of days schools shall remain open, the number of years of compulsory school attendance, the minimum salaries to be paid to teachers, the types of schools to be operated by the local boards, the number of grades to be taught, the qualifications of teachers, and the general content of curricula. In addition, many states choose the textbooks, establish course outlines, recommend teaching methods, establish statewide examinations, fix minimum teacher–pupil ratios, and stipulate course content in great detail. In short, the responsibility for public education is firmly in the hands of state governments.

State responsibility for public education is no mere paper arrangement. States ensure local compliance with state educational policy through (1) bureaucratic oversight, involving state boards of education, state commissioners or superintendents of education, and state departments of education, and (2) financial control through state allocation of funds to local school districts.

STATE BOARDS OF EDUCATION   Traditionally, state control over education was vested in state boards of education. In most states these boards are appointed by the governor; in some states they are composed of state officials; and in eleven states (Alabama, Colorado, Hawaii, Kansas, Louisiana, Michigan, Nebraska, Nevada, New Mexico, Ohio, and Texas) they are directly elected by the voters. These boards generally have the formal power to decide everything from teacher certification to textbook selection. However, in practice these boards rely heavily on the recommendations of the state commissioner of education and the state department of education.

STATE COMMISSIONERS OF EDUCATION   All states have chief education officers, variously entitled commissioner of education, state school superintendent, or superintendent of public instruction. In fifteen states this official is elected (Arizona, California, Florida, Georgia, Idaho, Indiana, Montana, North Carolina, North Dakota, Oklahoma, Oregon, South Carolina, Washington, Wisconsin, and Wyoming). In other states they are appointed by the governor or the state education board. The chief education officer may exercise the most important influence over education in the state, as public spokesperson for education, in testimony before the legislature, and as the head of the state department of education.

STATE DEPARTMENTS OF EDUCATION   State educational bureaucracies have greatly expanded in size and power over the years. They disburse state funds to local schools, prepare statewide curricula, select textbooks and materials, determine teacher qualifications, establish and enforce school building codes, and supervise statewide testing. Their principal tool in enforcing their control over local schools is the allocation of state educational money.

SCHOOL DISTRICT CONSOLIDATION   One of the most dramatic reorganization and centralization movements in American government in this century was the successful drive to reduce, through consolidation, the number of local school districts in the United States. In a thirty-year period (1950–1980), three out of every four school districts were eliminated through consolidation. Support for school district consolidation came from *state* school officials in every state. Opposition to consolidation was *local* in character.

STATE FINANCIAL CONTROL   States ensure the implementation of state educational policies through state grants of money to local school districts. Every state provides grants in one form or another to local school districts to supplement locally derived school revenue. This places the superior taxing powers of the state in the service of public schools operated at the local level. In every state, an equalization formula in the distribution of state grants to local districts operates to help equalize educational opportunities in all parts of the state. This enables the state to guarantee a minimum "foundation" program in education throughout the state. In addition, since state grants to local school districts are administered through state departments of education, state school officials are given an effective tool for implementing state policies, namely, withholding or threatening to withhold state funds from school districts that do not conform to state standards. The growth of state responsibility for school policy was accomplished largely by the use of money—state grants to local schools.

BATTLES OVER SCHOOL FINANCES

Public elementary and secondary schools enroll about 45 million students. Nationwide about $5,500 per year is spent on the public education of each child.[11] Yet national averages can obscure as much as they reveal about the record of the states in public education. Fifty state school systems establish policy for the nation, and this decentralization results in variations from state to state in educational policy. Only by examining public policy in all fifty states can the full dimension of American education be understood.

---

[11]*Statistical Abstract of the United States, 1995.*

VARIATION AMONG STATES   In 1995, for example, public school expenditures for each pupil ranged from $3,431 in Utah to $9,206 in New Jersey. (See Figure 15–2.) Why is it that some states spend more than twice as much on the education of each child as other states? Economic resources are an important determinant of a state's willingness and ability to provide educational services. Urbanization, education, and, especially, income, correlate significantly with variations among the states in per pupil expenditures for public education. Clearly, wealth is the principal determinant of the amount of money to be spent on the education of each child.

INEQUALITIES AMONG SCHOOL DISTRICTS   A central issue in the struggle over public education is that of distributing the benefits and costs of education equitably. Most school revenues are derived from *local* property taxes. In every state except Hawaii, local school boards must raise money from property taxes to finance their schools. This means that communities that do *not* have much taxable property cannot finance their schools as well as communities that are blessed with great wealth. Frequently, wealthy communities can provide better education for their children at *lower* tax rates than poor communities can provide at *higher* tax rates, simply because of disparities in the value of taxable property from one community to the next.

Disparities in educational funding among school districts *within* states can be quite large. A Congressional Research Service study reported disparities in excess of two to one (e.g., $8,000 versus $4,000) in per pupil spending among school districts in eleven states in the late 1980s (New York, New Jersey, Ohio, Pennsylvania, Texas, Montana, Missouri, Michigan, Indiana, Illinois, and Georgia).[12]

SCHOOL INEQUALITIES AS A CONSTITUTIONAL ISSUE   Do disparities among school districts within a state deny "equal protection of laws" guaranteed by the Fourteenth Amendment of the U.S. Constitution and similar guarantees found in most state constitutions? The U.S. Supreme Court ruled that disparities in financial resources between school districts in a state, and resulting in inequalities in educational spending per pupil across a state, do *not* violate the Equal Protection Clause of the Fourteenth Amendment. There is no duty under the U.S. Constitution for a state to equalize educational resources within the state.[13]

However, in recent years *state courts* have increasingly intervened in school financing to ensure equality among school districts based on their own interpretation of *state* constitutional provisions (see "The New Judicial Federalism" in Chapter 8). Beginning with an early California state supreme court decision requiring that state funds be used to help equalize resources among the state's school districts,[14] many state courts have pressured their legislatures to come up with equalization plans in state school grants to overcome disparities in property tax revenues among school districts. State court equalization orders are generally based upon *state* constitutional provisions guaranteeing equality.

---

[12]*Congressional Quarterly Weekly Report*, March 27, 1993, p. 752.

[13]*Rodriguez v. San Antonio Independent School District*, 411 U.S. 1 (1973).

[14]*Serrano v. Priest*, 5 Cal. 594 (1971).

Figure 15–2
RANKINGS OF THE STATES PER PUPIL SPENDING

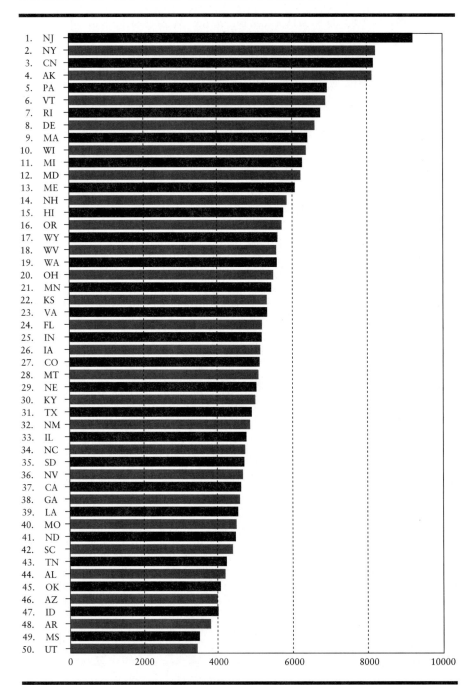

STATE FUNDS VERSUS LOCAL PROPERTY TAXES   Local school district reliance on property taxation, combined with inequalities in property values among communities, creates an equity problem: Should less money be spent on children in poorer districts because of where their parents live? Heavy reliance on local property taxes to fund schools generally ensures that fiscal disparities among school districts will exist. But many school districts across the country have sued their respective state governments, claiming that heavy reliance on local property taxes to fund schools discriminates unfairly against poorer communities. At least nine state supreme courts in recent years have agreed (Alabama, Kentucky, Louisiana, Massachusetts, Montana, New Hampshire, New Jersey, Tennessee, and Texas), and cases are pending in many other states. To achieve equity in school funding among communities, state courts are increasingly ordering their legislatures to substitute state general revenues for local property taxes. Michigan voters in 1993 approved a plan to abolish local school property taxes altogether and to replace their revenues by increasing the state's sales tax.

GOVERNING LOCAL SCHOOLS

Responsibility for many basic decisions in public education lies with the fifteen thousand separate school districts in America. In theory, these school districts are under local control. The people of the local school district are supposed to exercise that control through an elected *school board* and an elected or appointed *superintendent* who acts as the chief executive of the community schools. There is some variation to that pattern—in approximately a quarter of the nation's school districts, the boards are appointed rather than elected, usually by city councils, county commissions, mayors, or even judges. In theory, school boards exercise control over curriculum (that is, what should be taught in the schools), buildings and facilities, personnel (including both administrators and teachers), and perhaps most important of all, financing. In practice, however, as we have already seen, the concept of local control over education is heavily circumscribed by both state and federal laws.

WHO GOVERNS OUR SCHOOLS?   American schools face a dilemma in determining who should govern. Aside from the interference of federal and state administrative agencies, there is the recurring problem of "democracy" versus "professionalism." Is a democratically elected board, responsible to the citizens, an appropriate model of governance for the schools? Or should technical and policy issues be determined by professional educators who possess the necessary technical competence? Or should we continue to attempt to combine these two conflicting notions of governance?

Democratic theory assumes that schools are public institutions that should be governed by the local citizenry through their elected representatives. This was the original concept in American public education developed in the nineteenth century. However, as school issues became more complex, the knowledge of citizen school boards seemed insufficient to cope with the many problems confronting the schools—teaching innovations, curricular changes, federal and state mandates, multimillion-dollar building programs, special educational programs, and so forth. Over time, school superintendents and their administrative assistants came to exercise more and more control over day-to-day operations of the schools. Theoretically, superintendents only implement the policies of the board, but in practice they have assumed much of the policy making in local school districts. Superintendents keep in touch with the university schools of education; devote full time to their job; receive direct advice from attorneys, architects, accountants, and educational consultants; and generally set the agenda for school board meetings.

PROFESSIONALISM VERSUS DEMOCRACY   The resulting "professionalism" in education tangles directly with the "democratic" notion of control of schools. There are few meetings of local school boards that do not involve at least some tug-of-war between board members and the superintendent. (It is interesting to note that in European countries education has long been under the control of professionals, with little or no direct citizen participation in school governance.) Professional educators are frequently disdainful of the laypeople who compose the school board: The professionals must patiently explain matters of curriculum, faculties, personnel, and finance to citizen board members who are untrained in the matters about which they must decide. Professional educators often support the idea that "politics" should be kept out of education; to them, this means that nonprofessionals, even elected school board members, should not interfere in educational decisions.

THE SCHOOL DISTRICT SUPERINTENDENTS

The school district superintendents are usually professionally trained educators, either appointed by the local school board or separately elected on a nonpartisan ballot. The superintendent is responsible for the management of the public schools—hiring and supervising teachers and principals, planning and organizing the schools, preparing budgets and overseeing expenditures, and recommending policy to the board.

PROFESSIONAL DOMINANCE?   Superintendents are expected to bring professional expertise to the schools. But if citizen boards were once easily intimidated by professionally trained superintendents, such is seldom the case today:

> The American school superintendent, long the benevolent ruler whose word was law, has become a harried, embattled figure of authority. . . . Browbeaten by once subservient boards of education, teachers' associations and parents, the superintendent can hardly be blamed if he feels he has lost control of his destiny.[15]

School superintendents stress their professional expertise and rely heavily on their educational credentials to give weight to their policy recommendations. About three-quarters of school superintendents in large metropolitan areas hold doctoral degrees.[16] Those

---

[15]Harmon Zeigler, Ellen Kehoe, and Jane Reisman, *City Managers and School Superintendents* (New York: Praeger, 1985), p. 21.

[16]Ibid., p. 40.

without doctorates have at least a master's degree. Most superintendents earned their graduate degree *after* they had been employed several years as teachers.

RESPONSIBILITIES   School superintendents have three major responsibilities. First, the superintendents set the agenda for school board decisions. Second, the superintendent makes policy recommendations. Most agenda items will carry a recommendation. Third, the superintendent implements board decisions. In performing these responsibilities, superintendents, even more than city managers, provide strong leadership—advocating policy changes and selling programs to the community. Moreover, many superintendents, in contrast to city managers, involve themselves in school board elections, providing encouragement to candidates whom they respect.

LEADERSHIP   Professional superintendents do not expect to be overruled by their boards. Many of them have a "trust me or fire me" attitude that often makes compromise difficult. Nonetheless, the average tenure of appointed school superintendents is fairly long, about eight years. This is slightly longer than the average tenure of city managers (seven years).

A dominant role for school superintendents in educational policy, a role claimed on the basis of professional expertise and educational credentials, tends to minimize citizen participation in education decision making. But this role may be increasingly challenged. As one school superintendent acknowledged:

> The job of superintendent has changed radically over the past twenty years. . . . Now I have to deal with teacher militancy, closing schools, firing teachers, being more accountable for costs, and working with more active parents and citizens.[17]

However, school board members and interested citizens generally believe that popular control of education is a vital component of democracy. Schools should be "responsive" to community needs and desires. Frequently, citizen criticism has focused on the schools' failure to teach basic skills—reading, writing, and arithmetic. Another frequent source of citizen concern is the perceived retreat of the schools from traditional moral values. These issues have in turn raised the underlying question—who should govern our schools, professional educators or interested citizens?

SCHOOL BOARDS: RESPONSIBLE POLICY MAKERS?

Even if we accept the notion that schools should be governed by a democratically elected board, how can we know whether board members are accurately reflecting their constituents' desires and aspirations?

---

[17]Ibid., p. 158.

RECRUITMENT AND SELECTION   Like most decision makers, the nation's 85,000 school board members are unrepresentative of their constituents in socio-economic background. Specifically, board members are more often male, white, middle-aged, better educated, more prestigiously employed, Republican, and Protestant and have lived in the county longer than their constituents.[18] They come disproportionately from "educational families"; many members have relatives in education, usually their spouse. Many school board members report that they were first prompted to run for the school board by friends already on the board; this suggests a perpetuation of similar kinds of people on school boards. Most school board elections are nonpartisan. Many members originally came to the board as appointees to replace individuals who left the board with unexpired terms. Seldom are incumbents defeated for reelection; two-thirds of the board members who leave office do so voluntarily. The average tenure of board members is about five years, compared to over eight years for superintendents. School board members do not ordinarily aspire to, or gain, higher political office. All of this suggests "volunteerism" among board members and difficulty in holding members accountable through the threat of electoral defeat.

BLACK REPRESENTATION   Black membership on the nation's large central-city school district boards reflects fairly accurately the black population in central cities.[19] Black representation on school boards has been linked to a variety of school policies: increased employment of black teachers; fewer black students disciplined, suspended, or dropping out; fewer black students assigned to special education classes, and more black students in gifted programs.

TEACHERS' UNIONS   The struggle for power over the schools between interested citizens, school board members, and professional educators has now been joined by still another powerful force—the nation's teachers' unions. Most of the nation's 2 million teachers are organized into either the older, larger National Education Association (NEA) or the smaller American Federation of Teachers (AFT), an affiliate of the AFL-CIO. Since its origin, the AFT has espoused the right to organize, bargain collectively, and strike, in the fashion of other labor unions. The AFT is small in numbers, but its membership is concentrated in the nation's largest cities, where it exercises considerable power. Traditionally, the NEA was considered a "professional" organization of both teachers and administrators. However, today state and district chapters of the NEA are organized as labor unions, demanding collective bargaining rights for their members and threatening to strike to achieve them. Both AFT and NEA chapters have shut down schools to force concessions by superintendents, board members, and taxpayers—not only in salaries and benefits, but also in pupil–teacher ratios, classroom conditions, school discipline, and other educational matters. As the teachers' unions grow stronger, the traditional question of whether citizens or professional administrators should run the schools will be made more complex: What role should teachers' unions have in determining educational policy?

---

[18]See Trudy Haffron Bers, "Local Political Elites: Men and Women on Boards of Education," *Western Political Quarterly*, 31 (September 1978), 381–91.

[19]Kenneth J. Meier and Robert E. England, "Black Representation and Educational Policy," *American Political Science Review*, 78 (June 1984), 393–403.

FRUSTRATION ON THE BOARD   Yet, even school board members who try diligently to be responsive to their constituents are likely to face frustration in their job. Their friends, neighbors, and supporters in the community expect much more of them than they can deliver. As one frustrated board member lamented:

> America prides itself on local control of its schools; after four years on the board I have concluded that this notion of local control is a fallacy. . . . The state dictates graduation requirements and the minimum time to be spent on subjects . . . special education statutes require costly individualized educational plans for the mentally, physically and learning disabled. . . . In the critical matter of teacher performance, school boards are restricted statutorily by the state and contractually by the teachers' union. . . . Antiquated state certification [of teachers] laws hamper boards further. . . .[20]

The result is that school board members can do little to improve educational outcome—to raise SAT scores, for example. Indeed, gifted student programs, computer education, and foreign language classes are routinely eliminated when budget shortfalls occur in order to preserve state-mandated programs.

THE POLITICS OF HIGHER EDUCATION

States have been involved in public higher education since the colonial era. State governments in the Northeast frequently made contributions to support private colleges in their states. The first university to be chartered by a state legislature was the University of Georgia in 1794. Before the Civil War, northeastern states relied exclusively on private colleges, and the southern states assumed the leadership in public higher education. The early curricula at southern state universities, however, resembled the rigid classical studies of the early private colleges—with heavy emphasis on Greek and Latin, history, philosophy, and literature.

EARLY FEDERAL SUPPORT   It was not until the Morrill Land Grant Act of 1862 that public higher education began to make major strides in the American states. Interestingly, the eastern states were slow to respond to the opportunity afforded by the Morrill Act to develop public universities; eastern states continued to rely primarily on their private colleges and universities. The southern states were economically depressed in the post–Civil War period, and leadership in public higher education passed to the midwestern states. The philosophy of the Morrill Act emphasized agricultural and mechanical studies, rather than the classical curricula of eastern colleges, and the movement for "A and M" education spread rapidly in the agricultural states. The early groups of midwestern state universities were closely tied to agricultural education, including agricultural extension services. State universities also took over the responsibility for the training of public school teachers in colleges of education. The state universities introduced a broad range of modern subjects in the university curricula—business administration, agriculture, home economics, education, engineering. It was not until the 1960s that the

---

[20]Quotations from a local school board member in Connecticut, in *Newsweek*, September 14, 1992, p. 11.

eastern states began to develop public higher education (notably the State University of New York multicampus system).

PUBLIC HIGHER EDUCATION   Today, public higher education enrolls three-quarters of the nation's college and university students. Perhaps more importantly, the nation's leading state universities can challenge the best private institutions in academic excellence. The University of California at Berkeley and the University of Michigan are deservedly ranked with Harvard, Yale, Princeton, Stanford, and Chicago.

Higher education in America is mass education. No other nation sends so large a proportion of its young people to college. Over 15 million Americans are enrolled in colleges and universities. Over half of all high school graduates enroll in college. (See Table 15–4.)

ECONOMIC VALUE OF EDUCATION   An education may be its own reward, enhancing one's life regardless of economic circumstances. But there is also ample evidence that education improves one's earning potential. (See Figure 15–3.) At each level of advanced education, earnings are significantly enhanced.

COMMUNITY COLLEGES   In most states, community colleges are separate from state colleges and universities; the community colleges are really part of local government. They receive revenue from local property taxes as well as grants from the state and federal government. They are usually governed by a local board, whose members are elected or appointed from the communities served by the college.

Community colleges are the fastest growing sector of American higher education. (See Table 15–4.) These colleges are designed to reflect the local area's requirements for higher ed-

Table 15–4
HIGHER EDUCATION IN AMERICA

	1970	1980	1992
INSTITUTIONS			
Total	2,556	3,231	3,638
Four-year colleges and universities	1,665	1,957	2,169
Two-year colleges	891	1,274	1,469
Faculty (thousands)	474	686	840
ENROLLMENT (THOUSANDS)			
Total	8,581	12,097	14,491
Four-year colleges and universities	6,290	7,571	8,768
Two-year colleges	1,630	4,526	5,724
Public	5,800	9,457	11,388
Private	2,120	2,640	3,104
Graduate	1,031	1,343	1,670
Undergraduate	7,376	10,495	12,540

Source: Statistical Abstract of the United States, 1995, p. 182.

Figure 15–3

THE ECONOMIC VALUE OF EDUCATION

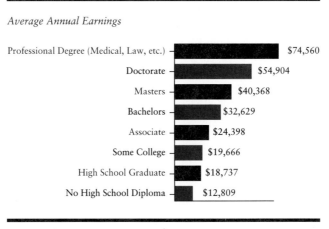

Average Annual Earnings

Professional Degree (Medical, Law, etc.) — $74,560
Doctorate — $54,904
Masters — $40,368
Bachelors — $32,629
Associate — $24,398
Some College — $19,666
High School Graduate — $18,737
No High School Diploma — $12,809

Source: Bureau of the Census, Statistical Brief SB-94-17, 1994.

ucation, and they usually offer both a general undergraduate curriculum that fulfills the first two years of a baccalaureate degree, and vocational and technical programs that fulfill community needs for skilled workers. Moreover, community colleges usually offer special programs and courses in adult higher education often in association with community groups.[21]

UNIVERSITY GOVERNANCE   The organization and governance of public higher education varies a great deal from state to state. Most states have established boards of trustees (or "regents") with authority to govern the state universities. One of the purposes of the boards is to insulate higher education from the vicissitudes of politics. Prominent citizens who are appointed to these boards are expected to champion higher education with the public and the legislature, as well as set overall policy guidelines for colleges and universities. In the past, there were separate boards for each institution and separate consideration by the governor's office and the legislature of each institution's budgetary request. However, the resulting competition caused state after state to create unified "university system" boards to coordinate higher education. These university system boards consolidate the budget requests of each institution, determine systemwide priorities, and present a single budget for higher education to the governor and the legislature. The stronger and more independent the university system board, the less likely that university and college funding will be distributed in a pork-barrel fashion by legislators seeking to enhance their local constituencies.

THE PRESIDENTS   The key figures in university politics are the presidents. They are the chief spokespersons for higher education, and they must convince the public, the

---

[21]Trudy Haffron Bers, "Politics Programs and Local Governments: The Case of Community Colleges," *Journal of Politics,* 40 (February 1980), 150–64.

regents, the governor, and the legislature of the value of state universities. The presidents' crucial role is one of maintaining support for higher education in the state; they frequently delegate administrative responsibilities for the internal operation of the university to the vice-presidents and deans. Support for higher education among the public and its representatives can be affected by a broad spectrum of university activities, some of which are not directly related to the pursuit of knowledge. A winning football team can stimulate legislative enthusiasm and win appropriations for a new classroom building. University service-oriented research—developing new farm crops or feeds, assessing the state's mineral resources, advising state and local government agencies on administrative problems, analyzing the state economy, advising local school authorities, and so forth—may help to convince the public of the practical benefits of knowledge. University faculty may be interested in advanced research and the education of future Ph.D.s, but legislators and their constituents are more interested in the quality and effectiveness of undergraduate teaching.

THE FACULTY   The faculty traditionally identified themselves as professionals with strong attachments to their institutions. The historic pattern of college and university government included faculty participation in policy making—not only in determining academic requirements but also in budgeting, the hiring and firing of personnel, building programs, and so forth. However, government by faculty committee has proven cumbersome, unwieldy, and time-consuming in an era of large-scale enrollments, multimillion-dollar budgets, and increases in the size and complexity of academic administration. Increasingly, concepts of public "accountability," academic "management," cost control, centralized budgeting and purchasing have transferred power in colleges and universities from faculty to professional academic administrators.

THE UNIONS   The traditional organization for faculty was the American Association of University Professors (AAUP); historically, this group confined itself to publishing data on faculty salaries and officially "censoring" colleges or universities that violated longstanding notions of academic freedom or tenure. (*Tenure* ensures that faculty members who have demonstrated their competence by service in a college or university position for three to seven years cannot thereafter be dismissed except for "cause"—a serious infraction of established rules or dereliction of duty, provable in an open hearing.) In recent years, some faculty have become convinced that traditional patterns of *individual* bargaining over salaries, teaching load, and working conditions in colleges and universities should be replaced by *collective* bargaining in the style of unionized labor. The American Federation of Teachers of the AFL–CIO, as well as the National Education Association and the AAUP have sought to represent faculty in collective bargaining. Many states now authorize collective bargaining with the faculty of public colleges and universities if the faculty votes for such bargaining. Faculty collective bargaining is complicated by the fact that faculty continue to play some role in academic government—choosing deans and department heads, sitting on salary committees, and so forth.

STATE LEGISLATURES   The costs of public higher education are borne largely by taxpayers. Rarely does tuition at state colleges and universities pay for more than one-quarter of the costs of providing an education. Public higher education spending per capita ranges from approximately $200 to over $500 per year in the states (see Figure 15–4). Each year's higher education appropriations bill provides state legislatures with the opportunity to exercise their oversight of the state university system.

In recent years, public higher education has faced increased austerity as the demands for state spending on Medicaid, social services, and prison construction have risen dramatically. In most states, higher education is today receiving a *smaller* share of the state budget than in previous years. Moreover, state legislatures are increasingly interjecting themselves into college and university policy making, often intruding on the traditional powers of independent trustees and regents, as well as presidents and faculty.

The thrust of legislative interventions is to increase teaching loads and responsibilities of faculty. State legislators are rarely impressed with the research activities of faculty, even when these activities are funded by grants and contracts from federal agencies or private foundations. And legislators are more concerned with teaching *under*graduates than graduate students. Legislators often receive complaints from parents about closed or overcrowded classes encountered by the sons and daughters of their constituents, or the inability of a state university to admit qualified students. So many state legislators are demanding greater faculty "productivity," usually defined as teaching more classroom hours each week to more undergraduate students.[22]

FEDERAL ROLE   Federal aid to colleges and universities comes in a variety of forms. Historically, the Morrill Act of 1862 provided the groundwork for federal assistance in higher education. In 1890 Congress initiated several federal grants to support the operations of the land-grant colleges, and this aid, although very modest, continues to the present. Federal support for scientific research has also had an important impact on higher education. In 1950 Congress established the National Science Foundation (NSF) to promote scientific research and education through direct grants to university faculty and departments. (In 1965 Congress established a National Endowment for the Arts and Humanities, but these fields receive only a fraction of the amounts given to NSF.) In addition to NSF, many other federal agencies—the Department of Defense, the Department of Education, the U.S. Public Health Service, the Department of Health and Human Services, the Department of Housing and Urban Development, and so forth—grant research contracts to universities for specific projects. Thus, research has become a very big item in university life.

FEDERAL STUDENT AID   The federal government directly assists students through Basic Educational Opportunity Grants, commonly called "Pell Grants" for its sponsor, Senator Claiborne Pell (D.–Rhode Island). The program offers college students in good standing a money grant each year that is based on the amount their families could reasonably be expected to contribute to their educational expenses. The Stafford guaranteed student loan program encourages private banks to make low-interest loans to students. The federal government pays the interest charges while the student is in school and guarantees repayment in the event the student defaults on the payment after graduation. The Perkins national direct student loan program allows students to borrow from the

---

[22]See Charles Mathesian, "Higher Ed: The No-Longer-Sacred Cow," *Governing* (July 1995), 20–26.

Figure 15–4
Per Capita Higher Education Spending

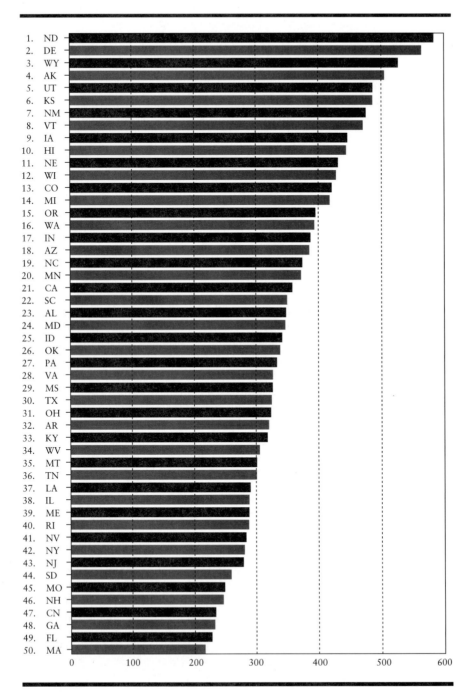

Source: U.S. Bureau of the Census, *Governmental Finance, 1992.* Washington, D.C.: Government Printing Office, 1994.

financial aid offices of their own universities. Again, no interest is charged while the student is in college; repayment is delayed until after the student leaves school. Finally, a national work-study program uses federal funds to allow colleges and universities to employ students part time while they continue to go to school.

READING, WRITING, AND RELIGION

The First Amendment to the Constitution of the United States contains two important guarantees of religious freedom: (1) "Congress shall make no law respecting an establishment of religion. . . ," and (2) "Or prohibiting the free exercise thereof." The Due Process Clause of the Fourteenth Amendment made these guarantees of religious liberty applicable to the states and their subdivisions as well as to Congress.

"FREE EXERCISE" AND PRIVATE RELIGIOUS SCHOOLS   Most of the debate over religion in the public schools centers on the *No Establishment Clause* of the First Amendment rather than the *Free Exercise Clause*. However, it was respect for the Free Exercise Clause that caused the Supreme Court in 1925 to declare unconstitutional an attempt on the part of a state to prohibit private religious schools and to force all children to attend public schools. In the words of the Supreme Court: "The fundamental theory of liberty upon which all governments in this Union repose excludes any general power of the state to standardize its children by forcing them to accept instruction from public teachers only. The child is not the mere creature of the state.[23] It is this decision that protects the entire structure of private religious schools in this nation.

THE MEANING OF "NO ESTABLISHMENT"   A great deal of religious conflict in America has centered on the meaning of the *No Establishment Clause*, and the public schools have been the principal scene of this conflict. One interpretation of the clause holds that it does not prevent government from aiding religious schools or encouraging religious beliefs in the public schools, so long as it does not discriminate against any particular religion. Another interpretation of the No Establishment Clause is that it creates a "wall of separation" between church and state in America, which prevents government from directly aiding religious schools or encouraging religious beliefs in any way.

SUPPORT FOR PUBLIC AID TO RELIGIOUS SCHOOLS   The Catholic Church in America enrolls over half of all private school students in the nation, and the Catholic Church has led the fight for an interpretation of the No Establishment Clause that would permit government to aid religious schools. As Catholic spokespeople see it, Catholic parents have a right to send their children to Catholic schools; and since they are taxpayers, they also expect that some tax monies should go to the aid of church schools. To do otherwise, they argue, would discriminate against parents who choose a religious education for their children. Those who favor government aid to religious schools frequently refer to the language found in several cases decided by the Supreme Court, which appears to support the idea that government can *in a limited fashion* sup-

---

[23]*Pierce v. The Society of Sisters*, 268 U.S. 510 (1925).

port the activities of church-related schools. In *Cochran* v. *Board of Education* (1930), the Court upheld a state law providing free textbooks for children attending both public and parochial schools on the grounds that this aid benefited the *children* rather than the Catholic Church and hence did not constitute an "establishment" of religion within the meaning of the First Amendment.[24] In *Everson* v. *Board of Education* (1947), the Supreme Court upheld the provision of school bus service to parochial school children at public expense on the grounds that the "wall of separation between church and state" does not prohibit the state from adopting a general program which helps *all* children, regardless of religion, to proceed safely to and from schools.[25] These cases suggest that the Supreme Court is willing to permit some forms of aid to parochial school *children* that indirectly aids religion, so long as this is not directly used for the teaching of religion.

Proponents of public aid for church schools argue that these schools render a valuable public service by instructing millions of children who would have to be instructed by the state, at additional expense, if church schools were not available. Moreover, there are many precedents for public support of religious institutions: Church property has always been exempt from taxation; church contributions are deductible from federal income taxes; federal funds have been appropriated for the construction of religiously operated hospitals; chaplains are provided in the armed forces as well as in the Congress of the United States; veterans' programs permit veterans to use their educational subsidies to finance college educations in Catholic universities; federal grants and loans for college construction are available to Catholic as well as to public colleges, and so on.

OPPOSITION TO PUBLIC AID TO RELIGIOUS SCHOOLS   Opponents of aid to church schools argue that free public schools are available to the parents of all children regardless of religious denomination. If religious parents are not content with the type of school that the state provides, they should expect to pay for the establishment and operation of special schools. The state is under no obligation to finance the religious preferences in education of religious groups. In fact, they contend that it is unfair to compel taxpayers to support religion directly or indirectly; furthermore, the diversion of any substantial amount of public education funds to church schools would weaken the public school system.

The Supreme Court has also voiced the opinion that the No Establishment Clause of the First Amendment should constitute a "wall of separation" between church and state. In the words of the Court:

> Neither a state nor the federal government can set up a church. Neither can pass laws which aid one religion, aid all religions, or prefer one religion over another. Neither can force nor influence a person to go to or to remain away from church against his will, or force him to profess a belief or disbelief in any religion. No person can be punished for entertaining or professing religious beliefs or disbeliefs, for church attendance or nonattendance. No tax in any amount, large or small, can be levied to support any religious activities or institutions, whatever they may be called, or whatever form they may adopt to teach or practice religion. Neither a state nor the federal government can openly or secretly, participate in the affairs of any religious organizations or groups, and vice versa.[26]

---

[24]*Cochran* v. *Board of Education*, 281 U.S. 370 (1930).

[25]*Everson* v. *Board of Education*, 330 U.S. 1 (1947).

[26]Hugo Black, majority opinion in *Everson* v. *Board of Education*, 330 U.S. 1 (1947).

TRIVIA
THE "BEST-EDUCATED" STATE POPULATIONS

Approximately 22 percent of the population over twenty-five of the United States has completed a bachelor's degree or more. But the college-educated population spreads itself unevenly across the states. (Actually the District of Columbia, with its hordes of federal bureaucrats, can boast of the largest proportion of college-educated adults—37.6%.)

STATES RANKED BY COLLEGE-EDUCATED POPULATIONS

Top Ten (25% or more)		Average (20 to 25%)		Bottom Twenty (Below 20%)	
1 Colorado	30.2	11 New York	24.2	31 Florida	19.8
2 Massachusetts	30.0	12 Kansas	24.1	32 Ohio	19.5
3 Connecticut	28.4	13 Minnesota	23.3	33 South Dakota	19.4
4 New Jersey	27.9	14 Alaska	23.1	34 Idaho	19.1
4 Washington	27.9	14 Vermont	23.1	34 Michigan	19.1
6 New Hampshire	26.4	16 Oregon	22.9	36 Pennsylvania	18.7
7 Maryland	26.1	17 Utah	22.7	37 North Carolina	18.5
8 Virginia	25.8	18 Arizona	22.4	38 Iowa	18.4
9 Hawaii	25.1	19 New Mexico	22.2	38 Wyoming	18.4
10 California	25.0	20 Delaware	22.1	40 Nebraska	18.2
		20 Illinois	22.1	41 Nevada	17.6
		20 Texas	22.1	42 Mississippi	17.5
		23 Montana	21.9	43 Kentucky	17.2
		24 Georgia	21.1	44 South Carolina	16.7
		25 North Dakota	20.8	45 Louisiana	16.5
		26 Oklahoma	20.5	46 Arkansas	15.8
		26 Rhode Island	20.5	47 Tennessee	14.9
		28 Maine	20.4	48 Alabama	14.6
		29 Missouri	20.3	49 Indiana	14.1
		30 Wisconsin	20.0	50 West Virginia	12.2

However, if "best-educated" is defined as the highest percentage of adult *high school graduates,* then Utah (90.0%) must be ranked number one, and West Virginia (68.5%) ranked number fifty.

The Supreme Court held in 1971 that it was unconstitutional for a state to pay the costs of teachers' salaries or instructional materials in parochial schools.[27] The Court acknowledged that it had previously approved the provision of state textbooks and bus transportation directly to parochial school children. Nevertheless, the Court held that state payments to parochial schools involved "excessive entanglement between government and religion" and violated both the establishment and free exercise clauses of the First Amendment. State payments to religious schools, the Court said, would require excessive government controls and surveillance to ensure that funds were used only for secular instruction. Moreover, the Court expressed the fear that state aid to parochial schools would create "political divisions along religious lines . . . one of the principal evils against which the First Amendment was intended to protect." However, in *Roemer* v. *Maryland* (1976) the Supreme Court upheld government grants of money to church-related *colleges and universities*: "Religious institutions need not be quarantined from public benefits which are neutrally available to all."[28]

PRAYER IN THE SCHOOLS   Religious conflict in public schools also centers on the question of prayer and Bible-reading ceremonies conducted by public schools. The practice of opening the school day with prayer and Bible-reading ceremonies was once widespread in American public schools. Usually the prayer was a Protestant rendition of the Lord's Prayer, and Bible reading was from the King James version. To avoid the denominational aspects of these ceremonies, the New York State Board of Regents substituted a nondenominational prayer, which it required to be said aloud in each class in the presence of a teacher at the beginning of each school day:

> Almighty God, we acknowledge our dependence upon Thee, and we beg Thy blessings upon us, our parents, our teachers, and our country.

New York argued that this prayer ceremony did not violate the No Establishment Clause, because the prayer was denominationally neutral and because student participation in the prayer was voluntary. However, in *Engle* v. *Vitale* (1962), the Supreme Court stated that "the constitutional prohibition against laws respecting an establishment of a religion must at least mean in this country it is no part of the business of government to compose official prayers for any group of the American people to recite as part of a religious program carried on by government."[29] The Court pointed out that making prayer voluntary did not free it from the prohibitions of the No Establishment Clause; that clause prevented the *establishment* of a religious ceremony by a government agency, regardless of whether the ceremony was voluntary or not:

> Neither the fact that the prayer may be denominationally neutral, nor the fact that its observance on the part of the students is voluntary can serve to free it from the limitations of the establishment clause, as it might from the free exercise clause, of the First Amendment, both of which are operative against the states by virtue of the 14th Amendment. . . . The

---

[27]*Lemon v. Kurtzman*, 403 U.S. 602 (1972).

[28]*Roemer v. Maryland*, 415 U.S. 382 (1976).

[29]*Engle v. Vitale*, 370 U.S. 421 (1962).

establishment clause, unlike the free exercise clause, does not depend on any showing of direct governmental compulsion and is violated by the enactment of laws which establish an official religion whether those laws operate directly to coerce nonobserving individuals or not.[30]

One year later, in the case of *Abbington Township* v. *Schempp,* the Court considered the constitutionality of Bible-reading ceremonies in the public schools.[31] Here again, even though the children were not required to participate, the Court found that Bible reading as an opening exercise in the schools was a religious ceremony. The Court went to some trouble in its opinion to point out that they were not "throwing the Bible out of the school," for they specifically stated that the study of the Bible or of religion, when presented objectively as part of a secular program of education, did not violate the First Amendment, but religious *ceremonies* involving Bible reading or prayer, established by a state or school, did so.

State efforts to encourage "voluntary prayer" in public schools have also been struck down by the Supreme Court as unconstitutional. When the state of Alabama authorized a period of silence for "meditation or voluntary prayer" in public schools, the Court ruled that this was an "establishment of religion." The Court said the law had no secular purpose, that it conveyed "a message of state endorsement and promotion of prayer," and that its real intent was to encourage prayer in public schools.[32] In a stinging dissenting opinion, Chief Justice Warren Burger noted that the Supreme Court itself opened its session with a prayer, that both houses of Congress opened every session with prayers led by official chaplains paid by the government. "To suggest that a moment of silence statute that includes the word *prayer* unconstitutionally endorses religion, manifests not neutrality but hostility toward religion."

---

[30]Ibid.

[31]*Abbington Township* v. *Schempp,* 374 U.S. 203 (1963).

[32]*Wallace* v. *Jaffree,* 105 S. Ct. 2479 (1986).

16

THE POLITICS OF PLANNING, HOUSING, AND TRANSPORTATION

CONTROLLING THE USE OF LAND

The most significant and far-reaching powers of local governments in the United States center on their control of land use. Land is a scarce and valuable resource. Historically, its use was determined by private owners responding principally to free market economic forces—putting their land to its most productive use. But over time, land use decisions have been largely removed from private property owners and placed in the hands of local government agencies. Local governments respond to both economic and political forces in determining how land within their communities is to be used.

EARLY CITY PLANNING   City planning began in antiquity with the emergence of the first cities. Governing authorities have long determined the location of streets, squares, temples, walls, and fortresses. Most early American cities were planned as a grid-iron of streets and squares in the fashion of William Penn's plan for Philadelphia in 1682. A notable exception to the gridiron pattern was Pierre L'Enfant's 1791 plan for Washington, DC, with radial streets slashing through the gridiron.[1] Until the early twentieth century, city planning was focused almost exclusively on the layout of streets and the location of public buildings and parks. A city's "master plan" was a map showing the location of present and future streets and public facilities. There was relatively little regulation of the use of private property.

COMPREHENSIVE PLANNING   But the reform movement of the early twentieth century (see "Reformers and Do-Gooders" in Chapter 10) brought with it a much broader definition of planning. "Comprehensive planning" involves not only the determination of the location of *public* facilities but also the control of *private* land uses.

Comprehensive planning involves the identification of community goals, the development of plans to implement these goals, and the use of governmental tools to influence and shape private and public decision making to serve these goals. Community goals are identified not only in land use and physical development policies, but also in those for population growth, health and safety, housing and welfare, education, transportation, economic development, culture, lifestyle and beautification, historic preservation, and environmental protection. According to the American Institute of Planners (AIP), planning is "a comprehensive, coordinated and continuing process, the purpose of which is to help public and private decision makers arrive at decisions which promote the common good of society."[2] Obviously this extended definition of planning plunges the planner deep into the political life of the community.

CONSTITUTIONAL CONCERNS—THE TAKINGS CLAUSE   How far can government go in regulating the use of property without depriving individuals of their property rights? The U.S. Constitution (Fifth Amendment) states clearly: "nor shall private property be taken for public use without just compensation." Taking land for highways, streets, and public buildings, even when the owners do not wish to sell, is known as *eminent domain*. A city or state must go to court and show that the land is needed for a legitimate public purpose; the court will then establish a fair price (*just compensation*) based on testimony from the owner, the city or state, and impartial appraisers. Eminent domain is a constitutional protection to American citizens against arbitrary government seizure of their land.

But what if a government does not "take" ownership of the property, but instead restricts the owner's use of it through regulation? Zoning ordinances, subdivision regulations, environmental regulations, or building and housing codes may reduce the value of the property to the owner. Should the owner be compensated for loss of uses?

Courts have always recognized that governments can make laws to protect the health, safety, and general welfare of its citizens. Owners of property have never been entitled to any compensation for obeying laws or ordinances with a clear public purpose. But it was

---

[1]See Anthony J. Catanese and James C. Snyder, *Urban Planning,* 2nd ed. (New York: McGraw Hill, 1988).

[2]American Institute of Planners, *AIP Planning Policies* (Washington DC: Author, 1977).

not clear that zoning restrictions were legitimate public purposes until 1926 when the U.S. Supreme Court upheld city zoning ordinances as "a proper exercise of police powers."[3] Cities are *not* required to compensate owners for lost value as a result of zoning regulations. Yet it was still argued that some planning and zoning provisions, especially those designed for beauty and aesthetics, had no relation to public health, safety, and welfare. They simply enacted somebody's taste over that of their neighbor. But in 1954 the U.S. Supreme Court upheld a very broad interpretation of the police power: "It is within the power of the legislature to determine that the community should be beautiful as well as healthy, spacious as well as clean, well-balanced as well as carefully patrolled."[4] So it is difficult to challenge the constitutionality of planning and zoning as a "taking" of private property without compensation.

"TAKINGS"—WHEN CITIES GO TOO FAR   However, the U.S. Supreme Court has held that a regulation that denies a property owner *all* economically beneficial use of land (e.g., a state coastal zone management regulation preventing any construction on a beach lot) was a "taking" that required just compensation to the owner in order to be constitutional.[5] The Takings Clause of the Constitution's Fifth Amendment was designed to protect private property from unjust taking by government. Its purpose is "to bar Government from forcing some people alone to bear public burdens which, in all fairness and justice, should be borne by the public as a whole."[6] If a community wants open spaces, wildlife preserves, environmental havens, historic buildings, or other amenities, these should be paid for by all of the citizens of the community. Property should not be taken from private owners, even for public purposes, without compensation. All citizens should share in the costs of providing community amenities, not just the owners of particular properties.

The question remains, however, how far can government go in regulating land use without compensating property owners? Depriving land owners of *all* beneficial uses of their land without compensation is clearly unconstitutional. But what if their use of their land is devalued by 50 percent or 25 percent? Are governments constitutionally required to compensate them in proportion to their losses? In the past, federal courts have ruled that "mere diminution" in the value of property is not a "taking" within the meaning of the Fifth Amendment and hence does not require government to compensate landowners. However, in recent years both Congress and the federal courts, as well as some states, have undertaken to reconsider "how far" government can go in depriving property owners of valued uses of their land. Increasingly, regulatory devaluations of 50 percent or more are becoming highly suspect, and property owners have a reasonable chance of recovering compensation from governments.

---

[3] *Village of Euclid, Ohio v. Amber Realty Company,* 272 U.S. 365 (1926).

[4] *Berman v. Parker,* 348 U.S. 26 (1954).

[5] *Lucas v. South Carolina Coastal Council,* 112 Sup.Ct. 2886 (1992).

[6] *Dolan v. City of Tigard* (1994).

PLANNERS IN POLITICS

State laws authorize and often mandate that cities develop comprehensive plans. Traditionally the comprehensive plan was prepared by semi-independent *planning commissions* composed of private citizens appointed by the mayor and approved by the city council. These commissions rely heavily on *professional planners* to prepare the comprehensive plan. Professional planners are mostly university graduates in city planning. They are organized into the American Institute of Planners (AIP), which publishes its own journal and grants professional credentials to planners. Over time however, independent, citizen planning commissions are gradually being replaced with planning departments within city government that are directly responsible to the mayor and council.

DEVELOPING SUPPORT   Citizen planning commissions are still retained in many communities to facilitate citizen input into the planning process and to develop political support for the comprehensive plan. Planning commissions often hold public hearings on the comprehensive plans and proposed changes to it.

The decisions of professional planners and planning commissions are officially considered advisory. That is, the comprehensive plan must be enacted by the city council to become law. The recommendations of the planning commission can be overturned by the city council. But the advice of a prudent planning staff, with the support of influential private citizens on the planning commission, cannot be easily ignored.

POLICY-MAKING ROLES   Planners, like reformers generally, claim to represent the welfare of the community as a whole. They are usually hostile to what they perceive to be narrow, self-serving interests in the community, especially business people, real estate developers, and property owners.

Planners can play a variety of roles in the policy-making process.[7] One role is that of the pure "technician," who develops plans strictly on the basis of professional planning theory, avoiding political entanglements and remaining aloof from struggles over the acceptance or implementation of plans. The technician-planner emphasizes neutral expertise. Another role is that of the "broker," who acts as confidential advisor to policy makers and considers the political "marketability" of the plans and recommendations. A third role is the "mobilizer," who actively seeks community support for the plans and enlists the backing of civic, business, professional, and service clubs. Yet another role is that of "advocate." Advocacy planning assumes that the poor and minority groups are largely unrepresented in community decision making, and therefore it is the responsibility of planners to represent them in the comprehensive planning process.

THE INFLUENCE OF PLANNERS   While the formal role of planners is advisory, they can have a substantial influence on community policy. In smaller cities, planners may be preoccupied with the day-to-day administration of the zoning and subdivision

---

[7]See John M. Levy, *Contemporary Urban Planning* (Englewood Cliffs, NJ: Prentice Hall, 1988).

control ordinances. They may have insufficient time or staff to engage in genuine long-range comprehensive planning. In large cities, the planning staff may be the only agency that has a comprehensive view of community development. Although they may not have the power to "decide" about public policy, they can "initiate" policy discussions through their plans, proposals, and recommendations. The planners can project the image of the city of the future and thereby establish the agenda of community decision making. Their plans can initiate public discussion over the goals and values to be implemented in the community. The comprehensive plan can be a tool for mobilizing public interest in community development.

LIMITS ON PLANNING   There are, of course, some limitations on the influence of planners. First of all, many important decisions in community development are made by private enterprise rather than by government. Real estate interests, developers, builders, and property owners make many of the key decisions that shape the development of the community. Their actions are often determined by the economics of the marketplace. Property owners will try to find a way to make the most profitable use of their land, the ideas of the planners notwithstanding. Second, the planners can only advise policy makers; they are just one voice among many attempting to influence public decisions about land use and physical development.

OPPOSITION TO PLANNING   The free market usually does a better job of allocating resources in a society than does government. Opponents of government planning and land use control argue that the decisions of thousands of individual property owners result in a better allocation of land than the decisions of government bureaucrats. Decentralized marketplace decisions allow more rapid adjustment to change and satisfy the preferences of more people than centralized bureaucratic decision making. Marketplace prices signal the most appropriate uses of land, just as they do the most appropriate uses of other resources.

Opponents also argue that requiring government permits for land uses—for new commercial, industrial, or residential developments and for new homes, buildings, or other structures—adds to the time and costs of development and the size of government bureaucracy (see Table 16–1). By adding to the costs of housing, planning places owning homes beyond the reach of many middle-class families. By adding to the costs of industry, or banning new industrial development altogether, planning limits the number of jobs created in a community. By empowering local officials to describe how land will be used, individual citizens are deprived of an important individual freedom.

PLANNING: INSTRUMENTS OF CONTROL

What formal powers do local governments have to control land use? Cities that choose to implement comprehensive planning and control land use have a variety of legal tools available to them: (1) zoning ordinances, (2) subdivision regulations, (3) an official map, (4) building and construction codes, (5) a capital improvement program, including locational decisions on public facilities and buildings, (6) environmental regulations, and (7) moratoriums on new construction. Planning agencies often have an important role in all

Table 16–1

THE PRIVATE COSTS OF LOCAL PLANNING AND PERMITTING
SO YOU WANT TO BUILD AN OFFICE?

The following cost estimates for planning and permitting were compiled by a CPA firm for the construction of a small (10,000 sq. ft.) office building on a two-acre site in Tallahasse, Florida. The estimates assume complete *conformity* with all existing planning, zoning, building, environmental, and land use requirements. These are costs of *planning and permitting*, not construction!

Requirement	Time	Compliance Costs
Submit land-use compliance inquiry to planning department	2 days	$530.00
Receive land-use compliance certificate	10 days	—
Complete traffic and stormwater studies	30 days	$10,948.00
Receive water, sewer, and traffic certificates	10 days	$35,800.00
Prepare preliminary site plan	3 days	$1,500.00
Pre-application conference with planning department	15 days	—
Environmental Impact Part I review	7 days	$3,360.00
Approval from environmental management department	21 days	—
Prepare final site plan	14 days	$9,100.00
Approval of final site plan by planning review committee	45 days	—
Environmental Impact Part II review	2 days	$1,410.00
Receive environmental and building permits	60 days	$23,220.00
Total	206 days (6–7 months)	$85,868.00

Source: Based on a report in *Tallahassee Democrat*, April 28, 1993, p. 4D. Estimates by Moore, Bass & Bibler.

these activities, even though the principal responsibility for these tools of implementation rests with the mayor and council.

ZONING   Planning agencies usually prepare the *zoning ordinance* for the approval of the city council. The zoning ordinance divides the community into districts for the purpose of regulating the use and development of land and buildings. Zoning originated as an attempt to separate residential areas from commercial and industrial activity, thereby protecting residential property values. The zoning ordinance divides the community into residential, commercial, and industrial zones, and perhaps subdivisions within each zone, such as "light industrial" and "heavy industrial," or "single-family residential" and "multifamily residential." Owners of land in each zone must use their land in conformity with the zoning ordinance; however, exceptions are made for people who have used the land in a certain way before the adoption of the zoning ordinance. An ordinance cannot prevent a person from using the land as one has done in the past; thus, zoning laws can only influence land use if they are passed prior to the development of a community. Many new and rapidly expanding communities pass zoning ordinances too late—after commercial and industrial establishments are strung out along highways, ideal industrial land is covered with houses, good park and recreational land has been sold for other purposes, and so on.

Since the planning agency prepares the zoning ordinances as well as the comprehensive plan, the ordinance is expected to conform with the plan. In many communities, the role of the planning agency is strengthened by the requirement that a city council *must* submit all proposed changes in the zoning ordinance to the planning agency for its recommendation before any council action.

Changes in the zoning ordinance usually originate at the request of property owners. They may wish to change the zoning classification of their property to enhance its value—for example, to change it from single-family to multifamily residential, or from residential to commercial. Usually the planning agency will hold a public hearing on a proposed change before sending its findings and recommendation to the city council. The city council may also hold a public hearing before deciding on the change.

City councils can and sometimes do ignore the recommendations of their planning agencies when strong pressures are exerted by neighborhood groups or environmentalists opposed to rezoning, or by developers and property owners supporting it. However, the recommendations of planning agencies prevail in the vast majority of rezoning cases, indicating the power of the planners in community affairs.[8]

A *zoning variance* is a request for a limited and specific variation from the strict standards in a zoning ordinance as applied to a particular piece of property. Some cities create special boards to hear requests for zoning variances, and other cities allow their planning agency to grant zoning variances. The zoning variance may be the most abused of all zoning procedures. It is not intended to encourage "spot" zoning, grant special privileges, or circumvent the interest of the zoning ordinance, but this is frequently what happens.

SUBDIVISION CONTROL   Another means of implementing the master plan is *subdivision regulations,* which govern the way in which land is divided into smaller lots and made ready for improvements. Subdivision regulations, together with the zoning ordinance, may specify the minimum size of lots, the standards to be followed by real estate developers in laying out new streets, and the improvements developers must provide, such as sewers, water mains, parks, playgrounds, and sidewalks. Often planning agencies are given direct responsibility for the enforcement of subdivision regulations. Builders and developers must submit their proposed "plats" for subdividing land and for improvements to the planning commission for approval before deeds can be recorded.

OFFICIAL MAP   The planning agency also prepares the *official map* of the city for enactment by the council. The official map shows proposed, as well as existing, streets, water mains, public utilities, and the like. Presumably, no one is permitted to build any structures on land that appears as a street or other public facility on the official map.

---

[8]See Arnold Fleischmann and Carol A. Pierannunzi, "Citizens, Development Interests, and Local Land-Use Regulation," *Journal of Politics,* 52 (August 1990), 838–53.

Many cities require the council to submit to the planning agency for their recommendation any proposed action that affects the plan of streets or the subdivision plan and any proposed acquisition or sale of city real estate.

BUILDING AND CONSTRUCTION CODES   Most cities have building codes designed to ensure public health and safety. These codes are lengthy documents specifying everything from the thickness of building beams and the strength of trusses, to the type of furnaces, electric wiring, ventilation, fireproofing, and even earthquake resistance that must be incorporated into buildings. No construction may be undertaken without first obtaining a building permit, which must be prominently displayed at the building site. Building inspectors are then dispatched periodically to the site to see if work is progressing in conformance with the building codes. The planning agency does not usually administer the code (that is normally the function of a building or housing department), but the planners are usually consulted about proposed changes in the building code.

Housing codes are designed to bring existing structures up to minimum standards. They set forth minimum requirements for fire safety, ventilation, plumbing, sanitation, and building condition. As with building codes, enforcement is the responsibility of city government, but the planning commission is normally consulted about changes in the code.

CAPITAL IMPROVEMENTS   Comprehensive planning can also be implemented through a *capital improvement program*. This program is simply the planned schedule of public projects by the city—new public buildings, parks, streets, and so on. Many larger cities instruct their planning agencies to prepare a long-range capital improvement program for a five- or ten-year period. Of course, the council may choose to ignore the planning commission's long-range capital improvement program in its decisions about capital expenditures, but at least the planning commission will have expressed its opinions about major capital investments.

ENVIRONMENTAL REGULATIONS   Governments have increasingly turned to environmental laws and regulations to assert control over community development. State laws or local ordinances may designate "areas of critical concern" in an effort to halt development. Designation of such areas is usually very subjective; they may be swamps, forests, waterfront, or wildlife habitats, or even historic, scenic, or archeological sites. "Critical" may also refer to flood plains or steep hillsides or any other land on which governments wish to halt construction.

States and cities are increasingly requiring developers to prepare "environmental impact statements"—assessments of the environmental consequences of proposed construction or land use change. These statements are usually prepared by professional consultants at added cost to builders and developers.

In most cities and counties enforcement of environmental regulations is the responsibility of separate environmental departments. This means that landowners and developers usually must deal with two separate bureaucracies. Planning departments are generally consulted in the preparation of environmental regulations.

MORATORIUMS   Moratoriums are temporary freezes on building or development pending the completion of a comprehensive plan or the construction of necessary public facilities—sewers, roads, and so on—to support the new development. Moratoriums are perhaps the most drastic action available to city and county governments to halt growth.

PLANNING PRACTICES

The formal instruments of land use control are often considered too inflexible for optimum planning. Local governments and private property owners frequently seek ways to avoid the rigidities of zoning and subdivision ordinances and construction codes. These regulations, when applied strictly and uniformly, often limit the freedom of architects and developers, produce a sterile environment through separation of land uses, and lead to excessive court litigation. So planners have increasingly turned to a variety of practices intended to minimize some of the worst consequences of land use regulation.

PUDs   One technique that has grown in popularity in recent years is planned urban development (PUD). PUD ordinances vary but typically they allow developers with a minimum number of acres (e.g., ten, twenty, or more) to have the option of abiding by conventional zoning, subdivision, and building codes, or alternatively submitting an overall site plan for the approval of the planning agency and council. PUD designs usually incorporate mixed residential and commercial uses, perhaps with single-family homes and apartments or condominimums, retail shops, hotels and restaurants, parks and open spaces, all included. Planners and councils often exercise considerable discretion in approving or rejecting or forcing modifications in PUDs, depending on their own preferences.

EXACTIONS AND IMPACT FEES   Many communities require developers to pay substantial fees or give over land to local government in exchange for approval of their land use plans. This practice, known as "exaction," is often defended as a charge to pay the local government's costs in connection with the new development, for example, additional roads or sewers needed or additional schools or parks required for new residents. A closely related practice is that of charging developers "impact fees" that are supposed to compensate the community for increased costs imposed by the development *beyond* the added tax revenues that the development will generate when completed. But it is virtually impossible to accurately calculate impact costs, if indeed a development actually does impose more costs on a community than the revenues it produces. So impact fees become just another cost to developers that are passed on to homebuyers and (through commercial tenants) to consumers.

DEVELOPER AGREEMENTS   Often conflict between local governments and developers are settled through developer agreements. Some states (e.g., California) specifically authorize municipalities to enter into such agreements, bypassing zoning, subdivision, and construction ordinances. In other states, often lawsuits, or the threat of lawsuits, by developers force municipalities into such agreements. The municipality benefits by being able to specify the details of a project. The developer benefits by obtaining a legally binding contract that cannot be changed later by the municipality as the project proceeds to completion.

NO-GROWTH POLITICS

"No-growth" movements in communities are citizen efforts to halt or restrict population growth and economic development. Generally, no-growthers prefer the phrase "growth management" to "no-growth," implying that not all growth or development is undesirable. However, these movements generally support restrictive zoning laws, costly requirements placed on builders and developers, strong environmental regulations, high "impact fees" on new housing or commercial developments, protection of trees, green spaces, historic sites, and so on. Unrestricted growth threatens the aesthetic preferences of upper-middle-class homeowners. It brings congestion, noise, pollution, ugly factories, cheap commercial outlets, hamburger stands, fried chicken franchises, and "undesirable" residents.

WHO ARE THE NO-GROWTHERS?   Opposition to growth is generally concentrated among well-educated, upper-middle-class, white residents who own their own homes and whose income does not directly depend upon the economic health of the community. College and university faculty are fertile grounds for antigrowth movements. Home-owning, elderly persons on Social Security or retirement income often join in opposition to community change.[9] Restrictions on development help inflate the prices of existing homes. Hence it is in the economic interest of homeowners, once they have acquired their own homes, to oppose further development. While the rhetoric of "growth management" usually cites environmental, scenic, or historic rationales for limiting growth, the deliberate inflation of existing property values provides an economic interest in opposition to new development.

Generally, the traditional "community power structure" supports growth (see Chapter 13). Real estate developers, builders, mortgage bankers, and retail merchants generally seek to encourage economic development. However, occasionally larger, better-financed developers may support costly and cumbersome planning restrictions as a means of forcing smaller developers out of the local real estate market.

TACTICS OF NO-GROWTHERS   "No-growth" movements are influential in many large and growing cities—for example, Denver, Phoenix, San Francisco, San Jose, and Tucson. More importantly, *many upper-middle-class suburban communities* (even those in metropolitan areas with declining core cities) view growth restrictions as in their own interest. These cities may restrict growth through zoning laws, subdivision-control restrictions, utility regulations, building permits, environmental regulations, and even municipal land purchases. Zoning laws can rule out multifamily dwelling or specify only large expensive lot sizes for homes. Zoning laws can exclude heavy or "dirty" industrial development, or restrict "strip" commercial development along highways. Opposition to street widening, road building, or tree cutting can slow or halt development. Public utilities needed for development—water lines, sewage disposal, fire houses, and so on—can be postponed indefinitely. High development fees, utility hookup charges, or building permit

---

[9]See Charles E. Connerly and James E. Frank, "Predicting Support for Local Growth Controls," *Social Science Quarterly,* 67 (September 1986), 572–86.

costs can all be used to discourage growth. Unrealistic antipollution laws can also discourage growth. If all else fails, a community can buy up vacant land itself or make it a "wildlife refuge."

EFFECTS ON THE POOR   Note that the burden of these policies falls not only on builders and developers (who are the most influential opponents of "no-growth" policies), but also on the poor, the working class, minorities, and non–property owners. These groups need the jobs that business and industry can bring to a community, and they need reasonably priced homes in which to live.

By restricting the supply of housing in a community, no-growth policies increase its costs. Higher housing costs restrict access for minorities and the poor. Indeed, many "growth-management" policies do not limit population growth but rather discourage the movement of minorities and the poor into a community.[10]

When suburban communities restrict growth, they are often distributing population to other parts of the metropolitan area.[11] The people kept out do not cease to exist; they find housing elsewhere in the metropolitan area. They usually end up imposing greater costs on other municipalities—central cities or larger, close-in suburbs—which are less able to absorb these costs than the wealthier upper-middle-class communities that succeeded in excluding them. What appears to be a local "growth" issue may be in reality a metropolitan "distribution" issue.

THE NIMBY SYNDROME   Opponents of growth can usually count on help from community residents who will be directly inconvenienced by particular projects. Even people who would otherwise support new commercial or housing developments or new public facilities may voice the protest, "Not in my back yard!" earning them the Nimby label. Many Americans want growth; they just do not want it near them.[12]

Nimbys may be the noisiest of protest groups. They are the homeowners and voters who are most directly affected by a private or public project. They can organize, sue, petition, and demonstrate to block projects. And virtually every project inspires Nimby opposition. Nimbys are particularly active regarding waste disposal sites, incinerators, highways, prisons, mental health facilities, low-income public housing projects, power plants, pipelines, and factories.

Nimbys are formidable opponents. While they may constitute only a small portion of the community, they have a very large stake in defeating a project. They have a strong motivation to become active participants—meeting, organizing, petitioning, parading, demonstrating. The majority of the community may benefit from the project, but because each person has only a small stake in its completion, no one has the same strong motivation to participate as the Nimbys. Government agencies and private corporations seeking to lo-

---

[10]See Todd Donovan and Max Neiman, "Local Growth Control Policy and Changes in Community Characteristics," *Social Science Quarterly,* 76 (December 1995), 780–93.

[11]For discussions of why suburban communities adopt growth controls, see Mark Baldasarre, *Trouble in Paradise* (New York: Columbia University Press, 1986); John R. Logan and Min Zhou, "The Adoption of Growth Controls in Suburban Communities," *Social Science Quarterly,* 71 (March 1990), 118–29.

[12]See Kent E. Portney, "Allaying the NIMBY Syndrome," *Hazardous Waste,* 1(1984), 411–21; and "Coping in the Age of Nimby," *New York Times,* June 19, 1988.

cate projects in communities are well-advised to conduct professional public relations campaigns well in advance of ground breaking. When the power of the Nimbys is added to that of "no-growth" forces, economic development can be stalemated.

HOUSING AND COMMUNITY DEVELOPMENT POLICY

For nearly a half century, the federal government has pursued a national goal of "a decent home and suitable living environment for every American family." And the nation has made impressive strides toward achieving that goal. Today nearly two-thirds of all Americans own their own homes. Yet problems remain. Low-cost housing is in short supply. Homeownership is declining, especially among younger families. Indeed, liberals and conservatives alike agree that "affordability" is the principal problem facing American housing today.

The national effort in housing is centered in the U.S. Department of Housing and Urban Development (HUD). HUD is the federal department concerned primarily with mortgage insurance, public housing, community development, and related programs.

MORTGAGE INSURANCE   The federal government began as early as 1934 to guarantee private mortgages against default by the individual home buyer. The Federal Housing Administration (FHA), now a part of HUD, insures home mortgages and thereby helps banks, savings and loan associations, and other lending agencies to provide long-term, low–down-payment mortgages for Americans wishing to buy their own homes. After checking the credit rating of the prospective buyer, FHA assures the private mortgage lender—bank, savings and loan company, or insurance company—of repayment of the loan in case the home buyer defaults. This reduces the risk and encourages mortgage lenders to offer more loans, lower down payments, and longer repayment periods. While these advantages in borrowing assist middle-class home buyers, note that the direct beneficiaries of mortgage insurance are the banks and mortgage-lending companies who are insured against losses. The Department of Veterans Affairs also provides VA insurance for veterans seeking mortgages.

FHA and VA mortgage insurance has been extremely successful in promoting homeownership among millions of middle-class Americans who have financed their homes through federally insured mortgages.

A great many of these mortgages financed suburban homes. In fact, the success of mortgage insurance programs may have contributed to the deterioration of the nation's central cities by enabling so many middle-class white families to acquire homes in the suburbs and leave the city behind. The FHA's mortgage insurance program is an entirely federal program, but its impact on city and suburban governments should not be underestimated.

HUD also subsidizes and insures apartment projects for low- and moderate-income families and housing projects for the elderly and handicapped. It also provides flood insurance and risk insurance in areas where private insurance is difficult to obtain.

FRAUD AND MISMANAGEMENT   Federal subsidies and insurance guarantees offer many opportunities for fraud and mismanagement. Real estate developers with "connections" at HUD have succeeded in the past into winning approval for mortgage insurance guarantees for large projects that banks would otherwise consider too risky for mortgage loans. But with government guarantees of payback in event of default by developers or owners, banks have proceeded to grant mortgages for poorly planned projects and unqualified buyers. When default occurs, HUD must pay the banks with taxpayers' money. Because both developers and banks do not fully share the risk in a project—HUD mortgage insurance assumes the risk—they may not exercise the same sound fiscal judgment they would if their own money was fully at risk. Moreover, the opportunities for fraud are many: HUD officials have been bribed to approve projects that are known to be unsound; credit checks and appraisals have been deliberately inflated; high-priced luxury projects have been approved under low-income or elderly assistance programs; political associates and campaign contributors have obtained preference for their projects over those that might better serve the community. Many of these problems have been uncovered in recent years.

THE TROUBLED HISTORY OF PUBLIC HOUSING   The Housing Act of 1937 initiated federal public housing programs to provide low-rent public housing for the poor who could not afford decent housing on the private market. The public housing program was designed for people without jobs or incomes sufficient to enable them to afford homeownership, even with the help of FHA mortgage insurance. HUD makes loans and grants to *local public housing authorities* established by local governments to build, own, and operate low-cost public housing. These housing authorities keep rents low in relation to their tenants' ability to pay. This means that local housing authorities operate at a loss and the federal government reimburses them. No community is required to have a public housing authority; it must apply to Washington and meet federal standards in order to receive federal financial support.

Public housing functioned fairly well in its early years. Its tenants were mostly working poor who sought temporary housing, could pay some rent, and moved on to the private housing market once their economic status improved. These were the people Congress intended to help when the program was originated during the Great Depression of the 1930s.

But by the 1950s the occupants of most big-city public housing projects were the chronically unemployed, female-headed households whose only source of income were welfare payments. These occupants could not afford any rent, even for building maintenance costs, and public housing across the country deteriorated. Some public housing projects became uninhabitable.

Very often, the concentration of large numbers of poor persons with a great variety of social problems into a single, mass housing project compounded their problems. The cost of central-city land required many big cities to build high-rises of ten to twenty stories. These huge buildings frequently became unlivable—with crime in the hallways, elevators that seldom worked, drugs and human filth in halls and stairways, and families locking themselves in and alienating themselves from community life. Huge housing projects were impersonal and bureaucratic, and they often failed to provide many of the stabilizing neighborhood influences of the old slums. Children could be raised in public housing projects and never see a regularly employed male head of a household going to and from work. The behavior and value patterns of problem families were reinforced.

Moreover, removing thousands of people from neighborhood environments and placing them in the institution-like setting of large public housing developments very often increased their alienation or separation from society and removed what few social controls existed in the slum neighborhood. A family living in public housing that successfully found employment and raised its income level faced eviction to make room for more "deserving" families. Finally, black groups often complained that public housing was a new form of racial segregation, and, indeed, the concentration of blacks among public housing dwellers does lead to a great deal of de facto segregation in housing projects.

EFFORTS AT PUBLIC HOUSING REFORM   Federal housing policy shifted somewhat under the "Great Society" banner of President Lyndon Johnson. The cabinet-level Department of Housing and Urban Development was created in 1965, and efforts began to move federal policy away from large publicly owned housing projects toward subsidies for private developers as well as local public housing agencies to build scatter-site low-income housing. Moreover, recognizing the fact that most public housing residents could not afford rents sufficient to maintain buildings adequately, HUD began subsidizing maintenance and operating costs, as well as capital expenditures, of local housing authorities. HUD limited rents to 25 percent (later raised to 30 percent) of tenants' income. To encourage the private market to provide low-income housing, a subsidy program known as "Section 8" paid rental vouchers to private apartment owners to house the poor. Some Section 8 money went directly to developers for new construction, but scandals eventually led to the elimination of construction subsidies, except for housing for the elderly and disabled.

During the Reagan and Bush presidencies, federal housing policy tilted toward "privatization"—greater efforts to encourage private developers to provide affordable low-income housing, as well as encouragement to tenants in public housing to manage their own developments and eventually purchase their own units. HUD Secretary Jack Kemp developed Home Ownership for People Everywhere (HOPE) to help public housing residents buy their units; but relatively few units were sold under HOPE, as residents confronted the problem of paying future maintenance costs of their purchased units.

PUBLIC HOUSING TODAY   Today there about 3,200 local public housing authorities nationwide. They house about 3.4 million residents who pay no more than 30 percent of their income in rent. These residents are among the nation's poorest citizens; in 1992 the average *family* income in public housing was $7,394.[13] Most of this income is in the form of government welfare payments; only about one-quarter of public housing residents depend primarily on earned income. Over 1 million eligible families are on the waiting list of public housing authorities for units to become available. Many "troubled" local housing authorities and projects have been taken over by HUD. Some of the worst buildings have been demolished, and HUD now encourages local authorities to evict drug dealers.

COMMUNITY DEVELOPMENT   In the original Housing Act of 1937, the ideal of "urban renewal" was closely tied to public housing. Slums were to be torn down as

---

[13]*Congressional Quarterly Weekly Report*, April 10, 1993, p. 970.

public housing sites were constructed. Later in the Housing Act of 1949, the urban re-newal program was separated from public housing, and the federal government under-took to support a broad program of urban redevelopment to help cities fight a loss in population and to reclaim the economic importance of the core cities. After World War II, the suburban exodus had progressed to the point where central cities faced slow decay and death if large public efforts were not undertaken. Urban renewal could not be un-dertaken by private enterprise because it was not profitable; suburban property was usu-ally cheaper than downtown property, and it did not require large-scale clearance of obsolete buildings. Moreover, private enterprise did not possess the power of eminent do-main, which enables the city to purchase the many separately owned small tracts of land needed to ensure an economically feasible new investment. For many years, the federal government provided financial support for specific renewal projects in cities.

COMMUNITY DEVELOPMENT BLOCK GRANTS   In the Housing and Community Development Act of 1974, federal development grants cities were consoli-dated into *community development block grant* (CDBG) programs. Cities and counties were authorized to receive these grants to assist them in eliminating slums; increasing the supply of low-income housing; conserving existing housing; improving health, safety, welfare, and public service; improving planning; and preserving property with special value. Community development block grants are based on a formula that includes popu-lation, housing overcrowding, and extent of poverty. No local "matching" funds are re-quired. Communities are required to submit an annual application that describes their housing and redevelopment needs, and a comprehensive strategy for meeting those needs.

To ensure that the CDBG program remains targeted on the poor, the legislation re-quires localities and states to certify that not less than 60 percent of their CDBG funds are spent on activities that benefit low- and moderate-income persons. Low- and moderate-income persons are defined as those persons whose income does not exceed 80 percent of the median income for the area.

Community development block grants can be used by local authorities to acquire blighted land, clear off or modernize obsolete or dilapidated structures, and make down-town sites available for new uses. When the sites are physically cleared of the old struc-tures, they can be resold to private developers for residential, commercial, or industrial use, and the difference between the costs of acquisition and clearance and the income from the private sale to the developers is paid for by the federal government. In other words, local authorities sustain a loss in their redevelopment activities, and this loss is made up by federal grants.

No city is required to engage in redevelopment, but if cities wish federal financial back-ing, they must show in their applications that they have developed a comprehensive pro-gram for redevelopment and the prevention of future blight. They must demonstrate that they have adequate building and health codes, good zoning and subdivision control reg-ulations, sufficient local financing and public support, and a comprehensive plan of de-velopment with provisions for relocating displaced persons.

ECONOMICS OF DEVELOPMENT   Urban redevelopment is best understood from an economic standpoint. The key to success is to encourage private developers to purchase the land and make a heavy investment in middle- or high-income housing or in commercial or industrial use. In fact, before undertaking a project, local authorities frequently "find a developer first, and then see what interests that developer." The city cannot afford to purchase land, thereby taking it off the tax rolls, invest in its clearance, and then be stuck without a buyer. A private developer must be encouraged to invest in the property and thus enhance the value of the central city. Over time a city can more than pay off its investment by increased tax returns from redeveloped property and hence make a "profit." Thus, many people can come out of a project feeling successful—the city increases its tax base and annual revenues, the private developer makes a profit, and mayors can point to the physical improvements in the city that occurred during their administrations.

RELOCATION   Relocation is the most sensitive problem in redevelopment. Most people relocated by redevelopment are poor and black. They have no interest in moving simply to make room for middle- or higher-income housing, or business or industry, or universities, hospitals, and other public facilities. Even though relocated families are frequently given priority for public housing, there is not nearly enough space in public housing to contain them all. They are simply moved from one slum to another. The slum landowner is paid a just price for the land, but the renter receives only a small moving allowance. Redevelopment officials assist relocated families in finding new housing and generally claim success in moving families to better housing. However, frequently the result is higher rents, and redevelopment may actually help to create new slums in other sections of the city. Small business owners are especially vulnerable to relocation. They often depend on a small, well-known neighborhood clientele, and they cannot compete successfully when forced to move to other sections of the city.

POLITICS AND DEVELOPMENT   Political support for redevelopment has come from mayors who wish to make their reputation by engaging in large-scale renewal activities that produce impressive "before" and "after" pictures of the city. Business owners wishing to preserve downtown investments and developers wishing to acquire land in urban centers have provided a solid base of support for downtown renewal. Mayors, planners, the press, and the good-government forces have made urban redevelopment politically much more popular than public housing.

NATIONAL TRANSPORTATION POLICY

Few inventions have had such a far-reaching effect on the life of the American people as the automobile. Henry Ford built one of the first gasoline-driven carriages in America in 1893, and by 1900 there were 8,000 automobiles registered in the United States. The Model T was introduced in the autumn of 1908. By concentrating on a single unlovely but enduring model, and by introducing the assembly line processes, the Ford Motor Company began producing automobiles for the masses. Today, there are nearly 200 million registered motor vehicles in the nation and 3.9 million miles of roads. (See Figure 16–1.)

HIGHWAY POLITICS   Highway politics are of interest not only to the automotive industry and the driving public, but also to the oil industry, the American Road

Figure 16–1
PUBLIC ROAD AND STREET MILEAGE

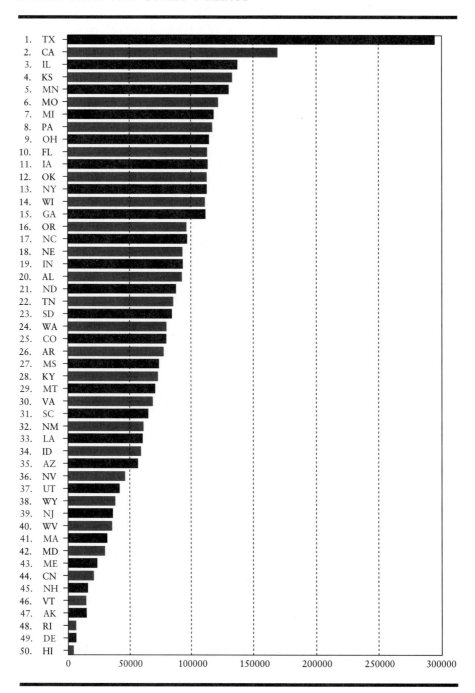

Builders Association, the cement industry, the railroads, the trucking industry, the farmers, the outdoor advertising industry, and the county commissioners, taxpayer associations, ecologists and conservationists, and neighborhood improvement associations. These political interests are concerned with the allocation of money for highway purposes, the sources of funds for highway revenue, the extent of gasoline and motor vehicle taxation, the regulation of traffic on the highways, the location of highways, the determination of construction policies, the division of responsibility among federal, state, and local governments for highway financing and administration, the division of highway funds between rural and urban areas, and many other important outcomes in highway politics.

EARLY FEDERAL AID   It was in the Federal Aid Road Act of 1916 that the federal government first provided regular funds for highway construction under terms that gave the federal government considerable influence over state policy. For example, if states wanted to get federal money, they were required to have a highway department, and to have their plans for highway construction approved by federal authorities. In 1921, federal aid was limited to a connected system of principal state highways, now called the "federal aid primary highway system." Uniform standards were prescribed and even a uniform numbering system was added, such as "US 1," or "US 30." The emphasis of the program was clearly rural. Later, the federal government also designated a federal aid "secondary" system of farm-to-market roads and provided for "urban extensions" of primary roads, in addition to the federal aid for the primary highway system.

THE INTERSTATE SYSTEM   Congress authorized a national system of interstate and defense highways in 1956 ("I" highways). The interstate system is the most important feature of the federal highway policy. Costs are allocated on the basis of 90 percent federal and 10 percent state. The Federal Highway Act of 1956, as amended, authorized 42,500 miles of highway, designed to connect principal metropolitan areas and industrial centers and thereby shifted the emphasis of federal highway activity from rural to urban needs. Although the system constitutes less than 2 percent of the total surfaced roads in the nation, it carries over 20 percent of all highway traffic. The U.S. Department of Transportation has been given strong supervisory powers, including the selection of routes, but administration and execution are still left to state highway departments. Federal monies are paid to the states, not to the contractors, as the work progresses.

FEDERAL HIGHWAY MONEY   Revenue from the federal gasoline tax has long been "earmarked" for the Federal Highway Trust Fund. Since 1970, federal highway trust fund money has also been allocated to urban mass transit. Although the current federal gasoline tax is now nine cents per gallon, the revenue from this tax alone is insufficient to repair and maintain the nation's highway system.

Congress generally recognizes the need to rebuild the nation's highways. The real political fireworks center on requirements that Congress attaches to the receipt of federal highway funds.

SPEED LIMITS   An example of the controversies generated by federal highway policy was the long battle over speed limits. Prior to 1974 most states had speed limits of 70 miles per hour on interstate highways. A national speed limit of 55 was enacted by

Congress during the Arab oil embargo as a means of saving gasoline. Congress mandated that a state be denied 10 percent of its federal highway aid if it failed to enact and enforce a 55-mph speed limit. But truckers and others who drive a great deal, particularly over long open stretches of interstate highway in the western United States lobbied hard to eliminate the 55-mph national speed limit. They argued that the costs in billions of additional hours spent on the road were unreasonable, that the 55-mph speed limit was widely ignored anyway, and that it eroded respect for the law. The national speed limit was also seen as symbolic of federal intrusion in state affairs and a threat to American federalism. However, insurance companies and consumer safety groups lobbied hard to keep the 55-mph speed limit. In 1987 Congress relented; the speed limit on rural portions of interstate highways was raised to 65 mph.

Finally in 1995, twenty-one years after first imposing a national speed limit, Congress returned control of speed limits to the states. Arguments over speed and safety will be heard now in state capitals across the county. Proponents of lower limits argue that "speed kills" and that drivers will always exceed posted limits by 10 mph. Opponents contend that most drivers exceed speed limits only when they are set too low, and that safety is more closely related to enforcement of drunk driving and seat belt laws, as well as with improved auto safety, than with speed limits. Most Eastern states are expected to retain the 65-mph limit, but Western states may up their limit to 70 or 75 mph.

THE TWENTY-ONE-YEAR-OLD DRINKING AGE   Currently federal law also mandates that the Department of Transportation withhold 10 percent of a state's highway funds if it fails to enact a twenty-one-year-old minimum age for the purchase of alcoholic beverages. (See "How Congress Raised the Drinking Age" in Chapter 3.)

TRAFFIC SAFETY   States have the responsibility for licensing drivers and vehicles and enforcing traffic laws. Prominent state efforts to improve traffic safety include mandatory seat belt laws, enforcement of laws prohibiting driving under the influence of alcohol (DWI), and the enforcement of maximum speed limit laws. Mandatory seat belt laws have been shown to more than double seat belt usage (from 20 to 50 percent or more); usage is higher in states where a violation is considered primary (where a driver can be ticketed for nonusage alone) rather than secondary (where a driver can be ticketed for seat belt violation only if stopped for another reason).[14] Studies have generally found that increased seat belt usage (as well as air bags) results in lower traffic fatality rates. Stepped-up enforcement of DWI laws has also been shown to reduce fatalities.[15]

AUTO SAFETY   Under pressure from consumer lobbies and the U.S. Department of Transportation, auto manufacturers gradually improved the safety of their products. The traffic death rate in the United States (the number of deaths from motor vehicle accidents per 100 million miles traveled) was 4.7 in 1970. This rate dropped significantly to

---

[14]Jerome S. Legge, "Policy Alternatives and Traffic Safety," *Western Political Quarterly*, 43 (September 1990) 597–612.

[15]For a summary of previous research on the effects of state traffic safety, as well as well-crafted original research, see David J. Houston, Lilliard E. Richardson, and Grant W. Neeley, "Legislating Traffic Safety," *Social Science Quarterly*, 76 (June 1995) 328–45.

3.2 in 1975 following the federally mandated 55-mph speed limit. But the traffic death rate continued to drop during the 1980s even as average highway speeds returned to previous levels. The number of accidents, about 34 million per year, remained the same, but the death rate dropped to 1.8 by 1993. These figures suggest that auto safety improvements are allowing more people to survive accidents.

STATE TRANSPORTATION POLITICS

The states retain the principal responsibility for building and maintaining the nation's highways. State and local governments also operate airports, port facilities, and mass transit.

HIGHWAY POLITICS   For many years, rural interests in state legislatures, together with representatives of the automobile, trucking, and oil industries, dominated transportation politics. Farmers wanted roads to move themselves and their products to cities; and auto, trucking, and oil interests wanted the states to build roads to subsidize their industries. The only opposition came from the railroads, which objected to the subsidization of their competitors, the truckers. But the railroads were an industry in decline, and the highway interests won most of the battles.

Highway interests in the states sought to separate highway departments from general state government and to separate gasoline tax revenues from general state revenues. Highway interests believed that their road-building programs would fare better when organization and funding were not in competition with other state programs. They succeeded in most states in obtaining (1) the creation of separate highway boards and commissions and (2) the establishment of separate highway trust funds to receive gasoline tax revenues "earmarked" for highway construction and maintenance. Indeed, some states passed constitutional amendments preventing the "diversion" of gasoline taxes for nonhighway purposes. These policies guaranteed a continual flow of road-building funds and gave highways preferential treatment over other public programs. Today some southern and western states retain these special organizational and funding arrangements for highways.

HIGHWAYS AND ECONOMIC GROWTH   Highway construction, and infrastructure development generally, is widely recognized as a key component of economic development.[16] Nonetheless, while overall government spending has skyrocketed in recent decades, spending for public infrastructure (highways, bridges, ports, airports, sewers, etc.) has stagnated. Despite evidence that spending for highways is linked to economic development,[17] state and local government spending for highway construction and maintenance has declined from about 20 percent of total spending in 1962 to less than 7 percent in 1990. Even the share of national income devoted to highways has declined, from 2.3

---

[16]Governing's Special Report, "The Public's Capital: A Forum on Infrastructure Issues," *Governing*, July 1992.

[17]See Thomas R. Dye, "Taxing, Spending, and Economic Growth in the States," *Journal of Politics*, 42 (November 1980), 1085–87.

percent in 1962 to 1.3 percent in 1990.[18] These figures suggest not only that the nation is failing to invest in *new* public infrastructure, but also that older existing highways, bridges, sewers, and water mains are deteriorating over time.

INFRASTRUCTURE INVESTMENT   Investment in public infrastructure—highways, bridges, sewage disposal and water treatment plants, airports, high-speed trains, communications, and even the electronic "superhighway"—is frequently praised by politicians in Washington. Indeed, early in the Clinton administration, "investment" (government spending) on worker training and infrastructure was offered as the means to moving America ahead in global economic competition. But it turned out to be very difficult to increase public works spending in a period of horrendous federal budget deficits. Total federal spending for highways, mass transits, and air and water transportation have remained stagnant in recent budget years. Most public infrastructure spending—over 80 percent of the nation's total—is undertaken by state and local governments.

METROPOLITAN TRANSPORTATION

City planners and transportation specialists argue that the only way to relieve traffic congestion and preserve central cities is to get people out of private automobiles and onto public transit, that is, "to move people, not cars." Automobiles on expressways can move about 2,000 people per lane per hour; buses can move between 6,000 and 9,000; rail systems can carry up to 60,000 people per hour. In other words, one rail line is estimated to be equal to twenty or thirty expressway lanes of automobiles in terms of its ability to move people. Nationwide many millions of hours are wasted by Americans sitting in traffic (see Table 16–2). The costs of this congestion exceed $90 billion a year, or $480 for every vehicle in the nation.

COMMUTING TO WORK   However, the average citizen has a large investment in the automobile. Few Americans want to see their financial investment sit in a garage all day. Americans clearly prefer private automobile transportation and costly expressways to mass transit, regardless of the arguments of transportation experts. Only 5 percent of Americans use buses or trains to commute to work (see Table 16–3). The result is that mass transit facilities almost always lose money.

CHANGING COMMUTING PATTERNS   Almost all cities now experience heavy expressway congestion at rush hour and a resulting increase in time and cost to the average automobile commuter. But predictions about future expressway "gridlock" may prove inaccurate. The proportion of daily commuters who drive from the suburbs to work in central cities is gradually decreasing as more businesses move to the suburbs. Intersuburban commuting is increasing over time; circumferential expressways circling cities now carry more traffic than expressways leading into central cities.[19]

---

[18]Advisory Commission on Intergovernmental Relations, *Significant Features of Fiscal Federalism 1992* (Washington, DC: Author, 1992), Table 55.

[19]U.S. Department of Transportation, *Demographic Change and Worktrip Travel Trends* (Washington, DC: Government Printing Office, 1985).

Table 16–2
THE MOST CONGESTED BIG CITIES[a]

Los Angeles, CA	1,780
New York, NY	1,508
San Francisco, CA	645
Washington, DC	553
Cincinnati, OH	529
Baltimore, MD	421
Honolulu, HI	390
Houston, TX	383
Detroit, MI	361
Boston, MA	337

[a]Total vehicle hours (000) of delay.
Source: Statistical Abstract of the United States, 1994, p. 631.

Rail-based mass transit facilities are usually designed for city–suburban commuting. As the central city fades as a center for employment and shopping, and more people travel from suburb to suburb, the ridership for mass transit decreases.[20]

THE CASE FOR SUBSIDIES   It is necessary to provide public subsidies to commuter-rail companies or to have governments operate these facilities at a loss if commuter service is to be maintained. Only a small portion of the costs of public transit come from the fares charged riders. However, it is argued that the cost of mass transit subsidies is very small in comparison with the cost of building and maintaining expressways. Thus, mass transit is considered cost-effective for many cities, even if fares do not meet operating expenses. Moreover, new, speedier, more comfortable, air-conditioned, high-capacity trains with fewer stops and more frequent trips may lure many riders back to public transportation.

Table 16–3
HOW AMERICANS GET TO WORK

Drive alone	73.2%
Carpool	13.4%
Mass transit	5.3%
Walk	3.9%
Work at home	3.0%
Other	1.2%

Source: Federal Highway Administration, reported in *USA TODAY,*
June 16, 1994.

[20]See Peter Gordon and Harry Richardson, "Notes from the Underground: The Failure of Mass Transit," *The Public Interest* (Winter 1989), 77–86.

TRIVIA
THE BIGGEST LANDOWNER IN THE STATES

Few people realize that the nation's largest landowner is the United States government. It owns nearly one-third of the total land area of the United States. Its land use polices are largely determined by the U.S. Department of the Interior. Federal land use policies are particularly important in those states where the U.S. Government owns half or more of the total land area.

FEDERAL LAND OWNERSHIP

By % of State

1. Nevada	82.3	10. New Mexico	33.1	19. Michigan	9.8
2. Alaska	67.8	11. Washington	29.0	20. Florida	9.7
3. Utah	63.8	12. District of Columbia	28.2	21. Virginia	7.5
4. Idaho	62.6	13. Montana	27.7	22. Georgia	6.1
5. California	60.6	14. Louisiana	22.6	23. Vermont	6.0
6. Wyoming	48.8	15. Hawaii	16.5	24. South Dakota	5.6
7. Oregon	48.2	16. West Virginia	13.6	25. Mississippi	5.5
8. Arizona	43.3	17. New Hampshire	13.1	26. Kentucky	5.5
9. Colorado	34.1	18. Arkansas	10.2	27. Wisconsin	5.4

Less Than 5%

Tennessee	South Carolina	Illinois
Minnesota	Pennsylvania	Kansas
Missouri	Indiana	Ohio
North Dakota	Oklahoma	Maine
North Carolina	Texas	Rhode Island
Maryland	Alabama	New York
New Jersey	Massachusetts	Connecticut
Delaware	Nebraska	Iowa

Source: U.S. Department of Commerce, Bureau of the Census, *Statistical Abstract of the United States, 1992* (Washington, DC: Government Printing Office, 1992).

Mass transit facilities are very costly, particularly for cities that do not already have commuter rail service. Proponents of greater federal aid for mass transit argue that cities and states do not have sufficient resources to build mass transit facilities. They argue that mass transit is cheaper than expressway construction and that expressways can never handle predicted traffic increases anyhow. They emphasize the costs of traffic jams in time and wages lost and their economic impact on central cities. Opponents of federal aid for mass transit object to the idea that the entire nation, including rural areas, should be asked to contribute to solving transportation problems of the nation's cities. Moreover, they are doubtful about the feasibility of convincing Americans that they should give up the convenience of their automobiles for mass transit.

FEDERAL MASS TRANSIT AID   For many years the federal government has subsidized the building of highways, particularly the interstate highways, where the federal government assumed 90 percent of the costs. It was not until the 1970s that the federal government showed any comparable interest in mass transit. (Indeed, the *interstate* highway system, despite its name, has carried a major share of *intra*metropolitan city–suburban traffic.) The energy crisis accelerated federal efforts in mass transit. In the Urban Mass Transit Act of 1974, the U.S. Department of Transportation was authorized to make grants to cities for both construction and operation of mass transit systems. In many cities, this simply meant the creation of a local mass transit authority and the purchase of buses. However, in some cities, massive new mass transit programs were developed with federal funds.

Among the most striking efforts in mass transit were San Francisco's BART (Bay Area Rapid Transit), Washington, DC's METRO, and Atlanta's MARTA (Metropolitan Atlanta Rapid Transit Authority). These are large projects into which the cities and the federal government pumped hundreds of million of dollars. They incorporated all of the latest features of modern, pleasant, rapid, convenient, and efficient mass transit. Nonetheless, ridership cannot pay for continuing operating costs, let alone the enormous costs of construction. Perhaps the worst example of federally subsidized mass transit is Miami's Metrorail. The costs were so great and the ridership so small that critics estimated it would have been cheaper for the federal government to buy every regular rider a Rolls-Royce.

THE POLITICS
OF POVERTY, WELFARE,
AND HEALTH

POVERTY IN AMERICA

Political conflict over poverty in America begins with disagreement over its nature and extent, and then it proceeds to disputes over it causes and remedies.

HOW MANY POOR?   How much poverty really exists in America? According to U.S. Bureau of the Census, there are between 35 and 40 million poor people in the United States. The official *poverty rate* (the number of people living in poverty as a percentage of the total population) has ranged between 13 and 15 percent in recent years (see Figure 17–1). This official definition of poverty includes all those Americans whose annual cash income falls below that which is required to maintain a decent standard of living. The dollar amounts of poverty level change each year to take into account the effect of inflation.[1]

---

[1]For example, the poverty level for an urban family of four in 1990 was $13,359; in 1993 it was $14,763. U.S. Bureau of the Census, *Statistical Abstract of the United States, 1995.*

Figure 17–1
THREE DEFINITIONS OF POVERTY

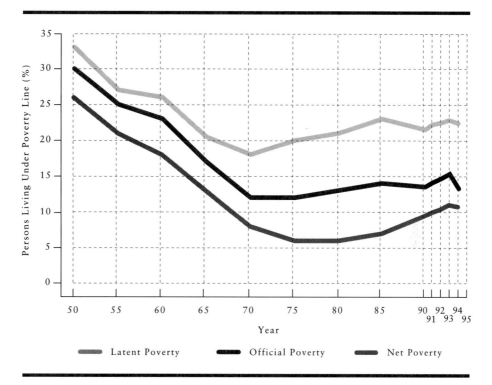

LIBERAL CRITICISM   This official definition of poverty has many critics. Some liberals believe poverty is underestimated because (1) the official definition does not take into account regional differences in the cost of living, climate, or accepted styles of living; (2) the "thrifty" food budget on which the poverty level is based is too low for good nutrition and health; (3) the official definition includes cash income from welfare and Social Security (without this government assistance, the number of poor would be much higher, perhaps 25 percent of the total population); and (4) the official definition does not count the many "near poor" there are nearly 50 million Americans or 19 percent of the population living below 125 percent of the poverty level.

CONSERVATIVE CRITICISM   Some conservatives also challenge the official definition of poverty: (1) It does not consider the value of family assets. People (usually older people) who own their own mortgage-free homes, furniture, and automobiles may have current incomes below the poverty line yet not suffer hardship; (2) there are many families and individuals who are officially counted as poor but who do not think of themselves as "poor people"—students, for example, who deliberately postpone income to secure an education; (3) many persons (poor and nonpoor) underreport their real income and this leads to overestimates of the number of poor; (4) more importantly, the official definition of poverty excludes "in kind" (noncash) benefits given to the poor by governments. These benefits include, for example, food stamps, free medical care, public housing, school lunches. If these benefits were "costed out" (calculated as cash income), there may be only half as many poor people as shown in official statistics.

THREE DEFINITIONS OF POVERTY   Thus, in addition to the "official" government definition of poverty, we can also consider "latent poverty"—the number of people who would be poor if there were no government welfare or Social Security programs—and "net poverty"—the number of people who fall below the poverty line after costing out the value of in kind government benefits. The official poverty rate, the latent poverty rate, and the net poverty rate are shown on Figure 17–1.

WHO ARE THE POOR?

Poverty occurs in many kinds of families and in all races and ethnic groups. However, some groups experience poverty in greater proportions than the national average.

FAMILY STRUCTURE   Poverty is most common among female-headed families. The incidence of poverty among these families in 1993 was over 50 percent, compared to only 7 percent for married couples (see Table 17–1). These women and their children comprise over two-thirds of all of the persons living in poverty in the United States. These figures describe "the feminization of poverty" in America. Clearly, poverty is closely related to the family structure. Today the disintegration of the traditional husband–wife family is the single most influential factor contributing to poverty.

Table 17–1
POVERTY IN AMERICA

Poverty definition 1993 (Nonfarm family of four)	$14,763
Number of poor	39.3 million
Poverty percentage of total population	15.1
RACE (% POOR)	
White	12.2
Black	33.1
Hispanic	30.6
AGE (% POOR)	
Under 18	22.7
Over 65	12.2
FAMILY (% POOR)	
Married couple	6.5
Single parent, mother only	53.7

Source: Statistical Abstract of the United States, 1995, pp. 482–83.

RACE   Blacks experience poverty in much greater proportions than whites. Over the years the poverty rate among blacks in the United States has been about three times higher than the poverty rate among whites. Poverty among Hispanics is also significantly greater than among whites.

AGE   The aged in America experience *less* poverty than the nonaged. The aged are not poor, despite the popularity of the phrase "the poor and the aged." The poverty rate for persons over sixty-five years of age is *below* the national average. Moreover, the aged are much wealthier than the nonaged. They are more likely than younger people to own homes with paid mortgages. A large portion of their medical expenses is paid by Medicare. With fewer expenses, the aged, even with relatively smaller cash incomes, experience poverty in a different fashion than young mothers with children. The lowering of the poverty rate among the aged is a relatively recent occurrence. Continuing increases in Social Security benefits over the years are largely responsible for this singular "victory" in the war against poverty.

WEALTH   Wealth is the net worth of all one's possessions—home value minus mortgage, auto value minus loan, business value minus debts, money in bank accounts, savings, stocks and bonds, and real estate. All calculations of poverty consider *income*, not *wealth*. It is theoretically possible for persons to have considerable wealth (e.g., to own a mortgage-free home and a loan-free automobile and have money in savings and investments), yet fall within the official definition of poverty because current cash income is low. Indeed, many of the *aged* who are counted as poor because their incomes are low have substantial accumulations of wealth. The U.S. Census Bureau estimates that in 1990 the net worth of the median family over age 65 was $91, 300, compared to a net worth of only $4,000 for householders under age 35.[2] This suggests that the elderly are twenty times wealthier than the young!

POVERTY AS INEQUALITY

It is also possible to defined poverty as "a state of mind"—some people think they have less income or fewer material possessions than most Americans, and they believe they are entitled to more. Their sense of deprivation is not tied to any *absolute* level of income. Instead, their sense of deprivation is *relative* to what most Americans have and what they, therefore, believe they are entitled to. Even fairly substantial incomes may result in a sense of relative deprivation in a very affluent society; commercial advertising and the mass media portray the life of the "average American" as one of high levels of consumption and material well-being.

INEQUALITY IN THE STATES   Economists have provided us with a way of measuring income inequality within political systems. Income inequality is measured by a Gini coefficient or a Gini index, which ranges from a plus 1.00 (theoretically perfect inequality) to 0.00 (theoretically perfect equality). Income inequality is greatest in Mississippi and least in Utah. (See Figure 17–2.) In general, income inequality is greater in the

---

[2]*Statistical Abstract of the United States, 1992*, p. 462.

Figure 17–2

POVERTY AND INEQUALITY IN THE STATES

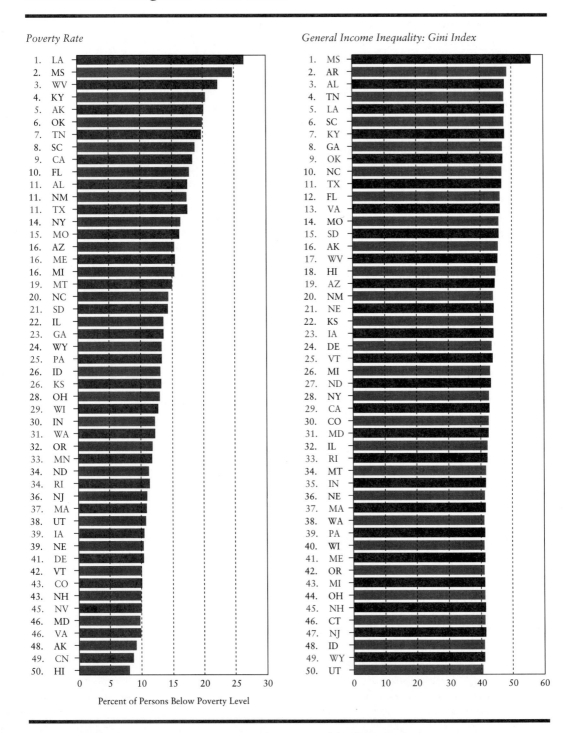

Poverty Rate

1.	LA	
2.	MS	
3.	WV	
4.	KY	
5.	AK	
6.	OK	
7.	TN	
8.	SC	
9.	CA	
10.	FL	
11.	AL	
11.	NM	
11.	TX	
14.	NY	
15.	MO	
16.	AZ	
16.	ME	
16.	MI	
19.	MT	
20.	NC	
21.	SD	
22.	IL	
23.	GA	
24.	WY	
25.	PA	
26.	ID	
26.	KS	
28.	OH	
29.	WI	
30.	IN	
31.	WA	
32.	OR	
33.	MN	
34.	ND	
34.	RI	
36.	NJ	
37.	MA	
38.	UT	
39.	IA	
39.	NE	
41.	DE	
42.	VT	
43.	CO	
43.	NH	
45.	NV	
46.	MD	
46.	VA	
48.	AK	
49.	CN	
50.	HI	

0   5   10   15   20   25   30

Percent of Persons Below Poverty Level

General Income Inequality: Gini Index

1.	MS	
2.	AR	
3.	AL	
4.	TN	
5.	LA	
6.	SC	
7.	KY	
8.	GA	
9.	OK	
10.	NC	
11.	TX	
12.	FL	
13.	VA	
14.	MO	
15.	SD	
16.	AK	
17.	WV	
18.	HI	
19.	AZ	
20.	NM	
21.	NE	
22.	KS	
23.	IA	
24.	DE	
25.	VT	
26.	MI	
27.	ND	
28.	NY	
29.	CA	
30.	CO	
31.	MD	
32.	IL	
33.	RI	
34.	MT	
35.	IN	
36.	NE	
37.	MA	
38.	WA	
39.	PA	
40.	WI	
41.	ME	
42.	OR	
43.	MI	
44.	OH	
45.	NH	
46.	CT	
47.	NJ	
48.	ID	
49.	WY	
50.	UT	

0   10   20   30   40   50   60

southern, rural, and poorer states. Income distributions are more equalized in the wealthy, urban, industrialized states.

INEQUALITY IN THE NATION   Inequality in America has decreased over most of the last century, although not very rapidly. Certainly poverty as relative deprivation is not disappearing at the same rate as absolute poverty. Table 17–2 divides all American families into five groups—from the lowest one-fifth of personal income to the highest one-fifth—and shows the percentage of total family personal income received by each of these groups over the years. (If perfect income equality existed, each fifth of American families would receive 20 percent of all family personal income, and it would not be possible to rank fifths from highest to lowest.) The poorest one-fifth received 3.5 percent of all family personal income in 1929; by 1947, however, this group had increased its percentage of all family personal income received by each of these groups over the years. (If percent income equality existed, each fifth of American families would receive 20 percent of all family persona income, and it would not be possible to rank fifths from highest to lowest.) The poorest one-fifth received 3.5 percent of all family personal income in 1929; by 1947, however, this group had increased its percentage of all family personal income to 5.0. (Most of this increase occurred during World War II.) The highest one-fifth receive 54.5 percent of all family personal income in 1929; by 1947, however, this percentage had declined to 46.0. Another measure of income equalization over time is the decline in the percentage of income received by the top 5 percent in America. The top 5 percent received 30.0 percent of all family personal income in 1929, but only 15.3 percent in 1980.

RECENT INCREASES IN INEQUALITY   While income differences in America have declined over the long run, inequality has increased in recent years. This reversal of historical trends has generated both political rhetoric and serious scholarly inquiry about its causes. The political argument that inequality increased because of miserly federal social welfare payments in the 1980s is untrue. Aggregate government social welfare transfer payments did *not* decline, either in real dollars or as a percent of gross national

Table 17–2

DISTRIBUTION OF FAMILY INCOME BY QUINTILES AND TOP 5 PERCENT, SELECTED YEARS

Quintiles	1929	1947	1954	1968	1974	1980	1990	1993
Lowest	3.5	5.0	4.8	5.7	5.4	5.1	4.6	4.2
Second	9.0	11.0	11.1	12.4	12.0	11.6	10.8	10.1
Third	13.8	16.0	16.4	17.7	17.6	17.5	16.6	15.9
Fourth	19.3	22.0	22.5	23.7	24.1	24.1	23.8	23.6
Highest	54.4	46.0	45.2	40.6	41.0	41.6	44.3	46.2
Total	100	100	100	100	100	100	100	100
Top 5 percent	30.0	20.9	20.3	14.0	15.3	15.3	17.4	19.1

Source. U.S. Bureau of the Census, Statistical Abstract of the United States, 1995, p. 475.

product. It is true that the *rate of increase* in social welfare spending declined in the 1980s, but total social welfare spending by governments remained at approximately 18.5 percent of GNP throughout the 1980s.

Recent increases in inequality in the United States are a product of several social and economic trends: (1) the decline of the manufacturing sector of the economy with its relatively high-paying blue-collar jobs, and the ascendancy of the communications, information, and service sectors of the economy with a combination of high-paying and low-paying jobs; (2) a rise in the number of two-wage families, making single-wage female-headed households relatively less affluent; and (3) demographic trends, which include larger portions of aged and female-headed families; and (4) global competition, which restrains wages in unskilled and semiskilled jobs while rewarding workers in high-technology, high-productivity occupations.

FEDERALISM AND WELFARE POLICY

The basic framework for social welfare policy in the United States for all levels of government was established by Congress in the Social Security Act of 1935. For over a half-century, the nation's major social welfare entitlement programs have been directed from Washington. The federal government has exclusive responsibility for Social Security and Medicare for the aged, and for Supplemental Security Income for the aged, blind, and disabled. The federal government, through the grant-in-aid mechanism, largely determines the nation's public assistance programs for the poor, including Aid to Families with Dependent Children, food stamps, Medicaid, and various social services. The states administer these programs, contribute matching funds to them, and enjoy some discretion in determining eligibility and benefit levels. States may also chose to provide some general assistance to persons who did not qualify for federal entitlement programs. And states may provide health care, housing, and social services, with the assistance of federal block grants for these purposes.

THE LOGIC OF NATIONALIZING   It is frequently argued that state and local governments cannot provide social welfare services effectively because both taxpayers and needy people can move freely from one jurisdiction to another. The reasoning is that if any state or local government raises welfare benefits or broadens eligibility, it will be flooded with needy people fleeing from more miserly jurisdictions. Moreover, the increased taxes required to pay for higher welfare benefits or broader participation would encourage affluent taxpayers and businesses to relocate to jurisdictions that did not impose these added tax burdens. Political scientist Paul Peterson describes this dilemma:

> One liberal Massachusetts town became a convenient locale for a range of social services, including apartments for poor families, group homes for recovery of drug and alcohol abusers, halfway homes, counseling centers, and other programs for the poor. . . . The growing number of agency clients [recipients of these benefits] eventually provoked complaints from town leaders that the community had become a "magnet for everyone else's problems" . . . "We can't afford this anymore." Even if local officials ignore such opposi-

tion and persist in efforts to assist the poor and the needy, their effort, if carried too far will almost necessarily fail. If no other force is able to stop [them], bankruptcy will.[3]

The smaller the local government, the less able it is to provide welfare services, not only because the cost of such services are directly felt by taxpayers, but also because affluent taxpayers can more easily move away if they wish to escape the burdens of providing these services. Some big cities may be able to undertake more extensive welfare services if they enjoy "natural" advantages that keep affluent taxpayers from fleeing their heavier tax burdens. States are better able to provide social welfare services than cities, but their ability to do so is still limited by the mobility of both affluent taxpayers and needy beneficiaries. It is argued that the needy will be attracted to generous states, while the affluent will be encouraged to move elsewhere.

Only the national government, it is argued, can provide adequate social welfare services and impose their costs on taxpayers without encouraging shifts in people and resources. If any *state* had attempted to provide social security by itself, it would have quickly become a haven for the aged and gone bankrupt. (Using the same logic, however, we might conclude that the openness of U.S. borders, combined with welfare benefits, encourages increased legal and illegal immigration of needy persons, while simultaneously encouraging corporations to locate their activities in less costly nations.) Thus, the logic of federalism dictates that the national government should have the principal responsibility for social welfare policy.

THE CASE FOR DECENTRALIZING WELFARE   Federal welfare policy is currently under heavy criticism. Federal entitlement programs, it is argued, actually encourage poverty by destroying incentives to work, encouraging families to break up, and condemning the poor to social dependency. The system sentences many millions of people to a life of poverty—people who would otherwise form families, take low-paying jobs, and perhaps with hard work and perseverance gradually pull themselves and their children into the mainstream of American life. Evidence for this thesis is found in the *rise* in poverty associated with the federal government's Great Society programs. Poverty in America had steadily *declined* from 1950, when about 30 percent of the population was officially poor, to about 11 percent in 1970. (See Figure 17–1.) During this period of progress toward the elimination of poverty, government welfare programs were minimal. (These were small AFDC programs for women with children who live alone; eligibility was restricted and welfare authorities checked to see if an employable male lived in the house. There were also federal payments for aged, blind, and disabled poor.) However, with the addition of many new Great Society welfare programs, the downward trend in poverty ended. Indeed, the numbers and proportion of the population living in poverty began to move upward in the 1970s and 1980s. This was a period in which AFDC payments were significantly increased and eligibility rules were relaxed. The foot stamp program was initiated in 1965 and became a major new welfare benefit. Medicaid was initiated in the same year. Federal aid to the aged, blind, and disabled was merged into a

---

[3]Paul E. Peterson, *The Price of Federalism* (Washington, DC: Brookings Institution, 1995), pp. 27–28.

new SSI (Supplement Security Income) program, which quadrupled in number of recipients.

The breakup of the family, nearly everyone agrees, is closely associated with poverty. The effect of federal entitlement programs, it is argued, has been to encourage teenage pregnancy by removing the disincentives of economic hardship and offering cash benefits, food stamps, public housing, and other means to economic independence. Moreover, federal entitlement programs, it is argued, discourage work and create dependency. The greatest increase in poverty in recent decades has been among families headed by *working-age* persons. (Social Security reduced poverty among the aged.) Generous welfare benefits discourage people from taking minimum wage jobs, and even acquiring the work habits to move into better-paying jobs later in their lives. Welfare may even help to create a dependent and defeatist subculture, lowering personal self-esteem and contributing further to joblessness, illegitimacy, and broken homes.

Welfare reformers have generally divided into two camps: (1) those who wish to impose reform from Washington, for example, by mandating time limits on welfare benefits and mandating work or job training requirements for beneficiaries, and (2) those who wish to "devolve" welfare responsibilities to the states. The argument for "devolution" of welfare policy to the state parallels the general arguments for federalism (see "Why Federalism?" and "Devolution: The New New Federalism" in Chapter 3). Specially with regard to welfare policy, it is argued:

- Decentralization will improve efficiency. The welfare system is a failure because it was built on the premise that Washington knows best, that the nation's welfare problems could be solved with a one-size-fits-all solution. State and local governments are in a better position to understand what really works.
- Decentralization will reduce bureaucracy. Streamlining federal welfare assistance into a single block grant would eliminate many federal bureaucrats and regulators. State and local welfare bureaucracies would survive, but costly federal oversight would be greatly reduced.
- Decentralization will encourage innovation and experimentation. Clearly the federal government has proven that it cannot deal effectively with poverty. Why not allow the states to experiment with various welfare reforms—time limits, restrictions on assistance to teenagers, job training programs, work requirements, and so on? Positive results from innovations in particular states would no doubt lead to widespread adoption; negative results would warn off legislators. Nationally mandated experiments are far more costly when they fail.
- Decentralization will reduce political conflict throughout the nation; differences over welfare policy can be accommodated by allowing different states to pursue different approaches. Wealthier states will provide more generous welfare benefits than poorer states (as they do now). But few welfare recipients migrate from state to state in search of higher benefits; when the poor move it is usually in search of jobs. And affluent taxpayers and wealthy firms usually do not wish to locate in area of squalor and poverty.

"Devolution" of welfare responsibilities to the states through block grants would end the federal "entitlement" approach to welfare. States themselves would undertake to determine eligibility for benefits as well as their levels. More importantly, perhaps, it would allow Congress to better control costs by deciding each year on the size of block grants. If the need began to outpace federal assistance, states would be forced to either reduce benefits or increase their own financial contributions. Finally, there are always arguments among states over the formula for determining the amounts of their block grants. States that are growing rapidly want growth factors built into the formula, while slower-growing states want to lock in federal support levels.

OVERVIEW OF WELFARE POLICY

Public welfare has been a recognized responsibility of government in the United States since colonial days. As far back as the Poor Relief Act of 1601, the English Parliament provided workhouses for both the "able-bodied poor" (the unemployed) and poorhouses for widows and orphans, the aged, and the handicapped. Today, as many as half of all families in America receive some type of government payments (see Table 17–3).

SOCIAL SECURITY   The key feature of the Social Security Act is the Old-Age, Survivors, and Disability Insurance (OASDI) program; this is a compulsory social insurance program which gives individuals a legal right to benefits in the event of certain occurrences that cause a reduction of their income—old age, death of the head of the household, or permanent disability.[4] Both employees and employers must pay equal

Table 17–3
SOCIAL WELFARE FOR EVERYONE

PERCENTAGE OF ALL FAMILIES RECEIVING GOVERNMENT PAYMENTS

Benefit	%
Social Security	26
Medicare	24
Medicaid	12
Food stamps	9
Unemployment	9
School lunches	8
Government retirement	5
AFDC	4
SSI	4
Energy assistance	4
Educational assistance	3
Public housing	3
Veterans' benefits	2
Any Benefit	52%

Source: Data from Statistical Abstract of the United States, 1995.

---

[4]The original act did not include disability insurance; this was added by amendment in 1950. Health insurance for the aged, "Medicare," was added by amendment in 1965.

amounts toward the employees' OASDI insurance. Upon retirement, an insured worker is entitled to monthly benefit payments based upon age at retirement and the amount earned during his or her working years. OASDI also ensures benefit payments to survivors of an insured worker, including the spouse if there are dependent children. However, if the spouse has no dependent children, benefits will not begin until he or she reaches retirement age. Finally, OASDI ensures benefit payments to people who suffer permanent and total disabilities that prevent them from working more than one year.

OASDI is a completely federal program, administered by the Social Security Administration in the Department of Health and Human Services. However, OASDI has an important indirect effect on state and local welfare programs, by removing people in whole or in part from welfare roles. Social Security has doubtlessly reduced the welfare problems that state and local governments would otherwise face.

UNEMPLOYMENT COMPENSATION   Another feature of the Social Security Act was that it induced states to enact unemployment compensation programs through the imposition of the payroll tax on all employers. A federal unemployment tax is levied on the payroll of employers of four or more workers, but employers paying into state insurance programs that meet federal standards may use these state payments to offset most of their federal unemployment tax. In other words, the federal government threatens to undertake an unemployment compensation program and tax if the states do not do so themselves. This federal program succeeded in inducing all fifty states to establish unemployment compensation programs. However, the federal standards are flexible, and the states have some freedom in shaping their own unemployment programs. In all cases, unemployed workers must report in person and show that they are willing and able to work in order to receive unemployment compensation benefits, and states cannot deny workers benefits for refusing to work as strikebreakers or refusing to work for rates lower than prevailing rates.

CASH ASSISTANCE: SSI AND AFDC   A third major feature of the Social Security Act was its public assistance provisions. Today, the federal government directly aids certain categories of welfare recipients—the aged, the blind, and the disabled—under a program called Supplemental Security Income (SSI). The federal government also provides *grants to the states* to assist the largest category—families with dependent children. Within broad outlines of the federal policy, states retain some discretion in the Aid to Families with Dependent Children (AFDC) program in terms of the amounts of money appropriated, benefits to be paid to recipients, and rules of the program, such as rules of eligibility. Each state may choose to grant assistance beyond the amounts supported by the national government. Each state establishes its own standards to determine "need." As a result, there is a great deal of variation among the states in ease of access to welfare rolls and in the size of welfare benefits. (See Figure 17–3.)

FEDERAL OVERSIGHT   Federal standards for state AFDC programs are established as a prerequisite to receiving federal aid. Federal law requires the states to make financial contributions to their public assistance programs and to supervise these programs either directly or through local agencies. The federal Department of Health and Human Services (HHS) demands periodic reporting from the states and oversees the enforcement

Figure 17–3
AFDC AVERAGE MONTHLY PAYMENTS IN DOLLARS PER FAMILY

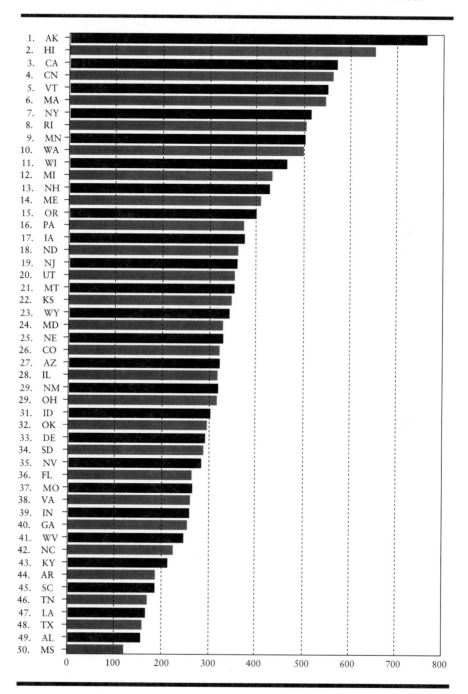

of federal rules and regulations. However, HHS may grant a "waiver" of some federal rules upon a state's request to experiment with welfare reform.

FOOD STAMPS   The food stamp program now distributes billions in federal monies to improve food and nutrition among the poor. Eligible persons may receive food stamps, generally from county welfare departments, which may be used to purchase food at supermarkets. This program has mushroomed very rapidly since its origins; eligibility for food stamps now extends to many people who are not poor enough to qualify for public assistance. Federal expenditures for food stamps are rapidly approaching federal expenditures for the AFDC program, making food stamps a major subsidy for low-income families.

OTHER SOCIAL PROGRAMS   Public assistance recipients are generally eligible for participation in a variety of other social programs. These include school lunch and milk; housing assistance; job training; various educational and child-care programs and services; special food programs for women, infants, and children (WIC); home heating and weatherization assistance; free legal services; and more.

WELFARE POLITICS IN THE STATES

Political conflict over welfare policy arises in part from a clash of values over individual responsibility and social compassion. As Harvard sociologist David Ellwood explains:

> Welfare brings some of our most precious values—involving autonomy, responsibility, work, family, community and compassion—into conflict. We want to help those who are not making it but in so doing, we seem to cheapen the efforts of those who are struggling hard just to get by. We want to offer financial support to those with low incomes, but if we do we reduce the pressure on them and their incentive to work. We want to help people who are not able to help themselves but then we worry that people will not bother to help themselves. We recognize the insecurity of single-parent families but, in helping them, we appear to be promoting or supporting their formation.[5]

While the social insurance programs (Social Security, Medicare, and unemployment compensation) are politically popular and enjoy the support of large numbers of active beneficiaries, the public assistance programs (AFDC, SSI, and Medicaid) are far less popular.

WORK DISINCENTIVES   In most states, if a recipient of assistance takes a full-time job, assistance checks are reduced or stopped. If the former recipient is then laid off, it may take some time to get back on welfare. In other words, employment is uncertain, while assistance is not. The jobs available to most recipients are low-paying jobs that do not produce much more income than does assistance, particularly when transportation, child care, and other costs of working are considered. Moreover, a family on the welfare rolls is generally entitled to participate in the food stamp program, to receive health care

---

[5]David Ellwood, *Poor Support: Poverty in the American Family* (New York: Basic Books, 1988), p. 6.

through Medicaid, to gain access to free or low-rent public housing, to receive free lunches in public schools, and to receive a variety of other social and educational benefits at little or no cost to themselves. These benefits and services are available to the poor and are not counted as income, yet the nonpoor must pay for similar services out of their own earnings. If a family head on welfare takes a job, he or she not only loses welfare assistance, but, more important perhaps, becomes ineligible for food stamps, Medicaid, public housing, and many other social services.

SOCIAL DEPENDENCY   About half of the people receiving welfare benefits at any one time are doing so temporarily; that is, they will leave the welfare rolls within two years. For these recipients, welfare payments are a relatively short-term aid that helps them over life's difficult times. But for others, welfare is a more permanent part of their lives. An "underclass" of persistently poor become dependent on welfare payments for much of their lives. About half of welfare recipients will receive aid for five years or more.

Many long-term welfare recipients are unable to get or keep full-time jobs under any circumstances. They have little or no work experience, no employment skills or aptitudes, and often no work habits or desire to work regularly. Disabilities, alcoholism, drug abuse, depressions, and emotional problems are common in this "underclass." While most express a desire to work, their desire does not extend to the menial, minimum-wage jobs that are the only ones open to them.

FAMILIES EFFECTS   Current welfare policies provide many disincentives to family life. Unwed parenthood has risen rapidly since 1970. Today nearly one-third of all births are to unmarried women (see Table 17–4). Many poor, young, unmarried, women become dependent on welfare payments as teenagers when they first give birth. It is argued that the availability of welfare cash payments, food stamps, Medicare, and housing encourages teenagers to have children, or at least removes the traditional hardships once associated with teenage pregnancy. Welfare benefits accompanying motherhood allow these young women to live independently of the families in which they were raised, and to live independently of the child's father, thus encouraging these men to abandon their child support responsibilities.

Table 17–4
RISING BIRTHS TO UNMARRIED WOMEN

	All Races	Whites	Blacks
1950	5.0	4.0	17.0
1970	10.7	5.6	37.0
1975	14.3	7.3	46.8
1980	17.8	10.2	55.5
1985	22.0	14.5	60.1
1990	28.0	20.1	65.2
1992	29.5	21.8	67.9

Source: Office of U.S. Senator Daniel Patrick Moynihan.

WORKFARE APPROACH   In the Family Support Act of 1988, liberals and conservatives joined in an effort to reform the largest cash assistance program, Aid to Families with Dependent Children. The goal was to end long-term dependence on welfare. The Family Support Act required that states

- Develop a federal job training program (JOBS) for most adults receiving AFDC payments; AFDC recipients who are not exempt because of age, illness, or disability may be required to participate.
- Provide child care for JOBS participants.
- Furnish transitional child care and Medicaid for 12 months after a participant leaves AFDC to take a job.
- Strengthen its child support enforcement programs.

TROUBLE WITH WORKFARE   But welfare rolls continued to rise in the 1990s despite the Family Support Act. Nationwide, welfare rolls increased from 10 million persons to nearly 15 million. No state "workfare" programs required all welfare recipients to take jobs, or even to enroll in job training programs. Most programs allowed mothers with preschool children to opt out altogether. No state provided enough money to fund the necessary counseling and job training, child care, and health insurance, to permit any sizable number of people to move off of welfare rolls. Only about 10 percent of AFDC recipient parents participated in any education, job training, or job placement programs, and even fewer actually found jobs. Effective "workfare" reform—moving people off welfare rolls into jobs—proved to be more costly than simply providing welfare assistance.

WELFARE REFORM IN THE STATES

In recent years there has been a growing consensus that long-term social dependency must be addressed in welfare policy. The fact that most nonpoor mothers work convinced many liberals that welfare mothers have no special claim to stay at home with their children. But liberals generally believe that spending on transitional assistance—education, job training, continued health care, and day care for children—is necessary to move welfare mothers into the work force. Conservatives are more likely to rely on welfare time limits, requirements that teenage mothers remain in their parental households, and denial of added benefits to women already receiving welfare who have additional children.

OBSTACLES TO REFORM   While nearly everyone agrees that getting people off of welfare rolls and onto payrolls is the main goal of reform, there are major obstacles to the achievement of this goal. First of all, a substantial portion (perhaps 25 to 40 percent) of long-term AFDC recipients have handicaps—physical disabilities, chronic illnesses, learning disabilities, alcohol or drug abuse problems—that prevent them from holding a full-time job. Many long-term recipients have no work experience (perhaps 40 percent) and two-thirds of them did not graduate from high school. Almost half have three or more children, making day-care arrangements a major obstacle. It is unlikely that any counseling, education, job training, or job placement programs advocated by liberals could ever succeed in getting these people into productive employment. Policy makers argue whether or not there are 5 million jobs available to unskilled mothers, but even if there are such jobs available, they would be low-paying, minimum wage jobs that would not lift them out of poverty.[6] And cutting off aid, advocated by many conservatives, would place millions of children at risk. Orphanages are not really an economic alternative; their costs per child are many times higher than welfare payments.

STATE EXPERIMENTS IN WELFARE REFORM   Under current federal law, states are permitted to devise their own experimental programs and apply to the U.S. Department of Health and Human Services for a waiver from standard federal regulations to implement them. The Clinton administration has granted a number of state waivers. Various states have experimented by requiring job training or unpaid community service as a condition of receiving cash assistance; requiring mothers to identify fathers of their children in order to initiate court proceedings for child support; requiring teenage mothers to live with a parent or guardian to receive benefits; conditioning welfare payments on progress toward high school graduation; allowing recipients to marry the fathers of their children and providing counseling and job placement for both parents; requiring welfare recipients to work part time in community service; threatening to reduce welfare payments if parents do not keep their children in school; stipulating that benefits do not increase with additional children born to recipients while on welfare.[7] While many of these experimental programs report success with limited numbers of welfare recipients, to date no major reductions in welfare rolls have been achieved.

HEALTH CARE POLICY

Good health correlates best with factors over which doctors and hospitals have no direct control: heredity, lifestyle (smoking, eating, drinking, exercise, stress), and the physical environment. Historically, most of the reductions in death rates have resulted from public health and sanitation improvements, including immunization against smallpox, clean public water supplies, sanitary sewage disposal, improved diets, and increased standards of living. Many of the leading causes of death today, including heart disease, stroke, cirrhosis of the liver, AIDS, accidents, and suicides, are closely linked to personal habits and lifestyles and are beyond the reach of medicine. Thus, the greatest contribution to better health is likely to be found in altered personal habits and lifestyles, rather than in more medical care.

COMMUNITY PUBLIC HEALTH AND HOSPITALS   Public health and sanitation are among the oldest functions of local government. Keeping clean is still one of the major tasks of cities today, a task that includes street cleaning, sewage disposal, garbage collection, and the provision of a clean water supply. Very often these services are taken for granted in the United States, but in many underdeveloped countries of the world, health and sanitation are still major concerns.

---

[6]Estimates by U.S. Department of Health and Human Services and the Urban Institute. Reported in *U.S. News and World Report*, January 16, 1995, pp. 30–40.

[7]See *Congressional Quarterly Weekly Report*, July 8, 1995, p. 2001–5.

Local public health departments are directly concerned with the *prevention* of disease. They engage in compulsory vaccination, immunization, and quarantine, as well as regulatory activity in the processing of milk and the safeguarding of water supplies.

In addition to the preventive activities of the public health departments, state and local governments also provide extensive, tax-supported hospital care. State and local governments provide both general and specialized hospitals, health centers, and nursing homes and very often subsidize private hospitals and medical facilities as well. New York City operates the nation's largest city hospital system, but almost every community subsidizes hospital facilities in some way. City and county hospitals and heavily subsidized private hospitals are expected to provide at least emergency care to indigent patients.

MEDICARE   The federal government added *Medicare* to the Social Security program in 1965. Medicare provides for prepaid hospital insurance for the aged, and low-cost voluntary medical insurance for the aged under federal administration. Medicare includes (1) a compulsory basic health insurance plan covering hospital costs for the aged, which is financed through payroll taxes collected under the Social Security system; and (2) a voluntary but supplemental medical program that will pay doctors' bills and additional medical expenses, financed in part by contributions from the aged and in part by the general tax revenues. Only aged persons are covered by Medicare.

MEDICAID   The federal government also provides federal funds under *Medicaid* to enable states to guarantee medical services to the poor. Each state operates its own Medicaid program. Unlike Medicare, Medicaid is a welfare program designed for needy persons; no prior contributions are required, and recipients of Medicaid services are generally welfare recipients. States can extend coverage to other medically needy persons if they choose to do so.

PAYING THE HEALTH CARE BILL   Government pays about 41 percent of all health care costs—through Medicare for the aged, Medicaid for the poor, and other government programs including military and veterans care. Private insurance pays for 32 percent of the nation's health costs; direct patient payments count for only 25 percent. (See Figure 17–4.)

HEALTH CARE INFLATION   The costs of health care in the United States have risen much faster than prices in general. Advances in medical technology have produced elaborate and expensive equipment. Hospitals that have made heavy financial investment in this equipment must use it as often as possible. Physicians trained in highly specialized techniques and procedures wish to use them. Physicians and hospitals are forced by the threat of malpractice litigation to use the most advanced tests and treatments.

COPING WITH COSTS   Various efforts have been made to counter rising costs. Private insurers have negotiated discounts with groups of physicians and with hospitals (so-called "preferred provider organizations") and have implemented rules to guide physicians about when patients should and should not receive costly diagnostic and therapeutic procedures (so-called "managed care"). The government has replaced payments to hospitals under Medicare based on costs incurred, with payment of fixed fees based on

Figure 17–4
WHO PAYS THE HEALTH BILL?

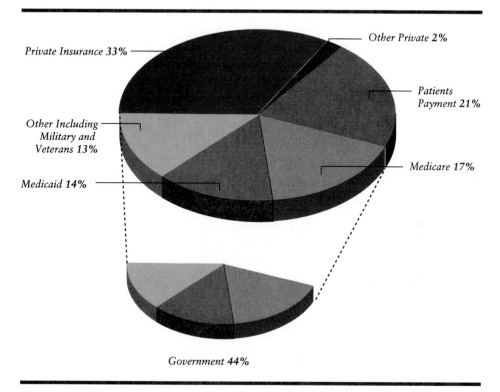

Private Insurance 33%

Other Private 2%

Patients
Payment 21%

Other Including
Military and
Veterans 13%

Medicare 17%

Medicaid 14%

Government 44%

Source: Statistical Abstract of the United States, 1995, p. 109.

primary and secondary diagnoses at the time of admission (the diagnosis-related group, or DRG system). Government and private insurers have encouraged the expansion of health maintenance organizations (HMOs) that promise to provide a stipulated list of services to patients for a fixed fee and that are able to provide care at lower total costs than can other providers.

Nonetheless, health care costs continue to rise. Whether this trend reflects the failure of cost control efforts or the strength of forces driving up costs is not clear. What is increasingly obvious is that payers, private and public, are finding health care costs increasingly burdensome and even insupportable.

MEDICAID IN THE STATES   Medicaid is the costliest of all public assistance programs. States must pay about 43 percent of Medicaid's costs, with the federal government paying the remainder. Medicaid is the most rapidly growing item in the budget of most states.

Medicaid is increasingly becoming the last resort for people who have no medical insurance and for those whose insurance does not cover long-term illness or nursing home care. People confronted with serious or "catastrophic" illness who exhaust their private insurance or Medicare coverage are often forced to impoverish themselves in order to qualify for Medicaid. (Medicare pays for only 60 days of hospital care and 100 days of nursing home care.) Moreover, as the number and proportion of the very old in society rise (those 80 years and over comprise the nation's fastest-growing age group), the need for long-term nursing home care grows. Medicaid is the only program that covers nursing home care, but middle-class people must first "spend down" their savings or transfer their wealth to others in order to qualify for Medicaid. Nursing home care is now the largest item in Medicaid spending. (See Figure 17–5.)

POLITICS AND HEALTH CARE REFORM

Health care reform centers on two central problems: controlling costs and expanding access. These problems are related: Expanding access to Americans who are currently uninsured and closing gaps in coverage require increases in costs, even while the central thrust of reform is to bring down overall health care costs.

No system of health care provides as much care as people want. Each individual, believing his or her health and life are at stake, will want the most thorough diagnostic testing, the most constant care, the most advanced treatment. Physicians have no strong incentive to save on costs; they want the most advanced diagnostic and treatment facilities available for their patients. Any tendency for physicians to limit testing and treatment is countered by the threat of malpractice suits. So both patients and physicians push up the costs of health care when public and private insurance, "third-party payers," foot the bill.

RATIONING–THE OREGON PLAN   In reforming its Medicaid program, Oregon sought to expand coverage to everyone at or below the poverty line, yet at the

Figure 17–5
MEDICAID EXPENDITURES

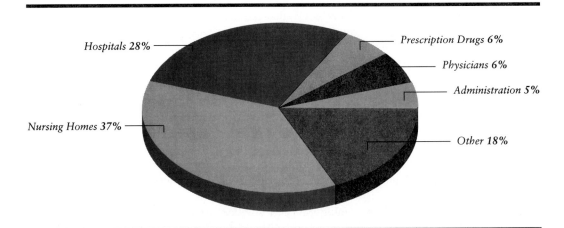

Source: Statistical Abstract of the United States, 1992.

same time to limit costs. It did so by engaging a panel of citizens and medical groups to draw up a list of 709 medical services ranked from highest to the lowest priority, based on both the seriousness of the condition to be treated and the likelihood that treatment would be effective. High priorities were awarded to treatments to prevent death in patients likely to recover (appendectomy, medications for heart disease) and to effective preventative care (mammograms, blood pressure screening). Low on the priority list were conditions that get better by themselves (head colds, flu) and conditions where treatment is generally futile (severe brain injuries, end-stage cancer). Medicaid patients are eligible for as many treatments as the state legislature decides to fund in any year. Thus, in the first year, legislature appropriations covered 587 of the 709 treatments (with low-back pain as the cutoff point at 588).

State innovations in Medicaid, as well as many other federal aid programs, usually require waivers from the federal government. The Bush administration initially denied the Oregon plan a waiver, but the Clinton administration did so, thereby encouraging health care reform.

"PLAY OR PAY"   States have also experimented with various methods of expanding health insurance coverage to those currently uninsured, including persons working for employers who do not provide insurance and persons who are unemployed. A "play or pay" approach requires all employers to either provide health insurance to all their workers and their dependents or alternatively pay into a state fund that would purchase insurance for uncovered workers. Rules are usually established concerning the proportion of premium costs paid by employers and employees and the range of services covered. While this approach expands coverage, it does little to control costs.

MANAGED COMPETITION   Some states have experimented with managed competition as an approach to health care cost containment. Management competition is an arrangement in which health insurance purchasing organizations (HIPOs) are organized to pool health insurance purchases (employers and individuals) in order to improve their bargaining power with insurers and providers. HIPOs are usually required to accept all applicants, including those with preexisting conditions. They receive government subsidies for members of groups expected to generate especially high costs. They negotiate costs either with insurance companies or directly with hospitals and physicians. Because of their size they are better able to collect information and identity providers that supply high-quality care at reasonable prices.

THE INTEREST GROUP BATTLE   While there is widespread public support for the general goals of health care reform—expanding coverage and reducing costs—there is no agreement among the principal interest groups on health care politics about the details of reform. *Insurance companies* are unhappy with the notion of health insurance purchasing organizations that would bargain down insurance premiums or even bypass insurance companies altogether and deal directly with hospitals and physicians' groups. *Physicians* strongly oppose price controls and treatment guidelines; they also oppose any program that takes away patient choice of physicians. *Hospitals,* both public and private profit making, oppose government payment schedules. *Drug companies* want to see prescription drugs paid for by government-sponsored insurance, but they vigorously oppose price controls on drugs. Powerful *senior citizens'* lobbies want added benefits for the aged, including coverage for drugs, dental care, and nursing homes, but they oppose folding Medicare into other health care systems. *Opponents and supporters of abortion rights* battle over whether abortion services should be included in taxpayer-paid programs. All of these groups have strong lobbying organizations in state capitals and in Washington, DC, and all have PACs that contribute heavily to state and national political campaigns.

NATIONAL HEALTH CARE REFORM?   The Clinton administration and Congress battled many months over a massive health care reform program developed by a committee headed by First Lady Hillary Clinton. Yet despite Democratic majorities in both the House and Senate in 1993–94, the program failed. The battle itself engendered intense rivalries and much bitterness among parties, interest groups, and individual policy makers in Congress and the executive branch. It is not likely that the federal government will be able to undertake national health care reform very soon. Whatever advances are made in expanding health care coverage or reducing costs must come from the states or the private sector.

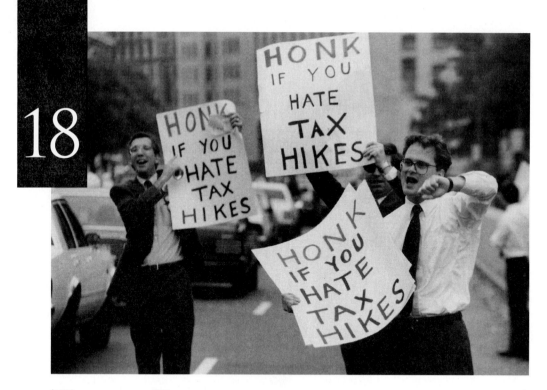

THE POLITICS
OF BUDGETING
AND TAXATION

AN OVERVIEW OF GOVERNMENT FINANCES

Governments do many things that cannot be measured in dollars. Nonetheless, government expenditures are the best available measure of overall government activity. The expenditure side of a government's budget tells us what public funds are being spent for, and the revenue side tells us how these funds are being raised.

GOVERNMENT FINANCES AND THE GDP   Dollar figures in government budgets are often mind-boggling. The federal government spends over $1.6 *trillion* each year, and all state and local governments combined spend an additional $1 *trillion*. To better understand what these dollar figures mean, it is helpful to view them in relation to the nation's gross domestic product (GDP), the sum of all the goods and services produced in the United States in a year.(See Figure 18–1.)

Over time governmental spending in the United States has grown faster than the

Figure 18-1

GROWTH OF GOVERNMENT SPENDING
EXPENDITURES AS A PERCENTAGE OF GDP

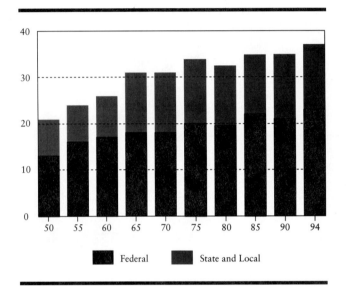

Source: Advisory Commission on Intergovernmental Relations, *Significant Features of Fiscal Federalism 1994.*

economy. In 1929 total governmental spending—federal, state, and local combined—amounted to only about 10 percent of the GDP. Today total governmental spending amounts to nearly 37 percent of GDP. *Federal* spending accounts for about 23 percent of GDP, and spending by all *state and local* governments adds another 14 percent.

STATE AND LOCAL GOVERNMENT SPENDING   State and local governments direct most of their spending toward education, social services (welfare and health), public safety (police and fire), and transportation.

Education is the most costly of these functions; health costs are rising more rapidly than any other function.

STATE AND LOCAL GOVERNMENT REVENUES   State and local governments in the United States derive revenue from a variety of sources. Of course, taxes are the largest source of revenue, accounting for nearly 60 percent of all state and local revenue. Federal grants are another major source of state and local government revenue (see Chapter 3), accounting for about 20 percent of total revenues. User charges of various kinds, from water and sewer, liquor store and electric utility revenues, to transit fares and admission fees, account for about 15 percent of all state—local revenue. Lotteries now bring in about 2 percent of all state–local revenue, and the remainder is derived from insurance premiums, licenses, fines, and miscellaneous sources.

TYPES OF TAXES AND TAX POLITICS

The politics of taxation often center on the question of who actually bears the burden or "incidence" of a tax, that is, which income groups must devote the largest proportion of their income to taxes. Taxes that require high-income groups to pay a larger percentage of their incomes in taxes than low-income groups are said to be *progressive*, while taxes that take a larger share of the income of low-income groups are said to be *regressive*. Taxation at equal percentage rates, regardless of income level, is said to be *proportional*.

LOCAL PROPERTY TAXES   Property taxes are the largest source of revenue for local governments in the United States. (See Figure 18–2.) However, property taxes are usually regressive. This conclusion is based on the assumption that renters actually pay their property taxes through increased rentals levied by the landlord, and the further assumption that high-income groups have more wealth in untaxed forms of property. Since the property tax is the foundation of local tax structures in every state, it is reasonable to conclude that states that rely largely upon local governments for taxes and services are

Figure 18–2
SOURCES OF TAX REVENUE

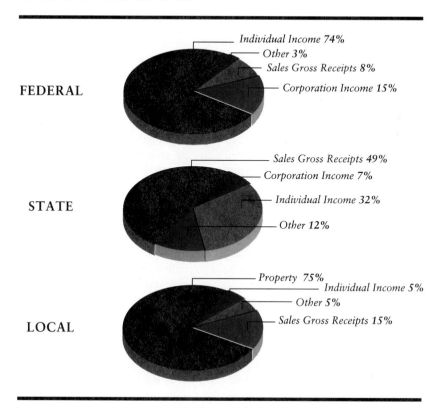

FEDERAL
- Individual Income 74%
- Other 3%
- Sales Gross Receipts 8%
- Corporation Income 15%

STATE
- Sales Gross Receipts 49%
- Corporation Income 7%
- Individual Income 32%
- Other 12%

LOCAL
- Property 75%
- Individual Income 5%
- Other 5%
- Sales Gross Receipts 15%

Source: Advisory Commission on International Relations, *Significant Features of Fiscal Federalism 1994.*

relying more upon regressive tax structures. Yet, in defense of property taxation, it is often argued that no other form of taxation is really feasible for local governments. Local sales and income taxes force individuals and businesses to leave the communities levying them; real estate, on the other hand, is less easy to move about and hide from local tax assessors. Real estate taxes are the only type of taxes that can be effectively collected by relatively untrained local tax officials.

Revenues from property taxation depend upon the property wealth of a community. Dependence upon property taxation means that wealthier communities will be able to raise more funds with less burden on taxpayers than communities without much property wealth. In other words, reliance on property taxation results in inequalities in burdens and benefits between wealthier and poorer communities.

The burden of property taxes depends on (1) the ratio of assessed value of property to the fair market value of the property; (2) the rate at which assessed property is taxed, which is usually expressed in mills, or tenths of a percent; and finally, (3) the nature and extent of tax exemptions and reductions for certain types of property. The ratio of assessed value to full market value may vary from one community to the next, even in states with laws requiring uniform assessment ratios throughout the state. The failure of communities to have periodic and professional tax evaluation means that taxes continue to be levied on old assessment figures, even while market values go up. The result, over time, is a considerable lowering of assessment ratios, and therefore taxes, on older homes and businesses and industries. Newer residents, whose sale price is generally known to tax assessors, must therefore pay taxes on the uniform assessment ratio. There are very few communities in which a suggestion of a reevaluation will not set off a heated debate between those who are enjoying a low assessment and those who are not. When a community tampers with reevaluation or a change in the ratio of assessed to market value, it threatens to change the incidence or distribution of tax burdens within a community. If new tax revenues are needed, it is much easier to simply increase the rate or millage to be applied against the assessed value of property. Many communities face state restrictions on maximum tax rates, or they are required to submit any proposed increase in tax rates to the voters in a referendum. These restrictions are usually favored by low-tax forces, which have succeeded in obtaining legislation at the state level that impairs the taxing abilities of local governments.

Some categories of property are exempt from taxation; these usually include properties that are used for nonprofit, charitable, religious, and educational, and other public purposes. Occasionally, such exemptions are attacked by those who feel that they are, in effect, subsidies to the exempted organizations; this is particularly true regarding exemptions for religious property. Exemptions for educational or public properties sometimes work a hardship on communities in which large public facilities or educational institutions are located. However, the exemptions that arouse the greatest controversy are usually those given by state and local governments to new business and industry, in an effort to induce them to locate in the state or community granting the exemption.

STATE SALES TAXES   While the property tax is the most important source of revenue for local communities, *the general sales tax is the most important source of tax revenue for state governments.* Consumers are a notoriously weak pressure group. It is difficult for them to count pennies dribbled away four or five at a time; the tax does not involve obvious payroll deductions, as in income taxation, or year-end bills, as in property taxation. As of 1995 only five states did *not* impose a general sales tax (Alaska, Delaware, Montana, New Hampshire, and Oregon).

State and local sales taxes are often considered *regressive,* that is, the poor are believed to devote a larger percentage of their income to paying these taxes than the wealthy. The regressivity of sales taxation is based upon the assumption that low-income groups must use most, if not all, of their income for purchases, while high-income groups devote larger shares of their income to savings. However, many states exclude some of the necessities of life from sales taxation, such as packaged food, rent, and medical expenses, in order to reduce the burden of sales taxation on the poor. Because of these exclusions, sales taxes in many states are not really regressive.

States generally rely more heavily on sales taxation than on income taxation. However, reliance upon one or the other type of tax varies from state to state. The decision to place primary reliance upon sales or income taxation is one of the most important policy choices facing state government. The yield from both types of taxation can be quite large.

There are several arguments on behalf of sales taxation in the states. The first is that sales taxation is the only major source of revenue left to the states—local governments must rely on property taxes, and the federal government has placed such a heavy tax burden on incomes that taxpayers will not countenance an additional state bite out of their paychecks. Moreover, sales taxes are not as visible as income or property taxes, since sales taxes are paid pennies at a time. Generally, the customer considers the sales tax as part of the price of an item. Taxpayers never add up the total they have paid in sales taxes, so sales taxation appears to be a relatively "painless" form of taxation. In addition, sales taxes ensure that low-income groups who benefit from public services will share in the costs of government. Actual hardships for the poor from sales taxes can be reduced by excluding food and other necessities from taxation, but the poor will pay taxes when purchasing luxury items. Finally, sales taxes are useful in reaching mobile populations, that is, tourists, commuters, and transients—people who derive benefits from a host state but who would not otherwise help pay for these benefits.

STATE INCOME TAXES   Wisconsin enacted the first modern, enforceable state income tax in 1911, and more than half the states had adopted income taxation by 1940. Today forty-one states tax all forms of individual income and two additional states tax nonwage income. But seven states eschew income taxation altogether, and two additional states do not tax wage income. (See Table 18–1.) Connecticut was the most recent state to enact an income tax in 1991. Fiscal pressures on state government continue to stir debate in the non–income tax states over the adoption of the tax.

Progressive state income taxes—income taxes with rates that rise with increases in income—are usually defended on the principle of "ability to pay"; that is, the theory that high-income groups can afford to pay a larger percentage of their income into taxation at no more of a sacrifice than that required of low-income groups who devote a smaller proportion of their income to taxation. The principle of a graduated income tax based on ability to pay, a principle accepted at the federal level in 1913 with the passage of the Sixteenth Amendment, together with the convenience, economy, and efficiency of income taxes, is generally cited by proponents of income taxation.

Personal income taxes in a few states are "flat rate" taxes of 3 percent (Illinois) or 5.0

Table 18–1

INCOME TAXATION IN THE STATES, 1995

States Without Income Taxes	States Taxing Interest, Dividends, and Capital Gains Only
Alaska	New Hampshire
Florida	Tennessee
Nevada	
South Dakota	
Texas	
Washington	
Wyoming	

States Taxing Adjusted Gross Income (rate ranges in parentheses)

Alabama (2.0–5.0)	Kansas (4.4–7.7)	New York (4.0–7.9)
Arizona (3.8–7.0)	Kentucky (2.0–6.0)	North Carolina (6.0–7.7)
Arkansas (1.0–7.0)	Louisiana (2.0–6.0)	North Dakota (2.6–12.0)
California (1.0–11.0)	Maine (2.0–8.5)	Ohio (0.7–7.5)
Connecticut (4.5)	Maryland (2.0–6.0)	Oklahoma (0.5–7.0)
Colorado (5.0)	Massachusetts (5.9–12.0)	Oregon (5.0–9.0)
Delaware (3.2–7.7)	Michigan (4.6)	Pennsylvania (2.8)
Georgia (1.0–6.0)	Minnesota (6.0–8.5)	Rhode Island (27.5% federal)[a]
Hawaii (2.0–10.0)	Mississippi (3.0–5.0)	South Carolina (2.5–7.0)
Idaho (2.0–8.2)	Missouri (1.5–6.0)	Utah (2.6–7.2)
Illinois (3.0)	Montana (2.0–11.0)	Vermont (25–34% federal)[a]
Indiana (3.4)	Nebraska (2.6–6.9)	Virginia (2.0–5.8)
Iowa (0.4–10.0)	New Jersey (2.0–7.0)	West Virginia (3.0–6.5)
	New Mexico (1.8–8.5)	Wisconsin (4.9–6.9)

[a]State income taxes determined as a percentage of federal income tax liability.

Source: Data from Council of State Governments, *Book of the States, 1994–95* (Lexington: Council of State Governments, 1994), p. 367.

percent (Colorado) of personal income. In other income tax states, the rates are "progressive"—rising from 2 to 3 percent, to 10 or 12 percent, with increases in income levels. A handful of states tie their *state* personal income tax to the *federal* income tax, by specifying that state taxes will be a specific percentage of federal taxes. Most states also have their own systems of exemptions.

CORPORATE TAXES   In addition to property taxes paid to local governments, corporations in forty-six states pay a corporate income tax. (Nevada, Texas, Washington, and Wyoming do not tax corporate income.) These taxes range from a 5 percent flat rate to sliding scales of 3 to 12 percent of net profits. Raising corporate taxes is popular with voters; individuals do not pay corporate taxes directly; but these taxes may be passed along to consumers in higher prices. The greatest barrier to higher state corporate taxes is the possibility that such taxes will cause corporations to locate in another state. It is difficult for a state to maintain a "good business climate" if its corporate taxes are high. Most studies find that industrial-location decisions are influenced by many factors other than taxes—for example, access to markets, raw materials, skilled labor, and energy. However, businesses expect their taxes to be kept in line with those of their competitors. In addition to corporate profits taxes, business looks at unemployment compensation and worker's compensation "premiums" (taxes) and the costs of environmental regulations.

LOTTERY AND GAMBLING REVENUE   More than half the states receive income from horse racing, gambling, or lotteries. Nevada leads the way with nearly a quarter of its revenue coming directly from gambling taxes. Most states restrict gambling to parimutuel betting on the racetrack. The total revenues raised from such sources, however, make up less than 0.5 percent of all state–local revenues.

Over half of the states now have public lotteries as a means of raising money. However, lotteries bring in less than 2 percent of all state–local government revenue. The administrative costs, including prize money, run about 50 percent of the gross revenue. This compares very unfavorably with the estimated 5 percent cost of collecting income taxes, and with the only slightly higher cost of collecting sales taxes.

USER CHARGES   User charges are currently the fastest-growing source of state and local government revenue. Today charges and miscellaneous revenues constitute nearly 25 percent of state–local revenue. (This figure is really a combination of user charges, utility and liquor store revenues, and miscellaneous revenues.) User charges directly link the benefits and costs of public goods in the fashion of the marketplace. Only those persons who actually use the government service pay for it. User charges include charges for water and sewer, garbage collection, electricity supplied by municipalities, transit fares, toll roads, airport landing fees, space rentals, parking meters, stadium fees, admissions to parks, zoos, swimming pools, and so on.

EXPLAINING STATE TAX SYSTEMS

What accounts for differences in tax policy among the states? Total state–local tax revenues in 1992 varied from a high of over $3,500 per person in New York, to a low of $1,323 in Mississippi (see Figure 18–3). This means that per capita tax levels of some states are over twice as high as those of other states. (Alaska and Wyoming receive most of their tax revenues from *severance taxes* on oil, gas, and coal extracted from the land. The burden of these taxes falls on consumers throughout the nation rather than directly on these states' residents.)

Tax burdens, that is, taxes in relation to personal income, also vary considerably among the states (see Figure 18–3). The concept of tax *burden* generally refers to taxes paid in relation to personal income; because of differences among the states in income levels, states with the highest *levels of taxation* (see Figure 18–3) are not necessarily the same states with the highest *tax burdens* (see Figure 18–3). The total tax burden in a state is measured by "total state and local tax revenues as a percentage of personal income." The state–local tax burden averages about 11 percent of personal income in the United States.

Figure 18–3

PER CAPITA STATE-LOCAL TAX REVENUE AND STATE AND LOCAL REVENUE AS A PERCENTAGE OF PERSONAL INCOME

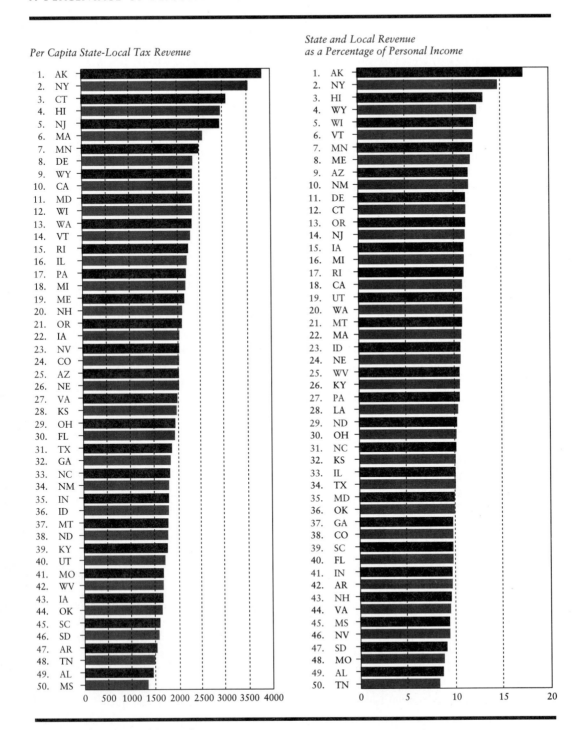

Per Capita State-Local Tax Revenue

State and Local Revenue as a Percentage of Personal Income

Source: Statistical Abstract of the United States, 1994.

TAX BURDENS   Among the fifty states, high levels of economic development usually reduce the burdens of taxation. Wealthy states can collect a great deal of tax monies without taking a very large percentage of personal income. High tax burdens are not necessarily a product of high tax levels, although, of course, there is some relationship between these variables (e.g., New York). Yet, high tax levels in an urbanized industrialized, high-income state may not necessarily be accompanied by a heavy tax burden (e.g., Connecticut). It is possible to have low tax levels that, because of the lack of industry and low income levels, may be very burdensome—that is, quite high in relation to low incomes (e.g., West Virginia).

RELIANCE ON LOCAL GOVERNMENT   Another important difference between richer and poorer states is in the degree of decentralization in state and local finance and administration. Local governments tend to play a greater role in the collection of taxes and the provision of public services in urban, high-income states, while state governments collect a greater portion of revenue and provide more services in rural, low-income states. Earlier, we observed that state governments in poorer rural states undertake more direct responsibilities in education, welfare, and highways. Low levels of economic development tend to force centralization upon these states. Wealthy urban states can afford to let local governments shoulder more responsibilities.

PROGRESSIVITY AND REGRESSIVITY   It is difficult to evaluate the overall progressivity or regressivity of state tax systems. It is generally believed that *overall* state and local government taxes are regressive; one estimate is that the lowest income group in America pays 12.6 percent of its income to state and local taxes, versus 8.4 percent for the highest income group.[1] This regressivity is largely attributed to state and local government reliance on sales and property taxation, rather than progressive income taxation. However, this estimate fails to consider the many types of exemptions to sales taxes found in various states (food, rent, medical care, etc.); these exemptions make sales taxes less regressive. They also fail to consider many property tax exemptions ("homestead" exemptions) found in many states that offer relief to owners of less expensive homes. Nevertheless, it is generally argued that states which rely more on income taxes (especially those states with progressive rate structures rather than flat rates) have more progressive tax systems[2] Progressivity *increases* with higher levels of state income. It appears to be easier to make tax systems more progressive when the size of the economic pie is expanding.[3]

REVOLTING AGAINST TAXES

The United States is the land of tax revolts. The national tradition of revolting against taxes includes the Boston Tea Party in 1773, a leading event in the movement toward independence; Shay's Rebellion in 1786, an important stimulus to creating the Constitution of the United States; and the Whisky Rebellion of 1794, forcefully extinguished by

---

[1]Rober McIntyre, *A Far Cry from Fair,* Washington DC: Citizens for Tax Justice, 1991.

[2]See David R. Morgan, "Tax Equity in the American States," *Social Science Quarterly,* 75 (September 1994).

[3]Neil Berch, "Explaining Changes in Tax Incidence in the States," *Political Research Quarterly,* 48 (September 1995), 629–42.

President George Washington. The political culture of the nation has always reflected a distrust of government power. The total tax burden in the United States is less than most other advanced industrialized nations of the world. Yet opinion polls regularly show that most Americans believe their taxes are "too high."

PUBLIC OPINION ABOUT TAXES   Much of the popular grievance about tax burdens is directed (accurately) against *federal* taxation. The federal income tax is most often mentioned as "the worst tax . . . the least fair" (see Table 18–2). Local property taxes are not very popular either.

POPULAR OPPOSITION TO RISING TAXES   Voters appear to be very sensitive to levels of state and local taxation. That is to say, popular dislike of taxes rises with increases in real levels of taxation. (This is not as obvious a conclusion as it might seem; state and local taxes are not as visible to most people as federal taxes, and few people are informed or attentive to state and local matters.) Indeed, as state income taxes rise about 4 percent, levels of dislike begin to rise exponentially.[4] Likewise, when sales tax levels rise about 5 percent, opposition increases rapidly. Homeowners are much more likely to object to property taxation than renters, while renters are more likely to object to sales taxes than homeowners.

TAX LIMITATION PROPOSALS   Tax limitation proposals fall into several general categories. Of course, any specific plan may vary in details from the outlines described here:

> *Property-Tax Limits*   Some proposals are specifically directed at property taxes. These proposals may limit allowable tax rates to 10 or 15 mills of full value of property, limit annual assessment increases, and/or allow reassess-

Table 18–2

TAX ATTITUDES

"Which do you think is the worst tax—that is, the least fair?"			
	1988	*1992*	*1994*
Federal Income Tax	26	25	27
Social Security Tax	17	10	12
State Income Tax	9	9	7
State Sales Tax	15	16	14
Local Property Tax	24	25	28
Don't Know	9	15	11

Source: Advisory Commission on Intergovernmental Relations, *Changing Public Attitudes on Government and Taxes, 1994.*

[4]Shawn Bowler and Todd Bowler, "Popular Responsiveness to Taxation," *Political Research Quarterly,* 48 (March 1995), 61–78.

ments only when the property is sold. This form of limitation applies mainly to local goverments and school districts and may actually increase state taxes if state governments simply take over local services.

Personal-Income Limits   A somewhat more complex scheme promises to limit state taxes to a certain percentage of the state's personal income. For example, if state taxes currently amount to 7 percent of a state's total personal income, a constitutional amendment could be offered to voters that limits all future state and local taxes to a total of no more than 7 percent of personal income. This prevents state government from growing at a faster rate than personal income, but it does allow tax revenues to rise.

Expenditure Limits   Similar restrictions can be placed on total state *expenditures*—limiting spending to a certain percentage of a state's total personal income. Presumably expenditure limits would hold down taxes over the long run, and therefore expenditure limits can be considered as an indirect form of tax limitation.

Prohibitions on Specific Taxes   State constitutions can be written or amended to prohibit certain types of taxes or require specific types of exemptions. For example, if the state constitution bars an income tax, this is a very effective tax limitation. States may also exempt specific items from sales taxes; some common exemptions include groceries, medicines, rents, and purchases by religious, educational, or charitable organizations.

Exemptions and Special Treatments   The *homestead exemption* is an increasingly popular method of excluding some part of the value of owner-occupied homes from property taxes. Homestead exemptions go only to homeowners, not to businesses; these exemptions may be expressed in dollar amounts of assessed value (where the first $5,000 or $10,000 of assessed value of a home is nontaxable), or in terms of percentages of assessed value (where the first 25 or 50 percent of assessed value of a home is nontaxable). *Personal property*-tax exemptions are common—exemptions of automobiles, boats, furniture, stock and bonds, and the like—in part because of the difficulty in identifying and assessing the true value of these types of property. Some states have adopted *circuit-breaker* programs that exempt property from taxation for individuals who are poor, aged, disabled, and so forth.

IMPACT OF LIMITS   What impact have tax limits had on the state and local government operations? The consequences of tax limits have been greater for *local* than for state governments. Constitutional provisions limiting state government taxing or spending have generally failed to have any discernible effect on state taxing or spending levels.[5] However, local property tax limits have had the effect of increasing reliance of local governments on state aid as well as fees and charges.[6]

---

[5]James Cox and Davie Lowery, "The Impact of the Tax Revolt Era State Fiscal Caps," *Social Science Quarterly,* 71 (September 1990), 492–509.

[6]Phillip G. Joyce and Daniel R. Mullins, "The Changing Fiscal Structure of State and Local Public Sector: The Impact of Tax and Expenditure Limits," *Public Administration Review,* 51 (May/June 1991), 240–53.

EXPLAINING TAX REVOLTS

Why do people support tax limitation measures? A variety of explanations have been offered and tested in opinion polls, but no single explanation seems to explain why people vote for or against tax limitations.[7]

THE SELF-INTEREST EXPLANATION   People who benefit most from government spending should oppose tax limitation measures, while people whose tax burdens are heaviest should support these measures. Despite the popularity of "rational" theory, this explanation finds only limited support in opinion surveys; high-income homeowners are only slightly more supportive of tax limits than beneficiaries of government services.

THE HIGH-TAX EXPLANATION   People who pay high taxes should support tax limitations, while people who pay modest taxes should show little interest in the tax revolt. Again, there is very little solid evidence to support this theory. Although people who say taxes are "high" tend to vote in favor of tax limitations, the states that have passed limitations are not necessarily the high-tax-burden states.

THE "WASTE-IN-GOVERNMENT" EXPLANATION   People who think government wastes a lot of money should support tax limitation proposals. Opinion polls do show a relationship between perceived waste and support for tax limits. This implies that tax limitation referenda can be defeated if people can be convinced that tax dollars are not wasted.

THE IDEOLOGICAL EXPLANATION   According to this explanation, conservatives should support tax limits, while liberals should oppose them. Indeed, according to this rationale, the tax revolt itself is a product of increasing conservatism of the electorate in the late 1970s and early 1980s. There is some support for this explanation in opinion polls: Conservatives and Republicans tend to support tax limitation measures more than liberals or Democrats.

THE FAIRNESS EXPLANATION   People who perceive the tax system as "unfair" should be more likely to vote for tax limitations than people who do not. Again, there is some limited evidence in opinion polls to support this explanation.

THE ALIENATION EXPLANATION   This explanation views the tax revolt as a reflection of declining confidence in government. Negative feelings about government

---

[7]The following discussion relies on the theoretical concepts and reports of opinion surveys in David Lowery and Lee Sigelman, "Understanding the Tax Revolt: Eight Explanations," *American Political Science Review*, 75 (December 1981), 963–74; James M. Buchanan, "The Potential for Taxpayers Revolt in American Democracy," *Social Science Quarterly*, 59 (March 1979), 691–96; Paul Allen Beck and Thomas R. Dye, "Sources of Public Opinion on Taxes," *Journal of Politics*, 44 (February 1982), 172–82; Carl Ladd, "The Polls: Taxing and Spending," *Public Opinion Quarterly*, 43 (Spring 1979), 126–35; Susan Hansen, *The Politics of Taxation* (New York: Praeger, 1983).

go beyond perceptions of waste, or fairness, or burdensome taxation, and tap deeply felt resentment and alienation from the political system. Again, there is some limited support for this explanation in opinion polls.

It is not surprising that no single explanation of the tax revolt can be offered. Indeed, even a combination of all of the explanations mentioned here does not fully explain voting on tax proposals. Other explanations may be derived from *the specific characteristics of politics in the states* in which tax limitation referenda have been voted on. Still other explanations may focus on *the specific provisions of the tax limitation amendments* being voted upon.

CITY FISCAL STRESS AND CUTBACK MANAGEMENT

Fiscal stress does *not* refer to the annual struggle to balance the budget without raising taxes or cutting services. This struggle occurs in every city. Fiscal stress refers to a financial condition so unfavorable as to impair borrowing ability, require reduction of municipal services, pose a threat to public health and safety, and thus diminish the quality and satisfaction of urban life.[8] Fiscal stress occurs when cities have large municipal payrolls, large socially dependent populations, and heavy tax burdens, yet an eroding tax base, a weak or declining economy, and population loss.

Fiscal stress has widespread impact.[9] As a city tries to solve its budget problems, it raises taxes; imposes fees; reduces its work force; cuts back on maintenance of streets, bridges, buildings, and parks; and postpones capital construction projects. These measures further hurt the local economy. Businesses move away and cancel plans to expand. Unemployment increases as well as demands for help from government. As a city's deficits grow, its bonds become hard to sell to banks and investors. This forces up interest costs that further hurt the city's budget.

Fiscal stress imposes new administrative tasks for mayors and managers. These tasks have been labeled as "cutback management." Managing organizational decline—cutting back on spending and organizational activity, deciding who will be let go, what programs will be scaled down or terminated, and what citizens will be asked to make sacrifices—is not as much fun as managing an expanding organization.

DIFFICULT DECISIONS   Cutback management presents a host problems for government officials. These include the following considerations:

> *Resist cutting or smooth the decline.*   Should officials resist cutting by claiming it cannot be done without great injury to the city? Should they cut vital

---

[8]David T. Stanley, "Cities in Trouble," in *Managing Fiscal Stress,* ed. Charles H. Levine (Chatham, NJ: Chatham, 1980).

[9]Various measures of fiscal stress have been devised and applied to American cities. See Richard P. Nathan and Charles Adams, "Understanding Central City Hardship," *Political Science Quarterly,* 91 (Spring 1976), 51–61; David T. Stanley, "Cities in Trouble," in *Managing Fiscal Stress,* ed. Charles H. Levine (Chatham, NJ: Chatham, 1980); Terry N. Clark and Lorna Crowley Ferguson, *City Money* (New York: Columbia University Press, 1983).

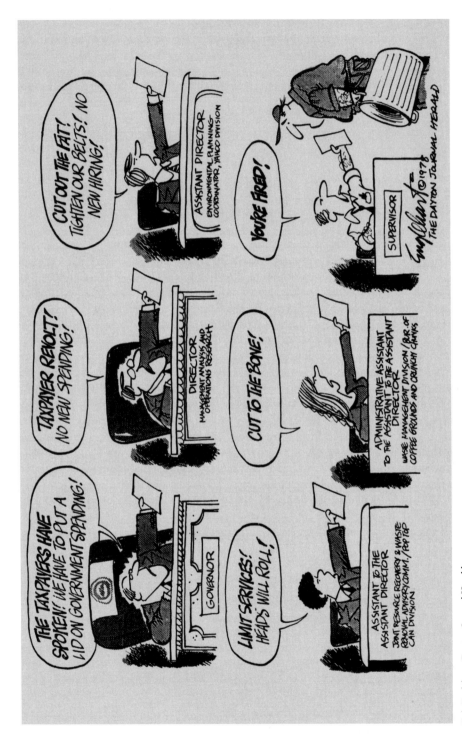

Bob Englehart, *Dayton Journal Herald.*

and popular programs first in order to stir opposition to the cut? By taking police and firefighters off the streets or closing the schools? By refusing to cut back until paydays are missed and loans are defaulted? Or should officials try to smooth the cutback but cutting low-prestige programs, administrative personnel, social programs, and less vital services?

Take one deep gouge or a series of decrements.   Should officials try to improve city finances with a single very difficult year by making one set of deep cuts in the budget? Or should they plan a series of smaller cuts over several years to minimize the impact of the cuts and hope that the financial condition of the city may turn around and the cutting can stop?

Share the pain or target the cuts.   Should city officials cut all programs "across the board" in order to minimize pain, avoid conflict, maintain morale, and build team spirit in the organization? Or should they make hard decisions about what programs are not really necessary? Targeting cuts requires officials to identify and rank priorities; it generates intense political conflict and tends to be avoided until things get very bad and across-the-board cuts are no longer feasible.

Promote efficiency or equity.   Should city officials favor the most efficient programs, usually police and fire protection, streets and sanitation, over the more costly social-service programs? Or should city officials act to protect the most dependent elements of the population?

CUTBACK STRATEGIES   What strategies can be employed by cities facing retrenchment? We have attempted to summarize some general strategies available to governments in confronting cutbacks:[10]

The no-change strategy: Across-the-board cuts, seniority retention, and hiring freezes.   Across-the-board cuts appear to be popular. They distribute the pain of budget reductions equally across agencies and among services. However, eventually across-the-board strategies must be abandoned "as officials become aware that the reductions are permanent . . . that equal cuts are not fair, as some programs are more important than others."[11] A hiring freeze is also a convenient and popular short-run strategy to minimize the pain of cutbacks. Hiring freezes rely on "natural attrition" through resignations and retirements to cut down the size of the work force. It does not require politically difficult decisions about which employees are most essential. If natural attrition does not occur fast enough to meet budget deficits, the next strategy is se-

---

[10]See Stephen C. Brooks, "Urban Fiscal Stress: A Decade of Difference," Midwest Political Science Association Meeting, Chicago, 1993; Cal Clark and B. Oliver Walter, "Urban Political Cultures, Financial Stress, and City Fiscal Austerity Strategies," *Western Political Quarterly,* 44 (September 1991), 676–97; Terry N. Clark and Lorna Crowley Ferguson, *City Money* (New York: Columbia University Press, 1983).

[11]Gregory B. Lewis, "Municipal Expenditures Through Thick and Thin," *Publius,* special issue (May 1984), 380–90.

niority retention. A "last-in–first-out" rule in layoffs may be viewed by most employees as fair, although it may result in disproportionate harm to women and minorities if they were recruited to government more recently.

A hierarchy of community-needs strategy   An alternative strategy is for cities to set priorities for essential services. Decisions about what services are essential may differ from city to city, but in general we can expect a ranking (from most essential to least essential): public safety (policy and fire), public works (streets, sewers, sanitation), administrative services, human services, leisure services.

A "privatizing" strategy.   Some city services are "priceable"—users can be charged for them. Cities can charge users for garbage collection, water supply, ambulance service, special police services, transit, licensing, libraries, recreation, and so forth. So one retrenchment strategy is to increase the number and types of user charges for city services. A related strategy is to transfer these services to private enterprise, which can usually perform them cheaper than can the city government. User charges are politically popular because citizens can "see" what they are buying and they are not forced to buy anything they do not want.

A reduction in capital spending strategy.   When tough times hit, one of the first responses is to cut back on capital spending—canceling or postponing new equipment purchases, new construction, major repairs. There are short-term advantages to this strategy; city employees can keep their jobs and service levels can be maintained. But over the longer term, this strategy can produce costly results, as streets, bridges, buildings, and equipment fail. Some capital investments can save money over the long run if they improve productivity and reduce labor costs.

A reduction in labor strategy.   Cities may finally confront the necessity to reduce personnel costs—hiring freezes, layoffs, renegotiated labor contracts. The most labor-intensive city functions are police and fire protection, together with hospitals and schools in those cities that have these responsibilities. Cutbacks in police and fire personnel are politically unpopular. Indeed, city officials may threaten such cutbacks to force a reconsideration of the rollbacks.

THE POLITICS OF BUDGETING

Too often we think of budgeting as the dull province of clerks and statisticians. Nothing could be more wrong. Budgets are political documents that record the struggles over "who gets what." The budget is the single most important policy statement of any government. There are very few government activities or programs that do not require an expenditure of funds, and no public funds may be spent without budgetary authorization. The budget sets forth government programs, with price tags attached. The size and shape of the budget is a matter of serious contention in the political life of any state or community. Governors, mayors, administrators, legislators, and interest groups, and citizens all compete to have their policy preferences recorded in the budget. The budget lies at the heart of the political process.

THE EXECUTIVE BUDGET   The budgetary process begins with the governor or mayor's budget office sending to each governmental agency and department a budget request form, accompanied by broad policy directives to agency and department heads about the size and shape of their requests. Very often these budget requests must be made six to twelve months prior to the beginning of the fiscal year for which the requests are made; state and local governmental fiscal years usually run from July 1 to June 30.[12] After all requests have been submitted to the budget office, the serious task of consolidating these many requests begins. Individual department requests are reviewed, revised, and generally scaled down; often departments are given more or less formal hearings on their budget request by the budget director. The budget agency must also make revenue estimates based upon information it obtains from the tax department.

Governors or mayors must decide whether their budget is to be balanced or not; whether particular departmental requests should be increased or reduced, in view of the programs and promises important to their administrations; whether economies should involve overall "belt tightening" by every agency or merely the elimination of particular programs; or finally, whether they should recommend the raising of new taxes or the incurring of additional debt. These decisions may be the most important that mayors or governors make in their terms of office, and they generally consult both political and financial advisors—budget and tax experts, party officials, interest group representatives, and legislative leaders. Ordinarily, these difficult decisions must be made before governors or mayors present their budget message to the legislature. This budget message explains and defends the final budget presented by the chief executive to his legislative branch.

THE LEGISLATIVE APPROPRIATION   The governor's budget generally appears in the legislature as an appropriations bill, and it follows the normal path of any bill. It is assigned to an appropriations committee, which often holds hearings on the bill and occasionally reshapes and revises the executive budget. The fate of the governor's budget in the legislature generally depends upon his or her general political power, public reactions to recommendations, the degree of support he or she receives from department heads, who are often called to testify at legislative budget hearings, his or her relationships with key legislative leaders, and the effectiveness of interest groups that favor or oppose particular expenditures.

After it is passed in identical form by both houses, the final appropriations measure is sent to the governor for signature. If the governor has an item veto, he or she can still make significant changes in the budget at that time.

"INCREMENTALISM" IN BUDGETING   What forces are actually involved in the budget-making process? Invariably, the forms provided by the budget office require departments to prepare budget requests alongside the previous year's expenditures. Decision makers generally consider the last year's expenditures as a base. Consequently, active

---

[12]The federal government's fiscal year is October 1 to September 30.

consideration of budget proposals is generally narrowed to new items or requested increases over the last year's base. The attention of governors and legislators, and mayors and councils, is focused on a narrow range of increases or decreases in a budget. A budget is almost never reviewed as a whole every year, in the sense of reconsidering the value of existing programs. Departments are seldom required to defend or explain budget requests that do *not* exceed current appropriations; but requested increases in appropriations require extensive explanation, and they are most subject to downward revision by higher political officials.[13]

The "incremental" nature of budgeting creates some interesting informal rules of the budget game:

- Spend all of your appropriation. A failure to use up an appropriation indicates that the full amount was unnecessary in the first place, which in turn implies that your budget should be cut next year.
- Never request a sum less than your current appropriation. It is easier to find ways to spend up to current appropriation levels than it is to explain why you want a reduction. Besides, a reduction indicates your program is not growing and this is an embarrassing admission to most government administrators.
- Put top priority programs into the base, that is, that part of the budget that is within current appropriation levels. Budget offices, governors and mayors, and legislative bodies will seldom challenge programs that appear to be part of existing operations.
- Increases that are desired should be made to appear small and should appear to grow out of existing operations. The appearance of a fundamental change in a budget should be avoided.
- Give the budget office, chief executive, and the legislature something to cut. Normally it is desirable to submit requests for substantial increases in existing programs and many requests for new programs, in order to give higher political authorities something to cut. This enables them to "save" the public untold millions of dollars and justify their claim to promoting "economy" in government. Giving them something to cut also diverts attention away from the basic budget with its vital programs.

POLITICS IN BUDGETING   Budgeting is very *political*. Being a good politician involves (1) the cultivation of a good base of support for one's requests among the public at large and among people served by the agency, (2) the development of interest, enthusiasm, and support for one's program among top political figures and legislative leaders, and (3) skill in following strategies that exploit one's opportunities to the maximum. Informing the public and one's clientele of the full benefit of the services they receive from the agency may increase the intensity with which they will support the agency's request. If possible, the agency should inspire its clientele to contact governors, mayors, legislators, and council members and help work for the agency's request. This is much more effective than the agency's trying to promote for its own requests.

CONSTRAINTS IN BUDGETING   As we have already seen, socioeconomic conditions further reduce the alternatives for budgetary action. Very often, local govern-

---

[13]For a discussion of the budgetary process at the federal level, see Aaron Wildavsky, *The New Politics of the Budgetary Process* (Boston: Little, Brown, 1988).

ments *begin* the budgetary process by estimating the amount of revenues that can reasonably be expected from the existing tax base, various service charges, and intergovernmental revenues; this estimate then becomes the ceiling for all budget requests. This practice, together with the conservative tendency of accepting past expenditure levels, seriously curtails policy change. This may be part of the reason why governors and mayors have a difficult time bringing about significant policy changes, and it contributes to the public's view of "politics as usual" and a feeling that nothing can be done, regardless of who is elected.

FRAGMENTED BUDGETING   Budgeting is also quite *fragmented*. In most of the states there is a great deal of constitutional and statutory "earmarking" of revenues. A common example is the earmarking of gasoline tax revenues for highway purposes. This practice fragments the budget and reduces executive control over the allocation of public funds.

NONPROGRAMMATIC BUDGETING   Finally, budgeting is *nonprogrammatic*. For reasons that accountants have so far kept to themselves, an agency budget typically lists expenditures under ambiguous phrases: "personnel services," "contractual services," "travel," "supplies," "equipment." Needless to say, it is impossible to tell from such a listing exactly what programs the agency is spending its money on. Obviously, such a budget obscures policy decisions by hiding programs behind meaningless phrases. Even if these categories are broken down into line items (for example, under "personnel services," the line-item budget might say, "John Doaks, Assistant Administrator $35,000"), it is still next to impossible to identify the costs of various programs. Reform-oriented administrators have called for budgeting by programs for many years; this would present budgetary requests in terms of end products or program packages, like aid to dependent children, vocational rehabilitation, administration of fair employment practices laws, highway patrolling, and so on. Many chief executives favor program budgeting because it will give them greater control over the policy. However, very often administrative agencies are hostile toward program budgeting; it certainly adds to the cost of bookkeeping, and many agencies feel insecure in describing precisely what it is they do. Moreover, there are some *political* functions served by nonprogram budgeting. Compromise comes much more readily when the items in dispute can be treated in dollars instead of differences in policy. Political bargaining and logrolling are made easier when discussions focus on increases and decreases in budgets rather than the desirability of whole programs.

WHEN ENDS DON'T MEET: STATE AND LOCAL DEBT

What happens when revenues fail to match expenditures in state and local government budgets? Most state constitutions require the operating budget of the state government, and those of local governments as well, to be balanced. In other words, most state constitutions prohibit deficits in *operating budgets*. Revenue estimates must match authorized expenditures in the appropriation act. If actual revenues fail to meet the estimates during the fiscal year, expenditures must be cut so that no deficit occurs at the end of the year.

CAPITAL FINANCING   However, state constitutions generally permit state and local governments to borrow funds for capital improvements, with provisions for repayment of the debt during the useful life of the project. State and local governments may sell bonds to finance traditional "essential functions"—roads, schools, parks, libraries, prisons, and government office buildings. These governments may also sell bonds to finance water and sewer systems, airports, ports, mass transportation facilities, solid waste disposal plants, hazardous waste disposal, single- and multifamily housing projects, and hospitals. In the world of municipal finance, these are referred to as "nonessential functions," even though we might argue that they are essential to a community. Finally, government may sell bonds to finance "private activities"—industrial development projects, trade and convention centers, sports arenas.

CONSTITUTIONAL RESTRICTIONS   State constitutions may place restrictions on these debts in the form of *debt ceilings,* limiting the total amount of money that a government can borrow (usually expressed as a percentage of the total assessed value of taxable property in the community); and *bond referenda* provisions, requiring that any bonded indebtedness (and the taxes imposed to pay off this indebtedness) be approved by the voters in a referendum. These restrictions usually apply only to general obligation bonds.

GENERAL OBLIGATION VERSUS REVENUE BONDS   Bonds issued by state and local government may be either general obligation bonds or revenue bonds. *General obligation bonds* are backed by "the full faith and credit" of the government that issues them. This pledges the full taxing powers of the government to pay both the principal and interest due on the bonds. Because these bonds are more secure, lenders are willing to accept lower interest rates on them. This saves the government (and the taxpayer) money in interest payments. *Revenue bonds* are not guaranteed by the issuing government but instead backed by whatever revenues the project itself generates. Both the interest and principal of revenue bonds are paid from fees, and charges or rents ("revenues") generated by the project, rather than tax revenues of the government. Because these bonds are not backed by the full taxing powers of the government, lenders face greater risks and therefore require higher interest payments. Revenue bonds are not usually subject to constitutional debt ceilings or referendum requirements.

INDUSTRIAL DEVELOPMENT BONDS   Competition between municipalities for economic development has led to a vast expansion in industrial development bonds. These are revenue bonds issued by a municipality to obtain funds to purchase land and build facilities for private businesses. Pollution control revenue bonds are issued by municipalities to obtain funds to provide industries with air and water pollution control facilities. Municipalities sometimes issue single-family mortgage revenue bonds to assist home buyers, builders, and developers. Municipalities may issue hospital revenue bonds to assist private as well as public hospitals in the community. These types of revenue bonds blur the distinction between public and private business. At one time most state and local indebtedness was in the form of general obligation bonds. But industrial development, pollution control, mortgage revenue, and hospital bonds, have become so popular that these nonguaranteed revenue bonds now constitute well over half of the outstanding municipal debt in the nation.

MUNICIPAL BOND INTEREST DEDUCTIBILITY   Traditionally the federal government did not levy individual or corporate income taxes on the interest that lenders received from state and local government bonds. All municipal bond interest income was deductible from gross income for federal tax purposes. The original rationale for this deductibility was based on the federal ideal: The national government should not interfere with the operations of state governments and their subdivisions. "The power to tax is the power to destroy,"[14] and therefore neither level of government should tax the instrumentalities of the other. Later this rationale was replaced by more practical considerations: By not taxing municipal bond interest, the federal government was providing an incentive for investment in public infrastructure—schools, streets, hospitals, sewers, airports. Because the federal government forgoes taxing municipal bond income, we might consider these lost federal revenues as a subsidy to state and local governments and the people who lend money to them.

The deductibility of municipal bond interest from federal income taxation makes these bonds very attractive to high-income investors. This attraction allows state and local governments to pay out less interest on their tax-free bonds than corporations must pay out on comparable taxable corporate bonds. Thus, for example, if average *corporate* AAA-rated 30-year bonds are paying 8 percent interest (taxable), average *municipal* AAA-rated 30 year bonds might only pay 6 percent interest (tax free). Many investors would prefer the lower rate because it is tax free. In short, federal deductibility allows state and local governments to borrow money relatively cheaply.

PUBLIC BONDS FOR PRIVATE USES   But controversy arises when private businesses ask municipal governments to issue revenue bonds on their behalf—bonds that businesses use to finance everything from the purchase of single-family homes and the development of luxury apartments, to the building of industrial plants and commercial offices. Business prefers municipal revenue bond financing over its own direct financing because municipal bond interest rates are cheaper owing to federal deductibility. In other words, the issuance of municipal "private purpose" revenue bonds is really a device to obtain cheaper interest rates for business at the expense of lost revenues to the federal government.

FEDERAL TAX REFORM AND MUNICIPAL FINANCE   The Federal Tax Reform Act of 1986 distinguished between "essential function" bond (bonds issued for roads, schools, parks, libraries, prisons, and government buildings), "nonessential function" bonds (bonds issued for water and sewer, transportation, multifamily housing, hazardous waste disposal, and health and education facilities), and "private activities" bonds (bonds for industrial development, pollution control, parking facilities, and sports and convention centers). Only essential function bond income is completely free of all federal income taxation. Nonessential bond income is subject to the federal alternate minimum tax (AMT), which means it may be taxable if the taxpayer has a large amount of

---

[14]*McCullogh v. Maryland*, 4 Wheaton 316 (1819).

tax-free income. And income from "private purpose" municipal bonds no longer enjoys tax-free status. These separate treatments complicate the municipal bond market for both governments and investors.

CITY DEBT PATTERNS   In examining total municipal indebtedness, we should consider both general obligation and revenue indebtedness. General obligation indebtedness of a city may range up to $1,000 per resident or more (New York City). Revenue indebtedness can range even higher, to over $3,000 per resident. Of course some cities avoid debt altogether. Indebtedness appears to be greater in cities in the Northeast, cities that undertake a wide variety of functions and services, and cities under fiscal strain.[15]

ORANGE COUNTY GOES BANKRUPT

With a population of over 2.5 million, Orange County, California, is the fifth largest county in the United States. And as the home of Disneyland and aerospace giants like the McDonnell Douglas corporation, it is one of America's wealthiest counties. Yet in 1994 it was forced to file for *bankruptcy,* unable to repay billions of dollars of loans that the county treasurer had borrowed from banks. How did it happen?

In addition to county funds, the Orange County treasurer managed a pool of short-term deposits by 185 municipalities, school districts, and local agencies in southern California. These were revenues that government bodies had collected but not yet spent; they were pooled in order to obtain higher interest rates, which would become an added source of revenue for these governments. The treasurer was expected to invest these pooled funds to obtain maximum returns with minimum risks.

For many years, the treasurer was praised for the high returns he produced from the investment pool; indeed, he was reelected to his post six times. But his investment strategy was, at the very least, "overly aggressive." He risked the $7.5 billion investment fund as collateral in order to borrow an additional $12.5 billion from banks in order to purchase bonds and other securities. His hope was that bond prices would rise, thus raising the value of the expanded $20 billion pool of bonds. But bond prices fell in 1994, shrinking the value of the pool. The treasurer had guessed wrong about the direction of the bond market. When he was unable to repay bank loans that he had used to buy bonds, the county was forced to declare bankruptcy. The county, plus all of the governments that had deposited their revenues in the pool, were obliged to postpone projects and cut back on services while the federal bankruptcy court tried to sort out the county's debts.

The lessons of the Orange County bankruptcy appear to be:

1. Treasurers must resist political pressures to produce unreasonably high returns on invested public funds.
2. Public funds must be managed conservatively, to preserve principal rather than maximize return.
3. Governments must provide full disclosure of public fund investments and provide continuous oversight of investment strategies.

---

[15]See Elaine B. Sharp, "The Politics and Economics of the New City Debt," *American Political Science Review,* 80 (December 1986), 1241–58.

WHEN A CITY GOES BUST

What happens when a city continually spends more than it receives in revenues, when its annual deficits pile up into a huge city debt, when banks and other lenders finally decide not to lend a city any more money? A number of large American cities have gone bust or come close to it, including New York City in 1975, Cleveland in 1979, Philadelphia in 1991, and Washington, DC, in 1995. But rather than officially declare bankruptcy and have federal bankruptcy courts take over fiscal control, these cities have been "rescued" by state and federal governments. Rescue, however, generally requires the city to turn over control of its financial affairs to a control board. Control board members are appointed by the state or federal government. In exchange for an infusion of state or federal money, the control board imposes fiscal discipline on the city. The mayor and council are required to win board approval for their annual budgets.

A Municipal Assistance Corporation, or "Big MAC," was established in 1975 to rescue New York City and oversee its finances. It was successful over time in reestablishing the city's credit ratings. Big MAC's powers can be reactivated if New York City again develops large operating deficits. Somewhat weaker boards were imposed by Pennsylvania and Ohio on Philadelphia and Cleveland, but both cities responded by lowering deficits. In 1995 Congress was obliged to impose a five-member control board over Washington, DC. It can reject the city's budgets, impose its own spending plans on the city, and even order changes in the organization and staffing of the city's government and school system.

PHOTO CREDITS

INDEX

ERNESTO "CHE" GUEVARA

ERNESTO "CHE" GUEVARA

Douglas Kellner

CHELSEA HOUSE PUBLISHERS
NEW YORK
PHILADELPHIA

31925

Chelsea House Publishers
EDITOR-IN-CHIEF: Nancy Toff
EXECUTIVE EDITOR: Remmel T. Nunn
MANAGING EDITOR: Karyn Gullen Browne
COPY CHIEF: Juliann Barbato
PICTURE EDITOR: Adrian G. Allen
ART DIRECTOR: Maria Epes
MANUFACTURING MANAGER: Gerald Levine

World Leaders—Past & Present
SENIOR EDITOR: John W. Selfridge

Staff for ERNESTO "CHE" GUEVARA
ASSOCIATE EDITOR: Jeff Klein
COPY EDITOR: Karen Hammonds
DEPUTY COPY CHIEF: Ellen Scordato
EDITORIAL ASSISTANT: Heather Lewis
PICTURE RESEARCHER: Nisa Rauschenberg
ASSISTANT ART DIRECTOR: Laurie Jewell
DESIGNER: David Murray
PRODUCTION COORDINATOR: Joseph Romano
COVER ILLUSTRATION: Michael Garland

First Printing

1 3 5 7 9 8 6 4 2

Library of Congress Cataloging in Publication Data

Kellner, Douglas, 1943–
Ernesto "Che" Guevara.

(World leaders past & present)
Bibliography: p.
Includes index.
   Summary: Traces the life of the revolutionary who joined Castro's
movement to overthrow Cuba's government, served as minister of
industry, and was killed while leading a Communist guerrilla force
in Bolivia.

1. Guevara, Ernesto, 1928–1967—Juvenile literature.
2. Guerrillas—Latin America—Biography—Juvenile
literature. 3. Latin America—Biography—Juvenile literature.
[1. Guevara, Ernesto, 1928–1967. 2. Guerrillas—Latin
America. 3. Latin America—Politics and government—
1948–] I. Title. II. Series.
F2849.22.G85   1988   980'.03'0924 [92]   87-32579

ISBN 1-55546-835-7

Contents

John Adams
John Quincy Adams
Konrad Adenauer
Alexander the Great
Salvador Allende
Marc Antony
Corazon Aquino
Yasir Arafat
King Arthur
Hafez al-Assad
Kemal Atatürk
Attila
Clement Attlee
Augustus Caesar
Menachem Begin
David Ben-Gurion
Otto von Bismarck
Léon Blum
Simon Bolívar
Cesare Borgia
Willy Brandt
Leonid Brezhnev
Julius Caesar
John Calvin
Jimmy Carter
Fidel Castro
Catherine the Great
Charlemagne
Chiang Kai-Shek
Winston Churchill
Georges Clemenceau
Cleopatra
Constantine the Great
Hernán Cortés
Oliver Cromwell
Georges-Jacques
  Danton
Jefferson Davis
Moshe Dayan
Charles de Gaulle
Eamon De Valera
Eugene Debs
Deng Xiaoping
Benjamin Disraeli
Alexander Dubček
François & Jean-Claude
  Duvalier
Dwight Eisenhower
Eleanor of Aquitaine
Elizabeth I
Faisal
Ferdinand & Isabella
Francisco Franco
Benjamin Franklin

Frederick the Great
Indira Gandhi
Mohandas Gandhi
Giuseppe Garibaldi
Amin & Bashir Gemayel
Genghis Khan
William Gladstone
Mikhail Gorbachev
Ulysses S. Grant
Ernesto "Che" Guevara
Tenzin Gyatso
Alexander Hamilton
Dag Hammarskjöld
Henry VIII
Henry of Navarre
Paul von Hindenburg
Hirohito
Adolf Hitler
Ho Chi Minh
King Hussein
Ivan the Terrible
Andrew Jackson
James I
Wojciech Jaruzelski
Thomas Jefferson
Joan of Arc
Pope John XXIII
Pope John Paul II
Lyndon Johnson
Benito Juárez
John Kennedy
Robert Kennedy
Jomo Kenyatta
Ayatollah Khomeini
Nikita Khrushchev
Kim Il Sung
Martin Luther King, Jr.
Henry Kissinger
Kublai Khan
Lafayette
Robert E. Lee
Vladimir Lenin
Abraham Lincoln
David Lloyd George
Louis XIV
Martin Luther
Judas Maccabeus
James Madison
Nelson & Winnie
  Mandela
Mao Zedong
Ferdinand Marcos
George Marshall

Mary, Queen of Scots
Tomás Masaryk
Golda Meir
Klemens von Metternich
James Monroe
Hosni Mubarak
Robert Mugabe
Benito Mussolini
Napoléon Bonaparte
Gamal Abdel Nasser
Jawaharlal Nehru
Nero
Nicholas II
Richard Nixon
Kwame Nkrumah
Daniel Ortega
Mohammed Reza Pahlavi
Thomas Paine
Charles Stewart
  Parnell
Pericles
Juan Perón
Peter the Great
Pol Pot
Muammar el-Qaddafi
Ronald Reagan
Cardinal Richelieu
Maximilien Robespierre
Eleanor Roosevelt
Franklin Roosevelt
Theodore Roosevelt
Anwar Sadat
Haile Selassie
Prince Sihanouk
Jan Smuts
Joseph Stalin
Sukarno
Sun Yat-sen
Tamerlane
Mother Teresa
Margaret Thatcher
Josip Broz Tito
Toussaint L'Ouverture
Leon Trotsky
Pierre Trudeau
Harry Truman
Queen Victoria
Lech Walesa
George Washington
Chaim Weizmann
Woodrow Wilson
Xerxes
Emiliano Zapata
Zhou Enlai

ON LEADERSHIP

Arthur M. Schlesinger, jr.

LEADERSHIP, it may be said, is really what makes the world go round. Love no doubt smooths the passage; but love is a private transaction between consenting adults. Leadership is a public transaction with history. The idea of leadership affirms the capacity of individuals to move, inspire, and mobilize masses of people so that they act together in pursuit of an end. Sometimes leadership serves good purposes, sometimes bad; but whether the end is benign or evil, great leaders are those men and women who leave their personal stamp on history.

Now, the very concept of leadership implies the proposition that individuals can make a difference. This proposition has never been universally accepted. From classical times to the present day, eminent thinkers have regarded individuals as no more than the agents and pawns of larger forces, whether the gods and goddesses of the ancient world or, in the modern era, race, class, nation, the dialectic, the will of the people, the spirit of the times, history itself. Against such forces, the individual dwindles into insignificance.

So contends the thesis of historical determinism. Tolstoy's great novel *War and Peace* offers a famous statement of the case. Why, Tolstoy asked, did millions of men in the Napoleonic Wars, denying their human feelings and their common sense, move back and forth across Europe slaughtering their fellows? "The war," Tolstoy answered, "was bound to happen simply because it was bound to happen." All prior history predetermined it. As for leaders, they, Tolstoy said, "are but the labels that serve to give a name to an end and, like labels, they have the least possible connection with the event." The greater the leader, "the more conspicuous the inevitability and the predestination of every act he commits." The leader, said Tolstoy, is "the slave of history."

Determinism takes many forms. Marxism is the determinism of class. Nazism the determinism of race. But the idea of men and women as the slaves of history runs athwart the deepest human instincts. Rigid determinism abolishes the idea of human freedom—

the assumption of free choice that underlies every move we make, every word we speak, every thought we think. It abolishes the idea of human responsibility, since it is manifestly unfair to reward or punish people for actions that are by definition beyond their control. No one can live consistently by any deterministic creed. The Marxist states prove this themselves by their extreme susceptibility to the cult of leadership.

More than that, history refutes the idea that individuals make no difference. In December 1931 a British politician crossing Park Avenue in New York City between 76th and 77th Streets around 10:30 P.M. looked in the wrong direction and was knocked down by an automobile—a moment, he later recalled, of a man aghast, a world aglare: "I do not understand why I was not broken like an eggshell or squashed like a gooseberry." Fourteen months later an American politician, sitting in an open car in Miami, Florida, was fired on by an assassin; the man beside him was hit. Those who believe that individuals make no difference to history might well ponder whether the next two decades would have been the same had Mario Constasino's car killed Winston Churchill in 1931 and Giuseppe Zangara's bullet killed Franklin Roosevelt in 1933. Suppose, in addition, that Adolf Hitler had been killed in the street fighting during the Munich *Putsch* of 1923 and that Lenin had died of typhus during World War I. What would the 20th century be like now?

For better or for worse, individuals do make a difference. "The notion that a people can run itself and its affairs anonymously," wrote the philosopher William James, "is now well known to be the silliest of absurdities. Mankind does nothing save through initiatives on the part of inventors, great or small, and imitation by the rest of us—these are the sole factors in human progress. Individuals of genius show the way, and set the patterns, which common people then adopt and follow."

Leadership, James suggests, means leadership in thought as well as in action. In the long run, leaders in thought may well make the greater difference to the world. But, as Woodrow Wilson once said, "Those only are leaders of men, in the general eye, who lead in action. . . . It is at their hands that new thought gets its translation into the crude language of deeds." Leaders in thought often invent in solitude and obscurity, leaving to later generations the tasks of imitation. Leaders in action—the leaders portrayed in this series—have to be effective in their own time.

And they cannot be effective by themselves. They must act in response to the rhythms of their age. Their genius must be adapted, in a phrase of William James's, "to the receptivities of the moment." Leaders are useless without followers. "There goes the mob," said the French politician hearing a clamor in the streets. "I am their leader. I must follow them." Great leaders turn the inchoate emotions of the mob to purposes of their own. They seize on the opportunities of their time, the hopes, fears, frustrations, crises, potentialities. They succeed when events have prepared the way for them, when the community is awaiting to be aroused, when they can provide the clarifying and organizing ideas. Leadership ignites the circuit between the individual and the mass and thereby alters history.

It may alter history for better or for worse. Leaders have been responsible for the most extravagant follies and most monstrous crimes that have beset suffering humanity. They have also been vital in such gains as humanity has made in individual freedom, religious and racial tolerance, social justice, and respect for human rights.

There is no sure way to tell in advance who is going to lead for good and who for evil. But a glance at the gallery of men and women in *World Leaders—Past and Present* suggests some useful tests.

One test is this: Do leaders lead by force or by persuasion? By command or by consent? Through most of history leadership was exercised by the divine right of authority. The duty of followers was to defer and to obey. "Theirs not to reason why / Theirs but to do and die." On occasion, as with the so-called enlightened despots of the 18th century in Europe, absolutist leadership was animated by humane purposes. More often, absolutism nourished the passion for domination, land, gold, and conquest and resulted in tyranny.

The great revolution of modern times has been the revolution of equality. The idea that all people should be equal in their legal condition has undermined the old structure of authority, hierarchy, and deference. The revolution of equality has had two contrary effects on the nature of leadership. For equality, as Alexis de Tocqueville pointed out in his great study *Democracy in America*, might mean equality in servitude as well as equality in freedom.

"I know of only two methods of establishing equality in the political world," Tocqueville wrote. "Rights must be given to every citizen, or none at all to anyone . . . save one, who is the master of all." There was no middle ground "between the sovereignty of all and the absolute power of one man." In his astonishing prediction of 20th-century totalitarian dictatorship, Tocqueville explained how the revolution of equality could lead to the *"Führerprinzip"* and more terrible absolutism than the world had ever known.

But when rights are given to every citizen and the sovereignty of all is established, the problem of leadership takes a new form, becomes more exacting than ever before. It is easy to issue commands and enforce them by the rope and the stake, the concentration camp and the *gulag.* It is much harder to use argument and achievement to overcome opposition and win consent. The Founding Fathers of the United States understood the difficulty. They believed that history had given them the opportunity to decide, as Alexander Hamilton wrote in the first Federalist Paper, whether men are indeed capable of basing government on "reflection and choice, or whether they are forever destined to depend . . . on accident and force."

Government by reflection and choice called for a new style of leadership and a new quality of followership. It required leaders to be responsive to popular concerns, and it required followers to be active and informed participants in the process. Democracy does not eliminate emotion from politics; sometimes it fosters demagoguery; but it is confident that, as the greatest of democratic leaders put it, you cannot fool all of the people all of the time. It measures leadership by results and retires those who overreach or falter or fail.

It is true that in the long run despots are measured by results too. But they can postpone the day of judgment, sometimes indefinitely, and in the meantime they can do infinite harm. It is also true that democracy is no guarantee of virtue and intelligence in government, for the voice of the people is not necessarily the voice of God. But democracy, by assuring the right of opposition, offers built-in resistance to the evils inherent in absolutism. As the theologian Reinhold Niebuhr summed it up, "Man's capacity for justice makes democracy possible, but man's inclination to injustice makes democracy necessary."

A second test for leadership is the end for which power is sought. When leaders have as their goal the supremacy of a master race or the promotion of totalitarian revolution or the acquisition and exploitation of colonies or the protection of greed and privilege or the preservation of personal power, it is likely that their leadership will do little to advance the cause of humanity. When their goal is the abolition of slavery, the liberation of women, the enlargement of opportunity for the poor and powerless, the extension of equal rights to racial minorities, the defense of the freedoms of expression and opposition, it is likely that their leadership will increase the sum of human liberty and welfare.

Leaders have done great harm to the world. They have also conferred great benefits. You will find both sorts in this series. Even "good" leaders must be regarded with a certain wariness. Leaders are not demigods; they put on their trousers one leg after another just like ordinary mortals. No leader is infallible, and every leader needs to be reminded of this at regular intervals. Irreverence irritates leaders but is their salvation. Unquestioning submission corrupts leaders and demeans followers. Making a cult of a leader is always a mistake. Fortunately hero worship generates its own antidote. "Every hero," said Emerson, "becomes a bore at last."

The signal benefit the great leaders confer is to embolden the rest of us to live according to our own best selves, to be active, insistent, and resolute in affirming our own sense of things. For great leaders attest to the reality of human freedom against the supposed inevitabilities of history. And they attest to the wisdom and power that may lie within the most unlikely of us, which is why Abraham Lincoln remains the supreme example of great leadership. A great leader, said Emerson, exhibits new possibilities to all humanity. "We feed on genius. . . . Great men exist that there may be greater men."

Great leaders, in short, justify themselves by emancipating and empowering their followers. So humanity struggles to master its destiny, remembering with Alexis de Tocqueville: "It is true that around every man a fatal circle is traced beyond which he cannot pass; but within the wide verge of that circle he is powerful and free; as it is with man, so with communities."

1

The Triumph of the Revolution

On the afternoon of January 2, 1959, Ernesto "Che" Guevara rode triumphantly into Havana, Cuba. The bearded 30-year-old revolutionary, wearing a beret over his unruly shoulder-length hair, captivated the wildly cheering crowds that lined the way.

Such was the culmination of more than two years of guerrilla fighting led by Fidel Castro who, with his trusted military strategist Che Guevara and others, had been waging a revolutionary war against the brutal and corrupt dictatorship of General Fulgencio Batista since November 1956. The revolution had grown from a tiny insurrection — with Castro and Guevara leading a band of fewer than 100 men — to a wave of popular resistance against the Batista regime. Only two days before his entrance into Havana, Guevara had engineered the most important military victory of the war. With only a few hundred troops, he had won control of Santa Clara, one of Cuba's largest cities. Batista, conceding defeat, fled the country on New Year's Day, 1959. On January 2, Guevara entered Havana to take final control of the capital and claim it for the revolution.

There is no life outside the revolution.
—CHE GUEVARA

Ernesto "Che" Guevara wearing his characteristic faded khaki uniform in 1964. The Argentinian-born Guevara, a leader in Cuba's socialist government, was dedicated to promoting revolution in Third World countries around the globe.

Guevara's troops, most of them thin and bearded after extended periods of time in the countryside as guerrilla fighters, moved through Havana to take possession of the government garrison at La Cabaña, an almost 200-year-old fortress with a commanding view of the city and harbor below. Guevara's troops expected a battle, but, instead, Batista's soldiers handed over the fortress to Guevara without combat. Elsewhere in Havana, Camilo Cienfuegos, another of Castro's commanders, occupied the military headquarters at Campamento Columbia. Other commanders took over the presidential palace and key military and police posts, all without firing a shot. The capital of Cuba was finally in the hands of the revolutionaries, secure for the impending entry of Castro and his men.

Guevara (bottom) and his fellow rebel leaders ride into Havana, the Cuban capital, on January 2, 1959, having brought down the dictatorship of General Fulgencio Batista.

Many of Havana's residents had lived through coups and the violence of several corrupt civilian and military regimes. They expected the rebels to "celebrate" their victory with bloodshed, but there was no violence other than some sporadic looting of houses and businesses closely identified with Batista's regime. Almost everyone professed admiration for the exemplary conduct of the rebel troops.

Che Guevara, an Argentinian by birth, had joined Castro's group of revolutionaries in Mexico in 1956 at the age of 28. The Cubans gave him the nickname "Che" — derived from the Argentinian expression *ché*, which means "hey, you!" or "hey, buddy!" — and it stuck with him for the rest of his life.

Guevara, satisfied with his victory, telegraphed his parents in Argentina, inviting them to come to Havana to see and experience the revolution. He knew that the war was essentially over; the work of rebuilding Cuban society was the next task. However, there was virtually no plan of action, and none could be made until the arrival of Fidel Castro, the 32-year-old leader of the Cuban revolution.

Guevara and Cuban premier Fidel Castro, both of whom enjoyed massive popular support during and after their defeat of the Batista regime, one year after taking power. At first Castro disavowed socialism, but soon, under the influence of Guevara, the regime fully adopted it.

The presidential palace in Havana, built in 1920. In 1957, during the early stages of the revolutionary war, it was the scene of a daring rebel attack that nearly resulted in Batista's assassination. Two years later, Castro's forces took it and other key buildings in the capital without firing a shot.

This was Castro's second attempt at overthrowing the government. On July 26, 1953, more than five years earlier, Castro, now a young lawyer, and approximately 130 of his comrades attempted to storm the Moncada military barracks in Santiago de Cuba, the country's second-largest city. They hoped to use the garrison as a base from which to launch a revolution against Batista's government. However, the attack quickly failed and many of the rebels died in the fighting. Some of those who were captured were summarily executed; others were held for trial. Castro was among those who escaped but he was later caught and arrested. At his trial Castro delivered a long defense of his action, later published under the title *History Will Absolve Me*. Despite his impassioned defense, he was condemned to 15 years in prison.

Castro was released two years later when Batista freed all political prisoners under a general amnesty in an attempt to win support and diminish political tensions. Soon after, Castro left the country and went to Mexico, where he founded the 26th of July Movement, dedicated to the overthrow of the Batista dictatorship. It was in Mexico that Castro met Guevara, who instantly decided to join the Cuban revolutionary movement.

Cuba, 90 miles south of Florida, with the largest population in the Caribbean (6.5 million), was no stranger to revolution. From its discovery in 1492 by Christopher Columbus until the end of the 19th century, Cuba was a Spanish colony. Throughout the 19th century, as countries all over Latin America gained their independence from Spain, Cuba remained a colony, producing sugar, tobacco, coffee, and copper for the mother country. By the middle of the 1800s, a number of revolts against Spanish rule had taken place. The bloodiest revolt of all occurred in 1868, the beginnning of the Ten Years' War, which claimed the lives of more than 200,000 Cubans and Spaniards. The war failed to secure Cuban independence, though it did result in the

In September 1933, Fulgencio Batista, then a sergeant in the Cuban army, led a military coup that made him the de facto leader of the nation's government. He remained Cuba's principal leader, presiding over a succession of corrupt and repressive regimes, until Castro ousted him in 1959.

Fidel Castro being sworn in as prime minister of Cuba on February 16, 1959; at left is Manuel Urrutia, a liberal judge chosen by Castro to serve as Cuba's president. Soon after, political parties were abolished, leaving Castro and Guevara to direct the government without opposition.

eventual emancipation from slavery of the island's large black population. Further reforms promised by Spain failed to materialize, and when in 1895 Spain suspended civil rights in Cuba, a second civil war broke out. The Cuban leaders of the Ten Years' War, including the poet José Martí and the former slave Antonio Maceo, took to the battlefield once again, seeking to make their country an independent democracy. Two more years of bloodshed followed, and by the beginning of 1898 the rebels were close to victory. In February of that year, the U.S. battleship *Maine* blew up in Havana harbor, and although no cause was ever established, the United

States reacted by entering the war on the side of the Cubans. The already staggering Spanish forces were easily defeated once the United States entered the war, and Cuba was finally free of Spain.

There was, however, a price. At the end of the war the United States occupied and ruled the island for three years. In 1902, the United States granted Cuba independence, but only on the condition that it could intervene militarily in Cuban affairs whenever it saw fit — and indeed the United States did intervene several times until the "agreement" was finally abrogated in 1934. During this period, communally owned land was subdivided and large sugar plantations, owned by a few wealthy landlords, were established in their place. After 1934, the United States continued to be Cuba's predominant trading partner. A succession of corrupt civilian and military governments ruled the island, always answerable first and foremost to American commercial interests. The last of these governments was Batista's dictatorship, which had just been overthrown by Castro's rebels.

Now in control of Havana, Guevara and Cienfuegos prepared for Castro's arrival by arresting those suspected of being enemies of the revolution. Guevara began organizing revolutionary tribunals for public trials of those who had committed "war crimes" against the Cuban people. Yet neither the leaders nor the followers of the Cuban Revolution had any definitive plans for the new government. For three years the rebels had concentrated on fighting a war; now they had to turn to a whole new set of problems — the building of a new social and economic order.

Cuba celebrated the rebels' victory. Fidel Castro, starting at the eastern end of the island, headed west on the Central Highway to make the 500-mile trip to Havana. Cheering crowds lined the route, and Castro stopped to give speeches that often lasted for hours. Mobbed by so many wildly enthusiastic supporters, it took him five days to reach Havana. Finally, on January 8, 1959, Castro triumphantly entered the capital with his brother Raúl, Camilo Cienfuegos, Che Guevara, and other heroes of the revolution at his side. The city exploded with joy — church bells rang, factory sirens whistled, boats in the harbor blew their horns, and hundreds of thousands of people poured into the streets to demonstrate their support for the revolution.

Castro stopped at the presidential palace to talk to the respected judge Manuel Urrutia, whom he had chosen to serve as president of the provisional government. Other politicians were also on hand, many of whom had just returned from exile in Miami to join the revolution. Castro then addressed the crowd of approximately a half million from the balcony of the building.

Throughout the late 19th century, the charismatic poet and patriot José Martí led the effort to free his country from Spanish rule. He died in 1895 during the early stages of Cuba's war of independence, but remains a powerful symbol of Cuban nationalism.

Castro and his entourage next drove to the military headquarters at Campamento Columbia, where he addressed an even larger and more ecstatic crowd. Castro introduced Guevara and his other military commanders, described the goals of the revolution, warned his supporters about their enemies, urged all political groups to lay down their weapons, and called for peace and order. Someone released two doves from the crowd and one alighted on Castro's shoulder; many took it as an omen of peace after so many years of violence and unrest.

Cuba was about to embark on an experiment with a new form of government, in which, for the next five years, the Argentinian rebel Che Guevara was to play a central role. Subsequently, Guevara would leave Cuba and turn once again to revolution, dedicating his brief life to fighting for the oppressed in underdeveloped nations around the world, dying before his 40th birthday. He would become the symbol of a new kind of revolutionary leader, and he would capture the imagination of the world for the next decade and beyond.

2

The Making of a Revolutionary

Ernesto Guevara was born in Rosario, Argentina, on June 14, 1928. His father, Ernesto Guevara Lynch, and mother, Celia de la Serna, were members of Argentina's privileged middle class. The elder Ernesto Guevara, a civil engineer and architect, failed in several business ventures, forcing the family to sell their estates in the countryside. Guevara's associate in later life, Ricardo Rojo, wrote in *My Friend Che* that given the world of business affairs, "Che's father [was torn] between two alternatives: money or continuing to be a gentleman, as his ancestors had been. He chose the second course, and it was this generous spirit that Che inherited."

The elder Guevara supported the resistance to the fascist General Franco in the Spanish civil war in

Very early young Ernestito developed an affinity for the poor.
—MARVIN D. RESNICK
Guevara biographer

Supporters and detractors alike recognized Guevara's complete personal commitment to socialism. Che espoused the concept of a "new Socialist man" and encouraged his followers "to struggle every day, so that the love for living humanity may be transformed into concrete deeds."

23

the 1930s and engaged in a campaign to stop Nazi propaganda in the Americas before World War II. During the war he belonged to several committees to aid the democratic countries, and after the war he opposed Juan Perón's neofascist dictatorship in Argentina and supported a Paraguayan revolutionary group. Che's mother, Celia, was equally outspoken. She had been arrested for her political activism on one occasion and, like her husband, would always support her son in his revolutionary career. During Che's youth, the Guevaras frequently played host to gatherings of Spanish republicans and other socialists, progressives, and liberals.

From the age of two, Guevara suffered from severe asthma attacks that were to plague him for the rest of his life. The family moved to Alta Gracia, a town in the Andean foothills where the high altitude would lessen the effects of Che's asthma. His mother tells how Che's father would sleep sitting on his young son's bed, the boy's head resting on his father's chest, to help Che cope with the asthma attacks.

Guevara had four brothers and sisters and an active and varied family life. His father recalled later: "We lived a good life. I spent all my time with the boy. I took him shooting, taught him to swim, and got him to play soccer and rugby. I saw to it that he spent about three hours each day in the pool in the summer, to relax his chest muscles and get him breathing well."

During grade school Guevara's asthma forced him to receive much of his education at home from his parents. He became frail because of his illness, yet he tried to overcome it by engaging in sports and vigorous exercise. Although Guevara never really excelled in these pursuits, he was able to build his stamina and became an untiring bicyclist.

Guevara was born on June 14, 1928, in Rosario, a city in southwestern Argentina. In his travels throughout South and Central America as a student, he saw firsthand the grinding poverty of most of the continent's inhabitants and resolved to dedicate his life to social change.

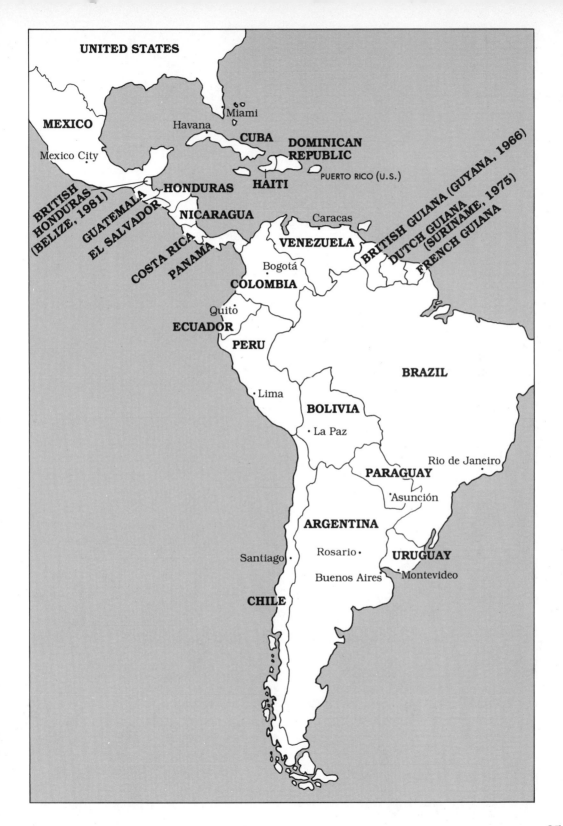

UNITED STATES

MEXICO

Miami

Havana

Mexico City

CUBA

DOMINICAN
REPUBLIC

HAITI

PUERTO RICO (U.S.)

BRITISH
HONDURAS
(BELIZE, 1981)

HONDURAS

GUATEMALA

NICARAGUA

EL SALVADOR

COSTA RICA

PANAMA

Caracas

VENEZUELA

BRITISH GUIANA (GUYANA, 1966)

DUTCH GUIANA
(SURINAME, 1975)

FRENCH GUIANA

Bogotá

COLOMBIA

Quito

ECUADOR

PERU

BRAZIL

Lima

BOLIVIA

La Paz

Rio de Janeiro

PARAGUAY

Asunción

ARGENTINA

Rosario

URUGUAY

Santiago

Buenos Aires

Montevideo

CHILE

When young Guevara reached the age of 12, the family moved to Córdoba, where they would live for many years. The family house stood across the street from a shantytown, home to many of the city's poorest people. Guevara mixed freely with the poor boys of the shantytown, behavior considered most unusual for a child of the middle class.

According to one family friend, the Guevara home contained more than 3,000 books. As a teenager Che became especially interested in poetry and literature, though he also read widely in philosophy, history, archaeology, and a variety of other subjects. Attracted to travel, Che went on a moped trip once that took him from one end of Argentina to the other. His excursion was cited later in an advertisement for the brand of bike he used. Whenever he went on one of his frequent trips, he always brought a load of books and usually kept a diary — both habits he would retain as a revolutionary fighter.

In 1944 the Guevara family moved to Buenos Aires, Argentina's sprawling capital, and Che enrolled in the medical school there in 1947. He graduated as an M.D. six years later.

At the end of 1944, when Guevara was 17, his family moved to Buenos Aires, Argentina's capital and largest city. There Guevara decided to study medicine at the university, but he seemed more interested in travel and adventure than in his studies. On December 29, 1951, Che and his friend Alberto Granados began a long motorcycle trip from Argentina to Chile and beyond. Their goal was to tour the entire continent to get to know the people, living conditions, geography, and history of South America. Guevara and Granados crossed the towering Andes mountain chain that separates Argentina from Chile. Nearing Santiago, Chile, their motorcycles broke down and could not be repaired, and they were forced to hitchhike into the city.

The two friends took a number of different odd jobs in the Santiago area to earn some money and quickly became accustomed to roughing it in the countryside. They set out for Peru to visit the famous Inca ruins at Machu Picchu, high in the Andes. On the way, and almost everywhere they went, they were struck by the crushing poverty, especially in remote rural areas, where peasant farmers worked small plots of land owned by rich landlords. In Peru they found a leper colony—Granados already had some experience working in leper colonies — so they decided to stay to offer their assistance. Guevara, who resolved to become a specialist in the treatment of leprosy, was especially impressed by the camaraderie among those living at the colony. Later he wrote, "The highest forms of human solidarity and loyalty arise among such lonely and desperate people."

Eventually they left the colony to travel down the Amazon River on a raft. They arrived penniless at Leticia, Colombia, and took jobs training a local soccer team that eventually won a regional championship. In Bogotá, Colombia, they were arrested by the police for lack of visible means of support and told to leave the country, but sympathetic students raised enough money for transportation to Venezuela, where Granados planned to work in another leper colony. Guevara promised to join him later but said that he had to return home first to finish his medical studies.

> *I got my children to seek the dangers and secrets of life very early. I had the firm conviction that they ought to . . . grow up in complete liberty.*
> —ERNESTO GUEVARA LYNCH
> Che's father

Guevara with his mother, Celia de la Serna, and father, Ernesto Guevara Lynch, in Havana in 1959. Though both of Che's parents came from upper-middle-class backgrounds, they held leftist political views and supported their son's revolutionary activities.

After a brief trip to Miami, Florida, Guevara returned to Argentina to finish medical school and take his final exams. He registered for compulsory military service but was classified as unfit for duty because of his asthma. In March 1953, at the age of 25, Guevara passed his exams and received his medical degree, but he was not ready to settle down and become a doctor. Instead, he took off with another friend to travel to Bolivia, arriving there in July 1953, the same month that Fidel Castro was to storm the Moncada barracks in Santiago de Cuba.

Guevara had not yet become politically committed, though he exhibited strong sympathies toward the poor and oppressed. He later wrote, "When I began my medical studies most of my ideals as a revolutionary did not exist. Like most other people, I longed for success. . . . But . . . I began to travel all over America, [where] I came into close contact with poverty and hunger and disease. . . . I saw the degradation of undernourishment and constant repression. Thus I began to realize that there was another thing that was as important as being [successful or] famous. . . . And that was to help those people."

In La Paz, the capital of Bolivia, Guevara began associating with more politically oriented people, especially a group of Argentinian exiles. One new friend, Ricardo Rojo, was an Argentinian lawyer who had been imprisoned for his opposition to the Perón regime in Argentina and had just escaped.

Guevara arrived in La Paz and joined this politically active circle at a propitious moment in Bolivian history. Bolivia's new, left-leaning government was taking the radical steps of nationalizing the country's tin mines and redistributing land to the impoverished Indian peasantry — policies with which Guevara was in total agreement. But when he witnessed the actual implementation, he grew doubtful. The Indians were given inferior land, and their treatment at the hands of government bureaucrats was less than dignified. Though the parliamentary government's land reform measures were well intentioned, Guevara felt that its efforts were not nearly significant enough.

Rojo convinced Guevara to travel with him to Guatemala. Guevara, who had been planning to join his friend Granados at the leper colony in Venezuela, was talked into changing his plans by Rojo's contention that "things are happening to Guatemala."

Rojo was right. Guatemala had been a democracy since 1944, when strikes by students, teachers, and workers forced the ouster of the country's military dictatorship. In the election that followed, a progressive, reform-minded government was voted into office and instituted a social security system and a series of pro-labor laws. In 1950, Guatemalans elected another progressive government, the president of which, Colonel Jacobo Arbenz Guzmán, promised to continue the dramatic program of reform begun in 1944. The Arbenz government, which had been true to its promise, was now under threat of overthrow.

> *By now our senses were well trained and we smelled something in the air, ready to explode.*
> —RICARDO ROJO
> on arriving with Che
> in Guatemala

Jacobo Arbenz Guzmán, a moderate leftist dedicated to land reform, was elected president of Guatemala in 1950. He was ousted four years later by a CIA-sponsored invasion and coup after he ordered the expropriation of large tracts of land owned by the U.S.-owned United Fruit Company.

Guevara, Rojo, and several other Argentinians made a difficult trip from Bolivia through Peru to Ecuador. There they got free passage to Panama on a boat owned by the United Fruit Company, a large American firm that handled the cultivation and exportation of fruit in several Central American countries. The free passage was arranged by a lawyer in Bolivia after seeing Rojo's letter of introduction from the prominent Chilean socialist Salvador Allende (who 20 years later would be elected president of Chile and then killed by the Chilean military in an American-backed coup).

After arriving in Panama, Guevara, Rojo, and some of the others made their way to Costa Rica, where they stayed among a community of exiles from several different Latin American countries — including some of the revolutionaries who had fled Cuba after the failed Moncada barracks attack a few months earlier. The Cubans in the group claimed they would return to Cuba to overthrow the Batista dictatorship, but according to Rojo, neither Rojo nor Guevara took them seriously.

By January 1954, Guevara and Rojo had arrived in Guatemala, where they met native and foreign radicals. Among such radicals was a Peruvian woman, Hilda Gadea Acosta, who came to live with Guevara in a boardinghouse in Guatemala City and whom he would eventually marry. She was a member of a radical Peruvian party and helped introduce Guevara to radical politics. Guevara also met Ñico Lopez, who had been one of Fidel Castro's closest advisers in the failed 1953 revolt in Cuba; Lopez would later introduce Guevara to Fidel and his brother Raúl Castro in Mexico.

Meanwhile, the government of President Arbenz — in office for more than three years and now receiving strong support from communists in the national assembly — had enacted a major land reform program. All uncultivated portions of large landholdings were to be expropriated and redistributed to landless peasants. The biggest landowner, and the one most affected by the reforms, was the United Fruit Company, from which the Arbenz government had already taken more than 225,000 uncultivated acres.

The United States, fearing the growth of the Gua-

A United Fruit Company plant in Guatemala in 1954, with a banner proclaiming President Arbenz's opposition to foreign intervention. One month later a U.S.-sponsored army invaded the country and installed a right-wing dictator. Che Guevara witnessed the coup, which convinced him that the United States was a repressive force in Latin America.

John Foster Dulles, the U.S. secretary of state under President Dwight Eisenhower, directed the anti-Arbenz coup. Like the government he represented, Dulles was vehemently opposed to communism and orchestrated efforts to suppress leftist movements throughout Latin America.

temalan communists and the breakup of United Fruit's large landholdings, moved to overthrow the Arbenz government. With the approval of U.S. president Dwight D. Eisenhower, the United States secretly organized and funded a small army of Guatemalan exiles and other Latin American mercenaries. The army, operating from neighboring Honduras, was directed by U.S. secretary of state John Foster Dulles and his brother, Central Intelligence Agency director Allen Dulles. The CIA, the agency in charge of the secret American effort, also secured the support of right-wing military officers within Guatemala itself.

On June 18, 1954, the anti-Arbenz forces invaded Guatemala. The Guatemalan army, many of its officers paid off by the CIA, offered no resistance. The only possible defense remaining rested among civilians. Guevara tried to organize armed resistance to the U.S.-sponsored invasion but none materialized. Within a week, the government was overthrown and a military dictatorship was installed in its place.

Guevara was outraged that a more resolute resistance was not offered. He later wrote, "The last Latin American revolutionary democracy — that of Jacobo Arbenz — still in power in this area failed as a result of the cold premeditated aggression carried out by the U.S.A. . . . Its visible head was the Secretary of State [John Foster] Dulles, a man who, through a rare coincidence, was also a stockholder and attorney of the United Fruit Company. When the American invasion first took place, I tried to get together a group of young men like myself to fight back. In Guatemala, it was necessary to fight and almost nobody fought. It was necessary to resist, and almost nobody resisted."

Hilda Gadea Acosta, Guevara's first wife, recalls: "During the aggression, Che volunteered for guard duty while there was a blackout and the city was being bombed. He asked to go to the front but was never sent." Guevara's repeated calls to resist the invasion went unheeded, but they were noted by supporters of the coup, who marked him for murder. The Argentinian ambassador discovered this and told Guevara that his life was in danger, and Guevara took refuge in the Argentinian embassy.

What Guevara witnessed in the overthrow of the Arbenz government convinced him that true revolution could only be brought about by force. According to Gadea, "It was Guatemala that finally convinced him of the necessity for armed struggle, for taking the initiative against imperialism." As Guevara himself later stated: "When I was in Arbenz's Guatemala, I had begun taking notes to try and assess what would be the duties of a revolutionary doctor. Then, after the United Fruit Company aggression, I realized one fundamental thing: To be a revolutionary doctor, you first need a revolution."

Che Guevara was indeed to become a revolutionary soon. First, however, he had to get out of Guatemala alive. He refused the offer of the Argentinian embassy of safe passage to Argentina and asked instead for passage to Mexico. It is not clear whether he had already decided to join the Cubans, who were gathering in Mexico for an invasion to free Cuba from Batista's rule, or whether he chose Mexico simply because it was the country most hospitable to political refugees.

In any case, Guevara arrived in Mexico City with a friend from Guatemala. Together they worked as street photographers, selling barely enough of their photos to rent a small, run-down apartment. Hilda Gadea Acosta soon arrived in Mexico and moved in with her husband and his friend. Subsequently, through some political connections, Guevara was able to get a job working in the allergy section of General Hospital in Mexico City. (In addition, he gave lectures on medicine at Mexico's Autonomous University and worked as a news photographer for the Latina News Agency.) One day at the hospital he encountered the Cuban Ñico Lopez. Lopez was delighted to see Guevara and took him to meet Raúl Castro, recently arrived in Mexico City.

Gadea recalls that Che brought Raúl to their apartment and that they became instant friends,

In July 1956, Fidel Castro (arrow) and Guevara (seated, second from left) were arrested in Mexico City with 20 other Cuban exiles for plotting to overthrow Cuban president Batista. They were released one month later and launched their invasion of Cuba in November.

meeting almost daily. She describes Raúl as "a dedicated revolutionary" who was "merry, open, sure of himself, [and] very clear in the exposition of his ideas." During the second week of July 1955, Raúl arranged for Guevara to meet his older brother Fidel Castro at the home of a Cuban woman who entertained and supported the young revolutionaries dedicated to overthrowing the Batista regime. Fidel and Che, both 27 years old, hit it off immediately, talking together through the night and agreeing that Guevara should join the 26th of July fighters on their expedition to Cuba to begin a revolution.

Guevara later wrote: "I met him [Castro] on one of those cold nights in Mexico City, and I remember that our first discussion was on international politics. A few hours later that same night — at dawn — I was one of the future expeditionaries. . . . After my experiences traveling all over Latin America and after Guatemala, it would have taken very little to persuade me to join any revolution against a tyranny; but Fidel made a very great impression on me. He would confront the most impossible situations and resolve them. He was absolutely positive that if we set off for Cuba, we would get there; that once we got there, we would fight; and that by fighting we would win. His optimism was contagious. We had to act, to fight, to consolidate our position. To stop moaning and to start the real struggle. And in order to prove to the Cuban people that they could trust his word, he made his famous speech, 'In 1956, we shall be free men or martyrs,' announcing that, before the year was over, he would land somewhere in Cuba at the head of an expeditionary force."

3
The Cuban Revolutionary War

Henceforth, Guevara would dedicate himself completely to the Cuban Revolution. Under the instruction of Alberto Bayo, a 63-year-old veteran of the Spanish civil war, Guevara and about 80 Cubans began combat training with newly bought rifles on a ranch 20 miles outside Mexico City.

The key portion of their training involved learning the hit-and-run tactics of guerrilla warfare, in which small groups of individuals draw regular enemy armies into the mountains or jungles where they can be attacked and demoralized. Guevara and the Cubans underwent arduous 15-hour marches over mountains, across rivers, and through dense undergrowth, learning and perfecting the procedures of ambush and quick retreat. From the start, Guevara was Bayo's prize student among the guerrillas-in-training, scoring the highest on all of the tests given.

It is the hour of the furnaces, and it is only necessary to see the glow.
—JOSÉ MARTÍ
19th-century Cuban patriot

Guevara's role in the Cuban Revolution made him an innovator in guerrilla warfare. He saw the guerrilla as the catalyst of armed revolution beginning in the countryside and later spreading to the cities. Guevara was the first and most committed Marxist among the rebels.

Of this initial training period, Guevara later recalled: "My almost immediate impression on hearing the first lessons was of the possibility of victory, which I had seen as very doubtful when I joined the rebel commander [Castro]. I had been linked to him from the outset by a tie of romantic adventurous sympathy, and by the conviction that it would be worth dying on a foreign beach for such a pure ideal." For the rest of his life, Guevara would harbor an idealized, "romantic" notion of revolution, as well as of the peasantry he sought to liberate.

The Mexican police, tipped off by Batista's secret police, raided the Cubans' ranch in July 1956. Twenty-four men, including Castro, Bayo, and Guevara, were arrested and charged with plotting to launch an invasion of a foreign country from Mexican soil. They were released within a month, but further pressure by the Mexican police, coupled with the fear that invasions planned by a number of other Cuban exile groups might overshadow his own, forced Castro to move up his invasion date to November 1956.

Castro recruiting peasants near a rebel camp in the Sierra Maestra mountains. The original guerrilla force consisted of only 82 men and soon fell to just 17, including Castro and Guevara. But after a year in the mountains, the rebel forces grew with the arrival of recruits from the cities and surrounding countryside.

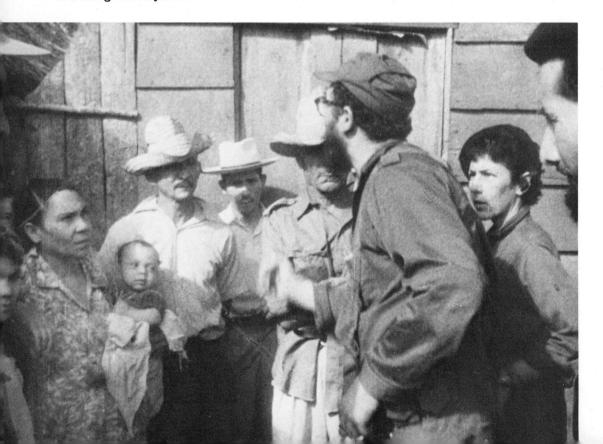

For over a year Castro had been traveling across Mexico and into the United States to raise money and support for his cause. Eventually, he was able to purchase a boat — the dilapidated, aptly named *Granma* (Grandmother) — and enough arms, ammunition, and medical supplies for a small band of guerrilla fighters.

On November 25, 1956, the *Granma* secretly set sail from the port of Tuxpan, Mexico, bound for Cuba. Eighty-two men, 28 of them veterans of the failed Moncada attack, were crowded onto the 58-foot-long boat. Guevara, the guerrilla band's medic, was one of only four non-Cubans aboard. Shortly after reaching the open sea, all but a handful of the men became violently seasick; Guevara later wrote that he suffered a severe asthma attack as well.

Castro's plan was to land, on November 30, near the town of Niquero in Oriente province, at the southeasternmost end of Cuba, more than 400 miles from Havana. The landing was timed to coincide with an uprising in Oriente's capital, Santiago de Cuba, led by the 24-year-old student leader Frank País. According to the plan, the Santiago insurrectionaries would combine with Castro's mountain forces to create a two-pronged, urban-rural catalyst to nationwide revolution, but poor navigation caused the *Granma* to be three days late in arriving. País's Santiago uprising began as scheduled and was crushed before Castro and his men reached shore on December 2, 1956.

Castro's invasion, already botched, proceeded to become a virtual disaster. After seven days at sea, the revolutionary army landed — but not at the designated site near Niquero, where supplies awaited them. Instead, they landed 10 miles too far to the south in swampland on Colorado Beach, near the village of Belic. The boat ran aground in mud several hundred yards from shore and was spotted by a government naval vessel. The rebels had to swim to shore, losing much equipment in the process, then were forced to wade through a mangrove swamp while government planes circled overhead. It was several hours before they reached firm ground.

Requested edition sold out.
—Castro's coded message meaning the revolution was about to occur

Rebel guerrillas making gasoline bombs on the eve of Castro's April 1958 offensive against government forces. Guevara became expert at leading hit-and-run ambushes against Batista's army and then fading back into the countryside before the army could launch a counterattack.

"We reached solid ground, lost, stumbling along like so many shadows or ghosts marching in response to some obscure psychic impulse," Guevara later wrote in his *Reminiscences of the Revolutionary War.* "We had been through seven days of constant hunger and sickness during the sea crossing, topped by three still more terrible days on land. Exactly 10 days after our departure from Mexico, during the early morning hours of December 5, following a night-long march interrupted by faintings and frequent rest periods, we reached a spot paradoxically known as Alegría de Pío [Rejoicing of the Pious]."

While Castro's bedraggled rebels paused near the fields of sugarcane at Alegría de Pío, a government army unit was closing in. Guevara recalls that, as troop doctor, he was attending to blisters and other injuries sustained in the landing and march when he became aware of planes circling the area, then a hail of bullets. A man next to Che dropped a cartridge box of ammunition. Guevara was confronted with a fateful choice: "This was perhaps the first time I was faced with the dilemma of choosing between my devotion to medicine and my duty as a revolutionary soldier. There, at my feet, was a knapsack full of medicine and a box of ammunition. I could not possibly carry both; they were too heavy. I picked up the box of ammunition, leaving the medicine, and started to cross the clearing, heading for the canefield."

As his comrades fell wounded or dead nearby, Guevara was hit in the chest and neck by gunfire. Though the wound proved superficial, at that moment he was certain it was fatal. He prepared to die in a "dignified manner," while around him "everything became a blur of airplanes flying low and strafing the field, adding to the confusion, amid Dantesque and grotesque scenes such as the one of a comrade of considerable weight desperately trying to hide behind a single stalk of sugar cane. In the turmoil someone kept on yelling, 'Silence!' "

Some 25 of the 82 rebels were killed in the ambush, among them Ñico Lopez, the man who introduced Guevara to Castro in Mexico City a year earlier. A number were wounded. Those who were able to escape — including Guevara, with the help of a fellow rebel — scattered in all directions. Some of the survivors formed small groups; several were captured by Batista's rural guards in the ensuing days and shot. Other survivors deserted. Guevara found himself with a band of five men; after several harrowing days of avoiding government forces and subsisting on what little food they could find, local peasants guided them to the Sierra Maestra mountains where they found Castro. There they discovered that of the original 82 men who had sailed with the *Granma*, only 17 remained.

The Sierra Maestra, where the rebels now planned to begin their revolution, is the highest mountain range in Cuba, a wild, rugged, sparsely populated region. In 1956, it was inaccessible to regular military forces due to the complete absence of paved roads. Most of the land was covered by thick tropical undergrowth, though there was some subsistence farming and a few coffee plantations. The inhabitants, at the time mostly illiterate, impoverished peasants, worked small plots of land, often as squatters. Batista's rural guards, whose main concern in the region was to protect the property of the few large landholders, were hated by the peasants. Yet when Castro's small band of guerrillas first arrived in the Sierra Maestra, most of the peasants kept their distance.

> *Many would call me an adventurer, and I am one of a different sort, one of those that risks his skin to demonstrate what he believes to be true.*
> —CHE GUEVARA

> *The attack on the small barracks at the mouth of the La Plata river in the Sierra Maestra brought us our first victory . . . it confirmed the possibility of our eventual triumph.*
>
> —CHE GUEVARA

By mid-January 1957, Castro, his rebel army numbering approximately 20 men, decided to carry out an attack to show the Cuban people that he and his 26th of July Movement were alive and active. Their first target was a small army garrison at the mouth of the La Plata River. Tricking a local informer for the rural guards into believing that they were government troops, the rebels entered the garrison and shot the informer as the battle began. Within an hour, the rebels had taken the post, killing two soldiers, routing the rest, and capturing some weapons without suffering a single casualty. Guevara found that "the effect of our victory was electrifying. It was like a clarion call, proving that the Rebel Army really existed and was ready to fight. For us, it was the reaffirmation of our chances for total victory."

In February 1957, two months after the *Granma* landing, *New York Times* reporter Herbert Matthews went into the Sierra and conducted a long interview with Castro. When it was published in the *Times*, the rebel movement gained worldwide notoriety, widespread sympathy, and, most important, legitimacy. The Batista government was forced to acknowledge that a rebel army was active within Cuba.

The revolutionaries impressed observers by following a new code of warfare. Though, like most armies, they generally dealt with deserters and civilian informers by executing them on the spot, they made a point of releasing all government troops taken prisoner and never practiced terror on the local population. This stood in sharp contrast to the conduct of the government troops, who tortured and executed rebel prisoners, and regularly rounded up, tortured, or shot civilians as a tactic of intimidation. The rebels also won the admiration of many observers by their stated adherence to the democratic principles of the Cuban poet and patriot José Martí.

For the rest of 1957, the rebel forces slowly increased their numbers and confidence. They survived ambushes, air attacks, desertions, betrayal by peasant guides, and the demoralizing effects of living isolated in the hills, all the while gathering experience and strength. Reinforcements arrived from the cities; like Castro, Guevara, and almost all of the original *Granma* men, they generally came from well-educated, middle-class backgrounds. But peasants, usually poor and illiterate, also joined the rebel army, making it more representative of the general population than it had been before. By the end of the year, Castro's forces controlled the Sierra Maestra mountains.

Guevara had emerged as one of Castro's most valuable men. In addition to serving as the troop doctor, he took an active part in the fighting, sometimes leading assaults. On July 12, 1956, six weeks after a major victory at the Battle of El Uvero, Castro gave Guevara the rank of *comandante* (commander), which had previously been assumed only by Castro himself. Guevara was put in charge of the Second Column of the Rebel Army.

Batista inspects arms seized after Castro's unsuccessful attack on the Moncada military barracks in July 1953. After Castro landed in Cuba in 1956, Batista's troops regularly harassed and shot civilians in an effort to intimidate them into withholding support from the rebels.

This rare photo shows the entire rebel command at its guerrilla base in the Sierra Maestra in 1957. Guevara (second from left), originally the guerrilla band's troop doctor, was promoted by Castro (center) to the rank of *comandante* (commander) and put in charge of the second column of the rebel army.

Guevara wrote: "It was a pleasure to look at our troop. Close to 200 men, well disciplined, with increased morale and armed with good weapons, some of them new. The qualitative change . . . was now quite evident in the Sierra. This was a true free territory; safety measures were not so necessary, and there was a little freedom to carry on conversations at night while resting in our hammocks. Authorization was given to move into the villages of the Sierra and establish a closer relationship with the people."

After almost a year in the Sierra Maestra, the rebels had gained the support of the peasantry. Elsewhere on the island during 1957, others — sometimes acting in concert with the rebels, sometimes acting independently — rose against the Batista dictatorship. In March, students launched an unsuccessful attack on the presidential palace in Havana. In Santiago de Cuba, where fighting was frequent and fierce, Frank País was killed. In September, an unsuccessful naval mutiny, reinforced by 26th of July fighters, broke out in Cienfuegos.

In October, a provisional government of prominent Cuban politicians in exile was formed in Miami, Florida. Batista and the army, sensing the imminent loss of their grip on Cuba, reacted with increasing violence, stepping up their campaign of terror and assassination.

By March 1958, the atrocities carried out by Batista's forces led the United States to announce that it would stop selling arms to the Cuban government — a blow to Batista's large but ill-equipped, poorly trained, and ineptly led army. Meanwhile, in the Sierra Maestra, Castro's army, now numbering 300, was firmly entrenched; he and Guevara had established a munitions works, schools, clinics, kitchens, workshops, a newspaper, and a radio station in the region. Land had been given to peasants, who were now free from the brutal harassment of Batista's rural guards.

In his later reflections on the eventual victory of the rebel army, Guevara wrote: "The dictatorship [of Batista] created the necessary ferment, with its policy of oppression of the masses and maintenance of a regime of privilege: privileges for the regime's lackeys, for parasitic *latifundistas* [big landowners] and businessmen, privileges for the foreign monopolies. Once the conflict broke out, the regime's repressive measures and its brutality, far from diminishing popular resistance, increased it. The demoralization and the shamelessness of the military caste facilitated the task. The ruggedness of the mountains in Oriente, plus our enemy's tactical ineptitude, also did their share. But this war was won by the people, through the action of its armed fighting vanguard, the rebel army, whose basic weapons were their morale and their discipline."

Guevara described the first year of the Cuban revolutionary war as the "nomadic phase," characterized by the constant mobility of the rebels. Now that the Sierra Maestra was firmly under rebel control, a new stage in the war was about to begin. In April 1958, anti-Batista forces in the plains and cities called for a general strike throughout the country to attempt to drive Batista out of office, but the strike was disorganized and failed. In May, Batista countered by mounting a 10,000-man offensive, supported by tanks and fighter-bombers, against the rebel stronghold. The offensive lasted for more than two months, but Batista's army, disorganized and led by corrupt and inept officers, was out of its element in the mountains. Unable to find the rebels, government forces contented themselves with dropping U.S.-made bombs on villages, killing scores of civilians.

By August, Batista's army had been decisively beaten back by Castro's outnumbered forces. Castro then began planning his own final offensive aimed at winning control of Cuba's largest cities. "The guerrilla war has ceased to exist," he announced; "it has become a war of positions and movements."

Castro had decided to move his forces out of the mountains and into the plains to confront Batista's army in the open. Fidel and his brother Raúl set out with 200 men for Santiago de Cuba, where they would join with 600 other guerrillas in an attempt to take the city. Meanwhile, Che Guevara, with 148 men, moved west through Las Villas province toward the Escambray Mountains and the city of Santa Clara. Camilo Cienfuegos led a column of 82 men, moving parallel to Guevara's forces; their ultimate goal: Havana.

Guevara and Cienfuegos began their advance with newly captured trucks, but the trucks were

Members of the Cuban army prepare to launch a counterattack on the rebel forces. Despite widespread reports of atrocities committed by Batista's regime, the U.S. government provided Batista's army with substantial military aid, extensive training, and nearly all of its weaponry.

destroyed by an aerial attack on the first day. Traveling on foot, and only at night to avoid ambush, the two columns often went several days without eating. After an extremely difficult seven-week march, they made it to Las Villas in the center of Cuba, where Guevara joined forces with groups composed of students, other 26th of July guerrillas, and communists.

Local 26th of July leaders objected to Guevara's increasing reliance on the communists. "Finally," according to British historian Hugh Thomas, "in the course of a heated argument, Guevara said that between him and the 26 July Movement there was a political chasm (*abismo político*) and that if in these moments they were united in the struggle against Batista, sooner or later they would end by going separate ways."

Batista had called elections for early November, intending to install a new, rubber-stamp president while he himself retained real power. Castro announced that anyone voting in the elections would be sentenced to 30 years or to death. In Las Villas, the presence of Guevara and Cienfuegos was enough to keep voter turnout very low, while across the island less than 30 percent of the Cuban population voted in the elections, which turned out to have been rigged well in advance by Batista anyway.

In December, Guevara's task was to cut the island in half by taking Las Villas province. In a matter of days, he executed a series of brilliant tactical victories that gave him control of all but the province's capital city of Santa Clara. It was defended by more than 2,000 government troops, air support, and an armored train; Guevara had 300 men. The outskirts of Santa Clara fell quickly as the government troops surrendered almost immediately, but it took nearly three days of house-to-house combat inside the city before the remainder of the government forces were routed. With Santa Clara finally taken, nothing stood between the rebels and Havana.

Meanwhile, Fidel and Raúl Castro had Santiago de Cuba surrounded, and Batista's troops frantically telephoned the dictator and told him they could not hold onto the city much longer. Guevara's as-

Camilo Cienfuegos, one of the original leaders of the 26th of July Movement, leads his cavalry unit to the victory celebration in Havana. He and Guevara led a dual offensive against Batista's army in late 1958, which brought about the dictator's final defeat on December 31.

tonishing victory at Santa Clara on December 31, 1958, coupled with the Castros' imminent victory at Santiago de Cuba, sounded the death knell for Batista's regime. His army disintegrating, Batista was certain of defeat; accordingly, he made arrangements to leave the country. At 3:00 A.M. on January 1, 1959, Batista boarded a plane in Havana and fled for the Dominican Republic, having amassed a fortune of more than $300 million through graft and payoffs.

Later that morning, Batista's flight was announced over Cuban radio. Castro, his victory all but complete, called a general strike for the next day to mobilize the people to resist a Batista military coup. He planned his entrance into Santiago and

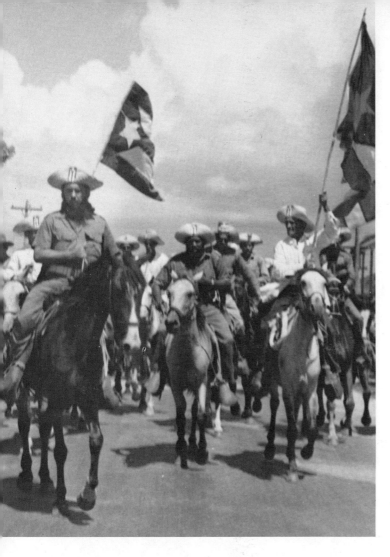

ordered Guevara and Cienfuegos to march on Havana.

Castro entered Santiago on January 2, and, soon after, Guevara and Cienfuegos entered Havana, where they took control of military installations to prevent the military from seizing power. Soon Castro would begin his triumphant march to the capital, consolidating his power as he drove from one end of Cuba to the other, making speeches and greeting rapturous crowds.

Against overwhelming odds, Castro, Guevara, and their rebel army had won the military phase of the Cuban Revolution. Next, the revolutionaries had to confront the difficult problems of creating a new society.

4

Cuban Socialism

The Cuban revolutionary war was over. A relatively small-scale conflict, it was vicious and bloody nonetheless. According to figures published 10 days after Batista fled the island, 900 people were killed in more than 2 years of fighting, about half of them rebels, rebel sympathizers, and civilians. In addition, government forces killed several hundred peasants in the countryside, bringing the final death toll to approximately 2,000 people in a nation of 6.5 million. The equivalent figure for a nation the size of the United States in 1959: more than 50,000 deaths.

In the first days after the victory, both Castro and Guevara were extremely concerned that remnants of the traditional Cuban military might attempt to seize power and set up a new dictatorship; it had been the pattern throughout Cuban and Latin American history. Guevara himself had witnessed an example less than five years before during the CIA-sponsored military coup in Guatemala. To prevent a right-wing coup from happening in Cuba,

Castro set out from his first day in power to destroy every vestige of the old social order in Cuba.
—TAD SZULC
Castro biographer

Guevara presiding over the Havana revolutionary court in which hundreds accused of war crimes were tried. Across the island, some 200 were found guilty of murder and torture and were executed. Although the U.S. government denounced the trials as barbaric, many Cubans supported the judgments.

Revolutionary officers listen to testimony from four of Batista's soldiers in January 1959. The trials were conducted by tribunals usually composed of two or three army officers, an assessor, and a respected local citizen.

Castro put his men in control of major military installations, resolving to substitute the rebel army for Batista's army as quickly as possible. He also decided to impose the death penalty on those of Batista's military leaders found guilty of committing crimes against the Cuban people. Revolutionary tribunals were set up to conduct the trials. Guevara, who had already arrested several of Batista's men upon entering Havana, was in charge of this process in the capital. Raúl Castro — whose men, according to some accounts, shot scores of prisoners upon entering Santiago de Cuba — was in charge of the tribunals in that city.

Fidel Castro called on the Cuban people not to resort to mob violence and personal vengeance as they had in 1933, when, with the overthrow of the hated Machado dictatorship, hundreds of Machado's supporters were killed by angry mobs. The Cubans heeded Castro's call, despite widespread sentiment that several of Batista's most notorious murderers and torturers be executed summarily — and indeed, in the first 10 days following the flight of Batista, approximately 100 of Batista's men captured by the rebels were condemned in summary courts-martial and shot.

By January 10, however, the formal revolutionary tribunals were established. The trials were quick, lasting just a few days. Presided over by rebel army officials, the accused were given a chance to fully state their case. Some confessed, some were found guilty and given jail terms, some were released. But those found guilty of murder or torture — approximately 200 in all—were executed.

In one famous case, for example, Major Jesús Sosa Blanco, who Herbert Matthews describes as "one of the worst torturers and killers of the Batista regime," was tried in a televised public spectacle in a Havana stadium. While witnesses recounted Sosa's crimes, thousands of spectators shouted "assassin"; Sosa replied by telling the court that the trial was "a Roman circus." He was found guilty, and after he lost a later appeal he was executed. Matthews, who was in Cuba at the time, writes, "I did not then, or ever, hear or read of an innocent man being condemned." But other American observers, including Secretary of State Dulles, several members of Congress, and many newspaper reporters, denounced the trials and executions as being a miscarriage of justice.

Major Jesús Sosa Blanco (in profile), a military commander under Batista, at his retrial in 1959 as a woman accuses him of having murdered her son during the war. Sosa's conviction at his first trial was voided under international pressure, but he was eventually found guilty of war crimes and executed.

Guevara, still dressed in army fatigues, being sworn in as head of the National Bank of Cuba in November 1959. He immediately made Cuba's currency world famous by signing the country's banknotes with his nickname, "Che." Earlier in 1959 he was made industries minister and put in charge of plans to diversify the Cuban economy.

The trials and executions soon ended and Castro subsequently outlawed the death penalty (though he would reinstate it two years later when Cuba was attacked by counterrevolutionaries). Now the business of actually governing Cuba began. Castro, by choosing as president Manuel Urrutia — the liberal judge who two years earlier had acquitted several 26th of July men over Batista's objections — effectively froze out once and for all the other moderate politicians who had formed a government-in-exile in Miami. Urrutia named his own cabinet, which included only a couple of Castro's men.

Although Castro (who held the post of prime minister), Guevara, and the other revolutionaries were formally on the sidelines, in reality they retained power. Castro appeared on television almost every night to explain the workings of the revolution to the people, becoming identified in the popular mind with the revolutionary process itself. He, Guevara, and other articulate rebel leaders also made frequent speeches in an attempt to try to win over the population to the revolution and to explain its goals and policies.

Perhaps the most significant speech was given by Guevara, when, on January 27, 1959, he spoke about "The Social Ideals of the Rebel Army." He began by explaining that the rebels' experiences with the peasants in the Sierra Maestra provided them with the concept of agrarian reform, which he described as "the first great social issue" of the revolution, adding that the "main concern" of the new government "is the social justice that land redistribution brings about." Guevara also stressed Cuba's need to diversify its agricultural production in order to move away from a dependence on sugar as its predominant export crop, and the necessity of developing industry to reduce the country's dependence on imported manufactured goods.

Such industrialization, he argued next, would require a merchant fleet, electricity, and modern roads and communications systems. Because the private enterprises that ran these key industries were either inadequate or nonexistent, they would have to be nationalized; that is, taken over by the state.

In effect, Guevara was calling for Cuban socialism. In a capitalist economy, agriculture, industry, communications, and so forth, are usually controlled by private corporations that produce a profit to be shared by owners and investors. In a socialist economy, the state owns and controls key sectors of agriculture, industry, communications, and transportation. Such a change would, of course, anger those Cubans, as well as foreign corporations and investors in Cuba, whose property would be taken over by the Cuban state.

With a socialist economy, the profits from any farm or industry are available for public, state-controlled projects, and are thus, in principle, owned and controlled by the people themselves. Such policies, Guevara reasoned, would make the Cuban economy, for the first time, independent from U.S. and foreign control.

Two other points in Guevara's speech were of central importance to the future evolution of Cuban society. Guevara called for the institution of a new people's army. "All the Cuban people," he said, "must become a guerrilla army. . . . Each and every Cuban must learn to handle and, if necessary, use firearms in the defense of the nation." Guevara

On July 10, 1960, Guevara addressed 100,000 workers in front of the presidential palace at a rally called to denounce U.S. "economic aggression" against Cuba. On July 7, U.S. president Eisenhower had sharply reduced the import of sugar, Cuba's main crop, as tensions between the two countries mounted.

Guevara, by this time a Cuban citizen, made his first official visit to the Soviet Union in November 1960 as part of a series of trips to communist countries. As a result of the visit, the Soviet government agreed to provide Cuba with substantial aid and to replace the United States as Cuba's main trading partner.

feared invasion from the United States, which opposed governments, especially socialist ones, that threatened the economic interests of American corporations. Both he and Castro believed that the United States, unable to tolerate a socialist government only 90 miles from its shores, would sponsor a right-wing coup, as it did in Guatemala, or perhaps send in its own troops to do the job.

Guevara also outlined his vision of Cuba's revolution as the beginning of the revolutionary process throughout Latin America. The Cuban Revolution, he said, "is not limited to the Cuban nation, because it has touched the consciousness of Latin America. . . . [It] has placed the dictators of Latin America on death row, because they, like foreign monopolies, are the enemies of popular government."

This remarkable speech provided the guidelines for the first five years of revolutionary Cuba's economic and political development. Less than two weeks later, on February 9, Castro announced that the government had decided to make Che Guevara a Cuban citizen as an act of gratitude for his services in the Cuban Revolution and as a legal step to enable him to hold government office.

By now, Guevara had clearly identified himself as a socialist — something Castro had not yet done. Throughout the revolutionary war, Castro denied that he was a socialist or communist, and the accounts of eyewitnesses both sympathetic to and critical of Castro agree that he was neither. On January 16, 1959, two weeks after the rebel victory, he denied it once again, and on a tour of the United States in April 1959, he repeated that neither he nor the revolutionaries were communists. Furthermore, the leaders of the Cuban Communist party had always been hostile to Castro, whom they mistrusted as an adventurer.

Guevara, on the other hand, had exhibited Marxist leanings long before his speech of January 27, 1959. Though never a member of an orthodox communist party, he was already familiar with the writings of Karl Marx and Vladimir Ilyich Lenin by the time he reached the Sierra Maestra. It would not be Castro, but Guevara — Castro's closest adviser — who would lead Cuba to left-wing politics.

In the spring of 1959, Guevara, suffering from illness and exhaustion, was confined to his suburban house under doctor's orders. Nevertheless, he played host to a series of secret meeetings attended by Fidel and Raúl Castro and other key members of the rebel hierarchy. They agreed that the restructuring of Cuban agriculture should be the first priority. Guevara was among those put in charge of drafting laws affecting agriculture.

On May 17, 1959, the Agrarian Reform Law called for by Guevara went into effect, limiting the size of farms to 1,000 acres (although a few extremely productive holdings were allowed to retain as many as 3,333 acres). Any holdings over these limits were expropriated by the government and either redistributed to peasants in 67-acre parcels or held as state-run communes. The law also stipulated that sugar plantations could no longer be owned by foreigners. A new government agency, the National Institute of Agrarian Reform (INRA), was established to administer the law.

> *We discovered . . . that everybody favored agrarian reform, but nobody really had mastered what needed to be done in that field.*
> —CHE GUEVARA

The government promised to pay individual property owners for land taken over by the state — which included as many as 480,000 acres owned by U.S. corporations — although it is not clear how far the Cuban government actually went in honoring this promise.

The U.S. financial community's reaction to the law was harsh, as was that of several wealthy Cuban families. On May 21 and 22, Castro reassured them publicly that despite the socialist nature of the law, he still opposed communism, but there was further opposition from Cuban cattle ranchers, who contended that 3,333 acres was insufficient for cattle ranching. On June 30, Pedro Díaz Lanz, the new head of the air force, gave a press conference in which he implied that Cuba was possibly headed for dictatorship and communism. Castro criticized him severely for his remarks, prompting Díaz Lanz to resign and flee to the United States.

Two weeks later, President Urrutia gave a speech attacking the Cuban Communist party, hoping Castro would follow suit. But Castro did not, saying instead, "I consider it not entirely honorable that if we are to avoid being called communists, we must embark on campaigns against them and attack them. . . . This is not done by self-respecting men. We . . . proclaim everyone's right to write as he thinks . . . " On July 17, Castro resigned as prime minister, shocking the nation with his unexpected move. That night he gave a long televised speech in which he completely denounced Urrutia; crowds gathered outside the presidential palace calling for Urrutia's resignation, even while the speech was still going on. The next day, he resigned. Ten days later, Castro, now ready to embrace the communists, reassumed the prime ministership; the Cuban people responded with wild enthusiasm.

INRA soon became the most important governing body in the country. Castro was named president of this body; Guevara was named minister of industries, which, in effect, put him in charge of the industrialization of Cuba. Castro and Guevara used INRA to give them and their closest associates virtual control of economic and political life in Cuba.

INRA created its own 100,000-person militia, used first to help the government seize control of the expropriated land, supervise its distribution, and set up cooperative farms; soon after, this militia was trained as a regular army. INRA also financed most of the highway construction in the country, built rural housing and even tourist resorts, and was the instrument for Guevara's industrialization plans.

Cuba was now proceeding rapidly down the path of socialist development, replacing a market economy controlled by private corporations with state-owned and state-managed industries. "There is a great difference between free-enterprise development and revolutionary development," Guevara explained. "In one of them, wealth is concentrated in the hands of a fortunate few, the friends of the government, the best wheeler-dealers. In the other, wealth is the people's patrimony." The government programs were popular with many Cubans because they meant lower rents, lower electric and telephone rates, and a sense of pride in the Cuban people's taking control of their economic and political life, free from foreign domination.

In November 1959, Guevara was named president of the national bank, which gave him even more executive power over the economy. Guevara immediately made Cuba's currency world famous by sign-

Third-graders stand to pledge their commitment to the revolution. In 1961 Guevara helped launch a massive program to reform Cuba's education system, sending hundreds of "literacy brigades" into rural areas and reorganizing the schools so that all children could attend for free.

ing the country's banknotes "Che." One of his first accomplishments was to negotiate a sugar quota treaty with the Soviet Union in February 1960, whereby the Soviets agreed to purchase one million tons of sugar annually from 1961 to 1965 at a fixed price. He arranged also for Eastern European countries to buy a fixed quota of Cuban sugar, and in July 1960 negotiated a similar five-year agreement with the People's Republic of China. These trade agreements and others he negotiated with the same socialist countries a few months later helped offset a stated U.S. threat to curtail sharply its purchases of Cuban sugar.

At home, Guevara worked around the clock planning the organization of the Cuban economy, often staying up almost until dawn studying economics and finance. He helped establish the Central Planning Board, which would control economic policy, and served as one of its five members. In addition, he helped implement an elaborate nationalization plan whereby the state would take over basic industries from foreign corporations.

As biographer Daniel James concludes, "Che was now at the zenith of his power. As Minister of Industries he was virtual czar of the Cuban economy, with all the political weight that that signified. . . . He had meanwhile blossomed forth as a theoretician, a champion of the Latin American revolution and of the Asian and African underdeveloped countries, a powerful ally of the 'socialist camp,' and an intransigent fighter against 'Yankee imperialism.' He had emerged, in short, as a revolutionary statesman of world stature."

As 1960 drew to a close, Guevara used his authority to carry through both the agricultural diversification and the industrialization that he had called for in his January 1959 speech. Meanwhile, two other projects of Castro and Guevara's, the revolutionary government's wide-reaching health and literacy campaigns, got under way. In 1961, dubbed the "Year of Education," the Cuban government sent hundreds of students and teachers out into the countryside in "literacy brigades" to teach the predominately illiterate peasants to read and write.

This campaign was remarkably successful. Before 1959, the official literacy rate for Cuba had been somewhere between 60 and 76 percent, and there was a serious shortage of both schools and teachers. By the completion of the campaign, 707,212 adults were taught to read and write, raising the literacy rate to 96.1 percent. Many new schools were built throughout the country; many new teachers were trained. Thus, by the early 1960s every Cuban citizen was guaranteed free education through the age of 14, and later, 16.

As the new programs moved forward, Castro appeared regularly on television to explain what the government was doing and why. Guevara also made speeches and television appearances frequently. On April 30, 1961, Guevara inaugurated the television series "The People's University" with a lecture on "Cuba's Economic Plan," explaining to viewers the government's reorganization of the country's economy.

Guevara opened the program by outlining the government's nationalization programs. He explained how the economy was based on central planning that required state control over the means of production — as he put it, a "socialist conception of the economy." He told viewers that the new economy would bring an end to private monopolies, which in Cuba "have very close ties to the U.S.A. In other words," he continued, "our economic war will be with the great power of the North."

The implementation of a centralized planned economy required a guiding body to assure "unity of direction and firmness of leadership"; this leadership was provided by the planning board chairman, Fidel Castro, and the vice-chairman, Raúl Castro. Thus, the "highest political authorities in this country directly manage the plan, guide it, and give it the unity of command necessary for its fulfillment. . . . The people must understand what we want, discuss our aims in each instance, present their counterviews. Once they understand and approve it, the plan can go forward. That is, the natural course is from the top down, but from there it returns to the top."

After detailing the difficulty of the task of reorganizing the economy, Guevara said, "What is fundamental is that this work would be impossible without two things: One is the country's own determination to do it, the other is the help of the socialist countries."

Guevara continually stressed the importance of changing individual consciousness and values to produce better workers and citizens; revolution was to produce a "New Man" who would overcome the egotism, greed, and selfishness characteristic of individuals in capitalist societies. As biographer John Gerassi writes, "From the outset Che's main concern was establishing [the] Socialist Man in Cuba. . . . Che felt that a socialist economy in itself is not worth the effort, sacrifice, and risks of war and destruction if it ends up encouraging greed and individual ambition at the expense of the collective spirit."

In this spirit, Guevara encouraged Cubans to work hard, to deeply involve themselves in the revolution, and to develop a new set of values that would place the importance of Cuban society as a whole above their own individual interests. To increase productivity, he introduced a structure of "moral incentives" that would reward individuals who excelled in work and social consciousness.

However, his critics contend that Guevara's economic system, though highly idealistic on the surface, was in reality a system designed to maintain strict control over workers. Each worker was required to meet a quota under which he or she had to produce a set number of goods. The "moral incentives" were used as a replacement for the pay increases abolished by Guevara; now if workers met or exceeded their quota, they were not allowed to receive more money for their extra labor, merely a certificate of commendation. Workers who failed to meet their quotas were given pay cuts. Furthermore, the government abolished independent trade unions, reserved the right to impose fines for lateness, and could even order the immediate and permanent transfer of a worker from one job to another without the worker's approval.

Cuban soldiers survey the U.S. military base at Guantánamo Bay on Cuba's southeastern coast. In early 1961, the United States, already preparing to overthrow Castro, cut off diplomatic relations with Cuba. Today, Guantánamo Bay is still a U.S. possession, despite the objections of the Cuban government.

Critics also contend that Guevara's program for central economic planning led to a situation wherein individual workers were turned into nothing more than instruments of the state. Guevara himself said that under Cuban socialism, the worker had "the duty and the right to make sure that all orders of the government, all the main lines of development established by the government, are accomplished." Elsewhere, he said that it was necessary to "categorically impose the principle of authority" upon workers. The French journalist Léo Sauvage, in his book *Che Guevara: The Failure of a Revolutionary*, writes that such statements marked Guevara as a "partisan of an all-powerful State, of a party obeyed to the letter."

Whatever the merits or demerits of Guevara's economic principles, his programs soon ended in failure. But his supporters and critics alike do agree that one important factor helped ensure that failure —the outright hostility of the United States.

5

The Bay of Pigs and Cuban Missile Crisis

The United States and Cuba were rapidly headed toward a confrontation. Relations between the two countries had started to degenerate from the first days of the Cuban Revolution in January 1959. Already, by March 10, 1959 — months before Castro had consolidated power, made known his intentions, or seized any American property — the National Security Council in Washington was discussing "bringing another government to power" and getting rid of Castro, Guevara, and the rest of the revolutionaries.

The presence of communists in the Cuban government alarmed the United States. Particularly irksome to the U.S. government was the high profile of Guevara as Castro's most trusted minister. Guevara, already an outspoken Marxist, was Cuba's leading diplomat, making continued visits and overtures to communist countries. He was also the chief architect of the new socialist Cuban economy, and, since the spring of 1960, the head instructor of Cuba's armed forces. Such combined evidence convinced the United States that Cuba was moving toward communism.

There's a good United States and a bad United States and . . . Latin America's fate depends on which of the two is in control.
—CHE GUEVARA

In 1960 Guevara traveled to Czechoslovakia, China, and North Korea, securing trade agreements from each. His overtures to communist countries greatly alarmed the U.S. government, which feared a "communist beachhead" in the Western hemisphere.

When John F. Kennedy (left) succeeded Eisenhower (right) as president in 1961, he inherited Eisenhower's plan to sponsor an invasion of Cuba and establish a pro-U.S. government there. Castro anticipated the invasion and began mobilizing thousands of troops in advance.

CIA director Allen Dulles — brother of John Foster Dulles, Eisenhower's secretary of state — helped direct the U.S.-sponsored coup in Guatemala in 1954. In 1960 and 1961, he oversaw the training of the Cuban exile force that was to attempt to overthrow Castro's regime.

Furthermore, the U.S. government was uncomfortable about the loss of its direct control over Cuban affairs. "Until Castro," former American ambassador to Cuba Earl Smith told the U.S. Senate in 1960, "the U.S. was so overwhelmingly influential in Cuba that the American ambassador was the second most important man . . . sometimes even more important than the [Cuban] president."

In response to the establishment of Cuba's Agrarian Reform Law in 1959, the United States first insisted that Cuba reimburse American owners for the value of the land confiscated, and then it cut back on the amount of sugar purchased from Cuba. In May and June of 1960, American-owned oil refineries in Cuba refused to refine Soviet oil purchased by Cuba. Castro retaliated by taking over the oil refineries. The United States retaliated in turn by completely cutting off all sugar purchases from Cuba. Throughout this period, airplanes departing from Florida and piloted by Cuban exiles made sporadic runs over the island to drop anti-government leaflets — and, on occasion, bombs — while U.S. authorities looked the other way.

Tensions between the United States and Cuba escalated in October 1960, when Castro nationalized 300 to 400 enterprises, many of which were American-owned. The U.S. government responded by putting into effect an economic embargo, making it impossible for Cuba to buy American products and spare parts. There were reports — confirmed more than a decade later during hearings before the U.S. Senate — that the CIA began making plans to assassinate Castro. It was also at this point that the CIA, acting under the orders of President Eisenhower, began training an exile army for the invasion of Cuba.

There were many Cuban exiles living in the United States, mainly in New York City and Miami, who lobbied for an invasion of Cuba. Some were right-wing supporters of the old Batista regime, others were moderates and liberals who had supported

Cuba, the largest country in the Caribbean, lies just 90 miles south of Key West, Florida. Cuba's proximity to the United States made the U.S. government anxious to oust Castro, particularly after he and Guevara had established close ties to communist nations.

Soldiers in the Cuban army march to meet the invading forces in southern Cuba. Some 1,500 Cuban exiles — trained, financed, armed, and directed by the CIA and traveling in U.S. merchant vessels — landed at the Bay of Pigs on April 17, 1961.

Castro during the revolution but had become disenchanted with the increasingly dominant control he and his advisers exercised over the Cuban government. Eisenhower's plan was to train a force of Cuban exiles for an invasion that was intended to be a repeat of the CIA's successful Guatemala coup of 1954. When John F. Kennedy became president in January 1961, he inherited the invasion plan, approved it, and moved to carry it out.

One of Eisenhower's last acts as president was to break off diplomatic relations with Cuba, clearing the way for Kennedy to initiate military action. On April 14, 1961, the exile force of about 1,500 men set sail from Puerto Cabezas, Nicaragua, aboard 6 ships. The plan was to invade Cuba at the Bay of Pigs, a large swamp on the south-central coast of the island. After the exile force had established a beachhead, the CIA was to fly in a new government with the recognition, aid, and support of the United States.

But Castro's agents had infiltrated the Cuban exile community and knew that an invasion was coming. To defend Cuba, the country was divided into three regional commands; Raúl Castro was in charge of forces in the eastern portion of the country; Guevara was in charge in the west; and Juan Almeida, another guerrilla leader from the Sierra Maestra days, was in charge of the center. Fidel Castro served as commander in chief.

One day before the invasion, a warship carrying U.S. Marines faked an invasion off the west coast of Pinar del Rio, drawing the forces commanded by Guevara to that region. Meanwhile, eight CIA-owned B-26 bombers attacked Cuban airfields; however, the World War II–era planes inflicted little damage. Late on the night of April 17, 1961, the landings themselves began, though they were badly mismanaged by the American CIA men leading the invasion.

Cuban militia ward off the invasion forces at the Bay of Pigs. The Cuban forces crushed the invasion within 72 hours, killing 129 of the exiles and taking the rest prisoner. Historians give Guevara, who was director of instruction for Cuba's armed forces, a share of credit for the victory.

Cuban soldiers celebrate their victory at the Bay of Pigs on April 19, 1961. The botched invasion was a public humiliation for the United States. A few days later, Castro declared for the first time that Cuba was a socialist state.

The exile force — disorganized, often firing on their own men, and coming under frequent aerial attack — was pinned down on the beach in the face of heavy resistance. Any hopes the invaders held that a wave of opposition inside Cuba would join them evaporated when Castro quickly and effectively ordered the arrest of 100,000 suspected counterrevolutionaries throughout the country. After three days of fighting, the defeated exile force surrendered, their casualties including 129 dead and almost 1,200 taken prisoner.

Guevara himself did not play a key role in the fighting, but Tad Szulc, in his explanation of the Cuban victory, assigns him partial credit: "The revolutionaries won because Castro's strategy was vastly superior to the CIA's, because the revolutionary morale was high, and because Che Guevara, as the head of the Instruction Department of the Revolutionary Armed Forces, in charge of the militia training program . . . had done so well in preparing 200,000 men and women for war."

Two weeks after the victory at the Bay of Pigs, Castro for the first time explicitly defined his revolution as socialist, stating in a speech that "the struggle in this country is for socialism." From then on, he openly defined himself as a socialist.

Just as important, the Bay of Pigs invasion confirmed in Guevara's mind the belief that U.S. foreign policy in Latin America was geared solely toward protecting the interests of American business without regard for the sovereignty of other countries. Guevara had personally witnessed the CIA coup in Guatemala, the U.S. government's support for the brutal Batista regime, the U.S. economic blockade of Cuba, and now the CIA-led attempt to fight a war intended to overthrow the Cuban government. He became utterly convinced that the United States was the enemy of freedom in Latin America.

In 1962, Castro, aware of continued U.S. efforts aimed at the overthrow of the Cuban government, sought military help from the Soviet Union. In the spring of that year, Guevara and Raúl Castro made trips to the Soviet Union to discuss possible military support. Details of negotiations between the Cubans and the Soviets are still sketchy, but it appears that Nikita Khrushchev, the Soviet premier, agreed to give the Cubans MiG jets and other advanced military equipment, which the Cubans eagerly accepted.

Guevara with Soviet premier Nikita Khrushchev in Moscow. In 1962, Guevara and Castro's brother, Raúl, made several trips to the Soviet Union for military aid, obtaining fighter aircraft and other advanced weapons. The Soviets also negotiated to deploy nuclear missiles in Cuba.

A U.S. Defense Department photo shows a medium-range ballistic missile site under construction in San Cristóbal, Cuba. The discovery of Soviet missiles in Cuba set off the Cuban missile crisis. For six days in October 1962 the world lived in fear of a nuclear war between the two superpowers.

The Soviets also decided to station nuclear missiles in Cuba. At the time, the Soviet Union lagged behind the United States in nuclear weapons and was faced with the presence of American missiles stationed in Turkey on the Soviet border. Seeking to counterbalance the presence of those missiles, the Soviets decided to install their own missiles in Cuba, 90 miles from the United States. The Cubans, who may actually have initiated the idea, believed that the presence of nuclear weapons on their soil would prevent the United States from trying another invasion.

In October 1962, American spy planes detected the presence of the Soviet missiles in Cuba. Kennedy made the news public and demanded that the missiles be withdrawn. The ensuing showdown, which came to be known as the Cuban missile crisis, led the world to the brink of nuclear war. For several tense days, Kennedy and Khrushchev negotiated to no avail, as both countries stood on alert for full-scale war. On October 22, as a large force of U.S. marines prepared to invade Cuba from Florida, Kennedy appeared before the television cameras to deliver a critical speech. He announced the establishment of a naval blockade against Cuba to prevent the arrival of more Soviet missiles and demanded that all missiles be removed from Cuban soil. If the Soviets refused to comply, he added, the United States would not hesitate to fight a nuclear war.

It was now clear that Khrushchev had only two alternatives: fight a nuclear war or back down. On October 28, he chose the latter, agreeing to remove the Soviet missiles from Cuba in exchange for an American removal of missiles from Turkey and a U.S. promise not to invade Cuba. The crisis was resolved but Castro was furious that Khrushchev had not consulted him about withdrawing the missiles. Cuban-Soviet relations cooled off immediately as a result.

Guevara's attitude to the Soviet Union changed as well. Convinced now that the superpowers treated developing countries, such as Cuba, as pawns, Guevara would soon devote most of his diplomatic efforts to uniting the countries of the Third World.

After the resolution of the missile crisis, Castro and Guevara had to deal with the deterioration of the Cuban economy. The economic plans developed by Guevara and his associates had produced many problems, aggravated by the U.S. blockade and the hostility of the capitalist world's financial community — as well as by workers' dissatisfaction with the spartan conditions Guevara's system imposed.

U.S. Marines off the coast of Florida train for a possible invasion of Cuba during the missile crisis. The crisis convinced Guevara that the two superpowers used Cuba as a pawn in their own global strategies; afterward, he denounced the Soviets almost as frequently as he denounced the Americans.

Under Guevara, the economy not only fell well short of projected goals, it was severely damaged. Ill-conceived attempts at agricultural diversification led to food shortages, which in turn led to the imposition of rationing. The income Cuba derived from the export of crops, already small, dwindled still further. The absence of spare parts and adequate technical training foiled industrialization efforts. The program of "moral incentives" for workers was causing a rapid drop in productivity and a rapid rise in absenteeism. The only demonstrable successes of Guevara's tenure at INRA were the great advances made in literacy and health care.

Guevara later admitted some of the mistakes he made as minister of industries, such as the failure of his program aimed at growing new cash crops to reduce Cuba's dependence on sugar. "Our first error," he wrote, "was the way in which we carried out diversification. Instead of embarking on diversification by degrees, we attempted too much at once . . . this meant a general decline in agricultural production. The entire economic history of Cuba had demonstrated that no other agricultural activity would give such returns as those yielded by the cultivation of sugar cane."

Despite his candor, Guevara stubbornly insisted to the end that "to build communism simultaneously with its new base, we must make the new man." He believed that Cuban society must produce new men and women — with better technical training, fervent commitment to building their society, and knowledge and ability to raise productivity — before Cuba could have a sufficiently strong economy and society.

The U.S. warship _Vesole_ draws alongside the Soviet freighter _Polzunov_ off the Cuban coast for a cargo inspection in November 1962. Khrushchev and the Soviets backed down in the face of American pressure and withdrew their missiles from Cuba.

Guevara's vision of socialism was different from that put forward in the Soviet Union and China. He placed emphasis not so much on the efficient management of the economy as on the spiritual awakening of morality among individual citizens. "The happiness of the people is the basis of our struggle," he once wrote, elsewhere saying, "This is not a matter of how many pounds of meat one might be able to eat, or how many times a year someone can go to the beach, or how many ornaments from abroad one might be able to buy with his current salary. What really matters is that the individual feels more complete, with much more internal richness and much more responsibility."

But however idealistic Guevara's socialist experiments were in theory, they resulted in increased hardship for the individual worker, a reduction in civil liberties, severe economic dislocations for a wide segment of Cuban society, and ultimately, in failure for the economy as a whole. By the end of 1963, Guevara was no longer president of the national bank and his role in the management of the Cuban economy had been greatly reduced. His duties were now more or less limited to diplomacy and international relations.

Cubans line up to buy bread in front of a Havana bakery. Guevara's spartan economic programs soon failed, leading to widespread food shortages and the rationing of many staples. By the end of 1963, he had been removed from all the key economic posts he once held.

6

Revolutionary Ambassador

From the start, the handsome and charismatic Guevara had been one of the Cuban Revolution's most effective ambassadors. In the summer of 1959, he undertook the new government's first diplomatic tour, visiting Egypt, India, Pakistan, Japan, and Indonesia to win good will and seek political and economic support for revolutionary Cuba. Guevara's reputation in official diplomatic circles grew in his five years as manager of the Cuban economy, during which time he traveled to three continents to negotiate trade agreements. His role as Cuban representative to the Inter-American Economic and Social Conference held in Punta del Este, Uruguay, in August 1961, was a testament to his growing importance in international diplomacy.

The Kennedy administration, just before it launched the disastrous Bay of Pigs invasion, sought to win support in Latin America by starting a massive aid program called the Alliance for Progress. After the failure of the invasion and the resulting loss of U.S. prestige and credibility, it became imperative for Kennedy to win support for his Alliance for Progress at the Punta del Este conference, where delegations from every Latin American country would be in attendance.

> *Along the way, Che made friends and enemies, the latter because of his usual blunt manner. No matter where [he] went, and no matter to whom [he] spoke, Che rarely contained his innermost thoughts.*
> —MARVIN D. RESNICK
> Guevara biographer

Guevara sips maté, a traditional herb tea, with Uruguayan president Eduardo Victor Haedo at Punta del Este, Uruguay, in 1961. Guevara's diplomatic efforts in the early 1960s were instrumental in creating the concept of the "Third World," an international coalition of developing countries.

Guevara as head of the Cuban delegation at the Punta del Este conference in August 1961. The conference was called to discuss President Kennedy's Alliance for Progress — a massive effort at cooperative economic and social development aimed at forestalling revolution in Latin America.

However, the big news at Punta del Este turned out to be the speech delivered by Che Guevara. Guevara criticized Kennedy's political motivations in offering the aid program, asserting that the United States was interested in upholding the status quo in Latin America, not in bringing about real reforms. "U.S. experts never talk about agrarian reform," Guevara told the conference at one point; "they prefer a safe subject, like a better water supply. In short, they seem to prepare the Revolution of the Toilets."

Guevara reminded the conference of the U.S. role in the Bay of Pigs invasion and demanded from the United States "a guarantee of non-aggression against our frontiers." He complained of U.S. efforts to isolate Cuba from other Latin American countries and asserted that the example of the Cuban Revolution would naturally spread throughout Latin America because it "is something spiritual that transcends all borders." At the same time, though, he pledged that Cuba would not export revolution by sending weapons to other countries — thus signaling that Cuba was willing to talk to the U.S. government about normalizing relations.

There are reports that President Kennedy's representative to the conference, Richard Goodwin, was ordered to avoid speaking with Guevara. Nevertheless, delegates from Argentina and Brazil arranged a meeting in which Goodwin and Guevara spent several hours discussing ways in which U.S.-Cuban relations could be improved. In addition, Guevara secretly flew from Punta del Este to nearby Buenos Aires, where he was met by the liberal president of Argentina, Arturo Frondizi. Shortly thereafter, Guevara attended another secret meeting, this time with the liberal president Janio Quadros of Brazil.

But ultimately, Guevara was too hot a subject for any of these governments to handle. When the U.S. Senate heard about the meeting between Guevara and Goodwin, most senators disavowed it as meaningless. Both Frondizi and Quadros were overthrown by right-wing military coups shortly after their meetings with Guevara, in part because they had had dealings with the avowed revolutionary. By January 1962, Cuba had been expelled from the Inter-American Conference for its adherence to communism. Thus nothing fruitful came of the negotiations, which otherwise might have led to friendlier relations between Cuba and the other governments of Latin America — and even the U.S. government.

The missile crisis followed. After the Soviets removed their missiles from Cuba without consulting the Cubans, Guevara became an outspoken critic of the Soviet Union. His stated ideology of promoting and supporting revolution anywhere in the world, whenever it might arise, was already at odds with official Soviet ideology (termed "peaceful coexistence"), which said, in effect, that most new revolutions would have to wait, perhaps for many generations.

Guevara had not always been a critic of the Soviets. Early in 1960 he had signed a trade agreement with the Soviet Union that made it Cuba's primary trading partner, hailing the pact as an act of "economic liberation." Now he was a critic — and to make matters worse, after the missile crisis the Cubans and the Soviets were not talking to each other.

In May 1963 and again in January 1964, Castro went to Moscow and patched up his differences with the Soviets, convincing them to sign new agreements to sponsor the flagging Cuban economy.

Guevara (far right) was the sole dissenter among the 21 U.S. and Latin American delegates who voted to approve Kennedy's Alliance for Progress. Guevara condemned the Alliance as "a vehicle . . . to sterilize the Cuban revolution" and subordinate Latin American countries to U.S. interests.

In December 1964 Guevara made a powerful speech before the United Nations General Assembly in New York, condemning the foreign policy of both the United States and the Soviet Union. He expressed Cuba's support for revolutionary struggles around the world and called for a global conference on nuclear disarmament.

After he returned, Castro made speeches in which he announced he would stop aiding revolutionaries in other countries if other countries would stop intervening in Cuban affairs — a pledge that the Soviets wanted to hear. Though Castro secretly continued to aid revolutionary movements in other countries, his public statements appeased the Soviets, upon whom Cuba was heavily dependent for economic assistance.

The country's economy suffered another setback when, in July 1964, Cuba was condemned by the United States and 14 Latin American countries for aiding revolutionaries in Venezuela. Practically every country in the hemisphere refused now to conduct trade with Cuba, leaving it almost totally dependent on the Soviet Union. Cuba's support for Latin American revolutionary movements — Guevara's most cherished belief—had cost it dearly.

By now, Cuba's economy was suffering greatly, prompting Castro to diminish Guevara's power as minister of industries. Despite the demotion, Castro chose Guevara to visit Moscow in November 1964. The trip was uneventful, and after he returned a few days later, a Cuban Communist party member was sent to Moscow to conduct the actual trade negotiations.

Guevara was next sent to represent Cuba at the United Nations General Assembly in New York. In his speech to the General Assembly on December 11, 1964, Guevara implied that the Soviet Union had reneged on its Marxist principles, ignoring Third World countries and revolutionary movements while paying attention only to its relations with the United States and the capitalist world. "If we are to ensure world peace," he said, "peaceful coexistence must not only be for the powerful. . . . As Marxists, we have maintained that peaceful coexistence among nations does not encompass coexistence between the exploiters and the exploited, the oppressor and the oppressed." He also called on the superpowers to dismantle their nuclear weapons and spoke of "the obligation of all states to respect the present frontiers of other states and to refrain from indulging in any aggression, even with conventional weapons," while presumably leaving open the right for armed struggle against oppression within any given country.

While Guevara obliquely attacked the policies of the Soviet Union, he overtly attacked the policies of the United States. As early as 1960, Guevara had told another high official in the Cuban government, "The Castro regime and Yankee imperialism are engaged in a death struggle and we both know that one of the two must die." Now, a few days after his United Nations speech, he appeared on the CBS News television program "Face the Nation," where he stated that Cuba's "freedom fighters" were battling oppression and imperialism in every country in Latin America and predicted that revolution would break out throughout the Third World.

Guevara had already become a hero to Third World revolutionaries, both for his outspoken public support of their efforts and for his actual accomplishments as a guerrilla in the Cuban revolutionary war. His manual, *Guerrilla Warfare*, which described the strategy and tactics that made the guerrilla war in Cuba a success, became the guidebook for thousands of insurgents in various countries around the world. In it, Guevara insisted that the only route to victory lay in first establishing a guerrilla army in the mountains and jungles, and then spreading out into the cities. Guevara advised visiting delegations of revolutionaries on these points, and it would not be too long before he himself would retest his theories.

His United Nations speech had made it clear that Guevara's hopes and sympathies in the battle against the United States lay not with the Soviet Union and orthodox communism but with the Third World and activist communism. Castro, on the other hand, had cast his lot with the Soviet Union and, at least publicly, moved closer to orthodox communism. There was another sticking point between Castro and Guevara: the bitter dispute between the Soviet Union and the People's Republic of China, which began to develop in 1960 and finally resulted in a complete break in 1963. Guevara supported China, which at the time had no relations

Guevara smokes a cigar as he listens to U.S. ambassador Adlai Stevenson speak before the UN Security Council in 1964. Guevara summed up his view of activist communism when he said, "the revolution will triumph in Latin America and the world, but this does not mean that revolutionaries should sit on their doorsteps."

Guevara greeting a Chinese delegation in Cuba in 1961, one year after he met with Mao Zedong, the Chinese leader, and established firm relations between the two countries. After the missile crisis, Guevara publicly scolded the Soviet Union and aligned himself with China, which led to a rift between him and Castro.

with the United States and exercised a policy of sending aid and advisers to several newly independent Third World countries, particularly in Africa. Castro had not yet publicly chosen sides in the Chinese-Soviet dispute, but when he did, in 1966, he came out squarely for the Soviets, vehemently attacking China in a number of speeches.

Meanwhile, Castro sought to expand contacts with other Third World countries. Late in 1964, he sent Guevara on a tour through Africa lasting several months. The purpose of the tour was to confer with the leaders of eight countries about the creation of a worldwide organization of developing nations. Guevara's first stop was Algeria, which had recently won its independence from France after long and bloody fighting. In Algeria, Guevara told a journalist, "Africa represents one of the most important, if not the most important, battlefields against all the forms of exploitation existing in the world, against imperialism, colonialism, and neo-colonialism."

Guevara went to Mali next, where he made several statements concerning efforts at armed revolution in Latin America. From Mali, Guevara traveled to Brazzaville, capital of the Congo Republic, then on to Guinea, Ghana, Dahomey, Tanzania, and finally Egypt, where he met with President Gamal Abdel Nasser on February 18, 1965. "After touring seven African countries," Guevara told Nasser, "I am convinced that it is possible to create a common front of struggle against imperialism, colonialism, and neo-colonialism."

Guevara briefly interrupted his African tour to make an unscheduled trip to China, which had just signed a trade pact with Cuba. The relationship between Guevara and the Chinese had been warm ever since his first trip to China late in 1960, which resulted in the first trade agreement between the two countries. On that occasion, Guevara had first indicated his admiration for the Chinese government, telling Vice-premier Zhou Enlai, "The great experience of the Chinese people in their 22 years of struggle in the backward countryside . . . revealed a new road for the Americas." After this, the Chinese looked on Guevara as their strongest ally in the Cuban government, and in 1965, Guevara was again received warmly.

On departing China, Guevara was ready to condemn its rival, the Soviet Union. In a speech he gave at the Afro-Asian conference in Algeria on February 26, 1965, Guevara sharply criticized what he saw as the failure of the Soviet Union to adequately support revolutionary movements. With an interna-

Guevara meets with Egyptian president Gamal Abdel Nasser during his tour of Africa in 1965. During the tour, Guevara spoke of the need for a worldwide organization of developing nations that would enable them to remain independent of the two superpowers.

Joseph Kasavubu, first president of the Democratic Republic of the Congo (now Zaire). Shortly after independence in 1960, civil war broke out among several different factions, with Kasavubu supported by the United States, and Prime Minister Patrice Lumumba by Cuba and the Soviet Union.

tional perspective on revolution, he said, "The socialist countries have a vital stake in making these acts of breaking away from the imperialist system successful." He continued by saying, "The socialist countries have the moral duty of liquidating their tacit complicity with the exploiting countries of the West." In effect, Guevara called upon the Soviet Union to break off relations with capitalist countries and to support worldwide revolution in underdeveloped countries. While the delegates at the Afro-Asian conference may have applauded such sentiments, the Soviet Union was not amused by Guevara's ultrarevolutionary demands.

One month later, during a trip to Egypt, Guevara openly criticized the economic policies of the Soviet Union and its allies in an official Egyptian publication. There were also reports that, throughout his trip, Guevara was privately criticizing the Soviet Union sharply for not giving enough aid to the developing countries and for not doing enough to support revolution in underdeveloped countries. On March 14, 1965, when Guevara returned to Cuba, Castro and other Cuban leaders were on hand to meet him, but their reception was cool. Castro was reportedly furious that Guevara had so explicitly criticized the Soviets when Cuba was so dependent upon the Soviet Union for military and economic aid. Shortly thereafter, Guevara gave a speech to youth leaders at the Ministry of Industries; he then disappeared from public sight for 18 months.

Guevara's disappearance was a mystery in Cuba and around the world. He had written his mother that he would spend a month as a fieldworker cutting sugarcane, then spend the next five years directing a nationalized industry, but neither of these turned out to be true. Where was Che? Speculation varied; he was reported dead, imprisoned by Castro, the victim of a nervous breakdown or fatal illness. Other reports claimed that he was alive and fighting a new revolution, and rumors surfaced throughout Latin America, Africa, and even Vietnam that he had been spotted in the jungles, carrying his rifle.

In fact, Guevara and Castro were attempting to define a new role for Guevara within the Cuban Revolution and in relation to the sort of world revolution that both supported. Guevara's economic programs had obviously failed; moreover, he had alienated many Cuban leaders over the years through his arrogance and his highly moralistic attitudes and policies. He was not a native Cuban and many of his enemies used this fact against him. Furthermore, Guevara's critical remarks about the Soviet Union on his recent trip had outraged many Cubans who either wanted their country to have a close relationship with the Soviets or, at the least, wanted to get as much aid from them as possible.

Consequently, it became impossible for Guevara to continue in his role in the Cuban Revolution either as economic manager or international diplomat — a fact of which both Castro and he must have been aware. In addition, it appears that throughout 1965 Guevara was becoming increasingly obsessed with world revolution and was probably yearning for more active participation in actual revolutionary struggles. Perhaps he was becoming bored as a government functionary and yearned for

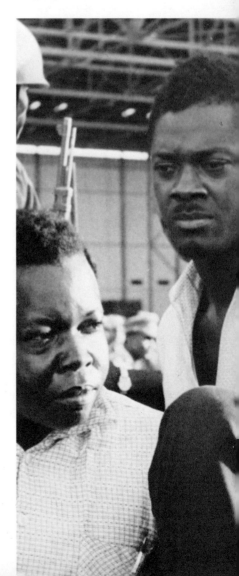

Patrice Lumumba (right) and an ally, Joseph Okito, being held by the forces of U.S.-backed army colonel Joseph Mobutu in December 1960; Lumumba was executed soon thereafter. Lumumba's leftist rebels continued to fight as a faction in the war, and in 1965 they were joined by Guevara and a Cuban brigade.

the heroic days of guerrilla warfare; perhaps he wanted to prove personally the validity of his theories of guerrilla war, which had been attacked by more orthodox communists and others and which had so far failed almost everywhere they had been implemented.

In any case, Guevara set out for Africa to join leftist forces in a civil war in the Democratic Republic of the Congo. Apparently he thought that the guerrilla movements there provided the best means for putting his theories into practice, and he evidently hoped that success in the Congo would help ignite revolution throughout Africa. The socialist government of Algeria — Cuba's closest ally in Africa — had just been overthrown, and, from this perspective, Guevara's return to Africa can be seen as an attempt to keep revolution alive on that continent.

Guevara, knowing that he was risking his life, wrote farewell letters to Castro, his parents, and his children. He asked Castro to make the letters public at an appropriate time. It was later revealed that in his letter to Castro, Guevara recalled their meeting and struggles together in the Cuban Revolution, then officially resigned all of his government posts and, with regrets, his Cuban citizenship.

"Other lands claim the help of my modest efforts," he wrote. "I can do what you can't, because of your responsibilities at the helm of Cuba, and the time has come for us to separate. Let it be known that I do so with a mixture of happiness and pain. Here I am leaving my purest hopes as a builder and the dearest of those who are dear to me . . . and I am leaving a people that accepted me as a son. This tears part of my spirit. To the new battlefields I shall carry the faith you taught me, the feeling that I am fulfilling the most sacred duty: fighting against imperialism, wherever it is. This is a source of comfort and more than heals any wound."

There is no official account of Guevara's Congo campaign, but it appears that with Castro's support, he traveled in July 1965 to Brazzaville, the capital of the Republic of the Congo. Accompanied by an elite corps of about 125 Cuban guerrillas, he crossed over into the adjoining Democratic Republic of the Congo (referred to here as the DRC; in 1971 its name was changed to Zaire), which had been wracked by civil war for five years.

The DRC had been granted independence by Belgium in 1960, and fighting between different factions erupted soon thereafter. The leftist prime minister Patrice Lumumba was killed by a Belgian mercenary in the employ of Colonel Joseph Mobutu, who was allied with the rightist Moise Tshombe. Tshombe and Mobutu — who held the mineral-rich Katanga province, where several European companies had productive mining operations — were both receiving aid from the CIA. By late 1964, Tshombe had emerged as the leader of the country, but now he was opposed by leftist rebels who were influenced in part by the memory of Lumumba. Guevara and the Cubans went to the DRC to join these rebels, while the United States openly supported Tshombe with direct military aid.

Guevara and the rebel forces he joined made no progress in their effort to overthrow Tshombe's regime. After some months of battle, Guevara concluded that the struggle was hopeless. Guevara later blamed the failure on the incompetence of the rebels, charging as well that they had committed a number of atrocities. "The human element failed," he told the Argentinian journalist Ciro Bustos in Bolivia two years later. "There is no will to fight, the leaders are corrupt; in a word, there was nothing to do."

There are also claims that Guevara was ordered home against his will by Castro due to pressure from the Chinese or the Soviets, both of whom had foreign policy objectives in the region that might have conflicted with Guevara's objectives. In any case, Guevara's Congo expedition remains shrouded in mystery to this day.

Around March 1966, Guevara returned to Havana. Once again, revolutionary guerrilla forces had failed. The stage was set for Guevara's last and most fateful adventure.

Guevara's overt criticism of the Soviet Union put him at odds with Castro, who was not willing to risk important trade agreements with the Soviets; by 1965, Guevara no longer appeared in public. He chose to abandon diplomacy and returned to the life of a guerrilla fighter.

7

The Bolivian Disaster

Guevara's already precarious position in the Cuban government was now hopeless. His economic policies had failed and his diplomacy had produced controversy. The principle with which he was most closely identified, actively aiding revolutionary movements, had yielded no success where he had personally intervened — neither in Venezuela first, nor in the Congo afterward. The policy of aiding revolutionaries had further isolated Cuba from the capitalist countries and threatened its relationship with the Soviet Union. Yet Castro was ready to finance still another attempt to ignite a revolution, this time in Bolivia.

Many observers have concluded that a major disagreement broke out between Guevara and Castro, and that Castro sent Guevara to Bolivia to get rid of him. Though Castro still firmly agreed with Guevara on the question of the Third World, Guevara's absence from what should have been his crowning achievement — the first Tricontinental Conference — added to speculation of a rift between Castro and him.

Bolivia seems to have been the country which both helped to inspire Che's political career and killed him.
—ANDREW SINCLAIR
Guevara biographer

Despite the failure of his Congo campaign, Guevara remained committed to the ideal of a global socialist revolution. "Create two, three, many Vietnams — that is the watchword," said Guevara, referring to his strategy of creating several small revolutions to break down the imperialist system.

Guevara in Bolivia at the start of his final guerrilla campaign. He arrived in November 1966 with 18 Cubans and set up headquarters in Nancahuazú, in the mountains. He hoped to repeat the formula of the Cuban Revolution, in which a small band of rebels gained the support of the peasantry and then overthrew the government.

Following up on the results of Guevara's Africa tour, in January 1966, Castro hosted the first Tricontinental Conference, in which representatives from the developing countries of Africa, Asia, and Latin America met for the first time. Castro and Cuba were instantly recognized as the leaders of the Tricontinental, which would eventually merge with other Third World groupings to become what is known today as the Nonaligned Movement.

Founded on the principle that the Third World should avoid too close a reliance on either the United States or the Soviet Union, the Tricontinental Conference was, in large part, the product of Guevara's ideology. Most speakers praised him, always to thunderous applause from the other delegates. For example, the Venezuelan delegate, a revolutionary opposed to that country's elected, pro-U.S. government, told the conference, "We are following the heroic example of Comandante Ernesto 'Che' Guevara." In the conference's closing address, Castro, too, praised the conspicuously absent Guevara, but used his speech to denounce rumors that he had had him eliminated. This served only to provoke even more conjecture on the whereabouts of Guevara, who at the time of the conference was still in Cuba, secretly planning his Bolivian insurgency.

In 1972, when confronted with the charge that he had sent Guevara to Bolivia to get rid of him, Castro told the American newspaperman Herbert Matthews: "No one knows how deeply I felt for him. I kept silent at his request for six months, and it was difficult. People were even saying that I killed him! In Mexico, when he joined the *Granma* expedition, it was agreed that once the revolution succeeded, he would go away and fight other revolutions. I don't know how I was able to keep him in Cuba as long as I did, but I had promised that when he wanted to leave he could go and I would not hold him back."

From this perspective, at least, Guevara's Bolivian campaign was a logical step in his vision of Latin American and world revolution. Furthermore, some speculate that it had become a psychological need for Guevara to participate in an actual struggle in

Latin America — whatever the odds against its succeeding. And there is much evidence that Guevara wanted to try to prove once again his theories of guerrilla war and to participate in his lifelong obsession: the liberation of Latin America.

Latin American revolution always had been one of Guevara's primary concerns, perhaps his single most important concern. His first wife, Hilda Gadea, reports that in Mexico Guevara had said that the upcoming struggle in Cuba was to be "just one stage in his Latin American struggle." Others told Matthews that from the beginning Guevara wanted to help create the Cuban Revolution and then move on to other tasks, and that in the autumn of 1964 he had told Castro of his desire to leave Cuba.

Throughout the 1960s, Guevara, the champion of Third World revolution, had supported almost every guerrilla movement that came to Cuba for support. An essay he wrote in 1965, "Vietnam and the World Struggle for Freedom," provides perhaps the best evidence of his mindset.

At the time he wrote the essay, American involvement in Vietnam was escalating and a worldwide antiwar movement was attacking U.S. intervention in Vietnam. Using the widespread opposition to the U.S. involvement in Vietnam as a starting point,

A group of Bolivian peasant women. During Guevara's guerrilla campaign in the Bolivian Andes, most of the peasants, who were Quechua-speaking Indians, did not support the rebel forces. The Indians tended to view the guerrillas as white foreign intruders intent on inciting warfare.

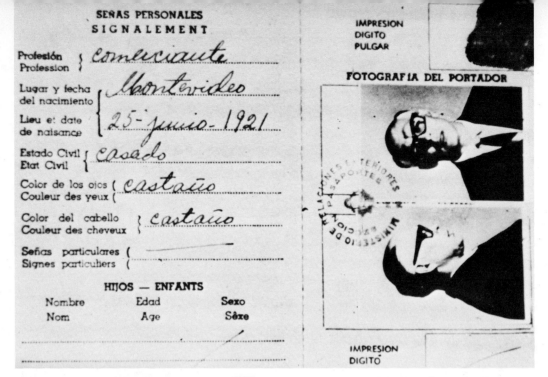

SEÑAS PERSONALES
SIGNALEMENT

Profesión } *comerciante*
Profession

Lugar y fecha } *Montevideo*
del nacimiento

Lieu et date } *25-junio-1921*
de naisance

Estado Civil } *casado*
Etat Civil

Color de los ojos } *castaño*
Couleur des yeux

Color del cabello } *castaño*
Couleur des cheveux

Señas particulares (
Signes particuliers (

HIJOS — ENFANTS

| Nombre | Edad | Sexo |
| Nom | Age | Sêxe |

IMPRESION
DIGITO
PULGAR

FOTOGRAFIA DEL PORTADOR

IMPRESION
DIGITO

This forged passport was used by Guevara to enter Bolivia disguised as an Uruguayan businessman. The passport photos show him bald and clean-shaven and sporting heavy-rimmed glasses.

Guevara discussed the prospects for revolution in Latin America, Africa, and Asia. "In Latin America," he wrote, "the struggle is going on, arms in hand, in Guatemala, Colombia, Venezuela, and Bolivia, and the first buds are already appearing in Brazil."

Guevara then pointed to the common heritage of oppression on the continent and the closeness in language and customs, all of which provided a basis for unity. He asked what sort of rebellion was appropriate to these conditions and answered: "The struggle in the Americas will in time acquire continental dimensions. It will be the scene of many great battles in behalf of humanity, in behalf of its liberation. Measured against the scope of this continent-wide struggle, the present struggles keeping it going in an active way are only episodes, but they have already provided their martyrs who will figure in the history of the Americas for having given their quota of blood in this final stage of struggle for the full freedom of mankind."

Guevara's apocalyptic vision of revolution spreading like wildfire throughout Latin America concluded with a vision of "two, three, many Vietnams" exploding all over the world, bringing about the final destruction of imperialism.

There is no doubt that world revolution in general and revolution in Latin America in particular were the major political goals for Guevara. Castro and he chose Bolivia because it is in the center of South America, surrounded by Argentina, Chile, Peru, Brazil, and Paraguay. Guevara often indicated that his deepest ambition was to carry out a revolution in his native Argentina, so he might have viewed Bolivia, on Argentina's northern border, as a stepping stone.

Yet even among radical leftists, Guevara and Castro have been roundly criticized for choosing Bolivia as a site from which to ignite a continental revolution. Guevara's strategy, it seems, was to initiate guerrilla struggles in Bolivia and, once they were under way, to organize struggles in neighboring lands. He, and perhaps Castro as well, seemed to believe that success in Bolivia and elsewhere in Latin America would elicit U.S. intervention, provoking outrage and fueling further revolution throughout the continent.

Bolivia's president was General René Barrientos, who had been part of a military junta that seized power in 1964. In 1965, the military government used the army to violently suppress opposition mining unions, and in 1966 Barrientos was elected president. Guevara's gamble was that the Bolivian military and government were weak enough to be defeated and overthrown, and that his efforts would receive adequate support from Bolivian miners and leftists, other Latin American revolutionary forces, and from the native Indian population. All such hopes of Guevara's would be dashed.

Much initial planning went into the expedition and Castro committed substantial amounts of personnel, resources, and money. Although details of the planning stage have not been officially revealed, it appears that Guevara might have gone to Bolivia to make preliminary investigations sometime during the first half of 1966. He then apparently returned to Cuba to help organize the expedition and sent Cuban operatives to Bolivia to purchase a ranch that would serve as a base for the guerrilla

The Cuban revolution totally engaged Fidel, while Che remained preoccupied with extending the war to Latin America and to the whole world.
—ANDREW SINCLAIR
Guevara biographer

Guevara at one of the guerrilla camps in September 1967. During the last three months of their Bolivian campaign, Guevara's small band was constantly on the run, while Guevara himself continually suffered from severe asthma attacks. Finally, on October 8, 1967, the rebels were defeated and Guevara was captured.

operations sometime near July 1966. Other Cuban forces began arriving in the fall, and Guevara himself appears to have entered Bolivia on November 3, 1966, disguised as a Latin American businessman, his long hair cut short and beard shaved off.

We have a full account of Guevara's activities from the time he arrived at the guerrilla base in Nancahuazú, Bolivia, on November 7, 1966, because, as usual, he kept a full diary of his activities, subsequently published as *The Bolivian Diary of Che Guevara*. His diary was supplemented by the notes of several other Cuban guerrillas there who emulated Guevara's practice of keeping a diary.

On November 7 the diary reads, "A new stage begins today." Guevara had arrived at the guerrillas' ranch in the highland region of central Bolivia. He began training his men, soliciting Bolivian recruits, and negotiating with leftists in the country for more support. His major disappointment was recorded on January 1, 1967, when he reported that Mario Monje, the leader of the Bolivian Communist party, had declined to support the expedition because Guevara insisted on command of the operation. This was a blow to the small guerrilla force, in serious need not only of more guerrilla fighters, supplies, and arms, but support in the cities as well.

Guevara was able to enlist some support from Bolivian Communist party dissidents and other political groups in Bolivia, but his main support consisted basically of a handful of volunteer recruits. He was never able to organize enough forces to carry out a revolution.

In January, he continued training his forces, stockpiling supplies that he and his men hid in caves in the area. They were ill frequently, and there was much quarrelling and dissension among his troops. On February 1, he began a training march that was supposed to last 25 days but which actually lasted 48 days because the guerrillas were constantly getting lost and fighting bad weather, sickness, and inexperience; Guevara himself suffered badly from asthma. By now Castro had announced to the world that Guevara was "somewhere in South America," leading a revolution. Right-wing regimes across the continent trembled; meanwhile, Guevara's small band of men struggled to stay alive.

In March, the operation began unravelling. Two of Guevara's Bolivian rebels who deserted were caught by the military and revealed the existence of the base camp in Nancahuazú. Some speculate that Guevara was betrayed by one of his chief contacts in Bolivia, "Tania," who had left incriminating documents in a jeep while she was carrying supplies to the base camp; the documents were found by the Bolivian military. "Tania" was the code name for Tamara Bunke Bider, an Argentinian woman of German parentage. Guevara had known her for years and was romantically involved with her; author Daniel James and others claim that she was an agent for the East Germans and the Soviets who perhaps had sabotaged Guevara's mission, but this theory is unproven.

The Bolivian army found the base camp on March 17 and discovered one of the guerrilla's diaries and some photos of Guevara. There were also a number of supplies and documents that Guevara had neglected to destroy. This constituted conclusive proof that the notorious Che Guevara was in the area trying to start another revolution.

French leftist journalist Régis Debray (left) and Argentinian socialist Ciro Bustos await the verdict of a Bolivian military tribunal in November 1967. They were both convicted of supporting Guevara's guerrilla movement and sentenced to 30 years in prison.

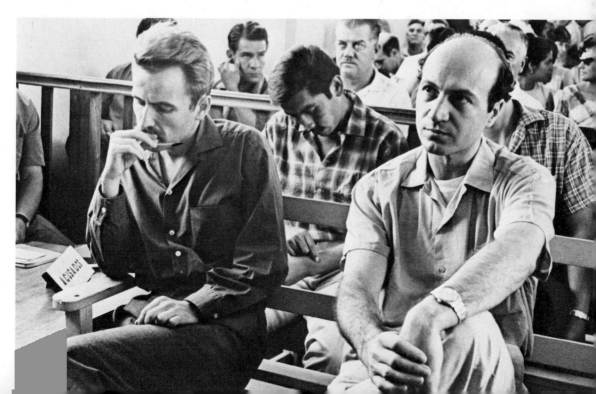

> *Guerrilla war is a people's war, a mass struggle. To try to carry out this type of war without the support of the population is to court inevitable disaster.*
>
> —CHE GUEVARA

Two days later, Guevara's group arrived in the vicinity of the camp and successfully ambushed Bolivian troops at Nancahuazú. At this point, Guevara reported that his forces had moved from the first to the second stage of guerrilla warfare. The first stage involved becoming familiar with the terrain and setting up supply operations. The second stage involved active aggression, and from then until his death in October, Guevara and his men engaged in several skirmishes with the Bolivian army and their American military advisers.

But Guevara's expedition was already doomed to failure. In the Sierra Maestra, the rebels had won the support of the peasants, who were fellow Cubans. In Bolivia, however, Guevara was unable to recruit a single Bolivian peasant to his cause. The Bolivian peasants were Indians who spoke little Spanish. Some interpreted Guevara's attitude toward them as condescending; he had idealized them as incipient socialists who, through a basic, child-like goodness, would naturally support his revolution. In reality, the peasants were highly suspicious of the bearded guerrillas, most of whom were white, foreign, educated, middle class, and not conversant with the specific situation in the area.

Many of the Bolivian peasants reacted to Guevara and his guerrillas as interlopers intent on inciting warfare, not as the "liberators" Guevara believed himself and his comrades to be. Thus, the peasants cooperated with government forces, regularly informing on the whereabouts of the guerrillas. Guevara, at first baffled by the peasants' unwillingness to help, became increasingly bitter toward them. In an April 1967 entry in his diary, he wrote, "The peasant base is still not developing, although it seems that by means of systematic terror we will obtain the neutrality of most of them."

Guevara, though, never resorted to the use of terror, and, as in the Sierra Maestra, he ordered the release of all government troops the guerrillas captured. But he also violated some of his own rules on the conduct of guerrilla warfare. His men were oversupplied, which made it difficult to move swiftly through the mountains. His mobility was further hampered by having a single headquarters, Nancahuazú. And his obsession with keeping a diary and having photographs taken revealed the identity of many guerrilla sympathizers; when the Bolivians captured this evidence, it led to the arrest and execution of dozens of his comrades elsewhere in Bolivia.

There was another reason for the failure of the Bolivian insurgency: Substantial help from left-wing political parties inside Bolivia never materialized. The Bolivian Communist party refused to provide any support at all, and the smaller leftist parties did not have much to offer. At one point, a violent labor dispute in Bolivia's tin mines caused the diversion of many government troops from Guevara's region and threatened the existence of the Bolivian government. But without assistance from Bolivian leftists, Guevara was unable to take advantage of the situation; the strike was brutally crushed, the governmental crisis ended, and the troops returned to resume the hunt for Guevara.

Although Guevara's guerrillas never numbered more than 47, they won several skirmishes against Bolivian troops in the spring and summer of 1966, leading the government to overestimate the true size of Guevara's army. In April, Guevara's forces were accidentally cut in half and the Bolivians seemed to interpret this as the presence of two separate fronts in the war. In May 1966, 16 American advisers from the CIA arrived to train the Bolivian army in their campaign against Guevara.

Guevara was never able to reunite with the other half of his small guerrilla army. On August 31, the Bolivian military found the other guerrilla group, capturing and killing its men. Guevara was now completely isolated.

He was left with 17 guerrillas. His communications equipment had broken down, cutting him off from the outside world. The peasants were against him. The Bolivian military was tracking him down and encircling his group in rough and unfamiliar country. They had already captured the guerrillas' supplies, including Guevara's asthma medicine. The end was near.

Bolivian General René Barrientos overthrew the social reform government of Paz Estenssoro in an army-backed coup in 1964. During his five-year rule, Barrientos and the army crushed all opposition to his conservative regime — including Guevara's small, poorly organized insurgency.

Guevara's forces fought a few more skirmishes against Bolivian troops in September and October. In a final battle on October 8, 1966, the Bolivian military surrounded and trapped them in a canyon. After fierce fighting, several guerrillas were killed. A few escaped. Guevara himself was wounded in the leg and, as Bolivian soldiers closed in to shoot him, he is reported to have said: "You shouldn't. I'm Che Guevara. I'm worth more to you alive than dead." He was taken prisoner and marched two miles to the hamlet of La Higuera.

The Bolivian government had a choice: They could execute Guevara, or they could try him. To put the renowned Che Guevara on public trial would almost certainly expose the government to a worldwide campaign for his release. That settled the issue. The next morning, President Barrientos sent a message to La Higuera: Kill Guevara.

On October 9 Guevara was interrogated by CIA and Bolivian intelligence agents. Then, according to an account given by the journalist José Alcazar, when the Bolivian warrant officer assigned to execute Guevara hesitated to pull the trigger, Guevara looked at him and said, "Well, go ahead then, you son of a bitch, kill me." The warrant officer fired several times. Che Guevara was dead.

This photo of Guevara in disguise was released in Cuba in April 1966 to dispel rumors that the guerrilla leader, unseen in public for more than a year, had been executed by Castro. Ironically, the release of this and other photos by Castro helped the Bolivian government track down Guevara.

A few hours later, fewer than a dozen journalists and one photographer were flown in to La Higuera. They were ushered into a small laundry shed, where Guevara's body had been put on display. After recording the evidence that Guevara was dead, they were led out and flown back to La Paz.

Guevara's body was buried in an undisclosed location, but just prior to that, the hands were cut off, packed in formaldyhyde, and sent to fingerprint experts in Argentina to make certain that the dead guerrilla was really the famous Che Guevara.

For several days there was international debate as to whether Che Guevara was or was not really dead; was it a double, and not Che, who had been killed? The speculation ended when Fidel Castro announced on October 15 that he was convinced. Che really had been captured and executed in Bolivia.

"Rarely," said Castro, "can one say of a man with greater justice, with greater accuracy, what we say of Che: that he was a man of extraordinary revolutionary virtues . . . he was an extraordinary human being, a man of extraordinary sensitivity."

A Bolivian air force colonel points to a bullet hole in Guevara's chest on October 10, 1967. Guevara had been executed two days before; the Bolivian government displayed his body to journalists to prove that the famous guerrilla was truly dead.

8

Che's Legacy

After his death as a revolutionary guerrilla, Che Guevara was instantly transformed into a symbol of revolutionary commitment and heroism. Signs proclaiming Che Lives! appeared in demonstrations and on T-shirts all over the world. Posters and likenesses of Che appeared on all continents. Even in the United States, the government of which Guevara so vigorously denounced, students began to emulate his style of dress, donning military fatigues, berets, and growing their hair and beards to show that they too were opponents of U.S. foreign policy. Few political leaders in history have had their image so worshipfully reproduced in so many different parts of the world.

Guevara's opposition to orthodox communism and his genuine concern for the impoverished of the Third World made him a seminal figure in the last years of the 1960s and throughout the 1970s,

If we wish to express what we want the men of future generations to be, we must say: "Let them be like Che."
—FIDEL CASTRO

A huge portrait of the late Guevara towers over a military parade in Havana's Revolutionary Plaza during the 20th anniversary celebration of Castro's regime in 1978. Following his death, Guevara was absolved of his economic failures in Cuba and proclaimed a national hero.

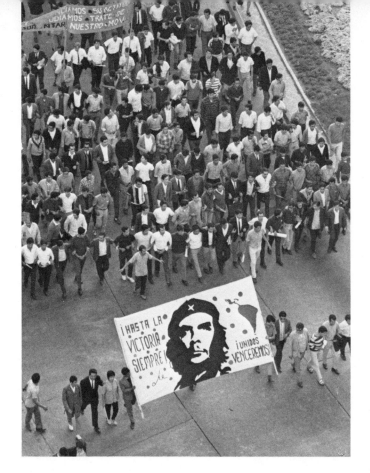

A student demonstration in Mexico City in 1968. Guevara was regarded as a hero by millions during the leftist protests that swept the world in the late 1960s. In Cuba, Castro declared 1968 the "Year of the Heroic Guerrilla" in honor of Guevara.

not only in politics, but in philosophy, too. Those years saw the rise of "the New Left" — a political-philosophical grouping of Marxists, socialists, and liberals who shared many of Guevara's beliefs. The members of the New Left movement, which was strong and influential throughout North America and Europe, rejected what they saw as grim Soviet-style communism as well as violent U.S. imperialism in Southeast Asia and Latin America.

With Guevara as their inspiration, leftist activists and students organized strikes and protests throughout the Western world. In France, they brought down the conservative government of Charles de Gaulle. In the United States, they turned the tide of public opinion against the war in Vietnam and forced President Lyndon Johnson to eschew his bid for reelection. In Mexico, they carried out the first demonstrations in decades against that country's conservative, single-party rule. And when the Soviet Union invaded Czechoslovakia to quash a liberalization program that allowed free speech and open political discussion — an invasion applauded by Fidel Castro — communists throughout Western Europe resigned their party membership and formed new communist parties independent of Soviet direction. All such events happened in 1968, just one year after Guevara's death.

Perhaps even more important, Guevara's memory fueled Third World consciousness. By the 1970s, the Nonaligned Movement of developing nations had become one of the world's most important international organizations; for the first time, the poorer countries were given a concerted voice and a chance to play a role in their own development. In Africa, guerrilla warfare would be waged in almost every country in the 20 years following Guevara's death, sometimes between socialist governments and right-wing revolutionaries, sometimes between socialist revolutionaries and right-wing governments — such as the Zairean government of Mobutu, still in power more than two decades after Guevara fought against him.

Cubans in straw hats wave flags and banners at the 15th anniversary of the Moncada attack in 1968. Castro dedicated the celebration to the memory of Guevara, whom he termed "a man of extraordinary revolutionary virtues . . . an extraordinary human being."

Meanwhile, Cuba itself continued to feel the effects of Guevara's legacy. Throughout the 1970s and 1980s, Castro sent arms and troops to new socialist governments in Angola, Ethiopia, and Yemen with far more success than he had had in Venezuela, the Congo, and Bolivia in the 1960s. While Cuba's relations with the rest of the capitalist world normalized, relations with the United States remained bitter through both the Carter and Reagan administrations.

Guevara's dream of continental liberation moved closer to reality for several South American nations in the first two decades following his death. Dictatorships in Bolivia, Brazil, Uruguay, and Guevara's home country of Argentina were overthrown, and all of them fell, at least in part, because of leftist

A plaster monument to Guevara was erected by three leftist sculptors in Santiágo, Chile, in 1968. In 1970, Chile elected a Marxist president, Salvador Allende, but he was overthrown and killed in 1973 during a U.S.-backed coup and replaced by a right-wing dictator, General Augusto Pinochet.

guerrilla insurgencies. Although Guevara would not have approved of the pro-American, capitalist orientation of these new governments, each of them did institute socialist programs aimed at redressing some of the same problems that he had identified in his travels through the continent in the 1950s: the inequitable distribution of land and the huge disparity between the few rich and the many poor. In Chile in 1970, a Marxist government closely in line with Guevara's philosophy was elected and came to power. It was headed by Salvador Allende, the same man whose letter of introduction 16 years earlier had expedited Guevara's trip to Central America. Allende instituted dramatically socialist land reform programs and nationalized several major industries. But as Guevara would have predicted, the CIA sponsored a military coup that overthrew the government, killed Allende, and resulted in the institution of a harshly repressive military regime that would rule Chile for more than 15 years.

In Central America, close to his adopted country of Cuba, the situation 20 years after Guevara's death remained much the same. Although the Sandinista movement — a revolutionary grouping of various socialist and liberal forces much like Fidel Castro's original 26th of July Movement — succeeded in winning a guerrilla war that ousted a 50-year-old U.S.-backed military dictatorship in Nicaragua, the United States would soon reply by financing counterrevolutionary forces in much the same manner as it had in Guatemala in 1954. Throughout the rest of Central America, right-wing governments sent death squads to harass, torture, and kill leftists, liberals, and impoverished peasants, while attempts at democracy did little to improve the overall conditions. Ironically, Guevara's manual on guerrilla warfare was required reading for U.S.-sponsored counterinsurgency groups dedicated to defeating the very movements that Guevara had championed.

Thus the world continued to be moved by the same forces Che Guevara fought for and against,

His choice to leave Cuba and his martyrdom for his cause set him above Fidel Castro or Ho Chi Minh or Mao Tse-Tung as a symbol of revolution.
—ANDREW SINCLAIR
Guevara biographer

and often these battles were fought in his name. So strong are the passions aroused by his memory that 20 years after his death, most of what is written about him either treats him as a monster or as a saint. In France alone, writers have produced a wide range of opinions. To biographer Léo Sauvage, "a fanatic as absolute as Che Guevara . . . can be contagious, but only for other fanatics, or for weaklings." To Régis Debray, a journalist who fought alongside Guevara in Bolivia, "the adventure of Guevara was a mystical adventure, and the last months of his life, a Passion. He brought to mind irresistably the image of Christ." To the great philosopher Jean-Paul Sartre, Guevara was simply "the most complete man of his time."

The British historian Hugh Thomas assessed Guevara, as follows, in his book *The Cuban Revolution*:

> Guevara was a brave, sincere and determined man who was also obstinate, narrow and dogmatic. At the end of his life, he seems to have become convinced of the virtues of violence for its own sake: "How close could we look into a bright future should two, three, or many Vietnams flourish throughout the world with their share of deaths and their intense tragedies . . . " Hatred, for Guevara, was indeed a praiseworthy emotion which could transform man into "an effective, violent, selective and cold killing machine". Guevara became in his last years a man for whom the sweetest music was the "staccato singing of the machine guns and new battle cries of war and victory". In an article written during the missile crisis but published posthumously, he even remarked "we must proceed along the path of liberation, even if that costs millions of atomic victims."
>
> Yet he was candid, and on the whole, he deceived neither himself nor others. His quarrel with the Soviet Union . . . was expressed without much care for his own future. . . . His influence over Castro, for good or evil, has grown after his death, for Castro has since taken up many of his views. As in the case of Martí, or Lawrence of Arabia, failure has brightened, not dimmed, the legend.

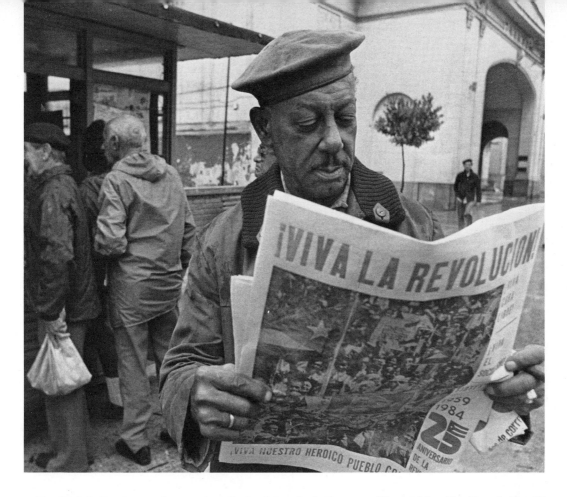

To Fidel Castro, who instantly befriended Guevara one night in Mexico City in 1955, Che Guevara was

> a man of total integrity, a man of supreme sense of honor, of absolute sincerity — a man of stoic and Spartan living habits, a man in whose conduct not one stain can be found. He constituted, through his virtues, what can be called a truly model revolutionary.

Che Guevara's major success was his participation in the Cuban revolutionary war. Despite his many contributions to the Cuban Revolution, his subsequent economic programs, diplomacy, and guerrilla campaigns abroad were for the most part failures. Yet Guevara himself served as a compelling symbol of the dedicated revolutionary whose actions were always consistent and in harmony with his moral ideals. He died fighting for those ideals.

"Long Live the Revolution!" proclaims a 1984 headline of *Granma*, Cuba's Communist party newspaper, in recognition of the 25th anniversary of the Cuban Revolution. Guevara's role in the revolution has become legend, and he remains a powerful symbol for left-wing movements throughout the world.

Further Reading

Alexandre, Marianne, ed. *Viva Che.* London: Lorrimer, 1968.

Cantor, Jay. *The Death of Che Guevara.* New York: Knopf, 1983. [Fiction]

Castro, Fidel. *Revolutionary Struggle: Selected Works of Fidel Castro.* Cambridge: MIT Press, 1972.

Ebon, Martin. *Che: The Making of a Legend.* New York: Universe Books, 1969.

González, Luis J., and Gustavo A. Sánchez Salazar. *The Great Rebel: Che Guevara in Bolivia.* Translated by Helen R. Lane. New York: Grove, 1969.

Guevara, Ernesto. *Che Guevara on Guerrilla Warfare.* New York: Praeger, 1961.

———. *Che Guevara Speaks.* New York: Merit, 1967.

———. *Che: Selected Works of Ernesto Guevara.* Cambridge: MIT Press, 1969.

———. *The Complete Bolivian Diaries of Che Guevara and Other Captured Documents.* New York: Stein and Day, 1968.

———. *Reminiscences of the Cuban Revolutionary War.* New York: Monthly Review Press, 1968.

———. *Venceremos! The Speeches and Writings of Ernesto Che Guevara.* New York: Macmillan, 1968.

James, Daniel. *Che Guevara.* New York: Stein and Day, 1969.

Lockwood, Lee. *Castro's Cuba, Cuba's Fidel.* New York: Macmillan, 1967.

Lowi, Michael. *The Marxism of Che Guevara.* New York: Monthly Review Press, 1973.

Matthews, Herbert. *Castro: A Political Biography.* New York: Simon & Schuster, 1968.

———. *Revolution in Cuba.* New York: Scribners, 1975.

Resnick, Marvin D. *The Black Beret: The Life and Meaning of Che Guevara.* New York: Ballantine, 1969.

Rojo, Ricardo. *My Friend Che.* New York: Dial, 1968.

Sauvage, Léo. *Che Guevara: The Failure of a Revolutionary.* New York: Prentice-Hall, 1973.

Sinclair, Andrew. *Che Guevara.* New York: Viking, 1970.

Szulc, Tad. *Fidel.* New York: Morrow, 1986.

Thomas, Hugh. *The Cuban Revolution.* New York: Harper & Row, 1977.

Vail, John J. *Fidel Castro.* New York: Chelsea House, 1986.

Zeitlin, Maurice, and Robert Scheer. *Cuba: Tragedy in Our Hemisphere.* New York: Grove, 1963.

Chronology

June 14, 1928	Born Ernesto Guevara de la Serna in Rosario, Argentina
1951–52	Takes motorcycle trip through Latin America; travels to United States
1953	Receives medical degree at Buenos Aires University
Dec. 1953–54	Travels from Argentina to Bolivia to Guatemala
1954	Leaves Guatemala; lives in exile in Mexico
1955	Meets Fidel Castro in Mexico
Nov. 1956	Accompanies Castro on *Granma* expedition
1956–58	Fights in the Cuban Revolution as military commander
Jan. 1959	Triumphantly enters Havana and claims it for the revolution
June–Sept. 1959	Travels through Europe, Asia, and Africa as the ambassador of the Cuban Revolution
Oct. 1959	Appointed director of industries for the National Institute of Agrarian Reform
Nov. 1959	Appointed head of the National Bank of Cuba
Oct.–Dec. 1960	Visits Czechoslovakia, the Soviet Union, the People's Republic of China, North Korea
1961	Named minister of industries
Aug. 1961	Participates in OAS economic summit in Punta del Este, Uruguay
1962–63	Travels to Soviet Union, China, Africa
1965	Visits Africa again
July 1965–March 1966	Participates in civil war in the Congo
Nov. 1966–Oct. 1967	Participates in the revolutionary guerrilla war in Bolivia
Oct. 9, 1967	Executed in Bolivia

Index

Douglas Kellner is professor of philosophy at the University of Texas at Austin and is the author of *Karl Korsch: Revolutionary Theory* and *Herbert Marcuse and the Crisis of Marxism*, and coauthor of *Camera Politica: The Politics and Ideology of Contemporary Hollywood Film*. He is currently at work on a book of critical theory and a biography of Jean Baudrillard. He is the author of *Kwame Nkrumah* in the Chelsea House series WORLD LEADERS—PAST & PRESENT.

Arthur M. Schlesinger, jr., taught history at Harvard for many years and is currently Albert Schweitzer Professor of the Humanities at City University of New York. He is the author of numerous highly praised works in American history and has twice been awarded the Pulitzer Prize. He served in the White House as special assistant to Presidents Kennedy and Johnson.

PICTURE CREDITS